RESEARCH METHODS FOR STUDYING GROUPS AND TEAMS

"Going beyond the description of abstract principles, *Research Methods for Studying Groups and Teams* uses the experience and insight of practicing researchers to help readers think about the concrete steps involved in the actual "doing" of research. As such, it is a resource for students wanting to learn about the rudiments of a wide array of different methods and for practicing researchers wishing to expand their horizons beyond their preexisting expertise. Although explicitly geared toward the study of groups, it has value for scholars interested in studying any aspect of human interaction."
—Dr. Charles Pavitt, Professor, Department of Communication, University of Delaware

This volume provides an overview of the methodological issues and challenges inherent in the study of small groups from the perspective of seasoned researchers in communication, psychology, and other fields in the behavioral and social sciences. It summarizes the current state of group methods in a format that is readable, insightful, and useful for both new and experienced group researchers. This collection of essays will inspire new and established researchers alike to look beyond their current methodological approaches, covering both traditional and new methods for studying groups and exploring the full range of groups in face-to-face and online settings.

The volume will be an important addition to graduate study on group research and will be a valuable reference for established group researchers, consultants, and other practitioners. The essays in this volume when considered as a whole will be a contemporary interdisciplinary integration on group research methods.

Andrea B. Hollingshead is Professor of Communication in the Annenberg School for Communication and Journalism at the University of Southern California. She has joint appointments in the Marshall School of Business and the Department of Psychology and is co-director of the Annenberg Program for Online Communities Research Initiative. Professor Hollingshead's research concerns the factors and processes that lead to effective and ineffective knowledge sharing in work groups. Her research also addresses how groups collaborate and create community using communication technologies.

Marshall Scott Poole is a professor in the Department of Communication and Director of the Institute for Computing in the Humanities, Arts, and Social Science at the University of Illinois Urbana–Champaign. His current research foci include team behavior in massive multiplayer online games, the use of information technology in emergency response, and integrating theories of small groups and social networks in the explanation of large, dynamically changing groups and intergroup networks.

Routledge Communication Series
Jennings Bryant/Dolf Zillmann, Series Editors

Selected titles include:

- Frey: *Group Communication in Context: Studies of Bona Fide Groups, Second Edition*
- Bucy/Holbert: *The Sourcebook for Political Communication Research*
- Heath/Bryant: *Human Communication Theory and Research, Second Edition*
- Stacks/Salwen: *An Integrated Approach to Communication Theory and Research, Second Edition*
- Rubin et al.: *Communication Research Measures II*
- Frey/Cissna: *Routledge Handbook of Applied Communication Research*

RESEARCH METHODS FOR STUDYING GROUPS AND TEAMS

A Guide to Approaches, Tools, and Technologies

Edited by
Andrea B. Hollingshead and
Marshall Scott Poole

Routledge
Taylor & Francis Group

NEW YORK AND LONDON

First edition published 2012
by Routledge
711 Third Avenue, New York, NY 10017

Simultaneously published in the UK
by Routledge
2 Park Square, Milton Park, Abingdon, Oxon OX14 4RN

Routledge is an imprint of the Taylor & Francis Group, an informa business

© 2012 Taylor & Francis

Library of Congress Cataloging in Publication Data
Research methods for studying groups and teams : a guide to approaches,
tools, and technologies / editors, Andrea B. Hollingshead & Marshall Scott
Poole. — 1st ed.
     p. cm. — (Routledge communication series)
   Includes bibliographical references and index.
   1. Small groups—Research—Methodology. 2. Small groups—Study and
teaching. I. Hollingshead, Andrea B. II. Poole, Marshall Scott, 1951–
   HM736.R47 2011
   302.3′4072—dc23

                                                            2011022519

ISBN: 978-0-415-80632-9 (hbk)
ISBN: 978-0-415-80633-6 (pbk)
ISBN: 978-0-203-80577-0 (ebk)

Typeset in Bembo
by Cenveo publisher services
Printed and bound in the United States of America on acid-free paper
by Edwards Brothers, Inc.

This book is dedicated to the memory of Joseph E. McGrath and his profound and lasting contributions to the study of groups and research methods.

CONTENTS

GROUP RESEARCH METHODS

An Introduction

Andrea B. Hollingshead

UNIVERSITY OF SOUTHERN CALIFORNIA

Marshall Scott Poole

UNIVERSITY OF ILLINOIS AT URBANA-CHAMPAIGN

Because you are reading this introduction, it is likely you need little convincing that groups are a worthwhile topic to study. In fact, this book presupposes that you are already interested in studying groups, and are looking for some guidance or ideas about how to study them.

Defining a "group" is not a simple task, and there is some disagreement among group scholars across disciplines about what constitutes a group. Hence, we take a broad and inclusive view of groups in this volume. We define groups as collectives with more than three people whose members share a common goal or purpose, have some degree of interdependence, interact with one another, and generally perceive themselves as a group. Groups have an internal structure and are embedded in larger social systems, members have various types of relationships with one another, and varying levels of influence on the group and vice versa. As a result, studying groups is often difficult and complex: substantively, logistically, and statistically. Group scholarship is on the upswing, and with this comes the need to understand methods specifically designed for group research. That is the purpose of this volume.

This volume is devoted to describing the challenges of studying groups, and strategies for meeting those challenges. There has never been a better time to study groups. With the rise of social networking, online communities, wikis, distributed work, crowd sourcing, and virtual worlds, there are many new forms of groups to study and new contexts in which to study them. The internet has also provided researchers with more access to information about traditional groups through publically available transcripts, databases, archives, and knowledge management systems. Powerful new methods and tools for voice recognition, social network analysis, interaction and content analysis, and statistics have reduced the costs in money, time, and labor to analyze group process. There is an increasing number of funding opportunities through governmental, corporate, and private foundations for studying collaboration and the social aspects of new media.

Structure and Organization of the Book

The objective, content, and approach of this book are different from those of most methods books. The book's major objective is to summarize the current state of group methods and tricks of the trade in a relatively brief volume that is readable, insightful, and useful for both new and experienced group researchers. In a sense, this volume features a backstage view of group research with tips, guidance, and suggestions. It covers topics related to both traditional and new methods for study-ing groups in face-to-face and online settings. Our hope is that the collection of essays in this book will inspire new and established researchers alike to look beyond their current methodological approaches.

We recruited a set of authors who are highly regarded experts and well known to group researchers across disciplines. Each author team has many years of expe-rience with the method described in their chapter. Taken together, the authors study a wide range of groups: top management teams, sports teams, political action groups, families, juries, support groups, friendship cliques, emergency response teams, project teams, ad-hoc laboratory groups, and game guilds in face-to-face and online settings.

Each chapter provides a general introduction and an overview of the method that describes its strengths and weaknesses, noteworthy examples, and latest inno-vations. The authors relate their personal experiences in conducting research and present aspects not usually reported in the method section of research articles. As a result, the chapters come alive with personal anecdotes about conducting research in the given domain: the authors' great successes as well as their grave errors.

The chapters of this volume are ordered chronologically to parallel the way in which a typical group research project unfolds. We considered dividing chapters into sections based on type of method (quantitative, qualitative, modeling) or locus of research (laboratory, field, simulation), but these categories seemed artifi-cial and restrictive. The orthodox position that there is "one best way" to conduct social and behavioral research has given way to an increasingly common tendency to employ multiple methods in programs of research. So we decided to put cate-gories to the side and invite readers to sample a variety of methods and research experiences.

Some Thoughts on Selecting Methods for Group Research

Identifying a problem of interest

> He who seeks for methods without having a definite problem in mind seeks for the most part in vain. (David Hilbert, mathematician, 1862–1943)

Research necessarily involves a problem of interest: a phenomenon, context, situation, condition, or issue that needs to be described, explained, predicted, or understood. Group research method selection often comes after you have determined the problem, and formulated a research question that is informed by the relevant literature. Generally, the research question should guide the selection of the method. However, there are notable exceptions to this rule, for example, researchers who develop new methods and statistical techniques may search for a problem domain or dataset that meets that method's underlying assumptions and requirements.

Finding a problem to tackle can be the easiest step of the research process but it takes time, effort, and perseverance. There are myriad problems to study, and multiple paths for locating one. First, by reflection through engaging with the literature on groups, you may discover a theory that you would like to test in a novel situation, generate an alternative explanation for a finding in an empirical article, or become inspired by an idea for future research directions from a discussion section. By browsing the table of contents of journals in your home discipline, and in the many interdisciplinary journals focusing on the topic of groups such as, *group dynamics, group and intergroup relations, group decision and negotiation, small group research* among others, you can identify the contemporary issues of the field and strategically select a topic that would interest your target audience.

A second path to discovering a problem is through direct observation where you detect an unusual occurrence or interesting practice and seek to understand why and how it occurred. For example, you may have come across an online community of competitors where members share information freely when the incentive structure, at least on the surface, suggests that members should not or you may have watched a charismatic person convince a group to act in ways that are clearly outside their collective interest. A third path is through direct experience, which can be the most rewarding as it is personally relevant and you may also have some insight that can help guide (and sometimes hinder) your quest. For example, perhaps you were a member of a group that exceeded expectations and won a competition despite very small odds or were a member of a team that failed miserably despite having very talented members.

The path becomes more treacherous once you have determined your problem of interest. The next step is forming a research question. A good research question defines the problem, describes the context, sets boundaries, and provides a direction for your investigation in the form of a question. Forming a research question is an iterative process that requires narrowing, clarifying, and redefining the problem through reading the relevant literature. Some researchers develop research questions inductively by creating a concept map that links together topics, theories, and findings (O'Leary, 2004). Others use a set of criteria or a checklist. The most important criterion on most checklists is whether it will sufficiently engage and motivate you through the research process, which can be long and arduous. Other often mentioned criteria include: (a) the potential contribution (is it novel and important, how will it add to existing knowledge, will it inspire future studies, and what are the policy or practical implications?); (b) feasibility (is it doable; and do you have access to the necessary resources?); and (c) ethical considerations (do the benefits for the participants and for society outweigh the risks and costs?).

Selecting an appropriate method

> Every research method is flawed. (Joseph E. McGrath, pioneering group scholar (1927–2007)

So far, the first two steps on the path to group research method selection, finding a problem and developing a research question, are similar for researchers with different epistemological orientations, although the form of the question and the approach taken in formulating it may be quite different. The next step is choosing the most appropriate method given the research question. As Runkel and McGrath (1972) suggest, there is no single best method: each has its inherent weaknesses and threats to validity, although some methods may be less well suited for some research questions than others. For example, a laboratory experiment may not be the best method for understanding how city council members deal with controversial topics during public hearings.

McGrath, Martin, and Kukla (1982) described research design as a three-horned dilemma. The three horns are: *precision* (control and measurement of behavior), *realism* (observing behavior in the context in which it naturally occurs), and *generalizability* (generalizing findings across actors and populations). All horns are equally important in the research process, but they are impossible to achieve in a single study. For example, laboratory experiments score high on precision, but score low on realism and generalizability. In contrast, field studies score high on realism, but low on precision and generalizability. However, there is a solution: by examining a given phenomenon using multiple methods and looking for convergence and triangulation of findings across methods. Although it is uncommon and difficult for any single researcher to do so in a single article (especially when the topic involves groups), a community of scholars using multiple methods engaged on a common research question can solve the three-horned dilemma. It is our hope that this edited book will encourage small group researchers to look beyond their current approach for new ideas, new methods and new techniques.

The central role of theory

Theory should play a central role in the method selection process. Edmondson and McManus (2007) provide a useful framework for understanding the relations between theory and method fit, and provide three archetypes of methodological fit (mature, intermediate, nascent) based on the state of theory in the problem domain. In a nutshell, they propose that theory falls along a continuum from mature theory that has well-developed constructs and established relations based on many studies by different researchers to nascent theory that proposes tentative answers for novel questions regarding the how and why behind a given phenomenon. Intermediate levels of theory development fall along the continuum. Research questions based on mature theory tend to describe relations between established constructs whereas research questions based on nascent theory tend to be more open-ended about the problem of interest. Hypothesis testing using quantitative methods is a more powerful approach for research questions based on mature theory, whereas qualitative, exploratory methods are more powerful for research questions based on nascent theory where theory generation comes after data collection and analysis.

A good place to find the current state of theory in group research across disciplines is in our first edited volume: *Theories of small groups: interdisciplinary perspectives* (Poole & Hollingshead, 2005). In fact, working on that volume inspired the present volume, which focuses on method and serves as a companion volume.

A Final Word of Thanks

We are very grateful to the authors for their outstanding contributions to the book. We heard from more than one author that writing their chapter was one of their most enjoyable writing projects ever. Their knowledge and passion for research shine in this volume and we hope you find the chapters as inspirational, insightful, and useful as we do.

Authors' Note:

We thank Peter Carnevale for his helpful comments on this introduction.

References

Edmondson, A. C., & McManus, S. E. (2007). Methodological fit in management field research. *The Academy of Management Review, 32,* 1155–1179.

McGrath, J. E., Martin, J., & Kulka, R. A. (1982). *Judgment calls in research.* Beverly Hills, CA: Sage Publications Inc.

O'Leary, Z. (2004). *The essential guide to doing research.* London: Sage.

Poole, M. S., & Hollingshead, A. B. (Eds.) (2005). *Theories of small groups: Interdisciplinary perspectives.* Thousand Oaks, CA: Sage Publications Inc.

Runkel, P. J., & McGrath, J. E. (1972). *Research on human behavior: A systematic guide to method.* New York: Holt, Rinehart and Winston, Inc.

1

DESIGNING FOR DRIFT

Planning Ethnographic Qualitative Research on Groups

Michael G. Pratt and Najung Kim

BOSTON COLLEGE

> Ethnographic research is guided as much from drift as design, and is perhaps the source of far more failures than successes.
>
> *(Van Maanen, 1979, p. 539)*

As the epigraph suggests, ethnographic research may be the source of more failures than success. Clearly it would not be unique in this regard; especially if you consider that the rejection rate by top-tier organizational studies/management journals can exceed 90 percent. But as we discuss below, ethnographic research has its own unique challenges that make it a high-risk/high-reward endeavor. We think it is worth the risks. We challenge the reader to find a more engrossing, energizing, and personally world-changing methodology for studying a group – be it a small team, an organization, an occupation, or a "people." Part of its allure may be in its subject matter – better understanding the cultures of groups. Its fun may similarly derive from the engrossing nature of its methods, such as actual participation in group life and the use of broad, largely unstructured interviews. Or perhaps its appeal is in the challenge in navigating the tension John Van Maanen raises: the pull between design and drift.

The design part is not that difficult to describe. In brief, to examine a group in an ethnographic fashion you have to: (a) select a research question; (b) locate a group to examine this question; (c) design your study; (d) obtain approval for your study through an Institutional Review Board (IRB); (e) gain access; (f) collect data; (g) analyze the data; and (h) write it up. Essentially, it is not that different, in abstract, to how you would approach other examinations of groups. However, as we will discuss below, *how* these steps are enacted in ethnographies may be unique. For example, engaging in "commitment acts" (Feldman, Bell, & Berger, 2003), finding key informants, asking grand tour questions, and the like are central to ethnographic studies. Moreover, what is more difficult to describe, but no less equally important, is the "drift" – taking advantage of where the study takes you. To be able to best "catch the drift," requires tactics, tips, and training often not found in "how to" books on ethnography (e.g., Fetterman, 1998; Spradley, 1979). Our charge is to cover those topics that are the least well covered by existing texts and articles. In this spirit, we discuss the design of an ethnographic group study including gaining access, and preparing for observations and interviews. Before turning to these topics, we first provide an overview of ethnography.

Ethnography: What it is, when you do it, and why

While definitions vary, at their core, ethnographies are the study of a group's culture (Fetterman, 1998; Rosen, 1991; Spradley, 1979; Van Maanen, 1979). These groups may vary in size – from teams (Bechky & Okhuysen, 2011), to occupations and organizations (Kayser-Jones, 2002; Pratt, 2000a; Rosen, 1991; Van Maanen, 1973), to people living in certain areas (Mead, 1928; Venkatesh, 2002). Ethnographies also have specific ways of gathering data, such as participant observation and ethnographic interviews. Some studies are relatively "pure" ethnographies, which typically involve long periods (e.g., over 6 months) of being "in the field" (Fetterman, 1998). To illustrate, the first author's (Mike's) study of Amway distributors was his most pure ethnography: he spent over 9 months in the field working as a distributor and interviewing other current and former distributors. In organizational research, there are relatively few ethnographies that are pure, but several which contain some ethnographic elements (e.g., Hinds & Cramton, this volume). Mike's work, for example, often uses ethnographic interviews or some limited participant observation, such as rounding with doctors (Pratt, Rockmann, & Kaufmann, 2006) or being involved in a nurse's dress code task force (Pratt & Rafaeli, 1997).

Ethnographies should be used when you are interested in getting the perspective of the cultural participants or "informants." The term "informant" rather than "subject" (as in a lab study) or a "respondent" (as in a survey) is not accidental, but speaks to the nature of the researcher to the researched. Informants, as the name describes, inform you. They are the cultural experts. You are not manipulating the conditions around them as you might for a "subject;" and "respondents" are often limited to answering questions on the topics and concepts that you deem critical. In the lab and when giving surveys, you are the expert; and you have a fair amount of control over what your subjects do and the kinds of questions they answer. Ethnography puts the researcher, who might have or be getting a PhD, into the unenviable position of often having to appear, or actually be, ignorant. Because you do not know what an informant will say or do, and where the study will "drift," you may also feel like you have very little control. For some researchers, these conditions may be enough to dissuade them from doing ethnography!

Moreover, because you are getting the informants' perspective, and are not testing concepts or constructs, you have ultimately to translate these understandings into "academese" to get published. This is both a daunting and exhilarating task. Part of the challenge is that you have to be careful not to do too much "violence to experience," that is, you need to translate your research in such a way as to do justice to how your informants' view the world. And if that is not enough of a challenge, your results will be detailed and specific, but gored on the horn of "generalizability" (McGrath, 1982). Thus, it is not clear whether your results will be comparable to any other group. All this and you often have to take hundreds of pages of data and fit them into a research article of roughly 40–50 pages in length.

High probability of failure, relatively low control, putting yourself into a situation where you are not the expert, and being placed between two worlds – that of your informants and that of your academic colleagues – where do I sign up? If you are still reading this chapter, you may have some of the critical characteristics of an ethnographer: persistence, self-confidence, and a desire to learn continuously. And in the spirit of mentioning the "high rewards," at the time of this writing, Mike's ethnography has been the most fruitful – at least in terms of leading to publications (Barnett & Pratt, 2000; Pratt, 2000a, 2000b, 2003; Pratt & Rosa, 2003) – when compared to any other methodology he has used.

Getting back to the issue of when to do ethnography, we have stated that ethnographies are great for exploring the mindsets of individuals within a group – insights that can enrich, support, or even challenge our existing ways of knowing. Like other inductive qualitative approaches, it is good for understanding "why" individuals do things (e.g., their motivations) and "how" they do them (e.g., the process). It is not good for describing the prevalence of some attitude or behavior (e.g., how many Fortune 500 employees express high degrees of affective, normative, and calculative commitment towards their organizations). It is good for building theory, but not as good for testing it. It can also elaborate or change how we see existing theories. For example, "organizational commitment" in Amway looked very different from many of the existing models in the literature (Pratt & Rosa, 2003). Finally, ethnographies ground our knowledge and our claims. Most articles suggest that "organizations are changing" – but how can we really know this is true without taking the time and energy to figure out how the people we study are viewing the world around them?

First things first? The question and the group

In the beginning there is the research question; sometimes. While it is indeed the case that it is helpful to have a general idea of the kinds of questions you are interested in, sometimes a research question does not crystallize until one finds the appropriate group to study. We'll give you an example. When Mike was completing graduate school, he was struggling to put together a viable dissertation project.

He knew he had an abiding interest in organizations that had "strong cultures" and conflicting belief systems, but he did not know where to go from there or how to narrow his focus. Fortunately, during this time of struggle, Mike saw his sister who had recently joined an organization he had never heard of: Amway. In their discussion, he became fascinated by the cultural/ideological elements of the organization, and his curiosity was piqued by what appeared to be identity changes in his sister; see Pratt (2003) for details. After reading about the organization, and attending a rally, he knew this was the organization he wanted to study. Once that decision was made, he was able to hone in on a research question around the issues of ideological contradictions, ambivalence and member attachments.

Ethnographic questions are not only of a certain form, they also tend to be of a certain type. As noted above, for qualitative research, the best research questions revolve around questions of "how?" or "why?" rather than "how many?" or "to what degree?" In addition, these research questions often deal with an issue or problem rather than a specific theory. That is, ethnographic research, like much qualitative research, is often problem centered rather than theory centered. Problem-centered research, as the name implies, is motivated by some conundrum in actual life. In Amway, Mike wondered how people could so strongly attach to a group that appeared to contradict itself in its most fundamental beliefs (e.g., put family before work, but miss kids' birthdays to "build the business"). Because ethnographies attempt to look at the world through the informants' eyes – and informants often do not think in theories – it is perhaps natural for ethnographies and problem-centered research to be related. If you start a study with a specific theory in mind, chances are you are simply going to get responses to and from your own perspective. Problem-centered research, however, carries with it at least two unique challenges.

First, problems lie at the intersection of multiple theories. Thus, going back to Mike's dissertation study, conflicting belief systems may be discussed in treatments of ideological conflicts, hybrid organizational identities, and differentiation perspectives on culture, just to name a few organizational examples. It may also require moving beyond the organizational literature. This is challenging when one needs to write up a proposal for an IRB, or possibly for a dissertation committee, because it means that you will be reading widely and integrating multiple theories when writing up your research.

Second, since problem-centered research lies at the intersection of multiple theories, you have to do an extraordinary amount of work, before you even go into the field, to show that the research question you are addressing has not been sufficiently examined before. This often involves writing an introduction to your research (or proposal) by crafting "theoretical frames" (Pratt, 2008). Creating theoretical frames involves constructing the argument that multiple theories imply, but do not directly address, the problem or issue with which you are concerned. For example, in Mike's dissertation proposal, he argued that conflicting belief systems should lead to ambivalence among members. However, reactions to ambivalence were that individuals might be more positive or more negative towards their organization, and that they might react by vacillating between beliefs or possibly by being paralyzed. Hence, in his proposal, he showed that extant research had proposed that almost any reaction can follow from ambivalence; but as importantly, he also was able to argue that no one had yet uncovered the conditions under which one response might be more likely than another.

Whether it precedes, follows, or is somehow iteratively involved with the construction of your research question, you must choose a group to study. For an effective ethnographic study, the group you choose is one that *you should not be too familiar with*. Thus, if you were a consultant before entering into academia, you should not attempt an ethnographic study of consultants. As noted above, you need to get your informants' perspective on their culture and "how they do things." If you have a fair amount of experience with a group, then (a) you are likely to come into the group with a lot of preconceptions and (b) it is more difficult to get away with asking the types of "dumb" questions that a newcomer would ask – and those needed to get at the group members' world view. That said, it is unlikely that you will be entering a culture that is totally foreign to you. Thus, Rosen (1991, p. 14) writes:

> The ethnographically inclined organizational researcher, on the other hand, must be concerned not with understanding the clearly strange or exotic, worrying about the truly foreign might never be made familiar, but with staying at home and claiming sufficient bravado to transform what is culturally familiar into a subject upon which to interpret understandings.

While admitting that working in organizations may not be as exotic as going to a foreign land to study a little-known people, the level of familiarity one has with an organization can vary greatly. For Mike, while Amway was not an entirely foreign culture (e.g., they spoke English and wore recognizable clothing), the culture was nonetheless quite different from what he was used to, and thus he could more easily apply ethnographic techniques.

Other issues that are critical to choosing a group, and which may be more obvious, are finding: (a) groups that will allow you to get the data you need; and (b) groups that will allow you access. With regard to the former, if Mike was interested in examining how office layouts influence group interactions, Amway distributors would be the wrong group to study as they are largely a geographically dispersed group. With regard to the latter, it is helpful before launching into a full project to have some idea of whether or not you will be able to get access to a group, and what kind of access you will get. For both of these criteria, it may help to informally "hang out" with the group before beginning your official studies. Mike attended an Amway convention to get a sense of what kinds of individuals he was likely to meet, what challenges studying the group might entail, and to help him hone the types of research questions that could be answered by this particular group. He even started building connections with existing distributors.

In general, if you are using ethnography to build theory, you should review the tenets of theoretical sampling, which is different from statistical sampling common to quantitative methods. In brief, theoretical sampling involves choosing a sample for theoretical reasons, such as finding a group that is an extreme example of the phenomena you want to study (and thus where the dynamics you want to study will be clearer), or possibly a prototypical case where a specific group well represents a broader type of group. Mike's ethnography of Amway represented an "extreme case" (Pettigrew, 1990). His study of physicians, which was not a pure ethnography, was done because physicians are believed to be a prototypical profession; see Marshall and Rossman (1989), Miles and Huberman (1994), and Patton (1990) for a discussion of different sampling logics in qualitative research. One word to the wise before we leave this subject: as with most decisions in ethnographic research, choosing whom to talk to or observe in a group is an ongoing task. As the epigraph which begins this chapter suggests, you may have to "drift" a bit before finding out who is best to talk to and observe.

Gaining access: International Review Boards, gatekeepers, key informants, and commitment acts

With question and context in hand, the design of the study is well under way. However, even brilliant designs are useless unless you can actually "get in" to study the group. Typically, access involves managing a local IRB process and gaining official entrée into the group itself. If this group is embedded in a larger organization(s), or if you are doing research with someone at another university, then gaining access may involve a more complex process involving multiple IRBs. IRBs and some elements of access happen iteratively, often starting with an official statement by the group allowing access, getting IRB approval, and then negotiating more details about access with the group; for more information on access, see Feldman et al., 2003).

International Review Boards

The primary university gatekeeper to any group is your local IRB. While there is some controversy over the role of IRBs, especially for social science research that largely involves talking and observing (see Gunsalus et al., 2007), you should always check in with your local IRB − even if they typically find that your research is ultimately exempt from review. Please know that, depending on your institution, IRBs may not know much about qualitative work, much less, ethnography. For IRBs used to seeing clear hypotheses, established measures, and the like, requesting permission to participate in the activities of the group, and to interview them – with no specific hypotheses in mind – may be troubling. From our own personal experience, IRBs may think that you are simply too early in your thinking to collect your data! From their standpoint, the institution would have to place a lot of trust in a researcher who is going into a situation without clear hypotheses. Thus, we found it is often helpful to (a) do a little method training with your IRB representatives; and (b) keep in touch with them throughout the process.

With regard to the former, you might write up a paragraph or two on what ethnographies are and how they are to be conducted. Ample "legitimizing" citations from academic books and articles are strongly encouraged. Some IRB reviewers may need to learn that there is a methodology involved and you are not simply, "hanging out with people and having conversations." You should also be clear with the IRB that ethnography is not the same as investigative reporting. For one, investigative reporting is often about finding the sensational, whereas ethnography is about translating what everyday life is for a group (Fetterman, 1998). In addition, investigative reporters often want to reveal the identities of those involved in a particular situation (e.g., a crime or a scandal), whereas in an ethnography, you work to protect the identity of those whom you are studying. Both, however, use the term "informant," and it is the investigative informant – who is expected to "snitch" on someone – that individuals often think of when using this term. This only adds to the confusion – and not just for the IRB. Again from personal experience, we would suggest not calling your ethnographic informants, "informants." They will likely not only be startled, but will be less willing to talk with you (or will use the interview to complain or "snitch.")

With regard to keeping in touch with your IRB, know that your "materials," such as interview protocols, change and evolve, by design, over the course of data collection. At least some university IRBs, and perhaps all of them in the US, would like to see and approve any changes in such materials. Thus, you may be going back to your IRB multiple times. Develop a good relationship with at least one of your IRB representatives. You might be able to work out an arrangement whereby such constant updates are waived or limited (e.g., limited to very major changes); alternatively, they may be willing to expedite the review of any changes. Without a good relationship, expect significant added time on to your data collection process.

Gatekeepers and key informants

Once approved, gaining access to a group requires at least two "roles" which may or may not be found in the same person. To begin, you need someone who can actually grant you access to the group in question (i.e., a gatekeeper). In the study of medical residents, Mike and his colleague followed primary care physicians for three years, radiologists for four years, and surgeons for as many as six years.

This would not have been possible without buy-in from one of the deans, and the department heads of every group studied. While these particular gatekeepers allowed the researchers wonderful access, they were "costly." During interviewing, it became clear to the researchers that some of the residents were wondering if they were "spies" for the administration. The nice thing about extended stays in an organization is that they were able to dissuade them of this belief; however, it does point out the need to pay attention to unintentional effects of power and politics when choosing gatekeepers.

Moreover, the deans and department chairs were not actually residents, and would not have been good for the second role: a key informant. A key informant (or informants) is your "tour guide" – the person of whom you can ask a lot of questions at various points throughout your study. Non-key informants may simply be observed or possibly interviewed. However, the key informant helps you to decipher language, fill in missing pieces, and the like.

In his book on ethnographic interviewing, Spradley (1979) devotes an entire chapter to the characteristics of a good informant, such as a key informant. These characteristics include someone who is "enculturated" or is an expert in the culture. This person should also be *currently involved in the group*. Former group members may not be aware of what is currently going on in the group, and depending on how they exited, may be overly biased towards the group. For these reasons, the department heads would have been bad key informants: they had not been residents for a long time and how they thought about residency training may have changed over the years, especially now since they were responsible for residency training themselves. Key informants should also be *able and willing to speak to you in their "native" tongue*, that is, you do not want an informant trying to translate what is going on in academese, which they might do in order to be helpful. For example, two of Mike's key informants among Amway distributors sometimes tried to talk about what was happening at events in academic language. For example, at Amway conventions, more successful distributors get to sit closer to the stage, and often wear very formal attire, such as tuxedos and ballroom gowns. The majority of distributors (those who are not at the highest levels of sales) are made to wait in line to be seated, are not dressed as formally, and sit toward the back of the room at conventions. Telling him that the successful distributors "represent the dream and create a burn in people to be more like them" is much more helpful than, "I think the psychology behind what they do is that they want us to suffer a bit so as to better motivate us to sell more products." The latter way of speaking means that the key informant is no longer representing his or her culture, but attempting to represent the researcher's. Thus, although these key informants were well intentioned, Mike had to always bring the conversation back to "distributor" language. A final characteristic of a good key informant is that they have to be *able and willing to take the time necessary to answer your questions* throughout what could be a very lengthy process. Cultivating a key informant(s) involves a lot of work, and a lot of trust. Thus, be sure to maintain this relationship.

It is extremely difficult to "start over" with someone once you are well into a project.

Commitment acts

A final issue concerning access involves becoming accepted by the group as a whole. While this may be facilitated by a gatekeeper or a key informant, gaining access may also involve *commitment acts*. Commitment acts (Feldman et al., 2003) are activities you have to perform to be trusted by the group at large. For example, to truly be accepted as an Amway distributor, Mike had to have a sales meeting. This involved inviting his friends from graduate school to come over to his house and hear an Amway sales pitch. As Mike has written about elsewhere (Pratt, 2003), this was very uncomfortable for him as it violated social norms – using friendship ties potentially to make money. However, this is exactly the kind of discomfort that all distributors feel. In fact, this tension is cultivated: upon joining as a new distributor, you are supposed to make a list of all of your family and friends so that you can contact them to either buy or distribute products. Thus, this commitment act had two benefits: (a) it showed his Amway "upline" sponsors that he was serious about Amway, and (b) it gave him unique insights into the psychology of distributing.

The notion of commitment acts brings to the forefront a tension or challenge that he did not foresee, but had to deal with in the field. Commitment acts are often referred to in the plural because they are ongoing. Thus, at some point, the researcher has to decide how far they are willing to go in order to join the community. For example, Peshkin (1984), a Jewish man who studied an evangelical Christian school, decided that while he would act in a Christian manner while on site (e.g., dress appropriately, not swear), he would not go as far as becoming converted to Christianity, despite his informants' numerous and sincere attempts to convert him. For Mike, while he was willing to sell products and even sell the Amway lifestyle, he referred all individuals who wanted to distribute actively to his sponsor. Since he was leaving the field within a year, he did not think it was ethical to take on the potentially long-term mentoring role in this organization.

We want to close this section on gaining access with one strong proviso. Gaining access is not a dichotomous variable. You aren't "without" access one day and fully immersed the next. There may be false starts when entering (e.g., your gatekeeper really isn't a gatekeeper and you have to find someone else). In addition, the need for commitment acts may be ongoing, and the trust that others feel toward you (and vice versa) may ebb and flow throughout your study. So think of access – as well as leaving the scene – as an ongoing activity, not a "one shot deal." It will, if nothing else, keep you focused on the need to maintain your relationships when in the field, and not burn your bridges for a short-term gain (e.g., you get some interesting "confession" from an informant, but turn him or her and the larger group against you).

I'm in, now what? Choosing and using your tools

While you will select which tools you are going to use before getting through an IRB, you will actually have to use them once you get in. Once upon a time, the methodological techniques you would bring to bear would comprise largely or entirely participant observation and ethnographic interviewing – with the possibility of some archival data gathering. However, ethnographic approaches have expanded to include new "tools." Communication technology, for example, allows ethnographers to observe video recordings (video ethnography) or to view online groups via the internet (netnography); thus, you don't even need to be in the field with your informants! We will briefly discuss video ethnography and netnography after first reviewing two skills that are central to ethnography: interviewing and observation. We'll start with and spend the most time on observations as we believe that there are fewer guides for good observing, and because observations are central to each of these forms of ethnography.

Observations

Observation can vary in whether other informants know you are a researcher (overt) or not (covert). While a classic distinction, we are not sure whether or not an IRB will allow for fully covert observations. Observation can also range in terms of whether you actively participate in group activities (participant observation) or not (nonparticipant observation). So one choice you'll have to make is what *kind of observation(s)* you want to do. Historically, some have distinguished among four forms of participant observation: complete participant, participant-as-observer, observer-as-participant, and the complete observer (Angrosino & Perez, 2005; Gold, 1957/1958). The complete observer is just that: they do not interact at all with the people they observe. As noted above, this does not tend to be the stance taken by ethnographers. Observer-as-participant means that you interact somewhat with those you study, but the interactions are more casual and passive. The closest example to this approach that we note above is rounding with physicians without asking or answering questions. Participant-as-observer means actually engaging in the work being done by the group. Gold's (1957/1958) description bears similarities to Whyte's (1984) discussion of semi-overt participant observation where one joins a group but all know that the researcher is collecting data. This is the stance Mike took as an Amway distributor. Complete participants are covert and fully immerse themselves in the activities of the group. Traditional ethnographies favor the more participative approaches. However, the more you move toward complete participation, the greater the danger you will "go native" or completely adopt the values and goals of the group – essentially becoming a full member of the group you were studying. In Amway, informants encouraged Mike to go "native:" they hoped that he would eventually become so successful a distributor that he could leave his academic job.

We should be clear that, although we have discussed different ways to observe across studies, one can switch approaches within a study. For example, some days you may be more "participant" than "observer;" while at other times the "observer" role may dominate. We found that alternating between these two stances helps us alternatively to learn and engage (participant as fore) and to reflect and comprehend (observer as fore).

A second issue involves getting the *proper training* to observe, especially as a participant. Such training normally comprises coursework, if available, and apprenticing with someone experienced in the methodology. Most generally, learning qualitative methods often occurs by doing: by actually observing it in the field. Training, however, is an especially interesting issue when one is a participant observer in organizational groups.

Rosen (1991), for example, suggests that those studying organizations may want to pursue an MBA first. However, we suggest that such a course of action depends on the kind of group you are studying and what skills you need to attain a desired level of membership (e.g., marginal or full). For example, Van Maanen took police training before riding along with police officers (Van Maanen, 1973). Mike went to conventions, talked, observed, and modeled his upline distributors, and bought books and tapes in order to sell Amway products and Amway opportunities effectively. Neither required an MBA. However, if your group has specialized business skills, such as an accounting department, getting an MBA may make more sense.

What makes the issue trickier, though, are the dual needs of (a) examining groups that are sufficiently different from what you know, and (b) participating productively in said groups. Fulfilling both can be highly problematic. Rosen (1991, p. 17) further suggests a related tension: "researching while one 'should be' working [at your 'new' job]." Thus, before entering the field, you should think carefully about the amount of training you need to receive in order to engage in a participant role in such a way that you do not harm the productivity or the safety of the group.

One way to minimize these tensions is to participate in an entry position, where the skills needed are low, and where asking "dumb questions" – as the kind an ethnographer might – is acceptable. In addition, one can choose a participant role that is not highly interdependent on others' roles. For example, while not a pure ethnographic study, Anat Rafaeli's and Mike's "participant observation" roles on the rehab unit involved being part of a dress task force for the unit. This allowed them to use their expertise in the area of dress and to engage in and observe activities of the rehabilitation unit; however, at the same time, these activities were buffered from the main tasks that the unit performed: patient care.

A third but related theme in the area of training is how you *prepare yourself mentally* for joining a new group. Some preparation is relatively straightforward. For example, we have discussed how Mike prepared extensively for joining Amway: he not only attended a convention, he also read about Amway, and listened to Amway tapes and read Amway books. But another thing that Mike did to prepare himself for entering Amway was create a type of psychologi-cal "time capsule" before he started. He wrote a snapshot of how he viewed himself – as well as the preconceptions, apprehensions, and opinions he had about his research project – before entering the field. He did not read it again until he had completed his research. At that point, he could see how, and in what way, that the experience had changed him. While there are certainly benefits poststudy, this self-reflective practice also helps to make you aware of potential biases or baggage you may be bringing into a study beforehand.

For a lack of a better phrase, participant observation also takes a certain type of "mental toughness." For example, when studying Amway distributors, Mike had to navigate academic, familial, friendship, and distributor roles constantly. These were difficult to do physically, cognitively, and emotionally; see Pratt (2003) for a descrip-tion of these struggles. Thus, one word of advice is to plan out where you can rest or periodically "escape" during the ethnographic process. For example, Mike's com-mittee was worried that he might defect to Amway. Thus, they encouraged him to be highly skeptical. In the role as a distributor however, he had to engage in "positive thinking" and essentially suspend disbelief and "fake it until he made it." In other words, his Amway colleagues wanted him to be a true believer. This tension was intense enough that Mike decided to not communicate with his committee mem-bers for weeks at a time (at least about the project) so that he could engage fully in his distributor role without the accompanying academic pressures. [Side note: this did not, of course, help assuage concerns that he was defecting.] Other tensions, however, he did not want to escape because these were the ones experienced by distributors. Thus, the tension between using family and friend networks for busi-ness deals were ones that all distributors face. To make sure he had the energy to deal with some tensions, however, he needed to find some respite from the others.

Fourth, and the one you are most likely to find in other written texts, is how you will *actually conduct your observations*. One major divide is whether your obser-vations will follow a protocol and be structured, or whether they will be more unstructured. While we have found moving from an unstructured to structured approach is often helpful, this insight still does not help someone to figure out what they actually have to do during observations. It is not as obvious or as easy as you might think. We have found two resources, in particular, to be useful on this front. To start, Wolcott (1994, pp. 161–163) makes a distinction among "observe and record everything," "observe and look for nothing in particular," "look for paradoxes," and "identify the key problem confronting a group." As the descriptive titles imply, the first is very unstructured and involves recording everything you can. This process will provide a broad view of events and will help you realize what you are interested in: because you cannot record everything, looking at what you actu-ally do record may be indicative of what you find most interesting. The second is more structured and forces you to look at discontinuities or surprises in the social landscape; and is great when you have a high degree of familiarity with the setting or when the field is overly complex. Looking for paradoxes is also structured, and involves looking for contradictions in behaviors, goals, and the like. This may help you understand key issues in the life of that group. For Mike, the apparent tension in Amway between putting "family before work" but "working on kid's birthdays" helped him to eventually ask questions about how such paradoxes were perceived (they really weren't) and resolved (i.e., through beliefs about how working hard now will allow you to spend more time with your family later). Finally, since cultures are often about how groups solve problems (Schein, 2004), looking for the key issue confronting a group can give you insight into what is important to the group and what is foundational to their world view. Again, this is somewhat structured, but offers a slightly different focus from looking at paradoxes or discontinuities.

Another resource for guiding observations is Whyte's (1984) *Learning from the Field*. Whyte has two terrific suggestions regarding the observation of groups. To begin, he suggests mapping the scene, paying special attention to where people stand or sit, who talks with whom, etc. Najung has successfully used this tactic. When she was observing an annual board meeting for a housing cooperative, she took note of where key board members sat, whether the employees were standing or sitting, how they set up the tables and chairs. In mapping out the territory, she noticed that employees were standing literally at the fringes of the group – at the corner by the door taking care of things and facilitating things. This observation was key in crafting interview questions about the relationship between board members, other house owners, and employees. A second tactic is to examine interactions, such as who proposes a specific action and who supports it (this is especially good for examining leadership and influence). Both verbal (e.g., speech content) and nonverbal (e.g., gaze, posture) are critical to watch.

Before closing this section, know that exiting the scene after observing as a participant is often very difficult. Douglas (1976) refers to field research as a "traitorous activity." While we are not sure we would go quite that far, Mike does discuss (Pratt, 2003) the twin burdens of (a) the guilt he felt in leaving the field, and (b) the tremendous responsibility he felt to not do "violence to experience:" describing his experience among the distributors in a way which honored how they saw the world. While certainly a more intense an experience than what you will likely experience during an ethnography, we suggest that you watch the movie *Donnie Brascoe*, where Johnny Depp plays an underground FBI agent that infiltrates the mob, to understand better how one can come to identify closely with the group in which one is participating, and the difficulties of exit.

Interviewing

If done well, interviewing can be fun for both you and the informant, and even therapeutic for the latter. Before starting interview, it is often wise to make an interview "guide" or "protocol." This protocol is used to provide some structure for the questions you will ask during an interview, and it is likely something that your IRB will want to see before you enter the field. There are now quite a few resources on how to prepare for and conduct an interview (Kvale & Brinkmann, 2008; Rubin & Rubin, 2005; Seidman, 1998). However, we like Spradley's (1979) book, *The Ethnographic Interview*; it is a wonderful resource. His book outlines the kinds of questions you might want to ask during an interview. We've outlined these question types in Table 1.1. Please note that the purpose of these questions is to get a better sense of what an informant thinks is important. Moreover, mirroring the tension between design and drift, and the "structured-ness" of observations, there is also some tension inherent in deciding how much to structure an interview. In Table 1.1, descriptive questions are the least structured; and the answers to these questions are often used as the basis for asking more structured questions.

While we would refer you to Spradley (1979) for a greater treatment of these question types, we would like to point out one in particular, the "grand tour question." Mike has found that no matter what type of interview he is doing, he likes to start with a grand tour question whereby the informant is asked to describe some aspect of their life. For example, acknowledging that few people have a "typical day," he will then ask "can you take me through a day at work?" While this is sometimes used to "warm up" the informant and get him or her talking, the answers to these have provided a trove of useful information in studies. For example, in the physician study (Pratt et al., 2006), the grand tour questions elicited detailed descriptions of what the residents did during their shifts. These descriptions made it clear that the work they *were* doing did not align with what they thought they *should be* doing as residents (e.g., surgery residents getting paged in the middle of the night to put down a toilet seat). From this realization, Mike and his colleagues came up with the idea of work–identity integrity violations: an idea that became the heart of the paper.

In addition to the wonderful resources out there, there are a few practical things to consider while interviewing individuals. To begin, *know that the protocol is just a guide, and that it is okay to ask questions in a different order.* Ideally your interview will be experienced more like a conversation than a series of questions to be rattled off in a rigid order. Sometimes to make this more natural, you might follow up with questions in a way that fits how the informant is already talking. For example, pretend you have one section in your protocol that asks about the work that an individual does at work, and another about what he or she does at home. In the course of answering a grand tour question where a person is taking you through a typical day, the informant might mention that before work he takes his son to school, and that he has some of his best conversations with his son at that time. He may then choose to discuss this aspect of his morning routine for a while. Rather than pulling him back to what goes on at the office, you might talk more about this part of his morning, essentially skipping to later questions. Once you come to a natural end to that conversation, you can go back to the grand tour question about what happens at work.

Table 1.1 Spradley's (1979) a sample of interview question types

Interview question types	Descriptive	Structural	Contrast
What it is	• Asking informants broad questions whereby they need to describe something (e.g., an event, a typical day, how someone would say something)	• Asking informants about how they organize information (e.g., how many ways can a project succeed?)	• After discovering the differences in two terms (i.e., "folk terms") you ask informants to confirm or disconfirm what you have found.
Specific interview question types	• Grand Tour questions ○ Typical (e.g., typical day) ○ Specific (e.g., last night) ○ Guided (e.g., show me around the office) ○ Task-related (e.g., draw me a map)	• Verification (e.g., is this right?)	• Contrast verification questions (e.g., can you tell me if I have got this right – that you do 'y' when doing 'x' but 'b' when doing 'a'?)
	• Mini-Tour (smaller scale than grand tour – e.g., how do you "let someone go?")	• Cover questions (e.g., are there other types of ....?)	• Directed contrast questions (e.g., in looking at all cases of 'x', under which circumstances will you need to do 'r' in order to do 'x'?)
	• Example (e.g., can you give me an example of ...?)	• Included domain (e.g., is 'x' a type of 'y'?)	• Dyadic contrast questions (e.g., what, if any, differences exist between 'a' and 'b'?)
	• Experience (e.g., you must have had some experience in ....)	• Substitution questions (e.g., you find 'x' people in organizations. What other types do you find?)	• Triadic contrast questions (e.g., of 'a', 'b', and 'c', which two are most similar and which one is most dissimilar?)
	• Native Language ○ Direct language (e.g., how would you refer to...?) ○ Hypothetical-Interaction (e.g., if you met another CEO, would you say it this way?) ○ Typical-Sentence: use a term in a typical sentence	• Card sorting structural questions (take native terms and have informants respond to them).	• Contrast set sorting questions: make a pile of terms and ask informants to sort them into two or more piles based on how the terms are similar and dissimilar • Rating questions: rate 'a' through 'e' by which is the most to least difficult to do

Second and similarly, *feel free to go "off roading" and ask questions that are not on your protocol.* Mike has seen many new interviewers (himself included) who were afraid to go beyond the questions asked in the protocol in fear that one would not get to all of the questions in the allotted time. Part of this anxiety stems from the fact that people want to ask similar questions of everyone in order to compare them during data analysis. However, one critical part of the ethnographic experience is changing your questions to fit your emerging knowledge. How then do you compare individuals if you do not ask them all the same questions? There are a few ways to do this. To begin, remember that in ethnographies, you may be interviewing the same person (e.g., a key informant) multiple times. If you interview multiple people, multiple times, it is easier to go back and ask them questions that are similar to those that you asked of others. Barring that, you might be able to go back to people you interviewed to ask some follow-up questions. Another approach is to ensure that, while you might not ask everyone the same questions, be sure to that every question is asked of at least a few informants. In addition, it is important to remember that not every question needs verification by *all* members. For example, questions about the ordering of an event may be relatively established after asking a handful of informants, so there may not be a need to keep asking the question. Other questions, such as how the group defines its purpose, or which groups are seen as the "competition" (and why), may be worth getting a broader set of informants. As a rule of thumb, the more contested or complex the issue, the more people you might like to ask about it.

When considering where to interview, you might want to consider meeting somewhere on or near where the group normally works. Being at work may "cue" work-related memories and identities. Ideally, you can interview the person in her or his office, if that person has a door or works in a quiet/low-traffic area. This may allow for a private conversation. However, if you are interviewing someone in an office, ask that the person to forward his or her phone calls (if possible), try to ensure that the computer in the office is not on, and ask the person if they could block out the time as "unavailable" on a public schedule or let his or her administrative assistant know. These will cut down on the potential interruptions during an interview. Depending on the status of the informant (and your own status), it may not be appropriate or comfortable to demand too much in this arena, but you can always ask politely. For those whose time is at a premium, you might suggest that the interview will be shorter if there are fewer interruptions.

If an office is not available, you might try for a small conference room. Big conference rooms may play havoc, acoustically, with your recording equipment. [As an aside, we always try to record our interviews – and Mike has learned the hard way to use both a primary and back-up recording device (see also Hinds & Crampton, this volume). There may be some debate over the use of such recording devices and how they influence how people answer questions, but we tend to find that people ignore these devices once the interview has started.] No matter what the size of the conference room is, be sure to set it up before the informant enters. For example, always be sure to arrange the seats so that the informant does not sit very far from you. It is awkward to set up at one end of the table and have your informant enter and sit at the opposite end. If there are multiple chairs, Mike will often put off to the side all of the "extra chairs" so that the informant has only one place to sit.

Najung found out the hard way about meeting in an office or private conference room. An informant told her that the only place she could be interviewed was a common area near the entrance of her workplace building. Despite it being after work hours, several colleagues passed through the common area during the course of the interview. Not surprisingly, the informant stopped speaking each time someone passed by, significantly interrupting the flow of the conversation and likely influencing the quality of the data obtained.

If there is not an office or a small conference room where the group perform their jobs, then you might consider an off-site area. *Do not*, unless you absolutely have to, interview at a restaurant or public café. It may sound convenient for the informant to "do lunch" during an interview, but it is a huge hassle for the interviewer. Here are our top five reasons for avoiding these places for interviews (not in any particular order). First, voice recorders often pick up background noise in restaurants, making the quality of the voice record difficult to transcribe. Second, it is hard to establish rapport with an informant when someone is coming up periodically to ask you "how things are" and "whether you want some more iced tea." Invariably, such interruptions come during the discussion of sensitive topics. Third, and especially if you are in a small town, you might get a visit from someone you or the informant knows – even the person's co-worker/team mate. While you might be able to extricate yourself quickly, it is more difficult once they see the tape recorder and want to know what you are doing. And if the person you are interviewing was hesitant to interview before, especially if they are concerned with anonymity, then such an encounter can be devastating. Fourth, the informant may find it difficult to eat and talk – and may prioritize the former over the latter. Last, but not least, people may be hesitant to talk about sensitive topics in public during the interview. So if you need to find a place off-site, you might use your own office or a small conference room in your own building.

Finally, there are unique issues that arise when you are interviewing intact teams, especially if you know that team members talk with each other frequently. Perhaps the biggest issue is that you have to be even more careful about the interview process in these situations, because you can quickly get a reputation based on how earlier interviews go. While it is rare that we would ever challenge an informant (e.g., bring up the inconsistencies in their own stories, confront them about a known lie), it would be an especially bad thing to do during the first interviews with a cohesive group. If you get a reputation as a "jerk" with one team member, you'll likely have it with most or all of them. You should also be wary that the content of your interview protocol may spread. When Mike was studying residency groups, there were times during interviews when someone would say, "I heard you were going to ask me this." Sometimes team members will even come up with theories about why you are asking certain questions, so be open to "listening" for them. In one interview, for example, an informant whom Mike had interviewed multiple times was acting strangely. When he explored the reasons for this, it became clear that people in his cohort were convinced that he was trying to get "dirt" on their residency program chairs. He addressed the concern with this informant, and soon this information spread to others in this person's cohort.

New "tools" for ethnographic studies: Video ethnography and netnography

As we indicated at the start of this section on "tools," there are two relatively new ways to conduct ethnography that sometimes bypass a fundamental aspect of traditional ethnographies: physically being in the field with your informants. However, like traditional ethnographies, both video ethnography and netnography are focused on studying the cultures of groups.

Video ethnography

Video ethnography is an ethnographic analysis of video recordings that allows researchers to analyze detailed physical and verbal interactions in great depth. While it is possible to do the video recording yourself, it is more common that the video you analyze has been filmed by someone else. If taking the more common route, you can opt simply to analyze a video that someone else collected for a study, similar to an archival analysis. Alternatively, you may have someone film your own interactions with a group, allowing yourself the chance to observe your own behavior and interactions with others in the group and analyze them. This ability to see your own interactions with a group is a unique opportunity afforded by video ethnography. Another unique strength of video ethnography is that video technology allows you to repeat, revisit, and thus "re-observe" the same scene multiple times. Consequently, video ethnography is a good option if your research question requires interaction analysis (Goffman, 1961, 1966, 1971, 1981; Hughes, 1971): a type of analysis premised on the notion that "talk and bodily conduct are … the primary vehicles through which people accomplish social activities and events" (Heath & Hindmarsh, 2002, p. 104).

Given its strength in capturing verbal and nonverbal interactions, video ethnography has been extensively used in communication research, qualitative sociology, and educational psychology to examine: (a) nonverbal cues, such as behavioral, physical movements, facial expressions; (b) relationships between these nonverbal cues and utterances; (c) the interactive relationship between physical settings and human interactions; as well as (d) the verbal communication that people generate while talking or interacting with others. [See the following for an overview of this method: Ellis & Bochner (2002); Gottman & Notarius (2000); Hall, Murphy, & Mast (2006); Lebaron & Streeck (1997); MacMartin & LeBaron (2006); Maynard (1992); Perakyla (1998); Pilnick & Hindmarsh (1999); Rich & Chalfen (1999); ten Have (1991); and Weingart, Olekalns, & Smith (2004).] While good in these situations, video ethnography also comes with some unique drawbacks as well.

To illustrate, this form of ethnography has the potential to lead to the depersonalization of your informants. During the data collection process and also the data analysis stage, researchers can detach themselves from the actual human beings filmed in video tapes, which hinders one's ability to see the world through the eyes of an informant. Moreover, bogged down by the detailed movements and verbal cues in the video, researchers can easily think of these individuals as objects rather than thinking about them as humans. There are also technical issues involved, whether one does the actual filming (e.g., checking cameras, recorders, videotapes, lighting, location of the camera, etc.) or not (e.g., assessing proper speed of playback functions, decisions regarding the use of software to code data). Finally, video ethnography also raises some unique ethical issues. It is important to keep in mind that these individuals are exposed (i.e., vulnerable to identification) whenever you play the video. Thus, its use requires a greater effort to protect the anonymity of an informant's identity than it would if you were doing a more traditional ethnography. Consequently, there may be heightened concerns from one's local IRB, unless of course the videos you are analyzing are in the public domain.

Netnography

Netnography is a "qualitative research methodology that adapts ethnographic research techniques to study the cultures and communities that are emerging through computer-mediated communications" (Kozinets, 2002, p. 62). More specifically, netnographies most often involve observation of electronic bulletin boards (e.g., newsgroups), web-pages, listservs, email exchanges, multiuser games (dungeons), and chat rooms. Because it was created by a consumer and marketing researcher (Kozinets, 1998), most studies have focused on behaviors and attitudes of online consumer groups (e.g., Beaven, 2007; Daugherty, Lee, Gangadharbatla, Kim, & Outhavong, 2005; Giesler, 2006; Jeppesen & Frederiksen, 2006; Kozinets, 2001, 2006; Maulana & Eckhardt, 2007). However, netnographies have potential for examining organizational groups as well (e.g., internal message boards of companies). The data one gathers in netnographies are typically textual (e.g., conversations among members of an online forum saved as text files and/or the researcher's written field notes); but one may also gather visual data (e.g., print screens). As one moves towards gathering more visual data, the pros and cons of this approach become similar to those of video ethnography.

When employing this method, researchers can range in terms of how overt or covert one is, or how active a participant one is, in the online community being examined. As with traditional ethnographies, your choice of how to observe depends on your research question. Beyond that, there is some differing advice given about what is the best way to observe online groups. For example, some suggest that your default should be to identify yourself as a researcher when observing an online community (Kozinets, 2002). Langer & Beckman (2005), however, suggest that one may want to be more covert when examining sensitive topics; but as we have discussed above, covert observation is often frowned upon by IRBs. Given the public nature of online groups, such concerns may be attenuated somewhat. Kozinets (2002) suggests that covert observation should only be considered when one can access the online group without having to apply for membership, that is, the group is fully in the public realm. Of course, one's local IRB may have its own guidelines. Regarding how active one should be in group activities, the general tendency has been to conduct netnographies using nonparticipant observations (e.g., lurking). But more recent thinking on netnographies involves more active participation (Kozinets, 2006), bringing netnographies more in line with ethnography's participant observation focus.

There are several strengths of the netnography. First, in contrast to traditional ethnographies, time and resources spent on collecting data are often much less. For example, not only is access often easier to negotiate, the extent of your travel may be walking to your office computer, and some of your data comes to you "transcribed." Also, depending on the size of the community as well as one's observational status (e.g., covert versus overt), the researcher may have to worry less that his or her presence in an online community will unduly influence the behaviors and attitudes of the members of that community. Third, because these members in the online communities can use pseudonyms or go incognito, they may feel more comfortable talking about sensitive issues, and may be more willing to share their true thoughts regarding an issue without pressure to answer in a socially desirable way.

One of the more unique limitations of netnographies, however, includes the lack of informant identifiers. This anonymity may have at least three undesirable consequences. First, in contrast to arguments that individuals may be more honest online, it may that individuals use their online personas to lie about their attitudes or behaviors, or to manipulate others' perceptions on them. Second, because you cannot track down the informants, it is harder to ask them follow-up questions. And without follow-ups, you have to rely more on your own interpretation of informants' statements rather than their own. Third, it is often difficult, if not impossible, to assess characteristics which may supplement one's interpretation of data. For example, pretend you are assessing a reaction to a new organizational policy on a corporate intranet. It would be interesting to know if "ReginaN", "SmithM" and "WangL" are male or female and whether they are relatively young or old in order to better understand trends in group members' responses.

The ethnographic study of online communities is currently a growing and contested domain, often using different terms to describe their studies, for example, "webnography" (Puri, 2007), or "online ethnography" (Markham, 2007). While netnography appears to be the best developed in terms of its methods at this time, it will be interesting to see how they and similar approaches develop when applied to organizational groups.

Concluding thoughts

At this point, we've discussed what you need to do in order to prepare yourself to do an ethnographic study of a group (although all ethnographies are, at some level, group ethnographies). Of course, one must go beyond preparation. Once you have constructed a research question, designed your protocols, gained access, passed through your IRB, and obtained any technology you might want to use (e.g., voice recorder, video camera, transcribing aids) for collecting observations and interviews, you actually have to collect the data, analyze it, and write it up. Explaining all of these would take us well beyond our page limits. However, we would like to close by suggesting the following three books that we have found to be particularly good regarding ethnographic research.

- Spradley (1979) *The Ethnographic Interview*. As noted above, this is a great source on doing ethnography, especially designing, conducting, and analyzing ethnographic interviews.
- Fetterman (1998) *Ethnography*, 2nd edition. Written by an anthropologist, this book mixes traditional ethnography with other techniques; not a "purist's" guide, but handy for the beginning ethnographer.
- Van Maanen (1988) *Tales of the Field: on Writing Ethnography*. A great book about the different kinds of voices you can use when writing up qualitative research – even if journals may want you to write in the dispassionate, third person "realist" voice.

In addition, when writing up any or all qualitative research, we could encourage you to read Golden-Biddle and Locke's (2006) *Composing Qualitative Research*. And if you want to publish your research in a top-tier North American management journal, you might take a peek at Mike's (Pratt, 2008, 2009) musings on the topic as an editor, author, and reviewer.

Finally, we noted at the start that ethnographies involve both drift and design. Perhaps by the nature of writing these things down, we tended more toward design than drift. However, we truly believe that you need to *design for drift*. We believe that by thinking through and planning for some of these issues, this allow you to free up some "head space" so that you can follow up interesting leads, be creative in your observations, and allow the research project to take you in new and potentially fruitful directions.

Authors' Note:

We'd like to thank Beth Bechky, Lakshmi Balachandra, Andrea Hollingshead, and Scott Poole for their comments on earlier drafts of this chapter.

References

Angrosino, M., & Perez, K. (2005). Rethinking observation: From method to context. In N. Denzin, & Y. Lincoln (Eds.), *Handbook of qualitative research* (2nd ed., pp. 673–715). Thousand Oaks, CA: Sage.

Barnett, C. K., & Pratt, M. G. (2000). From threat-rigidity to flexibility: Toward a learning model of autogenic crisis in organizations. *Journal of Organizational Change Management, 13*(1), 74–88.

Beaven, Z. (2007). 'Never let me down again': Loyal customer attitudes towards ticket distribution channels for live music events: A netnographic exploration of the US leg of the depeche mode 2005–2006 world tour. *Managing Leisure, 12*(2), 120–142.

Bechky, B. A., & Okhuysen, G. A. (2011). Expecting the unexpected? How SWAT officers and film crews handle surprises. *Academy of Management Journal, 54*(2), 239–261.

Daugherty, T., Lee, W. N., Gangadharbatla, H., Kim, K., & Outhavong, S. (2005). Organizational virtual communities: Exploring motivations behind online panel participation. *Journal of Computer-Mediated Communication, 10*(4), article 9.

Douglas, J. (1976). *Investigative social research: Individual and team field research.* Beverly Hills, CA: Sage.

Ellis, C., & Bochner, A. P. (2002). Symbolic interaction in restrospect: A conversation with Norma Denzin. *Studies in Symbolic Interaction, 25*, 179–198.

Feldman, M. S., Bell, J., & Berger, M. T. (2003). *Gaining access: A practical and theoretical guide for qualitative researchers.* Walnut Creek, CA: Rowman Altamira.

Fetterman, D. M. (1998). *Ethnography: Step by step* (2nd ed.). Thousand Oaks, CA: Sage.

Giesler, M. (2006). Consumer gift systems. *Journal of Consumer Research, 33*(2), 283–290.

Goffman, E. (1961). *Asylums.* New York: Doubleday.

Goffman, E. (1966). *Behavior in public places.* New York: Free Press.

Goffman, E. (1971). *Relations in public: Microstudies of the public order.* New York: Basic Books.

Goffman, E. (1981). *Forms of talk.* Philadelphia, PA: University of Pennsylvania Press.

Gold, R. L. (1957/1958). Roles in sociological field observations. *Social Forces, 36*(1/4), 217–223.

Golden-Biddle, K., & Locke, K. (2006). *Composing qualitative research.* Thousand Oaks, CA: Sage.

Gottman, J. M., & Notarius, C. I. (2000). Decade review: Observing marital interaction. *Journal of Marriage and the Family, 62*(4), 927–947.

Gunsalus, C. K., Bruner, E. M., Burbules, N. C., Dash, L., Finkin, M., Goldberg, J. P., et al. (2007). The Illinois white paper: Improving the system for protecting human subjects: Counteracting IRB "mission creep." *Qualitative Inquiry, 13*(5), 617–649.

Hall, J. A., Murphy, N. A., & Mast, M. S. (2006). Recall of nonverbal cues: Exploring a new definition of interpersonal sensitivity. *Journal of Nonverbal Behavior, 30*(4), 141–155.

Heath, C., & Hindmarsh, J. (2002). Analysing interaction: Video, ethnography and situated conduct. In T. May (Ed.), *Qualitative Research* (pp. 99–121). London: Sage.

Hughes, E. C. (1971). *The sociological eye: Selected papers on work, self, & the study of society.* Chicago, IL: Aldine-Atherton.

Jeppesen, L. B., & Frederiksen, L. (2006). Why do users contribute to firm-hosted user communities? *Organization Science, 17*(1), 45–63.

Kayser-Jones, J. (2002). The experience of dying: An ethnographic nursing home study. *The Gerontologist, 42*(3), 11–19.

Kozinets, R.V. (1998). On netnography: Initial reflections on consumer research investigations of cyberculture. *Advances in Consumer Research, 25*(1), 366–371.

Kozinets, R.V. (2001). Utopian enterprise: Articulating the meanings of star trek's culture of consumption. *Journal of Consumer Research, 28*(1), 67–88.

Kozinets, R.V. (2002). The field behind the screen: Using netnography for marketing research in online communities. *Journal of Marketing Research, 39*(1), 61–72.

Kozinets, R.V. (2006). Click to connect: Netnography and tribal advertising. *Journal of Advertising Research, 46*(3), 279–288.

Kvale, S., & Brinkmann, S. (2008). *Interviews: An introduction to qualitative research interviewing.* Thousand Oaks, CA: Sage.

Langer, R., & Beckman, S. C. (2005). Sensitive research topics: Netnography revisited. *Qualitative Market Research: An International Journal, 8,* 189–203.

Lebaron, C. D., & Streeck, J. (1997). Built space and the interactional framing of experience during a murder interrogation. *Human Studies, 20*(1), 1–25.

MacMartin, C., & LeBaron, C. D. (2006). Multiple involvements within group interaction: A video-based study of sex offender therapy. *Research on Language & Social Interaction, 39*(1), 41–80.

Markham, A. N. (2007). The methods, politics, and ethics of representation in online ethnography. In L. K. Denzin and Y. S. Lincoln (Eds.), *Handbook of qualitative research* (3rd ed., pp. 793–820). Thousand Oaks, CA: Sage.

Marshall, C., & Rossman, G. (1989). *Designing qualitative research* (2nd ed.). Newbury Park, CA: Sage.

Maulana, A. E., & Eckhardt, G. M. (2007). Just friends, good acquaintances or soul mates? An exploration of web site connectedness. *Qualitative Market Research: An International Journal, 10*(3), 227–242.

Maynard, D.W. (1992). On clinicians co-implicating recipients' perspective in the delivery of diagnostic news. In P. Drew, & J. Heritage (Eds.), *Talk at work: Interaction in institutional settings* (pp. 331–358). Cambridge, MA: Cambridge University Press.

McGrath, J. E. (1982). Dilemmatics: The study of research choices and dilemmas. *American Behavioral Scientist, 25*(2), 179–210.

Mead, M. (1928 [2001]). *Coming of age in Samoa.* New York: HarperCollins.

Miles, M. B., & Huberman, A. M. (1994). *Qualitative data analysis.* Beverly Hills, CA: Sage.

Patton, M. 1990. *Qualitative evaluation and research methods* (2nd ed.). Newbury Park, CA: Sage.

Perakyla, A. (1998). Authority and accountability: The delivery of diagnosis in primary health care. *Social Psychology Quarterly, 61*(4), 301–320.

Peshkin, A. (1984). Odd man out: The participant observer in an absolutist setting. *Sociology of Education, 57*(4), 254–264.

Pettigrew, A. (1990). Longitudinal field research on change: Theory and practice. *Organization Science, 1*(3), 267–292.

Pilnick, A., & Hindmarsh, J. (1999). "When you wake up it'll all be over": Communication in the anaesthetic room. *Symbolic Interaction, 22*(4), 345–360.

Pratt, M. G. (2000a). The good, the bad, and the ambivalent: Managing identification among Amway distributors. *Administrative Science Quarterly, 45*(3), 456–493.

Pratt, M. G. (2000b). Building an ideological fortress: The role of spirituality, encapsulation, and sensemaking. *Studies in Cultures, Organizations, and Societies, 6*(1), 35–69.

Pratt, M. G. (2003). Access as relating: On the relationship aspects of different types of access. In M. S. Feldman, J. Bell, & M. T. Berger (Eds.), *Gaining access: A practical and theoretical guide for qualitative researchers* (pp. 150–154). Walnut Creek, CA: Rowman Altamira.

Pratt, M. G. (2008). Fitting oval pegs into round holes: Tensions in evaluating and publishing qualitative research in top-tier North American journals. *Organizational Research Methods, 11*(3), 481–509.

Pratt, M.G. (2009). For the lack of a boilerplate: Tips on writing up (and reviewing) qualitative research. *Academy of Management Journal, 52*(5): 856–862.

Pratt, M. G., & Rafaeli, A. (1997). Organizational dress as a symbol of multilayered social identities. *Academy of Management Journal, 40*(4), 862–898.

Pratt, M. G., Rockmann, K. W., & Kaufmann, J. B. (2006). Constructing professional identity: The role of work and identity learning cycles in the customization of identity among medical residents. *Academy of Management Journal, 49*(2), 235–262.

Pratt, M. G., & Rosa, J. A. (2003). Transforming work–family conflict into commitment in network marketing organizations. *Academy of Management Journal, 46*(4), 395–418.

Puri, A. (2007). The web of insights: The art and practice of webnography. *The Market Research Society, 49*(3), 387–408.

Rich, M., & Chalfen, R. (1999). Showing and telling asthma: Children teaching physicians with visual narrative. *Visual Studies, 14*(1), 51–71.

Rosen, M. (1991). Scholars, travelers, and thieves: On concept, method, and cunning in organizational ethnography. In P. J. Frost, L. F. Moore, & M. R. Louis (Eds.), *Reframing organizational culture* (pp. 271–284). Newbury Park, CA: Sage.

Rubin, H. J., & Rubin, I. (2005). *Qualitative interviewing: The art of hearing data.* Thousand Oaks, CA: Sage.

Schein, E. H. (2004). *Organizational culture and leadership* (3rd ed.). San Francisco, CA: Jossey-Bass.

Seidman, I. (1998). *Interviewing as qualitative research: A guide for researchers in education and the social sciences.* New York: Teachers College Press.

Spradley, J. (1979). *The ethnographic interview.* New York: Holt Reinhardt.

ten Have, P. (1991). Talk and institution: A reconsideration of the "asymmetry" of doctor–patient interaction. In D. Boden, & D. H. Zimmerman (Eds.), *Talk and social structure* (pp. 138–163). Cambridge, UK: Polity Press.

Van Maanen, J. (1973). Observations on the making of policemen. *Human Organization, 32*(4), 407–418.

Van Maanen, J. (1979). The fact of fiction in organizational ethnography. *Administrative Science Quarterly, 24*(4), 539–550.

Van Maanen, J. (1988). *Tales of the field: On writing ethnography.* Chicago, IL: University of Chicago Press.

Venkatesh, S. A. (2002). "Doin' the hustle:" Constructing the ethnographer in the American ghetto. *Ethnography, 31*(1): 91–111.

Weingart, L. R., Olekalns, M., & Smith, P. L. (2004). Quantitative coding of negotiation behavior. *International Negotiation, 9*(3), 441–455.

Whyte, W. H. (1984). *Learning from the field: A guide from experience.* Beverly Hills, CA: Sage.

Wolcott, H. (1994). Confessions of a "trained" observer. *Transforming qualitative data* (pp. 152–172). Thousand Oaks, CA: Sage.

2

EXPERIMENTAL DESIGNS FOR RESEARCH ON SMALL GROUPS

The Five Ps

Patrick R. Laughlin

UNIVERSITY OF ILLINOIS AT URBANA–CHAMPAIGN

As richly attested in the chapters of this book, small groups are studied in many disciplines, including anthropology, behavioral accounting, behavioral economics, communications, management, media studies, organizational behavior, political science, social psychology, social work, and sociology, and by many methods, including laboratory experiments, surveys, participant and external observation, discourse analysis, archival research, and increasingly in our technologically integrated world, by the vast resources of the World Wide Web and the internet.

This chapter considers illustrative experimental designs for laboratory experiments on small groups. Laboratory experiments entail the full power and logic of the scientific method: (a) test of hypotheses, whether point predictions mathematically derived from quantitatively formulated theory, predictions deductively derived from well-formulated theory, less formal predictions suggested by previous results, plausible intuitions, or pure exploratory curiosity; (b) random assignment of participants to experimental conditions; (c) accepted methods of analysis of the results; and (d) accepted criteria of inference from the analyses.

Experimental designs in small group research are embedded within the "Five Ps:" Problems, Procedures, Processes, Performances, and Principles. *Problems* are questions about small group phenomena. For example, do groups perform better than individuals on logical reasoning? How do groups combine or aggregate the different beliefs or preferences of the group members, such as correct or incorrect on a geometric proof, or guilty or not guilty in a jury trial, in a collective group response? What is the effect of group experience on subsequent group member learning, beliefs, or preferences?

Procedures include the research setting, the group task and objective, the structure of the group such as roles of formal leader or group recorder, demographic and personality variables such as gender and extroversion, and the norms of expected behavior such as careful consideration of the views of other members.

Processes are how the group members interact with each other and influence each other in achieving the objective of the group task. Processes may be assessed as in classical rhetorical theory and current discourse analyses by who says what to whom under what circumstances with what effect. Processes may also be assessed by proposing formal models such as unanimity or majority by which groups combine the beliefs or preferences of the group members in a collective response and competitively testing the predictions of the models against the obtained data. Baron and Kerr (2002) call these two approaches to understanding group processes the social influence approach and the social combination approach.

Performances are what the groups do, such as propose a solution, make a judgment, decide guilt or innocence, or write a report. The correspondence between what the groups do and the objective of the group task defines the degree of success or failure.

Principles state the generalized relationships between independent and dependent variables. Sets of principles may then be incorporated into theories that provide understanding of the phenomena of interest. Principles are also called postulates or propositions.

We now consider illustrative problems that have motivated experimental research on small groups and present corresponding experimental designs.

Problem One: Do Groups Perform Differently from Individuals?

Symbolizing a group condition as G and an individual condition as I, we may schematize the design of an experiment to investigate Problem One as Design 1.

Condition 1:   G   Design 1
Condition 2:   I

Each participant is randomly assigned to either the group or individual condition.

Design 1 has been widely used in research on group versus individual performance on memory, learning, problem solving, decision making, evaluative judgments (attitudes), allocation of resources, and other tasks. For example, extensive research on group versus individual problem solving has supported the robust generalization that groups perform better than the average individual on a wide range of tasks (for illustrative reviews, see Hastie, 1986; Hill, 1982; Kerr & Tindale, 2003; Levine & Moreland, 1998; Stasser & Dietz-Uhler, 2001).

Problem Two: What are the Social Combination Processes by which Groups Map a Distribution of Group Member Beliefs or Preferences to a Collective Group Response?

Many groups combine or aggregate the preferences of their members for different alternatives by some process such as unanimity, majority, or truth wins (a single correct member suffices for a correct group response) to formulate a collective response. What are these social combination processes?

Assume that a number of individuals first respond to some measure of memory, problem solving, decision making, attitudes, allocation of resources, and so forth. Some of these individuals are then randomly assigned to respond to the same measure as a cooperative group, and some to respond again as individuals. We may schematize this as Design 2.

	Administration		
	One	Two	Design 2
Condition 1:	I	G	
Condition 2:	I	I	

Since the individual responses at Administration One are known, the composition of the groups (e.g., in a six-person group, five members are correct and one member is incorrect) at Administration Two are known, Design 2 therefore can test different social combination models such as majority wins or truth wins. For example, both Laughlin and Ellis (1986) and Stasson, Kameda, Parks, Zimmerman, and Davis (1991) found that five-person groups followed a truth-wins process on elementary algebra, geometry, and probability problems, where a single correct individual at Administration One sufficed for a correct group response on Administration Two. In general, tests of social combination models have found that the proportion of group members that is necessary and sufficient for a collective group response (problem solution, decision, judgment, choice, etc.) is inversely proportional to the demonstrability of the proposed group response (Laughlin & Ellis, 1986).

Competitive tests of the social combination processes may also be conducted from the control individuals on Administration Two; see Davis (1973) for the underlying logic and analytic methods.

Problem Three: What is the Effect of Group Experience on Subsequent Group Member Responses?

We now expand Design 2 to a third individual administration measure of memory, problem solving, decision making, attitudes, allocation of resources, and so forth.

	Administration			
	One	Two	Three	Design 3
Condition 1:	I	G	I	
Condition 2:	I	I	I	

Design 3 addresses *group-to-individual transfer.* Transfer may be *specific,* where the same task is repeated on the third administration, or *general,* where the third task is a new problem, decision, or judgment, etc. of the same general class. For example, Laughlin and Ellis (1986) demonstrated specific transfer with Design 3 when the same ten algebra, geometry, and probability problems were administered three times, and Stasson et al. (1991) demonstrated general transfer with Design 3 by using the same five algebra, geometry, and probability problems for the first two administrations, and then new problems that could be solved by the same general equation or approach on the third administration.

Problem Four: What is the Effect of Repeated Group Experience on Group-to-Individual Transfer?

The previous illustrative studies of Laughlin and Ellis (1986) and Stasson et al. (1991) on group-to-individual transfer used a single training session and a single transfer session, assessing two issues: (a) group versus individual training perform-ance (Problem Two); and (b) group-to-individual transfer (Problem Three). Laughlin, Carey, and Kerr (2008) used Design 4 to address two further issues: (c) sufficiency and (d) completeness. Sufficiency is the issue whether one training session is sufficient for group-to-individual transfer. Completeness is the issue whether group-to-individual transfer is complete (i.e., whether individual per-formance on the transfer problems is at the level of performance by comparably experienced groups on the same problems).

	Administration				Design 4
	One	Two	Three	Four	
Condition 1:	G	G	G	G	
Condition 2:	G	G	G	I	
Condition 3:	G	G	I	I	
Condition 4:	G	I	I	I	
Condition 5:	I	I	I	I	

The group or individual task was to solve letters-to–numbers problems as presented on an interactive computer terminal. The ten letters A, B, C, D, E, F, G, H, I, J were randomly coded without replacement to the ten numbers 0, 1, 2, 3, 4, 5, 6, 7, 8, 9 (e.g., A = 3, B = 5, etc.). Instructions explained that the objective was to identify the complete coding in as few trials as possible. Each trial for the groups consisted of four stages: (a) the group members discussed and proposed an expression in any number of letters and the operators of addition and subtraction (e.g., A + B =?, AB + G =?, D + E + J − C =?); (b) the computer gave feedback on the answer in letters (e.g., A + B = G); (c) the group discussed and proposed a number for one or more letters (e.g., A = 6, J = 4); (d) the computer indicated whether proposed numbers were correct or incorrect. The full correct coding solved the problem, whereas anything less than the full correct coding required another trial.

Sets of three persons solved four problems as cooperative groups or individuals on separate terminals. For example, in Condition 2 they solved three problems as a group and then separated to solve the fourth problem as individuals. The groups performed better than the individuals on each problem. Group-to-individual transfer occurred on each of Problems Two, Three, and Four. One group experience was sufficient for transfer to occur. Transfer was complete on Problems Two and Three, but not on Problem Four, due to exceptional performance by the groups in Condition 1.

Problem Five: Do Groups Perform Better than the Best of an Equivalent Number of Individuals and Does This Depend upon Group Size?

Recall the well-established finding that groups perform better than individuals on a wide range of problems. Virtually all of this research has compared an equal number of groups and individuals (say, 40 three-person groups and 40 individuals). With random assignment to group and individual conditions, this compares groups and the average individual. A more stringent test of group versus individual performance would compare groups of a given size with the best of an equivalent number of individuals (say, 40 three-person groups and the best 40 of $(40 \times 3) = 120$ individuals).

Laughlin, Hatch, Silver, and Boh (2006) used Design 5 to address Problem Five by comparing 40 two-person groups with the best 40 of 80 individuals, 40 three-person groups with the best 40 of 120 individuals, 40 four-person groups with the best 40 of 160 individuals, and 40 five-person groups with the best 40 of 200 individuals.

Condition 1:	200 individuals	Design 5
Condition 2:	40 two-person groups	
Condition 3:	40 three-person groups	
Condition 4:	40 four-person groups	
Condition 5:	40 five-person groups	

The 40 five-person groups had significantly fewer trials to solution than the 40 best of the 200 individuals. Four of the five individuals were randomly selected from each of the 40 replications, and the four-person groups had significantly fewer trials to solution than the 40 best individuals. Similarly, three of the five individuals were randomly selected from each of the 40 replications, and the three-person groups had significantly fewer trials to solution than the 40 best of 120 individuals; two of the five individuals were randomly selected from each of the 40 replications, and the two-person groups performed at the level of the best 40 of the 80 individuals and better than the second-best individuals. In summary, groups of size three, four, and five performed better than the best of an equivalent number of individuals, but groups of size two performed at the level of the best of two individuals.

Design 5 also addresses the effect of increasing group size. The groups of size three, four, and five performed better than groups of size two but did not differ from each other. In conclusion, groups of size three were necessary and sufficient to perform better than the best of an equivalent number of individuals on the highly intellective letters-to-numbers problems.

Problem Six: What is the Relative Importance of Multiple Hypotheses and Multiple Evidence in Collective Induction?

Collective induction is the cooperative search for generalizations, rules, and principles. Groups such as scientific research teams or auditing teams observe patterns, regularities, and relationships, propose hypotheses to explain them, and conduct experiments to evaluate the predictions from the hypotheses. If the observations and experiments support the predictions, the hypotheses become more plausible; if the results fail to support the predictions, the hypotheses are revised or rejected.

In an experiment by Laughlin and Bonner (1999) four-person groups induced a rule that partitioned ordinary playing cards of four suits (clubs, diamonds, hearts, spades) and 13 cards per suit (ace, deuce, … king) into examples and nonexamples of the rule. Aces were assigned the numerical value 1, deuces 2, treys 3, …, tens 10, jacks 11, queens 12, kings 13. The rule could be based on any characteristics of the cards, such as suit (e.g., diamonds; spades), number (e.g., eights; jacks; multiples of three), or any numerical and/or logical operations on suit and number of any degree of complexity (e.g., diamond or spade jacks; diamonds eight and above, or spades seven and below; two clubs alternate with two hearts; two even clubs alternate with two odd hearts).

The instructions to the groups explained that the objective was to induce a rule that partitions ordinary playing cards into examples and nonexamples of the rule in as few trials as possible. The problem began with a known positive example of the rule, such as the eight of diamonds for the rule "two diamonds alternate with two clubs," placed on a table. A trial consisted of the following four stages. First, each group member wrote his or her hypothesis (proposed correct rule) on a member hypothesis sheet. Second, the group members discussed until they reached a consensus on a group hypothesis, which a randomly selected group recorder wrote on a group hypothesis sheet. Third, the group members discussed to consensus on the play of any of the 52 cards on each of four arrays. Fourth, the experimenter classified the card on each array as either an example or nonexample of the correct rule. Examples were placed to the right of the known example on the table, and nonexamples were placed below the known example. As this cycle continued on successive trials, four progressive arrays of examples and nonexamples developed in the order of play. There were ten trials of hypotheses and card plays, with no feedback on either member or group hypothesis until after the final trial.

The groups solved rule-induction problems in one of the nine conditions of a 3 × 3 factorial design, inducing the rule from one, two, or four arrays (sets of card plays) and proposing one, two, or four hypotheses per trial, as in Design 6

	Hypotheses	Arrays	
Condition 1	One	One	Design 6
Condition 2	One	Two	
Condition 3	One	Four	
Condition 4	Two	One	
Condition 5	Two	Two	
Condition 6	Two	Four	
Condition 7	Four	One	
Condition 8	Four	Two	
Condition 9	Four	Four	

Performance improved with increasing arrays of evidence (card plays) but not with increasing hypotheses. This suggests that multiple evidence is relatively more important than multiple hypotheses in collective induction. Groups may be able to propose sufficient hypotheses to induce the rule, but they need evidence to evaluate the hypotheses.

Principles

Consideration of the aggregate body of findings from experimental research in an area may lead to the formulation of *Principles (Postulates, Propositions)*. For example, Laughlin and Hollingshead (1995) proposed a theory of collective induction in the form of eight postulates and Laughlin (1999) later formulated four further postulates integrating experimental research. Table 2.1 presents these 12 postulates. Postulates 1–6 set collective induction in a general theory of group decision making. Postulates 7–8 formalize the social combination processes in collective induction. Postulates 9–12 generalize research on collective versus individual

Table 2.1 Collective induction: 12 postulates (Laughlin, 1999)

Postulate 1: Cooperative decision making groups may resolve disagreement among their members in formulating a collective group response in five ways:
1. Random selection among proposed alternatives
2. Voting among proposed alternatives
3. Turntaking among proposed alternatives
4. Demonstration of preferability of a proposed alternative
5. Generation of a new emergent alternative.

Postulate 2: The five ways of resolving disagreement may be formalized by social combination models:
1. Random selection: equiprobability model.
2. Voting: majority and plurality models.
3. Turntaking: proportionality model.
4. Demonstration: truth-wins and truth-supported wins models.
5. Generation of a new emergent alternative: specified probability of an alternative not proposed by any member.

Table 2.1 (*Cont'd*)

Postulate 3: Cooperative group tasks may be ordered on a continuum anchored by intellective and judgmental tasks. Intellective tasks are problems or decisions for which there is a demonstrably correct response (e.g., algebra problems). Judgmental tasks are evaluative, behavioral, or aesthetic judgments for which there is no demonstrably correct response (e.g., jury decisions).

Postulate 4: A demonstrably correct response requires four conditions:
1. Group consensus on a conceptual system.
2. Sufficient information.
3. Incorrect members are able to recognize the correct response if it is proposed.
4. Correct members have sufficient ability, motivation, and time to demonstrate the correct response to the incorrect members.

Postulate 5: The number of group members that is necessary and sufficient for a collective decision is inversely proportional to the demonstrability of the proposed group response.

Postulate 6: Inductive tasks are both intellective and judgmental: nonplausible hypotheses may be demonstrated to be nonplausible (intellective) but correct hypotheses may not be demonstrated to be uniquely correct relative to other plausible hypotheses that also fit the evidence (judgmental).

Postulate 7: If at least two group members propose correct and/or plausible hypotheses, the group selects among those hypotheses only (demonstration); otherwise, the group selects among all proposed hypotheses.

Postulate 8: If a majority of members propose the same hypothesis, the group follows a majority social combination process (voting); otherwise, the group follows a proportionality process (turntaking) and proposes an emergent hypothesis with probability $1/(H + 1)$, where H is the number of proposed hypotheses (group members).

Postulate 9: Given sufficient information and time, collective induction is comparable to the induction of the best of an equivalent number of independent individuals.

Postulate 10: Collective induction is improved more by multiple evidence than by multiple hypotheses.

Postulate 11: There is more group influence on individuals than individual influence on groups in simultaneous collective and individual induction.

Postulate 12: Positive hypothesis tests are generally more effective than negative hypothesis tests in collective induction.

induction (Postulate 9), the relative importance of multiple hypotheses and multiple evidence (Postulate 10), influence in simultaneous collective and individual induction (Postulate 11), and the relative effectiveness of positive and negative hypothesis tests (Postulate 12). Similarly, Hollingshead (1998) aggregated her research on transactive memory in nine propositions.

Thus principles (postulates, propositions) are integrated in a theory of the phenomena of interest. Theory may be defined as "a set of interrelated constructs, concepts, definitions, and propositions that present a systematic view of phenomena by specifying relations among variables, with the purpose of explaining and predicting the phenomena (Kerlinger, 1988, p. 9)."

Summary

These illustrative experimental designs for research on groups may be considered within the framework of the five Ps: problems, procedures, processes, performances, and principles. Although the illustrations are largely from research in the broad substantive area of group problem-solving, the designs may be used for research on a wide variety of issues in small groups, including evaluative judgments (attitudes), jury decisions, decision under risk or uncertainty, allocation of resources, social dilemmas, and the other issues represented in the other chapters of this book. For example, the coding analyses of influence processes in small groups of Meyers and Seibold in this volume could be conducted for the groups within one or more of the illustrative designs.

Recommendations

Recommendation one: use experimental designs that address a number of problems in the same study

The illustrative designs address a number of problems in the same study. Similarly, we recommend that researchers design their experiments to address a number of different issues in their domain of interest. It is often informative to add an initial measure of knowledge, attitudes, personality traits, or preferences in order to conduct social combination analyses of the group process, possible covariance analyses, and regression analyses. Similarly, it is often informative to add a subsequent individual measure to determine the effect of the group interaction on the group members, such as group-to-individual transfer, or mere acquiescence in a group response that does not affect member change.

Recommendation two: use designs with more than two levels of the independent variables

Designs with more than two levels of independent variables are more likely than designs with only two levels to: (a) determine the form of the function that relates dependent variables to independent variables; (b) determine the relative importance of two or more independent variables; (c) discover relationships that may be integrated in principles; and (d) test competing theoretical predictions. For example, Kerr and Kaufman-Gilliland (1994) used eight equally spaced levels of share size in an endowment game to test the competing social identity and commitment theories of the effects of communication on cooperation.

Recommendation three: anticipate the data analysis when designing the experiment

Both data analytic methods such as analysis of variance or regression and accepted criteria of inference from the results are based on assumptions about the nature of the data. For example, it is frequently possible to design continuous response measures which allow more powerful data analytic techniques than dichotomous response measures. It is often possible to use randomized block designs and covariance designs to reduce the systematic variance from demographic, personality, or secular variables. Data periodontists may be helpful later, but we should brush and floss our experimental designs carefully in the planning stage.

Recommendation four: cooperate with other researchers

A major difficulty in conducting experimental research on small groups is obtaining sufficient participants for requisite statistical power when the group rather than the individual is the unit of analysis. Assuming limited allocations from departmental participant pools, group studies may be run in tandem with individual studies, both within and across laboratories and classes. Participant resources may be combined and groups or individuals run according to show–up rates. Studies which require periods of intervening activity or filler tasks, such as control individuals during the period when groups are interacting or delayed memory studies, may be coordinated and run cooperatively with other researchers: one researcher's filler task may be another researcher's task of interest. As with the previous recommendation, cooperation may be anticipated during the design stage and the appropriate data analyses may be incorporated in the research.

Coda

Our English word "problem" comes from the Greek προβαλλειν, to throw forward, literally a spear and by extension an ongoing situation. Our English word "decision" comes from the Latin *decidere*, to cut off, literally an arm with a sword and by extension our current more abstract meaning. Decisions in the design, conduct, analysis, and communication of experimental research on small groups are necessary cutoff points; the ongoing problems continue to motivate further research.

References

Baron, R. S., & Kerr, N. L. (2002). *Group process, group decision, group action* (2nd ed.). Philadelphia, PA: Open University Press.

Davis, J. H. (1973). Group decision and social interaction: A theory of social decision schemes. *Psychological Review, 80*, 97–125.

Hastie, R. (1986). Review essay: Experimental evidence on group accuracy. In G. Owen & B. Grofman (Eds.), *Information pooling and group accuracy* (pp. 129–157). Westport, CT: JAI.

Hill, G. W. (1982). Group versus individual performance: Are N + 1 heads better than one? *Psychological Bulletin, 91,* 517–539.

Hollingshead, A. B. (1998). Distributed knowledge and transactive processes in decision-making groups. In M. A. Neale, E. M. Mannix, & D. H Gruenfeld (Eds.), *Research on managing groups and teams* (Vol 1, pp. 103–123). Greenwich, CT: JAI.

Kerlinger, F. N. (1988). *Foundations of behavioral research.* New York: Holt, Rinehart, and Winston.

Kerr, N. L., & Kaufman-Gilliland, C. M. (1994). Communication, commitment, and cooperation in social dilemmas. *Journal of Personality and Social Psychology, 66,* 513–529.

Kerr, N. L., & Tindale, R. S. (2003). Group performance and decision making. *Annual Review of Psychology, 56,* 623–655.

Laughlin, P. R. (1999). Collective induction: Twelve postulates. *Organizational Behavior and Human Decision Processes, 80,* 50–69.

Laughlin, P. R., & Bonner, B. L (1999). Collective induction: Effects of multiple hypotheses and multiple evidence in two problem domains. *Journal of Personality and Social Psychology, 77,* 1163–1172.

Laughlin, P. R., Carey, H. R., & Kerr, N. L. (2008). Group-to-individual problem-solving transfer. *Group Processes and Intergroup Relations, 11,* 319–330.

Laughlin, P. R., & Ellis, A. L. (1986). Demonstrability and social combination processes on mathematical intellective tasks. *Journal of Experimental Social Psychology, 22,* 177–189.

Laughlin, P. R., Hatch, E. C., Silver, J. C., & Boh, L. (2006). Groups perform better than the best individuals on letters-to-numbers problems: Effects of group size. *Journal of Personality and Social Psychology, 90,* 644–651.

Laughlin, P. R., & Hollingshead, A. B. (1995). A theory of collective induction. *Organizational Behavior and Human Decision Processes, 61,* 94–107.

Levine, J., & Moreland, R. L. (1998). Small groups. In D. T. Gilbert, S. T. Fiske, & G. Lindzey (Eds.), *The handbook of social psychology* (Vol. 2, pp. 415–146). New York: McGraw-Hill.

Stasser, G., & Dietz-Uhler, B. (2001). Collective choice, judgment, and problem solving. In M. A. Hogg & R. S. Tindale (Eds.) *Blackwell handbook of social psychology: Group processes* (Vol. 3, pp. 31–55). Oxford: Blackwell Publishers.

Stasson, M. F., Kameda, T., Parks, C. D., Zimmerman, S. K., & Davis, J. H. (1991). Effects of assigned group consensus requirements on group problem solving and group members' learning. *Social Psychology Quarterly, 54,* 25–35.

3

RUNNING LABORATORY EXPERIMENTS WITH GROUPS

Gwen M. Wittenbaum

MICHIGAN STATE UNIVERSITY

Fledgling scholars who want to understand groups by conducting laboratory experiments will find many sources of information about how to design experiments (e.g., Haslam & McGarty, 2004; Kirk, 1995; Laughlin, this volume; Smith, 2000). Graduate students in social sciences typically learn about experimental design in their research methods courses and benefit from having an advisor or graduate committee assist with their experimental design for a degree-required project. When embarking to conduct the laboratory experiment, however, the fledgling scholar may have few sources of support for how to run it. Graduate students may compare notes with their peers for advice on how to run an experiment or use procedures typically used by the faculty advisor. There appears to be a dearth, however, of published tutorials on how to run a laboratory experiment, let alone one on groups. The purpose of this chapter is to demystify the process of conducting laboratory experiments on groups by highlighting personal research examples and behind-the-scenes procedures that rarely are reported in the method section of a journal article.

I began conducting laboratory experiments on groups as a graduate student in the field of social psychology 20 years ago. Throughout this time, I have studied both laboratory groups that interact face-to-face and groups that are imagined or anticipated. There are many ways to examine group dynamics in a laboratory experiment. First, I will offer a typology of commonly used groups in laboratory experiments. Second, I will provide research examples of these different types of laboratory groups. Third, I will detail the step-by-step procedures that will help to make a laboratory experiment on groups run smoothly the first time. Finally, I finish with conclusions about lessons learned.

Types of Laboratory Groups

Some fields have used laboratory experiments to understand group dynamics more than others. Social psychologists who study groups heavily rely on the laboratory experiment. In a content analysis of the top social psychology journals, Moreland, Hogg, and Hains (1994) reported that 76 per cent of published studies on groups utilized laboratory experiments. A similar content analysis of organizational psychology journals reported that 50 per cent of the group research in this field used the laboratory experiment method (Sanna & Parks, 1997). Likewise, communication scholars have been criticized for relying too heavily on laboratory experiments (Frey, 1994). Other fields, such as management, sociology, kinesiology, and political science may rely less than psychologists and communication scholars on laboratory experiments as a way to understand groups. However, nearly every social scientific field that houses group research uses the laboratory experiment. The ubiquity of the method suggests that there are many approaches to studying laboratory groups.

When scholars study group dynamics in a laboratory experiment, they typically examine groups that fall into one of the following four categories: (1) anticipated groups; (2) imagined groups; (3) confederate groups; or (4) interacting groups. In *anticipated groups*, participants complete tasks on their own with the expectation that they will interact with fellow group members at a later time. Often, the interaction expectation is fabricated on the part of the experimenter who wants to study how people think and behave when they expect to interact in a group, even though no group actually exists. This type of group is similar to *imagined groups*, which only exist in the mind of the participants. However, participants in imagined laboratory groups believe that they are interacting with fellow group members. In actuality, those group members do not exist, yet their behavior is simulated by fabricated messages transmitted typically through a mediated channel (e.g., note passing, online chat). In *confederate groups*, participants believe that they are interacting with other unsuspecting participants. In actuality, one or more other group members are trained accomplices (i.e., confederates) of the experimenter, constrained to act in a certain way. To participants, these confederate groups appear to be *in interacting groups*. However, an interacting group is used here to mean natural, in-person group interaction of several participants working toward a common goal. The interacting group simulates in the laboratory the type of groups that we typically think of in natural contexts, such as committees, juries, and teams. Interacting groups can communicate face to face or using a range of media such as video, phone, computer conferencing, email or text messaging, or in virtual worlds or social networking sites. As most of my research has been conducted in face-to-face groups, I will focus on face-to-face groups (FTF) in this chapter. See Wirth Feldberg, Schouten, van den Hooff, and Williams (this volume) for a discussion of experimental research using computer games and virtual worlds.

For each group type, I will provide a research illustration from the area of group decision-making – a foundational area of study that lends itself to investigation across the different types of laboratory groups. Table 3.1 provides a description of each type of laboratory group along with a summary of the following research examples.

Table 3.1 Summary of types of laboratory groups

Group type	Description
Anticipated groups	*Purpose*: For understanding how individuals think, feel, and behave in anticipation of joining a group *Challenge*: Deception or false feedback to participants may be challenging to make believable *Research examples*: Group decision-making (GDM): tacit coordination (Wittenbaum et al., 1995) Social ostracism (SO): rejection by a group (Nezlek, Kowalski, Leary, Blevins, & Holgate, 1997)
Imagined groups	*Purpose*: For simulating group interaction with complete control over other members' behaviors (because they are fabricated by the experimenter). Useful for behaviors that are difficult to facilitate in FTF groups, as a less resource-intensive alternative to confederate groups, or when complete control is desired *Challenge*: Making the procedures believable given that the other members do not exist *Research examples*: GDM: mutual enhancement (Wittenbaum, Hubbell, & Zuckerman, 1999) SO: cyberball (Zadro, Williams, & Richardson, 2004)
Confederate groups	*Purpose*: For facilitating group interaction when one or more other members' behaviors need to be controlled (in the form of a confederate), yet a somewhat realistic interaction is desired *Challenge*: Training confederates and scheduling them for each experimental session is labor intensive and sometimes results in only a single participant per session *Research examples*: GDM: minority influence (Hart, Stasson, & Karau, 1999) SO: ball-toss game; being ignored during a conversation (Williams, 1997; Williams, Govan, Croker, Tynan, Cruickshank, & Lam, 2002)
Interacting groups	*Purpose*: For understanding processes and outcomes within natural group interaction, such as communication and collaboration between members *Challenge*: Participant recruitment and data collection can be slow and time-consuming *Research examples*: GDM: collective information sharing (Wittenbaum, 1998) SO: ostracism in task groups (Wittenbaum et al., 2010)

Research Examples

Anticipated groups

Group decision-making requires members to integrate information to achieve a consensus. Efforts toward reaching a consensus, however, may begin before the group meets. This was the premise behind Wittenbaum, Stasser, and Merry's (1995) research on tacit coordination. I was a graduate student when I worked on this project, and it was an eye-opening introduction to the creative ways of studying groups in the laboratory. We reasoned that group members form expectations about other group members' likely areas of expertise and assume what kind of information other members likely will attend to before discussion based on their expertise. Group members may help to facilitate group task completion before the group's meeting by adjusting the kind of information that they attend to and remember. We thought, however, that the kind of information to which group members would attend would depend on the anticipated group task. When members anticipate a group decision-making task, they would attend to similar information as others in order to facilitate agreement. Whereas, when members anticipate a collective recall task, they would try to remember information that others likely would not, in the interest of maximizing the group's recall output. This idea lent itself perfectly to a laboratory experiment using anticipated groups.

Participants in Study 1 were told that they would interact with others on a group task but would have the opportunity to share surface information (in the form of a college life questionnaire) with each other before the group convened. After completing the college life questionnaire, the experimenter returned with copies of questionnaires presumably completed by the other eventual group members. These bogus questionnaires were designed so that each of the other members appeared to be expert in one of the domains relevant to the materials used for the group task. Participants perused these bogus questionnaires and then anticipated one of two group tasks (i.e., the experimental manipulation): a group decision regarding the best of three student body president candidates or collective recall of the candidates' information. After participants read the information about the three hypothetical candidates, they unexpectedly were asked to remember, individually, as much of the candidate information as possible within six minutes. From the researcher's perspective, the study was over after the free recall task. Participants, nevertheless, were placed into groups with others from that experimental session to follow through with the guise of the study. Just as expected, those who anticipated a group decision-making task better remembered information in the others' areas of expertise, whereas those who anticipated a collective recall task better remembered information outside of others' areas of expertise. This study showed that group member efforts to facilitate a group decision begin before the group meets.

Imagined groups

The research of Wittenbaum et al. (1995) showed that group members who anticipate a group decision-making task focus on knowledge that others probably know. This finding is consistent with research that shows that members of decision-making groups favor discussing *shared information* that all members know over *unshared information* that a single member knows (for a review, see Wittenbaum, Hollingshead, & Botero, 2004). Wittenbaum et al. (1999) reasoned that group members may prefer to discuss shared information because that information can be socially validated (as accurate and important), leading members to positively value such information when mentioned. Likewise, group members who communicate much shared information may receive more positive evaluations from others compared to those who communicate much unshared information.

We wanted to begin our investigation in a setting that was more controlled than FTF groups, where members could not see one another and potentially form evaluations based on other member features (e.g., physical appearance, nonverbal behavior). We also needed to control the information communicated by the target group member. Therefore, we generated a paradigm using imagined groups. Participants were seated in a room and expected to exchange written information with a dyadic partner in another room within the same social interaction laboratory. Participants read information about two hypothetical academic job candidates and indicated their preferred candidate. "Discussion" occurred via the exchange of written information. Participants listed ten pieces of candidate information to share with their dyadic partner, which was collected by the experimenter and presumably delivered to the dyadic partner across the hall. The experimenter returned with a list of ten pieces of candidate information, presumably handwritten by the participants' partner, but actually fabricated by the experimenter to have mostly shared information or mostly unshared information (i.e., the experimental manipulation). The lists of information were written in shorthand and contained a slight mix of shared and unshared information to enhance their perceived authenticity. After reading the bogus list of information, participants rated the knowledge, task competence, and credibility of their dyadic partner and themselves and indicated their preferred candidate. Results from Experiment 2 showed that participants gave not only their dyadic partner but also themselves higher ratings of task competence and knowledge when the partner communicated mostly shared rather than mostly unshared information – an effect called *mutual enhancement*. Although participants did not engage in group decision-making, this study showed that group members form evaluations of one another based on the information that they share en route to consensus formation.

Confederate groups

One of the challenges of achieving group consensus is the ability to resolve disagreement among members. Inevitably, some group members have more influence in changing the preferences of others. Social impact theory (Latane, 1981) predicts that a member with higher immediacy (e.g., physical proximity) and strength (e.g., status) will exert greater influence on the group. To isolate the impact of a single group member, Hart et al. (1999) tested the immediacy and strength components of social impact theory using confederate groups.

In their study, Hart et al. (1999) composed three-person groups of two participants and one confederate, where the immediacy and strength of the confederate were experimentally manipulated. A rigged seat assignment ensured that the confederate sat either 4 ft (*high immediacy*) or 10 ft (*low immediacy*) away from the two participants. The group task was to reach a consensus on the aptitude ratings of 40 hypothetical graduate school applicants. An ice-breaking exercise before the group started this task permitted the confederate to state his status as being either *high* (a senior who had applied to graduate programs) or *low* (a freshman merely doing the experiment for class credit). First, participants individually rated the graduate school applicants. Then, the group discussed the applicants to achieve consensus on the ratings of each. The confederate took a minority position in this discussion by arguing that, contrary to most students, he believed that research experience was the most important criterion and GPA was the least. After discussion, group members again rated the applicants so that the researchers could determine whether participants' postdiscussion ratings shifted toward the confederate's position (when compared to their prediscussion ratings). Results showed that participants' ratings shifted closer to the confederate's position when the confederate had high rather than low status, but only in the low immediacy condition. Contrary to social impact theory, the confederate was not more influential in the high than the low immediacy condition. As this research shows, the confederate group is a useful tool for understanding the influence of a minority opinion holder in decision-making groups.

Interacting groups

Much of the research on group decision-making has used FTF groups (for a review, see Kerr & Tindale, 2004). FTF groups allow researchers to study natural communication and influence processes among members as well as the type and quality of group decision. Although it may be more difficult to isolate or control a certain communication or influence process in FTF groups, the beauty of studying such groups is the ability to examine processes as they naturally occur and relate to one another. An article adapted from my dissertation (Wittenbaum, 1998) provides an illustration. I wondered whether high-status group members, compared to low-status members, were less likely to fall prey to the discussion bias favoring shared information and more likely to influence the group's decision.

I recruited students to participate in four-person, mixed-sex groups of two men and two women. To manipulate member status experimentally, I assigned two (*experienced*) members to work on a practice task similar to the eventual group's task and two (*inexperienced*) members to work on an unrelated task. Because I wanted to control for the effects of member sex, the two members within the same experience condition were always the same sex (so, either the two experienced members were women, or they were both men). Participants drew slips of paper from a bag that indicated the task on which they would work individually. Although this drawing appeared random, it was rigged to permit assignment to member status and to control for member sex. Specifically, the bag contained only slips intended for members in the experienced condition. The experimenter let either the two women choose first or the two men choose first, claiming that the final two slips were obviously assignments to be inexperienced, so there was no need for the final two members to reach into the bag. If they did challenge the experimenter, however, there was a secret compartment at the bottom of the bag where the experimenter could reach in and grab two slips of paper that indicated inexperienced assignments. Members were separated to work on their practice task individually. After doing so, the group was reunited to commence their group decision-making task. First, they read individually information about two hypothetical job candidates, which biased experienced members to prefer a different candidate than the inexperienced members. After indicating their preferred candidate in private, the experimenter removed the materials and audio-recorded the group's discussion and arrival at a decision. After discussion, members indicated their postdiscussion candidate preference.

Results showed that inexperienced members mentioned more shared than unshared information, replicating the typical pattern seen in groups. Experienced members, however, mentioned shared and unshared information equally often. It was more difficult than expected to get group members to prefer the intended candidate. In 35 of the 56 groups, the experienced and inexperienced members preferred the intended job candidate before discussion. Note that this is one of the limitations of FTF groups relative to confederate groups: in the latter, the researcher is able to guarantee the confederate's position and arguments. Ignoring the 21 groups where the preference distribution among members did not work out, the data showed that experienced members were no more likely than inexperienced members to have their preferred candidate adopted as the group's decision. Interestingly, when examining group decisions as a function of information mentioned, inexperienced members mentioned more information than experienced members when the group chose the candidate preferred by inexperienced members. Experienced members did not have to do the same when they won. So, even though both types of members were equally influential, inexperienced members had to work harder to get their way. This experiment highlights the benefit of FTF groups in helping to understand the communication processes of different types of group members and how such communication relates to group decisions.

Summary and caveat

The preceding research examples highlight how different types of laboratory groups aid the understanding of different aspects of group decision-making dynamics. Although most group decision-making research uses FTF groups, other group types can isolate processes regarding how members prepare for group discussion, form impressions of other group members, or respond to a minority opinion holder. Researchers who want to conduct experiments on group decision-making can select the group type that best enables them to answer their questions of interest.

It would be a mistake, however, to assume that the different types of laboratory groups must be used to answer different research questions. Research on social ostracism (i.e., being ignored or excluded by an individual or group) shows, to the contrary, that researchers can test the same hypothesis across the different laboratory groups. Replication of a common effect across laboratory group types demonstrates the validity of an effect across different procedures and manipulations. According to Williams (1997, 2001, 2007), being ostracized results in an immediate reduction in psychological needs for self-esteem, belonging, control, and meaningful existence. I will illustrate how this effect has been demonstrated using all four types of laboratory groups.

Nezlek et al. (1997) studied the effects of rejection on nondepressed individuals who anticipated possibly joining a group (i.e., anticipated groups). False feedback from imagined others indicated that either participants were one of the three chosen for the upcoming group task (*inclusion condition*) or they were not chosen and would work alone (*exclusion condition*). Participants felt more positive and accepted when they were in the inclusion rather than the exclusion condition. Williams, Cheung, and Choi (2000) developed an imagined-group paradigm, Cyberball, to establish a baseline of when ostracism effects occur. In it, participants believe that they are playing a game of ball-toss over the internet with other players (who, in actuality, do not exist). Zadro et al. (2004) showed that participants who were included in a three-person game of Cyberball (i.e., received the ball one-third of the time) reported higher self-esteem, control, belonging, and meaningful existence compared to those in the exclusion condition (who received the ball twice early on but not again during the six-minute game). Williams et al. (2002) showed that ostracism hurts when using a confederate group paradigm. Two trained confederates discussed euthanasia with a single participant, either including or ignoring the participant during the last ten minutes of discussion. Participants who were included reported higher mood, self-esteem, belonging, control, and meaningful existence compared to those who were ostracized. Finally, Wittenbaum, Shulman, and Braz (2010) established a FTF group paradigm for studying social ostracism. In groups of three, one member lacked (by random assignment) task-relevant information relative to the other two members. This uninformed member was less involved (based on observer ratings) in the group discussion while working on the task relative to the two more informed members and, as a result, felt lower self-esteem, belonging, control, and meaningful existence compared to informed members.

Like group decision-making research, social ostracism can be studied using the different types of laboratory groups. Including the latter research examples as a counterpoint to group decision-making research highlights two conclusions. First, the different types of laboratory groups can examine two important aspects of group life: task and social–emotional, with group decision making exemplifying the former and social ostracism the latter. Second, different laboratory approaches can help both to unveil various processes related to a particular group phenomenon and to replicate a common effect across paradigms. In the case of group decision-making, researchers used different types of laboratory groups to understand different aspects of the process, whereas in the case of social ostracism, the same effect was demonstrated across the different group types. Most researchers, however, will select a particular laboratory group type because of its unique ability to enable the investigation in question and its suitability given available resources.

Researchers who want to understand interaction dynamics in natural group discussion, such as nonverbal and verbal communication between members, are best served by using FTF groups. In Wittenbaum et al. (2010), despite wanting to replicate classic ostracism effects, we also wanted a FTF group paradigm that would allow us to examine the dynamic communication between included and excluded group members – something that the more artificial group types did not permit. In this way, FTF groups resemble the kind of group dynamics we encounter in everyday life (i.e., high ecological validity) more than the other laboratory group types. Confederate groups work well for understanding how group members respond to particular behaviors of others that may be difficult to promote naturally (e.g., a minority opinion holder). Moreover, researchers can record participant behavior in response to confederates, like Williams and Sommer (1997), who observed more smiling and laughing among participants who were included rather than excluded in a ball-toss game with two confederates. Because confederate groups are resource intensive (as I will argue later), imagined groups often can be used in their place to answer similar questions and offer more experimental control over others' behavior. This is, in part, why Williams et al. (2000) developed the Cyberball version of the confederate ball-toss game. Finally, anticipated groups lend themselves toward understanding group member thought and behavior before group interaction, such as how members prepare for group task completion or respond to being chosen (or not chosen) for group membership.

Laboratory Set-up and Data Collection

A great research idea and design is no guarantee that the laboratory experiment will run without a hitch. Numerous considerations regarding personnel, experimental materials, participant recruitment, laboratory set-up, and data collection will help to make the laboratory experiment on groups run smoothly. I personally have found it helpful to be a bit anally retentive and obsessive compulsive when setting up and running a laboratory experiment. Others may mock my excessive tendency toward organization, but after trial and error, they typically come to see the benefits of my ways. The following section reveals my tips for how to run a laboratory experiment on groups as well as some of the challenges and frustrations.

Personnel

The best way to run a laboratory experiment on groups is to have a team of capable personnel to assist with various aspects of the work. Research assistants can help to recruit participants, collect the data in the laboratory, code and enter the data, and act as confederates. For an experiment using FTF groups, for example, I might have six research assistants to assist with data collection in the laboratory and two to four different assistants to code data from recorded discussions. I typically recruit the best students from my group communication courses and a few who seek me requesting to do an independent study. Qualities that I look for depend on the type of work that needs to be done.

For data collection, I look for socially skilled, graceful, well-spoken, responsible undergraduate students who have an ability to act. These students also make great confederates and, fortunately for me, are easy to find in a communication department. The field of communication tends to attract students who enjoy public speaking and social interaction. All of the group experiments that I have run require the research assistant to deliver verbal instructions to an individual or group. Because some studies using anticipated or imagined groups require giving false feedback to participants or pretending that other group members are in neighboring rooms when they actually are not, theatrical skills are helpful. For example, we were able to run the tacit coordination (Wittenbaum et al., 1995) and mutual enhancement (Wittenbaum et al., 1999) experiments with a single participant if the experimenter opened and closed doors to neighboring rooms and spoke in these rooms as if other participants were in there. In addition, research on FTF groups often involves coding group discussion. For this type of investigation, I seek some assistants who exclusively will code and not collect data (because I do not want coders to know the study's purpose or manipulations). An undergraduate student who is very smart, meticulous, focused, self-motivated, and enjoys working alone is the prototype for an assistant who codes and enters data. Often, the kind of student who would be a great assistant collecting data in the laboratory is not the same kind of student who would make a great coder. As a result, I recommend matching assistant interests and personality to the best-fitting role and taking time to train them properly.

Confederate groups require some research assistants to play the role of confederate. Finding people to play the confederate role convincingly and training them to do so takes time. Confederate paradigms are resource intensive, as one or more confederates must attend each experimental session in addition to the other research assistants who run the session. Williams et al. (2000) developed an imagined-group paradigm for studying social ostracism (i.e., Cyberball), in part, because the confederate procedure was resource intensive. Prior to Cyberball, Williams (1997) used a ball-toss paradigm with two trained confederates who ignored the lone participant in a game of ball-toss. Only one participant could be run per session and required the attendance of two trained confederates. In this way, confederate groups can be a slow and resource-intensive method of studying groups compared to using imagined groups.

Design and organization of materials

Fledgling laboratory experimenters may focus their efforts on developing the experimental manipulations, questionnaires, and measurements to the neglect of support materials that aid research assistants in collecting data. These support materials include such things such as the experimenter log, verbal instructions, detailed procedure, procedural summary and reminders, and organization aids. The researcher needs to think about every detailed aspect of the experiment. Which questionnaires are written on and which are reused? Where are completed questionnaires stored? How do research assistants coordinate with each other in the laboratory? How do they keep track of which groups are recorded on which tapes or DVDs? How are recordings stored? Are there times when participants are sitting idle and a filler task would be helpful? If the laboratory is shared, how should materials be stored when other researchers are using the laboratory? The list of questions seems endless. To the extent that these details are worked out in advance, the laboratory sessions will run much smoother.

Office supplies will help to organize the materials. I begin with a three-ring binder with added sleeves to house the experimenter log (e-log). This log includes a table of the experimental design where assistants can place a tally in the box where a participant or group was run. For each session, assistants complete a sheet that summarizes the activities. The procedures are sufficiently complex typically to require a pair of assistants to run each session. So, they write their names, the date, and time of the session. For each group, they indicate the group number, condition, room, and assistant who ran it. There is a comments area where assistants can write anything out of the ordinary (e.g., participant suspicion, lack of compliance, experimenter errors, late arrivals). The e-log houses a detailed document of the procedure and verbal instructions read by the research assistants. The experiment is divided into steps, starting with pre-session preparation (e.g., determining condition to be run) and ending with postsession clean-up (e.g., coding conditions on the data, storing data). For each step, the procedure

Table 3.2 A Sample list of top ten recommendations for laboratory research assistants

10. Close the door when delivering verbal instructions. Open it when not.
 9. Take your time. Do not rush the procedure or participants.
 8. Be obsessive-compulsive! Check to make sure you deliver the right forms to the right participants at all times! Check to make sure you put them back in the right folder.
 7. Prepare for the next step while you're waiting.
 6. Be vigilant and mindful of what you're doing, not complacent and mindless!
 5. Be quiet so participants can work.
 4. Communicate clearly to coordinate with your lab partner.
 3. Leave the lab as you found it.
 2. Stick to the script!
 1. Act like a flight attendant! Put participants at ease. Be warm and friendly!

identifies what the assistant should do and say. The e-log also contains a printed list of the students who signed up for each laboratory session. Hanging on the wall in the experimenter's room is a single-page chart depicting a brief summary of the procedure and my infamous top ten list (see Table 3.2).

Because the social interaction laboratory that I use is shared with other researchers, I have become adept at making experiments well organized, yet compact. A plastic file box with a handle can house all of the materials. Each hanging folder inside the box is labeled with a step number in the procedure and contains the materials for that step. For example, the folder for Step 1 houses the informed consent forms. Steps that require an aggregation of materials, for example, the bogus questionnaires from the Wittenbaum et al. (1995) tacit coordination study, already have those materials compiled into a labeled folder ready to hand to participants. The box also contains envelopes for completed questionnaires (e.g., group decisions) and scanner sheets on which participants record responses for (typically postdiscussion) questionnaires that are reused. A compact CD case holds the mini-DVDs from the video recording of group discussions, and there is room for storing the e-log. The operation feels a bit like Dr Seuss's "The Cat in the Hat" in that all of research materials come out of the box and fill the laboratory during the session but neatly pack up into the box when it is time to go.

Several other practices can help research assistants to prepare and organize materials. Colors can make the experimental procedure run more smoothly. In FTF group studies where each member receives different instructions or information, we often color-code each member's materials to keep them straight. Our social interaction laboratory contains several small rooms with doors on which we hang an expandable folder that can be used for placing the materials that the group or individual will receive for the next experimental step. When recording group discussion, research assistants write the group's number on a dry erase board and display it at the start of the recording. This will let eventual coders know which group they are watching. Research assistants are less likely to forget to record groups if instructions to do so are integrated with the verbal instructions and if a pair of assistants who can catch each other's mistakes run each session. All of these organization tools may seem a bit excessive, but they do ease complex procedures for research assistants and help to minimize errors.

Participant issues

Prior to data collection, researchers should obtain approval from their organization's Institutional Review Board (IRB). The IRB will assure that the proposed experimental procedures abide by the standards of ethical treatment of human participants. Researchers will have to specify to the IRB all procedures used with participants, including methods of recruitment, research materials, informed consent, use of deception, and debriefing. If recording group discussions, consent forms may require two signatures from participants – one indicating their consent to participate and the other, their consent to be recorded. For experiments that use deception (e.g., those using anticipated groups, imagined groups, or false feedback), experimenters must perform a thorough debriefing. In all of the ostracism experiments, for example, the experimenters help to restore participants' sense of well-being by admitting that inclusion vs. exclusion was randomly assigned. It is assuring to know that the discomfort felt during cyberostracism dissipates by the end of an experimental session, even before debriefing occurs (Zadro, Boland, & Richardson, 2006). All of the experiments provided as examples in this chapter used college students as participants, a common procedure for laboratory experiments on groups. Some academic departments have subject pools where undergraduate students participate in research in exchange for class credit. Many of these pools today use internet-based computer software as the interface where researchers post sessions for their experiments and students sign up to participate. These websites make participant recruitment a breeze, as students can make and cancel appointments at their convenience. Researchers without access to a subject pool may need to recruit participants by visiting college classrooms or posting advertisements around campus or in newspapers.

When studying FTF groups, participant recruitment can be frustrating. The collective information sharing described in Wittenbaum (1998) was a part of my dissertation. The project was larger than described in that article, requiring over 500 participants. Fortunately, I had grant funding that allowed me to pay each participant $12 for nearly two hours of research participation. Still, the undergraduate students at Miami University were not terribly motivated to offer two hours of their time for $12. I supplemented participants from the psychology department subject pool with other students from across campus whom I painfully recruited by going door-to-door in residence halls. I would collect data by day, recruit participants in the evening, and call students the night before their scheduled appointment to remind them to come. It was a grueling schedule. Part of the challenge was the requirement to have exactly two women and two men in each group. For each session, I needed to ensure not only enough participants to achieve four-person groups, but also a mixture of men and women to achieve the desired group composition. As in all of my laboratory group experiments, I overbook one or two additional students to guard against a couple failing to show up to their appointment. If the additional students show up, however, there must be an alternative task that they can complete individually for the same amount of compensation or credit as those who work in groups. The procedure for my dissertation tried my patience because I could have four students show up, but if they were three women and one man, I could not obtain the sex composition that I needed. The result, in this case, was two hours of my scheduled time without any group data collection. At other times, I would have three students show up. In desperation, I would run to the building's lobby trying to recruit an additional student on the spot to achieve my desired group size of four. Some sessions would go unfilled and therefore were cancelled. Collecting data on FTF groups can be frustrating to achieve enough participants to form the desired group size and obtain the desired number of groups. Admittedly, working at a large university is helpful in this regard. The subject pool in my current department can have upwards of 1,000 students in it within any given semester. Additionally, the subject pool software sends automatic reminders by email the day before a student's appointment to reduce the likelihood of absence. This has made research on FTF groups more feasible.

Laboratory set-up

Before conducting laboratory experiments on groups, researchers should make sure that they have the necessary space and resources. All of my group experiments were conducted in social interaction laboratories that contained three or four smaller rooms used by individual participants or small groups and an additional small room for the experimenter and materials. The small rooms enable the study of anticipated and imagined groups. Individuals seated in one room can be told that the other group members are scattered throughout the various other rooms. Some theatrics are required to make this cover story believable. FTF groups usually are placed at a round or rectangular table in a small room. Dividers can be placed on the tables during periods of the session when members complete tasks individually and in private. If studying the interaction dynamics within FTF groups, the small rooms can be equipped with concealed recording devices or allow space for a video camera atop a tripod. It is important to position the video camera so that all members easily can be viewed, although problems still can result. A group member can move to block the view of another member, preventing the observation of the blocked member's nonverbal behavior. Likewise, when two or more members speak at once, inability to see a member in the recording can make it difficult to know who is speaking. Having group members wear lapel microphones using a multichannel recording device can help to distinguish speakers.

To help coders determine the speaker when watching the recording, begin discussion with each member introducing themselves and their member number or label each member with a numerical placard affixed to the table. Sound-proofing in the laboratory is helpful. Without it, noise from closing doors and delivering experimental instructions in other rooms may be picked up during the recording of a group's discussion. To make sure that the first experimental session will run smoothly, I recommend performing a dry run with the research assistants. During the dry run, the research assistants walk through the entire laboratory procedure without participants. This practice session often reveals whether the space, materials, and research assistants are ready for the study to begin.

Data collection

Now that the study is ready to go, when should data collection commence? If using a subject pool, timing during the semester is important. Students who participate in research at the beginning of the semester tend to be more engaged and motivated compared to those during the final weeks. If possible, try to collect data during the beginning of the semester. Group research tends to be more demanding of participants compared to other topics of study, so the more engaged participants are in the laboratory procedure, the more likely the experiment will work out as hoped. If recruiting participants from a more advanced class, make sure that the topic of investigation has not yet been covered in class. For this reason, my group communication students can participate in group decision-making research during the first half of the semester, before I cover that topic in class. Naïve students are less likely to guess the purpose of the study. As described earlier, data collection can be painstakingly slow, so the ability to achieve the desired sample size can be a blessing. If data collection is strained, as sometimes occurs during the middle of the semester, I will postpone it for another time. Peeking at the results at this point may reveal, surprisingly, that the effects are stronger than expected and emerging as statistically significant with a smaller-than-anticipated sample size. This occurred when running the social ostracism research (Wittenbaum et al., 2010), where the effects of being ignored were quite strong on the measures of threatened needs. Happily, we ended data collection sooner than expected.

Conclusion

Running laboratory experiments on groups can be both a rewarding and trying experience. The purpose of this chapter was to provide examples of how groups can be studied using laboratory experiments, illustrate best practices in running experiments on groups, and establish realistic expectations about what to expect from the process. I close with four distilled lessons from my experience conducting laboratory experiments on groups.

First, it is important to match the method to the research question. Assuming that the researcher wants to understand causal relations within group dynamics in a controlled environment, the researcher must determine which type of experimental laboratory group best fits the question of interest. Although I have always been interested in understanding group dynamics, sometimes this involves studying individuals who merely anticipate or think about other group members. At other times, it involves creating a small group to complete a shared task. Although the types of laboratory groups mentioned herein are commonly used methods of studying groups experimentally, there are countless other ways.

This leads to the second lesson: experimenting on laboratory groups requires creative thinking. It took time and many brainstorming sessions to generate a paradigm for studying social ostracism using FTF groups or one for how members tacitly coordinate in anticipation of group task completion. With clever thinking, it may be possible to study just about any group dynamic using a laboratory experiment.

Third, successfully pulling off a laboratory experiment on groups requires a lot of planning, organization, and, occasionally, some theatrics. The team of research assistants is critical for helping to make that all happen.

Finally, studying laboratory groups requires patience. It will take longer to complete than laboratory experiments on individual phenomena. However, the richness of data from group interaction and individuals who believe or expect to be a part of such interactions is difficult to exceed.

References

Frey, L. R. (1994). Introduction: Revitalizing the study of small group communication. *Communication Studies, 45*, 1–6.

Hart, J. W., Stasson, M. F., & Karau, S. J. (1999). Effects of source expertise and physical distance on minority influence. *Group Dynamics: Theory, Research, and Practice, 3*, 81–92.

Haslam, S. A., & McGarty, C. (2004). Experimental design and causality in social psychology research. In C. Sansone, C. C. Morf, & A. T. Panter (Eds.), *The Sage handbook of methods in social psychology* (pp. 237–264). Thousand Oaks, CA: Sage.

Kerr, N. L., & Tindale, R. S. (2004). Group performance and decision making. *Annual Review of Psychology, 55*, 623–655.

Kirk, R. E. (1995). *Experimental design*. Pacific Grove, CA: Brooks Cole.

Latane, B. (1981). The psychology of social impact. *American Psychologist, 36*, 343–356.

Moreland, R. L., Hogg, M. A., & Hains, S. C. (1994). Back to the future: Social psychological research on groups. *Journal of Experimental Social Psychology, 30*, 527–555.

Nezlek, J. B., Kowalski, R. M., Leary, M. R., Blevins, T., & Holgate, S. (1997). Personality moderators of reactions to interpersonal rejection: Depression and trait self-esteem. *Personality and Social Psychology Bulletin, 23*, 1235–1244.

Sanna, L. J., & Parks, C. D. (1997). Group research trends in social and organizational psychology: Whatever happened to intragroup research? *Psychological Science, 8*, 261–267.

Smith, E. R. (2000). Research design. In H. T. Reis, & C. M. Judd (Eds.), *Handbook of research methods in personality and social psychology* (pp. 17–39). Cambridge: Cambridge University Press.

Williams, K. D. (1997). Social ostracism. In R. M. Kowalski (Ed.), *Aversive interpersonal behaviors* (pp. 133–170). New York: Plenum.

Williams, K. D. (2001). *Ostracism: The power of silence*. New York: Guilford.

Williams, K. D. (2007). Ostracism. *Annual Review of Psychology, 58*, 15.1–15.28.

Williams, K. D., Cheung, C. K. T., & Choi, W. (2000). CyberOstracism: Effects of being ignored over the Internet. *Journal of Personality and Social Psychology, 79*, 48–62.

Williams, K. D., Govan, C. L., Croker, V., Tynan, D., Cruickshank, M., & Lam, A. (2002). Investigations into differences between social- and cyberostracism. *Group Dynamics, 6*, 65–77.

Williams, K. D., & Sommer, K. L. (1997). Social ostracism by one's coworkers: Does rejection lead to loafing or compensation? *Personality and Social Psychology Bulletin, 23*, 693–706.

Wittenbaum, G. M. (1998). Information sampling in decision-making groups: The impact of members' task-relevant status. *Small Group Research, 29*, 57–84.

Wittenbaum, G. M., Hollingshead, A. B., & Botero, I. C. (2004). From cooperative to motivated information sharing in groups: Moving beyond the hidden profile paradigm. *Communication Monographs, 71*, 286–310.

Wittenbaum, G. M., Hubbell, A. P., & Zuckerman, C. (1999). Mutual enhancement: Toward an understanding of the collective preference for shared information. *Journal of Personality and Social Psychology, 77*, 967–978.

Wittenbaum, G. M., Shulman, H. C., & Braz, M. (2010). Social ostracism in task groups: The effects of group composition. *Small Group Research, 41*, 330–353.

Wittenbaum, G. M., Stasser, G., & Merry, C. J. (1996). Tacit coordination in anticipation of small group task completion. *Journal of Experimental Social Psychology, 32*, 129–152.

Zadro, L., Boland, C., & Richardson, R. (2006). How long does it last? The persistence of the effects of ostracism in the socially anxious. *Journal of Experimental Social Psychology, 42*, 692–697.

Zadro, L., Williams, K. D., & Richardson, R. (2004). How low can you go? Ostracism by a computer lowers belonging, control, self-esteem, and meaningful existence. *Journal of Experimental Social Psychology, 40*, 560–567.

4

GROUP RESEARCH USING HIGH-FIDELITY EXPERIMENTAL SIMULATIONS

Franziska Tschan and Norbert K. Semmer

UNIVERSITY OF NEUCHÂTEL, SWITZERLAND AND UNIVERSITY OF BERN, SWITZERLAND

Sabina Hunziker and Stephan U. Marsch

UNIVERSITY HOSPITAL OF BASEL, SWITZERLAND

The Group Researcher's Dream

As a young group researcher interested in small group productivity, the first author daydreamed about the "paradise for a small group researcher," most often while waiting for undergraduate student participants who did not show up for her laboratory experiments. She imagined a close to real-life situation with a number of characteristics: competent and highly motivated participants; a research-friendly room (not too noisy, so that communication could be recorded; well lit, so there could be video recording); a task that was highly interdependent (thus inducing group processes) and complex (so there would be variance in performance); necessity of overt behavior, so group processes could be observed and coded. She wished for a rather short group process (as transcribing and coding is time-consuming), and finally she dreamt that there would be ample communication going on that could be related to group performance. It seemed much too much to ask for. However, some years later, she stumbled across the website of a group of physicians at a nearby hospital, presenting the "high-fidelity patient simulator" they used for training and research. The description surpassed the dream. The pictures showed medical professionals in a well-lit room gathered around a patient and obviously working in a highly interdependent way as a group. She wrote a mail. So, for a number of years, the authors of this chapter (two psychologists and two physicians) have been collaborating in research projects using a high-fidelity patient simulator that is situated in the Intensive Care Unit of the Basel University Hospital in Switzerland.

In this chapter, we share our thoughts and experiences on how to do group research using experimental simulation with high-fidelity simulators. Because we draw on our own experiences, most of the examples will be related to patient simulators, but the general lessons apply to research with simulators in other fields, too. (1) We will first give a short introduction into experimental simulation, what simulators are and how they are used. (2) In the main part, we discuss the characteristics of group research with simulators. We will present how research designs and methods may have to be adapted to characteristics of the tasks and the participants involved. (3) Research with simulators requires most often interdisciplinary cooperation. Again, drawing from our experiences, we will talk about the different backgrounds, interests, and research and publication strategies of group researchers and physicians, as we experience them.

What are simulators, who uses them and for what purpose?

Simulation in a broad sense is really nothing new in small group research. Group researchers have "simulated" political committees (Stasser & Titus, 1987) jury deliberations (Kerr & MacCoun, 1985; Tindale, Nadler, Krebel, & Davis, 2004); mechanical assembly groups (Moreland & Myaskovsky, 2000), or business negotiations (Weingart, Bennett, & Brett, 1993), to name just a few. However, most laboratory tasks are rather simple and only faintly resemble 'real' tasks, because the experimenter wants to control as much of the situation as possible. The use of simple tasks has many advantages; it generates, however, the problem of limited generalizability of the results to more complex situations. One obvious solution to this problem is to study real groups working on real tasks. This is, however, very difficult to do, and often, the complexity and variety of real tasks and situations make it difficult to draw conclusions from field research (e.g., Brehmer & Dörner, 1993). It thus seems to be a good idea to work with settings that simulate reality, but can still be standardized and controlled by the researchers (Vincenzi, Wise, Moula, & Hanckock, 2009).

In the continuum between artificial laboratory tasks and real situations, Gray (2002) distinguishes different types of simulated task environments with increasing complexity and realism. (1) Microworlds are computer game-like dynamic tasks that require rather complex decision making. For example, one has to be the mayor of a city, make decisions of allocating money; give advice to an African tribe (Brehmer & Dörner, 1993), or manage a forest fire (Granlund & Johanssoin, 2004). Although researchers usually try to present these tasks in a realistic context, the main goal is to study specific task requirements rather than being representative of the context that is chosen to embed the task. (2) Scaled worlds (also called synthetic task environments) are constructed to recreate important aspects of a real task, but are not necessary realistically to match the whole task and its environment. Cooke and Shope (2004) describe how to design a scaled world; theirs is based on the analysis of real military operations, and maps the most important aspects of these operations. When constructing a scaled world, researchers do not try to achieve high realism of all aspects of the task and its environment.

Rather, they strive for "psychological fidelity;" this is to present tasks so that they trigger the psychological or group processes the researcher wants to train or to study (Gurtner, Tschan, Semmer, & Nägele, 2006; Kozlowski & DeShon, 2004). (3) Finally, high-fidelity simulators are closest to real tasks because they are designed to provide an as-realistic-as-possible task in a realistic environment. High-fidelity simulators often map real tasks and their environments very closely. For example, power-plant simulators can not only simulate most of the states and potential problems of the plant: many are also located in a room that exactly matches the real control room of the plant, including the layout of all the work stations, screens, and even phones, printers, and noises. Flight-simulators do not only map the outline of the cockpit and display realistic computer animations of what pilots would see in the windows, but they are built on a platform that can simulate motion; and simulator stations for firefighters might include constrained paths, smoke, and even heat (McFetrich, 2007). This realism is useful, because high-fidelity simulators are most often designed for training of complex and difficult situations.

In our research, we work with high-fidelity patient simulators, which will be described next. In medicine, artificial full-sized patient simulators have been used as early as 1874 for nursing education (Good, 2003; Nehring & Lashley, 2009). However, only the recent technological development has allowed constructing high-fidelity patient simulators. The one we are working with is a real life-size rubber mannequin, full of mechanical and electronic devices that are controlled by a computer. He (most of the time our 'patient' is male) can open his eyes; he blinks regularly, and when doctors shine a flashlight into his pupils, they contract, unless the simulator is programmed otherwise. He breathes, and when he does, his chest moves. When he exhales, one can feel the air coming out of his mouth, and carbon dioxide levels can be measured; they map those of a real person exhaling and change depending on the condition of the patient. One can palpate pulse at many different locations, and little microphones in his chest can be programmed to display a wide array of different breathing and heart sounds. He can even twitch his thumb. Although a closer look makes very apparent that he is artificial, he looks stunningly human. The patient can even talk, with loudspeakers in his head being connected to an intercom operated from behind a one-way mirror. The simulator recognizes administration of medication and responds to it in real time. Parameters such as blood pressure, heart rate, and blood oxygen levels can be displayed on a monitor. The number of interventions medical professionals can perform is large. There are also many other medical simulators on the market – simulators of body parts, baby and infant simulators, or a simulator of a woman giving birth, to name just a few.

High-fidelity patient simulators are a relatively recent development; they are still expensive, but their use is growing rapidly. Cooper and Taqueti (2004), who present the history of medical simulators, estimate that the "tipping point" has not yet been reached; so one can expect more and more hospitals and universities to acquire high-fidelity simulators in the future. These simulators are mainly used for training medical professionals, ranging from basic training for medical students to continuous education of experienced physicians, nurses, and other medical professionals (McGaghie, Siddal, Mazmanian, & Myers, 2009). In simulators, medical professionals often train tasks or situations that are either uncomfortable or dangerous for the patient, if not correctly performed. Take the example of an intubation, which involves sticking a plastic tube through the patient's mouth down to the lungs for artificial ventilation. It seems indeed a good idea to perform such an intervention on a plastic mannequin before trying it on a real patient. Simulators are also useful to prepare for situations that occur infrequently (Wang et al., 2008). Real life often may not provide enough opportunities to practice the required reactions to the point at which they become sufficiently routinized. This situation is similar to training in flight-simulators, where pilots repeatedly practice events that they may never encounter, such as emergency landings on water, or in power-plant simulators, where operators train for situations that will hopefully never happen in reality.

Participants in a *simulator session* are confronted with a *scenario* that has been developed and programmed beforehand. In the case of our medical simulator, it can be programmed to be a male or female patient of a certain age with a specific basic condition. In our experimental laboratory, each "patient" has a regular patient file that lists his or her previous conditions. Typically, the scenario unfolds into an emergency situation, usually with the patient developing a specific condition characterized by several distinct phases. For example, in one of our scenarios (Marsch et al., 2005), Mr Bortolotti, the patient, is a 52-year-old male that had been admitted to intensive care after an acute myocardial infarction. He is already branched on to a monitor, and he has an intravenous drip, this is a needle access directly to the vein allowing the delivery of fluids and medication. The hospital bed with Mr Bortolotti is in a room that is furnished like a regular single patient room in an intensive care unit (with the possibility to branch all medical devices). The only difference to a regular patient room is that the room has no windows but a large one-way mirror.

When the participants (physicians) have been with the patient for two minutes, the patient suffers a sudden cardiac arrest; his heart stops pumping blood, but still displays electrical activity (a pulseless ventricular tachycardia). When this happens, we expect the physicians to start resuscitation, which includes defibrillation (applying an electrical shock to the patient's heart using two paddles). After the third defibrillation attempt, the programmer that runs the simulator changes the heart rhythm of the patient for a short time, and then heart activity stops (asystole). At this moment, the physicians are expected to inject a specific drug, and one minute after they do, the heart beat changes again, and can be converted to a normal rhythm with another defibrillation. This is a typical scenario;

it includes several phases, and the transition into a next phase depends on the physicians' interventions. The patient's state depends on the interventions of the team. For example, if the team misses a step, the patient becomes worse. However, there is always a nurse from the simulator team in the room, who intervenes if the physicians are lost for a long time and helps them to save the patient (see Figure 4.1).

High-fidelity patient simulators permit simulating rather complex situations and tasks. This includes tasks that require close collaboration of several people, offering excellent opportunities to train cooperation, communication, and teamwork. Although team training is not yet explicitly one of the core uses of simulators (Rosen et al., 2008), more and more authors stress the potential of simulators for training and assessing teamwork (Aggarwal, Undre, Moorthy, Vincent, & Darzi, 2004; Fernandez et al., 2008; Lane, Slavin, & Ziv, 2001).

In sum, patient simulators allow presenting very realistic medical situations (our participants rate the realism of the scenario at 8.5, on a scale from 1 to 10); they are used increasingly, most often for training technical skills. In addition, their potential for team training and assessment is being recognized, and presents an excellent starting point for the psychologist interested in group and team research.

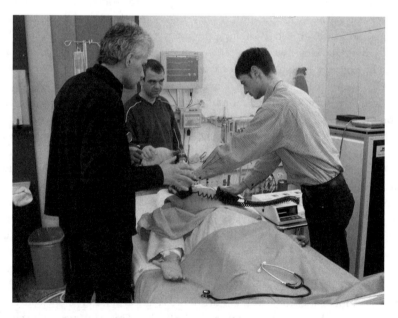

FIGURE 4.1 Cardiopulmonary resuscitation in a high-fidelity simulator setting.

Doing Small Group Research with High-fidelity (Patient) Simulators

Research topics and designs

Research topics

Given that the main use of high-fidelity simulators is skills training, research most often evaluates training success with regard to technical skills, often comparing simulator-based training with other teaching protocols. For medical simulations, the Agency for Healthcare Research and Quality (Marinopoulos et al., 2007) provides a good overview for this research, as does a paper by McGaghie and colleagues (2009).

Group and team-related research using simulators is on the rise and covers a wide variety of research questions. However, a literature search in psychology or communication journals may convey the impression that not much has yet been done, since many simulator-based studies on teamwork are published in journals of the respective field, rather than in psychology or communication journals. Research with patient simulators is found in many different medical journals, but there is also a medical journal that is entirely devoted to simulation-based medical research, called *Simulation in Healthcare*. Research with flight-simulators or military simulators may be published in human factors or ergonomics journals (Burke, Salas, Wilson-Donnelly, & Priest, 2004; Gaba, Howard, Fish, Smith, & Sowb, 2001; Helmreich & Davis, 1997; Salas, Sims, Klein, & Burke, 2003; Sexton, Thomas, & Helmreich, 2000), or domain-specific journals, such as aviation or military psychology journals. The literature search is even more difficult because some of the relevant research is not found under the keywords "groups" or "teams," as scholars use other keywords, such as "nontechnical skills," "communication" or "leadership." To find research topics and assess previous research, scholars may thus have to do literature searches beyond their field.

Research designs

What research designs are particularly well suited for simulator-based research? In principle, the same rules and methods as for other (group) research apply. Simulators seem well suited for *experimental research*, because they allow presenting the same task and situation with the same problem and the same temporal development to all participants. However, achieving a fully controlled experimental situation is not easy, because rigorous control of all important influences is often limited. This has to do with the fact that "laboratory experiments are inherently artificial" (Brewer, 2000, p. 15), whereas one of the main objectives (and strengths) of high-fidelity simulators is the possibility to model complex and highly realistic tasks. Experimental psychologists may thus be confronted with several factors limiting experimental control, which we illustrate here with regard to patient simulators.

First, participants are experienced medical professionals; even medical students are by no means "naïve subjects" (McGathie, 2008). In our research, we try to control for differences in expertise by asking physicians about their levels of training and experience. Medical students will also answer a knowledge test; physicians, however, will often not consent to such a test (remember, they come for training purposes, not primarily to participate in research). Furthermore, too specific questions may entail cues about the scenario to be expected. Thus, it is difficult to control for differences in pre-existing knowledge and expertise, which tend to be rather large.

Second, our participants expect training that is interesting and useful, and also provides them with credits for continuous education; therefore, the scenarios have to be meaningful and complex enough so that even experienced physicians can learn something. Certain interventions we would sometimes like to do are therefore not feasible; for example, we cannot interrupt the group after partial task fulfillment to give them self-report questionnaires. Third, our tasks can be solved in very different ways. For example, the guidelines for treating a "simple" cardiac arrest describe more than 30 different potential steps to consider or to carry out (e.g., Nolan, Deakin, Soar, Bottiger, & Smith, 2005). Although the guidelines suggest an ideal sequence of interventions, there are several reasonable ways to proceed, implying that different groups take different steps at different times. In order to stay realistic, the patient's reactions to all these variations has to be adapted, even if this was not planned initially. So occasionally, there are deviations from the standardized protocol, which may create less standardization than is needed for fully controlled experiments. Furthermore, a so-called scripted nurse (a confederate) participates in most simulator sessions to assist the physicians and help in case of technical problems. Although the nurse is instructed to act and react in a prescribed manner, he or she has to adapt his or her behavior to the actual situation and may not be able to stick to the script entirely.

All this creates threats to validity. These threats could be at least partially overcome with large sample sizes, which allows including more control variables without losing too much statistical power. However, simulator-based studies often have relatively small sample sizes. Participants cannot be recruited *ad libitum*, and running scenarios takes a lot of time and resources. Sample size concerns are even more important for group research, where often the group is the unit of analysis, implying small N values even though many participants may be involved.

Researchers who are not working with patient simulators may encounter similar practical limitations. We emphasize these aspects because, although simulator studies seem to be the experimental group researcher's dream at first sight, there may be important limitations for conducting highly controlled experiments.

Nevertheless, experimental designs are possible. For example, in one of our studies we randomly assigned medical students to groups with a technical debriefing (emphasizing the importance of some technical skills) or a leadership debriefing (emphasizing the importance of teamwork aspects) after the session. Four months later, we tested the students a second time, assigning them to groups at random but always within the same debriefing condition. This allowed us to test the influence of debriefing type on later group performance (Hunziker et al., 2010). In another study, we randomly assigned physicians to conditions where they received standard information plus a short leadership instruction prior to meeting the patient, or standard information only, in order to test effects of the different instructions (Tschan, Semmer, Windlinger, Hunziker, & Marsch, 2009). In these studies, the experimental manipulations were relatively simple, and we could test their influence on behavior and performance.

Simulators also present many possibilities to conduct *quasi-experimental research* (Shadish, Cook, & Campbell, 2002) where groups are not randomly assigned to experimental conditions. For example, in one study, we compared performance of general physicians and advanced medical students for the same scenario (Lüscher et al., 2010).

Simulator settings are particularly well suited for *observational studies* (Kerr, Aronoff, & Messé, 2000; Runkle & McGrath, 1972), where processes that are occurring "naturally" are reported, and hypotheses about these processes can be tested. The high realism of simulator settings offers many possibilities to investigate phenomena that have not yet been extensively studied in small groups, or to investigate phenomena well known from group research in a more realistic environment, with participants acting in their everyday roles. For example, we are currently investigating treatment interruptions in groups confronted with a cardiac arrest. This is particularly important, as each minute of untreated cardiac arrest diminishes survival chances by 7–10 per cent (von Planta, 2004). In a first study, we simply measured and counted interruptions – and were astonished by their number and length (Marsch et al., 2005). Given that the physicians told us that they were not aware of having interrupted treatment, in a later study we coded what groups actually did when interrupting patient care. We found that they are often so actively involved in monitoring the patient's condition or in resolving technical or knowledge problems that their attention was diverted from immediate treatment requirements (Tschan, Vetterli, Semmer, Hunziker & Marsch, in press). We are now evaluating which parts of the resuscitation process are most vulnerable for interruptions, what triggers them, and how they are overcome.

Simulator studies are also well suited for *qualitative research or a combination of quantitative and qualitative analyses*. Many researchers, particularly psychologists, shy away from including qualitative aspects into their research; it is difficult to do, and many psychology journals seem reluctant to publish studies based on qualitative data. However, qualitative research can be very useful for domains where theories are not well developed; and a combination of qualitative and quantitative research can be interesting if theories are "nascent", that is, not yet fully developed or mature (Edmondson & McManus, 2007). For example, in one scenario we observed that important information from the patient file often was not communicated to the group, despite the fact that at least one group member had consulted the patient file. Qualitative analyses of who handled the patient file in which manner suggested a phenomenon we called an "illusory transactive memory system." Transactive memory systems imply that members know about each other's competences, and rely on this knowledge. If one group member obviously has access to potentially important information (in this case, the patient file) but does not communicate anything, the group may erroneously assume that there is no important information in the file (Tschan et al., 2009). Another reason for qualitative data analysis for simulator-based studies is the occurrence of rare events, such as errors (Burke et al., 2004).

In sum, simulators provide good opportunities for experimental research, although there might be more confounding factors and unwanted influences than in classical laboratory experiments. Simulations are also well suited for observational and qualitative research, thus allowing a wide combination of methods.

Running a simulator study

Getting access to a (patient) simulator

For researchers, the first step is to establish cooperation with the professionals that run the simulators. This may be difficult in some cases, for example, access to powerplant simulators or military or police simulators may not be easy. In our case, we have found physicians and nurses to be very open for such a collaboration: after the first author initiated the contact, the physicians invited us to visit the simulator center; after some visits and discussions, the current research group formed. So, a first task for a researcher may be to make contact with simulator centers. Good sources of information where medical simulators are located are the websites of the Society for Simulation in Healthcare (SSIH) (www.ssih.org) in the US, and the Society for Simulation Applied to Medicine (SESAM) (www.sesam-web.org) in Europe. The annual conference of the SSIH provides an excellent opportunity for getting information, learning about 'hot' research topics, and for networking.

If the possibility for running a group study with a simulator is established, the general steps are the same as for any group research; however, some adaptations may be necessary. The process starts with scenario development and adaptation.

Scenario development and adaptation

Developing scenarios is a central aspect of simulator studies (Good, 2003). Obviously, good scenarios require profound knowledge in the domain studied; the scenario has to be realistic, the time frame has to be adequate, reactions of the system have to be plausible, etc. This has to be done by the domain specialists, but group researchers can contribute in terms of criteria for task requirements. For example, from a medical point of view, different illnesses may be worlds apart. From a psychological point of view, more general task requirements may be prominent, for instance, with regard to communication, planning, leadership, and coordination, or with regard to common errors in diagnosis, decision making, etc.

To give an example, our research involves two basic types of tasks. The first one (cardiac arrest) refers to a situation where the diagnosis is clear and unambiguous; the main question is whether participants perform the necessary (and well-known) intervention in a timely and adequate manner. Good team coordination in this scenario requires decisive leadership and timely task distribution. The second scenario refers to a situation where the diagnosis is ambiguous, as we provide cues pointing to a diagnosis that is wrong yet plausible (pneumothorax), sharing some (but not all) symptoms with the correct diagnosis (anaphylactic shock). The main question in this scenario is whether the team will adequately consider the information available, and good team coordination requires sharing of deliberate reasoning rather than quick decisions (cf. Tschan et al., 2009). The challenge in developing this scenario was to construe a case where some of the patient's symptoms could plausibly be interpreted in terms of two different diagnoses. Also, we had to construct a patient history that made sense for both diagnoses. Sometimes, in planning scenarios for simulations, researchers conduct a cognitive task-analysis (Gugerty, 2004), based on real situations (Klein, 2000) that helps to identify important task requirements of a situation. Once the basic scenario is developed, one has to consider possible adaptations, either for specific training goals (see Beard and colleagues, 1995, for guidelines), or for research goals. In some cases, relatively small adaptations suffice; others require more extended variations.

For example, in two of our studies we investigated errors in information transmitted to a physician who joined an ongoing emergency situation (Bogenstätter et al., 2009). The design for the first study was relatively easy: we simply asked the physicians to wait outside and join the situation only when called by the nurses who witnessed the emergency. We could then assess the adequacy of information transmitted to the physicians after they joined the group. In the second study, we wanted to test the hypotheses that (a) unusual information, (b) shared information, and (c) information about interventions would have a greater chance to be transmitted. For this, we had to change the patient history and to adapt the beginning of the scenario in a way that allowed us to provide some information to one group member only, and some to all. For the ambiguous diagnosis scenario mentioned above, (Tschan et al., 2009), we had to construe a variant without distracting cues in order to demonstrate that it was indeed the distracting information, rather than the complexity of the anaphylactic shock reaction, that was responsible for the difficulty in determining the correct diagnosis.

Running a simulator study

Running a simulator study typically requires especially long preparation time, and often more people are involved in each session than in other group experiments. For example, to run one of our experiments, we need a scripted nurse, someone who plays the patient (in terms of talking as the patient and at the same time controlling the simulator), a physician who hands the patient over to the group, and one person who organizes and runs the experiment. Otherwise, a simulator study is not very different from any other group experiment; we therefore refer to the respective chapters in this book. As with all research, it is advisable to obtain early Institutional Review Board (IRB) permission. Our participants sign up for training sessions, and they are informed in advance that we would like to use their data for research. We ask participants after the session to sign a sheet permitting us to use their data for research purposes; so far, only a few people declined. The IRB gave its consent to our procedure.

Data coding

Typically, in simulator centers, video cameras are installed, and sessions are taped for training debriefing. Thus, group process data are easily accessible. In our simulator room one of two cameras is focused on the patient bed, the other one, a wide-angle camera, is overlooking the whole room, so that all participants can be observed. A picture of the patient surveillance monitor is displayed on the screen, which allows for coding information about the patient's condition over time.

There is a variety of methods for behavioral coding in small group research. Generally applicable systems are the International Process Analysis (IPA) coding system by Bales (1950), the time-by-event method by Futoran and colleagues (Futoran, Kelly, & McGrath, 1989), or the function-oriented interaction coding system (Hirokawa, 1988) to name just a few. However, these systems are better suited for communication tasks than for tasks with high manual components. Most often, researchers adapt observational systems to their specific needs; such adaptations are explicitly encouraged in introductory texts on group process methods (McGrath & Altermatt, 2001; Weingart, 1997; Weingart, Olekalns, & Smith, 2004). Coding schemes have been developed and adapted for different simulator settings, such as powerplant simulations (Stachowski, Kaplan, & Waller, 2009), or aviation (Kanki, Lozito, & Foushee, 1989). Examples from the medical field are the observational coding systems by Kolbe, Künzle, Zala-Mezö, Wacker, and Grote (2009), and by Manser, Howard, and Gaba (2009) that are designed for observation during anesthesia inductions. These systems include measures for explicit and implicit coordination, for heedful interrelating, but also for task distribution and other important aspects of cooperation. Most importantly, these systems suggest coding not only for communication, but also for actions, and they provide examples of how to do this.

Another, more general, approach for observational systems has been proposed by Flin and Maran (2004). Their method allows developing and adapting behavior categories (called behavioral markers) for various cooperative situations in medicine, such as anesthesia or surgery. Their approach is based on similar systems used in aviation research (Fletcher et al., 2004; Helmreich, 2000). To develop behavioral markers for an observational system, they interview and survey specialists (Flin, Yule, Paterson-Brown, & Maran, 2006) and draw on existing observation systems (Fletcher et al., 2002, 2003; Klampfer et al., 2001; Yule, Flin, Paterson-Brown, Maran, & Rowley, 2006). Although their systems are mostly used for on-site assessments (Yule et al., 2008), they also are a valuable source for developing observational categories for video-based data.

To provide an example, we shortly describe parts of the coding system we used for one of our first studies. It investigated a resuscitation scenario, with medical professionals joining an emergency situation sequentially (Tschan et al., 2006). The goal of this study was to assess the relationship between communication and performance before and after new group members joined. We first transcribed all communication word by word, indicating who said what when. These transcripts were done by a medically trained person. Although on-line coding systems exist that would not require transcription, transcribing all communication helped, since often, communication was not easy to understand and participants used medical jargon. Since we hypothesized that directive leadership should be important for this task, we then coded each communication utterance with regard to directive leadership and other, more indirect strategies, such as a strategy we called "structuring inquiry." As in many other studies, we also initially coded some other aspects that did not make it into the paper. After training, coding could be done reliably, but was time consuming. We still use spreadsheets for transcripts and coding, but many others use observational software.

Our first experiences with behavioral coding taught us some seemingly trivial yet important lessons. For instance, we learned that automatic alarms from the surveillance monitor were so dominant (as alarms should be) that they masked some of the communication; the same applied to noisy equipment (e.g., an artificial breathing machine). Currently, we avoid having noisy equipment in the room whenever possible. Also, it was sometimes difficult to distinguish people and voices based on the video tapes, another problem for completing transcripts. Now, participants can be identified by the use of large numbers on their front, arms and back (as they move around in the room), facilitating the transcription of communication.

Students who work with us, by transcribing and coding, often underestimated the extent to which they needed to understand the medical terms used. Nurses and physicians use specialized vocabulary including, for example, abbreviations for drugs and doses; they discuss highly technical aspects, or ask questions about patient conditions that only medically trained people understand. They also use jargon, such as "filling up the patient" (i.e., increase the speed of the saline solution dripping into the patient's arm in order to increase the volume of fluid in the patient's body). This expert communication requires that the researchers understand the task and the possible interventions well, and transcripts cannot be done by untrained students. Even so, the physicians were required to help in interpreting the communication. This necessity to have at least a basic understanding of the task to be able to do reliable transcripts and coding may be even more of a challenge when using other simulators, for example, powerplant or flight simulators, and researchers have to be aware of the training requirements for coders.

Assessing group performance

We usually are interested in predicting group performance, so we need group performance measures. One way to assess performance is to rely on specialist's overall judgment, for example, by having experienced physicians rate the performance. This has been done successfully in powerplant simulation studies (Waller, 1999) and in flight simulator studies (Brannick, Prince, & Salas, 2002; Waller, 1996). However, this requires several domain specialists to review each session, which often is not feasible.

For our research, we develop performance markers for each scenario (Tschan et al., 2011), based on recommendations by Gaba and colleagues (1998). For some cases, this was easy. In the study on ambiguous diagnostic information, for instance (Tschan et al., 2009), we simply assessed whether and when the group communicated the correct diagnosis and started the appropriate first intervention; this could be easily coded based on the video tapes. For other scenarios, developing performance measures was more complicated. For example, in the cardiac arrest scenario, patient survival is not a feasible performance measure, as patients may well die even if the resuscitation is done perfectly (White & Guly, 1999). In addition, for didactic and ethical reasons, we never let the patient "die." In the rare cases where the groups do not treat the patient in an appropriate way for a very long time, the scripted nurse intervenes. We thus had to develop process performance measures. For this, we perform a task analysis (Tschan et al., 2011) and often develop several performance measures. For cardiac resuscitation, task analysis is based on the published treatment algorithms (Nolan et al., 2005) that describe "appropriate treatment during a cardiac arrest." We thus code for every second whether someone ventilated the patient, did cardiac massage, defibrillated or intubated the patient.

Given that time is critical in cardiac arrest situations, we often use performance measures that are time-related. For instance, we calculate the time the patient received appropriate treatment as a percentage of the time he needed treatment (i.e., had no pulse). Using such a performance measure, we can compare the performance across different phases or time-segments (e.g., before and after a physician joins). In the literature, one finds performance markers or performance checklists for many different medical scenarios. For example, Forrest and colleagues (2002) describe a performance assessment for anesthesia, based on text-book descriptions and guidelines, as well as on their own experience and expert advice.

Data analysis

Analysis of simulator-based data is, again, very similar to that of other group behavioral studies, and we refer to the respective literature (McGrath & Altermatt, 2001; Weingart, 1997). As the tasks we study are quite complex, we often do not analyze the process as a whole, but only specific phases. It has been shown, for instance, that a first organizing and planning phase should occur early in an emergency (McGrath & Tschan, 2004; Tschan, McGrath et al., 2009). Therefore, we often assess only initial leadership behavior, for instance, during the first three minutes. Indeed, in one of our studies we could confirm the hypothesis that performance was predicted only by directive leadership behavior that occurred during the first 30 seconds after the first physician joined an emergency (Tschan et al., 2006).

Often, specific events, such as for interruptions, or information transmission episodes, are of special interest. As such events may occur multiple times, multilevel modeling may be the appropriate methodological approach for such a data structure (e.g. Bogenstätter et al., 2009).

In sum, group research with (patient) simulators is not fundamentally different from other group research. However, whereas researchers in social psychology often can choose a task and therefore avoid specificities of tasks exerting a dominant influence, our research with such realistic and complex tasks constantly reminds us of the need to develop a good understanding of the tasks involved (Hackman & Morris, 1975; McGrath, 1984; Tschan & von Cranach, 1996).

Interdisciplinary collaboration

Simulator research requires interdisciplinary collaboration with domain experts. In our case, we collaborate with physicians and nurses. Each profession speaks a different professional language, and brings different competences, but also different research interests and research traditions to the table. It is thus important to get to know each other's perspectives and to negotiate interests. For example, medical professionals have the knowledge about patient conditions, diseases and intervention possibilities necessary for developing scenarios and interpreting participant behavior. On the other hand, social scientists typically have detailed knowledge about group processes, running experiments, data coding, and analysis. In the following, we list a few aspects where we became aware of the differences between disciplines. Again, we limit the discussion to the collaboration between physicians and psychologists, but assume that there are similar issues when cooperating with pilots, firefighters, or powerplant operators.

Maintaining realism versus standardization of the scenario

Physicians often are more concerned about the medical realism of the scenario than are psychologists. Thus, when a group did something unexpected, the physicians sometimes applied short-term changes to the scenario in order to adapt to the group's behavior. The psychologists were less worried about main-taining realism under all circumstances, but more concerned about standardiza-tion of the experimental situation. In our studies, given that physicians attend simulator sessions for training, in case of doubt, realism has to be more important than standardization. If important deviations from the protocol are necessary, we deal with this rare, but recurring issue by excluding those groups from analysis, similar to the exclusion of participants that do not follow instructions in a classical experiment. In one scenario that required flexible adaptations more fre-quently, the physician steering the simulator kept to the standardization as long as possible in each session, and signaled with a very short change of the patient's heartbeat (visible on the screen) that from this point forward he had to deviate from the standardized protocol. We then analyzed the group process data only up to this point.

Standardization of instructions and experimenter behavior

Similar problems arose for standardizing behavior such as instructions, informa-tion given to the participants, 'patient' verbal behavior, and the behavior of the scripted nurse. Careful instruction of all people involved was necessary. Often, physicians who happened to be on duty on the ward when we ran simulator sessions helped by playing the role of the physician handing over the patient to the group. All of them would have made great actors, but we had to limit their improvisation talents and to require that they act strictly in accordance with the instructions. Standardization of behavior was even more of a challenge for the scripted nurses and for the physician who represented the patient's voice, because they had to react flexibly but within prescribed limits to the actions of group members, and still play their role realistically. They thus had to maintain an "ad-hoc" equilibrium between standardization and adaptation.

Research traditions

Analyzing data and publishing follows different traditions in medicine and social sciences. Papers in medical journals are usually much shorter than publications in psychology; they have a somewhat different structure, and medical journals require a less extensive theoretical introduction than is customary in psychology. The psychologists in our group had thus to learn to refrain from suggesting long theoretical introductions when collaborating on a paper for a medical journal, and the physicians sometimes expressed concern about the rather extensive theorizing and the length of the papers for psychology journals. In our group, the physicians take the lead for publications in medical journals (often focused on aspects of medical training or medical performance with a strong emphasis on results that are immediately relevant for medical practice), the psychologists for publications in psychological journals (in our case focused on aspects of team processes, with a strong emphasis on basic research). This works very well.

There are also some differences in the statistical methods used in the two fields. For example, mediation analysis *à la* Baron and Kenny (1986) is not widely known or used in medical research. On the other hand, physicians use analyses that are not well known in other fields, such as survival analysis, and they often tend to divide continuous variables into discrete groups, for instance, by dichotomizing. Also, citation rules are strict in both medicine and psychology, but they differ in important ways.

Publications

Interdisciplinary collaboration is very enriching, but also has its costs, and these may be important, especially for young researchers. Running simulator-based studies requires substantial contributions of many people: specialists are needed for scenario development, for running the studies, and for coding, analysis, and writing. Therefore, most of our publications have many authors, sometimes more than six, and this is not uncommon in medicine. Publishing with many co-authors may, however, imply a disadvantage for young scholars who may be confronted with a selection committee that only partly acknowledges multiauthor publications. In addition, it may also be a disadvantage for social scientists to publish in medical journals, because colleagues may not easily find these publications, and journals of other fields are sometimes not recognized when publications or citations are counted in order to assess performance of a researcher. However, there is increasing awareness for the need of interdisciplinary research; thus, having publications in different fields may also be an advantage. Nevertheless, especially young researchers need to consider these aspects.

Conclusion

In our experience, research with simulators is one of the most fascinating opportunities for group researchers. In our research, we could show how directive leadership is important in unambiguous situations, and how explicit reasoning is important in ambiguous ones; we could show that some leadership interventions may be effective despite being very short; or we could show that quantitative information will be transmitted more accurately if encoded exactly as is needs to be transmitted (see Hunziker et al., 2010, for an overview of our research). This research is continuing, and there are many more issues we will be investigating.

Young researchers need to be aware that simulator-based research may take somewhat more time than classical experiments run with in-house subject pools, and they may have to reflect on possible publication strategies. However, running simulator sessions and observing the group processes is fascinating; the tasks have high external validity, and there are many different topics worth studying.

Authors' Note:

This paper was supported by a grant from the Swiss National Science foundation #325130-113429 to S. U. Marsch, N. K. Semmer, and F. Tschan.

References

Aggarwal, R., Undre, S., Moorthy, K., Vincent, C., & Darzi, A. (2004). The simulated operating theatre: comprehensive training for surgical teams. *Quality and Safety in Healthcare* (suppl 1), i27–32.

Bales, R. F. (1950). *Interaction process analysis. A method for the study of small groups.* Cambridge, MA: Addison-Wesley Press.

Baron, R. M., & Kenny, D. A. (1986). The moderator–mediator variable distinction in social psychological research: Conceptual, strategic, and statistical considerations. *Journal of Personality and Social Psychology, 51*, 1173–1182.

Beard, R. L., Salas, E., & Prince, C. (1995). Enhancing transfer of training: Using role-play to foster teamwork in the cockpit. *International Journal of Aviation Psychology, 5*, 131–143.

Bogenstätter, Y., Tschan, F., Semmer, N. K., Spychiger, M., Breuer, M., & Marsch, S. (2009). How accurate is information transmitted to medical professionals joining a medical emergency? A simulator study. *Human Factors: The Journal of the Human Factors and Ergonomics Society, 51*, 115–125.

Brannick, M., Prince, C., & Salas, E. (2002). The reliability of instructor evaluations of crew performance: Good news and not so good news. *The International Journal of Aviation Psychology, 12*, 241–261.

Brehmer, B., & Dörner, D. (1993). Experiments with computer-simulated microworlds: Escaping both the narrow straits of the laboratory and the deep blue sea of the field study. *Computers in Human Behavior, 9*, 171–184.

Brewer, M. B. (2000). Research design and issues of validity. In H. T. Reis, & C. M. Judd (Eds.), *Handbook of research methods in social and personality psychology* (pp. 3–16). Cambridge: Cambridge University Press.

Burke, C. S., Salas, E., Wilson-Donnelly, K., & Priest, H. (2004). How to turn a team of experts into an expert medical team: Guidance from the aviation and military communities. *Quality and Safety in Health Care, 13*(suppl 1), i96–104.

Cooke, N. J., & Shope, S. M. (2004). Designing a synthetic task environment. In S. Schiflett, G., L. Elliott, R., E. Salas & M. D. Coovert (Eds.), *Scaled worlds: Development, validation, and application* (pp. 263–278). Aldershot: Ashgate.

Cooper, J. B., & Taqueti, V. R. (2004). A brief history of the development of mannequin simulators for clinical education and training. *Quality and Safety in Health Care, 13*(suppl 1), i11–18.

Edmondson, A. C., & McManus, S. E. (2007). Methodological fit in management field research. *Academy of Management Review, 32*, 1155–1179.

Fernandez, R., Vozenilek, J. A., Hegarty, C. B., Motola, I., Rezneck, M., Phrampus, P. E., & Kozlowski, S. W. (2008). Developing expert medical teams: Toward an evidence-based approach. *Academic Emergency Medicine, 15*, 1025–1036.

Fletcher, G., Flin, R., McGeorge, P., Glavin, R., Maran, N., & Patey, R. (2003). Anaesthetists' Non-Technical Skills (ANTS): Evaluation of a behavioural marker system. *British Journal of Anaesthesia, 90*, 580–588.

Fletcher, G., Flin, R., McGeorge, P., Glavin, R., Maran, N., & Patey, R. (2004). Rating non-technical skills: Developing a behavioural marker system for use in anaesthesia. *Cognition, Technology and Work, 6*, 165–171.

Flin, R., & Maran, N. (2004). Identifying and training non-technical skills for teams in acute medicine. *Quality and Safety in Health Care, 13* (suppl 1), i80–i84.

Flin, R., Yule, S., Paterson-Brown, S., & Maran, N. (2006). Attitudes to teamwork and safety in the operating theatre. *The Surgeon, 4*(145–51).

Forrest, F. C., Taylor, M. A., Postlethwaite, K., & Aspinall, R. (2002). Use of a high-fidelity simulator to develop testing of the technical performance of novice anaesthetists. *British Journal of Anaesthesia, 88*, 338–344.

Futoran, G. C., Kelly, J. R., & McGrath, J. E. (1989). TEMPO: A time-based system for analysis of group interaction processes. *Basic and Applied Social Psychology, 10*, 211–232.

Gaba, D. M., Howard, S. K., Fish, K. J., Smith, B. E., & Sowb, Y. A. (2001). Simulation-based training in Anesthesia Crisis Resource Management (ACRM): A decade of experience. *Simulation Gaming, 32*, 175–193.

Gaba, D. M., Howard, S. K., Flanagan, B., Smith, B. E., Fish, K. J., & Botney, R. (1998). Assessment of clinical performance during simulated crisis using both technical and behavioral ratings. *Anesthesiology, 89*, 8–18.

Good, M. L. (2003). Patient simulation for training basic and advanced clinical skills. *Medical Education, 37*(suppl 1), 14–21.

Granlund, R., & Johanssoin, B. (2004). Monitoring distributed collaboration in the C3 fire Microworld. In S. Schiflett, L. Elliott, E. Salas, & Coovert (Eds.), *Scaled worlds: Development, validation, and application* (pp. 37–48). Aldershot: Ashgate.

Gray, W. D. (2002). Simulated task environments: The role of high-fidelity simulations, scaled worlds, synthetic environments, and laboratory tasks in basic and applied cognitive research. *Cognitive Science Quarterly, 2*, 205–227.

Gugerty, L. (2004). Using cognitive task analysis to design multiple synthetic tasks von uninhabited aerial vecile operatoin. In S. Shifflett, L. Elliott, E. Salas, & M. Coovert (Eds.), *Scaled worlds: Development, validation, and applications* (pp. 240–261). Aldershot: Ashgate.

Gurtner, A., Tschan, F., Semmer, N. K., & Nägele, C. (2006). Getting groups to develop good strategies: Effects of reflexivity interventions on team process, team performance, and shared mental models. *Organizational Behavior and Human Decision Processes, 102*, 127–142.

Hackman, J. R., & Morris, C. G. (1975). Group tasks, group interaction process, and group performance effectiveness: A review and proposed integration. In L. Berkowitz (Ed.), *Advances in experimental social psychology* (Vol. 8, pp. 45–99). New York: Academic Press.

Helmreich, R. L. (2000). On error management: Lessons from aviation. *British Medical Journal, 320*, 781–785.

Helmreich, R. L., & Davis, J. M. (1997). Anaesthetich simulation and lessons to be learned from aviation. *Canadian Journal of Anaesthesia, 44*, 907–912.

Hirokawa, R. Y. (1988). Group communication and decision-making performance: A continued test of the functional perspective. *Human Communication Research, 4*, 487–515.

Hunziker, S., Bühlmann, C., Tschan, F., Balestra, G., Legret, C., Schumacher, C., Semmer, N. K., Hunziker, P., & Marsch, S. U. (2010). Brief leadership instructions improve cardiopulmonary resuscitation in a high fidelity simulation: a randomized controlled trial. *Critical Care Medicine, 38*, 1086–1091.

Kanki, B. G., Lozito, S., & Foushee, H. C. (1989). Communication indices of crew coordination. *Aviation, Space, and Environmental Medicine, 60*, 56–60.

Kerr, N. L., & MacCoun, R. J. (1985). The effects of jury size and polling method on the process and product of jury deliberation. *Journal of Personality and Social Pschology, 48,* 349–363.

Kerr, N. L., Aronoff, J., & Messé, L. A. (2000). Methods of small group research. In H. T. Reis & C. M. Judd (Eds.), *Handbook of research methods in social and personality psychology* (pp. 160–189). Cambridge: Cambridge University Press.

Klampfer, B., Flin, R., Helmreich, R. L., Häusler, R., Sexton, B., Fletcher, G., Field, P., Staender, S., Lauche, K., Dieckmann, P., & Amacher, A. (2001). Enhancing performance in high risk environments: Recommendations for the use of behavioural markers. Presented at the Behavioural Markers Workshop sponsored by the Daimler–Benz Stiftung GIHRE-Kolleg, Swissair Training Center, Zurich, July 5–6, 2001.

Klein, G. (2000). Cognitive task analysis of teams. In J. M. Schraagen, S. Chipman, & V. Shalin (Eds.), *Cognitive Task Analysis.* Mahwah, NJ: Lawrence Erlbaum.

Kolbe, M., Künzle, B., Zala-Mezö, E., Wacker, J., & Grote, G. (2009). Measuring coordination behavior in anaesthesia teams during induction of general anaesthetics. In R. Flin & L. Mitchell (Eds.), *Safer surgery. Analysing behavior in the operating theatre* (pp. 203–223). Burlington, VT: Ashgate Publishing Company.

Kozlowski, S. W., & DeShon, R. P. (2004). A psychological fidelity approach to simulation-based training: Theory, research and principles. In S. G. Schifflet, L. Elliott, E. Salas, & M. D. Coovert (Eds.), *Scaled worlds: Development, validation and applications* (pp. 75–99). Aldershot: Ashgate.

Lane, J. L., Slavin, S., & Ziv, A. (2001). Simulation in medical education: A review. *Simulation Gaming, 32,* 297–314.

Lüscher, F., Hunziker, S., Gaillard, V., Tschan, F., Semmer, N. K., Hunziker, P., & Marsch, S. U. (2010). Proficiency in cardiopulmonary resuscitation of medical students at graduation: A simulator-based comparison with general practitioners. *Swiss Medical Weekly, 140,* 57–61.

Manser, T., Howard, S. K., & Gaba, D. (2009). Identifying characteristics of effective teamwork in complex medical work enviorments: Adaptive crew coordination in anaesthesia. In R. Flin & L. Mitchell (Eds.), *Safer surgery.* Burlington, VT: Ashgate Publishing Company.

Marinopoulos, S. S., Dorman, T., Ratanawongsa, N., Wilson, L. M., Ashar, B. H., Magaziner, J. L., Miller, R. G., Thomas, P. A., Prokopowicz, G. P., Qayyum, R., & Bass, E. B. (2007). *Effectiveness of continuing medical education. Evidence Report/Technology Assessment No. 149 AHRQ Publication No. 07-E006.* Rockville, MD: Agency for Healthcare Research and Quality.

Marsch, S. U., Tschan, F., Semmer, N., Spychiger, M., Breuer, M., & Hunziker, P. R. (2005). Unnecessary interruptions of cardiac massage during simulated cardiac arrests. *European Journal of Anaesthesiology, 22,* 831–833.

McFetrich, J. (2007). A structured literature review on the use of high fidelity patient simulators for teaching in emergency medicine. *Emergency Medical Journal, 23,* 509–511.

McGathie, W. C. (2008). Research opportuniites in simulation-based medical education using deliberate practice. *Academic Emergency Medicine, 15,* 995–1001.

McGaghie, W. C., Siddal, V. J., Mazmanian, P. E., & Myers, J. (2009). Lessons for continuing medical education from simulation research in undergraduate and graduate medical education. *Chest, 135,* 62S–68S.

McGrath, J. E. (1984). *Groups, interaction and performance.* Englewood Cliffs, NJ: Prentice-Hall.

McGrath, J. E., & Altermatt, W. T. (2001). Observation and analysis of group interaction over time: Some methodological and strategic consequences. In M. A. Hogg & R. S. Tindale (Eds.), *Blackwell handbook of social pschology: Group processes* (pp. 525–556). Oxford: Blackwell Publishers.

McGrath, J. E., & Tschan, F. (2004). Dynamics in groups and teams: Groups as complex action systems. In M. S. Poole & A. H. van de Ven (Eds.), *Handbook of organizational change and development* (pp. 50–73). Oxford: Oxford University Press.

Moreland, R. L., & Myaskovsky, L. (2000). Exploring the performance benefits of group training: Transactive memory or improved communication? *Organizational Behavior and Human Decision Processes, 82*, 117–133.

Nehring, W. M., & Lashley, F. R. (2009). Nursing simulation: A review of the past 40 years. *Simulation & Gaming, 40*, 528–552.

Nolan, J. P., Deakin, C. D., Soar, J., Bottiger, B. W., & Smith, G. (2005). European resuscitation council guidelines for resuscitation 2005: Section 4. Adult advanced life support. *Resuscitation, 67*(suppl 1), S39–S86.

Rosen, M. A., Salas, E., Wu, T. S., Silvestri, S., Lazzara, E. H., Lyons, R., Weaver, S. J., & King, H. B. (2008). Promoting teamwork: An event-based approach to simulation-based teamwork training for emergency medicine residents. *Academic Emergency Medicine, 15*, 1190–1198.

Runkle, P., & Mc Grath, J. E. (1972). *Research on human behavior: A systematic guide to method.* New York, NJ: Holt.

Salas, E., Sims, D. E., Klein, C., & Burke, C. S. (2003). Can teamwork enhance patient safety? *Forum, 23*, 5–9.

Sexton, J. B., Thomas, E. J., & Helmreich, R. L. (2000). Error, stress, and teamwork in medicine and aviation: Cross sectional surveys. *British Medical Journal, 320*, 745–749.

Shadish, W. R., Cook, T. D., & Campbell, D. T. (2002). *Experimental and quasi-experimental designs for generalized causal inferences.* Boston: Houghton-Mifflin.

Stachowski, A. A., Kaplan, S. A., & Waller, M. J. (2009). The benefits of flexible team interaction during crises. *Journal of Applied Psychology, 94*, 1536–1543.

Stasser, G., & Titus, W. (1987). Effects of information load and percentage shared information in the dissemination on unshared information during discussion. *Journal of Personality and Social Psychology, 53*, 81–93.

Tindale, R. S., Nadler, J., Krebel, A., & Davis, J. H. (2004). Procedural mechanisms and jury behavior. In M. B. Brewer & M. Hewstone (Eds.), *Applied social psychology. Perspectives on social psychology* (pp. 136–164). Malden, MA: Blackwell Publishing.

Tschan, F., & von Cranach, M. (1996). Group task structure, processes and outcome. In M. West (Ed.), *Handbook of work group psychology* (pp. 95–121). Chichester: Wiley.

Tschan, F., McGrath, J. E., Semmer, N. K., Arametti, M., Bogenstätter, Y., & Marsch, S. U. (2009). Temporal aspects of processes in ad-hoc groups: A conceptual scheme and some research examples. In R. Roe, M. J. Waller, & C. Clegg (Eds.), *Doing time. Advancing temporal research in organizations.* (pp. 42–60). London: Roudlege.

Tschan, F., Semmer, N. K., Gautschi, D., Hunziker, P., Spychiger, M., & Marsch, S. C. U. (2006). Leading to recovery: Group performance and coordinative activities in medical emergency driven groups. *Human Performance, 19*, 277–304.

Tschan, F., Semmer, N. K., Gurtner, A., Bizzari, L., Spychiger, M., Breuer, M., & Marsch, S. U. (2009). Explicit reasoning, confirmation bias, and illusory transactive memory: A simulation study of broup medical decision making. *Small Group Research, 40*, 271–300.

Tschan, F., Semmer, N. K., Vetterli, M., Gurtner, A., Hunziker, S., & Marsch, S. U. (2011). Developing observational categories for group process research based on task analysis: Examples from research on medical emergency driven teams. In M. Boos, M. Kolbe, P. Kappeler, & T. Ellwart (Eds.), *Coordination in human and primate groups.* Berlin: Springer.

Tschan, F., Semmer, N., Windlinger, R., Hunziker, S., & Marsch, S. U. (2009). *Enhancing leadership and performance by minimal invasive training: The case of medical emergency driven groups treating a cardiac arrest in a high fidelity simulator* Paper presented at the 4th Annual INGRoup Conference, Colorado Springs, July 2009.

Tschan, F., Vetterli, M., Semmer, N. K., Hunziker, S., & Marsch, S. U. (in press). Activities during interruptions in cardiopulmonary resuscitation: A simulator study. *Resuscitation*.

Vincenzi, D. A., Wise, J. A., Moula, M., & Hanckock, P. A. (2009). *Human factors in simulation and training*. Boca Raton, FL: Taylor & Francis.

von Planta, M. (2004). Wissenschaftliche Grundlagen der kardiopulmonalen Reanimation (CPR) [Scientific bases of cardiopulmonary resuscitation]. *Schweizerisches Medizin Forum, 4,* 470–477.

Waller, M. J. (1996). Multiple-task performance in groups. *Academy of Management Proceedings*, 303–306.

Waller, M. J. (1999). The timing of adaptive group responses to nonroutine events. *Academy of Management Journal, 42,* 127–137.

Wang, S. S., Quinones, J., Fitch, M. T., Dooley-Hash, S., Griswold-Theodorson, S., Medzon, R., Korley, F., Laack, T., Robinett, A., & Clay, L. (2008). Developing technical expertise in emergency medicine – the role of simulation in skill acquisition. *Academic Emergency Medicine, 15,* 1046–1057.

Weingart, L. R. (1997). How did they do that? The ways and means of studying group processes. *Research in Organizational Behavior, 19,* 189–239.

Weingart, L. R., Bennett, R. J., & Brett, J. M. (1993). The impact of consideration of issues and motivational orientation on group negotiation process and outcome. *Journal of Applied Psychology, 78,* 504–517.

Weingart, L. R., Olekalns, M., & Smith, P. L. (2004). Quantitative coding of negotiation behaviour. *International Negociation, 9,* 441–455.

White, S. P., & Guly, H. R. (1999). Survival from cardiac arrest in an accident and emergency department: use as a performance indicator? *Resuscitation, 40,* 97–102.

Yule, S., Flin, R., Paterson-Brown, S., Maran, N., & Rowley, D. (2006). Development of a rating system for surgeon's non-technical skills. *Medical Education, 40,* 1098–1104.

Yule, S., Flin, R., Rowley, D., Mitchell, A., Youngson, G. G., Maran, N., & Paterson-Brown, S. (2008). Debriefing surgical trainees on non-technical skills (NOTSS). *Cognition, Technology & Work, 10,* 265–274.

5

COMPUTER SIMULATION METHODS FOR GROUPS

From Formula Translation to Agent-based Modeling

James R. Larson, Jr

LOYOLA UNIVERSITY, CHICAGO

One danger in writing a chapter about computer simulation methods is that it will be read only by the cognoscenti: those who already know a great deal about the topic. Book chapters and journal articles describing particular computer simulations too often are either so abstract that it is hard for anyone but an expert to imagine how those simulations are actually implemented, or so technically detailed that nonexperts are quickly overwhelmed by the thick catalog of particulars. As a consequence, both types tend to be ignored by those with little or no background in computer simulation methods.

In this chapter I try to find a middle ground between the extremes of broad abstraction and excruciating detail that I hope will appeal to those who are unfamiliar with computer simulation, but who nevertheless are curious about (a) how computers can be made to simulate group behavior, and (b) how such simulations can benefit theory development. Toward this end, I emphasize just a few central concepts related to the use and implementation of computer simulations. In doing so, I hope to encourage those who have not tried it before to consider using this valuable research tool.

Preliminaries

In the broadest sense, a computer simulation is simply a program that has been written to emulate some aspect of behavior. The target behavior might be that of human individuals or groups, but could also be the behavior of nonhuman physical or imaginary objects, groups of objects, or large systems. Computer simulations are increasingly used for all sorts of purposes, ranging from gaming and education, to industrial design and product testing. We encounter computer simulations and their results on a near-daily basis, for example, in weather forecasts and highway travel-time projections. Computer simulations can entertain, enlighten, and be of great practical value. And more to the point of the present chapter, they can also be very useful as a tool for developing theory about group behavior.

Computer simulation is sometimes called computational modeling. Computational modeling should not be confused with constructing and testing statistical models using behavioral data, such as might be done with computer programs for hierarchical linear or structural equation modeling. The latter are techniques for discerning regularities in the already observed behavior of individuals and groups. Computational modeling (computer simulation), by contrast, is done for the purpose of generating *predictions about* behavior, given (a) a set of input parameters and processes, and (b) one or more theoretical ideas concerning how those parameters and processes combine to produce the target behavior. Once generated, those predictions can be evaluated for their match to the actual behavior of real people. A close match can increase our confidence that the theory expressed in the simulation is an accurate portrayal of reality, whereas a poor match suggests the need to revise the theory/simulation. Or, the simulation might yield interesting results under conditions (parameter values) for which no empirical data currently exist. In this case, the simulation gives direction to future research with real individuals and groups.

Several points are worth highlighting here. First, the purpose of computer simulation is not to test theory, it is to *express* theory (Ostrom, 1988; Simon, 1992; Sun, 2009). Computer simulation thus serves the same function as do natural language and mathematics, the other two common modes of theoretical expression. Second, a computer simulation's predictions about behavior are obtained simply by running the program. Thus, it is the computer, not the theorist, that deduces the theory's consequences. In this sense, the computer is a "derivation machine" (Latané, 1996), cranking out the logical implications of the theoretical ideas written into the programming code. Those implications take form as the simulation's output. Third, theories expressed as computer simulations are tested in exactly the same way that natural language and mathematically expressed theories are tested, by comparing their predictions (output) to empirical observations of real individuals and groups. Depending on the results of this testing, the simulation (and so the theory) might be modified and retested until known empirical benchmarks are matched.

These similarities to natural language and mathematical theories notwithstanding, expressing theory via computer simulation offers several advantages (see also, Davis, Eisenhardt, & Bingham, 2007; Hastie & Stasser, 2000; Lewandowsky, 1993; Myung & Pitt, 2002). One is that computer simulations can handle substantially greater complexity than is possible with either natural language or strictly mathematical theories. Increasingly, we seek to understand complex behavior. Complexities arise from the interaction among the manifold intrapersonal and interpersonal processes presumed to drive behavior, and from the repeated (and sometimes recursive) operation of those processes through time. The ability of computers to handle such complexities, and to derive unambiguous predictions in light of them, far exceeds that of humans using theories expressed in natural language. Mathematically expressed theories, too, are better than natural language theories at handling complexity. But it can sometimes be quite difficult, if not impossible, to formulate theory in terms of precise mathematical expressions (cf. Estes, 1975; Krause, 1996). And even when such formulations are possible, the equations themselves can become extremely complex, and so impose their own challenges when it comes to deducing behavioral predictions. Not surprisingly, and as will be described more fully in the next section to follow, complex mathematical formulations are often translated into computer simulations so that their less-obvious implications can be seen.

Computer simulation also encourages the identification and elimination of ambiguities, voids, and other theoretical insufficiencies. At the very least, the vagaries typically found in natural language theories must be given specific definition in a computer simulation. Consider, for example, the term "combined" in the following statement from a theory about group decision making: "The members' individual decision preferences are determined by the *combined* valence of the information that the group discusses about each choice alternative." Although this statement may be adequate as one element of a natural language theory of group decision making, it is too imprecise to be useful in a computer simulation. What exactly does "combined" mean? Computers cannot "combine" in the abstract; they can "combine" only in specific ways, for example, by summing or averaging. So, should the valences of discussed information be summed, averaged, or combined in some other manner when simulating the formation of members' decision preferences? Questions like this must be answered if a simulation is to be made operational. The answers can sometimes be found in the extant empirical literature (e.g., Anderson, 1991). But even then, several competing answers might turn up, in which case it would be prudent to implement each in a different version of the simulation, then test those versions competitively to determine which one provides the best fit to empirical data (cf. Stasser, 1988). Either way, the computer simulation will end up a more specific, detailed theory. The real behavior of individuals and groups arises from specifics, not generalities. Theories that are stated more specifically would therefore seem to have an advantage over those that are stated only generally, other things being equal.

But how are these advantages of computer simulation achieved? How does one actually go about getting computers to simulate human behavior? In the remainder of this chapter I describe three generic approaches to computer simulation. Although these approaches emerged at different points in the history of computer simulation, it should not be inferred that each one simply supplanted what had gone before. A more accurate description is that each new approach added a layer of capabilities not previously available, and that computer simulations employing one of the later-developed approaches often contain elements of the earlier approaches as well. My use of this tripartite division is thus mainly a pedagogical convenience that helps draw attention to several distinct features of contemporary simulation methods. Below I describe each approach in turn, and illustrate them with examples from my own work.

Formula Translation

The earliest use of computers for simulation purposes was to perform the often-tedious calculations required to solve complex mathematical equations. Many theories in both the natural and behavioral sciences are expressed mathematically – formulae are used to describe how particular sets of variables are presumed to be related to one another. Such theories are tested by solving for one of the variables in the equation given known values for the remaining variables, and then comparing the computed solution to values observed in the real world.

An historically significant example comes from the world of physics, and involves simulating the ballistic trajectory through the air of a launched, batted, or thrown projectile. Such trajectories are understood by theory to be a function of the projectile's initial velocity and launch angle, gravitational acceleration, time, and atmospheric conditions that affect drag (e.g., air temperature and humidity). The relationship among these variables is usually expressed in a system of linked equations. An important military application of this theory is computing (predict-ing) the launch angle needed to hit a target with an artillery shell when all of the other variables listed above (along with the distance to and elevation of the target, and the direction and velocity of the wind) are known. These computations can all be done by hand, of course. But the task becomes much easier and more useful with the aid of a computer, particularly when many such calculations are required in a short period of time. The first programmable digital electronic computer, ENIAC,[1] was developed specifically to perform this task (Goldstine, 1972), though any laptop computer in existence today can be made to do the same thing. To accomplish this, it is necessary only that the mathematical formulae describing the theory of trajectories be translated into the symbolic code understood by these computers.[2]

Thus, as I use the term, a formula translation approach to computer simulation is merely an extension of how predictions from mathematically expressed theories have always been derived. Computers are employed to perform the same calcula-tions that would otherwise be done by hand, but with greater speed and accuracy. When used in this manner, the computer makes the theory's predictions more accessible, which by itself can be of substantial benefit. Speedier access to a theo-ry's predictions offers improved visualization and understanding, and can lead to insights that would be difficult to obtain if all of the computations had to be done (slowly) by hand.

A contemporary example from the realm of group behavior is a computer simulation that predicts the content of group decision-making discussions. If we assume that group decisions are determined in part by what groups discuss, it makes sense to inquire about factors that affect the content of discussion. One such factor is the number of members who were aware of the decision-relevant information in advance. It is often the case that some of that information will have been known to everyone in the group prior to discussion. This commonly held knowledge is referred to as *shared information*. However, there may also be certain pieces of decision-relevant information that were known to just one member or another before discussion started. This uniquely held knowledge is called *unshared information*.[3] When members each hold a certain amount of unshared information, and when the best choice alternative can be identified only by taking account of that information, the decision they make as a group has the potential to be far superior to the decision that any one of them would have made acting alone. But this potential can be realized only if members actually mention during discussion the unshared information they hold (cf. Winquist & Larson, 1998).

Interestingly, there is much empirical evidence that groups tend to discuss significantly more of their shared than of their unshared information (for recent reviews, see Brodbeck, Kerschreiter, Mojzisch, & Schulz-Hardt, 2007; Larson, 2010). This difference is quite robust, with groups sometimes discussing twice as much shared as unshared information, and it occurs even when members do not know in advance what information they hold is shared and what is unshared. The latter fact rules out motivation as a necessary cause of this phenomenon: members cannot intentionally choose to discuss one type of information more than the other if they do not know what is shared and what is unshared.

But if motivation does not account for this phenomenon, what does? Stasser and Titus (1987, 2003) offered a simple but elegant explanation in their Collective Information Sampling (CIS) model of group discussion. The CIS model conceptualizes group decision-making discussions as a sampling process, wherein the content of discussion is obtained by members sampling from the pool of decision-relevant information they collective hold. This sampling is accomplished simply by them recalling and then mentioning the individual items of decision-relevant information. However, because shared information initially is held by more members than unshared information, there are more opportunities for the group as a whole to sample a given item of shared rather than unshared information. As a result, shared information is more apt than unshared information to be mentioned during discussion, even when group members are equally motivated to surface both types, and even when they are equally (though not necessarily perfectly) able to recall both types.

One way to represent these ideas mathematically is as follows:

$$p(D) = 1 - [1 - p(R)]^n, \tag{5.1}$$

where $p(D)$ is the probability that a given piece of decision-relevant information will be discussed by the group, $p(R)$ is the probability that any one member who was aware of that information prior to discussion will both recall and mention it during discussion, and n is the number of members who were aware of that information prior to discussion. If we assume that the available decision-relevant information is all equally memorable (i.e., $p(R)$ is invariant across items),[4] then the CIS model's prediction about the overall proportions of shared and unshared information that will be discussed given any particular value of $p(R)$ can be obtained by computing $p(D)$ when n is set equal to group size for shared information (because everyone in the group was aware of the shared information prior to discussion), and to 1 for unshared information (because only one group member was aware of the unshared information). One implication of this formulation is that $p(D_{shared}) > p(D_{unshared})$ for all values of $p(R)$ except 0 and 1.

Equation 5.1 is relatively simple, and its predictions are easily derived without the aid of a computer. However, the CIS model itself makes additional predictions that Equation 5.1 does not reveal. Specifically, it predicts the likelihood of each new piece of information raised during discussion being either shared or unshared information.[5] To anticipate, it suggests that over the course of discussion the probability of mentioning additional items of shared information gradually declines, while the probability of mentioning additional items of unshared information gradually increases. By way of analogy to the ballistic trajectory example discussed above, the CIS model is able to predict the entire "discussion entry trajectories" of shared and unshared information, not just the cumulative effect of those trajectories (i.e., the total amounts of shared and unshared information that will be discussed).

These additional predictions are derived by applying a computational algorithm that takes into account the sequential nature of group discussion: the fact that information is brought into discussion one piece at a time. The calculations required by this algorithm are not difficult when considered individually. They entail nothing more than addition, subtraction, multiplication, and division (for a full description, see Larson, 1997, especially Case 3 in the Appendix). What is difficult is the very large number of them that is needed, even for problems of modest proportion. For example, when three people each hold just nine shared and three unshared items of decision-relevant information, as many as 136,135 intermediate calculations are necessary, the results of which, when cumulated, yield the handful of probabilities (18 in this case) that fully describe the predicted discussion entry trajectory of shared information.[6] This surprisingly large number arises because of the very large number of possible orders in which nine items of shared information and $3 + 3 + 3 = 9$ items of unshared information might be raised during dissuasion. Obviously, this is well beyond what reasonably can be calculated by hand.

The problem is quite manageable, however, when the computational algorithm is translated into a computer simulation. I wrote just such a simulation using a general purpose computer programming language called BASIC (Larson, 1997).[7] That simulation solves the complete discussion entry trajectory predicted by the CIS model, given specific values for several input parameters (e.g., group size, number of shared items, number of unshared items, $p(R)$, etc.). The solutions computed by this simulation can be evaluated by comparison to empirical observation.

Figure 5.1 illustrates such a comparison. It displays the computer simulation predictions for, and the empirical results actually obtained from, 24 three-person teams of physicians that worked together to diagnose two hypothetical patient cases (Larson, Christensen, Franz, & Abbott, 1998). The information about each case was presented in three specially constructed video-taped interviews with the patient, with each physician in the team seeing a different interview. These video tapes were designed so that the physicians all learned some information about the case that the other two members of their team also learned (shared information) and some that no one else learned (unshared information). However, the physicians were not told which of the information they saw was shared and which was unshared. After viewing privately their separate video tapes, the three physicians met in a conference room to discuss each case and to decide as a group what disease was most likely to be producing the symptoms displayed by the patient.

The horizontal axis in Figure 5.1 refers to the sequential order in which the various items of case information were initially mentioned during discussion (i.e., the first item mentioned, the second item, the third, etc.), with each successive position referring to the introduction of a new, not-yet-mentioned piece of information. The solid circles are the computer simulation predictions about the proportion of teams in which shared information would be introduced at each item serial position (equivalent to the probability of mentioning shared information at each position). As can be seen, that proportion was expected to be high

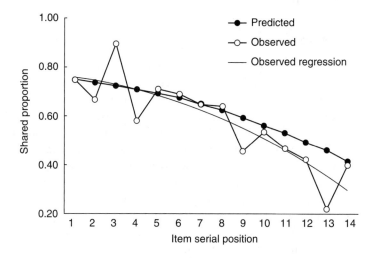

FIGURE 5.1 Predicted and observed proportion of group discussions in which shared information was brought out in each item serial position. Reprinted from Larson et al. (1998) with permission of the American Psychological Association.

initially, but gradually decrease as more and more information was brought into discussion. By contrast, the proportion of teams in which unshared information would be introduced at each item serial position was predicted to be low initially, but gradually increase (the introduction of unshared information is not shown in Figure 5.1, but can be computed by subtracting each of the plotted values from 1.00). These predictions are close to what was actually observed. The proportion of teams that introduced shared information at each item serial position (open circles), and in particular the quadratic regression line that best fits those observations (thin line without markers), follow closely, and are statistically indistinguishable from, the curve defined by the computer simulation predictions. Overall, the computer simulation predictions account for 73 per cent of the variance in the observed proportions shown in Figure 5.1.

In sum, the principal advantage of the formula translation approach to computer simulation is that it allows one to "do the math" much more quickly than would otherwise be possible. This, in turn, makes it easier to "play with" the parameters written into the simulation in order to uncover their expected effects. When the CIS model is implemented as a computer simulation, for example, it becomes easy to vary the recall parameter, $p(R)$, and so examine the model's predictions about how the discussion entry trajectories of shared and unshared information might change when the decision-relevant information is either more or less difficult to remember. Epistemologically, there is no difference between (a) using a computer program to predict the content of group discussion under varying conditions of member recall, and (b) using a (different) computer program to predict the trajectory of an artillery shell under varying atmospheric conditions (cf. Simon, 1992).

Generative Process Modeling

A rather different approach to computer simulation is to model directly the operation of key processes hypothesized to generate a given type of behavior, then allow those processes to "run" (by running the program) so that the simulated behavior (program output) they produce can be observed. If this is done a large number of times, simulating in each instance the behavior of a single individual or group, then the simulation's predictions for individuals or groups in general can be obtained by cumulating the results across those many instances (i.e., just as inferences drawn from observations of real behavior are based on results cumulated across many instances). For example, predictions about the development of outgroup stereotypes might be obtained by modeling in each of a large number of simulated individuals a learning process, a memory storage process, and a sequence of encounters with different members of the outgroup (e.g., Kashima, Woolcock, & Kashima, 2000; Linville, Fischer, & Salovey, 1989; Queller, 2002; Read & Urada, 2003; Van Rooy, Van Overwalle, Vanhoomissen, Labiouse, & French, 2003). Likewise, predictions about the brainstorming productivity of groups might be obtained by modeling in each of a large number of groups the retrieval of ideas from long-term memory, the waxing and waning of attention paid to ideas put forth by others, and the forgetting of ideas held too long while waiting for a speaking turn (e.g., Brown, Tumeo, Larey, & Paulus, 1998; Coskun, Paulus, Brown, & Sherwood, 2000).

Three points should be noted here. First, simulations that follow the generative process modeling approach do not try to emulate every conceivable mental and behavioral process at play in real individuals and groups. Rather, they model only those processes presumed essential for explaining the phenomenon in question, and then only the most relevant features of those processes. Thus, like any theory, computer simulations are both a simplification and an abstraction of reality.

Second, although the modeled processes need not be represented in every detail, those details that are represented should be realistic, in the sense of being consistent with the current state of knowledge in the field. It is generally accepted, for example, that humans have two memory systems – long-term and working memory – and that the latter has a limited, though elastic, capacity. A simulation that includes as one of its components a model of group member memory should not be inconsistent with these facts. At the same time, computer simulation is valuable as a theory development tool precisely because it permits alternative theoretical ideas about the operation of underlying processes to be implemented and tested competitively. Thus, the theorist must be clear about which aspects of the simulation do and do not follow conventional wisdom.

Finally, the individual or group behavior being simulated is an emergent product that arises from the underlying process(es) modeled in the simulation. The generative process modeling approach to computer simulation explains behavior as a direct consequence of these underlying processes. This stands in contrast to the formula translation approach, which explains behavior in terms of mathematical or statistical relationships among variables (cf. Smith & Conrey, 2007).

To illustrate these points, I describe here a simulation that predicts the same discussion entry trajectories of shared and unshared information as predicted by the formula translation simulation outlined above, but does so via a generative process modeling approach. As will be seen, the predictions made via the two approaches are similar, but the generative process modeling approach is both easier and more practical to implement.

Thus, let us consider once again a three-person group in which each member holds nine shared and three unshared items of decision-relevant information. For simplicity, we will assume that during discussion the members can recall all of the information that they individually hold (i.e., $p(R) = 1.00$). As previously described, the CIS model views group discussion as a sampling process, wherein the content of discussion is obtained by members sampling from the pool of information they collectively hold. Taking a generative process modeling approach, we might try to simulate the essential details of this process. That is, we might simulate the successive, random selection (without replacement) of one discussion item after another, continuing until there is either no more information left that has not already been sampled, or until some other stopping criterion is reached.[8] By simulating a large number of group discussions in this way, each involving the same number of people, with the same recall capacity, and holding the same mix of shared and unshared information, inferences can be drawn about what the CIS model predicts for such discussions in general under these conditions. Specifically, the probability of the first, second, third, etc., new discussion item being either shared or unshared information can be inferred directly from the proportion of simulated group discussions in which the first, second, third, etc. new piece of information sampled actually was either shared or unshared information, respectively.

To see how this sampling process might be simulated, it is important first to recognize that in real three-person groups there are three opportunities to sample (i.e., mention during discussion) each piece of shared information (again, because every member holds that information), but only one opportunity to sample each piece of unshared information (because only one member holds it). Thus, in a discussion among three people who collectively hold nine pieces of shared and $3 + 3 + 3 = 9$ pieces of unshared information, there are initially $3 \times 9 = 27$ opportunities to sample shared information, but only $1 \times 9 = 9$ opportunities to sample unshared information.

Now, suppose we let the integers 1–27 represent each of the 27 opportunities to sample shared information, and the integers 28–36 represent the nine opportunities to sample unshared information. Next, consider the following two lines of pseudo programming code:[9]

(1) Let X be any random integer between 1 and 36, inclusive.

(2) If $X \leq 27$, then [Discuss Shared]; Otherwise [Discuss Unshared].

I will refer to "≤ 27" in the second line above as the decision rule, and set aside for the moment the question of where X might come from. Let us suppose, however, that at any given moment X, whatever its source, can be depended upon to be one of the integers 1–36, with each of those integers being equally likely to occur (i.e., $p(1) = p(2) = p(3) = \cdots = p(36) = 1/36$).

Next, let us imagine in a single execution of this pseudo code that X happens to be an integer in the range 1–27 (e.g., suppose it is 15), so that the computer performs the action "[Discuss Shared]." We will take this as a simulation of actually sampling and mentioning shared information during group discussion. But if one piece of shared information has now been mentioned, then the pool of not-yet-mentioned information from which the *next* discussion item will be drawn has decreased in size by one piece of shared information (i.e., it now comprises eight shared and nine unshared items). Consequently, there remain only $3 \times 8 = 24$ opportunities to sample another item of not-yet mentioned shared information, but still $1 \times 9 = 9$ opportunities to sample an item of not-yet mentioned unshared information. Paralleling what was done above, we might now use the integers 1–24 to represent the 24 remaining opportunities to sample shared information, and the integers 25–33 to represent the (still) nine opportunities to sample unshared information. To obtain the second discussion item, we would then simulate sampling from this slightly shrunken pool of information by executing a modified version of the pseudo code given above, one that uses the decision rule "≤ 24," and where the value of X is constrained to be one of the (again, equally likely) integers 1–33.

Of course, in the original execution of the pseudo code as described in the first sentence of the preceding paragraph, X might have been in the range 28–36, not 1–27 (e.g., suppose it was 31 instead of 15). Had that occurred, the computer would have performed the action "[Discuss Unshared]," which we would have taken as a simulation of sampling and mentioning unshared information during group discussion. Further, the pool of not-yet-mentioned information would have decreased by one piece of unshared (not shared) information, so that for the *next* discussion item there would still be $3 \times 9 = 27$ opportunities to sample shared information, but only $1 \times 8 = 8$ opportunities to sample another item of not-yet-mentioned unshared information. In this case, we would continue to use the integers 1–27 to represent the (still) 27 opportunities to sample shared information, but use the integers 28–35 to represent the eight remaining opportunities to sample unshared information. Thus, to obtain the second discussion item in this alternative scenario, we would simply execute again the original version of the pseudo code given above (i.e., with the decision rule "≤ 27"), but this time constrain the value of X to be one of the integers 1–35.

The same basic routine would be used to obtain all subsequent discussion items. In each case, we would keep track of how the pool of not-yet-mentioned information shrinks as a result of removing the item selected, and change accordingly the decision rule and/or the constraints on X in the pseudo programming code. In this way, it is possible to simulate the sequential entry of shared and unshared information into a single group discussion. And by repeating this entire procedure from the beginning, we can simulate any number of such discussions. Importantly, with this approach it is unnecessary to perform all of the many thousands of computations needed to derive the exact probabilities associated with the formula translation approach. Rather, by modeling the step-by-step sampling process that is posited by theory to generate the content of group discussion, and by doing so for a large number of simulated discussions, we can closely approximate those probabilities simply by observing the proportion of times the computer actually performs the actions "[Discuss Shared]" and "[Discuss Unshared]" when sampling the first, second, third, etc. discussion items.

All of this hinges, however, on the critically important assumption that X can be depended upon to be one of n equally likely integers within a specified range, where n is the total number of sampling opportunities (shared plus unshared) that exist at any given moment. This assumption is made plausible by obtaining X from a random number generator. A random number generator is a utility (function) embedded within many programming languages that furnishes, on demand, a sequence of numbers, one after another, that do not have a discernable pattern to them – for all intents and purposes they are randomly ordered.[10] The values produced by random number generators are often decimal numbers in the range 0–1 (including 0 but excluding 1), with all values in that range being equally likely to occur. Simple arithmetic operations can be performed on these values in order to transform them to the range required by the simulation (e.g., to obtain integers in the range 1–36, compute $[X \times 36] + 1$, then drop the decimal portion of the number). Thus, in the present example, the first line of pseudo code given above implies obtaining a value for X from a random number generator, then transforming that value as necessary to yield an integer within the required range.

Random number generators are invaluable to generative process modeling, as they supply the stochastic feature that is central to how we understand all behavioral phenomena. Besides the tendency of groups to discuss one type of information more than another (e.g., shared vs. unshared), random number generators are critical for modeling such phenomena as the proclivity of individuals and groups to recall certain kinds of information more readily than others (e.g., attitude consistent vs. inconsistent information), to forget information with the passage of time, to be more or less talkative, and to choose certain courses of action (e.g., cooperation vs. competition) more often than others. In each case, randomly generated numbers, along with judiciously chosen decision rules about the values of those numbers, are used to instantiate a probabilistic element in the simulation.

I employed a random number generator – and several of the other ideas described above – in a second version of the computer simulation that predicts the discussion entry trajectories of shared and unshared information (Larson, 1997). Called the Dynamic Information Sampling Model of Group Discussion (DISM-GD), this generative process modeling simulation, just like the formula translation version, relies on inputs about group size, the amounts of shared and unshared information available, $p(R)$, and several other parameters. Unlike the formula translation version, however, the generative process modeling version does not yield the exact, mathematically computed probabilities of shared and unshared information entering discussion at each item serial position. Rather, those probabilities are estimated from the observed proportion of simulated groups in which the actions "[Discuss Shared]" and "[Discuss Unshared]" are actually performed at each item serial position.

Figure 5.2 displays output from both versions of the simulation. The top panel displays the exact discussion-entry probabilities computed via the formula translation version, and the bottom panel displays the proportions obtained when the generative process modeling approach was used to simulate 1,000 separate

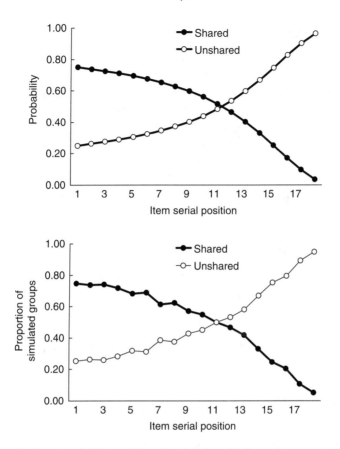

FIGURE 5.2 Predicted probability of shared and unshared information entering discussion in each item serial position derived from the formula translation-based (top panel) and generative process modeling-based (bottom panel) computer simulations. Both simulations assume a three-person group that collectively holds 9 shared and $3 + 3 + 3 = 9$ unshared items of information, and where the members are able to recall and mention all of that information during discussion (i.e., $p(R) = 1.00$).

group discussions. As can be seen, the two versions yield similar results. Both predict that shared information is more likely than unshared information to be brought up early in discussion, whereas the reverse is predicted later on. The one obvious difference between them is that the formula translation version yields a pair of smooth curves, whereas the curves produced by the generative process modeling version contain small irregularities. Those irregularities are a natural consequence of the stochastic nature of the generative process modeling approach, but their magnitude tends to decrease as the number of simulated group discussions increases.

What is not obvious from Figure 5.2, is that the formula translation version of the simulation took nearly 300 times longer to run than did the generative process modeling version: it took just 5 seconds to generate the proportions on the bottom, but nearly 25 minutes to calculate the probabilities on the top. This difference increases exponentially as the size of the problem increases (e.g., increasing by just 33 per cent the amounts of available shared and unshared information increases the run time to 6 seconds for the generative process modeling version, but to more than 24 hours for the formula translation version!). Further, the formula translation version took substantially longer to program initially. Thus, even when a theory can be expressed fully in mathematical form, there may still be significant practical advantages to using a generative process modeling approach.

Agent-based Modeling

The most recently developed approach to computer simulation is agent-based modeling. Agent-based modeling is an evolutionary outgrowth of generative process modeling. An agent-based model is one that simulates simultaneously multiple agents, or actors, who behave in ways that impact one another. Each agent is endowed with its own generative processes, and each can act autonomously vis-à-vis its environment. That environment might include various resources (e.g., food, money, information), along with opportunities for reward and punishment, but always includes the other agents in the simulation. Agents are thus a key element of the environment for one another, in the sense that their actions affect – and are affected by – the actions of others. Depending on the simulation, agents might affect one another either directly or indirectly. They affect one another directly when, for example, they exchange task-relevant information, engage in cooperative help-giving, or put forth arguments to persuade others. By contrast, agents affect one another indirectly when they act in ways that change some nonagentic feature of the environment that in turn impacts others (e.g., by consuming a nonrenewable resource). It is the central purpose of agent-based modeling to understand the cumulative effects of these direct and indirect influences over time.

Several characteristics of the agents that inhabit this type of computer simulation are worthwhile noting (cf. Gilbert, 2008; Smith & Conrey, 2007). First, they are self-contained, discrete entities with flexible behavioral repertoires: they usually can act in more than one way. Second, agents typically possess local rather than global knowledge of their environment. For example, in a simulation involving many agents, each might be aware only of the actions of its closest neighbors, and may have access to information only about those resources and rewards that are near at hand. Third, agents display bounded rationality, gathering information and generating behavior by means of relatively simple rules. Complex computational routines, like those typical of the formula translation approach to computer simulation, generally are not used. Fourth, each agent acts autonomously according to its own objectives – agents are not under the command of a central authority. Finally, a given agent's behavioral repertoire may or may not be able to adapt to changes in its environment. Depending on the purpose of the simulation, the rules by which agents generate behavior might be fixed in advance and immutable during a given run of the simulation, or they might instead be learned and modified as a function of experience.

Agent-based modeling is well suited for simulating behavior both in large social networks (e.g., Axelrod, 1997; Kalick & Hamilton, 1996; Kennedy, 2009; Kenrick, Li, & Butner, 2003; Latané & Bourgeois, 2001; Schelling, 1971) and in small groups (e.g., Feinberg & Johnson, 1997; Kameda, Takezawa, & Hastie, 2003; Reimer, & Hoffrage, 2005, 2006; Ren, Carley, & Argote, 2006; Rousseau & Van Der Veen, 2005; Stasser, 1988, 2000; Stasser & Taylor, 1991). Here I illustrate its application in the latter domain with a simulation I created to explore the effects of diversity among members' problem-solving strategies on group problem-solving performance (Larson, 2007a, 2010).

The simulation is called ValSeek, after the value-seeking problems with which it is concerned. A value-seeking problem is one that requires problem-solvers to search for a solution from among a set of alternatives that vary in their underlying value or desirability. The goal is to find the alternative with the highest value. A real-world example is designing a portable consumer electronics product (e.g., a smartphone). A product's design refers not only to its visual and tactile features, but also to its functionalities. Each possible combination of features and functionalities represents a unique solution to the design problem. Because the combination of design elements ultimately selected will determine the product's appeal to customers, and so its success in the marketplace, finding an appealing design that can also be built reliably and inexpensively is a value-seeking problem.

The individual elements of a given solution alternative sometimes contribute additively to that alternative's value, but sometimes they contribute multiplicatively. The latter implies that some elements may be more (or less) useful when certain other elements are also present. Consequently, solving value-seeking problems requires that solution elements be considered in combination, not separately. But often the number of possible combinations is very large, so much so that it is impractical to evaluate all of them. Under these conditions, the strategies that problem-solvers use to sift through the myriad possibilities – considering some combinations, while ignoring others – can significantly affect the value they ultimately find.

Value-seeking problems are represented abstractly in the ValSeek simulation. A problem consists of nothing more than a set of solution alternatives that vary in their underlying value. Each alternative is represented as a string of binary digits (e.g., 1–1–0–0–1), with each digit being a different solution element, and each possible combination of elements being a different solution alternative. No particular meaning is given to either the solution elements or the solution alternatives, except that each alternative is randomly assigned a different value (expressed in arbitrary units). Thus, in a particular run of the simulation, 1–1–0–0–1 might be assigned more value than 1–1–0–1–1. Given a set of solution alternatives involving the same number of elements (e.g., there are $2^5 = 32$ alternatives involving five binary elements), the problem is to sift through the alternatives in search of the one with the highest value.

ValSeek simulates group problem-solving as a collaborative activity among a small number of agents (up to six). Beginning at a randomly selected starting point, each agent independently searches through the set of solution alternatives in serial fashion, considering them one at a time, comparing each to the alternatives examined before it. As they go, agents can also communicate with one another when they make progress toward finding a high-value solution (see later). For each new alternative considered, the agent first determines its value (by looking it up in a table; ValSeek is not concerned with *how* value is determined, only *that* it is determined), then compares that value to the value of the best alternative previously considered. If the current alternative has more value, then that previous alternative is abandoned, and the current alternative becomes the (new) best alternative considered so far. On the other hand, if the current alternative has less value than the previous one, the previous alternative is retained (i.e., it remains the best alternative considered so far), and the current one is abandoned. Once the outcome of this comparative evaluation is known, the alternative to be considered next is determined.

The solution alternative that is considered next depends partly on the binary code of the alternative retained in the just-completed comparative evaluation, and partly on the agent's strategy for selecting to-be-considered alternatives. That strategy is implemented in the ValSeek simulation simply as an instruction for changing the elements of the binary code of the retained (best so far) solution alternative. An example is "flip one randomly selected element of the code," where "flip" means change that element to its other possible state (i.e., from 0 to 1, or vice versa).[11] For example, if as a result of the just-completed evaluative comparison the retained solution were 1–1–0–0–1, then a single execution of this strategy instruction might lead the agent to consider next the solution alternative 1–0–0–0–1 (i.e., the second element was randomly selected and flipped). The value of that new alternative would then be determined in the same manner as before, and it would be compared to the value of 1–1–0–0–1. Depending on the outcome of this new comparative evaluation, one of the two alternatives would be retained, the strategy instruction would be executed again, and another comparison of values would be made. This process would be repeated over and over until no new alternative can be found that has more value than the previously retained alternative.

This evaluation process has several important features. First, an agent's strategy instruction will, in general, permit it to consider only a subset of all possible solution alternatives – some will be considered, but some will be overlooked.

Second, a group of agents may be endowed either with the same strategy instruction or with different instructions. For example, some agents might be given the instruction "flip *all except one* randomly selected element of the code" (e.g., 1–1–0–0–1 might become 0–1–1–1–0, where only the second element was *not* flipped). Different strategy instructions cause agents to move through the solution alternatives differently, considering different (though often overlapping) subsets of those alternatives as they go. Third, even when endowed with exactly the same strategy instruction, agents do not necessarily evaluate the same subset of solution alternatives, or do so in the same order. This is because each agent starts the process with a different, randomly selected alternative, and because the strategy instruction itself contains a strong stochastic component (e.g., given the retained solution 1–1–0–0–1 and the strategy instruction "flip one randomly selected element," there are five equally likely solution alternatives that might be considered next).

Fourth, agents can communicate with one another whenever they find a solution alternative that has more value than the value of the best alternative they previously considered. These are occasions when communication often occurs in real groups, as they are the moments where it is most evident that progress is being made toward finding the solution with the highest value. Communication is operationalized in the ValSeek simulation as agents passing the identity (binary code) of their newly identified best solution alternative to the other agents in the simulation, who then compare its value to that of their own currently best alternative (that value might be either higher or lower). Depending on the outcome of this comparative evaluation, those other agents might either retain or abandon this new alternative, and then consider additional alternatives in the same manner as before. In this way, agents can influence the solution alternatives that other agents consider next. The agents' propensity to communication about newly identified solution alternatives is treated as a variable in the ValSeek simulation. Consequently, the results from simulated groups with a high propensity to communicate (e.g., those with extroverted, highly verbal members) can be compared to the results from groups with a low propensity to communicate (e.g., those with introverted, taciturn members).

Finally, the group's problem-solving activity terminates when no agent can find a new alternative that has more value than the value of its own currently best (retained) alternative. The group's collective solution is then defined simply as the best of the agents' best alternatives. One consequence of this process is that while groups will choose the solution with the highest discovered value, they will not necessarily discover the solution that is objectively best, simply because they will not always evaluate every possibility. An important output from the ValSeek program is thus the proportion of simulated groups that do in fact identify the solution that is objectively best.

An example of the output from the ValSeek simulation is shown in Figure 5.3. It illustrates the simulation's predictions about the joint effect of

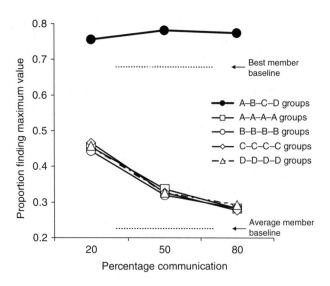

FIGURE 5.3 Predicted performance for four-person groups with either heterogeneous or homogeneous problem-solving strategies, and whose members have either a weak (20 percent), moderate (50 percent), or strong (80 percent) propensity to communicate. Adapted in part from Larson (2007b).

two variables: (a) the degree of diversity among agents with respect to their problem-solving strategies; and (b) the agents' propensity to communicate with one another when they find higher-value solution alternatives. In these simulations, groups of four agents each solved value-seeking problems involving five binary elements (like those described above). The diversity variable had two levels: agents were all endowed either with the same strategy instruction (homogeneous groups), or with different strategy instructions (heterogeneous groups). The instructions employed in the simulation were the two mentioned previously, along with two others: "flip *two* randomly selected, adjacent elements of the code," and "flip *all except two* randomly selected, adjacent elements of the code." The communication variable had three levels: agents exchanged information about newly discovered solution alternatives either 20 percent, 50 percent, or 80 percent of the time, to simulate groups whose members have either a relatively low, moderate, or high propensity to communicate, respectively.

Each data point in Figure 5.3 represents the proportion of simulated groups (out of 10,000) that identified the objectively best solution from the full set of 32 alternatives. Four different versions of the homogenous group condition are represented in the figure, one for each different strategy instruction employed. These are labeled "A–A–A–A," "B–B–B–B," "C–C–C–C," and "D–D–D–D" groups, respectively. As can be seen, regardless of the strategy instruction used, given the same propensity to communicate, homogeneous groups all perform similarly.

More importantly, the homogeneous groups all performed considerably worse than the heterogeneous groups (the "A–B–C–D" groups). Further, and somewhat surprisingly, the performance of homogeneous groups worsened with increased communication. This is because increased communication among agents who all have the same problem-solving strategy increases the degree to which they all search through the solution alternatives in exactly the same way. Said differently, increased communication makes it more likely that four similar agents will perform as if they were just one agent. This does not occur, however, in heterogeneous groups – varying their propensity to communicate, at least within the range simulate here, does not harm their performance (though neither does it improve their performance much). Finally, across all conditions, simulated groups tended to perform better than their average member would have performed working completely alone (marked in the figure with the dotted line labeled "Average member baseline"). However, only the heterogeneous groups perform better than their *best* member would have performed working alone (marked with the dotted line labeled "Best member baseline"). The ValSeek simulation thus predicts that heterogeneous groups should demonstrate what I referred to elsewhere as a strong synergistic performance gain when solving value-seeking problems (Larson, 2007a, 2010). This and the other predictions shown in Figure 5.3 would have been extremely difficult to deduce had the ideas underlying ValSeek not been expressed as a computer simulation.

Lessons Learned

A theorist who wants to begin using computer simulation as part of his or her work faces several challenges. The biggest, I believe, is overcoming in one's own thinking the habits of mind associated with conventional modes of theorizing about individual and group behavior. As I hope the present chapter has made clear, modern computer simulation methods, particularly those that employ a generative process and/or agent-based modeling approach, emphasize the emergent nature of behavior, and call attention to the repeated and persistent interplay over time of the often manifold underlying processes that give rise to it. These approaches explain behavior by reference to the ability of the simulated processes actually to generate a facsimile of that behavior. In other words, when using a computer simulation to express theory, explanation inheres in *generation*. To create such a simulation it is therefore necessary that the theorist himself or herself learn to think in dynamical generative terms. In my experience, this is much easier said than done.

The difficulty is that "generative thinking" is largely incommensurate with traditional modes of theorizing. Like most researchers who study small group behavior, I was originally trained in variable-based theory construction, where explanation is rooted in *covariation*, not generation. That is, in a variable-based approach, emphasis is placed on the observed (or hypothesized) pattern of covariation among variables across cases, and it is the structural (usually causal) relationships among those variables that take center stage. These relationships are often depicted in diagrams with boxes and arrows, and are the basis for understanding behavior. Although theories of this sort have been extremely useful, they do not offer a complete picture of behavior. Importantly, because they are mostly static and cross-sectional, theories that focus on covariation do not speak in a very direct way to the inherently dynamic and longitudinal character of behavior generation. Despite this shortcoming, the variable-based approach has become so firmly entrenched as *the* way to theorize about behavior that it is difficult for most researchers to think in other potentially useful ways.

All of this makes it tough for anyone who wishes to get started in computer simulation actually to do so. Particular troublesome is developing a computer simulation in a topic area where none currently exists, simply because it is hard to know how even to approach the problem. A more workable strategy, at least until one has gained some experience with computer simulation methods, is to create simulations in areas where there is already some form of template that can be used for guidance. Each of my own simulations described in this chapter initially took shape in this way.

For example, the development of DISM-GD, the simulation that predicts the complete discussion entry trajectories of shared and unshared information, was guided by the ideas in Stasser and Titus (1985, 1987). They described in natural language the core elements of the generative process assumed to produce the summary results they observed (i.e., the total amount of shared and unshared information eventually discussed by groups). I set out initially to express those same ideas in a computer simulation that modeled the underlying generative process, and found in the first few runs of that simulation that it made the same summary predictions as did the mathematical formulation given by Stasser and Titus (i.e., Equation 5.1). Once the nucleus of the simulation was written, it was relatively easy to add to it the ability to report the intermediate values associated with the full discussion entry trajectories of shared and unshared information, like those shown in Figures 5.1 and 5.2. I then further modified the simulation in order to explore other interesting issues, such as what happens when, instead of participating equally in the group's discussion, members participate differentially.[12]

In similar fashion, development of the ValSeek model was strongly influenced by the ideas in Hong and Page (2001), who published their work in an economics journal. They were concerned with sequential problem-solving situations, wherein one person first works alone on a value-seeking problem to find the best solution he or she can, then a second person takes over from where the first left off, then a third takes from where the second left off, and so on. My goal initially was to replicate with an agent-based model the predictions they made for this scenario via a mathematical analysis. Once that was accomplished, my next step was to make the agents more fully interactive, and so better simulate what actually occurs in real groups. Thus, like DISM-GD, ValSeek started out as a replication of what already existed in another form, but then went beyond the ideas that gave rise to it.

A final challenge worth mentioning here concerns software. There are a number of dedicated software platforms for creating computer simulations, including agent-based models (cf. Alessa, Laituri, & Barton, 2006). These can be very useful, especially for the novice, as they typically do not require any special programming skills. On the other hand, each of these platforms is designed for a particular genre of simulation, and so may or may not be suited to the needs of a theorist who wishes to construct a specific type of simulation. If an appropriate platform does not currently exist, it will be necessary to program the simulation from scratch using a general-purpose programming language.

I wrote the ValSeek simulation using the Visual Basic® programming language, and I wrote DISM-GD using its predecessor, Basic 7.0®. For anyone who does not already know a general-purpose programming language, but who would like to learn one in order to develop a computer simulation, Visual Basic is a good place to start. Visual Basic is a relatively easy-to-learn, object-oriented language that is taught in many high schools, colleges, and universities. I recommend taking a one-semester course in Visual Basic, although some may be able to learn it on their own with the aid of a good introductory textbook (e.g., Schneider, 2009).[13] But be patient. You will not learn much about computer simulation *per se* from an introductory course. What you will learn instead is a set of skills that will be very useful later on when you do start your first computer simulation project.

Alternatively, rather than writing the program yourself, you might consider hiring a programmer. This tack presents its own set of challenges, however. In computer simulation, as in many areas of life, the devil is in the details. One particularly devilish problem in creating computer simulations is that, as suggested previously, ideas must be expressed with much greater precision than is normally found in natural language theories. As a consequence, when deciding how to implement an idea in a simulation, there are often important programming choices to be made about which our natural language theories offer little guidance. Further, these choices sometimes appear trivial on their face, despite having profound implications for the way the simulation operates. A programmer hired by the theorist to write the code – especially someone who is unfamiliar with the relevant natural language theories – may not always be able to tell the difference between trivial and theoretically significant programming choices, and so may not know when it is important to seek advice from the theorist. This, in turn, makes it difficult for the theorist to know for sure that the simulation has been implemented in exactly the way he or she intended. My own experience in communicating theoretical subtleties to hired programmers (mostly students from computer science departments) has been sufficiently frustrating that I usually prefer to do the programming myself.

Next Steps

For those who want to learn more about the details of computer simulation methods, there are a number of useful resources available, though little in the way of textbook treatments, and not much that focuses specifically on simulating behavior in small groups. Still, many of the techniques used to simulate behavior in larger social networks are readily adapted to simulating behavior in small groups. Axelrod and Testfatsion (2006) provide a helpful annotated bibliography, and Testfatsion (2010) maintains a companion website with many useful links to downloadable resources and demonstration software. Davis et al. (2007), Elliott and Kiel (2004), Frantz and Carley (2009), Gilbert (2008), Harrison, Lin, Carroll, and Carley (2007), Macy and Willer (2002), and Miller and Page (2004) also provide valuable insights. Among these, Davis et al. (2007) offer a particularly useful roadmap for developing theory using computer simulation methods. Their treatment, and that of the other works cited here, also elaborate a number of the themes introduced in the first section of this chapter.

Authors' Notes:

I would like to thank Nick Aramovich, Olga Goldenberg, Ryan Leach, Jared Majerle, and the two editors for their helpful comments on an earlier draft of this chapter. Correspondence regarding this chapter can be sent to the author at jlarson4@luc.edu.

Notes

1 ENIAC is an acronym for the Electrical Numerical Integrator And Computer. It was built at the University of Pennsylvania between 1943 and 1945, and operated until the mid-1950s. ENIAC contained 18,000 vacuum tubes, weighted 30 tons, and could solve in 25 seconds the complete trajectory of an artillery shell that, when fired, took 30 seconds to reach its target (Burks & Davidson, 1999). Although remarkably slow by today's standards, in 1945 ENIAC was 1,000 times faster than any other calculating machine then in existence (Goldstine, 1972).

2 The translation process involves two main steps. The first is performed by the programmer when he or she translates the mathematical formula as expressed on paper into the notation required by the programming language that he or she is using. Anyone who has entered a formula into an Excel® spreadsheet is familiar with this. The second, more challenging step is performed automatically by the programming language itself. All computers operate on instructions expressed in binary code – long strings of 0s and 1s – often referred to as machine language. The primary function of any programming language is to translate the notation input by the programmer into the specific arrangement of 0s and 1s that is required to get the computer to perform the desired function. Thus, the formula translation process is ultimately one of converting an arrangement of symbols understandable to humans into the binary code understandable to machines. It is no coincidence that one of the first widely used programming languages developed to help accomplish this formula translation task draws its very name from that use: FORTRAN.

3 Between these extremes are various degrees of partially shared information: information that is held by more than one, but not every, group member. Although I focus here on

the extremes, the principles involved are perfectly general, and so can be applied as well to these intermediate levels of sharedness.

4 This assumption may be unrealistic in absolute terms, but there is no reason to presume that shared information is inherently any more or less memorable than unshared information.

5 It is important to realize that the CIS predicts only the entry into discussion of information that has not previously been mentioned. It does not predict either the thoroughness with which that information is discussed or its likelihood of being repeated (but see Larson & Harmon, 2007).

6 The trajectory for unshared information can then be obtained by subtraction.

7 I will have more to say about the ease and usefulness of learning a programming language near the end of this chapter.

8 One interesting stopping criterion is the total amount of information brought into discussion, with discussion terminating when some fixed quantity, Y, has been reached (regardless of whether that information was originally shared or unshared). Y might be set to a high value to simulate groups whose members are all high in need for cognition, and a low value to simulate groups whose members are all low in need for cognition, under the assumption that high need for cognition groups will discuss more information than low need for cognition groups (cf. Cacioppo, Petty, Feinstein, & Jarvis, 1996).

9 Pseudo programming code, or simply pseudo code, is an informal way of expressing the instructions contained in a computer program. Pseudo code does not have the syntax of a real programming language, but is more easily understood by humans. In principle, different programmers using different programming languages should be able to translate the ideas expressed in pseudo code into real computer programs that all perform the same function.

10 Different random number generators use different algorithms to produce numbers. One involves computing the sequence of digits to the right of the decimal point in the irrational number π (3.141592635589793238462643...). Of course, because they are mathematical algorithms, random number generators are deterministic – given the same set of initial conditions, the same sequence of numbers will be produced each time the generator is started. An important initial condition for most random number generators is a starting value called a "seed." Given the same seed, the same string of numbers will be produced. But given different seeds, different strings of numbers will be produced. One way to improve the "randomness" of a random number generator is to change the value of the seed in a way that is itself hard to predict. For example, many generators consult the computer's internal clock for the current time of day (usually expressed to a fraction of a second) and base the seed on this value. By doing this, the generator will have a different seed each time it is started, unless it happens to be started at exactly the same time each day – a very unlikely event. Thus, whereas the algorithms employed by random generators are deterministic, and so the numbers they produce can never be truly random, those numbers are nevertheless exceptionally difficult to predict, which makes them very similar to random numbers. For this reason, these deterministic but hard-to-predict numbers are often called pseudo random numbers.

11 The stochastic feature of this instruction ensures that no special priority is given to any one element of the binary code. This is consistent with the generic nature of the value-seeking problems being modeled, where no inherent priority among solution elements is assumed.

12 As it turns out, there is a hidden assumption underlying the model expressed in Equation 5.1. It implicitly assumes that members contribute equally to the group's discussion. In reality, this is hardly ever true. Relaxing this assumption yields results that predict an even stronger discussion bias in favor of shared information than is predicted by Equation 5.1 (cf. Larson, 1997, Table 2). The existence of this hidden assumption

became clear only when I began using DISM-DG to explore the impact of differential participation rates among members.

13 I was fortunate as an undergraduate student in the early 1970s to have taken an elective course in FORTRAN programming. Although I have not used FORTRAN in nearly 30 years, that course gave me a fundamental understanding of how programming languages work, which has since allowed me to learn several new languages on my own, including Visual Basic. There are many differences among programming languages, of course, but there are also commonalities, so learning a new language is not as difficult as it might seem – certainly it is a lot easier than learning a new natural language.

References

Alessa, L. N., Laituri, M., & Barton, M. (2006). An "all hands" call to the social science community: Establishing a community framework for complexity modeling using agent based models and cyberinfrastructure. *Journal of Artificial Societies and Social Simulation, 9*(4), 6. Downloadable at: http://jasss.soc.surrey.ac.uk/9/4/6.html.

Anderson, N. H. (1991). *Contributions to information integration theory.* Hillsdale, NJ: Erlbaum.

Axelrod, R. L. (1997). The dissemination of culture: A model of local convergence and global polarization. *Journal of Conflict Resolution, 41,* 203–226.

Axelrod, R., & Testfatsion, L. (2006). A guide for newcomers to agent based modeling in the social sciences. In K. Judd, & L. Testfatsion (Eds.), *Handbook of computational economics*, Vol. 2: *Agent-based computational economics* (pp. 1647–1658). Amsterdam: North-Holland.

Brodbeck, F. C., Kerschreiter, R., Mojzisch, A., & Schulz-Hardt, S. (2007). Group decision making under conditions of distributed knowledge: The Information Asymmetries Model. *Academy of Management Review, 32,* 459–479.

Brown, V., Tumeo, M., Larey, T. S., & Paulus, P. B. (1998). Modeling cognitive interaction during brainstorming. *Small Group Research, 29,* 495–526.

Burks, A. W., & Davidson, E. S. (1999). Introduction to "The ENIAC." *Proceedings of the IEEE, 87,* 1028–1030.

Cacioppo, J. T., Petty, R. E., Feinstein, J. A., & Jarvis, W. B. G. (1996). Dispositional differences in cognitive motivation: The life and times of individuals varying in need for cognition. *Psychological Bulletin, 119,* 197–253.

Coskun, H., Paulus, P. B., Brown, V., & Sherwood, J. J. (2000). Cognitive stimulation and problem presentation in idea-generating groups. *Group Dynamics, 4,* 307–329.

Davis, J. P., Eisenhardt, K. M., & Bingham, C. B. (2007). Developing theory through simulation methods. *Academy of Management Review, 32,* 480–499.

Elliott, E., & Kiel, L. D. (2004). Agent-based modeling in the social and behavioral sciences. *Nonlinear Dynamics, Psychology, and Life Sciences (Special Issue: Agent-Based Modeling), 8,* 121–130.

Estes, W. K. (1975). Some targets for mathematical psychology. *Journal of Mathematical Psychology, 12,* 263–282.

Feinberg, W. E., & Johnson, N. R. (1997). Decision making in a dyad's response to a fire alarm: A computer simulation investigation. In B. Markovsky, M. J. Lovaglia, & L. Troyer (Eds.), *Advances in Group Processes, 14,* 59–80.

Frantz, T. L., & Carley, K. M. (2009). Agent-based modeling within a dynamic network. In S. J. Guastello, M. Koopmans, & D. Pincus (Eds.), *Chaos and complexity in psychology: The theory of nonlinear dynamical systems* (pp. 475–505). New York: Cambridge University Press.

Gilbert, N. (2008). *Agent-based modeling.* Thousand Oaks, CA: Sage.

Goldstine, H. H. (1972). *The computer: From Pascal to von Neumann.* Princeton, NJ: Princeton University Press.

Hastie, R., & Stasser, G. (2000). Computer simulation methods in social psychology. In H. Reis & C. Judd (Eds.), *Handbook of research methods in social and personality psychology* (pp. 85–114). Cambridge: Cambridge University Press.

Hong, L., & Page, S. E. (2001). Problem solving by heterogeneous agents. *Journal of Economic Theory, 97,* 123–163.

Harrison, J. R., Lin, Z., Carroll, G. R., & Carley, K. M. (2007). Simulation modeling in organizational and management research. *Academy of Management Review, 32,* 1229–1245.

Kalick, S. M., & Hamilton, T. E. (1986). The matching hypothesis reexamined. *Journal of Personality and Social Psychology, 51,* 673–682.

Kameda, T., Takezawa, M., & Hastie, R. (2003). The logic of social sharing: An evolutionary game analysis of adaptive norm development. *Personality and Social Psychology Review, 7,* 2–19.

Kashima, Y., Woolcock, J., & Kashima, E. S. (2000). Group impressions as dynamic configurations: The tensor product model of group impression formation and change. *Psychological Review, 107,* 914–942.

Kennedy, J. (2009). Social optimization in the presence of cognitive local optima: Effects of social network topology and interaction mode. *Topics in Cognitive Science, 1,* 498–522.

Kenrick, D. T., Li, N. P., & Butner, J. (2003). Dynamical evolutionary psychology: Individual decision rules and emergent social norms. *Psychological Review, 110,* 3–28.

Krause, U. (1996). Impossible models. In R. Hegselmann, U. Mueller, & K. G. Troitzsch (Eds.), *Modeling and simulation in the social sciences from the philosophy of science point of view* (pp. 65–75). Dordrecht: Kluwer.

Larson, J. R., Jr (1997). Modeling the entry of shared and unshared information into group discussion: A review and BASIC language computer program. *Small Group Research, 28,* 454–479.

Larson, J. R., Jr (2007a). Deep diversity and strong synergy: Modeling the impact of variability in members' problem-solving strategies on group problem-solving performance. *Small Group Research, 38,* 413–436.

Larson, J. R., Jr (2007b). A computational modeling approach to understanding the impact of diverse member problem-solving strategies on group problem-solving performance. Invited paper presented at the annual *Society for Experimental Social Psychology Small Groups Research Preconference.* Chicago, IL.

Larson, J. R., Jr (2010). *In search of synergy in small group performance.* New York: Psychology Press.

Larson, J. R., Jr, Christensen, C., Franz, T. M., & Abbott, A. S. (1998). Diagnosing groups: The pooling, management, and impact of shared and unshared case information in team-based medical decision making. *Journal of Personality and Social Psychology, 75,* 93–108.

Larson, J. R., Jr, & Harmon, V. M. (2007). Recalling shared vs. unshared information mentioned during group discussion: Toward understanding differential repetition rates. *Group Processes and Intergroup Relations, 10,* 311–322.

Latané, B. (1996). Dynamic social impact: Robust predictions from simple theory. In R. Hegselmann, U. Mueller, & K. G. Troitzsch (Eds.), *Modeling and simulation in the social sciences from the philosophy of science point of view* (pp. 287–310). Dordrecht: Kluwer.

Latané, B., & Bourgeois, M. J. (2001). Successfully simulating dynamic social impact: Three levels of prediction. In J. P. Forgas & K. D. Williams (2001). *Social influence: Direct and indirect processes* (pp. 61–76). New York: Psychology Press.

Lewandowsky, S. (1993). The rewards and hazards of computer simulations. *Psychological Science, 4,* 236–243.

Linville, P. W., Fischer, G. W., & Salovey, P. (1989). Perceived distributions of the characteristics of in-group and out-group members: Empirical evidence and a computer simulation. *Journal of Personality and Social Psychology, 57,* 165–188.

Macy, M. W., & Willer, R. (2002). From factors to actors: Computational sociology and agent-based modeling. *Annual Review of Sociology, 28,* 143–166.

Miller, J., & Page, S. E. (2004). The standing ovation problem. *Complexity, 9*(5), 8–16.

Myung, I. J., & Pitt, M. A. (2002). Mathematical modeling. In J. Wixted (Ed.), *Stevens' handbook of experimental psychology* (3rd ed., Vol. 4, pp. 429–460). New York: Wiley.

Ostrom, T. M. (1988). Computer simulation: The third symbol system. *Journal of Experimental Social Psychology, 24,* 381–392.

Queller, S. (2002). Stereotype change in a recurrent network. *Personality and Social Psychology Review, 6,* 295–303.

Read, S. J., & Urada, D. I. (2002). A neural network simulation of the outgroup homogeneity effect. *Personality and Social Psychology Review, 7,* 146–159.

Reimer, T., & Hoffrage, U. (2005). Can simple group heuristics detect hidden profiles in randomly generated environments. *Swiss Journal of Psychology, 64,* 21–37.

Reimer, T., & Hoffrage, U. (2006). The ecological rationality of simple group heuristics: Effects of group member strategies on decision accuracy. *Theory and Decision, 60,* 403–438.

Ren, Y., Carley, K. M., & Argote, L. (2006). The contingent effects of transactive memory: When is it more beneficial to know what others know? *Management Science, 5,* 671–682.

Rousseau, D., & Van Der Veen, A. M. (2005). The emergence of a shared identity: An agent-based computer simulation of idea diffusion. *Journal of Conflict Resolution, 49,* 686–712.

Schelling, T. C. (1971). Dynamic models of segregation. *Journal of Mathematical Sociology, 1,* 143–186.

Schneider, D. I. (2009). *An introduction to programming using Visual Basic 2008* (7th ed.). Upper Saddle River, NJ: Prentice Hall.

Simon, H. A. (1992). What is an "explanation" of behavior? *Psychological Science, 3,* 150–161.

Smith, E. R., & Conrey, F. R. (2007). Agent-based modeling: A new approach for theory building in social psychology. *Personality and Social Psychology Review, 11,* 87–104.

Stasser, G. (1988). Computer simulation as a research tool: The DISCUSS model of group decision making. *Journal of Experimental Social Psychology, 24,* 393–422.

Stasser, G. (2000). Information distribution, participation, and group decision: Explorations with the DISCUSS and SPEAK models. In D. R. Ilgen, C. L. Hulin (Eds.), *Computational modeling of behavior in organizations* (pp. 35–156). Washington, DC: American Psychological Association.

Stasser, G., & Taylor, L. A. (1991). Speaking turns in face-to-face discussions. *Journal of Personality and Social Psychology, 60,* 675–684.

Stasser, G., & Titus, W. (1985). Pooling of unshared information in group decision making: Biased information sampling during discussion. *Journal of Personality and Social Psychology, 48,* 1467–1478.

Stasser, G., & Titus, W. (1987). Effects of information load and percentage of shared information on the dissemination of unshared information during group discussion. *Journal of Personality and Social Psychology, 53,* 81–93.

Stasser, G., & Titus, W. (2003). Hidden profiles: A brief history. *Psychological Inquiry, 14,* 304–313.

Sun, R. (2009). Theoretical status of computational cognitive modeling. *Cognitive Systems Research, 10,* 124–140.

Testfatsion, L. (2010). *On-line guide for newcomers to agent-based modeling in the social sciences.* http://www.econ.iastate.edu/tesfatsi/abmread.htm

Van Rooy, D., Van Overwalle, F., Vanhoomissen, T., Labiouse, C., & French, R. (2003). A recurrent connectionist model of group biases. *Psychological Review, 110,* 536–563.

Winquist, J. R., & Larson, J. R., Jr (1998). Information pooling: When it impacts group decision making. *Journal of Personality and Social Psychology, 74,* 371–377.

6

STUDYING GLOBAL WORK GROUPS IN THE FIELD

Pamela J. Hinds

STANFORD UNIVERSITY

Catherine Durnell Cramton

GEORGE MASON UNIVERSITY

Together and separately, we have been studying geographically and globally distributed work teams for over a decade. Fortunately, our work (and the work of others) has evolved considerably over that time and we enthusiastically share in this chapter some of the methodological insights we have had and experimentation that we have tried along the way. Our focus in this chapter is on qualitative *field research* in *real organizations*. We are not talking about studies using quantitative methods (which open up a whole different set of issues), nor about laboratory experiments or studies of student teams. All of those are valid methods (and between us, we've used them all), but we focus here on qualitative field studies designed to build theory about global work.

Why does research on global teams warrant its own chapter in this book? In our experience, the study of global teams presents unique methodological challenges in four ways. First, by definition, team members are not located together. If one wants to study the entire team, one cannot use traditional methods of going out to a single field site and remaining there for the duration of the study. Even if one travels to multiple sites, it is impossible to be in both (all) places at the same time, thus observations are not conducted at exactly the same time (or phase) in a project and cross-site comparisons become suspect. Second, on global teams, team members at different sites are almost guaranteed to have quite different perspectives. Members at one site may feel insulted and devalued as a result of their distant team members' behavior without anyone at the distant site being aware of it. If one wants to conduct team-level research on the dynamics of global teams, we believe it is imperative to understand the perspectives of team members at all sites. Third, globally distributed teams are generally culturally diverse. This isn't unique by itself, but coupled with the geographic distribution, it becomes more challenging because team members are not only *from* different cultures, they are embedded *in* different cultures. Taking culture into consideration is particularly difficult because there is so much variation within a given culture and there is interpenetration of the influence between culture and other factors in the workplace. Finally, to understand intercultural collaboration, researchers are inevitably hampered by their own cultural lenses. As a result, the research team and the data collection approach must be sensitive to these cultural nuances.

We describe the method that we have developed over the last 5 years to study globally distributed teams. It is not perfect and we talk about the challenges later in the chapter, but this approach yields extremely rich data that we believe captures relatively well the experience of the teams and team members we study. Using these methods, we have gained insights into the dynamics of intercultural collaboration and adaptation on teams (Cramton & Hinds, 2007, 2009), the role that site visits play in global work (Hinds & Cramton, 2007), how emotionally charged language issues can derail a team (Beyene, Hinds, & Cramton, 2005), what factors affect team members' sense of having power and influence on the team (Hinds & Cramton, 2008), and how teams deal with the pressure to design global solutions by reconciling local differences (Xu & Hinds, 2009).

Our method is in many ways traditional qualitative research (ethnographic, if we're permitted to use that term loosely), but with our own pragmatic spin. We conduct interviews *in situ* by traveling to the locations of our informants and talking with them. We are generally hosted by a local manager who has agreed to invite us into the site, provide us with badges and work space, and get us acquainted with the location. We also conduct observations of team members as they go about their day-to-day work. Where our method departs from traditional ethnographic research in organizational behavior is in: (a) our use of a multicultural research team to conduct field interviews and provide insight into the data collected; (b) our conduct of concurrent observations in which we have a researcher at each of the sites during the same time period; and (c) the length of time we spend in the field, which is necessarily short due to the resources required to travel to and remain in multiple countries.

Although one might study global work at the individual level (e.g., people's experience of collaborating with distant colleagues) or dyadic level, our approach is to identify project teams that are split across at least two locations and focus on the dynamics of the team. Our interview protocols focus on team dynamics and our observations are explicitly focused on the social dynamics on the teams.

We have conducted one large field study together. This included 12 software development teams split between two locations: three teams split between the US and Germany, three split between Germany and India, and six split between India and the US. We interviewed 181 informants during a four-month period, observed six of the teams for the next four months, then returned the following year to interview a subset of the team members again. This was the big project on which we "cut our teeth," but we have continued to conduct field research over the last few years. Pam, for example, led a study of global product integration activities in six teams spread across the US, Germany, Sweden, India, and Australia. She is also in the midst of another study focused on design practices in different regions of the world. The insights and anecdotes we present in this chapter reflect the intersection of all of the studies on which we have worked together and separately. We hope that you enjoy reading it as much as we enjoy doing the research.

A General Description of the Method

Selecting the research team

Selecting the research team for these in-depth, long-term field studies is one of the most important decisions to be made. We knew, for example, at the beginning of our joint project that we needed to have research team members who could speak the local languages and understand the cultures of those countries in which we would be conducting research. This is in keeping with the embedded intergroup relations perspective championed by Alderfer and his colleagues (e.g., Alderfer, 1987; Alderfer & Smith, 1982) in their studies of race relations. Alderfer argued that composing teams of researchers that encompass the diversity of the groups being studied helps to establish a more empathic understanding of the underlying group dynamics. In the cross-cultural domain, we projected that working as a multicultural research team would increase the likelihood of our being included in sensitive, culturally nuanced communications and arriving upon culturally balanced understandings. In our joint research project on global teams, we had an idea, based on our initial conversation with the field sites, that Germany and India were likely countries for the teams we would be studying. We were extremely fortunate to find outstanding graduate students from Germany and India and a third "multicultural" student who had lived in multiple countries and spoke many languages. In all cases, we strive to compose our research teams so that they mirror the cultural backgrounds of the team members in our studies.

The cultural mixes in our teams are imperative and orchestrated. The personality mix, however, is equally important and can be harder to orchestrate. What makes it work? Deep interest in culture and understanding others' perspectives, thirst for adventure, adaptability (to time zones, ambiguity, food, etc.) are all necessary ingredients. In our studies, the research team has to live and travel together for an extended period of time. We also have to collaborate together across our own cultural differences as we collect and interpret data from the field. Traveling together is stressful, we are often exhausted (but invigorated), and a resilient team with a good attitude makes an enormous difference to the experience and to the quality of the data that are collected.

Selecting (and being selected by) the field site

Selecting the right field site is also key in this type of work. This is true of any organizational field study (as described in Pratt & Kim, this volume), but it is especially so in studies of global teams because there is less time on-site to build rapport and negotiate access due to the duration of the visits and cultural differences make the probability of a cultural blunder much higher. The groundwork has to be in place prior to arriving so that the time *in situ* can be used most productively. In most cases, the companies that we have studied have approached us asking for our insights about globally distributed work, so we have had the good fortune to work with receptive field sites. In our experience, studies go most smoothly if there is an insider who acts as host at each site and can ensure that the research team knows how to get to the field site, has access to the building, has a desk at which to sit, has access to the internet, knows where to meet people, etc. Some of these conveniences may seem minor, but it is possible to spend an enormous amount of time and energy sorting out these details if there is no insider to help.

As with all field studies, the commitment at all levels of the organization opens doors and makes the research possible. In advance of our visits, we make sure that teams are identified and contacted by the informant granting access to the organization. We then contact the team leaders and make sure that they understand the study and are committed to having their team participate, and find out if there are any issues or concerns about which we should be aware. Building rapport, as much as possible, using email ahead of time paves the way for our visits. Finally, we try to schedule interviews prior to arriving on the site.

We have developed a simple scheduling application that allows participants to schedule and reschedule themselves in the interview appointments that we have made available. We found that this is enormously helpful because there are inevitably changes that are needed and we have more certainty that the schedule reflects the actual availability of informants. We also found that getting access to the organization's internal scheduling system ahead of time can make a huge difference. We can then send invitations through the internal company system which legitimizes our requests and makes it easier for informants to accept our requests. One little snafu with this, however, was that we once forgot that we were in Europe and sending invitations to team members in India who were on a different time zone. We, for example, made available a 10am appointment, but the calendaring system automatically converted this to 1:30pm Indian time because it assumed that we would remain in our respective locations. We ended up with about 30 percent of our interviews scheduled 3.5 hours later than we expected during one of our visits. This would have been fine except for the fact that we were using two systems concurrently, one that adjusted (the company's internal calendaring system) and the other that didn't (our home-grown interview scheduling system). In future projects, we learned to use a single system and be more aware of the automatic time-zone conversions embedded in today's advanced calendaring systems.

A final point about the field sites is about our responsibility to the organizations we study. Again, as with most field studies, there is a significant cost to the organization in hosting us and allowing us to interview and observe team members. We generally offer to present our preliminary insights to the organization multiple times in order to enable participants in multiple time zones to hear about our findings. We have found that written reports do not get read and have little hope of affecting change in the organization, so presentations, generally via a system like WebEx, seem to do the trick. We also try to return to all field sites and make in-person presentations of our results. This not only fulfills our responsibility to the informants, but allows us to enter into dialog with them, find out what has changed since we were last there, and obtain their insights about our preliminary findings.

Conducting *interviews* in situ

A key element of our approach to the study of global teams is to talk with people. We are generally interested in team dynamics, including attitudes, perceptions, and behaviors. To obtain information about how people feel about their team dynamics, their perceptions of and concerns about how the team is working together, and their attributions about the sources of challenges and opportunities, we have to talk with them. We use unstructured interviews (see Spradley, 1979), but spend a great deal of time researching the prior literature, identifying questions of interest, and thinking about how we might follow up on, or probe, thoughts interviewees express in order to learn more (see more on this in Pratt & Kim, this volume). We do this for several reasons. First, it helps us to think more deeply about how to approach the interviews. Second, as a research team, it forces dialog about our research goals and how this translates into the interviews themselves. Third, it helps us to identify potentially inappropriate questions or approaches for the cultures we plan to study. When preparing for our interviews in Germany, for example, our German research assistant informed us that asking about the nature of the "relationships" between team members in Germany would be tantamount to suggesting that they were intimate with each other. We quickly changed our wording to "relations" for that setting.

With unstructured interviews of members of global teams, we worry about having our research team calibrated and avoiding systematic bias based on the researcher conducting the interview. We deal with this in several ways. First, we always begin our studies by interviewing in pairs so that we can get a sense of others' interviewing styles. We generally conduct 3–4 interviews (or more, if needed) in pairs and discuss the interviews afterward to calibrate with one another. Second, we plan carefully for who will be interviewing which team members in which locations. So, for example, in our joint study we considered having one or two team members interview all members of a team. That would have had the advantage that those researchers would know the project, the language, and have a sense of the issues pertinent to that team. Despite its potential advantages, however, we did not do this because it makes cross-team comparisons potentially difficult due to concerns about systematic differences in the interviewing styles, interests, and interpretations of the interviewer. Similarly, having interviewers segmented by site or country has the advantage of being logistically much less complicated (and less expensive), but also makes it difficult to know if any differences by site are merely a result of the perspectives of different interviewers. Instead, we opt whenever possible for the more complicated and resource-intensive approach of having all researchers interview members of multiple teams and at multiple sites, often in the course of an intensive data collection trip.

On occasion, we have also had an insider accompany us on the interviews. On the whole, we have found this to work extremely well because the insider knows the language of the organization (e.g., acronyms, projects, people, etc.), can ask more sensitive questions that we may not know to ask, and can reaffirm the importance of the study to the organization. In Pam's study of global product integration teams, for example, our four-person research team included two insiders from the research laboratory in the field organization. The insiders worked in tandem with Pam and a PhD student in the data collection as well as the early data analysis and were responsible for making the results actionable for the organization.

Armed with an interview protocol and probes, a well-calibrated team, and a schedule, we sit down with each informant in a private office or meeting room (or on some occasions in break areas or a corner of a cafeteria), and proceed to talk with them about their experience of being a global team member. Although we always have a broad research question that shapes our study design (e.g., who we talk with, number of sites, cultures represented, etc.), we allow the informant to use our open-ended queries to communicate what *they* think is important. In Pam's study of global integration teams, for example, we started with questions about the role of the informant in the team and the goals of the team. We also generally asked about the extent to which there were different requirements for the project in different regions and how compromises affected the way things were done locally. We use our protocol as a guide, varying the order in which questions are asked and dropping questions if an informant has seized upon a particular topic and is showing us a new dimension of the situation. In our joint study of global teams, however, we wanted to be sure to ask about cross-cultural learning, so we had a single question at the end of the protocol that we usually posed ten minutes prior to the end of every interview. The interview could proceed in any direction, but we always brought it back at the end to ask if they had learned anything in the process of working with people from the other countries as represented on the teams.

This achieved a nice balance between the two objectives of finding the particular informant's deep knowledge and getting a well-rounded picture of a particular critical topic.

Finally, on the logistics side, we always record the interviews (with the permission of the informant, see Pratt & Kim, this volume, for more on Institutional Review Board considerations) and we always use two recorders just in case of equipment failure. On numerous occasions we have had batteries die, found that we neglected to turn on a recorder, had the adjustments set so that the recording was poor, accidentally deleted a recording, etc. So far, using our overly conservative method of dual recorders, we have managed to acquire at least one high-quality recording of every interview we have conducted. Back in the days of tape recorders, we had to carry around suitcases filled with tapes and we always had the completed tapes carried by two researchers on different flights to avoid possible loss. We now use DAT (digital audio tape) recorders, download our files at the end of each day, and send our DAT files nightly through a password-protected website to our transcriptionist who can start transcribing our files right away. A good transcriptionist will also provide immediate feedback about the quality of the recordings, problems with accents, background noise, etc., so that we can immediately correct any problems. This approach, however, has not been without problems. In Pam's recent work in China, we discovered that our secure transmission website was blocked by the Chinese government and the bandwidth available in the hotel was such that it took hours to upload a single file. Our attempts to transmit our files regularly to our transcriptionist were therefore stymied. Instead, we downloaded files on to external hard drives for safe transport back to the US.

A final comment regarding interviews is that language is inevitably a challenge. Even if the lingua franca of the organization is English, we quickly learned that informants may be uncomfortable expressing themselves, may not be as forthcoming, and may be unable to understand the subtleties of the questions when interviewed in English. In planning the interviews, we try to make sure that, even if the informants are fluent in English, they have the option of being interviewed in their native tongue. We then translate the interviews after transcribing them. Pam has also experimented with having an interpreter present in the interview, but this is not as straightforward as it may seem. Nonsimultaneous (sequential) interpretation refers to cases where one person at a time speaks, so the interviewer asks a question in English, it is interpreted into the interviewee's native language, then their response is translated for the interviewer, and so forth. Such an approach poses several difficulties for ethnographic interviews. First, the interview takes far longer, so much less ground can be covered in the time available. Second, and most importantly, it can disrupt the flow of the interview and the ability of the interviewer to build rapport with the informant because the informant and the interpreter end up talking directly with each other while the interviewer is the "odd man out." Simultaneous interviewing holds much more promise, but it requires a highly skilled interpreter who is able to "fade into the background" so that the interviewer and informant have the feeling of talking directly. Such expertise, however, can be hard to find and tends to be expensive, thus pushing the costs of the project even higher.

Conducting concurrent observations

The second prong of our data collection strategy, and perhaps the most exciting for us, is conducting *concurrent observations* at distributed field sites. Concurrent observations refer to observing and recording the activities of team members at multiple sites during the same time period. Although observing sequentially at different sites is valuable for understanding the perspectives of all team members, concurrent observations enables us to see how events and perceptions are similar and different during exactly the same time period. Thus, we are assured that the differences we are seeing are not the result of different project phases, or reorganizations or external events that occurred between observation periods. During the observations, we take detailed field notes paying particular attention to what is salient, the rhythms of the day, the information team members at each location have, and how cross-site meetings are prepared for, engaged in, and interpreted at each site. We record how events that affect both sites are interpreted and handled. During observation in the US of a US–Indian team, for example, Catherine mentioned to a US-based team member the Indian subgroup's impending move the next day into a new building. The US team member had not known his colleagues were moving and wondered aloud whether this then explained why they had not been responding to his emails that day. During another observation period of our joint project, a massive reorganization, the largest in the history of the firm, was announced. At the headquarters location in Germany, this was a dominant topic of conversation and speculation during the observation week. At the Indian site, however, this topic never came up in conversation among the team members that Pam observed. Toward the end of the week, she asked the local team leader and he said that he knew about it, but didn't want to stir up the team, so he didn't discuss it with them. As a result, we were able to learn about how differently this reorganization was handled at the two sites and to gain insight into how the information flows varied.

One of the ways that we manage concurrent observations is to have regular communication between the locations being observed. We try to communicate to one another the topics of conversation that seem to be important so that the observer at the other site is aware of these issues and can make sure to notice their presence or, as interesting, their absence. We also notify each other of important cross-site meetings that will be taking place so that we can observe these from both locations. Finally, although we rarely have time to read them while on site, we have a practice of sending completed field notes to the entire research team at the end of each day. Continual updating across sites is a way of keeping the research team calibrated and making sure that we are capturing comparable sets of field notes.

There is, of course, a practical challenge in conducting team-level observations. The main one, we think, is that there are multiple people of whom to keep track. Rarely do our informants conveniently remain in a single location (even the sub-teams that are collocated) so that we can observe them all at the same time. We handle this by stationing ourselves at a desk as close to the team members as possible and wandering around to pick up on any action that is occurring. Oftentimes, we are observing knowledge workers, so they are sitting at their computer screen for a significant portion of the day. We ask the team members we are observing to invite us to meetings and we stroll the halls looking for social interaction involving the team members we are studying. In some locations, this is quite easy. India, for example, tends to have a work culture that invites interruption and frequent discussion. Germany, in contrast, tends to be more "heads-down" work with scheduled conversations. As a result, we found it more challenging to get insight into what people were doing in Germany and had to resort to different methods. For example, while observing the German members of a team housed in several adjoining offices, Catherine set up shop in different offices each half day and learned to read body language concerning when German team members were receptive to questions and conversation.

In preparing for our observational work, we anticipate having far more to observe than we can ever capture in our field notes. Although we want to remain open to surprises, we find that determining the level of the observation a priori (at least provisionally) is essential to ensure that our distributed research team takes similar approaches. We make decisions, for example, about the priority of capturing individual work vs. social interaction, within team interaction vs. interactions outside of the team, leader vs. team member behavior, and whether or not to capture general rhythms or focus on the minute details of day-to-day work. Our field notes are inevitably a mixture, but setting priorities ahead of time helps to focus us when we have to make choices in the field about what to capture (see Pratt & Kim, this volume, for further discussion of observation strategies).

Analyzing the data

Once the data are collected, we begin our analysis. Although we send our DAT files to our transcriptionist nightly, we rarely see the transcripts before we return home and never before we go into the field the next day. This presents a challenge to ethnographic research, particularly grounded theory building, which relies, in part, on ongoing analysis of the data and adjustment of the research strategy and sampling based on the insights that are emerging (Lofland, Lofland, Snow, & Anderson, 2005; also Charmaz, 2006; Strauss & Corbin, 1990). When we only have 1–4 weeks at each site, we simply cannot approach the study in this way.

To help alleviate this (if only a little), we hold meetings with the research team each day and talk about what we are learning and what we are seeing. Based on these meetings, we get a sense of the themes that are emerging and are able to talk with the members of the research team from the local culture about their interpretations. We continually adjust our interview approach based on these meetings. In our joint study of global teams, for example, we noticed early in the interviews that there were numerous informants talking about language issues. One of the informants in Germany, for example, told us about how stigmatizing it was to ask her management's approval to attend English training because she was expected to be fluent in English as a prerequisite for the job she held. As a team, we talked about this interview and were more attentive to probing if similar issues surfaced in other interviews.

Once we get home and start receiving interview transcripts, we begin our analysis by open coding (see Strauss & Corbin, 1990). We generally have multiple members of the research team open code all of the data so that we have better insight into what themes are robust across readers (especially readers from different cultures). We then generate team-level summaries by having one researcher read all of the material for a single team. The summaries typically include a description of the team, the dynamics of the team, and insights about particular themes identified in open coding (e.g., power dynamics, communication patterns, etc.). Working with our German research assistant, Catherine checked for cultural bias in interpretation by conducting and comparing independent reviews of all the materials from several of the teams, particularly those teams that appeared to experience the greatest cultural tensions. From that point, we begin delving deeper into the data and iterating with the literature to develop grounded theory on topics that emerge.

Strengths, Surprises, and Challenges

Strengths

There are several strengths of this method. One is that we are building on a method that is well developed. Although we have our own spin on it, the foundation for what we do has been established elsewhere by management scholars (e.g., Barley, 1986; Orlikowski, 2002). There are classes that students can take on ethnographic methods, books that researchers can read (see Pratt & Kim, this volume, for suggestions), and symposia that deal with the opportunities and challenges of the method. Further, the method is an established approach in many fields of study, so gaining acceptance is not problematic. More importantly, the method yields incredibly rich data. We find that we have more data and insights than we can possibly manage after a study of the type we describe. We learn an amazing amount and, because of the method, we trust that what we learn has meaning.

Surprises and challenges

There have been numerous surprises and challenges in data collection, data analysis, and writing papers based on the method we describe. One obvious challenge is that it requires a great deal of traveling and careful planning. Although traveling has the ring of adventure, it takes time away from family and other obligations, so it predictably takes its toll on all members of the research team. Globetrotting also brings with it jetlag, unusual food, medical considerations (e.g., malaria medication, shots, etc.), and the inevitable missed flight or lost luggage. In a nutshell, it is exciting, but it is also stressful and exhausting. Finally, with regard to travel, it is extremely expensive, so one must have a large research budget to do what we describe. In addition, the carbon footprint is significant and the cost of transcriptions, translations, interpreters, and so forth, mounts quickly. The bottom line is that it is a resource-intensive approach.

Another challenge is the intensity of the work on site. Because of the short duration of our stays at each location, we try to accomplish as much as we possibly can while there. This translates into long hours of intense work. Catherine, for example, ended up with tendinitis as a result of writing and typing observation notes in the field during our joint study. There is a delicate balance to be reached between the resources expended for this type of research and the burden on the researchers. Each additional day of observation requires, for example, another day on site (and away from home) for at least two researchers.

Another challenge is when concurrent observations breed identification with the subteam being observed. As with most ethnographic work, identification with members of the field site is to be expected (Lofland et al., 2005). This means that, in the case of concurrent observations, research team members may become identified with the people or subteams at the particular site they are observing. We prefer to have observers at a given site who are fluent in the local language, and, as a result, observers are also likely to either be natives of or have a particular affinity for the country in which they are conducting observations, thus exacerbating the likelihood of identification. Tension between the distant subgroups being observed also can intensify identification on the part of the researchers at each site. Because the researcher is seeing the world through the eyes of the particular site she or he is observing, she or he can form attributions about the distant team members in the same way as the team members she or he is observing. Although this may generate tension within the research team at some points, we also recognize it as an opportunity to better understand team dynamics, consistent with the notion of "parallel process" in the work of Alderfer and Smith (Alderfer & Smith, 1982; Alderfer, 1987; Smith, Simmons & Thames, 1989; Smith & Zane, 1999).

This happened to Pam and one of our research assistants in our joint study. Pam observed in the US and our German research assistant observed in Germany during the same week. Pam found herself defending the US-based team against the criticism of the research assistant who had observed in Germany and the researcher assistant defended the seemingly aggressive behavior of the Germans to Pam. Once we realized what was happening, we were able to use ourselves and our internal dynamics to better understand the perspectives of the different parts of the team.

The stability of the teams is also a challenge in organizational research. In our joint study, we were surprised (perhaps naively) by a massive reorganization that took place mid-way through our study. Several of the teams that we were studying were no longer intact and we were not able to (easily) return to continue our research with them. We believe that reorganizations are particularly challenging for team researchers, especially those hoping to do longitudinal research on intact teams, because the teams become disrupted. Fortunately, in our joint research project, we had more or less finished the first wave of data collection when the reorganization occurred. As a result, it affected our ability to obtain longitudinal data, but not the first phase of interviews and observations. We were also lucky because we had two organizations in that study, one of which did not undergo reorganization. Having a second organization, it turns out, is a good risk-mitigation strategy for longitudinal field studies of teams.

One of our biggest challenges in all of this work is the massive amount of data that we collect and analyze. Because we are studying teams, and not individuals, our sample is at the team level. So, we may have only 12 teams (our joint study) or six teams (the study of global product integration teams), but that amounts to 15–20 times that number in individual interviews. In addition, because we risk getting into the field and finding that a team does not match our requirements, we err on the side of larger samples, further increasing the number of interviews required.

We have been told that we do too many interviews for a grounded theory method because we interview beyond saturation, but we feel that we do not have a choice because we need to do all of the interviews while we are on the road. It just is not feasible to interview, analyze, and go back to India the next week if we have more questions or need more material. We could, of course, follow up with telephone interviews, which we do on occasion, but time-zone differences, language and accent considerations, reorganizations, and the difficulty of building rapport over impoverished media can make this less appealing. Grounded theory really demands iterative analysis and our method reduces opportunities to develop and test theory along the way. We see this as the weakest link in our approach.

In terms of the most frustrating aspect of our research, it is without question the amount of time it takes to analyze and write papers based on the mass of data that we have. It is not unusual for it to take three, four, or five years to submit a paper from our data. Reading data, coding, recoding, summarizing, analyzing, reanalyzing, and writing dominates our research time. When we are fortunate enough to be asked to revise and resubmit a paper, it can take a year or more to recode and reanalyze the data and revise the paper. In all seriousness, given how research activity is rewarded, at least in the US, we would not recommend this style of research to someone working toward tenure. For all of its rewards, it is time-consuming and risky. In addition, it is rare that a granting agency will fund multiple years of analysis work, so the analysis and writing ends up, ultimately, getting squeezed into smaller and smaller amounts of available time as we feel pressure to find funding.

A final challenge is fulfilling our responsibility to the field site. Organizations generally are not happy waiting three to five years to get feedback on the studies in which they participate. We have found that a presentation following the open coding stage seems to work well for all involved. Our insights at this point may not be deep and penetrating, but they hopefully provide some new knowledge for the organization and the informants. We sometimes follow up a year later with additional insights and try to stay in touch with the organizations, but the preliminary feedback is when we find that our organizational contacts are most likely to hold the same positions and the organizations are most receptive to hearing our results.

Appropriate and Inappropriate Uses

The method we describe is appropriate for any study in which a researcher cannot observe the entire group in one location. This includes distributed teams, global teams, and cross-organizational teams where the goal of the study is to understand the dynamics of the team and thus it is vital to understand the perspectives of all team members. As with much qualitative work, it is best for theory building, not theory testing. It requires a significant commitment from the research team and from the organization, although the number of teams can be relatively small. Our studies have not yet spanned more than four sites and we have only conducted concurrent observations with teams split between two locations. As the number of locations increases, it may not be practical to employ concurrent observations and it may become cost prohibitive to visit all locations. Thus, where consistent with the research goals, limiting teams to fewer locations is preferred.

Opportunities, Latest Innovations, and Ethical Issues

In this chapter, we have described what we have done thus far in our research. As the study of global teams is relatively new and evolving, so is our approach. Although we have yet to leverage these opportunities, we envision several ways to improve upon these methods and address some of the challenges. First, there is an obvious opportunity to leverage local researchers who have language skill and cultural insight. Although we have not used this approach to study a globally distributed team, Pam is currently working with researchers in China and

The Netherlands in a similar way. She has developed research relationships, for example, with faculty and industry researchers in China and is jointly conducting cross-cultural research. These types of research relationships have great potential to enable studies of globally distributed teams with research teams that mirror the characteristics of those being studied. In such arrangements, however, we advise that the research team conduct some joint data collection activities prior to working in a distributed fashion so that the team can calibrate its efforts. We think that some overlap between researchers and sites helps in detecting and minimizing biases. For data analysis and interpretation, it is important that each researcher have a good understanding of all contexts in which the research is being conducted.

Another opportunity that we have yet to integrate into our studies of global teams is a diary method. Diaries involve informants keeping track of specific behaviors, thoughts, or feelings over a period of time specified by the researcher. Sometimes they involve triggers (such as emails, phone calls, or pages) for the informant to record a particular behavior or answer a question provided by the researcher. So, for example, a diary on a distributed team might ask team members to record every interaction they have with a distant team member or the researcher might email the informants asking them to describe their biggest challenge that day, depending on the goals of the research. Diary methods enable the researcher to acquire records of informant behaviors, attitudes, and thoughts over a longer period of time than it may be feasible to observe. Combined with interviews, diaries can be a powerful method for collecting detailed behavioral data (Conrath, Higgins, & McClean, 1983). Members of a team can be invited to keep logs of their behavior for a specified period of time so that the data collection period, as in the concurrent observations, is held constant. Diary methods are challenging because the researcher must compel the informants to complete the diaries and must specify precisely what is desired, but if done correctly, may be a less resource-intensive way to gather data during the same time period from multiple perspectives on global teams.

There are several ethical considerations in our research on globally distributed teams. One, which we have already discussed, is the resource requirements. We believe it is important to explore less resource-intensive approaches to gain the same (or nearly the same) insights. Diaries, for example, as we discussed above, is one possible way to increase the amount of behavioral data collected with less travel. As with all ethnographic studies, we also feel we have an obligation to represent the interests of the informants to the organization. This is not always straightforward because organizations have competing interests, for example, not paying for team members to travel when our findings suggest that it is necessary to healthy team dynamics. Still, our ethical responsibility includes gaining access to executives to make sure that our informants' voices are heard.

In Closing

Our goal in this chapter has been to describe how we approach research on global teams in a way that enables us to gain empathy for the team members at all sites. In developing our research, we think it is important to give the considerable time that is necessary to produce a generalizable scholarly product that remains faithful to the complicated reality that our informants encounter in their day-to-day work lives. Our research suggests that trying to study global teams without visiting the distant sites is likely to be biased. Although there are many challenges, we find this research to be incredibly rewarding. We gain a deep understanding of the perspectives of team members and the dynamics of these teams and we have yet to embark upon a study where we were not surprised and excited by what we learned.

References

Alderfer, C. P. (1987). An intergroup perspective on group dynamics. In J. Lorsch (Ed.), *Handbook of organizational behavior* (pp. 190–122). Englewood Cliffs, NJ: Prentice Hall.

Alderfer, C. P., & Smith, K. K. (1982). Studying intergroup relations embedded in organizations. *Administrative Science Quarterly, 27*, 35–65.

Barley, S. R. (1986), Technology as an occasion for structuring: evidence from observations of CT scanners and the social order of radiology departments, *Administrative Science Quarterly, 31*, 78–108.

Beyene, T., Hinds, P., & Cramton, C. (2005). Language challenges in international work: The impact of uneven proficiency in the lingua franca. Presented at the *Academy of Management Meeting*. Honolulu, HI.

Charmaz, K. (2006). *Constructing grounded theory: A practical guide through qualitative analysis.* Thousand Oaks, CA: Sage Publications.

Conrath, D. W., Higgins, C. A., & McClean, R. J. (1983). A comparison of the reliability of questionnaire versus diary data, *Social Networks, 5*, 315–322.

Cramton, C., & Hinds, P. (2007). Intercultural interaction in distributed teams: Salience of and adaptations to cultural differences. *Academy of Management Best Paper Proceedings*, Philadelphia, PA.

Cramton, C., & Hinds, P. (2008). Being in the right place with the right people: How influence dynamics are disrupted in offshore collaborations. Paper presented at the *European Group for Organizational Studies (EGOS)*, Amsterdam.

Cramton, C., & Hinds, P. (2009). The dialectical dynamics of nested structuration in globally distributed teams. *Academy of Management Best Paper Proceedings*, Chicago, IL.

Hinds, P., & Cramton, C. (2007) Situated *knowing who:* Why site visits matter in global work. Presented at the *Academy of Management Meeting*, Philadelphia, PA.

Lofland, J., Snow, D., Anderson, L., & Lofland, L. (2005). *Analyzing social settings: A guide to qualitative observation and analysis.* Belmont, CA: Wadsworth Publishing.

Orlikowski, W. (2002). Knowing in practice: Enacting a collective capability in distributed organizing, *Organization Science, 13*(4), 249–273.

Smith, K. K., Simmons, V. M., & Thames, T. B. (1989). "Fix the women:" An intervention into an organizational conflict based on parallel process thinking. *Journal of Applied Behavioral Science, 25*(1), 11–29.

Smith, K. K., & Zane, N. (1999). Organizational reflections: Parallel processes at work in a dual consultation. *Journal of Applied Behavioral Science, 35*(2), 145–162.

Spradley, J. P. (1979). *The ethnographic interview*. Belmont, CA: Wadsworth Publishing.

Strauss, A., & Corbin, J. (1990). *Basics of qualitative research: Grounded theory procedures and techniques*. Sage Publications.

Xu, C., & Hinds, P. (2009). How do differences matter? Toward a theoretical framework of subjective diversity in work groups. Presented at the *Academy of Management Meeting*, Chicago, IL.

7

CROSSING PARTY LINES

Incorporating Measures of Individual Differences in Groups

Randall S. Peterson

LONDON BUSINESS SCHOOL

When asked to write a chapter on measuring personality and other individual differences in the context of groups research, I immediately said "yes" because I have been doing it for 20 years since I was in graduate school at Berkeley (see Tetlock, Peterson, & Berry, 1993). Then I recalled all of the problems, questions, difficulties, and challenges in publishing individual difference papers that cross the strong party line in our profession between individual and group levels of analysis and thought that perhaps I had agreed too quickly. However, I have also always believed that real progress is made by those who focus on interesting problems, regardless of, and in many cases especially because they focus on those problems that cross artificial professional boundaries. So, if I can help and encourage more researchers to span the divide and address the very important problems of how individuals interact to create group-level phenomenon, it will have been worth the time to write this chapter. In doing so, I have tried to outline my thinking through a series of questions that someone new to the profession might have. First, why are these questions of individual differences in the study of groups interesting? Second, what are the challenges of studying individual differences in groups? Third, how do I work through some of those challenges and the specific problems of publishing group-level papers with individual difference measures?

Why Are Individual Difference Variables Interesting?

The first question any reasonable person interested in studying groups should ask is why individual differences are interesting and important questions. If one looks at any one issue of journals like *Small Group Research* or *Group Processes and Intergroup Relations*, one will see a multitude of important group-level variables out there (e.g., polarization, conflict management, virtual teams, cohesion, group development, etc.). So if one is interested in groups, why address questions by moving down a level of analysis? This question is, I suspect, behind many colleagues who have over the years shrugged their shoulders at my work on personality and individual differences. For many of the problems in our field, moving to individual differences might well be reductionist and unnecessary. However, many of the key questions about groups are actually questions about either individuals, or about how individuals come together to create group phenomenon. My own interest in individual differences came from being interested in leadership within groups. Does group leadership matter? Are some individuals better group leaders than others? What do effective leaders do that is different from those who are ineffective? Each of these questions, and others like them, require the researcher to look at both the individual and group levels of analysis simultaneously.

Many other and less obviously individual-level questions being asked in the field of groups research also require a careful look at the individual level of analysis and an understanding of the interplay between individuals and groups. For example, one question that has interested many scholars in recent years is why two groups that report similar levels of conflict report very different levels of cohesion, satisfaction, and even levels of performance (e.g., Jehn, Rispens, & Thatcher, 2010). One explanation scholars have investigated looks at other related variables rather than individual differences: issues such as conflict resolution. Perhaps level of conflict experienced does not really predict these dependent measures reliably. Rather, what matters is not level of conflict, but how it is resolved. If it is resolved amicably, then the group will have a positive trajectory and, if not, then there will be a downward trajectory (e.g., Behfar, Peterson, Mannix, & Trochim, 2008). However, there is a long history of group-level research on conflict in groups and the data would seem to suggest that levels of conflict experienced *does* matter often. So, the questions have come back to looking at the individuals in the team.

In response, scholars have begun to investigate the individuals within the group. Perhaps there is an asymmetry of conflict assessments and this is what might explain the differences between groups. For example, a group of four people could assess the level of task conflict or debate at a moderate level within the group in one of two very different ways. One group could individually assess the level on a five-point scale as 3, 3, 3, and 3 while a second group could assess it as 1, 1, 5, and 5. The first group has uniformly experienced moderate task conflict, believed by most scholars in the area as generally healthy with enough conflict to bring out differences, but not too much to bring out the risk of task conflict mutating into relationship conflict and damaging group satisfaction; see Simons & Peterson (2000) for more detail. The second group has half of its members who have experienced a potentially debilitating level of debate that makes it difficult for them to work with the group, thus damaging group satisfaction and performance.

To the extent that individuals within the group assess the level of conflict within the group differently, this invites a whole series of questions about individual differences and what is happening within the group between individuals. (1) Is it the case that the two who score the group more highly are clashing between themselves within the meeting and take it more seriously than the other two? (2) Is it the case that the two who score the group more highly are arguing outside of the official meetings so that the other two do not see it? Or (3) might it be the case that the two who score the group more highly are more sensitive to expressions of conflict and see things that the other two are not noticing? To address the phenomenon, one needs to consider all of these questions, and then the relevant follow-on questions. For example, if the answer is (3) that some individuals notice more nuance of conflict behavior than others, one needs to understand whether this is an individual personality difference (e.g., high agreeableness people are more attuned to, and place a higher priority on, how people are feeling as they interact), or potentially a cultural difference (e.g., individuals from high context and collectivist national cultures are more likely to notice and prioritize conflict behaviors because overt conflict is generally socially unacceptable). Whatever the answer, one is now firmly into the issues of group composition and reliable individual differences.

My example started with a simple group-level question about why some groups perform better than others, despite reporting similar levels of conflict. Our research questions lead us to a series of individual difference questions, that when answered will allow us to work back up to the group level to address the original question. There are many such issues and questions within the field of groups. Sometimes we can get lucky and answer our group-level questions with exclusively group-level research. However, to answer many of the most interesting and practical questions about groups, we simply need to delve into individual-level research. That means that group researchers need to be prepared to measure individual differences within the groups that we study.

What Are the Challenges of Studying Individual Differences?

So, if studying individual differences in the context of studying groups is so obvious, why do so relatively few people actually publish this kind of work? For many years I thought that the answers were simple – scholars just did not want to move away from what they know, there were not many scholars doing this kind of work so it might be perceived as risky, etc. In more recent years I have to come to understand that the problem is much more complex. The story as I now understand it is that personality and social psychology (i.e., the historical disciplines for where individual difference and group research began) both went through a crisis period in the late 1960s and early 1970s. Social psychology was chastised for recording the history of how university undergraduates responded to questionnaires rather than being about science and identifying universal situational responses (e.g., Gergen, 1973). Social psychologists, including most group researchers, responded by conducting controlled experiments, thus ensuring scientifically valid conclusions. There was also a secondary emphasis on ensuring that ideas were relevant to the world rather than being only about students. The result of which is that social psychologists, including the vast majority of scholars conducting groups research at the time, came to put special emphasis on ideas to be tested in a "critical experiment" pitting one explanation against another.

As the mainstream study of groups broadened to include business schools, communication departments, etc., the emphasis on experimentation has faded away and a much broader array of methods has become acceptable (see the range within this volume, for example). Thus, the long-term impact on the study of groups has been a focus on theoretical ideas to be tested, and a re-invigoration of the idea of the importance of relevance in the study of groups. Ironically, the latter of which was where groups research began with the Lewin studies of the 1930s and 1940s.

At about the same time as social psychology was in crisis, the study of individual differences was also under attack by one of its own, suggesting that consistency across situations was not actually very helpful or likely (see Mischel, 1968, 1969). The challenge was never about the relevance of the work to the world, but whether it was a fruitful path for personality psychologists to be looking for consistency across situations. Personality psychologists responded to this critique by focusing on measurement and methods to demonstrate how, when, and where there are consistencies in behavior over time, and thus to show which individual differences matter over time and situation. It took 25 years to establish that there are five large cross-situational individual differences that account for significant variance, the aptly named "Big Five" personality dimensions, including neuroticism/emotional stability, extraversion/surgency, openness to experience/ intellectance, agreeableness, and conscientiousness (see McAdams, 1997). Thus, the legacy of the crisis in the study of individual differences and personality is a special emphasis on methods and measurement and a fascination with the five key personality factors.

The problem for us as scholars who might be interested in studying groups by occasionally looking at some individual difference measures, is that the reviewers we are likely to encounter will be a mix of scholars who come from these two very different traditions. Any manuscript looking at both group and individual differences variables is likely to get individual reviewers who are strongly focused on very different aspects of the manuscript. The reviewers who come more from the group-level tradition will be focused on the quality of the ideas (i.e., with a premium on whether it is new to the literature) and the reviewers who come from the individual differences tradition are more likely to be focused on precise and careful measurement. That is not to say that someone from the individual differences tradition will not be focused on theory and ideas or that someone from a groups tradition will not be focused on methods and measurement. However, every research study requires trade-offs between rigor and relevance, theory and practical, and the newness of an idea versus how well measured it is. If the reviewers come from very different places and would be willing to make very different trade-offs, this constrains the choices one can make (more later on that problem) and makes navigating the gauntlet of journal revisions extremely difficult indeed!

This problem of pleasing two very different sets of reviewers is what I mean by the title of this chapter "Crossing Party Lines." The reference here is to political parties. Political parties are defined not so much by specific policies: if they work, it is easy for both parties to join together and agree how to move forward. It is where there is no right answer, where it is a matter of taste or inclination, or more importantly guesswork as to what might succeed. Different political parties will start in different places when searching for answers to social problems. Similarly, individual difference and groups scholars will tend to start in different places when looking for answers and when needing to make judgment calls about how to address a problem. Neither is right all of the time, or probably even more of the time (i.e., do you not have findings because the idea is bad, or because it is measured poorly?).

On the other hand, where they both agree there is a problem (i.e., your "new" construct looks like and is measured similarly to an existing construct already in the literature), then as with political parties, the direction to be taken is probably fairly clear. The problem is that, as in politics, it is likely to be a relatively rare event. My experience in publishing papers with individual difference and group-level variables is that they tend to follow a hard road in the publishing process, with many papers taking many years from conception to publication; for instance, Peterson, Smith, Martorana, and Owens (2003) took 13 years from start to publication, most of which was spent in trying to appease these two very different sets of reviewers.

Before I go any further I do want to say categorically that it is possible to get individual difference and group-level measures published together, and in a reasonable time frame, if you are fully prepared to deal with the challenges. The third section of this chapter is specifically about those challenges, and includes my best advice for how to avoid making some of the big mistakes, where to stretch versus where to be more conservative, and how to approach the use of individual difference and composition variables in the study of groups.

How Do I Work Through The Specific Challenges?

I would suggest that there are four key sets of interrelated decisions you will be making that will affect your experience in trying to have the research published that includes both individual difference and group-level variables.

They are: (1) writing multilevel theory; (b) selecting an individual difference measure; (c) deciding how to aggregate the individual difference measure to the group level; and (d) choosing a statistical approach to analyzing data. I will address each of these questions in turn, drawing on my analysis of the challenges of publishing individual-difference variables in the context of groups research above.

Writing multilevel theory

Writing theory and developing novel hypotheses is never easy. When one combines it with the complications of working across levels of analysis, it becomes all the much harder. The key problem to avoid sounds simple enough, but is very difficult to avoid in practice. That is, assuming that how something works at the individual level is how it will work at the group level – just "add-up" the levels. For example, we know that extroverts talk more than introverts as individuals generally, but will a group where there is a mix of introverts and extroverts talk less than a group of all extroverts? It would seem obvious at one level to say "yes." However, that would not necessarily be a good assumption to make. All it takes is one extrovert in a group to talk and fill the air space. Alternatively, looking at individuals who score highly on neuroticism (i.e., defined by the experience of negative emotions such as stress, anxiety, worry, etc.), does a group with two individuals who score highly on neuroticism worry twice as much as a group with one? Similarly to extroversion, it takes only one person who scores highly on neuroticism at the individual level to create the demand characteristic for the whole group to operate at a higher level of response to their concerns (see Peterson, Davidson, & Moynihan, 2007). In both of these two cases, how the individual difference variable operates at the individual level is decidedly not how it operates at the group level. All it takes is one high scorer on extroversion to fill the airspace in a meeting, or one high scorer on neuroticism to make the entire group respond to their worries.

The net effect of trying to avoid the problem of assuming individual processes translate directly to group processes is the need to identify when and under what conditions individual differences will manifest themselves. Will this difference affect all behavior across all time? Or is it contingent on other processes, situational circumstances, or organizational culture? Or might the effects of personality depend on the configuration of people in the group such that the group will look like the average of the individuals in the group, the most extreme scorer in the group (i.e., as with neuroticism), or the dispersion in the group (i.e., heterogeneity versus homogeneity on an individual difference is key, e.g., homogeneity is helpful with agreeableness). This is what Lisa Moynihan and I called the contingent configurational approach to theory about the role of personality in groups (Moynihan & Peterson, 2001). When theorizing across individual and group level, one needs to be clear, careful, and consistent in explaining how each of the levels operates, and specifically how individual behavior will interact to create group-level behavior.

Selecting an individual difference measure

The first instinct for many groups scholars trained in the social psychology tradition (i.e., whether they are in a communication department, business school, etc.) is to invent or modify an existing scale to accommodate the theoretical innovation or, even more acceptably, to take a scale someone else has published with once, since if it is published that means it must be alright. This is standard practice for those most who engage in groups research, but would be a highly hazardous step in measuring personality or indeed most any individual difference variable. Remember from our discussion above about the importance of measures and methods within the individual differences tradition, reviewers are likely to want reassurance that your measure is both valid and reliable. So unless you want to engage in detailed scale construction yourself, which is highly technical and incredibly time consuming and data intensive (e.g., DeVellis, 2003; Rea & Parker, 1997), then one is best picking something "off the shelf." That is not to say one can never innovate, but it will not be as easy as it is when one is dealing only with group-level constructs.

The best guideline is to ask yourself whether you can defend the reliability and validity of the scale applying the exact same wording or use of your individual difference scale. If the answer is anything other than a strong "yes," then it is best to look further for other measures. There are literally hundreds of measures that have already been fully validated to the satisfaction of the profession. The most efficient way I have found to identify validated scales is to go to the International Personality Item Pool (IPIP) website (http://ipip.ori.org/; see also Goldberg, 1999; Goldberg, et al., 2006). This website shares hundreds of scales, along with their full validity information and cross-correlations with other scales. It provides invaluable assistance in helping to select individual difference variables that are appropriate for particular questions.

One thought about the timing of when you might collect your individual difference variable, based on which variable(s) you choose: if your individual variable is personality, which is conceptualized as stable across time, then in principle the timing of your data collection should not matter. However, reviewers from the group tradition will be uncomfortable with both personality and group-level data being collected on the same survey at the same time. They worry that the personality measures might be somehow tainted by the group experience and the questionnaires or both. So, ideally you will measure personality before the group interaction so that it is clearly unaffected by the group experience. If for some reason you can only administer it during or after the group experience, you will need to make the argument in the paper and to reviewers – another reason to stick with well-established scales. If your individual difference variable might be affected by situation (e.g., Integrative Complexity has been shown to be partly personality and partly situational; see Tetlock et al., 1993; Tetlock & Suedfeld, 1988), then the timing of when it is measured becomes critical and should be made in accordance with the predictions of your study.

Although personality questionnaires are standard practice in the profession and are able to handle most situations in which you might wish to measure personality, you may occasionally find yourself in a situation in which you cannot ask your participants to complete a personality questionnaire. I found myself in this situation when I wanted to study Chief Executive Officers. Hard as I have tried, they generally do not answer researcher personality questionnaires! Or perhaps more realistically, if you have conducted a study of groups, having interviewed group members individually, and a reviewer starts asking some difficult questions about personality or group composition. It is possible to study individual differences and derive measures of personality from archival material, provided one has data describing individual behavior (see Peterson, Smith et al., 2003). There is a fairly wide range of variables that can be coded from archival materials, ranging from the Big Five personality variables to measures of Integrative Complexity and counts of specific individual behaviors. Here you will need to engage multiple coders with a q-sort or other semi-projective measure of personality (see Meyers & Seibold, this volume, on engaging coders). Luckily, the IPIP does also have some help for you on these types of measures.

Deciding how to aggregate the individual difference measure to the group level

Building on the points above about how to write good multilevel theory, the next key decision is about how to aggregate your individual difference scores to the group level. In the old days (i.e., ten years ago or more) the answer was simple: create a mean score to represent the group-level construct. The simple days are, alas, long gone, and definitely for the better. This crude approach to creating group-level variables that could then be run in a simple regression or ANOVA obscured many important effects and implied what we now know are incorrect assumptions about how individual level variables combine to create group-level variables. If you have built your group-level theory carefully (as explained above), it should tell you how to aggregate individual variables to create/predict group-level effects. Much of the time this leads to straightforward answers. For example, if one is measuring the effects of neuroticism, based on the argument that the group operates at the level of the most neurotic individual (see earlier) the best way to represent this is by using the maximum score within the group, regardless of how the other members of the group score. Your group-level variable will be very different from that found if you had used the mean score or standard deviation for the group. And if your theory is correct, you are much more likely to find significant results. Sometimes the answers are not always obvious, however.

For help when the aggregation questions are much more complicated, see Harrison and Klein (2007) and Klein, Dansereau, and Hall (1994) for detailed help.

One additional complication has arisen in more recent years: group researchers are meant to provide justification for aggregating individual scores or individual assessments of group processes to the group level. Particularly if a mean-level score is used, the reviewers want to know that the variable does have meaning at the group level. The key question is whether there is more variance within or between groups in the sample. If the variable in question has group-level meaning, then one expects much less variation within groups than between groups (i.e., with people who have not interacted). Typically, this is established by providing a set of Intra-Class Correlation or ICC scores (see James, Demaree, & Wolf, 1984). However, this is not always relevant for individual difference variables (like personality) that are not expected to be affected by group interaction. It could be a useful measure of attraction, selection, and attrition in naturalistic groups, demonstrating how those processes have narrowed the range of personalities within a particular group or organizational culture. However, reviewers may become confused and expect measures of justification for aggregation for representing group-level personality effects with groups that have been assigned (i.e., where each group would start and end with a full range of personality scores). Do not get confused that some of your measures may need justification (i.e., those that are directly affected by group interaction) and others may not!

Choosing a statistical approach to analyzing data

Once you have written good multilevel theory, carefully selected an individual difference measure that is appropriate to your theory, and then thought carefully about how you will operationalize that individual difference variable at the group level, it is now time to think about the statistical and methodological approach to your data. Are your hypotheses all at the group level? If they are, then you can choose a relatively simple approach to analyzing your data: an ANOVA if you have done a controlled experiment, or a simple regression if you are in the field (see those chapters in this volume as well). However, if you have hypotheses at both the individual and group levels, you are going to need to engage in the newer multilevel methods (see Kashy & Hagiwara, this volume; Kozlowski, this volume; Klein & Kozlowski, 2000). These methods are much more complicated than the traditional ones you will see in older published work in the profession, but the rewards are in greater sensitivity to the data and the ability to hypothesize across levels of analysis.

A Few Final Thoughts

Having been trained as social psychologist to do groups research, rather than as a personality psychologist or individual differences person, my mistakes, and this chapter, have focused more on methodological issues than on issues of theory and idea development. If that is also your perspective, and for most readers I expect it will be since this is in a book about research methods for group research, I hope this chapter has highlighted the absolute necessity of getting better with methods, data, and levels of analysis issues if you are to incorporate individual difference measures successfully into your research. Fast. If you are already a methods and data guru, however, and you would like more on theory development in the area, I would recommend Kilduff (2006) for a punchy summary of what makes for good theory. There are many more resources out there to help you, but that summary will tell you succinctly what the idea-oriented people in the profession will be looking for.

Finally, I wanted to share one final thought about the party lines analogy. As frustrating as it can be to have reviewers giving you divergent advice on how to develop your research, the rewards of pleasing both sides are in creating exceptional scholarship that is recognized across a very wide array of social scientists. Some of the very best work in the study of groups today is happening in this area. This work is fundamental to understanding the nature of groups and group interaction. If we can fully get to grips with how individuals come together to create team-level outcomes, we will have unlocked the black box that holds many of the remaining answers about why groups are at the core of every human society. And like a great democracy that is open to many points of view, the study of individual differences in groups is frustrating and messy but somehow it works to create an excellent outcome. I encourage you to join into this fascinating research discussion.

References

Behfar, K. J., Peterson, R. S., Mannix, E. A., & Trochim, W. M. K. (2008). The critical role of conflict resolution in teams: A close look at the links between conflict type, conflict management strategies, and team outcomes. *Journal of Applied Psychology, 93*, 170–188.

DeVellis, R. F. (2003). *Scale development: theory and applications* (2nd ed.). London: Sage.

Gergen, K. J. (1973). Social psychology as history. *Journal of Personality and Social Psychology, 26*(2), 309–320.

Goldberg, L. R. (1999). A broad-bandwidth, public domain, personality inventory measuring the lower-level facets of several five-factor models. In I. Mervielde, I. Deary, F. De Fruyt, & F. Ostendorf (Eds.), *Personality psychology in Europe* (Vol. 7, pp. 7–28). Tilburg: Tilburg University Press.

Goldberg, L. R., Johnson, J. A., Eber, H. W., Hogan, R., Ashton, M. C., Cloninger, C. R., & Gough, H. C. (2006). The International Personality Item Pool and the future of public-domain personality measures. *Journal of Research in Personality, 40*, 84–96.

Harrison, D. A., & Klein, K. J. (2007). What's the difference? Diversity constructs as separation, variety, or disparity in organizations. *Academy of Management Review, 32*(4), 1199–1228.

International Personality Item Pool: A Scientific Collaboratory for the Development of Advanced Measures of Personality Traits and Other Individual Differences (http://ipip.ori.org/), Internet website.

James, L., Demaree, R., & Wolf, G. (1984). Estimating within-group inter-rater reliability with and without response bias. *Journal of Applied Psychology, 69*(1), 85–98.

Jehn, K., Rispens, S. & Thatcher, S. M. B. (2010). The effects of conflict asymmetry on workgroup and individuals outcomes. *Academy of Management Journal, 53*(3), 596–616.

Kilduff, M. (2006). Editors comments: Publishing theory. *Academy of Management Review, 31*(2), 252–255.

Klein, K. J., Dansereau, F., & Hall, R. J. (1994). Levels issues in theory development, data-collection, and analysis. *Academy of Management Review, 19*(2), 195–229.

Klein, K. J. & Kozlowski, S. (2000). *Multilevel theory, research, and methods in organizations: Foundations, extensions, and new directions* (pp. 512–553). San Francisco, CA: Jossey Bass.

McAdams, D. P. (1997). A conceptual history of personality psychology. In R. Hogan, J. Johnson, & S. Briggs (Eds.), *Handbook of personality psychology* (pp. 4–29). San Diego, CA: Academic Press.

Mischel, W. (1968). *Personality and assessment*. New York, NY: Wiley.

Mischel, W. (1969). Continuity and change in personality. *The American Psychologist, 24* (11),1012,8.

Moynihan, L. M., & Peterson, R. S. (2001). A contingent configuration approach to understanding the role of personality in organizational groups. *Research in Organizational Behavior, 23*, 327–378.

Peterson, R. S., Davidson, J., & Moynihan, L. M. (2007). Does one rotten apple spoil the barrel? Using a configuration approach to assess the conflict-inducing effects of a high neuroticism team member. In K. J. Behfar and L. L. Thompson (Eds.), *Conflict in Organizational Groups* (pp. 93–112). Evanston, IL: Northwestern University Press.

Peterson, R. S., Smith, D. B., Martorana, P. V., & Owens, P. D. (2003). The impact of chief executive officer personality on top management team dynamics: One mechanism by which leadership affects organizational performance. *Journal of Applied Psychology, 88*, 795–808.

Rea, L. M., & Parker, R. A. (1997). *Designing and conducting survey research: A comprehensive guide*. San Francisco, CA: Jossey-Bass Publishers.

Simons, T. L., & Peterson, R. S. (2000). Task conflict and relationship conflict in top management teams: The pivotal role of intragroup trust. *Journal of Applied Psychology, 85*, 102–111.

Tetlock, P. E., Peterson, R. S., & Berry, J. M. (1993). Flattering and unflattering personality Portraits of integratively simple and complex managers. *Journal of Personality and Social Psychology, 64,* 500–511.

Tetlock, P. E., & Suedfeld, P. (1988). Integrative complexity coding of verbal behavior. In C. Antaki (Ed.), *Lay explanation*. Beverly Hills, CA: Sage.

8

STUDYING TEAM COGNITION

The Good, the Bad, and the Practical

Susan Mohammed and Katherine Hamilton

THE PENNSYLVANIA STATE UNIVERSITY

As a newly minted assistant professor, I (first author) embarked on an ambitious study that had all of the hallmarks of academic fame and success (or so I thought!). The goal of the project was to examine the impact of two types of team training (task and team building) on two types of team mental models (teamwork and taskwork) and two types of team performance (task and contextual) over two time periods (mid-semester and the end of the semester). The attempt to directly measure the nascent notion of a team mental model (organized mental representations of relevant team knowledge that are shared across team members) longitudinally and position the construct in a nomological network of antecedents and consequences was cutting-edge research for this literature over a decade ago. In addition, we had the perfect context in which to test our model: student restaurant management teams that were required to plan and supervise the preparation of meals patronized by the public daily.

The setting constituted a real-life educational laboratory. Seven to nine individuals were arranged in teams and had to fulfill both kitchen and dining-room duties, including menu planning, purchasing food, cost accounting, testing recipes, decorating tables, marketing, serving customers, supervising student employees, and sanitation. Because teams managed their meals twice over the course of the semester, we had the opportunity to administer the two types of training to each team, but vary the order so that we could assess whether the task–team building or team building–task sequencing was most effective. In short, the study conceptualization and operationalization were brilliant!

The longitudinal nature of team data collection required the coordination of a large research team of graduate and undergraduate students who were first trained to deliver the two types of training and administer a complex array of measures in the correct sequence. Scheduling seven to nine students to come into the laboratory as an intact team for two hours turned out to be a significant undertaking. Twice during the semester for each team, training sessions were conducted a few days prior to the meal that they would be managing. Owing to the fact that the students were already taxed by course demands and understandably time pressured, extra efforts such as providing snacks and sodas were utilized to help them remain attentive during training and motivated to complete the measurement battery. Furthermore, because of the involved nature of the team project, class sizes were small, so data collection took three semesters in order to obtain even a minimal number of teams for quantitative data analysis.

Our research team was optimistic that the project would result in at least two or three top tier publications, so my hopes were high. I was banking on this study to fast track me through the tenure process. However, the descent of my lofty plans was fast and swift after data analysis revealed very few significant effects and abysmally low effect sizes for training and team mental models. Much to my surprise, neither type of training influenced teamwork or taskwork mental models or task or contextual performance. Because of the large amount of data collected, we were able to publish an empirical paper out of this dataset (Mohammed, Mathieu, & Bartlett, 2002), but not on the variables that we expected to be the primary story.

This early career disappointment was part of my introduction to the logistical trials and tribulations of collecting team data and the difficulty of measuring a concept as elusive as team cognition. Although not particularly fruitful from an outcome standpoint, this research experience was markedly beneficial from a process standpoint. The invaluable lessons that I learned have served me well over the years. For example, when designing a study, I am sensitive to issues of parsimony and recognize that less often turns out to be more. I understand the importance of having multiple streams of empirical work and not "putting all of your eggs in one basket." I am less excited about innovative research designs in and of themselves and more enthused about results that actually highlight the positive features of the innovative research design. Apart from these general research lessons, I also discovered a great deal about measuring team cognition, which I will be sharing throughout this chapter. Despite the challenging nature of team cognition research, I continue to be intrigued by the opportunity to contribute to a growing and constantly evolving area that has been identified as one of the most significant developments in the team literature over the last decade (e.g., Salas, Cooke, & Rosen, 2008; Salas & Wildman, 2009). Thankfully, subsequent successes in my research program and those of doctoral students have also bolstered my enthusiasm for this line of study.

This chapter is divided into two parts. First, we provide an overview of team cognition research and then focus on team mental models as a specific exemplar. For both constructs, we discuss conceptual issues, methodological choice points, strengths and weaknesses, as well as appropriate and inappropriate uses. We also offer specific recommendations for researchers interested in studying team cognition and team mental models.

Team Cognition

Overview

Team cognition is a broad term referring to the collective cognitions of a group (Tindale, Meisenhelder, Dykema-Engblade, & Hogg, 2001) or "processes at the intraindividual level that are dependent on and interact with process at the interindividual level" (Salas & Fiore, 2004, p. 138). Although cognition has traditionally been addressed at the individual level of analysis, it has become increasingly common to discuss the existence of group-level cognitive structures because of the increasing emphasis on teams in research and in organizations. Individual cognition is nested within team cognition, and both occur at the same time (Cooke, Gorman, & Rowe, 2009). Team cognition has been used as a mechanism to explain how successful teams are able to make more accurate predictions about team functioning and coordinate without explicit communication (Cannon-Bowers & Salas, 2001). On the flip side, investigations of many disastrous aviation and military incidents have been blamed on team cognition failures (Foushee, 1984; Wilson, Salas, Priest, & Andrews, 2007).

Over the past decade, there has been a proliferation of team cognition research across disciplinary boundaries, including psychology (Mathieu, Heffner, Goodwin, Salas, & Cannon-Bowers, 2000), management (Lewis, 2003), sports and exercise (Fiore & Salas, 2006), engineering (Badke-Schaub, Neumann, Lauche, & Mohammed, 2007), information sciences and technology (Carroll, Rosson, Convertino, & Ganoe, 2006), human factors (Kiekel & Cooke, 2005), and medicine (Undre, Sevdalis, Healey, Darzi, & Vincent, 2006). Shared cognition has been recognized as one of the hallmarks of expert teams (Salas, Rosen, Burke, Goodwin, & Fiore, 2006) and is prominently featured in recent reviews of team research (e.g., Ilgen, Hollenbeck, Johnson, & Jundt, 2005; Kozlowski & Bell, 2003; Kozlowski & Ilgen, 2006; Mathieu, Maynard, Rapp, & Gilson, 2008; Salas et al., 2008). Indeed, a recent meta-analysis of 65 independent studies found that team cognition positively predicted team motivational states, processes, and performance, confirming that there is a cognitive foundation for team effectiveness (DeChurch & Mesmer-Magnus, 2010a).

Conceptual framework

As an overarching, multidimensional construct, team cognition is comprised of many specific exemplars, including team mental models (team members' shared, organized understanding of teamwork and taskwork knowledge; Klimoski & Mohammed, 1994), transactive memory (shared awareness of who knows what within the team; Lewis, 2003), team/shared situation awareness (shared perceptions among group members concerning the meaning and projected status of environmental events; Wellens, 1993), cognitive consensus (similarity in the way that group members conceptualize key issues; Mohammed, 2001), group learning (sharing, storage, and retrieval of group knowledge that represents a change in the group's potential behavior; Wilson, Goodman, & Cronin, 2007), and strategic consensus (shared understanding of strategic priorities among managers; Kellermanns, Walter, Lechner, & Floyd, 2005). Although related through referencing some form of sharedness or similarity among group members, these constructs derive from different literatures and are distinct in their conceptualization and methodology (Cooke et al., 2009; Mohammed, Ferzandi, & Hamilton, 2010). For example, whereas the academic roots of cognitive and strategic consensus are in decision making, team mental models and transactive memory derive from psychology and team/shared situation awareness and group learning have strong traditions in the human factors and organizational behavior literatures, respectively (Mohammed & Dumville, 2001). While some forms of team cognition tend to assess forms of knowledge (e.g., team mental models, transactive memory, team/shared situation awareness, and group learning), others assess more subjective and evaluative beliefs (e.g., cognitive consensus and strategic consensus).

General description of methodology

The study of team cognition covers the range of laboratory experiments (e.g., Hollingshead, 1998), computer simulations (e.g., Mathieu et al., 2000), field work (e.g., Austin, 2003), and case studies (e.g., Carley, 1997). Several basic distinctions related to measurement can be made between the various types of cognition, including content only versus both content and structure, obtrusive versus unobtrusive measures, perceived versus actual sharing, and context-dependent versus generic assessments. Each of these distinctions is described in further detail below.

First, content refers to the knowledge that comprises cognition, while structure represents the way the content is organized in the minds of the participants. Several forms of team cognition such as transactive memory (e.g., Lewis, 2003), group learning (e.g., Edmondson, 1999), and strategic consensus (e.g., Knight et al., 1999) capture content via questionnaires (as well as other methods). In contrast, the assessment of team mental models involves the additional step of examining the structural relationship between concepts, necessitating the use of techniques such as scaling algorithms or concept mapping.

Second, whereas most team cognition measures are unobtrusive in that they assess constructs either before or after task completion, some are obtrusive in that they assess constructs during task performance. For example, the Situation Awareness Global Assessment Technique (SAGAT) is a popular type of query method that freezes the task at predetermined times to ask participants questions concerning their awareness of the current situation (e.g., "Enter the aircraft which are not in communication with you;" Endsley, 1995; Jones & Endsley, 2004, p. 349). An advantage of query methods is that they capture the dynamism fundamental to the notion of situation awareness, but a disadvantage is that their disruptive nature may significantly impact task performance (Salmon, Stanton, Walker, & Green, 2006).

Perceived versus actual sharing among team members is a third point of differentiation among the various types of team cognition. For example, some studies have ascertained the extent to which team members perceive that they are "on the same page" in their interpretations of cognitive content by asking items such as "We understand each other" (e.g., Swaab, Postmes, van Beest, & Spears, 2007, p. 191) and "Predictions on task-related outcomes are similar among team members" (Kang, Yang, & Rowley, 2006, p. 1707). In contrast, other studies have directly assessed each individual's knowledge structures and then compared them to the rest of the team to assess similarity (e.g., Lim & Klein, 2006; Marks, Zaccaro, & Mathieu, 2000). Specifically, Lim and Klein (2006, p. 417) asked team members to judge the relatedness of pairs of statements describing tasks (e.g., "Team members are proficient with their own weapons") or team interaction processes (e.g., "Team members communicate openly with each other"). The average similarity of each team's taskwork and teamwork mental models were then calculated by means of a network analysis program.

Fourth, team cognition is assessed using generic or context-dependent measures. Specifically, team mental model and cognitive consensus measures are context dependent, needing to be tailored to the team's task. However, generic scales are commonly used to measure transactive memory (Lewis, 2003), group learning (e.g., Edmondson, 1999), and strategic consensus (e.g., Ensley & Pearce, 2001). Some situation awareness measures, such as SAGAT, are context dependent (e.g., "Enter the location of all aircraft;" Jones & Endsley, 2004, p. 349). Others, such as the Mission Awareness Rating Scale (MARS), are generalizable across tasks (e.g., "How well did you understand what was going on during the mission?"; Matthews, 2002, p. 30).

Although not commonly made salient in empirical research, these basic distinctions help to highlight the theoretical and operational choice points inherent in team cognition research.

For example, the notion of accuracy (the degree to which team members' mental models converge with a "true score" or expert's mental model) would be relevant when measuring actual sharedness for knowledge structures, but not when measuring the perceived sharedness of belief structures. Methodologically, developing context-dependent measures and assessing actual sharedness and content as well as structure are more difficult than utilizing pre-developed scales and measuring perceptual sharedness and only content.

Strengths and weaknesses

A key advantage of studying team cognition is the opportunity to participate in a rapidly growing, multidisciplinary field that shows no signs of waning

anytime soon. According to Salas and colleagues (2008), two significant developments in the team literature over the past 50 years are the empirically established
links between shared cognition and team performance as well as the discovery
that shared cognition can be measured. Although researchers acknowledge the
usefulness of team cognition and recognize its potential as a promising line of
research, they are also quick to stress that there is much to be done before this
potential can be fully realized. Early on, lack of conceptual development and
confusion over how to measure cognitive structures at the group level were identified as two fundamental research needs (Mohammed, Klimoski, & Rentsch,
2000). Unfortunately, this concern still exists (e.g., Smith-Jentsch, 2009). As conceptual clarity is a prerequisite to measurement precision, ambiguity in defining
and differentiating shared cognition constructs has negative implications for
operationalization.

As gauged by a lack of coherence in terminology, conceptualization, and measurement, the maturity of this area of research is still relatively low. Therefore, there
are plenty of opportunities to make substantial contributions to this literature.
In addition, because there are no clearly established measurement paradigms,
opportunities for creativity and innovation are encouraged. On the flip side, however, studying team cognition can feel like wandering into a tangled, uncharted
forest of messy conceptualization and underdeveloped measurement. Rather than
following a road that has already been conveniently paved, the experience of
conducting team cognition research is more like first having to clear the brush
and weeds to get from point A to point B. Although it can be exciting to pioneer
new ground and go where no one has ventured before, the lack of well-defined
terms, strong theoretical frameworks, and standard methodological procedures
can easily produce uncertainty (and even some anxiety) regarding being on the
right track. We would not recommend team cognition research to those who are
low in tolerance for ambiguity!

Appropriate and inappropriate uses

As a broad, multidimensional construct, team cognition should be used as an
aggregate term and not as a substitute for specific types of collective cognition
(e.g., team mental models, transactive memory, and group learning). Similarly, a
pervasive problem in the shared cognition literature is that researchers use different terms to describe constructs that are conceptually similar or the same term to
describe constructs that are conceptually and/or operationally distinct. This was
identified as problematic from the literature's inception (e.g., Klimoski &
Mohammed, 1994) and is still recognized as troublesome a decade and a half later
(e.g., Mohammed et al., 2010). Given the state of the literature, Smith-Jentsch
(2009) concluded that a key challenge for researchers is to "achieve clarity and
parsimony with respect to the manner in which facets of team cognition are
operationally defined" (p. 492). To avoid construct proliferation, it is recommended

that team cognition researchers maintain conceptual integrity by thoroughly familiarizing themselves with relevant literatures, using existing constructs as intended, and only introducing a new construct when the value of the distinction can be demonstrated (Weingart & Cronin, 2009).

Recommendations

Our recommendations are organized around three basic questions that need to be addressed in studying team cognition. Each will be discussed below.

1. How do you decide what type(s) of team cognition to measure?

As noted above, there are several choices, including team mental models, team/shared situation awareness, transactive memory, strategic consensus, group learning, and cognitive consensus. Because they derive from distinct literatures and disciplines, it is important to be aware of the conceptual and methodological distinctions among the various types of team cognition (e.g., Mohammed & Dumville, 2001).

In preparation for my dissertation research, I (first author) had the opportunity to observe several mental health planning groups who had the complex task of determining the availability and financing of publicly funded in-patient services for their region. The membership of each group consisted of representatives from a range of constituencies, including boards, agencies, family members, and unions. From the outset, it was clear that various constituencies had conflicting assumptions underlying the key issues. Whereas the unions presumed that state hospitals would continue to exist indefinitely, boards and agencies assumed that the state hospitals would be phased out after a designated number of years.

This qualitative work stimulated my interest regarding how individuals entering a group with different "thought worlds" reconcile dissimilar assumptions underlying the issues. Although group members may have similar goals, such as reaching the best decision, their diverse perspectives may interfere with the ability of the group to view issues cognitively in similar ways. Whereas decision-making research has tended to focus on how groups negotiate to reach consensus on decisions, considerably less attention has been given to how group members negotiate to reach consensus on the fundamental interpretation of issues. Therefore, my co-author and I focused on cognitive consensus (similarity among group members regarding how key issues are conceptualized). While preferences reveal what members want out of the decision process, cognitive representations help to explain the reasons underlying their preferences (Mohammed & Ringseis, 2001). As seen in this example, selecting the type of team cognition to measure is intricately linked with the purpose and context of the research.

Several questions should be carefully contemplated when determining the type(s) of team cognition to examine. First, are knowledge structures or beliefs/

opinions most relevant to the purpose of the research? Knowledge is characterized by descriptive states of nature that one knows to be true, whereas beliefs are characterized by desired states of nature that are preferred or expected (Mohammed et al., 2000). For example, asking whether a member of the team has expertise in a certain area (knowledge) is distinct from asking one's opinion on whether a group member should be assigned to a particular task (belief). Because cognitive consensus focuses on the reasons underlying preferences and how key issues are conceptualized, beliefs were most relevant in the Mohammed and Ringseis (2001) study.

Second, what type of content is appropriate to capture (e.g., taskwork, teamwork, representations of key issues, situational context)? Taskwork (what needs to be accomplished) and teamwork (how work needs to be accomplished) are two types of content that are commonly used in the team literature (e.g., Lim & Klein, 2006; Mohammed et al., 2002). However, in the case of cognitive consensus, the focus is specific to the framing perspectives and underlying assumptions of decisions (Mohammed & Ringseis, 2001).

Third, is sharing conceptualized as distributed or overlapping? Extending beyond their content domains, types of team cognition also differ regarding their treatment of cognitive similarity. The term "sharing" can mean "having in common" (e.g., sharing the equipment; Cannon-Bowers, Salas, & Converse, 1993) or "dividing up" (e.g., sharing the workload; Resnick, 1991). Whereas some forms of team cognition subscribe more to the distributed definition of sharing (e.g., transactive memory), others subscribe more to the overlapping definition (e.g., team/shared situation awareness, group learning, team mental models; Mohammed & Dumville, 2001). On the other hand, cognitive consensus embraces both distributed and overlapping views of sharing. As discussed in Mohammed and Ringseis (2001), extreme diversity and extreme consensus in cognitive consensus is generally viewed as dysfunctional. Therefore, a balance of both agreement and disagreement is desirable, and the optimal level will depend on factors such as the nature of the team task and where the group is in the decision-making process (Mohammed, 2001).

If logistically possible, we would recommend measuring multiple types of shared cognition in the same study. Clearly, the potential for leveraging the multidisciplinary nature of team cognition research is large. However, analogous to "ships passing in the night," team cognition has been criticized for the lack of cross-fertilization among research streams occurring in parallel across the different constructs (DeChurch & Mesmer-Magnus, 2010a). Although there have been some conceptual and empirical advances in this area (e.g., Ellis, 2006; Mohammed & Dumville, 2001), integration among different types of cognition was recently noted as one of the top ten critical research needs for team effectiveness research (Salas & Wildman, 2009). Therefore, comparing and contrasting among two or more types of team cognition would be an excellent way to contribute to the literature.

2. How do you ensure that there is a good match between team cognition types and your intended sample?

Teams with distinct roles that have different expertise are well suited to the study of transactive memory, whereas teams facing dynamic environmental events are appropriate for the study of situation awareness. Focusing on goals and priorities, strategic consensus has traditionally been assessed using top management decision-making teams (e.g., Kellermanns et al., 2005). In addition to team type, task characteristics, interdependence, stage of development, and level of interaction should be considered in determining the suitability of a sample for the measurement of a specific type of team cognition. Although requiring more effort up front, we have found careful consideration of the research context to be a critical step in preventing problems down the road.

In Mohammed and Ringseis (2001), decision-making teams were clearly most appropriate for investigating interpretations of issues. Because we wanted to manipulate the conditions affecting the emergence of cognitive consensus, we designed a laboratory study adapting a multi-issue negotiation exercise called Towers Market. Participants played the role of store representatives (grocery, florist, liquor store, or bakery) who negotiated on the forming of a joint market. In order to measure cognitive consensus, the original task had to be altered in several ways. Specifically, participants were randomly assigned to constituency (store) groups in which they received role instructions. To maximize the variability of cognitive diversity across stores, the role instructions were constructed so that each store had different underlying assumptions concerning how the market should operate. It was important that the task had no obvious "right" solution so that differences of opinion could be generated prior to group discussion. After constituency groups discussed their store's viewpoints collectively, participants were then divided into decision-making groups consisting of one representative from each of the four store groups. The constituency and decision-making groups were designed to mirror the structure observed in the earlier qualitative research on mental health planning groups. All of these task design choices were critical to the measurement of cognitive consensus.

3. How do you select a team cognition measure?

Clearly the most challenging, the choice of assessment method is made difficult not only by the diverse measurement traditions across team cognition constructs, but also by the considerable variety within specific types of team cognition. However, determining the answers to the following questions provide general guidance.

a.   Does the research purpose necessitate measuring structure as well as content?

b.   Based on research goals, does the advantage of capturing the dynamic nature of the construct outweigh the disadvantage of disrupting the participant while they are performing the task?

c.   Is there perceptual or actual sharing of theoretical interest?

d.   Are generic scales available and relevant to your study setting or are context-dependent measures more appropriate?

Although logistically easy to administer, pre-existing measures may not be well suited to the team context that you are studying. Even if there is a good overall match, we have found that adjustments in terminology or tense (e.g., past, present) are generally necessary.

In the Mohammed and Ringseis (2001) study, there were no appropriate pre-existing scales because the measurement of cognitive consensus had largely been ignored in previous literature. Because we operationalized cognitive consensus as shared assumptions underlying decisions, a major challenge was to extract the key assumptions of the Towers Market exercise. After considerable thought and task analysis, we recognized that whether the market should operate interdependently (share personnel, resources, and costs) or independently (only share the building) was a primary issue at the core of many disagreements on specific decision options. Indeed, a common theme derived from multiple research experiences is that measuring team cognition often involves going beyond the surface and digging deeper to extract the underlying issues that are fundamental to cognitive constructs. In the end, we made significant adjustments to the original Towers Market negotiation exercise to effectively assess cognitive consensus. For example, we constructed confidential role information sheets so that each store had different underlying assumptions concerning how the market should operate as well as provided convincing rationale as to why the store had the stated views and issue positions. We also created a store group phase of the experiment so that participants could learn and discuss their store's assumptions and preferences prior to being divided into decision-making groups, which consisted of one representative from each of the four store groups. We then measured cognitive consensus both before and after discussions in the decision-making groups. Sample cognitive consensus items included, "Stores in the Market should operate independently, except for sharing a common building with other stores" and "Forming a Market should be a truly collaborative joint venture where personnel, resources, and costs are shared among the stores involved."

Given the number of team cognition constructs, it is beyond the scope of this chapter to cover all of them. However, in the service of providing a more in-depth discussion of a specific construct than an overview of team cognition allows, we focus on team mental models in the following section. In addition to measuring cognitive structure and accuracy as well as addressing a broader array of content than other forms of team cognition, the study of team mental models can be particularly challenging. Therefore, it is an appropriate construct to discuss in detail.

Team Mental Models

Conceptual framework

Team mental models (TMMs) are team members' shared, organized understanding and mental representation of knowledge about key elements of the team's relevant environment (Klimoski & Mohammed, 1994). Team members hold multiple mental models simultaneously, including models concerning taskwork (work goals, performance requirements) and teamwork (interpersonal interaction requirements; Mathieu et al., 2000). Whereas other types of team cognition capture either only taskwork (e.g., team/shared situation awareness, transactive memory, information sharing) or teamwork (e.g., group learning) knowledge, TMMs represent both content domains (Mohammed & Dumville, 2001). In addition, TMMs have two primary properties: sharedness (the degree to which members' mental models are consistent with one another) and accuracy (the degree to which members' mental models converge with experts' mental models or a "true score"), although sharedness has received more emphasis. The general thesis of this emerging literature is that team effectiveness will improve if team members are mentally congruent and have an adequate shared understanding of the task and team. Consistent with this thesis, empirical studies have consistently shown TMM similarity to be of substantial benefit to both team processes and performance (e.g., Lim & Klein, 2006; Marks et al., 2000; Mathieu et al., 2000; Rentsch & Klimoski, 2001; Smith-Jentsch, Mathieu, & Kraiger, 2005).

General description of TMM measurement

From its inception, the measurement of TMMs as team-level cognitive structures has presented the most significant stumbling block to progress in this area of study (e.g., Mohammed et al., 2000). There are several features that make TMM measurement more challenging than some types of team cognition constructs. First, there is no consistent methodology that has been used to measure TMMs. To illustrate a different model, the information-sharing literature has been marked by systematic, programmatic research due to a common hidden profile task and a similar laboratory-based research design (Stasser & Titus, 1985). In contrast, the TMM literature is characterized by a variety of quantitative and qualitative measures represented in a wide array of field and laboratory environments, including student teams performing PC-based command and control simulations (e.g., Mathieu et al., 2000), air traffic controller towers (e.g., Smith-Jentsch et al., 2005), military teams (e.g., Lim & Klein, 2006), nuclear powerplant control room crews (e.g., Waller, Gupta, & Giambatista, 2004), and government employee teams (e.g., Rentsch & Klimoski, 2001).

Second, because of their context-dependent nature, TMM measures need to be tailored to the specific task under investigation. A number of researchers desiring to measure TMMs have contacted me (first author) over the years and are disappointed to hear that I cannot provide a generalizable measure that they can easily import into their study. Much valuable time has been wasted wishing this was true!

Third, because organized knowledge (usually reflected as relationships between concepts), is central to the definition of TMMs, both content and structure are important components of their measurement (Mohammed et al., 2010). Whereas other forms of team cognition commonly use Likert scales to capture content, the assessment of TMMs involves the additional step of examining the relationship between concepts. Elicitation techniques derive mental model content and representation techniques reveal the structure or the pattern of relationships between elements (Mohammed et al., 2000).

Fourth, with its focus on knowledge structures and measuring actual sharedness, TMM measurement has given more attention to accuracy than forms of team cognition that emphasize evaluative beliefs and perceptions of sharing. Because shared teamwork and taskwork knowledge may turn out to be inaccurate, highly convergent mental models, in combination with those that are of high quality, are expected to yield the greatest team performance benefits (e.g., Edwards, Day, Arthur, & Bell, 2006; Mathieu, Heffner, Goodwin, Cannon-Bowers, & Salas, 2005).

Given that several reviews of TMM measurement have described the breadth of choices associated with assessing TMMs (e.g., Cooke, Salas, Cannon-Bowers, & Stout, 2000; Langan-Fox, Code, & Langfield-Smith, 2000; Mohammed et al., 2000), we only provide a brief description of two of the most commonly used techniques: similarity ratings and concept mapping. Similarity ratings (also referred to as relatedness judgments or paired comparison ratings) are a popular content elicitation method involving judgments of the relatedness between pairs of concepts or statements. In our work, we have found it helpful to present the concepts in tabular form (similar to a correlation matrix) with the terms listed across the top row and term descriptions listed in the left-hand column. Separate tables are needed to assess different categories of content (e.g., taskwork, teamwork).

In administering similarity ratings to student restaurant management teams, taskwork concepts included "costing the menu" and "ordering food," while teamwork concepts included "motivating and supporting employees" and "looking for and fixing problems as they arise." Participants rated how related the concepts or statements were to each other on a response scale (e.g., −4 (highly negatively related) to +4 (highly positively related)). A sample taskwork similarity matrix is shown in Appendix A. Respondents are generally not required to specify their definition of similarity, even though various options such as causation, contingency, or co-occurrence exist (Mohammed et al., 2000). Although it is important to include key concepts and adequately sample the content domain, it is also important to recognize that too many concepts can easily overwhelm participants. In our experience, we have found that 8–11 concepts in a single table works well and that more than 14 concepts becomes burdensome for student participants when multiple tables are administered multiple times. In fact, Shepard and Chipman (1970) have shown that it is noticeably more cognitively taxing to complete pairwise comparisons containing over 15 concepts.

To obtain a more interpretable representation, similarity ratings are then transformed by means of computerized scaling algorithms, including Pathfinder (e.g., Lim & Klein, 2006), multidimensional scaling (e.g., Rentsch & Klimoski, 2001) or the UCINET network analysis program (e.g., Mathieu et al., 2005). Despite differences in the representation of "structure," each program offers quantitative indices to evaluate cognitive structure and intra-team convergence. For example, Pathfinder graphically represents structure by closely linking concepts that respondents rate as high in similarity and assigning a numerical weight to the closeness of the link between concepts (Schvaneveldt, 1990).

In contrast to paired comparison ratings, concept mapping involves participants placing concepts in a pre-specified hierarchical structure depicting the sequence of activities required to perform the team's task (e.g., Marks, Sabella, Burke, & Zaccaro, 2002; Marks et al., 2000). The map is generally a series of boxes placed horizontally and linked together. In the case of the concept maps used for the student restaurant management teams, the rows represented the action sequences for each member's role, and the columns depicted a cross-section of the tasks team members should be doing at once. Therefore, each team member was not only asked to consider what they would be doing to accomplish the meal, but also what their team mates would be doing at the same time. A sample map is provided in Appendix B. We provided a list of concepts representing different task aspects, and respondents placed a subset of concepts on the map that best captured the expected actions of each team member. For example, concepts included various task duties including "ingredient check" and "decide on product substitutions" for roles such as the expeditor and the food production manager. Overlap between team members' concept maps was assessed via a point system representing the number of shared linked concepts, which is consistent with research done in previous studies (e.g., Ellis, 2006; Marks et al., 2000).

Measuring accuracy presents several methodological challenges regarding who determines accuracy as well as how it is determined. In the case of similarity ratings, subject matter experts (SMEs) are generally asked to complete the same TMM measure as the participants, and comparisons are then made between experts and team members. Alternatively, concept mapping SMEs rated each participant's concept map on an accuracy scale (Ellis, 2006; Marks et al., 2000).

Strengths and weaknesses of TMM measurement

Team mental models represent a broader content domain (e.g., teamwork, taskwork) than other types of team cognition and have the properties of both sharedness and accuracy. One of the key strengths, and a distinguishing feature, of TMMs is the measurement of both content and structure (e.g., Langan-Fox et al., 2000; Mohammed et al., 2010; Rentsch, Small, & Hanges, 2008). In comparison to rating scales that only assessed content, meta-analytic results from 23 independent studies found that structural measures had stronger relationships with team processes (DeChurch & Mesmer-Magnus, 2010b). Specifically, similarity ratings analyzed via Pathfinder evidenced the strongest relationships with processes (DeChurch & Mesmer-Magnus, 2010b).

In addition to a strength, the measurement of structure is also a weakness. As we can attest from personal experience, administering and analyzing similarity ratings and concept maps is far more labor intensive and time consuming than Likert scales. Participants are generally not thrilled (and sometimes downright annoyed!) to be presented with matrices or maps requiring more thought and effort to complete than more traditional questionnaire items. In addition, coding concept maps can be laborious, especially if too many boxes and linkages were included in the map.

Appropriate and inappropriate uses

As with team cognition in general, there is still confusion surrounding how to conceptualize and measure TMMs. Because they are defined as team members' shared and organized mental representations of team-relevant knowledge (Cannon-Bowers et al., 1993; Klimoski & Mohammed, 1994), TMM measurement should capture relationships between concepts through structural representation. However, several studies have used TMM terminology while only measuring content sharedness and/or accuracy (e.g., Chou, Wang, Wang, Huang, & Cheng, 2008; Levesque, Wilson, & Wholey, 2001; Millward, 2006; Webber, Chen, Payne, Marsh, & Zaccaro, 2000). Given that conceptual–operational alignment would significantly reduce perplexity and help to distinguish TMMs as a construct, researchers need to evaluate closely the appropriateness of their measurement of TMMs.

Recommendations for TMM measurement

1. Start with a team task analysis

In many TMM techniques, cognitive content is supplied by the researcher (e.g., similarity ratings, concept maps), which facilitates the comparison of structures across respondents, but requires careful sampling to ensure comprehensive coverage. Because TMMs are context specific, determining what content to measure is a critical step in the measurement process. A review of TMM measurement stated that "the task context must be specified before the issue of appropriate measurement strategies can even be approached ... Investigators of shared cognitive structures must clearly specify the performance domain of interest to evoke the right cognitive structures" (Mohammed et al., 2000, p. 127). The importance of this step is not to be underestimated and will in large part determine the success of TMM measurement. Therefore, though it does require time and effort, we strongly advise that researchers not rush this process, as fancy network analysis programs or maps in the representation phase do not substitute for poor choice of content in the elicitation phase.

With the benefit of hindsight, I (first author) attribute some of the failure of the study described at the beginning of the chapter to lack of attention given to proper content elicitation. In a later TMM study with student restaurant management teams (yes, I am persistent!), I derived a comprehensive list of concepts through conducting detailed interviews with instructors as well as observing students performing kitchen and dining room tasks. This step proved to be invaluable to creating a TMM measure with more favorable results.

2. Understand the pros and cons of measurement choices

Clearly, researchers should critically examine the strengths and weaknesses of each tool in light of the research question under examination and the team context. Significant distinctions exist between the assessment methods regarding their treatment of content as well as structure. To illustrate, while taskwork and teamwork content are assessed independently with similarity ratings (e.g., Lim & Klein, 2006), they are assessed simultaneously with concept maps when respondents are asked to list sequential task information for their role as well as other team member roles (e.g., Marks et al., 2000). Similarly, elicitation and representation are examined independently in similarity ratings and the subsequent network analysis programs used, but are combined in concept maps. With Pathfinder, Multidimensional Scaling, and UCINET, representation is determined by computerized metrics after participants provide similarity ratings. However, in concept mapping, a hierarchical map is pre-specified by the researcher and can therefore be imposed even if this structure does not exist in the mind of the participant. We refer authors to reviews of TMM measurement that offer more detailed evaluations of TMM analytic techniques than we have provided here (e.g., Langan-Fox et al., 2000; Mohammed et al., 2000).

Researchers are also advised to consider logistics when considering what TMM measure to use. Completing dozens of paired comparison ratings may be more feasible with students in a laboratory context than organizational employees being asked to take time away from performing business tasks. In my (first author) experience with the student restaurant management teams, concept maps were more successful in a later study than the similarity ratings used in the study described at the beginning of the chapter. Whereas similarity ratings primarily capture declarative knowledge (knowledge of *what* should be done), concept maps assess procedural knowledge (knowledge of *how* the task should be completed). Procedural knowledge was well suited to the nature of restaurant tasks; therefore, students perceived greater face validity for concept maps than similarity ratings in this context.

3. Sweat the small stuff

When it comes to TMM measurement, we agree that the "devil is in the details" (Smith-Jentsch, 2009, p. 491). In our experience, particulars like rating scales and the instructions provided to participants matter. In one study, we utilized a −4 to +4 response scale for similarity ratings, only to find out later that Pathfinder does not accept negative numbers (but UCINET does). Filling out similarity ratings and concept maps is not intuitively obvious to many participants and therefore requires careful explanation. For example, I (second author) found it helpful to provide participants with detailed instructions prior to completing a series of grids using paired similarity ratings. Specifically, students were encouraged to read through all definitions of the concepts before attempting to fill in any information. Once the participants understood the definition of each concept, they were encouraged to enter the extreme numbers of the scale first (not related and strongly related), followed by the values in the middle (Hamilton, 2009). In addition, a simplified football-related example was provided, in which the rationale for the high, low, and moderate ratings between the concepts were explained (Hamilton, 2009).

4. Maximize data collection within the boundaries of what is logistically possible

Unfortunately, the design features that will make the most contribution to the TMM literature are often the most difficult to implement. Have you ever wondered why the need for longitudinal investigation appears in so many "future research" sections instead of being a part of the methodology of a particular study? Obviously, collecting data over time is difficult to implement and therefore best passed on to more brave souls! TMMs are no exception in this regard, but a key research agenda item is to understand how team mates' knowledge structures develop over time (Mohammed et al., 2010). Similarly, owing to the laborious nature of measuring TMMs, it is understandable that many studies use only a single measurement method (e.g., Ellis, 2006; Mathieu et al., 2000). However, the simultaneous use of multiple measures is needed to capture varied cognitive content comprehensively.

Recent innovations

Although the broad categories of teamwork and taskwork are commonplace in representing TMM content, researchers are beginning to examine shared understandings of the situation to capture the dynamic context in which TMMs develop (e.g., Hamilton, 2009; Waller et al., 2004). In addition, more emphasis is being given to the temporal aspects of TMMs.

While an understanding of the "what" (taskwork) and the "how" (teamwork) have been emphasized in TMM measurement, failure to understand the "when" can seriously jeopardize final team outcomes (Mohammed, Hamilton, & Lim, 2009). With regard to the measurement of accuracy, the traditional assumption has been that there is a single, correct model. However, Mathieu and colleagues (2005) recently invoked the concept of equifinality to suggest that there may be "multiple *equally good* yet *different* mental models" (p. 39). This notion is especially applicable in field settings where many effective strategies may exist for accomplishing tasks.

We anticipate that the role of technology in shaping the development of TMMs will be at the forefront of innovation in the coming years. Technological tools should be created to assess the extent of overlap between team members on both taskwork as well as teamwork content. Therefore, technology can serve as a mechanism for improving the "real-time" assessment of team mental model similarity, but also as a feedback tool so that team members are informed when knowledge sharing has not occurred. Indeed, efforts in this direction are currently under way (e.g., Rentsch, Delise, & Hutchison, 2009; Yen, Fan, Sun, Hanratty, & Dumer, 2006) and will expand in the future to benefit teams practically. Clearly, increased efforts to create tools that assess the similarity and accuracy of teamwork and taskwork content in a logistically feasible and user-friendly manner are needed, especially for field applications. It will be exciting to see innovation in TMM measurement in the near future.

References

Austin, J. R. (2003). Transactive memory in organizational groups: The effects of content, consensus, specialization, and accuracy on group performance. *Journal of Applied Psychology, 88,* 866–878.
Badke-Schaub, P., Neumann, A., Lauche, K., & Mohammed, S. (2007). Mental models in design teams: A valid approach to performance in design collaboration? *CoDesign, 3,* 5–20.
Cannon-Bowers, J. A., & Salas, E. (2001). Reflections on shared cognition. *Journal of Organizational Behavior, 22,* 195–202.
Cannon-Bowers, J. A., Salas, E., & Converse, S. (1993). Shared mental models in expert team decision making. In N. J. Castellan, Jr (Ed.), *Individual and group decision making: Current issues* (pp. 221–246). Hillsdale, NJ: Lawrence Erlbaum.
Carley, K. M. (1997). Extracting team mental models through textual analysis. *Journal of Organizational Behavior, 18,* 533–559.
Carroll, J. M., Rosson, M. B., Convertino, G., & Ganoe, C. H. (2006). Awareness and teamwork in computer-supported collaborations. *Interacting with Computers, 18,* 21–46.
Chou, L., Wang, A., Wang, T., Huang, M., & Cheng, B. (2008). Shared work values and team member effectiveness: The mediation of trustfulness and trustworthiness. *Human Relations, 61,* 1713–1742.
Cooke, N. J., Gorman, J. C., & Rowe, L. J. (2009). An ecological perspective on team cognition. In E. Salas, G. F. Goodwin, & C. S. Burke (Eds.), *Team effectiveness in complex*

organizations: Cross-disciplinary perspectives and approaches (pp. 157–182). New York: Routledge, Taylor & Francis Group.

Cooke, N. J., Salas, E., Cannon-Bowers, J. A., & Stout, R. J. (2000). Measuring team knowledge. *Human Factors, 421,* 151–173.

DeChurch, L. A., & Mesmer-Magnus, J.R. (2010a). The cognitive underpinnings of effective teamwork: A meta-analysis. *Journal of Applied Psychology, 95*(1), 32–53.

DeChurch, L. A., & Mesmer-Magnus, J.R. (2010b). Measuring shared team mental models: A meta-analysis. *Group Dynamics: Theory, Research, & Practice, 14*(1), 1–14.

Edmondson, A. (1999). Psychological safety and learning behavior in work teams. *Administrative Science Quarterly, 44,* 350–383.

Edwards, B. D., Day, E. A., Arthur, W., & Bell, S. T. (2006). Relationships among team ability composition, team mental models, and team performance. *Journal of Applied Psychology, 91,* 727–736.

Ellis, A. P. J. (2006). System breakdown: The role of mental models and transactive memory in the relationship between acute stress and team performance. *Academy of Management Journal, 49,* 576–589.

Endsley, M. R. (1995). Measurement of situation awareness in dynamic systems. *Human Factors. Special Issue: Situation Awareness, 37,* 65–84.

Ensley, M. D., & Pearce, C. L. (2001). Shared cognition in top management teams: Implications for new venture performance. *Journal of Organizational Behavior, 22,* 145–160.

Fiore, S. M., & Salas, E. (2006). Team cognition and expert teams: Developing insights from cross-disciplinary analysis of exceptional teams. *International Journal of Sport and Exercise Psychology, 4,* 369–375.

Foushee, H. C. (1984). Dyads and triads and 35000 feet: Factors affecting group process and aircrew performance. *American Psychologist, 39,* 885–893.

Hamilton, K. (2009). *The effect of team training strategies on team mental model formation and team performance under routine and non-routine environmental conditions.* Unpublished doctoral dissertation, Pennsylvania State University, University Park.

Hollingshead, A. B. (1998). Communication, learning, and retrieval in transactive memory systems. *Journal of Experimental Social Psychology, 34,* 423–442.

Ilgen, D. R., Hollenbeck, J. R., Johnson, M., & Jundt, D. (2005). Teams in organizations: From input-process-output models to IMOI models. *Annual Review of Psychology, 56,* 517–543.

Jones, D. G., & Endsley, M. R. (2004). Use of real-time probes for measuring situation awareness. *International Journal of Aviation Psychology, 14,* 343–367.

Kang, H. R., Yang, H. D., & Rowley, C. (2006). Factors in team effectiveness: Cognitive and demographic similarities of software development team members. *Human Relations, 59,* 1681–1710.

Kellermanns, F. W., Walter, J., Lechner, C., & Floyd, S. W. (2005). The lack of consensus about strategic consensus: Advancing theory and research. *Journal of Management, 31,* 719–737.

Kiekel, P. A., & Cooke, N. J. (2005). Human factors aspects of team cognition. In R. W. Proctor & K.L.Vu (Eds.), *Handbook of human factors in web design* (pp. 90–103). Mahwah, NJ: Lawrence Erlbaum Associates Publishers.

Klimoski, R., & Mohammed, S. (1994). Team mental model: Construct or metaphor? *Journal of Management, 20,* 403–437.

Knight, D., Pearce, C. L., Smith, K. G., Olian, J. D., Sims, H. P., Smith, K. A., & Flood, P. (1999). Top management team diversity, group process, and strategic consensus. *Strategic Management Journal, 20,* 445–465.

Kozlowski, S. W. J, & Bell, B. S. (2003). Work groups and teams in organizations. In W. C. Borman, D. R. Illgen, & R. J. Klimoski (Eds.), *Handbook of psychology: Industrial and organizational psychology* (Vol. 12, pp. 333–375). New York: Wiley.

Kozlowski, S. W. J., & Ilgen, D. R. (2006). Enhancing the effectiveness of work groups and teams (Monograph). *Psychological Science in the Public Interest, 7*, 77–124.

Langan-Fox, J., Code, S., & Langfield-Smith, K. (2000). Team mental models: Techniques, methods, and analytic approaches. *Human Factors, 42*, 242–271.

Levesque, L. L., Wilson, J. M., & Wholey, D. R. (2001). Cognitive divergence and shared mental models in software development project teams. *Journal of Organizational Behavior, 22*, 135–144.

Lewis, K. (2003). Measuring transactive memory systems in the field: Scale development and validation. *Journal of Applied Psychology, 88*, 587–604.

Lim, B. C., & Klein, K. J. (2006). Team mental models and team performance: A field study of the effects of team mental model similarity and accuracy. *Journal of Organizational Behavior, 27*, 403–418.

Marks, M. A., Sabella, M. J., Burke, C. S., & Zaccaro, S. J. (2002). The impact of cross-training on team effectiveness. *Journal of Applied Psychology, 87*, 3–13.

Marks, M. A., Zaccaro, S. J., & Mathieu, J. E. (2000). Performance implications of leader briefings and team-interaction training for team adaptation to novel environments. *Journal of Applied Psychology, 85*, 971–986.

Mathieu, J. E., Heffner, T. S., Goodwin, G. F., Cannon-Bowers, J. A., & Salas, E. (2005). Scaling the quality of teammates' mental models: Equifinality and normative comparisons. *Journal of Organizational Behavior, 26*, 37–56.

Mathieu, J. E., Heffner, T. S., Goodwin, G. F., Salas, E., & Cannon-Bowers, J. A. (2000). The influence of shared mental models on team process and performance. *Journal of Applied Psychology, 85*, 273–283.

Mathieu, J. E., Maynard, M. T., Rapp, T., & Gilson, L. (2008). Team effectiveness 1997–2007: A review of recent advancements and a glimpse into the future. *Journal of Management, 34*, 410–476.

Matthews, M. D. (2002). *Assessing situation awareness in field training exercises.* Alexandria, VA: US Army Research Institute for the Behavioral and Social Sciences.

Millward, S. M. (2006). Do you know your stuff? Training collaborative modelers. *Team Performance Management, 12*, 225–236.

Mohammed, S. (2001). Toward an understanding of cognitive consensus in a group decision-making context. *Journal of Applied Behavioral Science, 37*, 408–425.

Mohammed, S., & Dumville, B. (2001). Team mental models in a team knowledge framework: Expanding theory and measurement across disciplinary boundaries. *Journal of Organizational Behavior, 22*, 89–106.

Mohammed, S., Ferzandi, L., & Hamilton, K. (2010). Metaphor no more: A 15-year review of the team mental model construct. *Journal of Management, 36*(4), 876–910.

Mohammed, S., Hamilton, K., & Lim, A. (2009). The incorporation of time in team research: Past, current, and future. In E. Salas, G. F. Goodwin, & C. S. Burke (Eds.), *Team effectiveness in complex organizations: Cross-disciplinary perspectives and approaches* (pp. 321–348). New York: Routledge Taylor and Francis Group.

Mohammed, S., Klimoski, R., & Rentsch, J. (2000). The measurement of team mental models: We have no shared schema. *Organizational Research Methods, 3*, 123–165.

Mohammed, S., Mathieu, J. E., & Bartlett, A. L. (2002). Technical-administrative task performance, leadership task performance, and contextual performance: Considering the influence of team- and task-related composition variables. *Journal of Organizational Behavior, 23*, 795–814.

Mohammed, S., & Ringseis, E. (2001). Cognitive diversity and consensus in group decision making: The role of inputs, processes, and outcomes. *Organizational Behavior and Human Decision Processes, 85*, 310–335.

Rentsch, J. R., & Klimoski, R. J. (2001). Why do 'great minds' think alike? Antecedents of team member schema agreement. *Journal of Organizational Behavior, 22*, 107–120.

Rentsch, J. R., Delise, L. A., & Hutchison, S. (2009). Team member schema accuracy and team member schema congruence: In search of the Team MindMeld. In E. Salas, G. F. Goodwin, & C. S. Burke (Eds.), *Team effectiveness in complex organizations* (pp. 241–266). New York: Routledge, Taylor & Francis Group.

Rentsch, J. R., Small, E. E., & Hanges, P. J. (2008). Cognitions in organizations and teams: What is the *meaning* of cognitive similarity? In B. Smith (Ed.), *The people make the place* (pp. 129–157). Mahwah, NJ: Lawrence Erlbaum Associates.

Resnick, L. B. (1991). Shared cognition: Thinking as social practice. In L. B. Resnick, J. M. Levine, & S. D. Teasley (Eds.), *Perspectives on socially shared cognition* (pp. 1–20). Washington, DC: American Psychological Association.

Salas, E., & Fiore, S. M. (2004). *Team cognition: Understanding the factors that drive process and performance.* Washington, DC: American Psychological Association.

Salas, E., & Wildman, J. L. (2009). Ten critical research questions: The need for new and deeper explorations. In E. Salas, G. F. Goodwin, & C. S. Burke (Eds.), *Team effectiveness in complex organizations* (pp. 525–547). New York: Routledge, Taylor & Francis Group.

Salas, E., Cooke, N. J., & Rosen, M. A. (2008). On teams, teamwork and team performance: Discoveries and developments. *Human Factors, 50,* 540–547.

Salas, E., Rosen, M. A., Burke, C. S., Goodwin, G. F., & Fiore, S. M. (2006). The making of a dream team: When expert teams do best. In K. A. Ericsson, N. Charness, P. J. Feltovich, & R. R. Hoffman (Eds.), *The Cambridge handbook of expertise and expert performance* (pp. 439–453). New York, NY: Cambridge University Press.

Salmon, P., Stanton, N., Walker, G., & Green, D. (2006). Situation awareness measure: A review of applicability for C4i environments. *Applied Ergonomics, 37,* 225–238.

Schvaneveldt, R. W. (Ed.). (1990). *Pathfinder associative networks: Studies in knowledge organization.* Ablex series in computational sciences. Westport, CT: Ablex Publishing.

Shepard, R. N., & Chipman, S. (1970). Second-order isomorphism of internal representations: Shapes of states. *Cognitive Psychology, 1,* 1–17.

Smith-Jentsch, K. A. (2009). Measuring team-related cognition: The devil is in the details. In E. Salas, G. F. Goodwin, & C. S. Burke (Eds.), *Team effectiveness in complex organizations* (pp. 491–508). New York: Routledge, Taylor & Francis Group.

Smith-Jentsch, K. A., Mathieu, J. E., & Kraiger, K. (2005). Investigating linear and interactive effects of shared mental models on safety and efficiency in a field setting. *Journal of Applied Psychology, 90,* 523–535.

Stasser, G., & Titus, W. (1985). Pooling of unshared information in group decision making: Biased information sampling during discussion. *Journal of Personality and Social Psychology, 48,* 1467–1478.

Swaab, R., Postmes, T., van Beest, I., & Spears, R. (2007). Shared cognition as a product of, and precursor to, shared identity in negotiations. *Personality and Social Psychology Bulletin, 33,* 187–199.

Tindale, R. S., Meisenhelder, H. M., Dykema-Engblade, A. A., & Hogg, M. A. (2001). Shared cognition in small groups. In M. A. Hogg & R. Tindale (Eds.), *Blackwell handbook of social psychology: Group processes* (pp. 1–30). Malden, MA: Blackwell Publishers.

Undre, S., Sevdalis, N., Healey, A. N., Darzi, S. A., & Vincent, C. A. (2006). Teamwork in the operating theatre: Cohesion or confusion? *Journal of Evaluation in Clinical Practice, 12,* 182–189.

Waller, M. J., Gupta, N., & Giambatista, R. C. (2004). Effects of adaptive behaviors and shared mental models on control crew performance. *Management Science, 50,* 1534–1544.

Webber, S. S., Chen, G., Payne, S. C., Marsh, S. M., & Zaccaro, S. J. (2000). Enhancing team mental model measurement with performance appraisal practices. *Organizational Research Methods, 3,* 307–322.

Weingart, L. R., & Cronin, M. A. (2009). Teams research in the 21st century: A case for theory consolidation. In E. Salas, G. F. Goodwin, & C. S. Burke (Eds.), *Team effectiveness in complex organizations: Cross-disciplinary perspectives and approaches* (pp. 509–524). New York: Routledge Taylor and Francis Group.

Wellens, A. R. (1993). Group situation awareness and distributed decision making: From military to civilian applications. In J. Castellan (Ed.), *Individual and group decision making: Current Issues* (pp. 267–291). Hillsdale, NJ: Lawrence Erlbaum Associates.

Wilson, J. M., Goodman, P. S., & Cronin, M. A. (2007). Group learning. *Academy of Management Review, 32,* 1041–1059.

Wilson, K. A., Salas, E., Priest, H., & Andrews, D. (2007). Errors in the heat of the battle: Taking a closer look at shared cognition breakdowns through teamwork. *Human Factors, 49,* 243–256.

Yen, J., Fan, X., Sun, S., Hanratty, T., & Dumer, J. (2006). Agents with shared mental models for enhancing team decision makings. *Decision Support Systems, 41,* 634–653.

Appendix A: Sample Taskwork Similarity Matrix in a Restaurant Context

−4		−3 −2 −1	0		1 2 3		4
Negatively related (doing the task means that the other will definitely not be done)			Unrelated (the two tasks are totally unrelated)				Positively related (doing one task means that the other will definitely be done)

	Ordering the food	Creating job descriptions	Monitoring production	Managing back of house	Managing front of house	Post-production analysis	Profit
Costing the menu and setting the selling price							
Ordering the food							
Creating job descriptions for self and employees							
Monitoring production (front of and back of the house)							
Managing the back of the house during service time							

	Ordering the food	Creating job descriptions	Monitoring production	Managing back of house	Managing front of house	Post-production analysis	Profit
Managing the front of the house during service time							
Doing the post-production analysis							
Making a suitable profit on your meal							

NOTE: Only white squares are rated.

Appendix B: Sample Concept Map for Restaurant Context

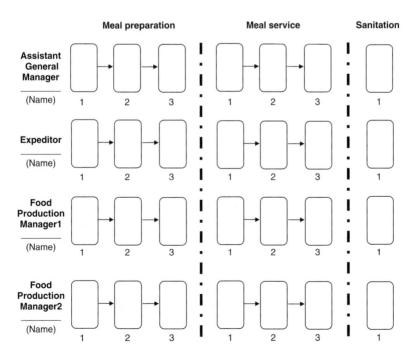

9

INVESTIGATING EMOTIONS AND AFFECT IN GROUPS

Janice R. Kelly

PURDUE UNIVERSITY

Eric E. Jones

SOUTHERN ILLINOIS UNIVERSITY CARBONDALE

It is the middle of March and the NCAA basketball tournament for both women and men are down to the Sweet Sixteen. As any of those who have watched (or endured) their favorite team advance (or not!) through the first two rounds of the tournament, the affective nature of groups is quite apparent. The teams themselves show the thrill of victory or the agony of defeat visibly on their faces and in their demeanor. The fans, as well, reflect their team's fate in their expressions of elation or dejection. Quite clearly, many aspects of group process and performance are indexed by the emotional outcomes exhibited by their members.

In other domains as well, we find evidence that emotions are an important input to, context for, and outcome of group interaction. Certainly, friendship groups exist at least in part because they provide a context for interpersonal interaction and the pleasurable consequences of such interaction. And such groups also disintegrate when those consequences turn unpleasant. Members of task groups feel such emotions as pride and joy when their pet project has been accepted and has succeeded, and feel sadness or even anger when those projects are rejected or fail.

However, despite the essential emotional quality of groups, research into their more socio-emotional side has been lacking – until recently. For the past 25 years, individual-level researchers have been documenting the important influences that moods and emotions have on people's cognitive functioning. Moods and emotions have been found to influence people's judgments, evaluations, and style of information processing (Schwarz & Clore, 1996). Moods and emotions are also widely acknowledged to be interpersonal in context and character (Wallbott & Scherer, 1986). As a consequence of this, group researchers are also becoming interested in the causes and consequences of moods and emotions in small groups and there is growing recognition of the importance of these affective influences on group process and performance (Barsade & Gibson, 1998; George, 2002; Kelly, 2001; Kelly & Barsade, 2001; Kelly & Spoor, 2006, 2007; Spoor & Kelly, 2004; Tiedens, Sutton, & Fong, 2004).

A quick search of the literature shows a growing number of empirical studies examining affective influences in small groups. For example, a number of studies have examined emotional contagion in groups (e.g., Barsade, 2002; Bartel & Saavedra, 2000; Spoor & Kelly, 2009; Totterdell, 2000; Totterdell, Kellett, Teuchmann, & Briner, 1998), and others have investigated affect and group performance (e.g., Bramesfeld & Gasper, 2008; Forgas, 1992; Grawitch, Munz, Elliot, & Mathis, 2003; Grawitch, Munz, & Kramer, 2003; Jones & Kelly, 2009; Kelly & Spoor, 2007). Leadership is another growing area in which the role of affect is being explored (e.g., Damen, van Knippenberg, B., & van Knippenberg, D., 2008; Damen, van Knippenberg, D., & van Knippenberg, B., 2008; Lewis, 2000; Pescolido, 2002; Sy, Cote, & Saavedra, 2005), and yet, many theoretically important affective influences in groups and subsequent consequences for groups in terms of member interaction and performance remain uninvestigated. It is our hope that, as a result of this chapter, we will be able to suggest and bring to bear methods that will be useful in addressing this important gap in our knowledge of group behavior.

General Description of the Method

Types of affective experiences

Many researchers have described the variety of affective states that individuals may experience (Forgas, 1995; Isen, 1984; Kelly & Barsade, 2000). For example, individuals have affective dispositions, or their characteristic ways of affectively responding to situations (Lazarus, 1991). Individuals may experience diffuse positive or negative low-intensity mood states (Forgas, 1992; Isen, 1984), or higher intensity emotions that are generally of shorter duration than moods and that are directed toward specific targets (Fridja, 1994). As individual members of interacting groups, we are all likely to experience any of these types of affective states during group interaction. But as group members interact over time, these individual affective states may be influenced by other members' states, and thus a group-level affect may also develop that ultimately shapes how the group operates and performs.

There are a number of existing group-level constructs that have affective characteristics, including group cohesion (Hogg, 1992; Mullen & Copper, 1994) and emotional contagion (Hatfield, Cacioppo, & Rapson, 1994). However, a number of more recent group-level affective constructs have been proposed. George (1990, 1996), for example, proposed that some groups develop a "group affective tone" or a group's characteristic level of positive or negative affect. By definition, a group affective tone only exists when group members report similarity in their affective reactions in the group. That is, a group has a group affective tone to the extent that consistency exists in the affective responses of group members, such as when interacting in a group setting leads members to all feel positive. Bartel and Saavedra (2000) demonstrated that groups can be characterized as a whole by mood states. Their investigation showed that both members of a group and outside observers can agree in their judgment of a group's mood. In addition to general mood states, emotions have been demonstrated at the group level as well. For example, Duffy and Shaw (2000) described the effects of group envy. Group envy led to reduced group performance as a consequence of social loafing, less cohesiveness, and diminished confidence in the group's ability to succeed.

As described, members of groups and perhaps groups themselves, experience moods and emotions, and these moods and emotions influence and are shaped by group performance and interaction. That is, moods and emotions can serve as inputs into the group experience, can be a measure of group process, and can serve as an outcome of a group experience. We examine next how affect serves in each of those roles in a group context, and describe how researchers manipulate, observe, and measure moods and emotions in groups.

Manipulating group members' moods and emotions to serve as inputs

As mentioned previously, a growing number of studies have examined the effect of member affective states on group performance (e.g., Bramesfeld & Gasper, 2008; Grawitch, Munz, Elliot et al., 2003; Grawitch, Munz, & Kramer, 2003; Jones & Kelly, 2009). In each of these studies, mood states served as an input to the group process. That is, group members' mood states were manipulated prior to group interaction in order to demonstrate how those mood states affected group process and performance.

In empirical research that explores these effects, researchers have primarily relied on traditional and individual-level methods of inducing mood (e.g., Forgas, 1992), such as exposing participants to films or music with sad or uplifting content (Hertel, Neuhof, Theuer, & Kerr, 2000), having participants read a series of increasingly positive or negative statements (e.g., Velten statements; Velten, 1968), or having participants recall and vividly describe recent happy, sad, or neutral events (Grawitch, Munz, Elliot et al., 2003; Grawitch, Munz, & Kramer, 2003).

Grawitch, Munz, and Kramer (2003), for example, had individuals imagine an event from their recent past that put them into a good mood or into a bad mood. Participants in a neutral condition imagined a neutral scenario (wandering through a grocery store). Hertel et al. (2000) showed participants video tapes in order to induce positive or negative moods. In the positive mood condition, participants watched a humorous video clip about ostriches roaming through the African steppe. Participants in the negative mood condition watched a sad video clip about a cruel killing of a tiger. Positive and negative music played in the background to support the intended emotional effects. Similarly, Sy et al. (2005) had participants in a positive mood condition view a humorous clip of David Letterman, whereas participants in the negative mood condition viewed part of a TV documentary about social injustice and aggression.

In our own recent research, we have often used film clips as a source of mood induction. We use a cover story such that participants are asked to rate various qualities of the video clip, including its vividness, memorability, and quality, to help us for an upcoming study. Then participants watch a series of short video clips and fill out rating forms in between each clip. For example, in Spoor and Kelly (2009; see also Jones & Kelly, 2009), participants watched a total of three clips (approximately seven minutes each). Everyone first watched a neutralizing clip from *The Mosquito Coast*, because we have found that the mood induction is more effective if all participants first watch a neutral movie scene. Using a neutral clip also serves to make the purpose of the procedure (to induce positive or negative moods) less obvious. Participants in the positive mood condition then watched humorous clips from *Good Morning, Vietnam* and *Ferris Bueller's Day Off*. Participants in the negative mood condition watched sad clips from *Sophie's Choice* and *Terms of Endearment*. The factors that participants rate each clip on can also be used to rule out possible alternative explanations for some mood results. For example, depending on one's research question, it might be important to show that the positive and negative clips were equally attended to or were equally arousing, and so the rating forms for the clips can include questions concerning attention and arousal. Finally, we follow the video clip rating task with a brief questionnaire, purportedly about impressions of the upcoming group interaction, in which we embed manipulation check questions designed to assess the participants' current mood states (see section on 'Dependent measures' later in this chapter).

The preceding manipulations are generally conducted at the individual level. Even though group members may experience the manipulation in the same room, each group member individually recalls a recent happy experience or watches clips of happy or sad movie scenes. For some research questions, it might be desirable for group members to enter the group situation in different moods, and therefore individual mood inductions are required. For example, Spoor and Kelly (2009) deliberately paired together dyad members where one person was in a happy mood and one was in a sad mood in order to examine mood convergence. Tiedens et al. (2004) have suggested that creativity may be higher in groups where there is diversity in affect across members, and to test this hypothesis empirically, affectively diverse group members would need to be created.

Nevertheless, for other research questions, it might be desirable for the group as a whole to experience a mood induction. For example, it may be particularly important for all group members to be in a similar or shared mood state if one is interested in questions of how group mood might affect task strategies or information exchange. Kelly (2003) proposed a group-level manipulation in which group members discussed neutral or uplifting topics before engaging in the primary task. Specifically, we had groups complete a ranking task, in which they rank ordered a series of humorous insurance claims (e.g., "The pedestrian had no idea which way to go, so I ran over him") in order of their humorousness, a task which generally results in much laughter by group members. This group-level manipulation produced smaller but reliable differences in participants' perceptions of the *group's* affective state. That is, when asked about their perception of how their *group* felt, rather than how they themselves felt, members of groups who had engaged in the uplifting task (rank ordering the humorous statements) perceived their group to be in a more positive mood than did members of groups who engaged in a neutral task (rank ordering neutral statements).

Barsade (2002) used a group-level manipulation of mood in an experiment exploring emotional contagion processes in groups. Specifically, she introduced a confederate into a group who was trained to portray pleasant or unpleasant, high- or low-energy emotions. For example, in the pleasant/high-energy condition, the confederate's behavior was characterized as acting pleasant, happy, warm, and optimistic in an energetic, active, and alert way. In contrast, the confederate in the unpleasant/low-energy condition was characterized as acting unpleasant and unhappy in a low-energy way. The mood of the groups in which they interacted was altered due to the transfer of mood (emotional contagion) from the confederate to other group members.

Other potential group-level manipulations of affect could be developed. Groups could be asked to engage in fun or boring tasks. For example, groups could engage in a game of charades or Pictionary, both of which are generally enjoyable, in order to induce a positive mood in the group as a whole. Neutral mood might be induced by engaging the group in a more serious task, such as recalling all US Presidents in chronological order. Groups with a history might be asked to discuss recent or negative events that have impacted the group as a whole. For example, task groups might be asked to recall a recent success or failure, and friendship groups might be asked to recall a recent pleasurable outing or falling out within the group. It should be noted, however, that group-level manipulations of negative mood may be complicated by the fact that group interaction often leads to increases in positive mood (Hinsz, Park, & Sjomeling, 2004). Manipulations of group-level emotions may also be somewhat difficult, as it might be challenging to create an intense emotional reaction in a laboratory setting. However, an emotional reaction might be produced by providing the group with a success or failure experience, or false feedback indicating success or failure. In addition, intergroup emotions, such as group pride, envy, or shame, might be induced by introducing some kind of intergroup competition or conflict.

How to observe mood and emotional processes in groups

The moods and emotions that group members experience can also be an index of group process. That is, the manner in which group members experience moods and emotions can mediate the relationship between group inputs and outcomes. One such process is emotional contagion, which is thought to occur in two stages. First, emotional expressions, including facial, postural, and vocal features, are automatically mimicked by interacting partners. Second, afferent feedback from facial, postural, or vocal expression produces the emotional experience in the mimicking partner (Duclos et al., 1989; Strack, Martin, & Stepper, 1988). The mimicry processes of the first stage have been observed in a number of studies including Chartrand and Bargh's (1999) study of smiling, Lakin, Chartrand, and Arkin's (2008) study of foot tapping in response to social exclusion, and Neumann and Strack's (2000) study of vocal mimicry.

Consistent with the notion of moods and emotions as a process, Spoor and Kelly (2004) suggested that mood convergence within groups can improve their ability to coordinate efforts and therefore improve performance. For example, Sy, Cote, and Saavedra (2005) found that group members who had positive mood leaders experienced more positive moods (through contagion processes), and group members who had negative mood leaders experienced more negative moods. More importantly, positive group affective tone fully mediated, and negative group affective tone partially mediated, the relationship between leader mood and group coordination. Barsade (2002) also found that positive emotional contagion was associated with improved cooperation, decreased conflict, and increased perceived task performance in groups.

How can the affective processes of group members be observed and recorded? A number of systems exist for coding nonverbal behavior in humans; see Harrigan, Rosenthal, and Scherer (2005) for a comprehensive review. It is fairly straightforward to train observers to code simple nonverbal behaviors exhibited by group members to an adequate degree of reliability (see Hall, 2010). For example, generally observers can accurately code the degree of smiling among group members. More complicated systems for coding facial expressions exist (see e.g., the Facial Action Coding System; Ekman & Rosenberg, 1997), but such systems are probably too cumbersome and time consuming for use in group research.

Alternatively, Bartel and Saavedra (2000) have shown evidence that group mood can be assessed more globally and can be reliably measured by those outside of the group through observation. They have developed a "Guide to Work Group Mood" that consists of a set of behavioral indicators of eight mood categories that comprise the mood circumplex (see further description of the mood circumplex in the later section on dependent measures). In their study, observers familiarized themselves with the guide, observed a work group actively engaged in a task, and indicated when any of the behavioral indicators of mood were exhibited by group members. Teams of observers then discussed to consensus the degree to which groups experienced each of the eight mood categories on scales from 1 (not at all) to 6 (a great deal). Bartel and Saavedra (2000) reported significant positive correlations between group members' self-reports and observer ratings of work group mood, validating their group mood assessment instrument as an accurate indicator of the group's mood.

Barsade (2002) also used observers to record emotional contagion processes in groups. Barsade first trained coders to recognize affective states using the list of behaviors that indicate work group mood provided by Bartel and Saavedra's (2000) work group mood system described above. Barsade's coders then recorded the emotional contagion process in her groups by watching participants' facial expressions, body language, and tone of voice throughout the experimental session and rating the level of each participant's pleasant mood every two minutes (at the sound of a beep) on a five-point scale ranging from 1 (not at all) to 5 (very much). Consistent with an emotional contagion process, coders rated the participants who interacted with a pleasant confederate as more positive than those who interacted with an unpleasant confederate.

In addition to the growing research that involves observations of nonverbal behavior that are indicative of affective states, there is the older tradition of interaction process analysis that has been used to assess social–emotional aspects of group interaction (Bales, 1950; Kelly, 2000; Ridgeway, 1994). Interaction Process Analysis is a technique whereby observers are trained to code the verbal acts of group members during interaction. These verbal acts are then coded into categories that are theoretically meaningful for the research question at hand. In its traditional form as proposed by Bales (1950), verbal acts are coded into categories reflecting task activities (e.g., gives suggestions, asks for orientation) or socio-emotional activities (e.g., seems friendly, disagrees). Bales (1950) proposed that socio-emotional communication serves to support task activities and that the two forms of communication operate in equilibrium. In a more recent examination of process that focused more specifically on socio-emotional (relational) communication, Keyton (2009) examined the role of relational communication in a cancer support group. In particular, she examined the type of communication that preceded and followed relational communication in order to understand more fully the function of the relational act (e.g., agreement to confirm, agreement to signal identification, disagreement). These acts can change the communication atmosphere of a group, both positively and negatively.

How to measure moods and emotions as an outcome or DV

The field of group research seems to be focused on task outcomes such as productivity and efficiency. With a few exceptions (e.g., Grawitch, Block, & Ratner, 2005), little research to date has looked at affective outcomes to group processes. Different group processes (e.g., conflict, cooperation, coordination failures or successes) probably lead to different emotions, and these emotions may vary across group members. Imagine how conflict during a group meeting can make members angry, or how a complete group failure can lead to group members feeling miserable and depressed. Furthermore, groups characterized by different affective states may approach future tasks differently. For example, Grawitch and Munz (2005) argue that positive emotions lead groups to adopt a promotion focus, while negative emotions lead groups to assume a prevention focus. At the individual level, emotions such as anger can lead people to feel stronger and more powerful, resulting in riskier behavior (Lerner & Keltner, 2001). These individual tendencies combined with other group dynamics could dramatically shape group processes.

Browsing the existing literature on affect in groups, one can see that mood and emotions have been measured in a number of ways. Think of the last time someone asked you, "How do you feel?" Perhaps you answered with a simple and general statement such as "bad" or "happy." Some research has used straightforward scales assessing the experiences of positive and negative feelings (e.g., Jones & Kelly, 2009). These scales ask group members to respond to a given statement (e.g., "What is your group's current mood?") on a Likert-type scale anchored with a negatively valenced word on one end (e.g., negative, sad) and a positively valenced word on the other end (e.g., positive, happy). However, other measures of mood and emotions allow the experiences of positive and negative affect to be orthogonal or independent of one another. Consequently, positive and negative emotions are measured individually. For example, Grawitch et al. (2005) asked group members to recall experiences that produced a variety of different emotions (e.g., eager, excited, tense, worried). Likewise, when completing the Positive and Negative Affect Schedule (PANAS; Watson, Clark, & Tellegen, 1988), participants rate the extent to which each of 20 words (e.g., upset, scared, excited, interested) reflect their feelings in the specified time frame (e.g., right now, today, in general). These ratings are indexed into scores for positive affect and negative affect, and are assumed to be independent.

The PANAS focuses only on emotions characterized by high arousal: those affective experiences characterized by high physiological stimulation. For example, imagine the increased heart rate associated with the excitement of your team successfully completing a challenging task or the increased blood pressure correlated with an angry feud with fellow group members. In contrast to the PANAS, other measures of affect differentiate between emotions on two independent dimensions: valence (positive vs. negative) and arousal (high vs. low). For instance, experiences of negative emotions are not all equal. In a bad economy, a work team may experience gloom as the financial health of their company declines or as they see fellow co-workers laid off. Although the work team's feelings are clearly negative, the physiological experience of gloom is more subdued. In contrast, consider a situation where the team members are all afraid that their team will be dismantled because the company is downsizing. Such an experience is not only negative, but also characterized by more physiological arousal as the team members feel stress and ruminate on their fears. Models of affect that differentiate between valence and arousal are called circumplex models, and such models have been proposed by Russell (1980) and Feldman Barrett (2004). The Brief Mood Introspection Scale (BMIS; Mayer & Gaschke, 1988) allows researchers to measure these two dimensions with only 16 questions.

We should note that, at the individual level, the arousal dimension of emotional states can be assessed through physiological measures. Typical measures include skin conductivity levels, facial electromyography, skin temperature, breathing frequency, and pulse frequency (Ekman, Levenson, & Friesen, 1983). However, we feel that it is unlikely that such measures will have much application for emotion assessment at the group level, given that the leads and connections that are used to monitor these responses are likely to interfere with interaction among group members.

When deciding which method to use for measuring moods and emotions, researchers should balance practical and theoretical concerns. Simple positive–negative scales may be best when brevity is important. In particular, when investigating moods and emotions as outcomes in field settings, researchers may face limits on the number of questions they can ask or may encounter time constraints for respondents. As previously described, to avoid tipping off their participants to the purpose of a laboratory study, researchers may also wish to use a few short scales embedded in other questions, rather than a whole series of questions related to moods and emotions. Conversely, theory may lead to predictions about differential outcomes for positive and negative affect or high and low affective arousal. Therefore, using longer scales that reliably measure these dimensions may be necessary. For example, Grawitch and Munz (2005) suggested that unsuccessful group procedures should lead to, above all, greater negative affective experiences. Moreover, one might be interested in the implications of groups characterized by high vs. low arousal or positive vs. negative affective states, which can differentially influence whether groups are promotion or prevention focused (Grawitch & Munz, 2005; Park & Hinsz, 2006). Although Barsade (2002) predicted that high-arousal emotions would transfer more easily than low-arousal emotions, no such differences occurred. Nevertheless, researchers may be interested in predicting contextual factors that could produce these differences, in which case using a scale that differentiated between high and low arousal affect would be necessary.

When measuring mood in groups, it is important to define what exactly constitutes group mood. At the individual level, the focus is on the emotional experience of one person. However, when groups are the unit of focus, one has to consider the emotional experience of multiple people. Imagine Group A whose three members report an emotional experience of 5, 5, and 5 on a seven-point scale. Consider Group B whose three members describe their individual emotional experiences as 3, 5, and 7. One way to conceptualize group mood is by calculating the mean level of its group members' affective experiences

(George, 1990). In the aforementioned Groups A and B, the mean level affect of both groups is 5. Nevertheless, a glance at the individual experiences of group members suggests a different climate in each group. In Group A, all group members shared the same emotional experience. However, in Group B, the emotional experiences of group members varied widely, with one group member experiencing elation (7) and another feeling relatively negative (3). As such, measures of agreement and disagreement of group members are an important consideration when calculating a group's mood and emotions.

Methods for assessing group mood have been recently developed. George (1990, 1996) argued that high levels of intermember consistency are necessary for group affective tone to exist. If such consistency exists, then individual-level reports of affect may be combined into a group average that reflects the group's affective tone. In the case of low intermember consistency, an affective tone does not exist for that particular group. To index within-group agreement on a single target (e.g., group mood), a measure of interrater agreement such as r_{WG} should be used. To address limitations with r_{WG}, Brown and Hauenstein (2005) proposed an alternative method of calculating interrater agreement called a_{WG} [See LeBreton and Senter (2008) for instructions on calculating these indices and for a discussion of how these measures differ from each other and from measures of interrater reliability]. For the previously mentioned groups, Group A would have a high r_{WG} value, whereas Group B would not.

Although researchers may be interested in group members' shared affect, they may also wish to consider the dispersion or diversity of affective experiences of group members (e.g., Barsade, Ward, Turner, & Sonnenfeld, 2000). Members of Group A experienced a homogeneous emotional tone, but Group B's experience was more heterogeneous. Tiedens et al. (2004) discuss several reasons why group members, such as those in fictitious Group B, may not have similar emotional responses. They note that group characteristics such as low cohesiveness could reduce a group's shared affective tone. In addition, norms for expressed affective similarity may vary in strength and some groups may actually be explicit about a desire for emotional heterogeneity. A focus on affective diversity could be used to examine development of shared affective tone over time or to determine antecedents of homogeneous vs. heterogeneous affective experiences in groups. Moreover, dispersion in affective experiences has implications for subsequent group processes (Tiedens et al., 2004). Rather then the aforementioned indices of agreement, calculating SD_X is more appropriate for dispersion composition models (Chan, 1998; LeBreton & Senter, 2008).

An alternative to considering dispersion composition may be to examine minimum and maximum levels of individual group members' affect. Investigating personality composition, Halfhill, Nielsen, and Sundstrom (2008) showed that minimum scores on conscientiousness and agreeableness predicted group performance better than a group's mean level on these dimensions. Consequently, researchers may be interested in the maximum and minimum levels of group members' affect, because of possible implications for later group interaction. For example, consider the effect that a single "toxic" group member with high negative affect and low positive affect could have on a group. Likewise, imagine the potential impact on a group's morale by a group member with high positive affect – bubbly and upbeat. Regardless of the group mean, groups with members at either extreme could greatly impact the group's overall performance and effectiveness.

Strengths and Weaknesses

Laboratory and field settings

To date, the research that has been conducted in this field consists of both laboratory and field-setting approaches. For example, in studies of emotional contagion or convergence, some have taken place in laboratory settings (e.g., Barsade, 2002; Spoor & Kelly, 2009; Sy et al., 2005; Chartrand & Bargh, 1999), whereas others have taken place in naturalistic settings (Totterdell, 2000; Totterdell et al., 1998). Given that there are strengths and weaknesses inherent in both settings, this multisetting approach is likely to provide a stronger set of research findings than if only one setting were utilized. It should be noted that our review of methods for manipulating mood tended to focus on techniques that would be used in laboratory settings. However, most of the process measures and dependent measures could be used equally well in laboratory and field settings.

The duration of affective experiences

One caveat that was mentioned previously concerning research in this area is that affective experiences, and especially intense emotional experiences, might be somewhat short in duration. As Hinsz, Park, and Sjomeling (2004) found, the simple experience of interacting in a group can alleviate negative moods. Therefore, when exploring questions of affect and group performance, and especially when using an approach where the mood states of group members are manipulated, the duration of the affective experience needs to be accounted for carefully. A host of mood-regulation processes can occur in groups (George, 2002; Kelly & Barsade, 2001; Kelly & Spoor, 2006) such that initial affective inputs can be quickly changed. Therefore, it is important to make periodic assessments of mood over time, or to include additional induction reminders in order to assure that mood states are still intact. For example, Bramesfeld and Gasper (2008) had participants engage in a mood-refresher task, where participants were asked to write for one minute about the most memorable aspect of the film clip that they were shown (the original mood manipulation) and then were asked to report how happy or sad they felt at this moment on a seven-point scale.

The dynamic nature of group affect

Another way of framing the duration question is in terms of the dynamics of affect in groups. In groups interacting over time, affective processes are likely to be dynamic and cyclical in nature. Affective inputs are altered by affect regulation processes in groups (e.g., emotional contagion, norms concerning affective display, etc.) resulting in new levels of affect or affective compositions. In addition, groups may experience sudden outcomes (e.g., success, failure) that can immediately alter the affect of a group. In order to understand affective processes in groups fully, future research will need to consider the dynamic nature of those processes.

Latest Innovations

Given that this is a relatively recent field of inquiry, the development of almost any technique for manipulating moods and emotions in groups, or for measuring affective group processes or outcomes can be considered an innovation. There are, however, a few innovative technologies that we have come across recently that we think could be adapted for use to study affective processes in groups.

One such technology involves a method for assessing online changes in mood over time. This technique has previously been used to assess moment to moment changes in people's attitudinal reactions to persuasive messages (Keim, 2008), and other moment to moment states. The technology involves a dial that can be turned up or down as the participant feels changes in some subjective affective state. In a recent application (Wirth, Wesselmann, Williams, & Mroczek, 2008), the technology was adapted so that it could be used to assess online changes in mood over time. In this new application, Wirth et al. trained participants to calibrate their use of the dial to changes in mood using short training exercises in which participants imagined themselves in various positive or negative scenarios. Participants turned the dial clockwise to record positive changes in mood and turned the dial counter-clockwise to indicate negative changes in mood. Participants then engaged in a game of Cyberball (see Wirth, Feldberg, Schouton, van den Hoof, & Williams, this volume), a virtual ball-toss game during which they were either included or excluded (ostracized) by two other (computerized) participants who also were supposedly playing the game. During the game, participants were instructed to turn the dial in accordance to how they felt during the Cyberball game. Dial values were converted to numeric form and could be graphically displayed. In Wirth et al. (2008), the dial output dramatically and graphically showed the tremendous negative impact of being ostracized, even under these relatively minimal conditions. We are particularly intrigued by the possibility of using such a dial technology to examine emotional contagion or mood convergence in groups.

A second device involves an existing piece of equipment called a video quadraplexor. A quadraplexor is a device that can take several video inputs and display them on a single screen. The most common Currently, use of the device is for surveillance, where input from several cameras focused on different areas can be viewed simultaneously on the same screen. We believe that this technology could be adapted for use in observing emotional contagion processes in groups, as well as other affective processes. For example, separate cameras could capture images of each of several group members working together on a task, and these images could be displayed (and recorded) together on a single screen. Trained coders could then make judgments about the level of affect displayed by the group members, or the degree to which group members displayed similar emotional expressions.

Finally, there is recent research that investigates the use of emoticons in computer-mediated interaction (Lo, 2008). This research demonstrates that Internet users use emoticons to enhance their communications, and specifically that emoticons are used similarly to other nonverbal cues to communicate emotions. In fact, emoticons have been referred to as quasi-nonverbal cues (Lo, 2008). An examination of the pattern of use of emoticons in computer-mediated communication may be an important clue to emotional exchanges in this medium.

Ethical Issues and Concerns

Although research on moods and emotions in groups has important implications for group processes and performance, there are important ethical issues to consider, especially when exploring moods and emotions as independent variables in laboratory research. The first issue has to do with how participants might react to a mood manipulation. The second issue concerns subsequent results of the mood manipulation after the experiment is complete. A final issue concerns the use of deception in some manipulations of affective states. Feedback from an institution's IRB may lead researchers to address these issues, but researchers should also actively consider the implications of their mood manipulations and use materials with which they feel comfortable. These concerns primarily deal with inducing negative mood.

First, researchers need to balance their desire to use a strong manipulation in order to test their theory with concerns about how participants might react to a particular mood induction. Clearly, a very strong negative mood manipulation will leave researchers with little doubt about the effectiveness of their manipulation, increasing the chances of finding significant results. However, even when mood inductions use mundane materials (e.g., Hollywood movies), it can be difficult to predict how any one person will respond. Each person comes with their own unique history. While a vast majority may not be affected by the mood manipulation in any extreme way, there is a chance that some individuals will. For example, a clip that shows the tragic outcomes of a traffic accident may be sad to a majority of participants, but traumatic for a participant who survived or caused such an accident (or knows someone else who did). On some of our consent forms, we have a statement to help in these circumstances: "If you experience anything during the experiment that disturbs you or makes you recall something that you would like to speak with someone about, there are services available at. ..." It is also possible that particular individuals may be reluctant to show evidence of experiencing a strong emotion due to norms of emotional constraint in the situation or due to personal norms about emotional expression. Inducing a strong emotional experience in such a person may be a particularly negative experience if it violates personal or social standards.

Second, at the completion of the experiment, the manipulated mood could continue to have an effect on the participant. Having experienced negative moods and emotions, participants may be more easily provoked or more likely to interpret ambiguous stimuli in a negative way. Being in a negative mood could also be a burden for someone who has had a bad day. For these reasons, before they leave the lab, all of our participants who experienced a negative mood induction complete a task designed to lift their mood. Sometimes, we have participants complete the insurance ranking task that we described in the manipulation section. Other times, we have had participants watch a segment from Jay Leno involving a phony photo booth. In this clip, a photo booth makes bizarre requests of people at an amusement park before they have a free picture taken. For example, the photo booth may be concerned about someone's drink and therefore says that the liquid is interfering with its camera. The person places the drink outside the booth, but the photo booth says the liquid is still too close. This continues a few more times until the person places the drink in the middle of the street. At that point, the photo booth says the liquid is too far away. The person looks down in dismay and the picture is taken. Our participants laugh out loud at these vignettes and it gives the experimenter a mood induction of their own to see the groups of participants laughing so hysterically. Finally, we should also note that some of the techniques that we have recommended for manipulating moods and emotions involve the use of deception. For example, we suggested that the mood of a group could be manipulated by providing the group with false feedback concerning their success or failure on a task. As with all research, the researcher must carefully weigh the necessity of the deception for the purposes of the research against the subsequent potential for resentment and anger on the part of research participants when they are informed of the deception. Deception should be avoided when possible, but if used, it is the responsibility of the researcher to debrief the participants carefully on the necessity of the procedures that were used.

Recommendations

When conducting research on mood and emotion, researchers may want to consider several issues when designing their research, to maximize the effectiveness of manipulations and the knowledge gained from their studies. First, one challenge is for researchers to manipulate moods that last the entire duration of the experiment. As previously mentioned, group interactions tend to increase positive affect (Hinsz, Park, & Sjomeling, 2004), which poses a challenge to maintaining a group's negative mood. Moreover, the task itself can interfere with the experienced mood. For instance, we developed a task where groups watched either a positive or negative movie clip and then ordered still images from the movie in sequence (Jones & Kelly, 2008). One challenge when creating this task was to find a proper task difficulty. The task needed to be difficult enough to allow for variability on performance scores, which was the main dependent measure. However, it could not be so difficult that groups were frustrated or bored and failed to notice the humorous or disturbing imagery in the stills.

Second, the use of proper control groups in research on mood and emotion will provide information about whether it is positive mood, negative mood, or both moods that impact group processes and performance. In research at the individual level, a neutral mood, generally defined as a mood state where the mean falls in between positive and negative moods, is often induced as a control condition (e.g., Hirt, Melton, McDonald, & Harackiewicz, 1996), although one might use a no-induced mood condition as a control instead. When examining mood and emotions in groups, given the importance of consensus when aggregating individual group members' responses to calculate group affective tone, it is strongly recommended that a neutral mood is induced, similar to negative and positive conditions (e.g., Grawitch et al., 2003), so that all group members are in similarly neutral moods.

Third, researchers may wish to not only consider how mood and emotion influence group processes themselves, but also how they can change the relationship between individual and group performance. For instance, research on social loafing shows that individuals working separately often outperform the same number of individuals working together as a group (Latane, Williams, & Harkins, 1979). Similarly, interacting groups often recall fewer words (Basden, Basden, Bryner, & Thomas, 1997) and are less creative (Mullen, Johnson, & Salas, 1991) than nominal groups. Different moods and emotions may exacerbate or attenuate these performance differences between individuals and groups (e.g., Jones & Kelly, 2009).

Conclusion

We have shown that moods and emotions can be studied in a variety of settings, such as the field and laboratory, and can be examined in a variety of ways, including as an independent variable, a mediator, and a dependent variable. Our hope is that this chapter will provide a set of techniques for future researchers who are interested in the many ways in which moods and emotions can influence groups.

It is exciting to participate in a growing area of research such as this one. As research findings reach a critical mass, more sophisticated theories can be developed to describe and predict the influence of moods and emotions on group process and performance. We hope that this chapter will serve to stimulate such future research.

References

Bales. R. F. (1950). *Interaction process analysis: A method for the study of small groups.* Oxford: Addison-Wesley.

Barsade, S. G. (2002). The ripple effect: Emotional contagion and its influence on group behavior. *Administrative Science Quarterly, 47,* 644–675.

Barsade, S. G., & Gibson, D. E. (1998). Group emotion: A view from top and bottom. In D. H. Gruenfeld, B. Mannix, & M. Neale (Eds.), *Research on managing groups and teams* (pp. 81–102). Stamford, CT: JAI Press.

Barsade, S. G., Ward, A. J., Turner, J. D. F., & Sonnenfeld, J. A. (2000). To your heart's content: A model of affective diversity in top management teams. *Administrative Science Quarterly. 45,* 802–836.

Bartel, C., & Saavedra, R. (2000). The collective construction of work group moods. *Administrative Science Quarterly, 45,* 197–231.

Basden, B. H., Basden, D. R., Bryner, S., & Thomas, R. L., III (1997). A comparison of group and individual remembering: Does collaboration disrupt retrieval strategies? *Journal of Experimental Psychology: Learning, Memory, & Cognition, 23,* 1176–1189.

Bramesfeld, K. D., & Gasper, K. (2008). Happily putting the pieces together: A test of two explanations for the effects of mood on group-level information processing. *British Journal of Social Psychology, 47,* 285–309.

Brown, R. D., & Hauenstein, N. M. A. (2005). Interrater agreement reconsidered: An alternative to the rwg indices. *Organizational Research Methods, 8,* 165–184.

Carter, K. A. (2004). Type me how you feel: quasi-nonverbal cues in computer-mediated communication. *ETC, 60,* 29–39.

Chan, D. (1998). Functional relations among constructs in the same context domain at different levels of analysis: A typology of composition models. *Journal of Applied Psychology, 83,* 234–246.

Chartrand, T. L., & Bargh, J. A. (1999). The chameleon effect: The perception-behavior link and social interaction. *Journal of Personality and Social Psychology, 76,* 893–910.

Damen, F., van Knippenberg, B., & van Knippenberg, D. (2008). Affective match in leadership: Leader emotional displays, follower positive affect, and follower performance. *Journal of Applied Social Psychology, 38,* 868–902.

Damen, F., van Knippenberg, D., & van Knippenberg, B. (2008). Leader affective displays and attributions of charisma: The role of arousal. *Journal of Applied Social Psychology, 38,* 2594–2614.

Duclos, S. E., Laird, J. D., Schneider, E., Sexter, M., Stern, L., & Van Lighten, O. (1989). Emotion-specific effects of facial expressions and postures on emotional experience. *Journal of Personality and Social Psychology, 57,* 100–108.

Duffy, M. K., & Shaw, J. D. (2000). The Salieri syndrome: Consequences of envy in groups. *Small Group Research, 31,* 3–23.

Ekman, P., Levenson, R. W., & Friesen, W. V. (1983). Autonomic nervous system activity distinguishes among emotions. *Science, 22,* 1208–1210.

Ekman, P., & Rosenberg, E. (Eds.). (1997). *What the face reveals: Basic and applied studies of spontaneous expression using the Facial Action Coding System (FACS).* New York: Oxford University Press.

Feldman Barrett, L. (2004). Feelings or words? Understanding the content in self-report ratings of experienced emotion. *Journal of Personality and Social Psychology, 87*, 266–281.

Forgas, J. P. (1990). Affective influences on individual and group judgments. *European Journal of Social Psychology, 20*, 441–453.

Forgas, J. P. (1992). Affect in social judgments and decisions: A multiprocess model. *Advances in Experimental Social Psychology, 25*, 227–275.

Forgas, J. P. (1995). Emotion in social judgments: Review and a new affect infusion model (AIM). *Psychological Bulletin, 117*, 39–66.

George, J. M. (1990). Personality, affect, and behavior in groups. *Journal of Applied Psychology, 75*, 107–116.

George, J. M. (1996). Group affective tone. In M. A. West (Ed.), *Handbook of work group psychology* (pp. 77–93). Chichester, UK: Wiley.

George, J. M. (2002). Affect regulation in groups and teams. In R. G. Lord, R. J. Klimoski, & R. Kanfer (Eds.), *Emotions in the workplace: Understanding the structure and role of emotions in organizational behavior* (pp. 183–217). San Francisco: Jossey-Bass.

Grawitch, M. J., Block, E. E., & Ratner, J. F. (2005). How are evaluations of positive and negative experiences related to the intensity of affect in workgroups? *Group Dynamics: Theory, Research, and Practice, 9*, 261–274.

Grawitch, M. J., & Munz, D. C. (2005). Individual and group affect in problem-solving workgroups. In C. E. Hartel, W. J. Zerbe, & N. M. Ashkanasy (Eds.), *Emotions in organizational behavior* (pp. 119–142). Mahwah, NJ: Lawrence Erlbaum Associates Publishers.

Grawitch, M. J., Munz, D. C., Elliot, E. K., & Mathis, A. (2003). Promoting creativity in temporary problem-solving groups: The effects of positive mood and autonomy in problem definition on idea-generating performance. *Group Dynamics: Theory, Research and Practice, 7*, 200–213.

Grawitch, M. J., Munz, D. C., & Kramer, T. J. (2003). Effects of member mood states on creative performance in temporary workgroups. *Group Dynamics: Theory, Research and Practice, 71*, 41–54.

Halfhill, T. R., Nielsen, T. M., & Sundstrom, E. (2008). The ASA framework: A field study of group personality composition and group performance in military action teams. *Small Group Research, 39*, 616–635.

Hall, J. B. (2010). Nonverbal research in social psychology: The good, the bad, and the ugly. In C. R. Agnew, D. Carlston, W. Graziano, & J. R. Kelly (Eds.), *Then a miracle occurs: Focusing on behavior in social psychological theory and research* (pp. 412–437). Oxford: Oxford University Press.

Harrigan, J. A., Rosenthal, R., & Scherer, K. R. (Eds.) (2005). *The new handbook of methods in nonverbal behavior research.* Oxford: Oxford University Press.

Hatfield, E., Cacioppo, J., & Rapson, R. L. (1994). *Emotional contagion.* New York: Cambridge University Press.

Hertel, G., Neuhof, J., Theuer, T., & Kerr, N. L. (2000). Mood effects on cooperation in small groups: Does positive mood simply lead to more cooperation? *Cognition and Emotion, 14*, 441–472.

Hinsz, V. B., Park, E. S., & Sjomeling, M. (2004). *Group interaction sustains positive mood and diminishes negative mood.* Paper presented at the meeting of the Midwestern Psychological Association, Chicago, II.

Hirt, E. R., Melton, R. J., McDonald, H. E., & Harackiewicz, J. M. (1996). Processing goals, task interest, and the mood-performance relationship: A mediational analysis. *Journal of Personality and Social Psychology, 71*, 245–261.

Hogg, M. A. (1992). *The social psychology of group cohesiveness: From attraction to social identity.* New York: Harvester Wheatsheaf.

Isen, A. M. (1984). Toward understanding the role of affect in cognition. In J. R. S. Wyer & T. Srull (Eds.), *Handbook of social cognition* (pp. 170–236). Hillsdale, NJ: Lawrence Erlbaum Associates.

Jones, E. E., & Kelly, J. R. (2008). *Turn that frown upside down: Suppressing negative emotions hurts performance.* Paper presented at the annual meeting of the Midwestern Psychological Association, Chicago, IL.

Jones, E. E., & Kelly, J. R. (2009). No pain, no gains: Negative mood leads to process gains in idea generation groups. *Group Dynamics: Theory, Research, and Practice, 13,* 75–88.

Keim, B. (2008). High-tech analysis obscures presidential debate. *WIRED.* Retrieved April 2, 2009, from, http://blog.wired.com/wiredscience/2008/10/high-tech-analy.html.

Kelly, J. R. (2000). Interaction process analysis in task-performing groups. In A. P. Beck & C. M. Lewis (Eds), *The process of group psychotherapy: Systems for analyzing change* (pp. 49–65). Washington, DC: American Psychological Association.

Kelly, J. R. (2001). Mood and emotion in groups. In M. A. Hogg & R. S. Tindale (Eds.), *The Blackwell handbook of social psychology* (Vol. 3, pp. 164–181). Oxford: Blackwell.

Kelly, J. R. (2003). *Group mood and group decision making.* Invited talk presented at the meeting of the Midwestern Psychological Association, Chicago, IL.

Kelly, J. R., & Barsade, S. G. (2001). Mood and emotions in small groups and work teams. *Organizational Behavior and Human Decision Processes, 86,* 99–130.

Kelly, J. R., & Spoor, J. R. (2006). Affective influence in groups. In J. P. Forgas (Ed.)., *Affect in social thinking and behavior* (pp. 311–325). New York: Psychology Press.

Kelly, J. R., & Spoor, J. R. (2007). Naïve theories of the effects of mood in groups: A preliminary investigation. *Group Processes and Intergroup Relations, 10,* 203–222.

Lakin, J. L., Chartrand, T. L., & Arkin, R. M. (2008). I am too just like you: Nonconscious mimicry as an automatic behavioral response to social exclusion. *Psychological Science, 19,* 816–822.

Latane, B., Williams, K., & Harkins, S. (1979). Many hands make light the work: The causes and consequences of social loafing. *Journal of Personality and Social Psychology, 37,* 822–832.

Lazarus, R. S. (1991). *Emotion and adaptation.* New York: Oxford University Press.

LeBreton, J. M., & Senter, J. L. (2008). Answers to 20 questions about interrater reliability and interrater agreement. *Organizational Research Methods, 11,* 815–852.

Lewis, K. M. (2000). When leaders display emotion: how followers respond to negative emotional expression of male and female leaders. *Journal of Organizational Behavior, 21,* 221–234.

Lerner, J. S., & Keltner, D. (2001). Fear, anger, and risk. *Journal of Personality and Social Psychology, 81,* 146–159.

Lo, S. (2008). The nonverbal communication functions of emotions in computer-mediated communication. *CyberPsychology and Behavior, 11,* 595–597.

Mayer, J. D., & Gaschke, Y. N. (1988). The experience and meta-experience of mood. *Journal of Personality and Social Psychology, 55,* 102–111.

Mullen, B., & Copper, C. (1994). The relation between group cohesiveness and performance: An integration. *Psychological Bulletin, 115,* 210–227.

Mullen, B., Johnson, C., & Salas, E. (1991). Productivity loss in brainstorming groups: A meta-analytic integration. *Basic and Applied Social Psychology, 12,* 3–23.

Neumann, R., & Strack, F. (2000). "Mood contagion:" The automatic transfer of mood between persons. *Journal of Personality and Social Psychology, 79,* 211–223.

Park, E. S., & Hinsz, V. B. (2006). "Strength and safety in numbers:" A theoretical perspective on group influences on approach and avoidance motivation. *Motivation and Emotion, 30,* 135–142.

Pescolido, A. T. (2002). Emergent leaders as managers of group emotion. *The Leadership Quarterly, 13,* 583–599.

Ridgeway, C. L. (1994). Affect. In M. Foschi & E. J. Lawler (Eds), *Group processes: Sociological analyses* (pp. 205–230). Chicago, IL: Nelson-Hall Publishers.

Russell, J. A. (1980). A circumplex model of affect. *Journal of Personality and Social Psychology, 39*, 1161–1178.

Schwarz, N., & Clore, G. L. (1996). Feelings and phenomenal experiences. In E. T. Higgins & A. W. Kruglanski (Eds), *Social psychology: Handbook of basic principles* (pp. 433–465). New York: Guilford Press.

Spoor, J. R., & Kelly, J. R. (2004). The evolutionary significance of affect in groups: Communication and group bonding. *Group Processes and Intergroup Relations, 7*, 398–416.

Spoor, J. R., & Kelly, J. R. (2009). Mood convergence in dyads: Effects of valence and leadership. *Social Influence, 4*, 282–297.

Strack, F., Martin, L. L., & Stepper, S. (1988). Inhibiting and facilitating conditions of the human smile: A nonobtrusive test of the facial feedback hypothesis. *Journal of Personality and Social Psychology, 54*, 768–777.

Sy, T., Cote, S., & Saavedra, R. (2005). The contagious leader: Impact of the leader's mood on the mood of group members, group affective tone, and group processes. *Journal of Applied Psychology, 90*, 295–305.

Tiedens, L. Z., Sutton, R. I., & Fong, C. T. (2004). Emotional variation in work groups. In L. Z. Tiedens & C. W. Leach (Eds.), *The social life of emotions*. Cambridge: Cambridge University Press.

Totterdell, P. (2000). Catching moods and hitting runs: Mood linkage and subjective performance in professional sport teams. *Journal of Applied Psychology, 85*, 848–859.

Totterdell, P., Kellett, S., Teuchmann, K., & Briner, R. B. (1998). Evidence of mood linkage in work groups. *Journal of Personality and Social Psychology, 74*, 1504–1515.

Velten, E. (1968). A laboratory task for induction of mood states. *Behaviour Research and Therapy, 6*, 473–482.

Wallbott, H. G. & Scherer, K. R. (1986). The antecedents of emotional experiences. In K. R. Scherer, H. G. Wallbott, & A. B. Summerfield (Eds.), *Experiencing emotion: A cross-cultural study* (pp. 69–97). Cambridge: Cambridge University Press.

Watson, D., Clark, L. A., & Tellegen, A. (1988). Development and validation of brief measures of positive and negative affectivity: The PANAS scales. *Journal of Personality and Social Psychology, 54*, 1063–1070.

Wirth, J. H., Wesselmann, E. D., Williams, K. D., & Mroczek, D. K. (2008). *A time-line of affective decline during an ostracism experience.* Poster presented at the Society for Personality and Social Psychology Conference, Albuquerque, NM.

10

USING VIRTUAL GAME ENVIRONMENTS TO STUDY GROUP BEHAVIOR

James H. Wirth

UNIVERSITY OF NORTH FLORIDA

Frans Feldberg, Alexander Schouten, Bart van den Hooff

VRIJE UNIVERSITEIT AMSTERDAM

Kipling D. Williams

PURDUE UNIVERSITY

Research on group behavior in virtual environments is needed, not only because people are spending more and more time in online virtual environments, but also because the distinction between real life and virtual life is blurring. Millions are entering online virtual worlds that simulate their everyday lives or are pure fantasy. It is clear that online games are ever growing in their popularity and the significance they play in everyday life. An incredible number of people have adopted fast-rising online virtual games like *World of Warcraft*™ (11.5 million),[1] *Second Life*™ (13.3 million),[2] and *EVE Online*™ (300,000).[3] Institutions are also flocking to virtual worlds. Universities are establishing their presence, even going to the extent of recreating their university in a virtual space (see Figure 10.1 for an example). Fortune 500 companies like IBM, Philips and ABN-AMRO are choosing to create virtual spaces[4] in online virtual games. Some of the high-tech titans of these Fortune 500 companies (e.g., founders of corporations, project managers, vice presidents) admit their game playing helped them excel in their roles as bosses (Widman, 2008). As more and more individuals enter online worlds, research should also establish its place within the virtual worlds.

Virtual game environments create opportunities to study group behavior in a variety of different ways. A researcher studying groups could ask: how are virtual games part of everyday group experiences? How do virtual games fulfill the need to belong to a group? Virtual games can be used to observe group behavior that may be difficult to capture in a real-life setting. How do groups form and dissolve? How are meeting spots established for groups to meet? Virtual game environments can also be used to create virtual laboratories where previously unobservable behavior might be explored. For instance, after an individual is ignored and

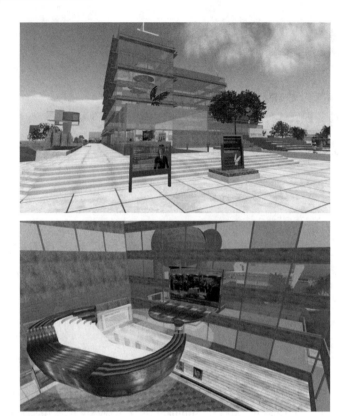

FIGURE 10.1 Examples of structures that can be created on a plot of land in *Second Life*. These figures depict a replica of Vrije Universiteit Amsterdam created in *Second Life*.

excluded (ostracized), how would he or she behave? Laboratory-based measures of behavior may constrain the participant's options and prevent a researcher from truly understanding the behavioral response to the ostracism. If an ostracized individual wants to behave aggressively, he or she may feel more comfortable aggressing against another avatar, but not another person. The goal of this chapter is to provide insights into the nuts and bolts of doing research that investigates any one of these topics.

The Role of Games

Games are often played as a form of entertainment, sometimes with friends or family. Alternately, games can be played for a variety of other purposes. For example, sports are played not only because they are enjoyable, but also because they are a form of exercise. The US Army uses games as a recruiting tool (www.americasarmy.com). Players get the experience of soldiering in the US Army through military elements such as training, technology, weapons, and by engaging in team-based, multiplayer, force-on-force operations. Virtual reality games are also used to help rehabilitate individuals with disabilities; for a review see McLaughlin (2006). Individuals might manipulate and move various objects around virtual environments to improve their motor abilities. In our case, we use games to study group behavior.

Games create the potential for individuals to interact, be mutually aware of each other, be interdependent, and anticipate interacting for a period of time, all defining criteria of a group (McGrath, 1984). We find games to be one of the best means to create an instant group and engage them in a task. Games were initially used by researchers studying group behavior to study social dilemmas (Hardin, 1968; Olson, 1965), such as cooperation versus competition in prisoners' dilemma-type games (Axelrod, 1980, 1984; Luce & Raiffa, 1957). In social dilemma games, one chooses between a behavior that benefits the group and a behavior that benefits oneself (Baron, Kerr, & Miller, 1992). Prisoner dilemma games were popular because researchers could control a variety of aspects of a game (e.g., payoffs and punishment, ability to communicate) to induce behaviors they want to investigate.

Games continue to be used to engage participants in a group task. However, they have evolved from being played face-to-face to now being played in virtual settings. For example, researchers recently created a virtual version of the board game *Clue*™ (Jones, Carter-Sowell, Kelly, & Williams, 2009). Participants ostensibly interacted with other game players online (actually the computer) who gave the participant all the available clues to solving who killed the Professor, or elected to give the participant only some of the clues. Only receiving some of the clues excluded the participant from pertinent information, giving researchers the ability to investigate how a person feels when he or she is "out of the loop." Additionally, a simple game of ball-toss was recreated in a virtual environment (e.g., Cyberball; Williams, Cheung, & Choi, 2000); for a virtual reality recreation, see Williams (2007). Online virtual game environments, referred to as Massively Multiplayer Online Role-playing Games (MMORPGs), are a new way researchers can study how groups form, complete a task, and dissolve. Virtual game environments have advanced to the extent that we use them to create virtual laboratories to study how members of a group interact. For the remainder of the chapter, we will discuss how to use virtual game environments to study group-based behavior.

Virtual Game Environments

A virtual environment can be defined as a three-dimensional, computer-generated simulated environment that is rendered in real time according to the behavior of the user (Loeffler & Anderson, 1994; see Figure 1 for an example). Games that utilize a virtual environment include a Massively Multiuser Online Games

(MMOGs), which refer to an environment where computer players come together to engage in a game activity, such as in *Halo*™. MMORPGs are large persistent virtual worlds that run independent of the user (Yee, 2006a). In these games, players take on the role of fictional characters, avatars, which move through worlds hosted by the game's publisher. These worlds are constantly evolving and changing. Players want to improve their character through completing tasks related to the game and often band together with other players creating long-term social groups. Some of the more popular MMORPGs include *World of Warcraft*, *The Sims Online*™, *Second Life*, *Lord of the Rings*™, and *EverQuest*™.

In a MMORPG, players can live a virtual life by means of their avatar and' dependent on the nature of the game, use their avatar to explore, compete, create content, collaborate, or socialize (see Figure 10.2 for an example avatar). An avatar is a graphical embodiment of a participant that conveys the participant's identity, presence, location, and activities to others (Benford, Greenhalgh, Rodden, & Pycock, 2001). Many MMORPGs offer an elaborate set of functions to edit avatar appearance. The default edit options allow for the development of human-like avatars, ranging from an accurate copy of the person operating the avatar, to the creation of an avatar that resembles the player's favorite movie character, as well as object-like avatars (e.g., cardboard box), and anthropomorphic animal-like creatures.

FIGURE 10.2 An example of avatars used in a *Second Life* experiment.

Why study group behavior in virtual worlds

"It's possible that one large category of human interactions in the future is going to be based on avatars." (D. Williams quoted in *Science*; Miller, 2007, p. 1341).

Attempting to answer the question of why study online games now, D. Williams argued the decline in civic and shared spaces, along with a decline in real-world places to meet to converse with people has created the backdrop for the rise of social gaming (Wiliams, 2006). The need to belong (Baumeister & Leary, 1995) has not been reduced, but the number of social outlets has, prompting social ties to be made in virtual communities (Rheingold, 2000). For example, rather than meeting at the local drinking establishment, friends might find themselves logging in to *World of Warcraft* and, while planning group tactics, they might catch up on important events in their real lives (Williams, 2006). Playing games online is not just where individuals simply go to "play," rather, games more and more are a reflection of naturally occurring phenomenon. As Ito put it, "Yes, it's just a game … the way the real world is a game," (*Newsweek*, September, 2006).

We now have a whole new arena to capture behavior of groups. Online virtual environment games have allowed us to investigate questions that may not be easily answered. Contractor points out, "virtual worlds provide an outstanding exploratorium for us to gather data and test models," (Miller, 2007, p. 1342). Contractor and his colleagues' work demonstrates a primary benefit to online research: complex questions can be investigated in a reduced amount of time compared to real-world studies. He spent 3 years and approximately $1.5M conducting in-depth surveys with more than 30 working groups from places such as NASA, Boeing, and Charles Schwab. In only months, the research team conducted similar experiments looking at *World of Warcraft*, and found similar results as organization-based studies. Virtual online games such as *The Sims Online* or *Guild Wars*™ present an unprecedented means to observe large-scale phenomena (e.g., hundreds organizing for battle) or to find enough instances of rarely occurring phenomena to make conclusive observations.

In conjunction with the fact that more people are flocking to virtual environments for social purposes, we use virtual environments to overcome some of the limitations we experience when studying groups in a laboratory setting. There are at least three methodological problems virtual environments help us overcome: (1) the experimental control–mundane realism trade-off; (2) the lack of replication; and (3) unrepresentative sampling (Blascovich et al., 2002).

Experimental control versus mundane realism

Experimental research traditionally requires a trade-off between experimental control (i.e., precise manipulation of independent variables) and mundane realism (i.e., the extent to which the experiment is similar to situations encountered in daily life); the higher the mundane realism the lower the experimental control

(Blascovich et al., 2002). We run studies in the laboratory, creating high experimental control, but we worry that the outcomes may no longer resemble how a group behaves in a more realistic environment. We use virtual environments to lessen this trade-off because they allow us to build elaborate and realistic experimental situations that still provide the experimental control we need to deduce what is causing an outcome.

Lack of replication

Replication is problematic because of the difficulties researchers studying groups experience in the exact application and implementation of procedures, methods, and settings used by other investigators. Sharing physically identical laboratories is impractical. However, by building laboratory settings in a virtual environment, we can export both the laboratory setting and the automated procedures to control the setting (e.g., scripts) to a digital file that can be imported in the environments used by other researchers. This process increases the portability and potential usage of existing experimental virtual laboratories. Additionally, we can invite other researchers directly into our virtual environment to conduct their research.

Nonrepresentative samples

We find one of the greatest benefits to using virtual game environments is the ability to have a random and representative participant sample, one greater in diversity than a college student sample. The use of internet-enabled virtual environments can level physical and geographical barriers to random and representative participant selection. Every person that has an internet connection can be invited to participate in an experiment that is hosted in a web-enabled virtual laboratory. We do not have to limit our scope of participants to the students in the classes we are teaching, but we can acquire a representative sample of participants, potentially by recruiting inhabitants of the virtual environments.

A typology of virtual game environments

We developed a typology to break down the different types of virtual game environments that can be used to study group behavior. We categorized virtual game environments by two dimensions: (a) whether they are based on a game or virtual life scenario; and (b) whether they are developed by designers or users. An individual playing any of the games within each of the typologies can either play alone or join others to form a group, such as warming up playing *Rock Band*™ alone before and joining others to form an impromptu band that goes on tour. Our typology may not neatly categorize every type of game that could be used to study group behavior, but it provides a starting point for deciding what game might work best to study a given behavior.

We first describe the distinction between game and virtual life scenario environments. They primarily differ in the way they give substance to the role-playing part of the games. The activities of players in game-scenario MMORPGs revolve around the rules of a built-in game scenario. Players have explicit goals, like "conquering land," "beating the enemy," "fighting monsters," or "completing a quest," and they behave in the context of story lines that are provided by the game (Yee, 2006b). Examples of game-scenario MMORPGs are *World of Warcraft* and *EVE Online.*

The primary purpose of virtual-life MMORPGs is to offer players the opportunity to live a virtual life independent of the rules of built-in game scenarios. In these environments people do the same things as they do in real life. Indeed, virtual game environments are a secondary form of life. Linden Lab, the creator and owner of *Second Life*, described *Second Life* as, "a world imagined, built and created by its Residents - people like you. Every minute, Residents assemble buildings, design new fashion lines and launch clubs and businesses."[5] *There.com*™, *Second life* and *Active Worlds*™ worlds are examples of these types of virtual games. Compared to game-scenario MMORPGs, virtual-life MMORPGs offer more advanced features to create and develop tailor-made virtual environments because this is inherent to their purpose. We find these features very helpful for doing research.

In some cases designers developed the virtual game environments. Often these worlds are created with a specific intent. For example, Sony's *Home*™ (accessible for Playstation 3 owners) allows users to go into a virtual environment to check out new media releases such as video games, movies, and music. Developments in these environments are based on additions that designers produce. Other virtual game environments are initially established by designers with the intent that users develop the virtual worlds. For example, in *Second Life*, users can purchase different land plots and develop them. Table 10.1 outlines the matrix of virtual game environments and gives an example of each type.

For the purposes of group behavior research, we will focus our discussion on virtual game environments that incorporate a game scenario (both designed and user developed) and user developed virtual life scenarios. These three types of virtual game environments have the greatest potential for investigating group behavior. All three provide a game element that causes groups to form quickly. In the case of a user-developed game, researchers can create virtual environments to study groups. These environments may be as formal as a virtual laboratory or informal, such as a park where avatars might want to hang out and observers can record their behavior.

Making observations of group behavior in virtual game environments

In this chapter we will share our experiences with laboratory experiments that were executed in virtual environments. However, we want to point out that

Table 10.1 Matrix of video game environments typology

	Designer developed	*User developed*
Game scenario	Designers specifically create a virtual environment intended to enhance a game playing scenario. Examples: *Rock Band*™, *The Legend of Zelda*™, *Madden NFL*™, and *Warcraft*™	Users develop the virtual environments by creating objects and modifying aspects of the environment. These objects become part of the ongoing game. Examples: *World of Warcraft*, *Guild Wars*, and *Lord of The Rings*
Virtual life scenario	Players cannot create the environment, but rather the designer can change the virtual environment as they see fit. The environment is designed so that players can live out their virtual lives by navigating through these worlds. One example is Sony's *Home*	Players can modify scenery and create objects, creating the worlds through wqhich players navigate. Players live out their virtual lives by doing a variety of activities and engaging with others as they would in everyday life. Examples: *Second Life* and *There.com*

the use of virtual worlds to study group behavior does not have to be limited to executing experiments in virtual environment settings. Virtual worlds, like *Second Life* and *Active Worlds*, host a great variety of communities that frequently organize and engage in online group activities. These activities can be used to study natural group behavior, both as a participant observer who is engaged in group activities while simultaneously noting group behavior, or through observational analysis.

Some interesting observational questions that might be investigated include: how do group members know where to meet? What happens to group members that get excluded from the group? How do larger groups function differently than smaller groups? How do groups initiate new members (this might be interesting to explore as a participant observer)? Large-scale observational questions can also be investigated. How are rules created and enforced? How are social norms established? Where are major locations where group congregate (e.g., cities) established? As Castronova (2006) observed, virtual worlds are Petri dishes for the social sciences.

There also exist several challenging research questions concerning the likeness between group behavior in the real versus virtual world including: are real-life social network dynamics also applicable in virtual environments? Do online groups form in a similar way to real-life groups? Do people share knowledge in the same way when hosted in a virtual office, compared to the way they share knowledge in a real life setting? What is the influence on group dynamics if the CEO is represented by his or her avatar, and will not be recognized as such by the other members in the team? Do virtual teams also socialize at the virtual coffee machine? It is also interesting to explore how group behavior in a virtual setting can enlighten group behavior in a real-world setting. It is exciting to see that companies like IBM study game settings to investigate if the leadership strategies that emerge in virtual games are also applicable in real-life business contexts (Miller, 2007).

Designing a Virtual Game Environment to Study Group Behavior

One way we study group behavior is to create a virtual environment where we can observe and measure a desired behavior. We created a virtual environment where participants could toss a ball around, called Cyberball. In our typology, this type of approach fits in the category of a designer-developed game scenario. We use this approach to study ostracism (being excluded and ignored) because it is optimal for efficiently conducting a variety of studies related to a single topic. Cyberball is an example of how a virtual game can be created to study numerous aspects of a specific phenomenon efficiently and effectively.

The development of cyberball

The first ostracism study involved confederate researchers playing ball-toss in a laboratory with participants (Williams, 1997). It was based on an experience Kip had at a park. After he returned an errantly thrown Frisbee, he was included in a game of toss only to have the players stop throwing it to him without an explanation why. To replicate this experience, participants sat in a triangle configuration with two other supposed participants (actually confederates) already seated across from each other (see Figure 10.3). At a certain point of the experiment, the confederate players took a ball out of a toy bin and tossed it around, initially including the participant. However, in one condition, the confederate players stopped throwing the ball to the participant, only to themselves (just like at the park). They additionally did not make eye contact or interact with the participant. Participants in this condition indeed felt ostracized.

Kip thought it was prudent to create a computer game that could address several limitations associated with face-to-face paradigm. The face-to-face ball-toss paradigm was cumbersome: only one participant could be run at a time, two confederates had to be present for every experiment session, and the confederates need to be trained on how to interact for each of the conditions. Confederates' behaviors may have varied between sessions. Of greatest concern was how the confederates felt when being asked to ostracize another individual. It was initially distressing for confederates to ignore and exclude another individual. Potentially to reconcile the distress of being asked to unfairly ostracize another individual, the confederate researchers began to ostracize participants with a sadistic glee. The face-to-face ball-toss paradigm turned into Cyberball,

FIGURE 10.3 Face-to-face ostracism and a virtual game of ball-toss, Cyberball.

a virtual game environment in which participants toss around a virtual ball (Figure 10.3).

Cyberball replicated the park experience and the face-to-face ball-tossing paradigm in a virtual game environment. By making the ball-tossing virtual, the need for confederates was eliminated and multiple participants could be run at a single time. During Cyberball (Williams & Jarvis, 2006; Williams et al., 2000), participants are instructed to visualize the ball-toss interaction, so as to avoid focusing on their ball-toss performance. The participant plays with two other players, similar to the face-to-face ball-toss, with both of these players being computer controlled. The participant is depicted by a hand at the bottom of the screen. Participants can play in either three- or four-player game.

Utilizing a designed virtual game environment

The features the designers included are critical to the utility of Cyberball and the ability to investigate ostracism's effects thoroughly. Initial ostracism studies investigated how ostracized participants felt compared to included participants (Williams et al., 2000). This included finding moderators of ostracism's impact, such as telling participants they were being ostracized by computer-controlled players compared to other players online (Zadro, Williams, & Richardson, 2004) or ostracized by a hated group (the Ku Klux Klan) compared to a more favored group (e.g., a mainstream political party to which one belongs; Gonsalkorale, & Williams, 2007). This last study involved manipulating pictures and names next to the confederate players. All of these questions utilized functions inherent in Cyberball or manipulations of instructions associated with the Cyberball game.

Small modifications to the virtual game environment can extend the ability to ask novel questions. Jim modified the characteristics of the Cyberball players, creating Cyberboys and Cybergirls, to study the impact of group membership on the recovery from an ostracism episode (Wirth & Williams, 2009). van Beest and Williams (2006) created €yberball (pronounced Euroball) where, in some conditions, participants lost money (Euros) when they received the ball, making it beneficial not to be included. A counter helped participants keep track of how many Euros they gained or lost. We evolved Cyberball by adding a new factor, control over how long it takes for the confederate players to decide to throw the ball (Wesselmann, Wirth, Pryor, Reeder, & Williams, 2009; Wirth, Wesselmann, Williams, Pryor, & Reeder, 2009). We find players that are burdensome to the group (i.e., take a long time to decide to throw the ball) are ostracized. Because Cyberball logs who is thrown to and how long it takes to throw the ball, we were able to make Cyberball a dependent measure. This slight modification now allows us to use Cyberball to investigate a new ostracism question, when does ostracism occur?

What is needed to create a virtual game environment

To develop a virtual game environment from scratch, researchers either need to be a designer (someone knowledgeable about computer programming), be willing to learn how to program, work with a virtual game designer who is willing to create the program for little or no money as a way to get more experience with virtual game programming (thereby needing to be patient as he or she makes mistakes), or be willing to spend a lot of money (although, this is not the case for virtual games like *Second Life*). Even if you have a designer there will be difficulties as you figure out what to include in the program, how to do it, what is reasonable for the scope of the project, and be able to communicate clearly with the programmer about desired aspects of the game. The difficulty creating the program will be a function of how complicated you want to make the design. Cyberball is a relatively straightforward program, but it includes a number of ways to manipulate characteristics of the game and several dependent measures.

For others to be able to use a computer program successfully, it needs to be designed to be user friendly and have clear instructions. It is important to share a virtual game so that other researchers can validate and extend your results. Cyberball is a game that is available for anyone to download freely.[6] It is also helpful to make the program one that can be modified to fit other researcher's applications. It was easy for Jim to create Cyberboys and Cybergirls, he simply changed the picture files that are used to show the Cyberball being tossed around. We were able to add the variable of how long a player took before throwing by adding lines of code to the Cyberball program. We worked with a computer programmer who was able to do it in a short amount of time for a minimal cost. Considering the costs that can be associated with creating an original virtual game, it may be worthwhile to first consider if using online worlds would achieve your goals. However, they have their own limitations.

Utilizing a User-developed Virtual Game Environment to Study Group Behavior

One means of understanding group behavior is to observe how groups interact while playing a game. Applying our typology, this type of research would focus on user-developed game-scenario virtual environments. In these games, groups form to complete various tasks as part of the game scenario. For example, in *World of Warcraft,* players might form a guild to go on a quest to secure valuable minerals. There are generally minimal requirements for doing research in these environments: essentially, access to the game and, in the case of a participant observation study, the ability to develop the avatar player as the game progresses (e.g., acquire new weapons, buy accessories). Conducting research within a user-developed game-scenario virtual environment is ideal for studies that require a large number of participants, for making observations that are difficult to capture in real life, or for capturing processes that take long periods of time to develop (Bainbridge, 2007).

Researchers can use virtual games to study behaviors that are difficult to capture. For example, Martey and Stromer-Galley (2007) explored the "digital dollhouses" of *The Sims Online*. Specifically, they investigated social norms of avatars in houses created by players in *The Sims Online*. The researchers visited several houses using their avatar and minimally engaged with others as they made observations (participant observation). They observed a wide range of norms associated with hosting others at a house, being a visitor, group projects, public conversations, and avatar action and interaction. *The Sims Online* is designed to engage players in a variety of group interactions, earning more points for a group task than doing a task alone. Group tasks can be business-like, such as two to four Sims operating a pizza machine, or more leisurely, such as dance parties or weddings.

Group phenomena that are nearly impossible to investigate in a real-world context may be possible to investigate in online worlds. For example, Castronova (2006) was interested in studying coordination equilibrium, or a point at which players agree to meet at and create a market to exchange goods. He studied where markets for goods were established inside the games *EverQuest* and *Dark Age of Camelot*™. Looking across similar worlds on several different servers, Castronova was able to test the theory of coordination. Similar to the prisoner dilemma games we discussed earlier, researchers use virtual environments to investigate how individuals can be induced to cooperate in producing public goods (Harrison & List, 2004). Online virtual games make is possible to observe large group behavior that otherwise would be nearly impossible to observe in a real-world setting.

Online worlds can potentially provide a large dataset to investigate questions where many observations are needed. They can also provide significant power to test for effects that may not be particularly large. For instance, Xiong, Poole, Williams, and Ahmad (2009) investigated the effects of group structure on group behavior and outcomes using data collected from *Everquest2*™. The researchers were able to demonstrate that structure and process at the group level can influence group behavior. They were also able to investigate direct and indirect effects due to the large sample size.

Researchers that are part of the Virtual Worlds Exploratorium offer additional examples of how online worlds can be used to study group behavior. These researchers forged a collaboration with Sony Online Entertainment to analyze data from the US-dedicated servers of *Everquest2*. This will allow them to investigate numerous dynamic group-based questions. Owing to vast social networks that are constantly changing, researchers (Xiong et al., 2009) are looking at who enters and leaves groups as they form, merge, and dissolve. They are also looking at how different levels of expertise can affect group outcomes. These researchers are capitalizing on the thousands of groups that can be observed.

Traditional field experiments can also be conducted in the virtual game environments. Eastwick and Gardner (2009) demonstrated that biases and processes in the real world carry over into the social world, despite the fantasy element of virtual worlds. They found the race of an avatar (light versus dark skinned) influenced the compliance with how willing individuals playing in *Second Life* would be to comply with a small request following a larger one (i.e., door-in-the-face technique; Cialdini et al., 1975). These results are similar to those found in laboratory-based research: the door-in-the-face technique was less effective for dark-skinned versus light-skinned avatars. Further simulating real-world field experiments, researchers using online games have found avatars will leave physical space between each other and female players made more eye contact and stood closer to other avatars than males (Yee, Bailenson, Urbanek, Chang, & Merget, 2007). Many of the approaches used to study group behavior in user-developed virtual game environments capitalize on how the online world reflects real-life interpersonal interactions.

Investigating Group Behavior by Utilizing User-developed Virtual Life Game Environments

The first two uses of virtual game environments involved researchers examining group behavior as it related to playing a game. This game may have been created to investigate a given group behavior, such as Cyberball, or group behavior may be observed as individuals participated in an online game, such as watching a group complete tasks in *World of Warcraft*. However, a third type of virtual game environment in our typology involves user-developed virtual life scenarios. These worlds are created to provide users a virtual second life. With this approach, rather than observing group behavior as a function of a game, researchers can create virtual scenarios, including a laboratory, within the virtual game environment. *Second Life* is an example of a virtual game environment we have adapted for the use of studying group behavior.

In user-developed virtual game environments, it is possible to create any type of scenario, including a virtual laboratory, in an undeveloped space. It is possible to own virtual estates in *Second Life* that can be used for any purpose the owner wishes to use it; in our case, we use them for research. The *Second Life* scripting language allows for the development of objects that can help to guide, control, and monitor key processes in experiments. Scripts in *Second Life* are a set of instructions that can be placed inside any object, or any object worn by or attached to an avatar. Scripts can make an object move, listen, talk, operate as a car or a plane, change size, shape, or color. A script can make an object react to your words as well as talk back to you. Scripts are written using an editor that is built into the *Second Life* user interface. *Second Life* offers a relative media rich environment including instant messaging, voice over IP, and avatar gestures. *Second Life* also supports the integration of streaming media (music and video). Controlling the availability of different cues allows for experiments that measure the influence of these cues on group behavior.

Frans, Alex, and Bart have already conducted group-based research in online virtual game environments, specifically, *Second Life*. They were interested in how virtual worlds influence group decision-making processes and their outcomes. They had four important reasons for conducting research in *Second Life*, including: (1) *Second Life* is a platform that hosts a variety of group processes; (2) based on prior experiences with *Second Life*, they knew that it was relatively easy to build an experimental setting and find participants familiar with *Second Life* (Verhagen, Feldberg, Van den Hooff, Meents, & Merikivi, 2011); (3) *Second Life* offers a great variety of features to modify avatar appearance easily; and last but not least, (4) at the time of the experiment, *Second Life* appeared to be a very popular virtual world attracting huge numbers of people as well as businesses all willing to explore the opportunities of virtual worlds.

The study Frans, Alex, and Bart conducted using *Second Life* involved participants, undergraduate students recruited from a class on business administration, who formed three-member teams representing a neighborhood council. The council had to make a decision among four different options on what would be built in a vacant space in the neighborhood they represented. The trio of researchers manipulated the degree the council was immersed in the virtual environment. Three levels of immersion were created for the experiment: (1) a text-chat only condition – participants in this condition could only make use of an instant messaging tool to communicate with each other, (2) a virtual decision room condition – participants in this condition were identified by an avatar and hosted in a small windowless meeting room containing only a table and chairs (see Figure 10.4); and (3) a virtual neighborhood condition – a digital representation of the neighborhood about which the team should make a decision (see Figure 10.5). In the virtual neighborhood condition, group members could move around the virtual space on which the group was making a decision. The findings of this experiment revealed that the participants felt more enveloped and included in the decision situation in the virtual laboratory they created for them in *Second Life*, than the participants who executed the decision task in a real-life setting and compared to those who used text-based communication only while not being in a three-dimensional (3D) virtual environment.

FIGURE 10.4 The virtual decision room.

FIGURE 10.5 Virtual neighborhood participants could navigate around while making a group decision on the use of the open space.

Requirements for creating an experimental environment in an online virtual game

To build the experimental setting in *Second Life*, they first needed to acquire space to establish a virtual laboratory. They did this by buying two so-called "virtual regions" from Linden Lab. Regions can be bought through the *Second Life* website. Linden Lab (the designers of *Second Life*) offers different types of regions, qualified according to the numbers of avatars that can be hosted simultaneously on a single region, and the maximum number of shapes (called primitives or prims in *Second Life*) that can be used to create a virtual setting. Linden Lab's pricing model includes a setup fee, and a monthly maintenance fee. The setup fee for the type of island we bought is $700, and the maintenance fee amounts to $150 per month (a discount pricing model is applicable for educational institutions and nonprofit organizations). As long as the research conducted does not violate legal conditions, no special permission from Linden Lab is needed to use *Second Life* for scientific research. In the end, scientific research fits Linden Lab's vision of "a world imagined, built and created by its Residents."

The virtual spaces they used were actually two "virtual islands," both owned by their research group. We decided to use two different regions, each measuring

65,000 square meters, in anticipation of three issues. The first issue was that the number of shapes (called primitives or prims in *Second Life*) that can be used to create a virtual setting is limited to 15,000 per region. Each object (e.g., building, table, car) in *Second Life* is basically a set of linked prims (building blocks). For example, a table can be built by using five prims: one box prim for the tabletop, and four cylinder prims, one for each of the four legs of the table. The second issue they contended with was performance. Each region in *Second Life* is linked to a certain amount of computer processing power. Performance is dependent on such factors as the number of prims used, the number of avatars present, and the scripting load. By using two regions that are joined together, the same avatar, prim, and scripting load will be dealt with by doubled processing power. The third issue was interaction between avatars in differing conditions. If the teams in the two different conditions get into each other's space they could potential "hear" each other and the discussions become mixed.

Expertise in building and scripting

An additional requirement for conducting experiments in *Second Life* is building know-how and expertise. Researchers will need people who are able to learn the skills of building in *Second Life*. However, the learning curve for mastering the *Second Life* tools appears rather steep, even for people who do not have experience in 3D building and modeling. If you do want to make use of scripts, people with more advanced programming skills must be part of the team. Most scripting languages that are used to write scripts are comparable to programming languages like Java or C. For Fran, Alex, and Bart, they recruited students to assist them in developing the environment. One call for *Second Life* building expertise, posted in our digital learning environment, appeared to be enough to create a pool of dedicated *Second Life* building experts. The full experimental setting was created by two builders in a lead time of four weeks.

The virtual laboratories

Conditions 2 and 3 of the experiment were developed on two different virtual regions of *Second Life*. The virtual decision room (condition 2) was a small windowless meeting room. A conference table with three chairs, one for each participant, was positioned at the center of the virtual room (see Figure 10.4). The chairs and table were not developed by the research team, but instead were obtained for free on one of the *Second Life* locations that offer a multitude of "freebee" objects. Every avatar has a so-called "inventory entry" in which objects can be stored. Objects that are not copy protected (dependent on the settings of the object) can be transferred to other avatars or can be placed in a virtual space. It is also possible to buy objects, like furniture, clothes, or gadgets, in one of the many shops hosted in *Second Life*. A multimedia object, including a streaming

FIGURE 10.6 The development of the virtual neighborhood in *Second Life* was based on buildings in the real-life neighborhood.

video of the neighborhood the team had to decide on, was attached to one of the walls of the decision room. Each participant could individually watch this video by touching the play button in the media section of the user interface.

The neighborhood (condition 3) was a representative reproduction of an existing urban neighborhood that consisted of a residential area, several office buildings, and small production and trade companies (see Figure 10.6). To create a setting that resembles reality as much as possible, the virtual neighborhood was an accurate copy of an existing neighborhood. The development of the virtual neighborhood was guided by pictures of the houses, buildings, and offices situated in the real-life neighborhood (see Figure 10.5). The vacant space in the center of the neighborhood in Figure 10.5 was the subject of the decision task. Avatars could explore the full virtual neighborhood, but could not leave it. Owing to the ability to control who enters and leaves the environment, no avatars other than the ones assigned by the research team were present.

Preparing the participants to use second life

Because most of the participants were not familiar with *Second Life* before the experiment, they had to be aware of so-called "novice effects." If technology is needed in support of a task to be performed, task performance might be dependent on the level of expertise with the relevant technology of the person performing the task (Venkatesh & Davis, 1996). To avoid novice effects they organized a one-hour tutorial for the participants that were assigned to the virtual environment conditions in the week prior to the actual experiment. In this tutorial session participants learned the basics of the *Second Life* user interface as well as the basic skills of movement, navigation, and interaction. For example, they taught participants the different ways of moving around: walking, running, and flying, as well as how to communicate with each other through the built-in instant messaging features.

Recruiting participants in a virtual game

Next to recruitment of participants in real life, virtual worlds offer the opportunity to recruit participants "in world" too ("in world" means in the virtual world setting). Populated virtual worlds offer different ways for "in world" participant recruitment. On the individual level, a researcher can use his or her own avatar to invite others directly to participate in a research project. It is important to pick an online game where you fit in and can comfortably participate. Virtual worlds include built-in search features like "top ten most popular places," "recommended events," or "destination guides," that can be used to select the right places for recruitment. Virtual worlds offer the opportunity to search for places and events. Researchers can use a keyword search to help select places and events that might be of specific interest for the researcher, or to compose a balanced sample of participants. A virtual place that has been tagged "shopping mall" by its owner, can be very interesting for a researcher exploring group decision-making in a commercial virtual settings. Crowded places offer both the opportunity to get in touch with other residents as well as being a venue for observational studies.

Participants can also be recruited for research at the community or group level. Most virtual worlds host groups or communities. In *Second Life*, for example, it is relatively easy to create a group and invite avatars to join the group you created. A researcher can also search through group profiles that are made available through a public directory. When a profile includes the name of the owner of the group, this owner can be asked to cooperate by asking the group members to participate through communication mechanisms like group notices. Group profiles can also be used to select special interest groups that might be of specific value for the researcher. Some virtual world communities even deploy activities in real life, have their own websites and maintain up-to-date mailing lists. These communities can be very valuable when it comes to participant recruitment. A combination of individual and group-level recruitment can be realized by asking an individual avatar to cooperate and ask all the members of the groups he or she had joined to participate in the research project too. Amy Bruckman (this volume) offers several tips for recruiting participants at the individual and group level.

Impressions of using Second Life for an experiment

What did Frans, Alex, and Bart learn from using *Second Life* to conduct group experiments? *Second Life* can be an appropriate platform to build virtual laboratories and support research projects without inducing huge investments. The opportunity to build and use scripts to control behavior was also valuable, as well as the built-in option to store the discussion logs. The opportunity to integrate multimedia objects relatively easily makes it possible to create lively and vivid virtual settings. *Second Life* offers a head start for creating an experimental labora-tory environment, not only due to its nature of being a platform for building custom-made settings, but also because of the availability of a great variety of objects that can be bought at relatively low prices (or for free) to furnish your laboratory. During the execution of the experiment, *Second Life* appeared to be rather stable and did not cause serious technical or performance problems. Are they going to use *Second Life* for future projects too? The answer is "yes," and they have already prepared a follow-up experiment that aims to address the research question: can 3D virtual environments contribute to individual and collective understanding of a decision problem?

Limitations to Using Virtual Game Environments

Researchers are limited in using online virtual game environments because they are dependent on the proprietors of the game. Using commercial virtual environ-ments that run on computer servers that are controlled by third parties may result in "unscheduled" maintenance and other changes in service that could interfere with conducting an experiment. The quality of the game environment may also vary. The high-resolution user interface of virtual game environments like *World of Warcraft*, for example, produces more sophisticated images than the relatively low-resolution interface of *Second Life*, making the latter virtual envi-ronment less realistic. Although higher resolutions are not always preferred above lower resolutions (Serviss, 2005), research findings indicate that more realistic game environments (higher resolutions) positively influence engagement, immer-sion, and focus (Sabri, Ball, Fabian, Bhatia, & North, 2007). Researchers are also limited because they may not be able to adapt the virtual environments in ways that would be helpful, such as integrating media from an external system (e.g., opening an interactive web page in the virtual environment itself). Finally, by using a virtual environment that is established by an external commer-cial party, the user will always be dependent on the commercial viability of the supplier.

One should always be aware of the fact that new virtual worlds may come and go, existing for a short time before interest wanes and the virtual world no longer exists. To make our research projects less dependent on third parties we are explor-ing open source solutions for virtual worlds. One such a solution is the so-called *OpenSimulator*™ (www.opensimulatior.org). *OpenSimulator* can be used to create a virtual environment similar to *Second Life* under your own control. It is even possible to use the *Second Life* client software to access virtual environments cre-ated in *OpenSimultor*. Content that has been created in *Second Life* can also be transferred to a virtual environment created in *OpenSimulator*. It is possible to make use of this open source solution by either creating your own virtual envi-ronment on your own computer servers, or to make use of a so-called *OpenSimulator* grid that hosts virtual worlds offered by third parties.

When you create your own virtual world based upon an open source solution, it will make you less dependent on third parties. In the end, you can always build and run your own environment by using the open source software. This independence, however, must be balanced against the effort, know-how, and investments needed to set up and run your own virtual environment. Another important issue to be considered in this context is the number of residents. If you set up your own virtual environment, initially this world is not inhabited. This can be a positive if you are planning for limited-scale laboratory experiments. However, if the set-up of your research requires large numbers of participants, the selection of an existing virtual world that is populated with huge numbers of residents might be a better choice.

Gathering data and conducting some experiments may be difficult in virtual game environments. It is difficult to gain access and work with data that a virtual game provider may share. A group of researchers worked closely with Sony to examine data structures of the servers, develop a data dictionary, and map the "in-game" actions, transactions, and interactions of game players (Williams, Contractor, Poole, Srivastava, & Cai, 2009). If access to information is gained, the data still needs to be organized as data logs do not identify groups, only characters, causing researchers to have to reconstruct groups as people in the same place, at the same time, and then link these data to character type, guild, and what experiences occur while in the group. Conducting field experiments in the virtual game can also be problematic as researchers do not want to do anything that is part of an experiment that could ruin the experience of a naïve game user. If a researcher is interested in how game players respond to unsociable behavior (e.g., aggression, abuse, rejection) or any behavior that could be irritating even to some, then conducting a study in an online world would not be the appropriate venue. Game players might complain and, moreover, game hosts and players may turn on researchers using these virtual environments.

Ethical concerns when using online virtual worlds

Risks associated with recruiting participants

There are some unique ethical challenges with recruiting participants online. The first of these begins with the online games themselves. Online games may have terms of service (TOS) that may state explicit rules on what studies would be allowed to be conducted. What is tricky is that TOS are selectively enforced. Researchers must also address ethical concerns with gatekeepers of certain areas of virtual games or the game designers themselves. The gatekeeper is someone who must be approached first before anyone else in the group can be addressed. Getting the gatekeeper's permission to conduct research is often needed. When recruiting participants it is important to depict yourself accurately. If you are a male, it could be considered unethical to depict yourself as a female to join a group of females for study purposes. Often researchers will put in their profile they are a researcher, or better still, they will create an avatar that depicts a researcher (potentially wearing a white lab coat). Getting informed consent may also be difficult. In some cases Institutional Review Boards (IRBs) may accept a click-to-accept consent form. Ultimately, it is best to consult with member of your institution's IRB before conducting extensive online research.

The ethical concerns for a virtual laboratory remain the same as the ethical concerns for traditional laboratory experiments. Ethical guidelines for this type of research are best guided by the American Psychological Association's (1992) ethical code of conduct. An additional ethical concern for both laboratory set-up in virtual environments and research conducted with naïve game players in virtual environments is related to using avatar representations of participants. If participants are put in a situation in which they feel uncomfortable during an experiment, it may be particularly difficult for an experimenter to identify a participant in distress based on the actions of an avatar. In a traditional laboratory experiment, the experimenter is able to interact face-to-face with participants and monitor social cues of distress. Participants may either hide their emotions or be unable to express them using their avatar, leaving an experimenter blind to any undue distress they cause participants.

To counter this ethical concern, additional safeguards might be established when using avatars. One might be putting a video camera on participants using an avatar in a study. Experimenters can watch the reactions of participants: re-establishing the ability to monitor social cues of distress (also recording nonverbal behavior). Additional directions at the beginning of an experiment might emphasize what participants should do if they feel distressed. Alternatively, participants can have their avatar leave the experiment if they become distressed, similar to if they were physically in an experiment and desired to leave. For those experiments where participants interact with naïve players, ethical guidelines indicate researchers cannot cause stress that is greater than everyday life experiences without obtaining the participants' consent.

Researchers observing or interacting with naïve participants in online virtual environments must consider a host of ethical issues that are unique from experiments conducted in the laboratory. Kraut and colleagues (2004) discussed ethical issues associated with collecting data online in the form of experiments using questionnaires, analyzing chat room comments, investigating posting on bulletin boards, group forums, or email distribution lists.

We will discuss these issues as they relate to doing observational research or field-like research within virtual environments.

Privacy

Making sure game players remain anonymous after being observed or following an interaction with the experimenter is central to reducing risk. When game players cannot be identified directly or indirectly, then this observation of public behavior is exempt from federal regulations protecting human subjects. If chat-room content or the responses of players that were interacted with are going to be analyzed, follow the suggestions of Kraut et al. (2004) concerning the use of pseudonyms and alter quoted text so it cannot be traced back to the original author. Game players do not want to have the sense that "Big Brother" is watching over their game play. Federal regulations dictate that electronic communication between individuals is not protected if the means of communication are readily accessible to the general public. However, to the advantage of researchers, norms in online games may include observing the actions of others and reading content that is posted in a chat room (e.g., Nonnecke & Preece, 2000). Lastly, game players may feel that what happens in the online world stays in the online world. Unbeknown to game players, gaming websites record essentially every move the players make. While this information is recorded to aid programmers in enhancing the experience of the game, to researchers' benefit, it can still be used for research purposes. Researchers can minimize harm by securing data acquired from game hosts and by de-identifying game players.

Risk associated with the experiment

The risk associated with any experiment conducted in an online world will be particular to the type of study being done. There are several initial restrictions on what type of studies can be conducted in online virtual game environments. First, investigators should not deceive participants in online virtual game environments research. In the case of Cyberball, Kip and Jim deceived participants in that they believed they were playing online with others, but because Cyberball is run in a laboratory setting, they were able to debrief participants fully. Recently, the American Psychological Association stated it would not publish research done online that involved deception due to concerns about participants being properly debriefed. Second, research using online worlds needs to be of minimal risk if an informed consent process is not used. Studies are considered minimal if the extent of harm or discomfort a researcher believes participants will experience is no greater than that during daily life.

Conclusion

The possibilities for researchers to study group behavior will only increase as virtual game environments expand in size, scope, and complexity. Virtual game environments can be created to examine a specific group behavior thoroughly. Even the simple virtual environment of Cyberball has led to researchers throughout the world downloading the program and running any number of studies. Group behaviors that a researcher could never imagine studying are now possible to explore in detail. By examining different worlds in a virtual game, by following groups over long periods of time, or even observing groups in action slaying a monster, researchers can learn about global group phenomenon and long-term group behavior. Using online game-scenario virtual worlds overcomes the limitations associated with a traditional laboratory. Regarding traditional laboratories, virtual laboratories, situated in virtual game environments, may revolutionize conducting research. Owing to virtual laboratories overcoming many limitations of group-based research, being easy to create, and requiring a minimal amount of resources, anyone can create a virtual laboratory and have access to a diverse group of participants. Virtual games will increasingly become a central feature of our everyday lives and an increasingly popular source for finding others with whom to interact. As this occurs, research will also increasingly become a greater part of the virtual online environments, opening up countless new ways to investigate how groups behave.

Notes

1 Based on statistics from December 2008. http://www.wired.com/gamelife/2008/12/world-of-warc-1
2 https://blogs.secondlife.com/community/features/blog/2009/04/16/the-second-life-economy–first-quarter-2009-in-detail
3 Based on statistics from April 2008. http://secondlife.com/whatis/economy_stats.php; http://www.activeworlds.com/info/index.asp
4 IBM developed a virtual business center in *Second Life* to host virtual meetings and learning sessions (http://www.ibm.com/3dworlds/businesscenter/us/en/) and Philips Design set up an immersive virtual environment in *Second Life* to support participation and co-creation activities in new product design (http://www.design.philips.com/sites/philipsdesign/about/design/designnews/pressreleases/secondlife.page)
5 http://secondlife.com/whatis/#Welcome (accessed: November 26, 2009)
6 Cyberball is freely available for download. The website for downloading Cyberball is: http://psyclops.psych.purdue.edu/~kip/Announce/cyberball.htm

References

American Psychological Association (1992). Ethical principles of psychologists and code of conduct. *American Psychologist, 47,* 1597–1611.
Axelrod, R. (1980). More effective choice in the prisoner's dilemma. *Journal of Conflict Resolution, 24,* 379–403.
Axelrod, R. (1984). *The evolution of cooperation.* New York: Basic Books.
Bainbridge, W. S. (2007). The scientific research potential of virtual worlds. *Science, 317,* 472–476.
Baron, R. S., Kerr, N. L., & Miller, N. (1992). Social dilemmas. In R. S. Baron, N. L. Kerr, & N. Miller (Eds.), *Group process, group decision, group action.* Pacific Grove, CA: Brooks Cole Publishing Company.
Baumeister, R. F., & Leary, M. R. (1995). The need to belong: Desire for interpersonal attachments as a fundamental human motivation. *Psychological Bulletin, 117,* 497–529.
Benford, S., Greenhalgh, C., Rodden, T., & Pycock, J. (2001). Collaborative virtual environments. *Communications of the ACM, 44,* 79–82.
Blascovich, J., Loomis, J., Beall, A. C., Swinth, K. R., Hoyt, C. L. & Bailenson, J. N. (2002). Immersive virtual environment technology as a methodological tool for social psychology. *Psychological Inquiry, 13,* 103–124.

Castronova, E. (2006). On the research value of large games: Natural experiments in Norrath and Camelot. *Games and Culture, 1,* 163–186.

Cialdini, R. B., Vincent, J. E., Lewis, S. K., Catalan, J., Wheeler, D., & Darby, B. L. (1975). Reciprocal concessions procedure for inducing compliance: The door-in-the-face technique. *Journal of Personality and Social Psychology, 31,* 206–215.

Eastwick, P. W., & Gardner, W. L. (2009). Is it a game? Evidence for social influence in the virtual world. *Social Influence, 4,* 18–32.

Gonsalkorale, K., & Williams, K. D. (2007). The KKK won't let me play: Ostracism even by a despised outgroup hurts. *European Journal of Social Psychology, 37,* 1176–1186.

Hardin, G. (1968). The tragedy of the commons. *Science, 162,* 1243–1248.

Harrison, G. W., & List, J. A. (2004). Field experiments. *Journal of Economic Literature, 42,* 1009–1055.

Jones, E. E., Carter-Sowell, A. R., Kelly, J. R., & Williams, K. D. (2009). "I'm out of the loop": Ostracism through information exclusion. *Group Processes and Intergroup Relations, 12,* 157–174.

Kraut, R., Olson, J., Banaji, M., Bruckman, A., Cohen, J., & Couper, M. (2004). Psychological research online: Report of board of scientific affairs' advisory group on the conduct of research on the Internet. *American Psychologist, 59,* 105–117.

Loeffler, T., & Anderson C. E. (1994). What is virtual reality? In T. Loeffler & C. E. Anderson (Eds.), *The virtual reality casebook.* New York: Van Nostrand Reinhold.

Luce, R. D., & Raiffa, H. (1957). *Games and decisions.* New York: Wiley.

McGrath, J. E. (1984). *Groups: Interaction and performance.* Prentice Hall, College Division.

McLaughlin, M. L. (2006). Simulating the sense of touch in virtual environments: Applications in the health sciences. In P. Messaris & L. Humphreys (Eds.), *Digital media: transformations in human communication.* Peter Lang Publishers.

Miller, G. (2007). The promise of parallel universes. *Science, 317,* 1341–1343.

Nonnecke, B., & Preece, J. (2000). Lurker demographics: Counting the silent. *CHI 2000, ACM Conference on Human Factors in Computing Systems, CHI Letters, 4,* 73–80.

Olson, M. (1965). *The logic of collective action: Public goods and theory of groups.* Cambridge, MA: Harvard University Press.

Rheingold, H. (2000). *The virtual community: Homesteading on the electronic frontier.* Cambridge, MA: MIT Press.

Sabri, J. A., Ball, R. G., Fabian, A., Bhatia, S., & North, C. (2007). High-resolution gaming: Interfaces, notifications, and the user experience. *Interacting with Computers, 19,* 151–166.

Serviss, B. (2005). Escaping the world: High and low resolution in gaming. *IEEE MultiMedia, 12,* 4–8.

van Beest, I., & Williams, K. D. (2006). When inclusion costs and ostracism pays, ostracism still hurts. *Journal of Personality and Social Psychology, 91,* 918–928.

Verhagen, T., Feldberg, F., Van den Hooff, B., Meents, S., & Merikivi, J. (2011). Satisfaction with virtual worlds: An integrated model of experiential value. *Information & Management, 48,* 201–207.

Venkatesh, V. & Davis, F. D. (1996). A model of the antecedents of perceived ease of use: Development and test. *Decision Sciences, 27,* 31.

Wesselmann, E. D., Wirth, J. H., Pryor, J. B., Reeder, G. D., & Williams, K. D. (2009). *Observing ostracism in groups: With whom do we side?* Presented at the Annual Meeting of the Midwestern Psychological Association, Chicago, IL.

Widman, J. (2008). Boss by day, gamer by night: Tech leaders' favorite video games. Retrieved from http://www.computerworld.com/s/article/print/9124143/Boss_by_day_gamer_by_night_Tech_leaders_favorite_video_games?taxonomyId=0&taxonomyName=Default

Williams, D. (2006). Why game studies now? Gamers don't bowl alone. *Games and Culture, 1,* 13–16.

Williams, D., Contractor, N., Poole, M. S., Srivastava, J., & Cai, D. (2009). *The virtual worlds exploratorium.* Manuscript in preparation.

Williams, K. D. (1997). Social ostracism. In R. M. Kowalksi (Ed.), *Aversive interpersonal behaviors* (pp. 133–170). New York: Plenum.

Williams, K. D. (2007). Ostracism. *Annual Review of Psychology, 58,* 425–452.

Williams, K. D., Cheung, C. K. T., & Choi, W. (2000). Cyberostracism: Effects of being ignored over the internet. *Journal of Personality and Social Psychology, 79,* 748–762.

Williams, K. D., & Jarvis, B. (2006). Cyberball: A program for use in research on interpersonal ostracism and acceptance. *Behavior Research Methods, 38,* 174–180.

Wirth, J. H., Wesselmann, E. D., Williams, K. D., Pryor, J. B., & Reeder, G. D. (2009). *When and why do we ostracize? To punish burdensome group members.* Poster presented at the Society for Personality and Social Psychology Conference, Tampa, FL.

Wirth, J. H., Williams, K. D. (2009). "They don't like our kind:" Consequences of being ostracized while possessing a stigmatizing group membership. *Group Processes and Intergroup Relations, 12,* 111–127.

Xiong, L., Poole, M. S., Williams, D., & Ahmad, M. (2009). *The effects of group structure on group behavior and outcomes in an online gaming environment.* Manuscript in preparation.

Yee, N. (2006a). Motivations for play in online games. *CyberPsychology and Behavior, 9,* 772–776.

Yee, N. (2006b). The demographics, motivations and derived experiences of users of massively-multiuser online graphical environments. *Presence: Teleoperators and Virtual Environments, 15,* 309–329.

Yee, N., Bailenson, J. N., Urbanek, M., Chang, F., & Merget, D. (2007). The unbearable likeness of being digital: The persistence of nonverbal social norms in online virtual environments. *Journal of Cyberpsychology and Behavior, 10,* 115–121.

Zadro, L., Williams, K. D., & Richardson, R. (2004). How low can you go? Ostracism by a computer lowers belonging, control, self-esteem, and meaningful existence. *Journal of Experimental Social Psychology, 40,* 560–567.

11

INTERVIEWING MEMBERS OF ONLINE COMMUNITIES

A Practical Guide to Recruiting Participants

Amy Bruckman

GEORGIA INSTITUTE OF TECHNOLOGY

In an interview study of members of an online community, one of the most daunting tasks is finding people who are willing to talk to you – and doing so ethically. Since 1997, I have taught a Georgia Tech class called "Design of Online Communities," in which students are assigned to interview at least three members of an online group and also engage in participant observation. The class began at the graduate level, and now is offered to undergraduates as well. Teams of three students study the same site and write up a detailed account of its design. The goal of the assignment is, first, to help students understand how designed features of an online site impact user behavior. Second, the project introduces them to interviewing and participant observation as research methods for understanding online behavior. As you might imagine, interesting things happen when I unleash 40 new student researchers each year.

Each semester, I repeatedly warn students that getting people to talk to you is hard work, and they should expect to spend a lot of time doing it. To further complicate matters, while you must be persistent, you may not annoy community members. And all activity takes place as governed by approval from our Institutional Review Board (IRB), the committee charged with protecting human subjects in research. In this chapter, I shall share the lessons learned from shepherding students through this process for the last 12 years. Those lessons are relevant not just for student projects but also for people working on research about this medium for publication.

In this chapter, I will focus primarily on the issue of how to get people to agree to talk with you. I will discuss issues of ethical conduct of online research, but not cover the subject in detail. For a more complete account from the ethics point of view, see (Bruckman, 2002, 2006).

Students in the class are required to read the book *Interviewing as Qualitative Research* by Irving Seidman (Seidman, 2006). Much of the advice relayed here builds on advice from Seidman's book, focusing on my students' experiences applying Seidman to studying online groups in particular.

Medium for the Interview

Students are instructed to conduct interviews on the telephone/skype or in person – *not* in text-based interaction. Students and potential interview subjects are often puzzled by this requirement. If we're talking about people's online experiences, why not talk with them in the medium itself? It's easier for both the researcher and subject, and seems appropriate given the topic of investigation. However, an online interview yields so few data that it is almost useless in comparison to a phone or in-person interview. When conducting an online interview, one develops a sense that you've had a profound conversation. But then looking back at the transcript later, you find there's little in it. The easiest way to demonstrate this is simply to compare a transcript of a text-based interview and a telephone one. The online interview transcript will typically fill a few pages, and the voice interview five to ten times as many. Each term I spread the pages out on the floor at the front of the classroom to make the point visually. When students see that the online/text transcript crosses the desk, and the phone/skype transcript goes across the room and back, they understand why the text-based interview is insufficient.

I will let students do text-based interviews as a backup for subjects who refuse to do a voice interview, though it doesn't "count" towards their interview assignment. As a result, for many years our informed consent form said "you are agreeing to do an interview in person, but telephone, or online." Many subjects agreed to a phone interview, saw the wording of the consent form, and then requested to do an online interview instead. As a result, we now have two separate, approved consent forms: one that says "in person or by telephone/skype," and another that says "online." We distribute the forms for audio-based interviews, and only send out the text-based forms when absolutely necessary.

Students in the online communities class are required to interview three subjects simply because time is limited. For publishable research, more are needed. How many interviews are needed is a subject of much discussion in qualitative methods literature. A good rule of thumb is that you are done when you "start to hear the same thing" over and over. For many studies, you may interview different kinds of participants (e.g., new users and "regulars.") For each category of user, you generally need 10–20 interview subjects. This is a very rough estimate, and the number, of course, differs depending on the goals of the particular study.

Although we interview people in person or on the phone, initial contact is made online. But before we do that, we first need to choose a site to study.

Challenges of recruiting subjects

The choice of site to study, of course, depends primarily on your research questions. Beyond that, researchers should also be aware that recruiting subjects is harder on some kinds of sites than others. The task is challenging for any site, but impossible if the site is poorly chosen.

To gain some insight into whether a particular site is a reasonable choice, try to imagine yourself as a participant on that site. Imagine someone asks if you'd talk to them about it. Under what circumstances will you say yes? List in your mind all the sites you personally use, and think about which ones you'd be willing or eager to discuss and which ones not. Most people will find they can immediately think of a special site they'd be willing to chat about (i.e., "I love that site – I spend way too much time there!") and many others they would not (i.e., "I posted a question there once, but I can't really comment on it in detail.")

For most people, it's a pleasure to talk about a site they're excited about. If a user is invested in a site, then telling someone about it is fun. It helps if being a member of the site makes them feel good about themselves – in other words, if being a member conveys a positive sense of social status. For example, if you are proud of the electronic music you make and share with friends, you'll be eager to talk to a researcher about the electronic music site where you post your work and get feedback from friends.

It is generally easier in to recruit subjects on a successful site (one that is growing, with users who appreciate it) than on a less successful one (one with a shrinking population, or a small site that appears to not be "taking off"). A site may also be problematic if it seems somewhat impersonal, for example, one where people participate but don't tend to form friendships.

Beyond the difficulty of getting people to talk to you, it is also more challenging to learn anything from a mediocre site. If it's not working well, it can be difficult to figure out why. There may be a dozen reasons why a site is less successful than others, or less successful than it used to be – and it's hard to figure out what the real reasons are. Furthermore, even if you can identify some of the reasons, they may be uninteresting (i.e., a site may be less successful because it has ugly graphics, slow performance, and poor user interface design). None of those observations contributes meaningfully to our understanding of online activity. On the other hand, there is usually something to learn from a site that is thriving – something is working, and that something is usually valuable to explore.

Terms of Service

Online sites have terms of service (TOS), and for many sites this may include explicit rules on what kind of studies are allowed there. Most ethics experts believe that researchers must comply with TOS, but the issue is complicated. In many cases, TOS are selectively enforced. If the rules are not followed by most site members, do researchers need to be held to them? TOS constitute a contract, and the legal standing of some provisions of those contracts can be drawn into question. Just because a company puts a clause in their policy does not mean the provision is legal and will hold up in court. The question of what research is ethical is arguably separate from the legal one concerning whether the terms of a TOS are legal and binding. On the other hand, some will argue that it is inherently unethical to break a contract, and hence the legal and ethical issues are the same.

If TOS of a particular site prohibit research, it is often possible to get permission to do the research with permission of the company. What the general public may not do, internal staff, summer interns, and collaborators with the company may do with permission. In these situations, some members of the research community argue that the independence of research is jeopardized. If activity on a particular online site becomes an important cultural phenomenon, it is ethically problematic if research on that site can only be conducted with the company's blessing and according to their restrictions.

In most cases, abiding by TOS is possible and is the wisest course of action. Studies that deviate from TOS can potentially be rejected from conferences and journals on those grounds. Before you invest time in exploring a potential study site, it is important to review its TOS and understand its terms. Deviating from those terms is not something to be done lightly. Note also that the wording of many sites' TOS are ambiguous, and it may be unclear what is permitted. In such cases, your IRB may be able to help you interpret the wording and decide what is permitted.

Gatekeepers

One of the trickiest concepts to understand is that of a gatekeeper. A gatekeeper is someone you legitimately must go through before approaching members of a group. A parent is a legitimate gatekeeper for their child – you must ask the parents' permission before approaching the child. A teacher is a gatekeeper for his or her class. For a small online group, particularly one with a strong and visible moderator, the moderator may serve as a legitimate gatekeeper for the group. Asking the gatekeeper's permission is often necessary. If the gatekeeper is enthusiastic about your study and willing to pass your request on to members, this may really get your study off to a strong start. On the other hand, it is not necessary or appropriate to ask permission of the site founder Jimmy Wales before starting to study Wikipedia. Many online sites do not really have gatekeepers. For a large site, you must comply with the TOS, but you do not need to obtain explicit permission from management. The size of the group and hands-on involvement of the group leader is a key to deciding whether a particular individual is a gatekeeper.

Sometimes a regular member of a group may see himself or herself as a gatekeeper when this is not really the case. In these situations, going through that person is not necessary, and may actually be damaging to your study. If the self-appointed gatekeeper is a busybody no one likes, then it will harm your study to have that person introduce you to the group; see Seidman (2006) for a discussion of "illegitimate" gatekeepers.

Choosing a community where you fit

Choosing a good site to study is not only about the site, but also about your fit for the site. Before you can begin studying a site, you need to participate there. People respond better to someone who has been a part of the group (at least for a little while), and seems to understand the community. In 2008, a team of students in the online communities class were having trouble getting interviews on bix.com, a site that presents itself as an amateur talent hour where members sing. However, once our student researchers started singing more themselves, interview subjects became much easier to recruit.

Students studying couchsurfing.com, a site where you stay on the couch at a stranger's house in another city, had no trouble at all finding interview subjects, because they went couch surfing. Their experiences staying on other people's couches and letting others stay with them built ties that made obtaining interviews trivial. The choice of the site made me nervous, because couch surfing seems risky to me. I personally would not do it, and was hesitant about the students trying. But they insisted that they had read enough to assure themselves that it was safe – couch surfers vouch for one another, so every host comes with references. Meeting people in person developed interpersonal ties, and they had one of the easiest jobs I have ever observed getting interviews. Everyone they stayed with was happy to be interviewed, and was eager to refer their couchsurfing friends.

It is easy to say, "if you're studying a talent site, start singing," but sometimes the stated purpose of a site is not its real purpose. One year a team of students chose to study a travel site – and travelling more was not the secret to getting users to participate in their interview study. The research team consisted of two single women in their 20s and one married man in his 30s. As they started their participant observation, the women had no trouble at all finding people to interview, but the man could not get anyone to respond to him. His team mates noticed that while they were talking about travel, there was a lot of flirting going on. Our male team mate took his marital status out of his profile and changed his picture from one of him and his wife to one of just himself, and suddenly interviews were much easier to get. In this case, the site seemed like a travel site, but functioned more as a dating site, with "people who like to travel" as a criteria for selection.

Note that removing his marital information was something he did only after great thought and discussion with myself and our teaching assistant. He did not in any way lie – he just removed irrelevant information. Every piece of information in his self-presentation was accurate, and he clearly disclosed that he was a student studying the site for a class. He just did not need to have his arm around his wife in his photo.

If you wish to study a site that contains sensitive information, you need to be even more careful. Lots of fantastic research is being conducted today on sites like health support sites. However, those researchers are generally educated about the topic of health support, and are usually part of a research team that includes physicians and other medical professionals. It is one thing to march into bix.com and start singing and see if anyone will talk to you, but quite another to join a cancer site and start talking with patients and their caregivers. I generally ask my students not to study sites with vulnerable populations unless it is necessary. We make exceptions for students who themselves suffer from a particular condition or have an immediate family member who is a sufferer. Personal experience gives one a sensitivity to the norms of the community that is hard to attain otherwise. Health support studies can be studied by outsiders with training and support, but it is advisable if possible to stick with something less sensitive where there are lower consequences to disturbing site activity accidentally.

Self-presentation

To conduct an ethical study, it is critical that you clearly disclose that you are a researcher studying the site. In sites that have a user profile, this fact can be placed prominently in your profile with a link to a URL with information about the study as approved by your IRB. In sites with a user-definable visual representation, you might consider looking like a researcher. Students in my class studying *Second Life* made avatars wearing white lab coats (see Figure 11.1). The fact that you are a researcher may even be put into your online name.

It is imperative that researchers avoid any kind of identity deception – even if identity deception is common on the site. Early in the history of the online communities class before sites selected had to be explicitly approved by our IRB and the instructor, one female student chose to study a site that was for men only. To gain entry into the site, she created a male avatar. When her true identity was unmasked, she was kicked off the site, and had to start her project over on a new site. (The requirement for explicit approval of site choice was added for the next class.) Defending her choice of self-presentation, she argued that gender swapping on the site was common – lots of women wanted to check out the site, and made male personas. However, a researcher is held to a higher standard than other participants of the site. It is not ethical (and not in the best interests of a successful study) to use deception in any form. Our student who took his marital status out of his profile is a rare case that stayed just on the right side of the ethical boundary: he merely omitted irrelevant information, and this even was a close call.

It is possible to do deceptive research studies. IRBs generally require that the deception be well motivated, and subjects be debriefed about the real purpose of

FIGURE 11.1 Avatar of Georgia Tech Ph.D. student, Susan Wyche, used for an online communities class project about *Second Life*.

the study. This is something to do only when necessary and with the supervision of an IRB. For an example of a deceptive study with a waiver of consent and exemption from debriefing, see Hudson and Bruckman (2004).

While we typically worry primarily about the researcher creating risks for community members, the opposite does rarely occur: sometimes the community can harass the researcher. In 2002 (a year after the 9/11 attacks), a student of Turkish descent chose to study an online site providing consumer advice. To everyone's surprise, the site turned out to be a politically charged "flame fest," with radically politically conservative members making a sport out of attacking consumer advocates as "leftists." Some of the more extreme members chose to attack our student with a Turkish name as being indirectly responsible for the 9/11 attacks. Their comments were racist and offensive. He used his real name on the site, and they found term papers he had written and posted online and used them as "evidence" of his status as a terrorist. While this kind of experience is rare (this is the only incident like it since 1997), it still is worth noting as a cautionary tale. It is important to get to know a site before committing to study it, and approach hate-filled sites with great caution. In special circumstances, extra precautions to protect the researcher may be advisable – with approval from your IRB. While we normally require students to use their real names and post links to Georgia Tech to show the legitimacy of their study, I would seriously consider having students studying contentious sites operate more anonymously in the future.

Our Turkish student responded politely but clearly to the ridiculous accusations against him. Having received a response from him, the racist site members provoked him more. The situation had already escalated when he first came to talk to the instructor and TA about what was going on. In general, the best advice for dealing with angry and contentious people online – sometimes referred to as "trolls" (Raymond, 1991) – is to simply not respond at all. It is hard to leave their accusations unanswered, but any reply will likely simply fan the flames. It is small consolation for the upsetting experience our Turkish student underwent, but it should be noted that all of this made for an extremely interesting (A+) study.

Dangers of being a "regular"

Every semester, at least one student asks to study a site where they have participated for an extended period of time – where they are a "regular" (Oldenburg, 1989). Knowing a site well certainly brings some benefits: the researcher has a depth of knowledge that can only be acquired over time. However, it is generally a bad idea for several reasons. First, it can be difficult to observe a site objectively when you are already familiar with it. You take things for granted, because they seem "normal." Anthropologists travel to remote villages to study human behavior to achieve that defamiliarization. What they observe about human relations in New Guinea ultimately helps us understand human relations in western culture: you can see phenomena better when they are unusual. The Level 70 Mage may have a hard time really understanding *World of Warcraft*, because they have already spent too much time there. Furthermore, studying your "friends" creates ethical tensions. They can't really say no to an interview if you have a longstanding relationship with them, and if they don't like what you ultimately write about them, you may jeopardize your friendship (see Pratt & Kim, this volume).

Last but not least, a "native" often finds things interesting that an outsider will not. To someone who is a longstanding community member, the history of internal squabbles among members may seem of great importance. To a neutral observer and the broader cause of research, such observations are usually decidedly uninteresting. The worst papers I receive each term are often by people studying sites they already knew too well.

Persistence in finding research subjects

Once you have chosen a site to study, and clearly marked your researcher status in your online representation, how do you recruit people to be interviewed? First, it is important not to jump right in but to "lurk" quite a bit first. It is a good idea to participate significantly before you ask anyone to speak with you at all.

There are multiple reasons for this. First, you will not appreciate the nature of the site until you have spent a nontrivial amount of time there. Our team studying the consumer advice site thought they were going to learn about peer production of content, but instead learned a whole lot about deviant behavior online. The site was something quite other than what they expected – and this necessarily shaped the questions they asked members and which members were approached for interviews. Second, people generally will not speak to you unless you have participated at least to some degree. Being an active participant creates a social context for approaching members of the group.

In sites that have synchronous communication, it is necessary to talk to someone for a while before asking if they would like to be interviewed. Then you may give them a URL with IRB-approved text describing the study. You will ideally talk with them on more than one occasion before making the request. This means you need to spend a lot of time talking with a lot of people. It is important to keep a record of who you have asked, and never ever ask the same person a second time.

In asynchronous communication, you again need to participate for a nontrivial amount before posting a message requesting study participation. It may be more effective to send individual requests than to make a public posting. Once you have made a public posting, you probably can not make a second posting to that same forum again. It is often strategic to have a private message conversation with an individual for more than one conversational turn before you make your request. You can start by complimenting someone on a post, or asking them a clarification question. The request to be interviewed will be more effective if you have already been interacting with them a few times over a period of weeks before you ask. This is a delicate business, because you do not want people to feel manipulated or used. It works better if you participate as a regular participant and then contact people with whom you have had genuine interactions.

Each term, some students fail to get any interviews at all. Typically these students did not participate or interact, but simply marched in and asked for interviews. They also typically send out one or two requests and then wait for an answer, doing nothing for a week or more. You can not simply wait – you need to assume that most requests will not be successful, and continue interacting and requesting interviews until you are successful. This is a labor-intensive process.

Even when someone agrees to be interviewed, you cannot assume that the interview will actually take place. Many people will agree to be interviewed, but then never return the consent form. Others will return the consent form and arrange a time, but then not answer the phone or show up at the time and place you have chosen. This is often passive aggressive behavior: they did not really want to be interviewed, but were reluctant to say so. Or perhaps they want to help, but are simply too busy. When a subject misses a scheduled meeting, you should follow up very lightly (i.e., you can say something like "I missed seeing you Tuesday. Let me know if you'd like to reschedule"). If they do not reply, do not contact them further. You should take the hint and give them an easy out if they are reluctant to follow through on their agreement to participate. Researchers should not take such rejections personally. It happens to everyone and is to be expected.

Although you must be persistent in requesting interviews, it is important not to disturb the site you are trying to study, and not to annoy people. The boundary between being sufficiently persistent to get results but not so persistent as to be annoying can be quite thin, and even the most experienced researcher may need to stop and talk over details of a plan with colleagues. People are more likely to get annoyed when they see the same request more than once. Thus, you may want to avoid public postings about your study, and focus more on approaching people individually. If you do post publicly, try to make sure any given user sees the posting only once.

The details of how to recruit subjects of course depend on what kinds of subjects you want to reach. That in turn depends on your research questions.

Sampling

The hardest interview to get is your very first. Once you have one interview subject, you can use "snowball sampling:" asking your subject who else you should particularly talk to (Seidman, 2006). This is particularly effective because then you have a de facto introduction to your next subject. You can say, "Pat suggested I talk with you." An introduction greatly increases the chance of someone agreeing to talk with you.

It is important to note that this biases your sample. If you talk only to one person and their friends and their friends' friends, you will not get a representative picture of activity on the site. Studies of this nature typically use "purposeful sampling" – you select people to represent certain types of participants. Think about what kinds of people should be in your purposeful sample, and work to recruit accordingly. What kinds of people you need will, of course, depend on your research questions.

Note that no matter what you do, you are more likely to talk to "regulars" – people who have spent a lot of time in the community and are invested in it. People who care less are less likely to agree to be interviewed. Incentives for participation (like small gift cards) may help you to reach a more diverse group of users. Those incentives will also often attract a few people with nothing relevant to say who just want the incentive. It is often acceptable to have a nonrepresentative sample, if this is clearly discussed in your methods and findings.

Consent, waivers of documentation of consent, and minors

After you make initial contact with a participant, you will need to obtain their consent to participate in the study. This paper will not deal with this topic in detail. However, note that we generally use a web form with a click-to-accept consent form. This process requires a waiver of documentation of consent from your IRB: clicking "OK" on a web form is not legal documentation. However, in most cases, the process of documenting consent can create more risk to the subject than participating in the study itself. There is often little or no risk to your privacy from participating in the interview – the risk is created by the consent form that contains your personal information. As a result, most IRBs will approve of a waiver of documentation of consent for such a study, particularly if the subject of the online site is not sensitive. A waiver of documentation of consent is not the same thing as a waiver of consent: the latter is much more rare.

Only adults can consent for themselves. Once someone has agreed to participate in your interview study, you need to ask if they are over 18 years of age. If they are a minor, then they need to provide assent and their parents need to sign a consent form. For minors, instead of a web form, we use paper assent and consent forms that are signed and returned to us by fax or surface mail.

Researchers are often surprised to discover that a particular subject is a minor. Teenagers often interact online with adults without acknowledging their age. In fact, Casey Fiesler studied Harry Potter role-playing groups, and found that some adults, who were role-playing romantic scenes with others, were not aware that they were interacting with teens (Fiesler, 2007). Age strongly shapes whom we interact with face to face, but these social conventions change online in ways that are complex and not yet sufficiently studied.

In some cases, researchers may wish to study a site that is explicitly for kids. It is nearly impossible for a strange adult to approach a child online and recruit them for an experimental study. It breaks too many taboos. One effective alternate approach is to leverage face-to-face contacts. For example, students in online communities class who wanted to study neopets.com found children of friends who were willing to participate, and then those children referred their friends and classmates who were also active on the site.

Summary

Getting members of online sites to agree to participate in an interview study is surprisingly challenging and complex – and the task has become more complex over time, as more and more users are annoyed by legions of internet researchers. To summarize, I offer these recommendations:

- conduct interviews in person or by phone – *not* online;
- study a successful site;
- study a site where you fit in, and can comfortably participate;
- avoid sensitive topics, if possible;
- do not study a site where you are a "regular;"
- get to know the site before you commit to study it;

- read your site's TOS, and abide by them;
- think carefully about whether your site has a legitimate gatekeeper and, if so, ask their permission to approach the group;
- go slowly – lurk before you participate, and participate before you start requesting interviews;
- be honest in your self-presentation – avoid any identity deception even if it is common on the site;
- clearly disclose your status as a researcher in your online self-presentation;
- use your real name, and provide links to your institution and officially approved details of your study;
- take extra precautions on contentious sites or those dealing with highly charged political content (you may consider not using your real name in those circumstances);
- do not respond to "trolls;"
- be persistent in requesting interviews (but not too persistent);
- do not do anything that disturbs natural activity on the site;
- never request an interview of the same person twice, and do not post interview requests in the same forum twice;
- interact with people (ideally more than once) before requesting an interview;
- do not send out requests and wait – keep working on recruiting until you are successful;
- use snowball sampling;
- use purposeful sampling;
- expect to be stood up now and then, and do not take it personally;
- if you need to interview minors, recruit them through face-to-face contacts.

References

Bruckman, A. (2002). Studying the amateur artist: A perspective on disguising data collected in human subjects research on the internet. *Ethics and Information Technology, 4*(3), 217–231.

Bruckman, A. (2006). Teaching students to study online communities ethically. *Journal of Information Ethics, 15*(2), 82–98.

Fiesler, C. (2007). Imagined identities: Harry Potter, roleplaying, and blogs. In *The Witching Hour: A Magical Compendium* (pp. 147–148). Xlibris Corporation.

Hudson, J. M., & Bruckman, A. (2004). "Go away:" Participant objections to being studied. *The Information Society, 20*(2), 127–139.

Oldenburg, R. (1989). *The great good place*. New York: Paragon House.

Raymond, E. (1991). *The new hacker's dictionary*. Cambridge, MA: The MIT Press.

Seidman, I. (2006). *Interviewing as qualitative research* (3rd ed.). New York: Teachers College Press.

12

BONA FIDE GROUPS

A Discourse Perspective

Linda L. Putnam and Cynthia Stohl

UNIVERSITY OF CALIFORNIA–SANTA BARBARA

Jane Stuart Baker

UNIVERSITY OF ALABAMA

In a special issue of *Communication Studies* (1990), we voiced concern that communication researchers were studying small groups as if they were separate from their social and temporal contexts. Challenging the research community to move beyond container models of group communication, we advocated that scholars should develop constructs and methods to enable an understanding of the multilevel and interpretive processes of groups. All groups, we argued, influence and are influenced by the environments in which they are embedded.

For almost 20 years, small group researchers have heeded this challenge and scholars have published a great deal of work that focuses on groups in context. The bona fide group perspective, first articulated in 1990 (Putnam & Stohl, 1990), has influenced this new direction and particularly in the ways that communication scholars approach the study of groups (see Frey, 1994, 2003; Poole and Hollingshead, 2005).

At its most basic level, this perspective sets forth a set of theoretical concepts that enable researchers to treat *all* groups as part of social systems linked to their contexts and past histories, shaped by fluid boundaries, and capable of influencing their environments. This approach, then, is not merely a descriptor of a certain type of group (as the term is sometimes used) or the equivalent of studying a group in its natural environment (as it has been posited), nor is it designed to distinguish among the populations from which groups are created (students, employees, strangers, or volunteers). Rather, its central purpose is to focus on the dynamic interplay among fundamental characteristics of group process that are often overlooked in the extant literature. These features highlight the diverse ways that groups form their identities through negotiating and socially constructing their boundaries, relationships, and contexts. The bona fide perspective advances the study of generative mechanisms of dynamic group process that are central to all groups, regardless of their formation, task, or composition.

Selecting methods that can capture these generative mechanisms is particularly challenging. One method, discourse analysis, provides the flexibility needed to analyze these features of groups. This chapter, then, illustrates the ways in which discourse methods are particularly appropriate for examining the interface between boundary permeability and interdependence with context, the two major features of the bona fide perspective. Using discourse methods is only one way to examine bona fide groups and we selected it because this approach provides a powerful lens for capturing both the characteristics and processes of groups in context. In doing so, however, we recognize that not all discourse studies of groups embrace a bona fide perspective and clearly not all studies that examine bona fide groups employ discourse methods.

Specifically, research that embraces a bona fide approach crosses a wide array of group settings (field, online, laboratory), group tasks (conflict management to decision making to social support), functions (creative performance, public deliberation, information dissemination), and methods. Some of the methodologies that scholars use to study groups in context include: ethnography (Kramer, 2002, 2005), in-depth interviewing (Mills & Walker, 2008), case study (Barge & Keyton, 1994), participation observation (Lammers & Krikorian, 1997), and experimental design (May & Stohl, 2009). Analytical approaches that examine features of the bona fide perspective also vary widely, including thematic and content analysis (Alexander, Peterson, & Hollingshead, 2003; Kramer, 2005), rhetorical approaches (Howell, Brock, & Hauser, 2003; Lesch, 1994), narrative analysis (SunWolf & Leets, 2004), and statistical assessment (Berteotti & Seibold, 1994). Even though these methods provide insights about the bona fide perspective, some are better than others in capturing the socially constructed boundaries, relationships, and context of groups.

This chapter proceeds in four sections. First, we briefly review the characteristics of the bona fide perspective, the different orientations that scholars bring to this work, and the methodological challenges in using this approach. Second, we define discourse analysis, describe key elements of it, explain different schools or approaches to discourse analysis, and then show how these features could be used to study groups at their boundaries. Third, we set forth steps for doing discourse analysis, illustrate their uses in studies with the bona fide perspective, and then we provide an extensive exemplar of a project, based on Jane Baker's (2009) dissertation, one that incorporates discourse analysis and a bona fide lens to study network groups. Finally, we conclude through examining ethical issues, providing an overview of the strengths and weaknesses of discourse analysis, and offering recommendations to meet the challenges of using the bona fide lens.

Characteristics, Tenets, and Challenges of the Bona Fide Perspective

As noted above, prior to the 1990s, most communication studies focused on the internal dynamics of groups without regard to how intragroup processes influence and are influenced by the contexts in which they are embedded. Group boundaries were taken for granted and viewed as static and unchangeable. The bona fide approach seeks to examine how group processes and outcomes (e.g., decision making, socialization, task completion, information processing, and conflict management) shape and are shaped by two interdependent dimensions, *permeable boundaries* and *interdependence with immediate context.*

Tenets and characteristics

We argue that the dynamic interplay between internal and external environments constitutes the essence of a group. *The first tenet of the bona fide perspective is that the ways in which groups create identities and negotiate their boundaries comprise the central mechanisms that define and constitute the nature of "groupness."*

Permeable boundaries

The first dimension, permeable boundaries, challenges the often unstated but critical assumption that groups have fixed locations, maintain static borders, and exist apart from their contexts. The bona fide perspective explicitly recognizes that boundaries are neither arbitrarily predetermined nor permanent; nor are they defined primarily by group tasks, goals, or the presence of members. Rather, boundaries are socially constructed through the interactive and recursive linkages among these characteristics: (a) multiple memberships and the enacting of member roles; (b) representative roles; (c) fluctuating memberships and affiliations; and (d) group identity that draws on collective history and shared relationships.

Following this premise, the second tenet of this perspective is that *the dynamic interactions among these four characteristics live out members' histories; shape group identity; create, reproduce, or sever connections with internal and external environments; and reflexively define the nature of a group.* Boundary construction, then, is an important group process that needs to be recognized and explored. This approach also posits a strong association between the ways that groups manage multiple and overlapping memberships and the maintenance of identity.

Interdependence with immediate context

The second dimension highlights the embeddedness of a group in its physical, task, cultural, political, historical, and social environment. The extent of a group's interdependence with its immediate context is not predetermined but rather socially constructed through the ways that groups interact in multiple environments. Thus, the bona fide perspective highlights the interconnections between communication processes and the ongoing social construction of boundaries linked to the immediate context. Interdependence is reciprocally negotiated through the following characteristics: (a) both intragroup and intergroup communication;

(b) coordinated actions within and across groups; (c) negotiation of jurisdiction and autonomy; and (d) collaborative sense-making activities, including the development of frames to interpret intergroup relationships. The concatenation of these four characteristics leads to the third tenet of the bona fide perspective: *contextual interdependence is multidimensional and waxes and wanes throughout a group's history, shaping group life through the mediation of identity, autonomy, and connectedness.*

Interdependence with immediate context shows how a group's internal processes, such as productivity, efficacy, and task accomplishment, are mutual dependent on external factors. For example, rather than seeing task dimensions, such as complexity, urgency, and accountability as static structural variables, we treat these features as socially constructed activities enacted at various points in time. Some groups actively define what they do and set their own priorities and criteria for decision making, whereas others have powerful external dependencies. Strong as well as weak external linkages may create communicative dilemmas for groups as they struggle to represent relevant stakeholder positions.

Within this perspective neither internal nor external relations are privileged. From the very conceptualization of what a group is to the methods used to study it, the bona fide perspective requires researchers to explore the production and reproduction of boundaries, the enactment of personal and collective identities, and the appropriation of historical and social context. This leads to the final tenet of the perspective: *group permeability and interdependence with context are articulated, interdependent, and interwoven processes that create, sustain, and dissolve group life.*

The many faces of the bona fide group perspective

The bona fide group perspective has generated a great deal of attention in the theoretical literature (e.g., Frey, 2003; Poole & Hollingshead, 2005) as well as in the empirical realm (e.g., Krikorian & Kiyomiya, 2003; SunWolf & Leets, 2004). We identify five distinct approaches that scholars employ in studying groups from a bona fide lens. These approaches have a direct relationship to the methods that researchers use and the ways that they incorporate the dimensions and characteristics of this perspective.

In the first approach, researchers employ the term bona fide as a *type of group.* Bona fide is an adjective or a marker that describes a category of groups, different from, for example, autonomous or experimentally created groups. For example, Galanes (2003) frames her investigation as "an exploratory study of bona fide group leaders" and Frey's award-winning text *Groups in Context* is subtitled *Studies of Bona Fide Groups.* The label of bona fide group would suggest that some groups have permeable boundaries and interdependence with context while others do not. Our argument, in turn, is that all groups enact these two dimensions.

In the second approach, scholars treat the bona fide perspective as *a catalogue* in which the characteristics form a checklist of variables that a study illustrates (Mills & Walker, 2009). These analyses describe or index how a particular group exemplifies the key characteristics of the bona fide perspective rather than exploring the dynamic processes that shape a group's trajectory. Researchers rely on excerpts from interviews (Oetzel & Robbins, 2003), components of models (Keyton & Stallworth, 2003), and checklists (Sherblom, 2003) to demonstrate the presence of bona fide group features.

In the third approach, researchers treat the perspective as *a rationale* or a framework to justify a particular type of study. Here the perspective provides a justification for selecting a project (see e.g., Frey, 1994; SunWolf & Seibold, 1998). Scholars often present the two central dimensions of the bona fide theory at the beginning and end of the articles, but the actual analyses of group process focus on other constructs. In this way the perspective becomes a research justification rather than an examination of ways that groups relate to their contexts.

The fourth approach casts the perspective as *a nascent group theory* in need of extension (e.g., Lammers & Krikorian, 1997; Stohl & Holmes, 1992; Waldeck, Shepard, Teitelbaum, Farrar, & Seibold, 2002). Scholars extend the perspective through creating new ways to enrich current dimensions and features of groups. Lammers and Krikorian (1997), for example, derived an expanded set of bona fide concepts, such as temporal control and contextual measures of degree centrality from a detailed set of observational records of surgical teams. These articles illustrate that the value of the bona fide perspective lies in the development of new features that embrace the dynamic interplay of boundary construction and interaction with context.

The final approach casts the bona fide perspective as *an enacted process* that focuses on how groups negotiate internal and external boundaries and socially construct their identities (Alexander, Peterson, & Hollingshead, 2003; Kramer, 2002, 2005; Stohl, 2007; Tracy & Standrefer, 2003). In these studies, scholars examine the ways that ongoing group processes create, maintain, and transform group identities based on the interplay of bona fide characteristics. The fundamental question that drives these studies is how do group members maintain their sense of *groupness* while negotiating their internal and external existence across time and space? This final approach fully embodies the tenets of the bona fide group theory and employs methods and processes designed to capture how boundaries and context reverberate with one another.

Methodological challenges in using the bona fide perspective

If a researcher chooses to embrace a bona fide perspective, such an investigation gives rise to four challenges that have direct bearing on research methods. First, utilizing a bona fide lens requires studying group processes in ways that capture both the internal and external communication. Specifically, researchers need to attend to a complex and dynamic network of intra- and intergroup communication simultaneously. Thus, defining the scope of relevant actors, identifying germane groups, and locating relevant contextual material are iterative processes in which a researcher moves back and forth interrogating group interactions and larger contextual sites. A second and related challenge is to identify and examine the multiple levels in which relevant interactions takes place. Groups are nested within other groups and the points of connection (i.e., the nexus) are often blurred and in flux. Research methods must be able to capture some aspects of these points of connection.

A third challenge relates to the study of boundaries; that is, it is important that researchers examine group boundaries as socially constructed features that members negotiate. Even if they construct a tightly bound group, members at some point determine how permeable or impermeable their boundaries will be. Since individual members may draw these lines differently, symbolic notions of membership infuse boundary constructions and the ways that members enact their roles. The research method must capture these symbolic boundary activities as they emerge within group interaction. A final challenge lies in the multifaceted, unfixed, and emergent nature of group identity that the bona fide perspective sets forth. As the pivotal feature of this theory, research designs and methods need to focus on the ways that groups work out their identities through negotiating their boundaries and roles within an interdependent context.

Using Discourse Methods to Meet the Challenges

As we noted in the epilogue to Frey's (2003) book, discourse methods are particularly suited to meeting these challenges (Stohl & Putnam, 2003). First, discourse analysis captures the process-orientation of negotiating boundaries within the group and in the larger intergroup context. Process refers to the ongoing features of group development and the dynamic interactions that constitute a group's context. Discourse centers on the "negotiation of meaning as it unfolds through the complex interplay of both socially and historically produced texts" (Grant, Hardy, Oswick, & Putnam, 2004, p. 22). In other words, discourse methods enable the researcher to oscillate between, within, and among groups and to track mutual influences across time and space. A related reason for using discourse analysis is to tap into the *nexus* or the nested intergroup relationships. Through a focus on texts that are drawn on and enacted in multiple arenas (e.g., intragroup, intergroup, organizational, and societal), discourse methods cross local and global levels.

Finally, discourse is a recursive process in which language both constructs and reflects back on the group process. Specifically, discourse brings "certain phenomena [in the social world] into being, including objects of knowledge, categories of social subjects, forms of self, social relationships, and conceptual frameworks" and these constructions reflect back on the intragroup process (Ainsworth & Hardy, 2004, p. 154). In effect, this method draws on and takes account of past interactions, historical practices, and social factors that exist beyond the words and actions under observation. In the enacted approach to bona fide groups, discourse analysis can capture *liminality* or those moments of flux in which a group exists in a state of suspended development as members shape, redefine, and make sense of boundary transitions (Stohl & Putnam, 2003). To show how this method can meet the challenges of studying groups with a bona fide lens, we present an overview of discourse analysis, apply this method to the extant literature, and articulate steps for using this method. Then we provide an extended example of how to analyze contradictions and dialectical tensions as a discourse method to study groups from the bona fide perspective.

Discourse Analysis

Discourse analysis focuses on the language, messages, texts, and symbols of inter-actions. It centers particularly on the forms and patterns of language use that surface in naturally occurring talk and written texts, such as documents, policies, and media publications. Discourse analysts are typically interpretive and view discourse practices as key features in the construction of social reality. Importantly, discourse analysis is not just a method or a set of techniques; rather, it assumes that words and texts both constitute and reflect back on structures and actions. High-quality discourse analysis stays close to the text and relies on language use to analyze concepts and group processes. Researchers select particular features of language under study and embrace a protocol for doing discourse analysis (e.g., speech acts, conversational analysis, or critical discourse analysis; see Putnam & Fairhurst, 2001). Scholars aim to discover patterns in the discourse use, ones that yield insights through tying them back to the group or the larger context in which groups are embedded.

As a basis for definition, discourse analysis is distinct from content or interac-tional analysis (Meyers & Seibold, this volume). Specifically, researchers who code transcripts of group interactions typically employ a priori category systems that center on message functions and characteristics. The process of coding breaks messages into units based on operationally defined categories while discourse analysis maps or charts types and interrelationships among discursive patterns, texts, and social contexts. In content analyses, overall frequency or number of occurrences of particular units drives functional and interpretive claims while in discourse analysis patterns emerge from what the language does and how mean-ings and patterns extend across time and space. The significance of an utterance is not rooted in its quantitative assessment but rather what language accomplishes in relationship to other locally-and/or globally-established texts. While the two approaches are closely related, we contend that discourse analysis is particularly suited to the bona fide group perspective because it functions recursively to link language to texts, taps into both local and global levels, and captures nested interactions that cross contexts. Moreover, the centrality of meaning in discourse analysis parallels a key characteristic of the bona fide perspective, that is, how members make sense of their boundaries and their intergroup relationships.

In effect, discourse analysis is a valuable method for examining how the dimensions and characteristics of the bona fide perspective are enacted and interpreted in an environmental context.

Units of discourse analysis

Discourse analysis typically draws on key units of language: codes, linguistic structures, language-in-action, text, context or intertexts, and meanings (Putnam & Fairhurst, 2001). Codes refer to the ways that discourse names, labels, or frames issues. For example, using the word "crisis" or "emergency" when calling for a decision, frames the situation differently than labeling it a "recurring problem." Thus, the choice of words influences how group members enact their processes and make sense of their deliberations.

Linguistic structure centers on the order, syntax, and sequence of language patterns, typically ones that evolve and change over time. Language patterns are ways to examine recurring use of discourse features. For instance, a study of the sequencing of messages in a town hall meeting focuses on the recurring question–answer patterns and how they relate to group deliberations (Tracy & Standerfer, 2003). Researchers also draw on other features of language, such as turn taking, topic shifts, qualifiers, and conversational repairs to examine how discourse enacts or accomplishes social processes. For example, Adkins and Brashers (1995) examined the role of disclaimers and powerless speech in computer-mediated groups. They observed that the use of words that function as qualifiers (such as *usually, sometimes, for the most part,* etc.) in conjunction with tag questions (i.e., statements that end with questions) reduce the credibility and persuasiveness of a group member's message.

In a similar vein, language is rooted in actions through the ways that words produce performances (e.g., speech acts), provide accounts and set forth explanations for current and past decisions, and negotiate rights and obligations. Specifically, conversational performances within and between cross-disciplinary teams demonstrate how members construct their identities in unique ways and balance tensions between groups and organizational departments (Donnellon, 1996). Examining the action features of language, like the use of directives from external agents, addresses the challenge to connect internal and external group process. Directives are speech acts that convey requests, instructions, orders, or commands (Putnam & Fairhurst, 2001). To illustrate, Jones (1992) compared gender differences in the frequency, targets, and types of directives given within a group and to a group. Finding no gender differences, she discovered that the use of solidarity expressions (e.g., *our team, we, together*) softened the face-threatening potential of giving directives within and to a group.

In discourse analysis, the notion of a text has two meanings. Specifically, a text refers to the type of data that a researcher uses, for example, transcripts, documents, reports, and a text also signifies the accumulation of social interactions.

When studying group processes, texts may include, material artifacts such as the minutes of past meetings, a tape recording of a particular decision-making session, the transcripts of interviews with group members, and the performance evaluation of a group by an external evaluator. These texts serve as records of past conversations that become assimilated and inscribed in collective forms, for example, organizational and group practices constitute texts, even when they are not in written form (Taylor, 1993). Texts, then, are also discourse units that exist in a reflexive relationship with ongoing interactions; that is, records and memories of past interactions both enable and constrain ongoing language use.

In the bona fide perspective, texts might consist of disagreements among members from past interactions, policies and practices that govern group jurisdiction; role episodes outside of the group; and/or the context features that members draw on to negotiate their group's identity. As a specific example, Tracy and Standerfer (2003) examined group interactions in a video-recorded, media-aired school board meeting. Their analysis of discourse units revealed that coalitions among members from past meetings, ways that nominations for new members were handled in the past, and the subtle challenges that one member made in the meetings were linked to the larger public audience and to future school board elections. Interactions in the present drew from discourse patterns in the past and became a resource for current deliberations that in turn shaped future interactions. Of particular note, the ways that texts crossed time and space provided an intriguing arena for examining contradictions and inconsistencies between what group members said and what they did over time.

Research on texts often focuses on macro- as well as micro-analyses, including the social and economic circumstances and the larger environments in which groups are embedded. For example, Hardy, Lawrence, and Nelson (1998) examined the discourse of a volunteer group called Community Partners, comprised of representatives of 13 different organizations that provided services (such as counseling, training, education, placement, etc.) for the unemployed. The group met monthly for over a year prior to engaging in a collaboration workshop. Their analysis centered on the discourse patterns that linked the context, the social and economic factors, and members' respective organizations (e.g., *leveling the playing field, not fighting for the pie, and forming a partnership*) that led the group members to move beyond simply sharing information to enact a shared identity. Discourse signaled which macro-level context features were salient and how members appropriated these features in their group deliberations prior to, during, and after the collaboration.

From a discourse approach, context also consists of the layering of texts, known as intertextuality. Intertexuality is defined as "a link in a chain of texts, reacting to, drawing in and transforming other texts" (Fairclough & Wodak, 1997, p. 262). Thus, a critical move that discourse analysts make is to draw on texts in the larger context to make inferences about language use, the significance of ongoing patterns, and the meanings of group interactions. To illustrate, the information-sharing process within the collaboration group in the Hardy et al. (1998) study drew on discourses from the 13 member organizations as well as the regulatory or legal environment in which this group worked. This layering or chaining together of texts across different arenas drew on intertextuality. Discourse researchers often sample across arenas (e.g., conducting a discourse analysis of legal texts or one on organizational documents) as ways of interpreting group member discussions about eligibility of clients. The linking together of texts from different arenas often provides a basis for making sense of group interactions. Of central importance in the bona fide perspective is how concepts such as interdependence with context and multiple memberships are enacted through texts that link internal and external discourses. Analyses that draw on these chains of texts, then, are particularly appropriate for examining the interface of multiple and nested intergroup processes.

Finally, most approaches to discourse analysis focus on meanings or how recurring patterns of language provide insights about interpreting a phenomenon under study. Meanings stem from the relationships among discourse use, texts, and contexts and are linked to insights about group process. Scholars who analyze particular symbolic forms, such as metaphors, narratives, rituals, and contradictions, also examine how meaning emanates through the interplay of discourse patterns, such as oppositional tensions or story plots. For example, Lesch's (1994) study of rituals in a consciousness-sharing group illustrated how story-telling episodes preserved the group's identity despite fluctuations in membership and inevitable change.

Types of discourse analysis

Four types of discourse analysis are common in the group literature: conversational analysis, pragmatics, rhetorical analysis, and critical-postmodern studies (Putnam & Fairhurst, 2001; Woodilla, 1998). Conversational analysis uses both verbal and vocal overtones, such as pauses, interruptions, topic shifts, and turn taking to analyze group interactions. Donnellon's (1996) study of the dimensions of team talk examines power differences among team members through analyzing the use of interruptions, repetition of questions, formal address, and topic changes. In a similar way, O'Donnell (1990) employs conversational analysis to examine how management exerted differential status over labor in quality of work life meetings. These studies track specific and detailed linguistic sequences that enact group differences.

Another type of discourse analysis, pragmatics, focuses on how language signals actions, for example, making a request, providing an account, giving a promise, stating an apology, or offering an excuse are activities that use language to enact these respective practices. For instance, the use of words, such as pronouns, adjectives, and verbs, can enact social distance or closeness among group members and reveal indicators of team identification through using such terms as "we" and "our" (Donnellon, 1996).

A third type of discourse analysis draws from rhetoric and focuses on argumentation, persuasion, and symbol use. Researchers center their analyses on broad-based language patterns, such as arguments, metaphors in language use, or group narratives. Bormann's (1996) symbolic convergence theory adopts a rhetorical approach to examine stories, visions, and fantasies in group interactions. Studies that investigate argument patterns in groups employ elements from rhetorical analysis and link them to argument quality, decision making, and influence processes (Seibold & Lemus, 2005; Seibold, Lemus, & Kang, 2010).

The fourth approach, critical and postmodern perspectives, examines how language exerts control or emancipates groups. Researchers study how groups are enabled or constrained in working out their identities in a social context. Analysts often focus on multiple and conflicting patterns of discourse that reveal how meanings are negotiated in ways that enable or constrain groups. For example, Barker (1993, 1999) showed how the discourse of discipline in a team enacted a form of control that was the opposite of its self-organizing mission. In a company that implemented a program of self-managed teams, he demonstrated how word choice, syntax, and language patterns in the Delta group pressured team members to conform to their own rules. Ironically, this member-imposed pressure (i.e., concertive control) constrained the group and undermined the vision of this self-organizing team.

In postmodern analyses, meanings emanate from what is present as well as absent in a text, in the ways that ambiguities open space for multiple discourses, and how discourse functions ironically to inscribe what it seeks to suppress (Mumby, 2004). Discourse units such as paradox, dialectical tensions, ambiguity, and irony are particularly useful in these analyses. Moreover, these approaches can capture the liminality of group processes, that is, the moments of transition in which a group exists in a suspended state or the ways that members enact their representative roles as simultaneously present and absent in a group's deliberations (Mumby & Stohl, 1991).

Thus, the study of discourse in groups varies from examining language-in-use to studying general and enduring systems of talk that are situated in historical and social practices (Alvesson & Karreman, 2000). Moreover, a study might examine talk and text in local interactions, such as conversational analysis and pragmatics, and relate these to historically situated texts, evident in rhetorical and critical analyses. For example, Geist and Chandler (1984) employ a pragmatic approach to investigate how members of a hospital executive group shared accounts about implementing group and organizational changes. Their focus on language use, however, was also tied to the discourse of role status embedded in group and organizational relationships. As suggested above, a scholar may combine several approaches to discourse analysis, even though his or her study centers primarily on one type. Deciding which type of analysis to use is mostly a matter of research questions, nature of the data itself, and personal preferences. Choices of theoretical frames, ways to connect to the intellectual community, and research strategy are important in selecting an approach for discourse analysis (Prichard, Jones, & Stablein, 2004).

Doing Discourse Analysis within the Bona Fide Perspective

Although a number of studies that use the bona fide perspective employ qualitative methods, only a few incorporate discourse analysis per se (Alexander et al., 2003; Barge & Keyton, 1994; Meier, 2003; Stohl, 2007; Parrish-Sprowl, 2006; Tracy & Standerfer, 2003). Discourse analysis requires selecting particular language features, engaging in systematic analysis of patterns, and linking these patterns to texts and contexts. Other qualitative approaches, such as thematic coding (Kramer, 2002, 2005), case studies with illustrative comments (Houston, 2003), and communication activity analyses (Krikorian & Kiyomiya, 2003) provide insights about the role that communication plays in studying groups in context, but discourse analysis focuses on particular language units.

Data selection and research questions

To conduct discourse analysis, researchers need to select the data, the research problem or question, and the particular features of language to analyze. Clearly, an array of textbooks offers guidance in conducting these tasks (Phillips & Hardy, 2002; Titscher, Meyer, Wodak, & Vetter, 2000; Wood & Kroger, 2000). For selecting data, textbooks typically favor naturally occurring talk; hence, transcripts of group interactions, either face-to-face or electronic ones, are certainly starting points to examine permeable boundaries and interdependence with context.

To capture the intergroup context, however, researchers may want to conduct interviews (Kramer, 2002), obtain blogs, on-discussions, bulletin boards, or newsgroups (Alexander et al., 2003; Krikorian & Kiyomiya, 2003), develop transcripts of video conferences (Meier, 2003) and media reports (Houston, 2003) or examine documents, such as training manuals (Mills & Walker, 2009), and field notes from participant observations (Kramer, 2005). Collecting data from multiple sources within and outside the group seems pivotal for examining the internal and external features of groups in context. Data that provides rich descriptors, for example, stories or reports about team coordination, incidents that reveal negotiations of jurisdiction and autonomy, and tales of enacting representative roles or multiple memberships provide excellent fodder for analyzing the concepts central to the bona fide group perspective.

The selection of data, however, is closely intertwined with the research goals and objectives that guide a particular project. Typically, we recommend selecting research questions from an interplay of the phenomena under study, the extant literature, and the overall aim of a project. For example, Barge and Keyton (1994) drew from verbatim transcripts of a City Council meeting, media accounts of the council's actions, and past reports of Council deliberations. Using a critical approach, their questions centered on the interrelationships between the Council and its immediate context, particularly regarding the role of power, coalition formation, and social influence. Moving away from the extant literature, they discovered that social influence in the bona fide perspective operated more as power issues rooted in previous decisions rather than as social influence attempts in the group's interactions. Specifically, they selected framing and reframing as discourse methods to examine the strategies that decision makers employed in defining issues and shaping the Council's identity.

In effect, interesting questions often arise from combining concepts with the bona fide group approach, understanding the extant literature, and teasing out puzzles that arise from the group experience. A "puzzle" is what seems peculiar, unpredictable, or contradictory in the situation. Interesting questions often challenge what participants or scholars hold to be true.

Discourse units and data analysis

Selecting which discourse units to analyze is often the most tedious step in the process. These choices come from moving back and forth through the data, with an eye to the research problem and the concepts under investigation. Knowledge of the context, the participants, and the larger picture of the group are crucial in selecting language units, tracking them, and linking them to social and organizational texts. For example, with the bona fide lens, researchers might target codes such as the use of pronouns, nouns, and identity markers that refer to external roles (Stohl, 2007), problem framing, such as how members name and label issues and then foreground them for the group (Barge & Keyton, 1994), or language structures such as sequences of questions and answers that expose hidden agendas and residues of past conversations (Tracy & Standerfer, 2003).

The research puzzle also draws the analyst to particular language units. For example, in a study of how groups resisted a new team system, Parrish-Sprowl (2006) was puzzled by the pervasiveness of such phrases as "management has tried these things before" and "the union is an obstructionist that creates suspicion." Working from a social/historical context, he discovered that a "discourse of failure" emanated from the texts of past change programs, oppositional rhetoric between labor-management, and weak links to a highly competitive market. These patterns helped him analyze how the labor groups enacted fixed boundaries and loose interdependence with context in ways that explained institutional resistance.

To make interpretations from the data, we recommend a systematic analysis of the discourse units through mapping, plotting, or counting them. This charting of exact phrases, words, and descriptors allows patterns to arise from the data. Patterns can also incorporate linguistic features of context, time, or development markers, provide links to texts and context features, and tap into the overall group process. Some analysts use such computer programs as ATLAS or NVivo to track units, their interrelationships, and patterns. These programs consolidate and plot different words, sort the patterns, and provide a way to index them. Although they are useful sorting techniques, they do not provide interpretations of the data or test research claims (Phillips & Hardy, 2002).

Making interpretations requires organizing discourse patterns in meaningful ways; moving back and forth between the patterns and the data, making potential claims, and testing out inferences about them. Some analysts rely on repetition of units, juxtaposition of patterns in the text, content of the interaction, and inter-relationships among texts (intertextuality) to make claims from the data. We view this step as a very messy process that requires considerable tolerance for ambiguity combined with a desire to tease out subtleties and insights in the data.

To illustrate how discourse analysts make claims, we use the example of Cynthia's (Stohl, 2007) study of an executive business retreat that focused on the succession of a company president. Her analysis was part of a larger project in which several researchers examined the transcripts of three days of meetings from a Canadian Broadcast Corporation's documentary film about Sam Steinberg's search for a successor. From a bona fide perspective, the first step was to understand the history of the group and the context in which the group was operating. Methodologically, this step enabled Cynthia to link specific features of the group discourse to other local, global, and institutional texts, that is, intertextuality. Virtually all the articles she reviewed (scholarly and popular press) as well as several case studies of the corporation made explicit reference to the Steinberg family's prominence as a highly successful Jewish-Canadian family. In the documentary neither the narrator nor any of the group members explicitly stated that the family was Jewish; however, the group interactions embodied the religious/ethnic identity in shared experiences, stories, rituals, and language use.

With this background knowledge, Cynthia began her analysis by focusing on the references to the organization's Jewish family heritage embedded in the discourse. Connecting her analysis of language-use patterns (e.g., pronouns, references to external context) with group members' representative roles, she drew interpretations about an individual's position as both an outsider and an insider, and the potential that this role offered for opening group boundaries within the organization's context and tightening interdependence to an external market. She read through the text repeatedly and tracked words that referred to external texts (e.g., Jewish heritage, Friday night dinners, and family relationships) as patterns that revealed the status of group members during the succession meetings. Then, she drew on her background and knowledge of Jewish customs to interpret these references as both organizational and Jewish-insider and outsider symbols.

This analysis raises a critical and often unacknowledged point about using discourse analysis to make social claims (Cunliffe, 2003). Reflexivity refers to the role of the researcher in selecting, analyzing, and interpreting the data. It advocates that an investigator needs to inform readers about his or her stance in a study. Thus, discourse scholars make no claims about objectivity, even though they argue for systematic, patterned, and detailed analyses of texts. Specifically, Cynthia, in her study of the executive business retreat, describes her own background and how it influences her selection of discourse methods and interpretations. Importantly, someone unfamiliar with the Jewish context of this group might miss the subtle references and the insider/outsider nature of group membership.

Thus, we see that doing discourse analysis with a bona fide group lens requires drawing data from a wide array of sources, particularly inside and outside the group. We urge scholars to select and map discourse units through moving back and forth among key concepts, puzzles, and knowledge of the extant literature. These patterns, when intertwined with relevant texts in the larger context, yield an understanding of group identity rooted in a bona fide perspective.

In the next section, we provide an extended exemplar of a project that adopted a bona fide perspective and discourse analysis to examine diversity groups in an organization. Through discussing the goal of her project, data collection, and data analysis, Jane examined how these groups negotiated their boundaries and identities in ways that both enabled and constrained their overall missions.

A study of employee diversity networks

Jane's (Baker, 2009) research focused on employee network groups as units aimed at creating awareness of organizational diversity and addressing issues of gender, race, disability, or sexual orientation in the workplace. Her overall research question was: how do members construct group boundaries in ways that enable and constrain their diversity goals? She selected groups as the primary unit of analysis because the diversity networks functioned as distinct units with executive committees and officers enacting tasks for their units. Thus, her study examined how each group communicated with its officers and its own members, with other network groups, and with corporate departments such as the Diversity Office. It also addressed how each group negotiated its identity and visibility within the company.

She studied two network groups, a Black and an Hispanic one, at a large international oil corporation called "Summit." The group members were employees who were part of multiple groups and connected with the diversity and human resources departments. She got access to the groups through an human resources officer, who was an acquaintance and knew the Vice-President of Diversity. Rather than beginning with a particular discourse approach, she developed initial research questions based on the bona fide group characteristics. In this way, Jane held group boundaries and interdependence together simultaneously without placing one as figure and the other as ground.

Then, Jane read over the texts multiple times and finally selected dialectical analysis as a discourse approach for the research. As a type of postmodern approach, dialectical analysis focuses on the ways that discourse signals the struggle to hold oppositional tensions together. In particular, it centers on how group members embrace the "both–and" of bipolar pairs. For example, when group members indicated a push–pull between wanting exclusive membership in one diversity group and preferring to belong to multiple groups, they expressed a contradiction or inconsistency between opposites that potentially negated each other. Dialectical analysis focuses on how participants see the opposites as interdependent, feel the tensions from the push–pull between them, struggle to hold them together, and make choices or take actions that manage these tensions in explicit or implicit ways. Deciding to do a dialectical analysis was not an easy one for Jane and she explored a wide array of options, including studying narratives and group rituals. But after multiple readings of the interview texts, field notes, and organizational documents, she was struck by the tensions that the groups faced in achieving their goals and crafting their unique organizational identities; hence, a dialectical analysis seemed isomorphic with the data and the group-related problems. In selecting this approach, she embraced a postmodern discourse stance to probe the puzzle of why these groups seemed to have problems achieving the fullness of their potential.

Data collection

Her main data consisted of 30 semi-structured interviews: 14 with members of each group and two with corporate diversity officers. She contacted the officers of the networks and asked them for names of members to interview. The interviews with diversity officers revealed the nexus between the groups and the relationship of the groups to the organizational context. Interviews captured how members made sense of their groups' identities, negotiated boundaries that defined their groups, and described the ways that groups embraced corporate values and vision. They also revealed the insights of the active and less active members.

In addition, she collected web documents and took field notes at several network events, including executive board meetings and two diversity conferences. She used the field notes of the executive board meetings to reveal tensions within the groups, namely, attracting versus losing members, focusing on group versus individual success, and prioritizing the network versus individual members' jobs. For example, she analyzed comments, such as "I have always looked at it [the network group] not like a volunteer opportunity, but as an extension of what I do." and "… anytime I need some time to … do something that's related to the network, if it doesn't contradict my job or put me behind …, then the staff here is more than willing to let [me] do it." These different quotations revealed the tensions among the members between either treating the network group as part of an employee's job or pitching in only when it would not interfere with day to day work.

Data analysis

To analyze the data, Jane took the comments from the interviews and put them into spreadsheets that represented the eight characteristics of the bona fide perspective. These charts basically plotted themes related to different organizational areas or targets (e.g., individual ties to the networks, intragroup communication with members, interactions with other network groups, and relationships with management). For example, if an officer discussed difficulties in retaining members, Jane positioned this theme under the characteristic of fluctuating group membership. This process revealed a number of contradictions and mixed messages. For example, members expressed pride in the autonomy of their networks, yet some of them felt that upper management policed them. They experienced uncertainty about their networks' positions in the company, yet they considered Summit to be supportive and rewarding of diversity groups. Networks boasted hundreds of organizational members, yet officers often felt a lack of employee involvement.

Discourse units and research findings

These contradictions pointed to the use of dialectics as a discourse unit. A contradiction referred to the enactment of seemingly antithetical group practices and dialectics centered on the struggle to embrace both of these bipolar pairs (Putnam, 1986; Tracy, 2004). Thus, Jane treated both poles in the contradictions as essential for social practices, examined how the groups experienced tensions, and focused on how members made choices in handling the tensions between the poles. To identify the contradictions, Jane selected words and key phrases that revealed oppositional stances in a group's practices, tensions in constructing its boundaries, and external dilemmas that arose in the intergroup context (Johnson & Long, 2002). For example, members used phrases like "including versus excluding outsiders," "participation in one versus multiple networks," and "similarities versus distinctions among the groups."

After Jane grouped these polar opposites into her charts, she created a tree that outlined overarching contradictions and alignment of opposite pairs. This practice produced a theme by examining how the network members struggled to connect the poles and multiple related tensions. Thus, she used the contradictions to make inferences about overarching and recurring tensions that the groups faced (e.g., autonomy versus control and tightly versus loosely coupled network groups). This step led to a list of major dialectical tensions involved in negotiating group boundaries, ones related to the characteristics of bona fide groups.

To illustrate, members experienced tensions in hosting both *narrow and broadbased* activities, in focusing on both *single and multiple* network memberships, and in advancing the *group as a whole while promoting the careers of individual members*. These tensions aligned with fluctuating and multiple memberships in that employees often belonged to more than one network group and groups planned programs that appealed to their own members as well as to employees outside their groups. Even though broad-based activities drew a large number of participants, active members often saw them as less relevant to their group's needs.

Moreover, since employees could belong to more than one network group, membership often fluctuated, a pattern that resulted in a less stable base of members. In effect, by examining the choices made to manage these dialectical tensions, Jane related them to the characteristics of stable but permeable boundaries.

After this initial stage of coding, Jane then classified the dialectical themes into targets: (1) intragroup, (2) individual-group, (3) group-organization, and (4) intergroup. She remained close to the discourse to make this classification by relying on descriptions of internal communication among members or relationships to the other network groups. She also identified two major types of intergroup tensions: (1) between network groups; and (2) between the group and the executive leadership of Summit. At the intergroup level, tensions often emerged through embracing both cooperation and competition between the networks, such as working together on key events while competing for the evaluation of premier group in the Diversity Office's performance appraisal. At the group-organizational level, tensions typically emerged because of struggles between organizational policies and a group's need for actions.

Overall, this type of analysis employed the constant comparison method, commonly used in grounded theory (Charmaz, 2006; Corbin & Strauss, 2008). Constant comparison relied on systematic comparison of similarities and differences between the themes. Hence, sets of dialectical tensions and themes were compared within targets (e.g., intergroup) and across targets (e.g., individual-group with intragroup). These comparisons yielded concepts based on core themes that operated at higher levels of abstraction above the unit of a discourse phrase and that integrated the dimensions and characteristics of bona fide groups to ways that group members managed the tensions. This step paralleled Strauss and Corbin's (1990) analytical approach of action–interaction strategies, that is, how a particular phenomenon was handled or carried out and the consequences of these actions.

To arrive at this final step, Jane drew from the theoretical work on dialectics to determine how members negotiated the push–pulls of competing tensions. She employed approaches from classic dialectical theory and compared interactions with actions to determine how the groups managed their tensions (Poole & Putnam, 2007; Seo, Putnam, & Bartunek, 2004; Tracy, 2004). For example, source splitting occurred when some members handled these tensions by favoring one pole while others selected the opposite one. Specifically, the officers and active members of the groups often felt controlled by the Diversity Office while the less active members believed that Summit empowered the groups. Thus, the groups managed the autonomy and control dialectic through source splitting among their members. Analyzing how dialectical tensions were managed aided in deciphering relationships among them and drawing conclusions about group boundaries and the intergroup context. In particular, Jane discovered a form of concertive control that operated at the intergroup rather than the group or the organizational levels (Barker, 1993). This type of control, in conjunction with highly permeable boundaries and loose interdependence with organizational context, resulted in silencing the groups from becoming advocates for radical change in corporate diversity practices.

Jane's journey through this project led to some important findings. Her use of multiple data sources and the comparison of the two groups allowed her to develop an understanding of how the interplay between contradictions and dialectical tensions influenced the construction of group boundaries and identities, as espoused in the bona fide group theory. Creating one spreadsheet for each bona fide characteristic allowed her to align dialectical tensions with a specific target for within and between group relationships. Since the same set of tensions could cross multiple characteristics, she experienced a challenge in deciding which dialectical tensions were most relevant to interdependence with context or permeable boundaries, but she relied on the definitions and explanations of the bona fide group characteristics to govern these choices.

In effect, this example demonstrated how a researcher could use discourse analysis to hold both dimensions, stable but permeable boundaries and interdependence with context, together in one project. A critical feature in her study was linking the dialectical tensions with particular targets, such as individual-group, intragroup, intergroup, and group-company relationships. In Jane's study, the interrelationships of dialectical tensions and bona fide characteristics illustrated a system of intergroup concertive control that both enabled and constrained the networks. Moreover, the powerful control system was completely outside the awareness of group members.

Concluding Recommendations

Discourse analysis, then, focuses on the features of language, messages, texts, and symbols. It is particularly appropriate for capturing interactive processes, negotiation of meaning, and local–global features of group life. Scholars interested in conducting discourse analysis in groups might consult Phillips and Hardy (2002) and Wood and Kroeger (2000) as primers for doing this type of research. As such, it provides an effective method for examining boundary negotiations, identity formation, and interdependence with context – key features of the bona fide perspective. Of particular note, discourse analysis is a very inductive process, even though researchers often cast their findings in deductive ways. Hence, teasing out puzzles through sticking close to the data requires ordering discourse units in ways that reveal patterns and promote discoveries.

This process, in turn, raises ethical issues, ones that create challenges for discourse analysts. Specifically, since discourse researchers use examples from written and oral texts to substantiate their claims, they need permission to make verbatim excerpts public. Hence, informed consent statements should contain clauses that indicate how discourse excerpts might be used. In a related way, researchers need to preserve anonymity and confidentiality of participants; hence, they should mask the identity of speakers when they use long verbatim quotes or they should edit and abbreviate quotes to disguise a participant's identity. Another ethical concern for discourse analysts relates to sticking close to the data and making inferences linked directly to the analysis. Researchers should rely on language patterns to make claims and should avoid speculating about a participant's unconscious internal motives. These ethical concerns, while generic for all researchers, pose particular problems in discourse analysis.

Ethical concerns in discourse research relate to the strengths and limitations of this method, ones rooted in the multilevel interpretive moves that characterize this method. As previously noted, discourse analysis is particularly effective at capturing the developmental and contextual features of groups. It is sensitive to a process orientation and the role of sensemaking in negotiating boundaries and identity formation. Through an emphasis on the role of language in different context arenas, it bridges local interactions with global texts and takes account of past practices. These strengths, however, should be balanced with significant challenges in using this method.

In particular, the method requires written or oral texts that are drawn from naturally occurring talk, interviews, media reports, video conferences, blogs, online discussions, or documents. Collecting these texts is one of the first challenges in doing this work. It is also labor intensive and requires detailed attention to word by word and sentence by sentence analysis; hence, it demands discipline and a zeal for finding patterns in a maze of data. This mass of data can overwhelm a researcher and stifle progress in data analysis. Thus, analysts need tolerance for ambiguity in plotting themes, selecting discourse units, and developing a systematic way to lay out the data. Above all, researchers need to be guided by a generic problem that might lead to a specific puzzle that arises from rather than being imposed on the data. In effect, discourse analysis offers a number of strengths that are conducive to studying bona fide groups, but researchers need to embrace the challenges and realize that qualitative studies necessitate time-consuming, systematic analyses.

Based on these strengths and limitations, several issues emerge as appropriate and inappropriate for doing discourse analysis, especially with the bona fide perspective. First, discourse analysis should be rigorous, systematic, and tightly interfaced with texts and layering of texts in the group environment. Most importantly, researchers need to ask what are the language patterns doing and how do they relate to negotiating a group's identity and boundaries? Specifically, discourse analysis works best if researchers draw together language and action. For example, how do references about intergroup interactions parallel reported and observed practices? How do these discourse patterns relate to the negotiation of a group's identity for its members and within its environmental context?

Second, discourse, as with any method, works most effectively when scholars have an interesting problem or a dilemma. Without an interesting puzzle, analysts often become lost in the micro-details of doing the analysis. For Jane's study, the interesting puzzle came through aligning dialectical tensions with the bona fide characteristics. Before Jane began her analysis, she wondered why the group members were so satisfied with their network experiences but felt that diversity issues at Summit had not changed much in the past decade. In trying to discover how these groups functioned, why members were so pleased with them, and why they were relatively ineffective in altering company diversity practices, she discovered a system of very permeable boundaries amid intergroup concertive control. Thus, the groups concentrated their energies on keeping each other in check rather than focusing on management practices and changing the patterns for promoting minorities. The initial puzzle guided her quest, but prior to the study, she could not identify or understand the dialectical tensions, how they worked, and how they produced concertive control.

Third, we recommend that analysts make interpretations that stick close to their data. The source and type of data provide clues as to the inferences that researchers can legitimately make. Researchers should avoid making inferences that are too global if no data are available to substantiate a particular claim. For example, Jane's reliance on the dialectical tensions that arose from her data led to the finding of concertive control through layering sets of tensions in relation to multiple targets and characteristics of the bona fide perspective. If she had employed a priori categories of types of dialectics used in previous research, she would not have discovered how group tensions functioned at the intergroup and organizational levels. Importantly, she drew on a generic category system for dialectical tensions and this practice to extends knowledge about dialectical theory. Hence, in discourse studies, the traditional notion of generalizability becomes transferability, that is, how might the claims from one setting generate concepts that would transfer to another setting. In Jane's study, the types of dialectics linked to bona fide characteristics, the management of these tensions, and the notion of intergroup concertive control sets forth concepts that might transfer to other research settings.

Finally, discourse analysis is not the same as a case study. Hence, analysts need to highlight language patterns, not the details of a case, the context, or the sequence of events. Language use should be examined through a particular approach, otherwise the patterns become lost in a play by play description of events. These recommendations provide direction for conducting discourse analysis, especially for studying groups in context. Hopefully, this chapter shows that integrating a bona fide perspective with discourse analyses will enhance our understanding of collective behavior in new and exciting ways.

References

Adkins, M., & Brashers, D. E. (1995). The power of language in computer-mediated groups. *Management Communication Quarterly, 8,* 289–322.

Ainsworth, S., & Hardy, C. (2004). Discourse and identities. In D. Grant, C. Hardy, C. Oswick, & L. Putnam (Eds.), *The Sage handbook of organizational discourse* (pp. 153–173). London: Sage.

Alexander, S. C., Peterson, J. L., & Hollingshead, A. B. (2003). Help is at your keyboard: Support groups on the internet. In L. R. Frey (Ed.), *Group communication in context: Studies of bona fide groups* (2nd ed., pp. 309–334). Mahwah, NJ: Lawrence Erlbaum.

Alvesson, M., & Karreman, D. (2000). Varieties of discourse: On the study of organizations through discourse analysis. *Human Relations, 53,* 1125–1149.

Baker, J. S. (2009). *Buying into the business case: A bona fide group study of dialectical tensions in employee network groups.* Doctoral dissertation, Texas A&M University. College Station, TX.

Barge, J. K., & Keyton, J. (1994). Contextualizing power and social influence in groups. In L. R. Frey (Ed.), *Group communication in context: Studies of natural groups* (pp. 85–105). Hillsdale, NJ: Lawrence Erlbaum.

Barker, J. R. (1993). Tightening the iron cage: Concertive control in self-managing teams. *Administrative Science Quarterly, 38,* 408–437.

Berteotti, C. R., & Seibold, D. R. (1994). Coordination and role-definition problems in health-care teams: A hospice case study. In L. R. Frey (Ed.), *Group communication in context: Studies of natural groups* (pp. 107–131). Hillsdale, NJ: Lawrence Erlbaum.

Bormann, E. G. (1996). Symbolic convergence theory and communication in group decision making. In R.Y. Hirokawa & M. S. Poole (Eds.), *Communication and group decision making* (2nd ed., pp. 81–113). Thousand Oaks, CA: Sage.

Charmaz, K. (2006). *Constructing grounded theory: A practical guide through qualitative analysis.* Thousand Oaks, CA: Sage.

Corbin, J., & Strauss, A. (2008). *Basics of qualitative analysis* (3rd ed.). Thousand Oaks, CA: Sage.

Cunliffe, A. L. (2003). Reflexive inquiry in organizational research: Questions and possibilities. *Human Relations,* 56, 983–1003.

Donnellon, A. (1996). *Team talk: The power of language in team dynamics.* Boston, MA: Harvard Business School Press.

Fairclough, N., & Wodak, R. (1997). Critical discourse analysis. In T. A. Van Dijk (Ed.), *Discourse as social interaction: A multidisciplinary introduction* (Vol. 2, pp. 258–284). London: Sage.

Frey, L. R. (Ed.) (1994). *Group communication in context: Studies of natural groups.* Hillsdale, NJ: Lawrence Erlbaum.

Frey, L. R. (Ed.) (2003). *Group communication in context: Studies of bona fide groups* (2nd ed.). Mahwah, NJ: Lawrence Erlbaum.

Galanes, G. J. (2003). In their own words: An exploratory study of bona fide group leaders. *Small Group Behavior, 34*(6), 741–770.

Geist, P., & Chandler, T. (1984). Account analysis of influence in group decision-making. *Communication Monographs, 51,* 67–78.

Grant, D., Hardy, C., Oswick, C., & Putnam, L. (Eds.) (2004). *The Sage handbook of organizational discourse.* London: Sage.

Hardy, C., Lawrence, T. B., & Phillips, N. (1998). Talk and action: Conversations and narrative in interorganizational collaboration. In D. Grant, T. Keenoy, & C. Oswick (Eds.), *Discourse and organization* (pp. 65–83). London: Sage.

Houston, R. (2003). In the mask of thin air: Intragroup and intergroup communication during Mt. Everest disaster. In L. R. Frey (Ed.), *Group communication in context: Studies of bona fide groups* (2nd ed., pp. 137–156). Mahwah, NJ: Lawrence Erlbaum.

Howell, S., Brock, B., & Hauser, E. (2003). A multicultural intergenerational youth program: Creating and sustaining a youth community group. In L. R. Frey (Ed.), *Group communication in context: Studies of bona fide groups* (2nd ed., pp. 85–107). Mahwah, NJ: Lawrence Erlbaum.

Johnson, S. D., & Long, L. M. (2002). "Being a part and being apart:" Dialectics and group communication. In L. R. Frey (Ed.), *New directions in group communication* (pp. 25–41). Thousand Oaks, CA: Sage.

Jones, K. (1992). A question of context: Directive use at a Morris team meeting. *Language in Society, 21,* 427–445.

Keyton, J., & Stallworth, V. (2003). On the verge of collaboration: Interaction process vs. group outcomes. In L. R. Frey (Ed.), *Group communication in context: Studies of bona fide groups* (2nd ed., pp. 235–260.). Mahwah, NJ: Lawrence Erlbaum.

Kramer, M. W. (2002). Communication in a community theater group: Managing multiple group roles. *Communication Studies, 53,* 151–170.

Kramer, M. W. (2005). Communication in a fund-raising marathon group. *Journal of Communication, 55,* 257–276.

Krikorian, D., & Kiyomiya, T. (2003). Bona fide groups as self-organizing systems: Applications to electronic newsgroups. In L. R. Frey (Ed.), *Group communication in context: Studies of bona fide groups* (2nd ed., pp. 335–365). Mahwah, NJ: Lawrence Erlbaum.

Lammers, J. C., & Krikorian, D. H. (1997). Theoretical extension and operationalization of the bona fide group construct with an application to surgical teams. *Journal of Applied Communication Research, 25,* 17–38.

Lesch, C. L. (1994). Observing theory in practice: Sustaining consciousness in a coven. In L. R. Frey (Ed.), *Group communication in context: Studies of natural groups* (pp. 57–84). Hillsdale, NJ: Lawrence Erlbaum.

May, R., & Stohl, C. (2009). *Destabilizing the information sampling bias: A bona fide group perspective on the hidden profile paradigm.* Unpublished honor's thesis, Department of Communication, University of California – Santa Barbara, Santa Barbara, CA.

Meier, C. (2003). Doing "groupness" in a spatially distributed work group: The case of videoconferences at Technics. In L. R. Frey (Ed.), *Group communication in context: Studies of bona fide groups* (2nd ed., pp. 367–397). Mahwah, NJ: Lawrence Erlbaum.

Mills, C. & Walker, K. (2009). Early intervention or early imposition: A bona fide group perspective analysis of the parent–child early intervention relationship. In T. Socha & G. Stamp (Eds.), *Parent–child communication outside the family: Exploring communication in parent–child–society relationships* (pp. 154–170). New York: Routledge.

Mumby, D. K. (2004). Discourse, power, and ideology: Unpacking the critical approach. In D. Grant, C. Hardy, C. Oswick, & L. Putnam (Eds.), *The Sage handbook of organizational discourse* (pp. 237–258). London: Sage.

Mumby, D. K., & Stohl, C. (1991). Power and discourse in organizational studies: Absence and the dialectic of control. *Discourse & Society, 2,* 313–332.

O'Donnell, K. (1990). Difference and domination: How labor and management talk conflict. In A. D. Grimshaw (Ed.), *Conflict talk* (pp. 210–240). Cambridge: Cambridge University Press.

Oetzel, J. G., & Robbins, J. (2003). Multiple identities in teams in a cooperative supermarket. In L. R. Frey (Ed.), *Group communication in context: Studies of bona fide groups* (2nd ed., pp. 183–208). Mahwah, NJ: Lawrence Erlbaum.

Parrish-Sprowl, J. (2006). Team facilitation of organizational change: A case study from a bona fide group perspective. In L. R. Frey (Ed.), *Facilitating group communication in context* (pp. 203–223). Cresskill, NJ: Hampton Press.

Phillips, N., & Hardy, C. (2002). *Discourse analysis as theory and method.* London: Sage.

Poole, M. S., & Hollingshead, A. B. (Eds.) (2005). *Theories of small groups: Interdisciplinary perspectives.* Thousand Oaks, CA: Sage.

Poole, M. S., & Putnam, L. L. (2007). Organizational paradox. In S. Clegg & J. R. Bailey (Eds.), *International encyclopedia of organizational studies* (Vol. 3, pp. 1146–1149). Thousand Oaks, CA: Sage.

Prichard, C., Jones, D., & Stablein, R. (2004). Doing research in organizational discourse: The importance of researcher context. In D. Grant, C. Hardy, C. Oswick, & L. Putnam (Eds.), *The Sage handbook of organizational discourse* (pp. 213–236). London: Sage.

Putnam, L. L., & Fairhurst, G. T. (2001). Discourse analysis in organizations: Issues and concerns. In F.M. Jablin & L. L. Putnam (Eds.), *The new handbook of organizational communication: Advances in theory, research and methods* (pp. 235–268). Newbury Park, CA: Sage.

Putnam, L. L., & Stohl, C. (1990). Bona fide groups: A reconceptualization of groups in context. *Communication Studies, 41*, 248–265.

Seibold, D. R., & Lemus, D. R. (2005). Argument quality in group deliberation: A structurational approach and quality of argument index. In C. A. Willard (Ed.), *Critical problems in argumentation* (pp. 203–215). Washington, DC: National Communication Association.

Seibold, D. R., Lemus, D. R., & Kang, P. (2010). Extending the conversational argument coding scheme in studies of argument quality in group deliberations. *Communication Methods and Measures, 4,* 46–64.

Seo, M. G., Putnam, L. L., & Bartunek, J. M. (2004). Dualities and tensions of planned organizational change. In M. S. Poole & A. H. Van de Ven (Eds.), *Handbook of organizational change and innovation* (pp. 73–107). New York: Oxford University Press.

Sherblom, J. C. (2003). Influences on the recommendations of international business consulting teams. In L. R. Frey (Ed.), *Group communication in context: Studies of bona fide groups* (2nd ed., pp. 263–290). Mahwah, NJ: Lawrence Erlbaum.

Stohl, C. (2007). Bringing the outside in: A contextual analysis. In F. Cooren (Ed.), *Interacting and organizing: Analyses of a management meeting* (pp. 185–198). Mahwah, NJ: Lawrence Erlbaum.

Stohl, C., & Holmes, M. (1992). A functional perspective for bona fide groups. In S. A. Deetz (Ed.), *Communication yearbook 16* (pp. 601–614). Newbury Park, CA: Sage.

Stohl, C., & Putnam, L. L. (2003). Communication in bona fide groups: A retrospective and prospective account. In L. R. Frey (Ed.), *Group communication in context: Studies of bona fide groups* (pp. 399–414). Mahwah, NJ: Erlbaum.

Strauss, A., & Corbin, J. (1990). *Basics of qualitative research: Grounded theory procedures and techniques.* Newbury Park, CA: Sage.

SunWolf & Leets, L. (2004). Being left out: Rejecting outsiders and communicating group boundaries in childhood and adolescent peer groups. *Journal of Applied Communication Research, 32*(3), 195–223.

SunWolf, & Seibold, D. R. (1998). Jurors' intuitive rules for deliberation: A structurational approach to communication in jury decision making. *Communication Monographs, 65,* 282–307.

Taylor, J. R. (1993). *Rethinking the theory of organizational communication: How to read an organization.* Norwood, NJ: Ablex.

Titscher, S., Meyer, M., Wondak, R., & Vetter, E. (2000). *Methods of text and discourse analysis.* London: Sage.

Tracy, S. J. (2004). Dialectic, contradiction, or double bind? Analyzing and theorizing employee reactions to organizational tensions. *Journal of Applied Communication Research, 32,* 119–146.

Tracy, K. & Standerfer, C. (2003). Selecting a school superintendent: Sensitivities in group deliberation. In L. R. Frey (Ed.), *Group communication in context: Studies of bona fide groups* (pp. 109–134). Mahwah, NJ: Erlbaum.

Waldeck, J. H., Shepard, C. A., Teitelbaum, J., Farrar, W. J., & Seibold, D. R. (2002). New directions for functional, symbolic convergence, structurational, and bona fide group perspectives of group communication. In L. R. Frey (Ed.), *New directions in group communication* (pp. 3–24). Thousand Oaks, CA: Sage.

Wood, L. A., & Kroger, R. O. (2000). *Doing discourse analysis: Methods for studying action in talk and text.* Thousand Oaks, CA: Sage.

Woodilla, J. (1998). Workplace conversations: The text of organizing. In D. Grant, T. Keenoy, & C. Oswick (Eds.), *Discourse and organization* (pp. 31–50). London: Sage.

13

UNDERSTANDING GROUP DYNAMICS USING NARRATIVE METHODS

SunWolf

SANTA CLARA UNIVERSITY

> In West Africa, when a person in the village becomes sick, the Healer will ask that person, "When was the last time that you sang? When was the last time that you danced? When was the last time that you shared a story?"
>
> *(Cox, 2000, p. 10)*

It was a dark and stormy night on the oncology ward of a large children's hospital when I first stepped into story. There was a room no doctors could enter, a room of sanctuary, where hospitalized children knew they would be temporarily free of painful intrusive treatments. The life battles these children confronted necessitated long periods of hospital-style incarceration – even the most engaging toys or creative crafts become too familiar. I was a trial attorney, also trained as a play therapist, who volunteered on weekend evenings on the oncology unit of a children's hospital where play is used to help children heal, rather than healing based on adult-favored conversations. Play is especially effective in groups of similarly struggling peers. Late one Saturday night, on duty as the play therapist in this special room, I found myself surrounded by six bored adolescent patients (it is the nature of cancer treatment that children spend a great deal of time in the hospital and soon exhaust the possibilities of available crafts).

Caught in a moment of epiphany, I (who did *not* consider herself to be a storyteller) asked my patient-companions if they'd like to turn out the lights and tell ghost stories. They were thrilled and fell to darkening the room. I gave them a scary story my father had given to me, stretching it as far as I could. The shivers and chills, shared in the community of group, were far different versions of *fear* than the ones these children faced daily. They were no longer afraid in this story-moment of dying, of pain, of questions no one was answering for them; it was healing-fear, safely stored in a story-container. They laughed, screeched, giggled. A trial attorney by day, my logical brain went into action and I set up camp in the local library until I had unearthed every book I could find about storytelling. I traveled the country to study with the best storyteller-teachers I could find. I knew more stories would always be needed (SunWolf, 2004a, 2005). The power of story began for me in the 1980s, as I awakened to the power of real-world face-to-face story-sharing in peer groups. When I later left the courtroom for graduate school and the study of small group communication processes, I found that I had "story eyes," narrative lenses for seeing the possibilities for understanding social behavior through story.

What is a Narrative Analysis Approach to Research?

> **story,** *n.* 1. a narrative, either true or fictitious, 2. a way of knowing and remembering information; a shape or pattern into which information can be arranged and experiences preserved, 3. an ancient, natural order of the mind, 4. isolated and disconnected scraps of human experience, bound into a meaningful whole.
>
> *(SunWolf, 2007, p. 445)*

It turns out that not all scholars are on the same page (or even reading from the same book) when it comes to narrative analysis. For Polkinghorne (1988), narrative analysis is linked to discourse analysis (discourse is a unit of utterance larger than a sentence). Berger (1997) takes on the question of how scholars distinguish between narratives and nonnarratives – excluding lists, pictures, drawings, and photographs. Narrative analysis is defined by Riessman (2008) as a *family of methods* for interpreting texts that have in common a storied format (oral, written, visual), with the actual analysis of data as only one component.

Stories offer a way of knowing and remembering experiences, providing a powerful structure for binding together seemingly isolated or confusing events in a meaningful way (SunWolf & Frey, 2001). Fisher (1987) suggested that people might be best understood as *homo narrans*, organizing experiences into stories with plots, central characters, and action sequences that carry implicit and explicit lessons. If, as Fisher (1985, 1987) argued, people do inherently pursue a narrative logic, and that all humans are essentially storytellers, it follows that stories will be embedded in group talk, culture, and task.

Narrative analyses may be thought of as involving one or more of three parts: (a) the data collected (narratives produced during group processes or shared by group members outside of group meetings); (b) the analytical or theoretical approach; and (c) research design tools the scholar uses to make sense of the narrative data about or from a particular group. All three, however, are aspects of the methodology of narrative analysis that can be applied to studying small group issues.

A narrative method might focus on the data collected

When a researcher's data consist of stories, the researcher has narrative data. For example, scholars who study family groups coping with illness often look at the stories that emerge from these groups:

> A family's or group's ongoing struggle to deal with a seriously ill member can be understood as the co-construction of a group story that allows them to cope with changes in identities, relationships, and duties imposed by an illness.
>
> *(Adelman & Frey, 1997; studying an AIDS hospice)*

They chose to capture on video the personal narratives of the residents about the challenges and rules of group living. In order to learn how childhood peer groups construct social boundaries, my collaborator and I collected retrospective narrative data from 682 adolescents (SunWolf & Leets, 2004, p. 208; research design described later in this chapter), using a survey instrument that asked, "Think of a time when a group of people excluded you and it hurt your feelings. What did someone in that group say or do that let you know you would not be included?" One white male teenager wrote, "They needed an extra person, so I offered. The person making the team said I was not good enough, even though we played on the same school football team."

A narrative method might focus on how data is analyzed

When a researcher examines collected data to make sense of it, narrative analysis occurs, in an attempt to lift meaning, qualitatively or quantitatively. A quantitative approach to analyzing data using narrative analysis might focus on creating a coding scheme, training coders for acceptable reliability on similar data using that scheme, and reporting, for example, frequencies of themes, metaphors, events, outcomes or the story-element of interest. SunWolf and Leets (2003), using an original narrative coding scheme, trained coders to analyze more than 600 adolescent personal stories about specific times they failed to speak up even when they disagreed with their peer group's decision to exclude an outsider (finding the narrative accounts revealed six reasons given for failing to voice disagreement with the social exclusion of outsiders by their peer groups, described below). Meyers and Seibold (this volume) describe specific methodological issues in developing coding schemes. An example of a qualitative approach to narrative analysis of small group behaviors is the work of Conquergood (1994), who used ethnography, moving into Chicago's tenements to gain access to group processes, symbols, and meaning-making of street gangs, as *participant-observer*.

A narrative method might focus on specific design tools that generate narrative data

Questions to participants intended to generate data in story format can be thought of as narrative research tools. "Tell us about a time when ..." is a format designed to produce stories about past events. Seibold and I (SunWolf & Seibold, 1998) used hypothetical story stems ("Imagine you are on a jury and ..."), for example, to generate story-thinking in citizens called for jury duty and waiting to be called in a jury assembly room (described later). Researchers at the US Center for Disease Control and Prevention, for example, used a narrative approach studying community groups in sub-Saharan Africa to change people's willingness to behave in healthier ways (Galavotti et al., 2005). In order to motivate increased participation in cervical cancer screening among Yakama Indian women, scholars at the University of Washington's School of Nursing and Yakama Indian Health Center joined existing storytelling circles of Alaskan Native American women (Strickland, Chrisman, Yallup, Powell, & Squeoch, 1996), listened to their cultural tales, then used those stories to create consistent interventions with the values of these women. In other words, narratives were gathered (data), then those stories were reformatted into health care advertising interventions.

All three aspects of narrative analysis, or only one, may be chosen by a group scholar as part of the methodology of studying small group processes and outcomes. Each of them, in addition, involve challenges and choices in the design, collection, or data interpretation, as illustrated by my experiences with a narrative approach to understanding small group dynamics.

Strengths and Tradeoffs of Narrative Methodologies for Group Scholars

Narrative methodologies can allow group scholars to connect more closely with the groups they study. The symbolic–interpretive perspective of group dynamics (Frey & SunWolf, 2004, 2005) argues that the vitality of any group relies upon the members' symbolic activities. Storytelling, in addition to ritual and symbols, are primary means by which a group's members bind themselves together as a group. Many peer groups, teams, and families also function as ongoing story circles, in which a collective point-of-view in that group is created and recreated. Members are both listeners and tellers. The power of small groups as story sharing has long been recognized, for example, in psychotherapy, self-help groups, and support groups. Ingroups and outgroups (critical to forming a sense of identity in small groups) are formed, in part, by the sharing of stories about "us" and "them" (SunWolf, 2008).

In addition, a narrative analysis of group talk, for example, offers scholars an opportunity to re-analyze existing transcripts, videos, or audio tapes of groups, in order to cast light upon the functions of personal, cultural, or co-created member stories that emerge during any group's task talk. Groups may tell identity stories (stories that describe "who we are"). Further, a narrative approach to understanding small groups can benefit from qualitative, quantitative, or triangulated methods (as illustrated later in this chapter). Another challenge of studying the dynamics of small groups is that the scholar is confronted with complex, multilayered data (such as member differences, group culture, embeddedness in community or organizations, member exits/entrances, conflict, creation and maintenance of group identity, leadership styles, rules, and multimember participation in group talk). Finally, as will be seen in the studies described in this chapter, a narrative approach acknowledges the many variables that impact narrative data. As a result, it both allows penetration of these variables by providing a focus (stories shared, stories co-created, and even story battles during group argument, for example) while, at the same time, being faithful to coexisting variables by including them in the research design or description of the results.

Three Exemplars of Studies that Used Narrative Analysis as a Component of Group Methodology

In this chapter, stories about my own narrative analysis of group data are shared, describing some of the challenges, choices, and findings that emerged from my research. I have drawn upon various forms of narrative analysis in studying three different types of small groups: social groups (childhood peer groups), decision-making groups (juries), and professional training groups (task groups). Drawing specifically upon the three-part framework of approaches used in narrative analysis introduced above (e.g., a focus on the actual data collected, an analytical or theoretical approach, or a research design tool), my studies of group dynamics in childhood peer groups incorporated a research design tool and the collection of narrative data, my study of jury deliberations focused on an analytical and theoretical approach to understanding naturally occurring group storytelling, and my work with professional training groups created a narrative research design tool to facilitate different group outcomes and experiences.

My goal is to offer specific scholarly experiences from the field, in order to encourage group researchers to feel better prepared to design and analyze research from a narrative perspective.

Studying social groups: childhood peer groups

When I became interested in childhood peer groups, it was the result of conversations I had with many of my students enrolled in group courses about the painful memories they had of being left out. I remembered my experiences in changing schools and being picked last for teams and I remembered, as well, excluding unwanted outsiders at school. I partnered with a fellow graduate student who was now on faculty at Stanford University and was interested in social justice issues. We wanted to learn how children and adolescents communicated social rejection, as well as how outsider children attempted to negotiate peer group inclusion. Our first methodological decision was to ask children directly about these events.

Research designs involving children are challenging because permission and consent at so many levels are required, as well as full review by university human subjects committees. It would be easier to design a study asking adults to remember these events, but the trade-off is that time has passed and distortions of painful events occur. We decided we wanted participants who were at the transitional cusp of childhood and adolescence, that is, those in their first year of high school. This would allow us to ask about current events for teens, as well as have them recall events only a few years before, in elementary school. The written permissions involved included: parents, student-participants, school administrators, and classroom teachers. Months later, we had university approval of the consent forms, only after showing them the survey that would be given. It took more than six months and many phone calls to get schools and classroom teachers to agree to participate.

Many considerations were involved in designing the survey, including using language that would be familiar to young teens, items that would be relatively easy to answer, and a length that would not generate fatigue and disinterest. We included narrative questions, frequency questions, and scaled questions: "Think of a time when a group of people excluded you and it hurt your feelings. What did someone in that group say or do (behavior and/or words) that let you know you would not be included?" followed by 1½ inches of white space. One frequency question asked, "How often have you experienced being left out? [Circle One]: never, not often, the same as most people, more than other people, constantly." This was in anticipation of the narrative analyses we wanted to do of the first question (e.g., did self-described frequently left out children respond differently than rarely-left out children?).

One question that generated narratives about social rejection was, "Sometimes we are part of a group that excludes somebody – even though we don't really agree and afterwards we regret that we didn't say anything. Think about a specific time when this happened. What happened?" We included a Likert scale on this same issue: "As you think about it now, how stressful was it for you to watch someone else be excluded when they wanted to be part of a group or activity?" followed by seven numbers, where 1 was "not at all stressful" and 7 was "definitely stressful." In all, we included questions that could generate narrative data for three separate studies that interested us: children's moral rules about peer group exclusion; the stress of watching or participating in social rejection; and specific words or behaviors used by children to exclude others.

Since we wanted to gather multiple datasets, this informed our decision to gather more than 500 participants, in order to generate enough data for multilevel analyses: the variety of stories gathered offers stronger support for findings, in addition to allowing for narratives to be analyzed by gender or ethnicity. We had decided to gather the data personally at each school and in each classroom, rather than use graduate students. As soon as we had full consent from a school and several classroom teachers (it would involve the students filling out the form in class), we went to the school with the consent forms, set a date for us to show up, and arranged with teachers for an alternative in-class activity for students who did not have permission. It did take large chunks of time, but it resulted in 682 adolescents (377 males, 301 females, four undeclared), from five high schools, from large urban school districts in northern California. The median age of students was 14, with 41.3 per cent Caucasian/White, 18.8 per cent Asian American, 24.2 per cent Hispanic American, 5.7 per cent African American, and 10 per cent other. We wanted to be able to analyze the stories gathered about social exclusion in peer groups by gender and ethnicity (although we elected to collapse these categories into "White" and "NonWhite," since there were not enough participants in specific non-Caucasian categories for statistical analyses).

We decided to do statistical as well as narrative thematic analyses in one study (SunWolf & Leets, 2004) to answer our research questions about how children and adolescents communicate peer group boundaries to unwanted children who attempt to join their groups and how stressful students reported it was to attempt to join a group or watch someone else be rejected by a group. Quantitative data were analyzed using nonparametric method, since we were not interested in central tendencies (peer rejection is not evenly distributed or similarly experienced); we wanted the relations between perceived elevated, moderate, and low levels of stress for various rejection events. Table 13.1 contains exemplars of the narrative data. To understand how peer group members communicated boundaries to outsiders, we analyzed the themes in participants' narratives using Owen's (1984) three-part criteria: recurring themes, repeated themes, or forcefulness. Both researchers made sense of the data in terms of first-order explanations from student answers and second-order explanations through our eyes as researchers. We took a bottom-up approach in analyzing responses by collecting short responses about similar events, then examining these responses for what they revealed about the communication of rejection. Once we identified broad themes, we looked for connections among them, collapsing several themes into single categories when similar communication dynamics were present.

For another part of our data, we trained undergraduate students to code narrative data from the survey. We were interested in the narratives participants shared about times when they were members of a group rejecting someone, but they disagreed with their group's rejection. What reasons did students give for specific storied events? An original coding scheme was developed, taking a grounded theory approach, that sought to build generalizations from the data collected (Frey, Botan, & Kreps, 2000), so we began an initial cycle of data analysis by reading each of the exclusion narratives for emerging themes that addressed words adolescents used to conceptualize their own failures to voice disagreements with

Table 13.1 Adolescents' responses to story prompts about peer group rejection

Response themes	Representative responses to: "What did someone in that group say or do that let you know you would not be included?"			
	Males		Females	
	White	NonWhite	White	NonWhite
Ignoring	I was new to the school and didn't know anyone. When it got time for recess I had nothing to do or anyone to lay with. In the class I had to do my work alone and was ignored by the other students.	When I was the only black person in a group they totally ignored me and whispered stuff to each other about me. I was talking and they would make a comment like, "is that the wind?"	The group wouldn't look at me, they seemed to be avoiding looking at my face and they turned their backs towards me. At recess in 5th grade there was a group of girls I always wanted to play with, but whenever I tried to they gave me dirty looks and ignored me or told me to go away.	They ignored me. I felt sad and wondered what I did. They don't acknowledge my presence, don't say hi or anything. They pretended I wasn't there.
Disqualifying	They needed an extra person, so I offered. The person making the team said I was not good enough, even though we played on the same school football team. They said my friends and I could not play because I was white. Their exact words were "no white boys allowed."	Because of some difficulty I have with my heart. They mocked me and made fun of my situation telling me that I'll die or have a heart attack. I went to the group and they said that I was dumb and asked me what did this word mean and so on.	They said I couldn't play cuz I wasn't good enough of a player. They were mean. They said I couldn't be in the group because I was too ugly and I wasn't German which made me "not good enough" to be in the group.	I was an athletic girl, so I was usually one of the first people picked. But that day I had to wear my Girl Scout dress to school. The boys saw that I was dressed too much like a girl and wouldn't let me play. Oh you don't even speak English.

Insulting	They told me to shut up and go away because I was stupid. Get out of here, stupid, you're gay. They said I was fat and stupid, so they didn't want to include me in anything. I walked away crying.	I was told no "Ghandhi's" were allowed. You ain't cool, you are weird. Someone was making fun of my head's shape. They were making fun of me by saying "E.T. phone home." They said that I was too stupid and ugly.	The boys said I couldn't play with them because I was a girl and I had cooties.	Other kids did not want to play with me because I had a mole on my nose. They would call me mole face. They said, hey, look at the ugly girl how she dresses.
Blaming	They said we have even teams and that I could not play very well. Because no one knew me and because of all my freckles. I wanted to play but they said no cause I wasn't good enough. They said no one liked me and I should just go away.	Because I don't look good enough. I'm not a good dresser kind of person. I was standing with who I thought were my friends and they told me don't hang out with them because I stutter. I was very hurt inside.	People do it all the time because I'm not like them or I'm not cool!!! Back in grade school I was really large (fat) and people would exclude me all the time. It hurt me a lot.	I wasn't a fun or smart person to be with. They said I wasn't popular enough. Once a group of girls didn't want me to hang around with them because I wasn't like a girly girl.
Creating new rules	They said I didn't get there in time and they already started. I would have to get another person in order to play. They ignored me and left me for last pick. Then they told me I couldn't play because it was uneven.	I went to the basketball courts and asked if I play and they said they were making teams. So as they chose I looked, there was 12 people so it would be 6 on 6. I waited then when I was the last one, the captain said, "It's already we'll make it 6 on 5, we have a better team."	They said "Sorry no more room" but I knew that there was about 5 spaces left. I saw someone else go up there to ask if they could play and the kids let that person in. They said that they had to go home because they were leaving, I thought it was cause they didn't like us.	One time in 8th grade we were supposed to be getting into groups of four people and then I was going over to this one group to ask them if I could be in their group because they only had three. When I asked them, they were like, "No, because Amanda was going to be in our group."

peer-group exclusion. Two senior undergraduate communication students were trained as coders, first practicing with a sample that used the same questionnaire (data generated only for purposes of coder training), then discussing their differences only during practice sessions; training sessions took a total of 12 hours, including individual practice. Finally, a written four-page "dictionary" that defined categories and offered examples was developed for the coders to use. Students coded every reason appearing in a response, with intercoder reliability per category calculated on a 20 per cent sample of actual data (ranging from a low of 0.90 to 1.00). As a result of this coding, a frequency table for each category in the coding scheme emerged from the analysis (see SunWolf & Leets, 2004, Table 1; for the reasons student offered for vignettes of failing to disagree with social rejection as a group member). We learned that however careful the coder training, narrative analysis that uses coding benefits enormously in terms of intercoder reliability with the development of a dictionary defining the categories, to insure all coders continue to use the researchers' definitions.

One further lesson in using survey instruments to gather narrative data emerged from my experience with research instruments that failed to allow respondents to add something important that related to the study. In other words, there are often stories triggered for some participants that would be of interest to researchers, but it was not specifically asked. Our survey instrument was three pages long (with plenty of white space for narrative answers), but at the end of the third page, we created a three-inch box that read:

> Optional Feedback: Sometimes a survey doesn't give people a chance to say everything they want to. We would be glad to hear more about any thoughts, opinions, or stories you have on being left out. Use this space in any way you like.

While only a few dozen used the space, those who did gave us gold: stories of a friend who committed suicide after being rejected so often, additional stories they had no space for, and many artistic renderings of children being rejected by a group, to name a few – priceless.

Studying decision-making groups: juries

As opposed to using a narrative approach by asking adolescents to recall stories about peer group events, I had the powerful experience of observing how stories emerged and were used by group members during their task.

At the time I was attempting to study juries for my master's degree, but there were no transcripts or tapes of jury deliberations to analyze (deliberations have been protected by the courts since the 1950s). Many studies existed using mock juries but, as a trial lawyer, I saw unacceptable research design issues (discussed in SunWolf & Seibold, 1998), including truncated deliberation times (often only

20–30 minutes), too few mock jurors (often 3–5) to replicate the more complex group dynamics of 12 jurors, no outcome saliency (mock jurors knew their "verdict" did not affect anyone and they were not hearing from real witnesses whose credibility they had to evaluate), and no real-world diversity among jurors (college students). My challenge, then, was to design a study that came closer to replicating real jurors and their deliberation task. What I really wanted was to be a fly on the wall of the jury room – I wanted access to the storied vignettes that I anticipated would occur during jury talk.

My research question did not involve narrative ("What rules about jury deliberations do citizens bring with them to jury duty?"), but the design used a narrative tool to get at those rules. Group members bring expectations, values, and rules with them to new group experiences; I wondered what rules citizens might have already formed about jury deliberations. I was also challenged by the issue of gaining access to the group of interest. I wanted to get to people as close to the moment *before* they became jurors as I ethically could. I drew upon my knowledge of what happens in jury deliberations (from talking to jurors as an attorney after verdicts) to create imaginary narratives and ask people to complete the story (story stems).

Narratives and stories can be used as stimulus materials in designing a study. Imaginary vignettes in a narrative format can be used to learn about the perspectives group members carry about possible future problems that may emerge in a group. (There are many small groups a scholar might not be able to sit in on or record, but a scholar may know the many issues that have faced similar groups, for example, in the military, in health care settings, or with police units designed to rescue hostages.) I talked to lawyers about the worst events they had heard happening in a jury for one of their trials and I remembered my own, because I wanted my data to help attorneys and judges think in new ways about the challenges of being a juror with a group task. I wrote five imaginary jury deliberation events that frequently occur in deliberations (choosing a leader, deciding how to vote, dealing with a member's misconduct, deciding whether or not to ask the judge a question during deliberations, and deciding how long to deliberate before giving up when no agreement had been reached). Pre-testing designs using narrative vignettes, however, is critical to uncovering misunderstandings and editing the vignette to its shortest salient format. Since attorneys were not the group of interest, I pre-tested the vignette on people I knew who could, conceivably, be called for jury duty. This resulted in useful editing. For example, my final vignette involved the dilemma facing jurors in deadlock. However, when I used that word, many people were uncertain what it meant. Jurors come in a wide variety of ages, ethnicities, professions, and educational backgrounds. After feedback, the final narrative vignette read:

> Time passes. The jurors have all been talking for a along time about what the best verdict would be. Some jurors want to announce that the group

cannot reach an agreement. They don't want to talk any more at all. Other jurors want to keep talking, because they think everyone will be able to agree if people keep talking. One juror says, "What should we do?" What do you say?

Potential jurors, I realized, did not need to hear the word "deadlock" or "hung jury," just the story of how that might develop.

The next issue was gaining access to relevant participants. What might be "as close to a real juror on a trial" as you can get, without being a real juror (who is, of course, not allowed to talk to outsiders, so ethically unavailable)? In the jury assembly room are people who have been summoned for jury duty from jury-eligible citizens in the judicial district. I knew people are generally bored waiting and might volunteer to help in a jury study. While attorneys are not allowed in a jury assembly room, I realized I was now a graduate student, instead. I knew that jury commissioners could grant permission, so I made a face-to-face appointment with the jury commissioner in a nearby county, described my study and empha-sized that the value to citizens might be that they would feel they had contributed to an interesting study, even if they never served. I not only received permission to come on as many days as I wished, but I was introduced by the jury commis-sioner to the citizens called for jury duty and they were told they could volunteer, if they liked. I had the use of a table inside the jury assembly room, in the back. (Bored groups of people "waiting," can be a rich source of data about group experiences, values, beliefs, rules.)

Since I wanted to capture the tone of voice, hesitancies, and linguistic cues of participants, I elected to use a tape recorder rather than a written survey. I read the stimulus vignettes (the citizen was asked to speak in the role of the imaginary juror); it took about five minutes per participant. The first vignette was:

> Imagine that you are a juror on a case and that the trial is coming to an end. The witnesses have testified. The evidence for both sides is completed. The attorneys gave their closing arguments. The judge told the jury the law that applies to the case. The jurors have just been sent into the jury room to talk and to reach a verdict. Each juror takes a chair and sits around the table. One juror says, "The judge told us to pick a foreperson before we do anything else. How are we supposed to do that?" One juror turns to you and says, "How should we decide who should be the foreperson?" Imagine that you are on the jury and that you are going to make a suggestion about picking the foreperson. Speak as if you were talking to the other jurors. What would you say?

> (SunWolf & Seibold, 1998, p. 292)

The subsequent decision was when to stop gathering data. As a master's stu-dent, I stopped at 100; today, it might be 500. Could I have used undergraduates and gathered more data? I rejected this possibility as injecting too many variables, including the fact that I wanted to experience the citizens myself and that I was, as a former attorney, entirely comfortable and familiar with courthouse protocols and rules.

My second study of jurors, however, did transport me into a real jury room during deliberations. As luck would have it, I was still looking for a way to study real jury deliberations for my doctorate two years later – at the same time that the Arizona Supreme Court agreed for the first time to allow television filming of four criminal trials (SunWolf, 2006b, 2007).[1] Since CBS was advertising the editing versions on their documentary of these trials, I became aware of them; one news article reported that scholars would later have access to the full tapes. Knowing data existed, however, and gaining access to it, turned out to be separate things.

After numerous calls to CBS, as well as the Arizona Supreme Court, I finally found out that two law schools were going to be given sets of complete tapes. I had recorded the CBS show, which provided background information on the trials, the charges, the issues, and clips from trial and deliberations. I needed the complete tapes, however. I called the head librarian at the first law school scheduled to receive the tapes, found out the tapes had not arrived yet; I was first on the list to get a copy. I paid for the physical copying of the tapes and they were shipped months later. (Learning lesson: consider a variety of people who may have authority to grant access to the data.)

I only wanted to analyze deliberations, but had to purchase the entire trials. I watched hours of tapes to find the point where deliberations began and made copies of those portions. At this point my research question involved both my roles as lawyer (Do jurors commit misconduct during deliberations?) and as group scholar (How do jurors structure themselves and communicate on their task during deliberations?). I started with the shortest tape and, using shorthand, created verbatim transcripts (none existed). Once the first stories started appearing in deliberative talk, I knew I wanted to use a narrative lens to learn about the types and functions of stories jurors told to one another during their deliberative task. I was now able to use the transcripts of deliberations.

These group deliberations contained both social and task talk, but were also were rich with shared storytelling:

> That happened to me once. Years ago, I was on the freeway and a guy, I was in real heavy traffic, and I couldn't move out of his way. He wanted to pass me. And I looked in my rear view mirror and he held a gun up like this. He didn't point it at me, but it scared the hell out of me.
>
> *(SunWolf, 2006, p. 118)*

Rather than counting the stories or frequencies of their occurrence, I chose to do a qualitative analysis, making many passes through the transcripts to find emerging themes and story types. I created a rough draft table of the stories that appeared, then plugging in each spoken example that I was able to think more deeply about how these stories were functioning for each group (both juries that reached a verdict and those that deadlocked). I needed to see the story talk across trials, side by side. As a result of many passes through the data, similar types emerged (e.g., jurors sharing personal stories). For a story typology to be valid, it should include all stories that emerged, as well as have data from more than one juror across all three trials. Some categories were expanded, for example "counterfactual" stories (in which a person imagines something that did not, in fact happen) were separated into "what-if" stories and "if-only stories," which allowed deeper understanding about a juror's story-thinking into imaginary past events of the trial (if-only) or imagined future events (what-if). At the same time, I collapsed some potential categories, relegating all personal stories into one category, no matter what the topic; this decision was based on the fact that myriad personal events were told, but it was the fact that the juror was sharing an experience which was the point of interest, not the content.

Finally, I looked at what happened after a story vignette was told in order to understand the effect narrative talk had on deliberative argument. I found, for example, that "story invitations" (e.g., What would your husband have done?) triggered story arguments about hypotheticals that were not part of the trial evidence. Further, "personal stories" or "common knowledge stories" had the effect of introducing improper out-of-court evidence for jurors to use as support for their positions. Throughout, however, I was aware that the data was rich with non-narrative talk and events (use of humor, for example); I made the decision to separate that for future study. With thick data it is seductive to analyze it all, but the resulting clutter can obscure the events of interest.

The story of jury deliberations did not end for me, however, with this first story-typology study. Several years later, I looked at this deliberation data again. I was now a professor, interested in how group theories might explain events during jury deliberations. In particular, I became interested in the counterfactual talk that was embedded in the narratives shared; that is, stories about what-might-have-been or what-might-yet-happen. Jurors were sharing counterfactual communication through the deliberations in all trials, imagining nonevidentiary events.

At this point, I stopped looking at the data and began a literature review of counterfactual thinking and regret, since jurors seemed to be trying to undo what did happen, as well as imagine unwanted outcomes of their verdicts (SunWolf, 2006b). I remembered that Bormann (1986, 1990) described developing Symbolic Convergence Theory while analyzing small group talk and I reread those articles. Studying naturally occurring group talk, Bormann found that a group's unique culture, task identity, and cohesiveness are created through shared fantasies, in story format. Bormann's Symbolic Convergence Theory explained how shared fantasies and imagined stories, shared by group members, functioned to shape a group's identity, which, in turn, influenced task and relational group processes. Bormann found group fantasy themes (shared stories group members tell one another), fantasy chains (or strings of connected stories), and convergence (during group talk, the private symbolic worlds of members will intersect, coming together). Communicated fantasies perform important functions for small groups in that they: (a) help to create a unique group identity; (b) allow difficult information to be dealt with indirectly; (c) direct a group's task by endorsing or condemning particular behaviors; and (d) provide entertainment and fun for group members. Shared fantasies, thus, help group members to make some sense of their group experience and to anticipate task demands.

This explained some of the imagined stories I was analyzing, prodding me to look at how they functioned in the group. One thing stood out: when a juror shared an imagined story about an unwanted outcome of a verdict (e.g., What if we find him not guilty and then he goes out and kills someone else?), other jurors would join the story and retell it with an acceptable outcome (e.g., What if we find him not guilty and the police realize they have to find the real gunman, who is still out there?). When jurors could not successfully retell a counterfactual story with an unwanted outcome from a verdict, the jury deadlocked. I decided to attempt a sequential outline for a new theory of group communication that explained the process by which a group member's imagined decisional regret impacted a decision-making group's task before analyzing the data further (SunWolf, 2006b).

Decisional Regret Theory is based upon the concept that people want to live in a predictable world, yet we all have a lifetime of having faced unwanted outcomes from our decision choices. It looks at the production, sharing, and reconstruction of pre-decisional imaginary narratives that allow alternative decisional outcomes to be anticipated a type of shared communication (counterfactual storytelling) under specific circumstances (anticipation of making a meaningful decision), also predicting how other group members will respond and various effects on the decisional task (group regret, for example, and deadlock). Returning to existing scholarship in the middle of analyzing data can be a powerful way of redirecting one's attentions; it was for me. Finally, using the lenses counterfactual thinking literature and this new theory that emerged from looking at storied data, I sorted all juror stories into pre-existing typologies of counterfactual thinking (see SunWolf, 2006b, Table 2). The narratives made sense as counterfactual talk attempting to avoid an unwanted outcome from group decision making (Table 13.2).

Studying task groups: professional training groups

In addition to using a narrative approach by asking adolescents to recall stories about peer group events and observing how stories emerged and were used by

Table 13.2 Story types emerging during jury deliberation talk

Story type	Trial A: Drug smuggling	Trial B: Shooting	Trial C: Store robbery	Trial D: Drug smuggling
What-if	Let's just say, for a moment, that she was a very bright person. Same actions, but bright. Calls up and says, "Tell Specta I'm at Madison County Jail. Good-bye." The whole case goes out the window.	What if Tho Tran was maimed, and what if he was blind, or if somehow it affected his spinal cord and he was, you know, in a wheel chair the rest of his life?	I'm the person that sat in the classroom and hated the "what if" people. "But what if-", and I would go, "Shut up!" But I'm not in school any more, and we're talking about a human life.	J #C: But see that's exactly my point. My thought is, it could have been reversed. There's no reason she couldn't have done the same thing.
If-only	What would have happened if, had she not had – if – how would we have decided, just for curiosity, if we didn't have any tapes from prison?	If he had not have gone right out there and shot at those people. If the natural course of events would have taken place, they would have just drive away.	It would have been nice to know, if she was a witness, if you could've asked her, "At which point is the helicopter being dispatched?"	If only the defendant had testified.
Common knowledge	If they already had the tickets when they went in, then you would check the luggage outside. If I already had my tickets, I'd check my luggage outside.	Even cops shoot accidentally. It's not that unusual. Because he has to make that decision so quick. And he's even been trained. And he made the wrong decision. And it's totally unfortunate.	It's hot, more than 100 degrees outside. I've gone to the grocery store and taken cans off the shelf and put 'em in my trunk, got home, picked it up, and it was cold. 'Cause when it's 100 degrees out, you know, 70 degrees is cold.	Common sense would tell you that she somehow came up with this money, very easily, and got bail. And he had to sit there.
Personal knowledge	Well, one thing, 'round trip on certain airlines, round trip tickets were more expensive than one-way. It depends on which airlines. I've flown on Frontier Airlines, to Missouri for $69 one-way. Got there, you know, $69 back. That was $130. Round trip was $200.	I've been in situations even where, I mean, you may not be directly involved, and it's like you can hardly talk. It's like it takes a minute. And then, all of a sudden, once you start talking, you can't – it's like [begins shaking] you're shaking, you can't stop. …	It's legal in Arizona to have a weapon in a holster. I've been in there more than once with guys, they weren't cops, just guys who had a holster and their gun was fully exposed. They'd walk in there and buy a candy bar and pay for it and leave.	The people that book them don't know what they're coming in for until they fill out that paper. They frisk them, they fingerprint 'em. "Give me your valuables." They might ask, "What're you here for?" But they would have no idea what the circumstances were.

Reasonable person	So, she comes back out and she tickets the baggage. He sees four tickets. She says, "Okay, I bought these tickets under Sarah Nunez and Marcos Bowdas." Why did they not use Urbano's name? I mean, if there's nothing to hide here, or whatever, why didn't we just use our real names?	What I would have done, as a reasonable person, would've gotten the license plate. There are cops in close proximity, because it only took one minute to get there. He could have had the license plate number. They would have been caught.	You just, you don't do it. You hope it will get by, you pause a little bit. You call 9-1-1. You go, "Yeah," and to me	The thing it goes back to for me is she said she knew the guy for a year. Well, I mean, if I know somebody for a year, I'm going to know what their job is, their family. Even if I know someone for three months, I'm at least going to know where they live, what they do for a living. I'm going to know if they do drugs.
What probably happened	Okay, they already miss the early flight. So, go in and find this next flight going to Newark. Takes care of the money end of it. All of a sudden you have two unemployed people and he's got a big wad of cash. Takes care of that. They go to check the luggage with the sky cap.	That always has been his role. Somebody's going to call down to their house, or that's his assumed role. Troy or Greg, whichever one was home, "This is your role. We want you to go and investigate."	So I'm trying to think what they were thinking. There's a good chance that they assumed that if there was no gun that the case was closed, no knowing that somebody else's testimony that they had a gun would be enough to sink them. I'm just guessing that …	Well, this is just a thing, might not make much sense, but I think that she's the one that was higher up on the ladder …
Story invitations	If I didn't know what was in those suitcases, I'd never say those were my suitcases. I wouldn't. Would you? Would you [to another juror]?	What if, six months down the line, he does it again – but this time, he kills somebody?	What would be an armed robbery that wasn't dangerous?	Example #1: Do you pick up hitchhikers? Example #2: Would you have been relaxed? [Answer: Yes, I would have.] After you found out?

group members during their task, I have also used narrative as an intervention to create new outcomes at the outset of small group processes.

As a group scholar, I recognize that I now have narrative eyes, so, even when working with task groups as a trainer/facilitator, I am likely to draw upon narrative tools to help those groups in their processes. Once upon a time, I was a trial attorney, appointed as a public defender to represent indigent clients who were charged with criminal acts. Seventeen years into this career, in the middle of a death penalty trial, I resolved that if I could save the life of that client, I would return to graduate school to study people, persuasion, and social thinking, so attorneys could learn more about real jurors. At the University of California, Santa Barbara, I studied group processes and communication, focusing on juries. After graduate school, I accepted a position at Santa Clara University, which has a law school; I was invited to participate as faculty in the law school's annual Death Penalty College,[2] so I did not face the challenge of gaining entrance to small groups of attorneys in training programs. I came with an insider's view of the stresses and demands of representing a client in a death penalty trial (SunWolf, 2006a). The goals of this program are to teach attorneys the skills, knowledge, and insights (into both themselves and other people) that are needed to defend a capital (death penalty) case successfully.

These attorneys, who have never met one another and come from various states, are assigned to work in the same group of eight members for six days. They are a task group. Each day, following lectures, attorney-participants meet in their small groups, performing, receiving feedback, and brainstorming various aspects of the mitigation portion of a death penalty trial (e.g., that portion of the trial that follows a conviction on the substantive charges of murder, including exercises on investigation, creating a compelling life story of clients). I became aware that these attorneys were often stressed and disconnected from their clients. Further, I was enrolled at my university's graduate counseling psychology program, with courses involving therapeutic tools for creating empathy and facilitating small therapeutic groups. I wanted to create an intervention for these attorneys that could enhance their work with one another during the week on the task of learning new trial skills, as well as create healthier relationships with their most challenging clients. I chose a narrative method, designed to be introduced in the first small group session. One reason for this choice was that there is little time in intensive continuing legal education programs to trigger new thinking. I combined my legal experience as a death penalty lawyer, my work with attorneys around the country on their criminal cases, my training as a group scholar, and my counseling psychology education to develop a group intervention based upon role-switching and storytelling in the first-person format. Group scholars are encouraged to draw upon their own multiple interests, training, and group memberships in this same way.

In this narrative intervention, for the first meeting, eight attorneys were challenged to "become" their current client, speak in that client's voice, then tell a small slice of that client's storied point-of-view. The technique (which I called empathic attunement, becoming connected with the emotions felt by another), involved the following steps.

1   At zero history (i.e., the first meeting of a small group of strangers), the facilitator (my role) places an empty chair in placed in the center of the group's U-shape of chairs.
2   Group members (attorneys) are told that they will be asked, one at a time, to sit in that chair and to respond to two specific prompts from the facilitator as the client would, adopting the behavior of that client as they have experienced it, but adopting as well the client's voice, emotions, and attitudes.
3   The facilitator poses the first prompt, "Who are you and what are you most afraid of?"
4   The attorney, as client, answers the question, as the group listens.
5   The facilitator poses a second prompt to the attorney, "Tell me about the lawyer you have on your case;" and the attorney, as client, answers.
6   After everyone has participated, the group is asked to share what was that like for them, as they role-switched with their client and as they listened to the mini-stories of others.

Each step was designed to reject the typical first session of these groups, in which people generally introduced themselves, talking about their legal practices. Instead, they were now listening to a dramatized client talking about facing death and dealing with a lawyer while in jail. I chose a U-shape rather than a circle, so that the person in the center did not have his/her back to anyone. I decided to delay any group discussion or feedback until everyone had participated, so as not to interrupt the drama of the experience across group members. One co-facilitator who watched this intervention for the first time offered his observation:

> I looked at the four [attorneys] nearest me, and they were *stunned!* I think they were speechless for a while. In those moments, they appeared to be making a mental shift from "the-world-revolves-around-me" to "let-me-see-what-my-client's-world-might-be."
>
> *(S. Harmon, personal communication, January 21, 2003)*

Some attorneys described feeling momentarily inadequate, even ashamed about how little they had thought about their clients before the narrative exercise, even though they saw themselves as extraordinarily people-oriented. As a co-facilitator explained, "It's an epiphany moment for them. For the first time, they realize there's a gap here, and they have been invited into a paradigm shift" (S. Harmon, personal communication, January 21, 2003). Comments from attorneys during the exercises included the following.

> I know they were doing *their* client, but I wanted to stop them and say, 'I've represented that guy!'

I was embarrassed to think I'd never asked him what he was scared of. It's such a "duh" on a death penalty case; you just never talk about it. Then I realized in my role-play that it wasn't dying he was afraid of!

I wanted to cry.

I felt so afraid, even when it was just my client that was talking about being afraid.

That's the first time I really *got* why he'd rather die than spend the rest of his life in prison.

I thought that if I could talk that way in closing argument, to the jury, they'd never be able to kill him. Is there a way I could do that?

I started liking my client again.

I remembered how long it had been since I visited him, and even longer since I looked him in the eyes. I'm so afraid I'll lose his case.

I am moved by what they share; the cohesion and insights help me tailor my teaching for the week every year.

For me, this group intervention using narrative represented the bridges I could build between various scholarly interests (in this case, counseling psychology, oral storytelling, and small group processes), my professional service (using my scholarship to help underresourced criminal defense attorneys more fully represent clients), and social activism (opposition to the death penalty), while learning more about the effects of group interventions on group processes and members. In particular, I came to understand more about the critical first moments of a group that set the stage for the climate and the task to follow.

Recommendations for Researchers Considering Learning about Groups Using Narrative Analysis

At the outset, group researchers new to narrative analysis can benefit by learning how narrative talk is embedded in group processes. In addition to reading the articles already referenced in this chapter from group scholars who observed group storytelling, such as Bormann (1986, 1990), there now exist in the public domain videos of real jury deliberations. In August 2010, a special issue of *Small Group Research* focused on jury deliberations, including five articles by group scholars who examined transcripts from a capital jury case (death penalty trial), addressing different aspects of the jury's deliberative talk from different scholarly perspectives. Jury deliberations are salient exemplars of group decision making, as community-based, single-event, conscripted groups of strangers face the task of reaching agreement on both law and facts (SunWolf, 2010). Access to those transcripts, as well as videos of the jury deliberations that may be purchased, are detailed in that issue, offering a valuable opportunity for scholars to practice retrieving, coding, and theoretically explaining the story types and functions during group deliberations. Drafts of coding instruments and attempts to obtain intercoder reliability on story typologies can be practiced on these and other existing exemplars of group talk. These transcripts and videos are also valuable tools in teaching university courses involving group processes or research methodology.

Further, group scholars might begin by experimenting with extraordinarily accessible narrative tools, the story vignette or the story stem question. They both can be used as story-gathering probes, focusing on group events, in group classes with students, with members of groups in which we are already embedded, or with colleagues or friends describing their group experiences. For example, a story vignette, as previously described, is a hypothetical mini-story about something that might happen in a group, which then asks the participant some form of, "What would you do or say if that happened?" On the other hand, a story-stem question focuses on a group event that did, in fact, happen to the participant, asking, in essence, "Tell me about a time when X happened in your group," The value for group scholars includes the fact that it becomes apparent that narrative data are created immediately by either tool, yet each gathers a different perspective, focusing back (it already happened) or forward (what might happen). Both offer access to group processes without the necessity of the group researcher being present when an event happens.

Finally, group scholars should ground themselves in some of the most respected and recent books describing narrative methods. These would include Riessman's (2008) *Narrative Methods for the Human Sciences*, as well as Gubrium and Holstein's (2009) *Analyzing Narrative Reality*. While narrative analysis, as already described, works well with quantitative methods, for qualitative researchers as a supplement to these two works I recommend *The Handbook of Qualitative Research* (2nd ed.) edited by Denzin and Lincoln (2000), which contains outstanding chapters on grounded theory for explaining narrative data, methods of collecting narratives, analyzing talk and text, case studies, co-constructed narratives, culturally situated narratives, interviews, and narrative evaluation, to name a few. These chapters help group scholars to anticipate methodological challenges embedded in narrative analysis, while also offering specific suggestions on research design and field work that involve collecting or interpreting stories.

Concluding Thoughts

Narrative methodologies can travel in time, retrieving past stories or provoking participants to imagine future group events, allowing group scholars access to what has already happened to the group or what might yet happen. Further, a narrative approach that acknowledges in the real world in which group members and groups are embedded adds value. Draw upon a bona fide groups perspective (Putnam & Stohl, 1990; Stohl & Putnam, 2003) to include investigation of the organization or community in which a group is embedded as you design your study. This perspective argues that group researchers should acknowledge all groups as embedded in multiple social systems, knowing that each group member also balances memberships in other groups, which is all a critical part of the environment necessary to understanding the dynamics of any particular group. When you know the group you wish to study, become familiar with the backstory, the prequels, and the community stories in which that group is embedded. Stories told by any culture function to persuade through generating new thoughts, triggering listener involvement, and modeling (SunWolf, 1999).

My group scholarship has and continues to benefit enormously when drawing upon existing narrative theories and perspectives. Fisher's (1986, 1990) Narrative Paradigm, Bormann's (1985) Symbolic Convergence Theory, and Decisional Regret Theory (SunWolf, 2006b) may suggest to you a narrative approach to designing group research. Why did a decision-making group fail to reach consensus (Decisional Regret Theory)? Why does discussion in a task group often get off track with humor and fantasies (Symbolic Convergence Theory)? Is it predictable that any group over time will generate stories and speak to one another in storied format (Narrative Paradigm)? The Symbolic Interpretative Perspective (Frey & SunWolf, 2004, 2005) invites group scholars to examine, among other group events, how groups use stories to socialize new members, recreate identity after loss of one or more members, create insider–outsider symbolic boundaries, or communicate unique group culture and rules.

While it has been traditional for many to speak of a methodology as having weaknesses, I argue that there are simply trade-offs with any methodology used to study groups. With a narrative approach, the richness of data gathered about specific group members' experiences might not be generalizable to other groups, for example, even though the data generate deeper understand of a particular group. Some methods of gathering narrative data, as well as analyzing it, are affected by the researcher (in particular interviewing, participant observation, ethnography), such that another researcher using the same design would produce different data or sense-making of that data. Further, the analyses of dense narrative data or the training of coders to analyze storied talk is time-consuming.

Groups, as entities, create storied rituals, use stories to socialize new members, share stories about group history and values. A narrative approach to studying groups offers a gateway into both the individual member experiences of group dynamics and the group processes that create and recreate narrative communication.

> We dream in narrative, daydream in narrative, remember, anticipate, hope, despair, believe, doubt, plan, revise, criticize, construct, gossip, learn, hate and live by narrative.
>
> *(Hardy, 1977, p. 13)*

Notes

1 In the midst of enacting major rules for jury reform, the Arizona Supreme Court granted permission to a national television network (CBS) to film both the trial and deliberations of four criminal trials after consent of all parties involved (attorneys, judges, defendants, and jurors) was obtained. The network agreed to make the tapes available for use by academic scholars. In Arizona, eight jurors are used on criminal trials. Trial A involved a possession of narcotics charge in which drugs were found in suitcases at the airport. Trial A jurors deliberated for twelve hours and ended in deadlock (6:2). Trial B involved assault charges resulting from a shooting in which one person died and another was wounded; the defense raised self-defense and defense of others. After 9-½ hours of deliberation, this trial resulted in a hung jury (6:2). Jurors in Trial C convicted a defendant charged with armed robbery, resulting from a convenience store robbery. Trial C jurors deliberated for 3 hours; seven jurors eventually convinced the holdout to change her vote and a guilty verdict was returned. Trial D was the retrial of Trial A, resulting in a conviction after 45 minutes of deliberation. Two cameras were used, both placed behind walls to minimize distraction (jurors knew about the cameras). Times were captured using a 24-hour clock.
2 Each small group was composed of eight lawyers, attending an intensive, week-long trial advocacy program, focused on the *aggravation/mitigation* portion of a capital defense trial (evidence and arguments supporting either a sentence of life or death, after considering the entire life of the defendant, as well as circumstances of the crime) rather than on the *guilt/innocence* portion (evidence and arguments supporting either a verdict of guilty or not guilty of the crimes charged).

References

Adelman, M. B., & Frey, L. R. (1997). *The fragile community: Living together with AIDS.* Mahway, NJ: Lawrence Erlbaum.
Bormann, E. G. (1986). Symbolic convergence theory and communication in group decision-making. In R.Y. Hirokawa & M. S. Poole (Eds.), *Communication and group decision-making* (pp. 219–236). Beverley Hills, CA: Sage.
Bormann, E. G. (1990). *Small group communication: Theory and practice* (3rd ed.). New York: Harper & Row.
Conquergood, D. (1994). Homeboys and hoods: Gangs and cultural space. In L. R. Frey (Ed.), *Group communication in context: Studies of natural groups* (pp. 23–52). Hillsdale, NJ: Lawrence Erlbaum.
Cox, A. (2000). A journey down the healing path through story. *Diving in the Moon, 1,* 10-23.
Denzin, N. K., & Lincoln, Y. S. (Eds.) (2000). *Handbook of qualitative research* (2nd ed.). Thousand Oaks, CA: Sage.
Fisher, W. R. (1985). The narrative paradigm: In the beginning. *Journal of Communication, 35*(4), 74–89.
Fisher, W. R. (1987). *Human communication as narration: Toward a philosophy of reason, value, and action.* Columbia: University of South Carolina Press.
Frey, L. R., Botan, C. H., & Kreps, G. L. (2000). *Investigating communication: An introduction to research methods* (2nd ed.). Boston: Allyn & Bacon.
Frey, L. R., & SunWolf (2004). A symbolic-interpretive perspective on group dynamics. *Small Group Research, 35*(3), 277–306.
Frey, L. R., & SunWolf (2005). The symbolic-interpretive perspective on group life. In M. S. Poole & A. Hollingshead (Eds.), *Theories of small groups: Interdisciplinary perspectives* (pp. 185–239). Thousand Oaks, CA: Sage.

Galavotti, C., Petraglia, J., Harford, N., Kraft, J. M., Pappas-DeLuca, K. A., & Kuhlmann, S. (2005). New narratives for Africa: Using stories to fight HIV/AIDS. *Storytelling, Self, Society: An Interdisciplinary Journal of Storytelling Studies, 1*(2), 26–37.

Gubrium, J.F., & Holstein, J.A. (2009). *Analyzing narrative reality*. Los Angeles: Sage.

Hardy, B. (1977). Narrative as a primary act of mind. In M. Meek, A. Warlow, & G. Barton (Eds.), *The cool web* (pp. 12–33). London: Bodley Head.

Leets, L., & SunWolf (2005). Adolescent rules for social exclusion: When is it fair to exclude someone else? *Journal of Moral Education, 34*(3), 343–362.

Owen, W. F. (1984). Interpretive themes in relational communication. *Quarterly Journal of Speech, 70*, 274–287.

Polkinghorne, D. E. (1988). *Narrative knowing and the human sciences*. Albany, NY: State University of New York Press.

Putnam, L. L., & Stohl, C. (1990). Bona fide groups: A reconceptualization of groups in context. *Communication Studies, 41*(3), 248–265.

Riessman, C. K. (2008). *Narrative methods for the human sciences*. Thousand Oaks, CA: Sage.

Stohl, C., & Putnam, L. L. (2003). Communication in bona fide groups: A retrospective and prospective account. In L. R. Frey (Ed.), *Group communication in context: Studies of bona fide groups* (pp. 399–414). Mahway, NJ: Lawrence Erlbaum.

Strickland, C. J., Chrisman, N. J., Yallup, M., Powell, K., & Squeoch, M. D. (1996). Walking the journey of womanhood: Yakama Indian women and Papanicolaou (Pap) Test screening. *Public Health Nursing, 13*, 141–150.

SunWolf (1999). The pedagogical and persuasive effects of Native American lesson stories, Sufi wisdom tales, and African dilemma tales. *Howard Journal of Communications, 10*, 47–71.

SunWolf (2004a). Stories as medicine. *Journal of Communication Studies, 21*(2). 5–14.

SunWolf (2004b). Once upon a time for the soul: A review of the effects of storytelling in spiritual traditions. *Communication Research Trends, 23*(3), 3–19.

SunWolf (2005). R_x Storytelling, prn: Storysharing as medicine. *Storytelling, Self, Society, 1*(2), 1–9.

SunWolf (2006a). Empathic attunement facilitation: Stimulating immediate task engagement in zero-history training groups of helping professionals. In L. R. Frey (Ed.), *Facilitating group communication: Innovations and applications with natural groups: Vol. 1: Facilitating group creation, conflict, and conversation* (pp. 3–32). Cresskill, NJ: Hampton Press.

SunWolf (2006b). Decisional regret theory: Reducing the anxiety about uncertain outcomes during group decision making through shared counterfactual storytelling. *Communication Studies, 57*(2), 1–29.

SunWolf (2007). *Practical jury dynamics2: From one juror's trial perceptions to the group's decision-making processes*. Charlottesville, VA: LexisNexis/Matthew Bender.

SunWolf (2008). *Peer groups: Expanding our study of small group communication*. Thousand Oaks, CA: Sage.

SunWolf (2010). Investigating jury deliberation in a capital murder case. *Small Group Research, 41*(4), 380–385.

SunWolf, & Frey, L. R. (2001). Storytelling: The power of narrative communication and interpretation. In W. P. Robinson & H. Giles (Eds.), *The new handbook of language and social psychology* (pp. 119–135). London: Wiley.

SunWolf, Frey, L. R., & Keränen, L. (2005). R_x Story-prescriptions: Healing effects of storytelling and storylistening in the practice of medicine. In L. M. Harter, P. M. Japp, & C. S. Beck (Eds.), *Narratives, health, and healing: Communication theory, research, and practice* (pp. 237–257). Mahwah, NJ: Erlbaum.

SunWolf, & Leets, L. (2003). Communication paralysis during peer group exclusion: Social dynamics that prevent children and adolescents from expressing disagreement. *Journal of Language and Social Psychology, 22*. 355–384.

SunWolf, & Leets, L. (2004). Being left out: Rejecting outsiders and communicating group boundaries in childhood and adolescent peer groups. *Journal of Applied Communication Research, 32*(3), 195–223.

SunWolf, & Seibold, D. R. (1998). Jurors' intuitive rules for deliberation: A structurational approach to the study of communication in jury decision making. *Communication Monographs, 65,* 282–307.

14

GROUPS AND TEAMS IN ORGANIZATIONS

Studying the Multilevel Dynamics of Emergence

Steve W. J. Kozlowski

MICHIGAN STATE UNIVERSITY

One of the biggest challenges of conducting insightful, informative, and impactful research on groups is effectively dealing with the multiple levels that comprise group phenomena. That is, group phenomena entail multiple levels of theory and constructs, measurement, and data analysis. What are you talking about, you may say. I want to study groups, that is the level I'm interested in, why should I care about other levels? My answer is, because the world is complex. Even the most "bare-bones" group situations entail a *minimum* of three levels: group (i.e., between group), individual (i.e., person within group), and time (i.e., within person over time). There are potentially other levels as well. Groups could be embedded in an organizational system with many higher, nested levels. One could be interested in dyadic relations embedded within groups, including families and work teams. You may not be interested in all these levels, but they nonetheless merit consideration in your theorizing, research design, and measurement.

First, groups typically exist in a broader context or setting. I am an organizational psychologist who is interested in team learning, problem solving, and effectiveness, so the groups I study are often in an organizational setting where they are subject to different contextual influences. These influences could include different types of leaders, exposure to different forms of training, or being in work units that use different technologies and administrative structures, among many other potential differences. Community psychologists might be interested in groups that exist in different neighborhoods or who have access to different services. Social psychologists might be interested in how influential group members, leaders, or other factors can shape group identities. Communication researchers might be interested in differences in group behavior and outcomes based on whether members discourse face-to-face or via virtual media. Finally, any laboratory study that manipulates conditions for groups in their research design – as I often do – has manipulated the context with the intent of observing differences across groups (i.e., between group differences) in those manipulated conditions.

Second, groups are comprised of individuals who differ on a variety of personal characteristics (e.g., cognitive ability, personality, interests, demographics, etc.). Collectively, this creates a group composition that can range from very homogeneous to heterogeneous. In addition, group members are exposed to the same contextual factors, share experiences, and interact with each other. Those common experiences and interactions may lead to very similar perceptions, feelings, and reactions, so that there is little within group variation (i.e., the data are dependent; see Kashy & Hagiwara, this volume). Such phenomena are collective. On the other hand, personal characteristics or other factors may lead people to have very different perceptions, feelings, and reactions such that there is a lot of within group variation. Such phenomena are individual level; differences lie between people.

Third, most psychological phenomena that are relevant to individual behavior within groups and to collective group-level behavior emerge over time. This within-person variation can be of interest in its own right. For example, experience sampling studies often examine how individual variation in mood over time can yield between-person differences in affect. Team researchers are interested in a variety of team process constructs that emerge over time (Kozlowski & Bell, 2003). For example, team members may share their reactions to contextual factors and, over time, converge on a shared perception of team climate or atmosphere (James & Jones, 1976), team cohesion, or their collective efficacy. The point is that many phenomena of interest in groups emerge over time from exposure to common events and group member interaction. Time needs to be considered theoretically and it has implications for research design. This is important because cross-sectional designs in the field and laboratory still dominate the groups and teams literature, but very few group phenomena are truly static.

The goal of this chapter is to provide an overview of multilevel theory (MLT) and methods, and to convince you that the principles of MLT have important implications for your theory building, research design, and measurement approach. As the contents of this volume makes clear, it is certainly not the only methodological consideration, but it is a very versatile framework that can help you to design and conduct cutting-edge research on groups. This chapter will highlight key conceptual and methodological challenges in studying groups from a MLT perspective. Although the primary focus of this volume is on methods, effectively using multilevel (ML) methods necessitates that you have a basic understanding of core theoretical principles. Research design and measurement are conditioned on the nature of the theoretical model you are evaluating.

I will begin with a brief overview of the development of MLT in organizational psychology, which is how I trace its application to group research. The primary MLT focus is on individuals, nested in teams, open to higher level contextual influences, with phenomena unfolding over time. I will then discuss key

262 Steve W. J. Kozlowski

theoretical principles for understanding primary linkages across levels of analysis and the implications of these principles for measurement and research design:

(a) the effects of higher-level contextual factors on lower-level entities (i.e., individuals and groups; *cross-level effects*);
(b) the way that dynamic interactions among individuals can coalesce, emerge, and manifest over time as higher level phenomena (i.e., *emergent phenomena*, as well as within-level process dynamics over time); and
(c) how some phenomena (e.g., antecedents, mediating processes, outcomes) can exhibit parallelism across levels of a system (i.e., *multilevel phenomena*).

One needs to begin with a solid, focused, and well-developed theoretical model. However, if one cannot realize the model with measures that appropriately represent constructs, then the model cannot be effectively evaluated. ML research typically assesses constructs at one level (frequently the individual level), but desires to have those measures represent a different (usually higher) level. Ensuring that the levels of origin (where constructs are fundamentally conceptualized), measurement (where data are assessed), and representation (where constructs reside in a specific model) are properly aligned requires careful research design. In addition, one of the complexities of ML research is that with constructs represented at different levels of analysis, researchers need to devise data collection designs that will yield sufficient variance for *each* of the constructs *at its level* in the model. "Business as usual" approaches to data collection are often inadequate to accomplish this and the wise researcher needs to plan this aspect of their project with care.

Finally, I do not address ML analyses because a detailed treatment is beyond the scope of this chapter, other authors in this volume address the topic (e.g., Kashy & Hagiwara, this volume), and there are excellent primers in the literature (e.g., Bliese & Ployhart, 2002; Hofmann, Griffin, & Gavin, 2000). However, it is important to note that problems with theory or methodology cannot be resolved by analyses. That is why theory (first) and methods (second, to mesh with theory) have primacy. I will also note at the onset that the material to be covered is abstract, although I will illustrate key points with examples. Being an organizational psychologist, my examples are about work teams; this is what I know. Hopefully, the reader can map the examples by analogy to your own research interests. An open mind and a spirit of conceptual adventure are essential!

The Nature of Work Groups and Teams: The Need for a Dynamic, Multilevel Perspective

Work groups and teams are like informal groups in that social interaction is a central aspect of group experience, but they also differ from informal groups in several important ways that have profound effects on team processes and outcomes.

These important differences can be summarized as the context, the task, and the interdependencies that arise from each. These differences are captured in the definitions of work teams and in the way teams are conceptualized as embedded in dynamic and interactive systems. Work groups and teams:

> (a) are composed of two or more individuals, (b) who exist to perform organizationally relevant tasks, (c) share one or more common goals, (d) interact socially, (e) exhibit task interdependencies (i.e., workflow, goals, outcomes), (f) maintain and manage boundaries, and (g) are embedded in an organizational context that sets boundaries, constrains the team, and influences exchanges with other units in the broader entity.
>
> *(Kozlowski & Bell, 2003, p. 334).*

The organizational context, team task, and interdependencies necessitates a conceptual approach that can capture the multilevel, dynamic, and emergent aspects of team functioning. The approach advanced by Kozlowski and Ilgen (2006, p. 80) conceptualizes teams

> as part of a *multilevel system* with individual, team, and organizational aspects; takes a central focus on *task-relevant processes*; incorporates *temporal dynamics* encompassing episodic tasks and developmental progression; and views team processes and effectiveness as *emergent phenomena* that unfold in a proximal task-social context that teams in part enact, while also embedded in a larger organization system or environmental context.
>
> *(Arrow, McGrath, & Berdahl, 2000; Ilgen, Hollenbeck, Johnson, & Jundt, 2005; Kozlowski & Bell, 2003; Kozlowski, Gully, McHugh, Salas, & Canon-Bowers, 1996; Kozlowski, Gully, Nason, & Smith, 1999; Marks, Mathieu, & Zaccaro, 2001).*

An Abbreviated Overview of Multilevel Theory

Precursors

My own interest in MLT was initially sparked when I was a graduate student and read a book entitled *Building a Multidisciplinary Science of Organizations* by Roberts, Hulin, and Rousseau (1978). It provided a succinct description of the fragmented nature of the organizational sciences (e.g., human factors psychology, organizational psychology, social psychology, sociology, management, etc.), presented a rudimentary framework for thinking about behavior as multilevel in nature, and discussed the data challenges involved. I was intrigued by this early call to move beyond the systems metaphor. My dissertation research incorporated both individual and higher-level contextual factors that influenced perceptions of the climate (i.e., work environment) in an effort to understand behavioral outcomes (cross-sectionally and over time; Kozlowski & Farr, 1988; Kozlowski & Hults, 1987).

A chapter by Rousseau (1985) provided a thorough scholarly treatment of levels of analysis challenges that, in the "early days," was the primary reference for ML research. A subsequent paper by Klein, Dansereau, & Hall (1994) helped to move interest in ML research towards mainstream awareness. In addition, the topic of climate in organizations, which distinguished between individual climate perceptions, or *psychological* climate, and a shared *organizational* climate (James & Jones, 1976), provided a systematic focus for research that eventually provided a foundation for the development of ML theory and methods (James, 1982; James, Demaree, & Wolf, 1984, 1993; Jones & James, 1979; Kozlowski & Hattrup, 1992; Kozlowski & Hults, 1987; Schneider & Bowen, 1985). By the mid to late 1990s, Katherine Klein and I planned and edited a book on ML theory, research, and methods (Klein & Kozlowski, 2000). Our goal was to extend ML theory and to push the ML perspective solidly into the mainstream of organizational psychology, organizational behavior, and human resources research. In particular, we sought to cut through the (then) confusion in the literature to create principles to guide theory development, measurement, and research design (Kozlowski & Klein, 2000). Much of what I will describe in what follows is based on that treatment. A basic primer on ML research, also based on Kozlowski and Klein (2000), is available in Klein and Kozlowski (2000).

The Influence of General Systems Theory

The roots of MLT are in General Systems Theory (GST; von Bertalanffy, 1968, 1972), albeit MLT is focused on human performance in organizational systems, which is bounded – individual, group, organization, and time – whereas the goals of GST are much broader. GST was intended to establish principles that generalize across phenomena, qualitatively different systems, and even scientific disciplines as a means to promote the unity of science. The orientation of GST is holistic, in that "*the whole is more than the sum of the parts*," and it sought to counter-balance the tendency toward reductionism that was viewed as prevalent in "normal science." There are several key principles from GST that have been important in the development and methods of MLT. *Isomorphism* is a principle of identity or similarity that has been applied in the conceptualization and representation of parallel constructs at different levels of analysis. *Functional equivalence* is a principle whereby a construct or a process linkage (i.e., a relationship between constructs) fulfills a similar role in a model or system at more than one level of analysis. *Logical homology* is a principle that there are phenomena whereby analogous constructs and linking processes hold at different levels or in qualitatively different systems. In essence, homology is a combination of the first two principles to envision constructs and processes that form parallel multilevel models. These principles are critical to establishing generality from one level of a system to another level of that system, or to a different system.

Although GST has had an important influence on theory in the organizational sciences throughout the twentieth century, the influence has not always been positive. Organizations as nested systems of individuals, groups, and subsystems in dynamic interaction over time are incredibly complex and impossible to grasp in their entirety. Thus, holism as a fundamental assumption has been a limiting factor. Indeed, the press for holistic thinking has had the opposite effect. Because the system could not be meaningfully bounded and disentangled, it was instead fragmented into level slices that represented core disciplines of organizational science (Roberts et al., 1978).

Conceptualizations of system behavior that have evolved from GST, such as complexity science, self-organization, and chaos theories, focus more on how simple elemental interactions over time can yield very complex behavior at the collective (system) level. The focus is on the emergence of complex system behavior, but the focus on the basic elements, entities, or agents is not reductionism. Rather, it is an effort to understand how the "wholeness" arises without reifying it. It is an effort "... to understand the whole, *and* keep an eye on the parts" (Kozlowski & Klein, 2000, p. 54). The goal of MLT is not to understand the system as a whole, but to decompose it selectively in meaningful ways to capture complex links at multiple levels. As I noted in the introduction, this is directly relevant to group researchers because group research inherently implicates at least three nested levels of analysis.

How Systems Are Coupled Across Levels: Types of Multilevel Linkages

There are three primary types of ML relationships: contextual, emergent, and multilevel. I have illustrated simple models of these relationships in Figure 14.1. It is important to recognize that these are basic types of multilevel relations. As a theorist, your model may combine these exemplars in myriad ways to craft a model that captures the group phenomena of interest. Contextual or top-down relationships are important because the setting in which an entity (i.e., a person, group) is embedded, if it is strong, will influence, constrain, and shape the entity. Situational strength trumps personality. Emergent or bottom-up phenomena are important because many team processes have their roots in individual cognition, affect, and behavior but, through social interaction and exchange, can take on collective properties. Constructs such as team efficacy, team cohesion, and team climate are emergent in nature. Indeed, a wide range of team phenomena are emergent. Being able to study such constructs requires methods to represent the constructs at the higher level of analysis appropriately. Multilevel relationships come in many forms. The classic homologous multilevel model captures a phenomenon that consists of parallel constructs and linking processes at more than

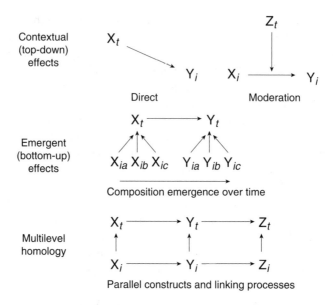

FIGURE 14.1 An illustration of contextual (cross-level), emergent, and multilevel models. (Note subscript *i* signifies the individual level; subscript *t* the team level.)

one level of analysis (e.g., goal effects on individual and team performance). However, complex multilevel models can also involve a mix of contextual, emergent, and parallel processes. I will discuss each type in turn. Because studying emergent constructs also entails some of the thornier conceptualization and measurement problems, I will address those issues in that section.

Contextual effects

Contextual effects are *top-down*, where factors at a higher level influence or constrain phenomena at the lower level. That is, they exert an effect that is *cross-level*. The hierarchical nature of social organizational systems is characterized by a nested structure. Individuals are nested in teams, teams are nested in subsystems, and subsystems are nested in the broader organization. Each level above is an embedding context for the level below that can exhibit potent effects on the lower levels. For example, the extent to which a control structure is more centralized vs. more decentralized will influence group and individual perceptions and behavior.

There are two kinds of possible cross-level linkages. One type of linkage is a direct effect in which a contextual construct at the higher level crosses down to account for variance in a construct at a lower level of analysis. For example, the nature of work unit technology (i.e., whether it is more complex or simple) can influence individual perceptions about the nature of their job (whether it is enriched or constraining, respectively; Kozlowski & Farr, 1988; Rousseau, 1978). Different types of leaders can influence group member feelings or how satisfied they are. In a now classic study, Lewin, Lippit, and White (1939) showed that different types of leadership climates influenced individual attitudes, so that "democratic" climates were associated with positive attitudes and "authoritarian" climates were associated with negative attitudes. These examples illustrate a simple cross-level direct effect.

The other kind of cross-level linkage is a moderating one in which a construct at the higher level changes the nature of a bivariate relationship at the lower level. For example, the well-established relationship between general cognitive ability and job performance at the individual level necessitates complexity and the discretion to utilize one's ability. Thus, a less centralized, formalized, and standardized structure is necessary to enable the relationship between ability and performance to hold. In highly structured contexts, because the context limits the discretion and the utility of ability, the relation is likely to decline or disappear (Hunter & Hunter, 1984); unit structure moderates the lower level relationship. Similarly, other higher level factors that might influence one's motivation to apply ability, such as leadership or team cohesion, could also evidence cross-level moderation.

Cross-level relationships – direct and moderating – tend to be most heavily represented in the literature, because there are well-developed exemplars, consensus on techniques for assessing contextual factors, and well-tailored analytical systems (e.g., multilevel random coefficient modeling; MRCM) that specifically examine these relationships (i.e., intercept differences for direct effects and slope differences for moderating effects). Because work groups and organizations are inherently hierarchical, research on contextual effects is important and useful. One key limitation is that much cross-level research relies on cross-sectional data, so that the (implied) causality inherent in most models cannot be examined. Moreover, cross-level models often assume a process of emergence of constructs from the lower level (e.g., team cohesion, team efficacy, team mental models), but rarely actually examine emergence as a process. It is the result of an assumed process of emergence (i.e., the manifestation of a collective construct) that is examined. Thus, one scientific challenge is that the attention devoted to cross-level relationships means that emergent *processes* that are also important get much less research attention.

Emergence

The nature of emergence

Emergence is the result of bottom-up processes whereby phenomena and constructs that originate at a lower level of analysis, through social interaction and exchange, combine, coalesce, and manifest at a higher collective level of analysis.

"A phenomenon is emergent when it originates in the cognition, affect, behaviors, or other characteristics of individuals, is amplified by their interactions, and manifests as a higher-level, collective phenomenon" (Kozlowski & Klein, 2000, p. 55). There are many exemplars of emergent constructs, what Marks, Mathieu, and Zaccaro (2001) describe as "emergent states," that are used as indicators of team processes in the literature such as team learning, team mental models, and team effectiveness (Kozlowski & Ilgen, 2006).

This view of emergence is rooted in complexity science, where the idea is to understand how complex, system-level phenomena can be produced by lower level entities operating according to a few simple rules or principles. It is not reductionism. Rather, it is an effort to understand the system not as a collective "whole," but as a phenomenon that emerges from the dynamic interactions of its behaving entities.

Craig Reynold's (1987) simulation of flock behavior in birds is a very elegant illustration of this perspective for modeling and understanding the dynamic inter-actions among individual entities that undergird complex collective behavior. In his simulation, "boids" are computer agents that simulate the motion of birds in a flock. Each boid is programmed to optimize a few simple rules: (a) separation – move away from other boids that are close to avoid collision; (b) alignment – fly in the average direction of the flock; and (c) cohesion – approach the center of the flock and avoid exterior exposure. Collective flock behavior is simulated by each agent maximizing the rule set in dynamic interaction with the other agents. As the simulation runs, the set of boids move essentially at random and, as they encounter other agents, the rules are applied dynamically. These three simple rules produce clumps of boids that flock together (see Figure 16.7 in Flake, 1998). The addition of one more rule, (d) view – move to the side of boids blocking the view (Flake, 1998), yields the classic V-formation of a migrating flock of birds (see Figure 16.9 in Flake, 1998). There is a compendium of useful information on Craig Reynold's website (http://www.red3d.com/cwr/boids/) and there are a variety of implementations of boids on the internet. A simple search will bring them up for your viewing pleasure and fascination. What is important is that the simulation provides a very palpable example of the emergence of a group-level phenomenon from dynamic individual interaction. Many analogous phenomena emerge in teams such as learning, coordination, and performance.

Computational modeling and simulation (the boids) are just beginning to make small inroads in organizational behavior research (Ilgen & Hulin, 2000; Larson, this volume; Tschan & Semmer, this volume). Meanwhile, we model most team phenomena by using measures that are designed to capture cognitive, affective–motivational, and behavioral constructs representing important aspects of team functioning (Kozlowski & Bell, 2003) that have emerged from the individual to the team level. How team constructs are represented is determined by the way or form in which they emerge. Different forms of emergence have implications for measurement and representation.

Forms of emergence

For the sake of keeping the discussion straightforward from here on out, there are a few caveats to note. First, I will focus on individuals as the lower level and teams as the higher level entities. However, it is important to note that the theoretical principles I describe apply to any other coupled lower and higher level relations. Second, I am describing phenomena that have emerged across levels. Thus, they originate in individual cognition, motivation–affect, and/or behavior, but through interaction emerge to manifest as team-level constructs. Representation at the team level has to be consistent with the form of emergence. Third, and this is important, it is the manifestation that is being represented, not the actual process of emergence. I shall touch on this issue more later. Fourth, there are obviously characteristics (e.g., group size, team function) or constructs (e.g., team diversity) that only have meaning and representation at the team level. Kozlowski and Klein (2000) describe these as global properties and I will not dwell on them further.

There are two "ideal" forms of emergence – composition and compilation – that represent distinctly different ways that a team construct can emerge from the individual level. One can think of these types as anchoring the ends of a continuum, with different emergent forms distributed between them (for more elaboration, see Kozlowski & Klein, 2000, pp. 52–77). As illustrated in Figure 14.2, each form of emergence has a different underlying theoretical model. Composition is based on the principle of *isomorphism*, where essentially the same construct exists at the individual and the team level (i.e., it has the same structure and function across levels). Composition captures emergent phenomena that are convergent. Compilation is based on the principle of *discontinuity*, where the construct has the same meaning and function across levels, but it is not measured or represented

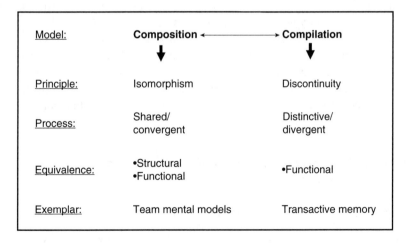

FIGURE 14.2 Characteristics of composition and compilation forms of emergence.

using essentially the same content (i.e., it is not structurally similar). Compilation captures emergent phenomena that are configural.

At one end of the continuum, *composition emergence* describes phenomena that combine, converge, and coalesce into a shared team property. A team mental model (Cannon-Bowers, Salas, & Converse, 1993), for example, is a shared property. Individual team members develop cognitive representations of their task, equipment, and how it is connected to other members' tasks. However, since individual team members are exposed to the same situations and task, and are prone to sharing their views, over time members come to agree on their team mental model and variation among individuals is reduced as team members share the same cognitive representation. This shared mental model allows them to coordinate implicitly, since they have a common understanding of how to accomplish the collective task.

The underlying theoretical principle is isomorphism in that the construct exhibits structural and functional similarity across levels (Morgeson & Hofmann, 1999). That is, individuals perceive the same elemental content (e.g., team mental model perceptions), it is shared in common, and it carries essentially the same meaning and function in a model at both levels of analysis (Kozlowski & Klein, 2000).

At the other end of the continuum, *compilation emergence* describes phenomena that are variable, patterned, or configural across members. Transactive memory (Wegner, 1995), for example, is a configural property. Because individual team members possess different types of expertise or hold different roles, they specialize in tracking information relevant to different aspects of the overall team task. Unlike the mental model example described previously, team members do not share all the same knowledge. Rather, they each possess distinct knowledge that can be accessed by members knowing "who knows what." In that sense, transactive memory is distributed across individual members in a pattern that is analogous to a network of memory nodes or pieces of a puzzle (Kozlowski & Bell, 2003).

The underlying theoretical principle is discontinuity in that the construct exhibits functional, but not structural, similarity across levels. That is, elemental content at the individual level is different (i.e., different knowledge or expertise), but the configuration and access to that knowledge at the team level is functionally equivalent to individual memory (i.e., it performs the same function at both levels of analysis).

Aligning the levels of construct origin, measurement, and representation

Levels of conceptualization and measurement

The level of origin for a construct is where it fundamentally exists. The level of measurement is the level at which data are collected to assess the construct.

The level of representation is the level within a theoretical model where a construct resides. The world is simple when one is interested in, say, cognitive ability. It originates at the individual level, it is assessed by having individuals take an intelligence test, and it is generally examined in models where individual ability predicts individual performance on intellective or cognitively loaded tasks. Origin, measurement, and representation are aligned.

Things become more complicated if one is interested in, say, team mental models (TMM) and their influence on team performance. TMMs originate at the individual level, but they need to be represented at the team level (predicting team performance) in a model. How does one make this leap? At what level should the construct be assessed?

Aggregation

Many (most even) team constructs are fundamentally rooted in individual cognition, affect, or behavior. Based on the theoretical principles of emergence, higher level constructs that originate at the individual level should be assessed at the level of origin. So, in the TMM example, individuals within teams should also be the level of measurement. Okay, fine, but how does one then bridge the levels gap for representation? In the previous section I described how TMMs emerge via a composition process. Since the process of convergence typically takes some time, groups should be mature enough for emergence to have occurred (note that we are not examining the hypothetical *process* of emergence, but rather the manifestation of the process). The researcher then has to establish that team members exhibit sharing on TMMs. This is typically accomplished by examining consensus (i.e., interrater agreement) or consistency (i.e., interrater reliability; see Kozlowski & Hattrup, 1992), or both. The basic idea is to justify aggregation of the individual level perceptions to the team level by establishing empirically that variance within teams is restricted. Evidence of restricted within-team variance is an indicator of sharing, thus it provides empirical support for the underlying model of composition *and* evidence for the construct validity of the aggregated measure. With that support in place, we can now aggregate the individual-level TMM measures to the team level. Typically, investigators use the group mean as the team level representation.

Consensus (i.e., interrater agreement) and consistency (i.e., interrater reliability) are conceptually related, but they are not interchangeable and investigators are advised to be aware of the differences when selecting an approach: Bliese (2000) and Kozlowski and Hattrup (1992) address this issue in detail. Consensus is generally indexed using r_{wg} (James, Demaree, & Wolfe, 1984, 1993; or one of its later-day variants), which indicates the degree of within-team agreement. High agreement provides evidence that the construct is shared.

Consistency is indexed using the intra-class correlation coefficient (ICC). There are two types of ICC and they tell us different things about consistency in the group. ICC(1) provides an indication of data clustering or nonindependence (i.e., the extent to which group membership exerts an effect on individual member responses). A significant and 'reasonably large' ICC(1) indicates that team members are essentially interchangeable and provides evidence supporting sharing. ICC(1) provides evidence to support aggregation. ICC(2) provides an indication of the reliability or stability of the group mean. A high ICC(2) can give us information regarding how confident we can be in the results of analyses. Prevailing practice is to accept r_{wg} and ICC(2) values using "rule of thumb" thresholds (i.e., values in excess of 0.70). ICC(1) values are more difficult to gauge by magnitude, although there is advice in the literature (e.g., Bliese, 2000). Some of the advice suggests that ICC(1) values in the neighborhood of 0.10 might be acceptable. Although the details are too complex to address in this brief essay, I would be wary of ICC(1) values lower than 0.30 and would prefer to see them well above 0.50. Remember, ICC(1) is an indication of the effect of group membership, so values below 0.50 are indicating that most of the variation is within groups, not between them. That is not strong support for aggregating data.

There is some inkling that item referents may play a role in agreement (Rousseau, 1985). Chan (1998) distinguished between aggregated measures based on items with a self-referent ("I perceive"), what he labeled as direct consensus, and aggregated measures based on items with a team referent ("My team perceives"), which he labeled referent shift. There has not been a great deal of research on this issue, but Klein, Conn, Smith, and Sorra (2001) reported that scales composed of team-level referents generally yielded higher agreement compared to scales with self-referents. I would add that my experience is consistent with this finding. So, if you are using individuals to assess team- or group-level constructs, you probably want to use the referent shift approach; I do.

Finally, what do you do if you do not find enough agreement to aggregate your data to the team level? In the mid-1990s Ken Brown and I were expanding some of the data simulations used by Kozlowski and Hattrup (1992) to see what the effects on agreement might be. One thing I was interested in was how different types of within-team social processes (e.g., leader–member exchange) could fragment a group and create really unusual patterns of within-team variance. We discovered that group polarization yielded observed variances that were much larger than would be expected from individuals responding in a purely random fashion. On that basis, we proposed that rather than using agreement as a criterion for aggregation that it instead should be treated as a construct (or more correctly, a phenomenon) and examined in its own right (Kozlowski, Brown, & Hattrup, 1996) since it could moderate the effect of the aggregated measure. In other words, when the variance is restricted, hence meaningful, the aggregated measure would have effects whereas when it was not restricted by group membership, the effect would be attenuated or reduced in magnitude. We later formalized this conceptualization as a dispersion theory (Brown & Kozlowski, 1999).

Subsequent applications of this idea in the area of group climate have been efficacious (e.g., Gonsalez-Roma, Piero, & Tordera, 2002; Schneider, Salvaggio, & Subirats, 2002).

Multilevel phenomena

Multilevel homology

Early on in this chapter I noted that an important goal of GST was to identify homologies – essentially analogous phenomena – across different levels of a system or even across qualitatively different systems. If one can identify homologies, then one can generalize a knowledge base that exists at one level to another without having to replicate all the basic research. It is an appealing prospect for leveraging knowledge. Perhaps one of the best examples of an effort to apply this logic is that of J. G. Miller (1978) who sought to construct a system of logical homologies transcending the subatomic to universal levels. It is an impressive exercise in scholarship, but by necessity a bit too abstract and general to be widely applicable as a knowledge generating framework.

In any case, the goal of MLT in organization science is more modest, but has the potential to be very powerful (Kozlowski & Klein, 2000). The focus is on identifying parallel phenomena in organizational systems. Until very recently, this exercise in multilevel thinking was confined primarily to conceptual exercises. One very nice and oft-cited example is the threat-rigidity model proposed by Staw, Sandelands, and Dutton (1981). In this model, the authors drawn on theory and research addressing how individuals become rigid in response to stressful inputs and generalize those principles to postulate how groups and organizations react. In other words, they extrapolate research at the individual level to build parallel propositions for how collectivities would react. Although analogy is a useful way to build multilevel theory, the real value of multilevel modeling is empirical evaluation so one can be confident in the generalization. Phenomena do not always replicate across levels. How can these sort of relationships be modeled with data?

With the turn of the new millennium, the advent of a more coherent approach to MLT and research (Kozlowski & Klein, 2000) allowed multilevel theorizing to develop an empirical foundation to begin actually to apply the logic beyond conceptual exercises. The basic problem that needed to be solved was how to capture a parallel phenomenon *simultaneously* at more than one level of analysis. There were methods in place, such as within-and-between-analysis (WABA), which allowed relations to be examined at multiple levels, but not simultaneously. Rather, WABA determined at what level a set of relations resided and then examined that level (Dansereau & Yammarino, 2000; Klein et al., 2000).

A key methodological development that enabled homology to be addressed was the conceptual distinction between measures referenced to the self and those that referenced a higher level entity. By conceptualizing the full model and parallel relations in advance, and then developing measures for each specific construct at its intended level of theoretical representation, researchers were able to begin probing homologous models empirically.

To my knowledge, the first successful example of validating a multilevel homology is represented by DeShon, Kozlowski, Schmidt, Milner, and Weichmann (2004). Note that there are many other examples of efforts to examine multilevel relations (cf. Chen & Bliese, 2002; Chen, Thomas, & Wallace, 2005; Chen et al., 2002; Gibson, 2001); I just think DeShon et al. (2004) was the first effort to validate homology that showed good evidence for parallelism across levels. The study provides a good illustration of application MLT to develop a model and method capable of examining contextual, emergent, and multilevel phenomena.

DeShon et al. (2004) were interested in the process of self-regulation (SR), and the potential for a homologous process of team regulation (TR) to emerge over time in a team context. SR is a useful conceptual heuristic for describing the process by which individuals initiate action, invest effort, and adjust their behavior to accomplish valued goals. In brief, SR involves an iterative process whereby individuals set goals, monitor progress, react to performance feedback, and adjust their effort and/or strategy to move toward goal accomplishment. SR is a dominant heuristic for explaining learning, motivation, and performance in psychology (Karoly, 1993), but it has largely been applied to individuals pursuing single goals. In most team task settings, individuals have their own goals and responsibilities to accomplish, but they also have requirements to back up team mates and to help accomplish the team objective. Thus, they actually have to regulate attention and effort to accomplish not just their own goal, but the team goal as well. At the individual level, this is a multiple goal model of regulation (DeShon et al., 2004).

Figure 14.3 illustrates the multiple goal model, with dual goal-feedback loops referencing both individual and team goals. As noted above, the basic idea is that individuals monitor discrepancies between their respective goals and current performance states. When a gap exists between the desired goal and the current state, the individual is expected to invest more effort or to modify their strategy to close the gap. In a team context, where the individual has discretion to work on their own goal or to contribute to the team, there is a second goal loop that has to be monitored. All things being equal (i.e., that both goals are important, valued, etc.), one would expect that the goal loop with the largest discrepancy would garner regulatory resources. As individuals work to accomplish both goals, one would anticipate that the discrepancies would be in flux and that team members would have to allocate their regulatory resources dynamically across both goal loops to manage the dual discrepancies.

If one imagines a set of team members simultaneously trying to accomplish their individual goals, while also contributing to team goal accomplishment, and

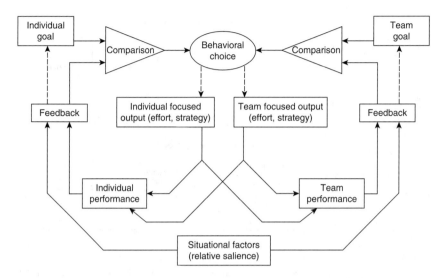

FIGURE 14.3 A multiple goal model of individual and team regulation. From: DeShon, R. P., Kozlowski, S. W. J., Schmidt, A. M., Milner, K. R., & Wiechmann, D. (2004). A multiple goal, multilevel model of feedback effects on the regulation of individual and team performance. *Journal of Applied Psychology*, *89*, 1035–1056. Published by the American Psychological Association. Reprinted with permission.

one plays out the dynamic resource allocation process described above over time, one can extrapolate that dynamic process yielding a process of individual SR and a parallel process of regulation that emerges at the team level. Figure 14.4 illustrates the resulting homologous multilevel of regulation.

How was the model evaluated? DeShon et al. (2004) had three-person teams perform a complex computer-based radar simulation over a series of multiple trials. All team members could view the same "synthetic world," and were responsible for monitoring a specific sector. The task was to monitor contacts, identify them, and take action to clear them. This contributed to individual performance. However, the task was designed to overload each team member systematically at different points such that team mates needed to help or the team would fail. Resource allocation to help a team mate constituted a contribution to team performance. Over the series of trials, teams performed the task iteratively, received feedback, and provided measures of the constructs. In addition to these task processes, the investigators manipulated feedback. In one condition, consistent with the multiple goal model shown in Figure 14.3, teams received individual and team performance feedback. In two other conditions, team members received only individual or team feedback only. The purpose of this design was to maximize variation across teams. Remember, if you want to be able to detect between team differences, you have to have variation and this was accomplished by manipulating

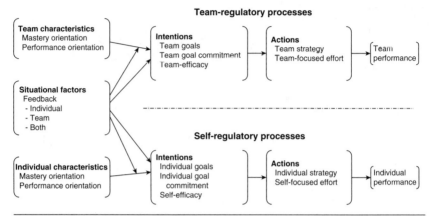

Team-regulatory processes

NOTE: Constructs above dashed line represent *team*-level constructs. Constructs below line represent *individual*-level constructs.

FIGURE 14.4 A multilevel homology of individual and team regulation. From: DeShon, R. P., Kozlowski, S. W. J., Schmidt, A. M., Milner, K. R., and Wiechmann, D. (2004). A multiple goal, multilevel model of feedback effects on the regulation of individual and team performance. *Journal of Applied Psychology, 89,* 1035–1056. Published by the American Psychological Association. Reprinted with permission.

sensitivity to the multiple goal loops. In other words, the context was manipulated to create variance between teams.

What levels are inherent in these data? Well, there is a temporal or within person element. Individuals provided repeated measures over time. Level 1 is within person. Next, individuals are nested within teams. Level 2 is the person within team. Level 3 is the between team level. How were the team construct measures modeled? To keep the discussion focused, I will simply describe the constructs within the team regulation and self-regulation "intentions" sections of Figure 14.4. At the individual level, the intentions of goals, commitment to goals, and one's self-efficacy to accomplish the goals (i.e., a self-perception of capability) were assessed by items that referenced the self. For the team level constructs, individual team members responded to parallel items that referenced the team as a whole (i.e., reference-shift; Chan, 1998). Because the team intentions were conceptualized as composition constructs, an indication of restricted within-team variance was used to justify aggregation of the data within teams to the team level. That is, we conceptualized the team-level regulation constructs as collective phenomena that would converge across team members. Significant ICC(1) values and indices of within team agreement (r_{wg}) provided the supporting evidence. Since there were multiple assessments of the SR and TR constructs over trials, this evaluation was conducted for each wave of data.

How was homology established? Principles based in GST indicate that to support a multilevel homology, one must establish that (a) constructs at both levels of analysis are parallel and (b) that the process linkages connecting parallel constructs are functionally equivalent (Kozlowski & Klein, 2000). As described previously, restricted within-team variance on core constructs provides evidence to support the construct validity, meaning, and aggregation of team constructs assessed via individuals' perceptions. This provided evidence for parallel constructs.

The second piece of support, to demonstrate that the linkages connecting constructs within each level are also parallel, was established by examining configural invariance or the pattern of significant and nonsignificant linkages across levels. This is essentially a demonstration of functional equivalence across levels. I should note that scholars have also identified more restrictive criteria for functional equivalence – metric and scalar invariance – that may be useful as our theories develop more precision (Chen, Bliese, & Mathieu, 2005; Chen et al., 2002). Since researchers are just beginning to examine multilevel models empirically, I think we have a ways to go before we get to the necessary level of precision.

Beyond homology

As I noted previously, homologous models have the potential to be a potent way for us to generalize knowledge about phenomena from one level where they may have been well explored to another level where they have not. In that sense, establishing homologies around meaningful phenomena can advance our science. Certainly, in the middle range focus on team processes, we can potentially generalize much of what we know about individual learning, motivation, and performance. However, I think it would be a mistake to think that homology per se is the only important focus for multilevel modeling.

It is important to remember that each level in a hierarchically structured social system serves as a context for the level below it. For example, for the DeShon et al. (2004) study, the individual is the context for within-individual variation over time, the team is the context for within-team variation, and the feedback manipulation (analogous to an organizational subsystem feature) is the context for between-team variation. Thus, one could argue that the team-level motivational processes in the homology act as contextual constraints (i.e., top-down effects) on their lower level counterparts. Thus, the phenomenon is not merely parallel, but it is also inexorably entwined. Indeed, Chen & Kanfer (2006) have proposed just such a model to account for team motivation, and individual motivation in the team context, that goes beyond homology per se. Here the focus is not just on the parallel processes, but rather on the interplay across levels over time as constructs emerge from the lower level to the team level and exert influence on subsequent motivational processes at the individual level. From an organizational systems theory perspective, this is a nice example of the duality of process and structure (Katz & Kahn, 1966). Perhaps more importantly, it begins to make salient the dynamic aspects of multilevel phenomena that are inherent but latent in homologous multilevel models (DeShon et al., 2004).

Indeed, Chen and colleagues (Chen, Kanfer, DeShon, Mathieu, & Kozlowski, 2009) evaluated the Chen and Kanfer (2006) model using two datasets that had previously been used to examine individual and team motivational homologies; a study by Chen et al. (2005) and DeShon et al. (2004). They found good support for the Chen and Kanfer model across both datasets. Given that the data had previously examined homology, that cross-level interconnections were established, and that the model was supported in both datasets (which each used different tasks and construct operationalizations), this is pretty solid support for broadening our view of inter-level linkages.

Dynamics, the next frontier

Although MLT has had a substantial influence on team and group research in terms of theoretical principles, research methods and measurement, and analysis, there is one important area that is changing only ever so slowly. The growing number of multilevel articles (see Figure 14.1) is still largely based on cross-sectional data. Although researchers apply MLT and hypothesize about process dynamics and emergent phenomena, for the most part the research is still focused on static models evaluated with static data. For MLT and team research to advance, this must change. We need to be serious about incorporating dynamic processes into our theory and then we need to be serious about modeling dynamic processes directly in our data. Our understanding of many phenomena is limited by the use of static models and between (without within) comparisons.

Dynamic within-person relationships

There are some good examples of modeling dynamic motivational processes in the literature that help illustrate my point. These examples are not team or group level, but they are multilevel because they examine within person variation over time. So, there are two levels, the within person level and between person level. One line of research that has led to an interesting debate is the work by Vancouver and colleagues, who have examined self-efficacy (SE) and performance relationships within persons over time (Vancouver, 2005; Vancouver, Thompson, Tischner, & Putka, 2002; Vancouver, Thompson, & Williams, 2001). Without trying to get into all the complexities, the research shows that, at the within-person level, SE tends to exhibit small negative correlations with subsequent performance. Essentially, when individuals perform well, they feel more confident. They then tend to reduce effort, and subsequent performance declines. This dynamic process playing out within persons over time yields, on average, a small negative relationship between SE and performance at the within-person level.

What is interesting about Vancouver's findings is that they are in stark contrast to the well-demonstrated (and widely accepted) positive relationship between SE and performance at the between-person level of analysis. As I noted, these differences have energized a vigorous debate (Bandura & Locke, 2003; Vancouver, 2005). However, although some frame this as a debate about "who is right," the differences in perspective are likely due to difficulty in understanding that between-person differences and within-person dynamics are very different types of relationships in the data. It is entirely reasonable for the relations to be quite different in form! They are different views of the phenomenon. In any event, there is small cadre of researchers doing some exciting work examining the within person dynamics of motivation (e.g., Schmidt & Dolis, 2009; Schmidt, Dolis, & Tolli, 2009; Yeo & Neal, 2006, 2008).

Modeling the dynamics of emergence

One of the caveats I noted at the beginning of the section on emergence is that representation of composition and compilation constructs generally treats the process of emergence as theoretical (i.e., it is not directly assessed) and then tries to verify the assumed theory checking assumptions in the measurement. That is, investigators check for composition measures for evidence of within-team sharing and compilation measures for evidence of within-team variance or configuration. This is, admittedly, the application of a somewhat circular logic. The tendency among researchers to use cross-sectional designs (let's face it, they are easier) is the primary culprit. Really to begin to extend a multilevel modeling perspective, researchers are going to have to move toward truly longitudinal designs and to model the dynamic process of emergence directly. I wish I could describe some exemplary research, but unfortunately, I'm not aware of any as yet.

As a point of departure, it would not be that difficult to model composition emergence or compilation emergence. What would you need to get started? Well, first you would need to identify phenomena that emerge over time. Socialization of new team members, team development, and team mental models vs. team transactive memory would be my top picks, but you can examine anything that fits the models and your interests. Next, you would need at least a rough idea of the relevant time frame for the phenomena of interest to emerge. Our theories tend to lack precision regarding time, if they treat it at all, so do not expect theory to be very helpful. A good research-guided guess, coupled with as many measurement periods as possible would be a good way to generate descriptive data that could then be used to build theory. With such data in hand, one could model how individual mental model perceptions or climate perceptions begin to converge over time, how antecedents such as team leadership or team training facilitate or inhibit convergence, and how convergence on some key constructs may have ripple effects on the convergence of others. Similarly, one could also model how transactive memory linkages develop over time, how antecedents can facilitate links, and how errors could potentially have catastrophic effects on team performance. This is an incredibly rich and important area for research inquiry and, at the moment, it is not garnering much attention from researchers. Time will tell.

Conclusion

Groups and teams in organizations are collective entities. Although one *can* study them holistically, such approaches tend to miss both the effects of the broader organizational (or other) system within which teams are embedded *and* the dynamic emergent contributions from team members that create collective properties. The purpose of this chapter was to describe basic principles from MLT and methods that enable researchers to study teams in ways that take account of (a) higher-level contextual factors that shape team phenomena *and* (b) lower level interaction and exchange that yield emergent collective phenomena. Although MLT is grounded in organizational systems, the principles are applicable to groups in a wide range of settings including education, communities, families, and friendship networks, among many others. I hope the chapter has conveyed the value of applying MLT to the study of group and team phenomena and that the astute reader will be sufficiently intrigued to delve into the source material.

References

Arrow, H., McGrath, J. E., & Berdahl, J. L. (2000). Small groups as complex systems: Formation coordination, development, and adaptation. Thousand Oaks, CA: Sage.

Bandura, A., & Locke, E. A. (2003). Negative self-efficacy and goal effects revisited. *Journal of Applied Psychology, 88*, 87–99.

Bliese, P. D. (2000). Within-group agreement, non-independence, and reliability: Implications for data aggregation and analysis. In K. J. Klein & S. W. J. Kozlowski (Eds.), *Multilevel theory, research, and methods in organizations* (pp. 349–381). San Francisco: Jossey Bass.

Bliese, P. D., & Ployhart, R. E. (2002). Growth modeling using random coefficient models: Model building, testings, and illustrations. *Organizational Research Methods, 5*(4), 362–387.

Brown, K. G., & Kozlowski, S. W. J. (1999). Toward an expanded conceptualization of emergent organizational phenomena: Dispersion theory. In F. P. Morgeson & D. A. Hofmann (Chairs), *New perspectives on higher-level phenomena in industrial/organizational psychology.* Symposium conducted at the 14th Annual Conference of the Society for Industrial and Organizational Psychology, Atlanta, GA.

Brown, K. G., Kozlowski, S. W. J., & Hattrup, K. (1996). Theory, issues, and recommendations in conceptualizing agreement as a construct in organizational research: The search for consensus regarding consensus. In S. Kozlowski & K. Klein (Chairs), *The meaning and measurement of within-group agreement in multi-level research.* Symposium presented at the 56th Annual Convention of the Academy of Management Association, Cincinnati, OH.

Cannon-Bowers, J. A., Salas, E., & Converse, S. A. (1993). Shared mental models in expert team decision-making. In N. J. Castellan, Jr (Ed.), *Current issues in individual and group decision-making* (pp. 221–246). Hillsdale, NJ: Lawrence Erlbaum.

Chan, D. (1998). Functional relations among constructs in the same content domain at different levels of analysis: A typology of composition models. *Journal of Applied Psychology, 83*, 234–246.

Chen, G., & Bliese, P. D. (2002). The role of different levels of leadership in predicting self and collective efficacy: Evidence for discontinuity. *Journal of Applied Psychology, 87*, 549–556.

Chen, G., Bliese, P. D., & Mathieu, J. E. (2005). Conceptual framework and statistical procedures for delineating and testing multilevel theories of homology. *Organizational Research Methods, 8*, 375–409.

Chen, G., & Kanfer, R. (2006). Toward a systems theory of motivated behavior in work teams. *Research in Organizational Behavior, 27*, 223–267.

Chen, G., Kanfer, R., DeShon, R. D., Mathieu, J. E., & Kozlowski, S. W. J. (in press). The motivating potential of teams: Test and extension of Chen & Kanfer's (2006) cross-level model of motivation in teams. *Organizational Behavior and Human Decision Processes.*

Chen, G., Thomas, B. A., & Wallace, J. C. (2005). A multilevel examination of the relationships among training outcomes, mediating regulatory processes, and adaptive performance. *Journal of Applied Psychology, 90*, 827–841.

Chen, G., Webber, S. S., Bliese, P. D., Mathieu, J. E., Payne, S. C., Born, D. H., & Zaccaro, S. J. (2002). Simultaneous examination of the antecedents and consequences of efficacy beliefs at multiple levels of analysis. *Human Performance, 15*, 381–409.

Dansereau, F., & Yammarino, F. J. (2000). Within and between analysis: The variant paradigm as an underlying approach to theory building and testing. In K. J. Klein & S. W. J. Kozlowski (Eds.), *Multilevel theory, research, and methods in organizations* (pp. 425–466). San Francisco: Jossey Bass.

DeShon, R. P., Kozlowski, S. W. J., Schmidt, A. M., Milner, K. R., & Wiechmann, D. (2004). A multiple goal, multilevel model of feedback effects on the regulation of individual and team performance. *Journal of Applied Psychology, 89*, 1035–1056.

Flake, G. W. (1998). *The computational beauty of nature: Computer explorations of fractals, chaos, complex systems, and adaptation.* Cambridge, MA: MIT Press.

Gibson, C. B. (2001). Me and us: Differential relationships among goal setting, training, efficacy, and effectiveness at the individual and team level. *Journal of Organizational Behavior, 22*, 789–808.

Homans, G. (1950). *The human group.* New York: Harcourt, Brace, and Company.

Hunter, J. E., & Hunter, R. F. (1984). Validity and utility of alternative predictors of job performance. *Psychological Bulletin, 96*, 72–98.

Ilgen, D. R., Hollenbeck, J. R., Johnson, M., & Jundt, D. (2005). Teams in organizations: From input–process–output models to IMOI models. *Annual Review of Psychology, 56*, 517–543.

Ilgen, D. R., & Hulin, C. L. (Eds.) (2000). *Computational modeling of behavior in organizations: The third scientific discipline.* Washington, DC: American Psychological Association.

James, L. R. (1982). Aggregation bias in estimates of perceptual agreement. *Journal of Applied Psychology, 67*, 219–229.

James, L. R., Demaree, R. G., & Wolf, G. (1984). Estimating within group interrater reliability with and without response bias. *Journal of Applied Psychology, 69*, 85–98.

James, L. R., Demaree, R. G., & Wolf, G. (1993). r_{wg}: An assessment of within group interrater agreement. *Journal of Applied Psychology, 78*, 306–309.

James, L. R., & Jones, A. P. (1976). Organizational structure: A review of structural dimensions and their conceptual relationships with individual attitudes and behavior. *Organizational Behavior and Human Performance, 16*, 74–113.

Jones, A. P., & James, L. R. (1979). Psychological climate: Dimensions and relationships of individual and aggregated work environment perceptions. *Organizational Behavior and Human Performance, 23*, 201–250.

Karoly, P. (1993). Mechanisms of self-regulation: A systems view. *Annual Review of Psychology, 44,* 23–52.

Katz, D., & Kahn, R. L. (1966). *The social psychology of organizations.* New York: Wiley.

Klein, K. J., Bliese, P. D., et al. (2000). An integrative perspective on multi-level analyses. In K. J. Klein & S. W. J. Kozlowski (Eds.), *Multilevel theory, research, and methods in organizations* (pp. 512–553). San Francisco: Jossey Bass.

Klein, K. J., Conn, A. B., Smith, D. B., & Sorra, J. S. (2001). Is everyone in agreement? An exploration of within-group agreement in employee perceptions of the work environment. *Journal of Applied Psychology, 86,* 3–16.

Klein, K. J., Dansereau, F., & Hall, R. J. (1994). Levels issues in theory development, data collection, and analysis. *Academy of Management Review, 19,* 195–229.

Klein, K. J., & Kozlowski, S. W. J. (Eds.). (2000). *Multilevel theory, research, and methods in organizations.* San Francisco: Jossey Bass.

Kozlowski, S. W. J., & Bell, B. S. (2003). Work groups and teams in organizations. In W. C. Borman, D. R. Ilgen, & R. J. Klimoski (Eds.), *Handbook of psychology: Industrial and organizational psychology* (Vol. 12, pp. 333–375). London: Wiley.

Kozlowski, S. W. J., & Farr, J. L. (1988). An integrative model of updating and performance. *Human Performance, 1,* 5–29.

Kozlowski, S. W. J., Gully, S. M., McHugh, P. P., Salas, E., & Cannon-Bowers, J. A. (1996). A dynamic theory of leadership and team effectiveness: Developmental and task contingent leader roles. In G. R. Ferris (Ed.), *Research in personnel and human resource management* (Vol. 14, pp. 253–305). Greenwich, CT: JAI Press.

Kozlowski, S. W. J., Gully, S. M., Nason, E. R., & Smith, E. M. (1999). Developing adaptive teams: A theory of compilation and performance across levels and time. In D. R. Ilgen & E. D. Pulakos (Eds.), *The changing nature of work performance: Implications for staffing, personnel actions, and development* (pp. 240–292). San Francisco: Jossey-Bass.

Kozlowski, S. W. J., & Hattrup, K. (1992). A disagreement about within-group agreement: Disentangling issues of consistency versus consensus. *Journal of Applied Psychology, 77,* 161–167.

Kozlowski, S. W. J., & Hults, B. M. (1987). An exploration of climates for technical updating and performance. *Personnel Psychology, 40,* 539–563.

Kozlowski, S. W. J., & Ilgen, D. R. (2006). Enhancing the effectiveness of work groups and teams (Monograph). *Psychological Science in the Public Interest, 7,* 77–124.

Kozlowski, S. W. J., & Klein, K. J. (2000). A multilevel approach to theory and research in organizations: Contextual, temporal, and emergent processes. In K. J. Klein & S. W. J. Kozlowski (Eds.), *Multilevel theory, research and methods in organizations: Foundations, extensions, and new directions* (pp. 3–90). San Francisco, CA: Jossey-Bass.

Levine, J. M., & Moreland, R. L. (1990). Progress in small-group research. *Annual Review of Psychology, 41,* 585–634.

Lewin, K. (1951). *Field theory in the social sciences.* New York: Harper.

Lewin, K., Lippitt, R., & White, R. K. (1939). Patterns of aggressive behavior in experimentally created social climates. *Journal of Social Psychology, 10,* 271–301.

Likert, R. (1961). *The human organization: Its management and value.* New York: McGraw-Hill.

Marks, M. A., Mathieu, J. E., & Zaccaro, S. J. (2001). A temporally based framework and taxonomy of team processes. *Academy of Management Review, 26*(3), 356–376.

Miller, J. G. (1978). *Living systems.* New York: McGraw-Hill.

Morgeson, F. P., & Hofmann, D. A. (1999). The structure and function of collective constructs: Implications for multilevel research and theory development. *Academy of Management Review, 24,* 249–265.

Roberts, K. H., Hulin, C. L., & Rousseau, D. M. (1978). *Developing an interdisciplinary science of organizations.* San Francisco: Jossey-Bass.

Rousseau, D. M. (1978). Measures of technology as predictors of employee attitude. *Journal of Applied Psychology, 63,* 213–218.

Rousseau, D. M. (1985). Issues of level in organizational research: Multi-level and cross-level perspectives. In L. L. Cummings & B. M. Staw (Eds.), *Research in organizational behavior* (Vol. 7, pp.1–37). Greenwich, CT: JAI Press.

Schmidt, A. M., & Dolis, C. M. (2009). Something's got to give: The effects of dual-goal difficulty, goal progress, and expectancies on resource allocation. *Journal of Applied Psychology, 94*(3), 678–691.

Schmidt, A. M., Dolis, C. M., & Tolli, A. P. (2009). A matter of time: Individual differences, contextual dynamics and goal progress effects on multiple-goal self-regulation. *Journal of Applied Psychology, 94*(3), 692–709.

Schneider, B., & Bowen, D. E. (1985). Employee and customer perceptions of service in banks: Replication and extension. *Journal of Applied Psychology, 70,* 423–433.

Schneider, B., Salvaggio, A. N., & Subirats, M. (2002). Climate strength: A new direction for climate research. *Journal of Applied Psychology, 87,* 220–229.

Staw, B. M., Sandelands, L. E., & Dutton, J. E. (1981). Threat-rigidity effects on organizational behavior. *Administrative Science Quarterly, 26,* 501–524.

Vancouver, J. B. (2005). The depth of history and explanation as benefit and bane for psychological control theories. *Journal of Applied Psychology, 90,* 38–52.

Vancouver, J. B., Thompson, C. M., Tischner, E. C., & Putka, D. J. (2002). Two studies examining the negative effect of self-efficacy on performance. *Journal of Applied Psychology, 87,* 506–516.

Vancouver, J. B., Thompson, C. M., & Williams, A. A. (2001). The changing signs in the relationships between self-efficacy, personal goals and performance. *Journal of Applied Psychology, 86,* 605–620.

von Bertalanffy, L. (1968). *General system theory.* New York: Braziller.

von Bertalanffy, L. (1972). The history and status of general systems theory. In G. J. Klir (Ed.), *Trends in general systems theory* (pp. 21–41). New York: Wiley.

Wegner, D. M. (1995). A computer network model of human transactive memory. *Social Cognition, 13,* 319–339.

Yeo, G., & Neal, A. (2006). An examination of the dynamic relationship between self-efficacy and performance across levels of analysis and levels of specificity. *Journal of Applied Psychology, 91,* 1088–1101.

Yeo, G., & Neal, A. (2008). Subjective cognitive effort: A model of states, traits and time. *Journal of Applied Psychology, 93,* 617–631.

15

UNDERSTANDING GROUPS FROM A NETWORK PERSPECTIVE

Noshir S. Contractor

NORTHWESTERN UNIVERSITY

Chunke Su

UNIVERSITY OF TEXAS AT ARLINGTON

There is a long-standing, albeit modest, tradition of applying network approaches to the study of groups starting with the launch of the Group Networks Laboratory at MIT shortly after World War II by Alex Bavelas. However, many group researchers, especially those not familiar with network research methods, are often frustrated and challenged by this methodological approach. Thus the goal of this chapter is to offer readers a pragmatic guidebook based on our experiences applying a social network approach to studying groups.

A fundamental commitment to incorporate relational and structural explanations along with individual and group level factors distinguishes the social network approach from other perspectives on analyzing groups (Contractor, Wasserman, & Faust, 2006; Katz, Lazer, Arrow, & Contractor, 2004; Kilduff & Tsai, 2003; Monge & Contractor, 2003; Wellman, 1988). This emphasis on incorporating relational explanations implies that the social network approach examines the group from a multilevel perspective by spanning the individual level (member attributes, such as expertise and satisfaction), the dyadic level (information retrieval, trust), and the overall group level (group density, centralization). We begin this chapter with a brief discussion of important research questions that motivate the use of a social network approach to study critical group processes. Second, we share with you our experiences on collecting network data from groups. The third section describes the "sausage-making" process of manipulating, visualizing, and analyzing network data. We conclude this chapter by addressing the challenges and limitations of network research in its current state, as well as its future.

Social Network Approach to Studying Groups

A social network is defined as a collection of social entities (termed as *nodes*) that are connected by one or more types of relationships (termed as *ties*) (Scott, 2000;

Wasserman & Faust, 1994). When a group is conceptualized as a network, the nodes typically include individual group members, and the network ties can be several types of relationships among group members: social communication, professional collaboration, trust, information retrieval and allocation, advice-seeking, perception of expertise, etc. Drawing upon our past research experiences, we suggest that a social network perspective would be particularly applicable and useful to examine four facets of group processes.

Group formation

We find ourselves increasingly participating in ad-hoc, distributed, virtual, and transient groups both at work and socially. Therefore, an increasingly important question is for us to understand why people form groups and how do those formation mechanisms influence the outcomes of these groups. Intuitively we can conjecture that our prior networks influence the groups we join and our experiences in these groups in turn shape our future networks. In the past half-decade, there has been some promising and intriguing research that have built on these intuitions by drawing on network approaches to address questions of group formation and assembly (Cummings & Kiesler, 2005; Guimerà, Uzzi, Spiro, & Amaral, 2005; Jones, Wuchty, & Uzzi, 2008).

Information retrieval and allocation

Propelled by the ongoing digital revolution, members of groups have unprecedented autonomy and choice in determining from whom (or from where) they can retrieve information or with whom they can share or to what repository they can allocate information. This unfettered ability does not imply that members engage in random acts of information retrieval and allocation. Instead, it underscores the importance of understanding the social motivations that explain these nonrandom behaviors. Research over the past decade has begun to uncover the motivations for information retrieval and allocation behaviors, and much of this research illustrates the ability of network approaches to address these questions (Casciaro & Lobo, 2005; Contractor & Monge, 2002; Cross & Borgatti, 2004; Palazzolo, 2005; Su & Contractor, 2011).

Leadership in groups

There is an increasing appreciation that in contemporary groups, leadership is more accurately investigated as an emergent phenomenon than formally designated. A social network approach is particularly desirable to study emergent and informal leadership, hidden from the formal organizational chart (Cross & Parker, 2004) or decentralized, transient, and shared (Burke, Fiore, & Salas, 2003). Therefore, not surprisingly, the complex interplay between members' positions in the network and their emergence in leadership roles has been the subject of growing interest in recent years (Balkundi & Harrison, 2006; Huffaker, 2010).

Outcomes of group processes

Finally, there is a growing awareness that social network approaches contribute additional explanatory variance in understanding the outcomes of group processes, such as performance and satisfaction. For instance, group members tend to be more satisfied with group work when actively retrieving information from others than passively receiving unsolicited information allocated from others in the network (Su, Huang, & Contractor, 2010). In a meta-analysis of 37 studies on naturally existent groups, Balkundi and Harrison (2006) concluded that groups with denser social networks among their members tended to achieve better performance and higher cohesiveness. At the group level, they found that groups that were central in their intergroup network tended to perform better as well (Balkundi & Harrison, 2006).

The four group phenomena summarized above illustrate why social network approaches have a growing relevance to the group research. Armed with this motivation, we next delve into the pragmatics of collecting network data.

Collecting Network Data from Groups

In this section, we share our experiences based upon a program of research over the past decade involving three large interdisciplinary projects investigating networks and groups. In the *first* project, we investigated how networks could help us better understand what motivated members of a team to retrieve or share expertise about certain topics with specific other members of the team. Our research, which investigated over two dozen teams from organizations in government, private, and public sector in the US and Europe, uncovered that members did not always go to those whom they identified as experts. There were other network motivations that explained their retrieval and allocation behaviors. In the *second* project, we have been investigating how networks can help us understand team formation in massively multiplayer online role-playing games. Our research, which is investigating thousands of online teams ranging in size from three to 70, indicate that decisions on whom to invite on to teams are driven both by social factors and the need to enlist members with specific skills. The networks among assembled teams have a systematic impact on the performance of these teams. Our *third* project is investigating the formation and leadership among virtual and co-located interdisciplinary research teams in the areas of nanoscience, translational science, and oncofertility. Here we find that co-authorship, citation, and prior collaboration have systematic but non-linear impacts on teams' success in submitting successful proposals, publishing highly cited articles, or developing highly utilized software. Next, we describe the approaches we adopted and our experiences with the collection of network data.

Broadly speaking, we can collect two types of network data: *whole-network* (or census network) and *egocentric* network data (Marsden, 2005). Whole-network data refers to the complete set of data available from each and every member within the group. The egocentric network concerns the focal (or "ego") member's network connections with others. In many cases, the "ego" members are also asked to provide information about their perceptions of network ties that might exist among their contacts. Egocentric research and whole-network research require different methods of data collection (for detailed distinctions between the two designs, see Marsden, 2005). In general, greater insights can be obtained by collecting whole-network data. For instance, if one is interested in investigating the extent to which a centralized group will have higher or lower performance, it would be essential to collect whole-network data. However, if one is interested in the extent to which an individual's satisfaction with the team is explained by the satisfaction of other team members whom they trust, it would be sufficient to collect egocentric network data.

From a practical standpoint, when conducting research in small groups, it would be prudent to collect whole-network data. Collecting whole-network data in large groups is more time-consuming and challenging than collecting individual data or group data that is based on individual attributes only. When studying a group as a whole network, researchers need to collect data about each individual, as well as how each individual is connected with everyone else in the same group. Further, in some instances, we have collected cognitive social structure (CSS) data (Krackhardt, 1987a) where we ask group members not only how they are connected with every other member in the group, but also their perceptions of how every other member is connected with one another. Therefore, in a group with a size of n, the unit number of relational data to be collected amounts to $n(n - 1)$ (directional network) or $n(n - 1)/2$ (undirectional network). An empirical example can be found in a study we conducted at a city's public works department (Heald, Contractor, Koehly, & Wasserman, 1998), where we investigated the predictors of co-workers' perceptual congruence (the degree to which people agree on their perceptions of the organization's social network structure). Our findings showed that department employees' perceptual congruence was influenced by their similarities in formal organizational structure, gender and racial homophily, as well as emergent network ties such as social communication, acquaintance, and workflow relationships (Heald et al., 1998).

In the next two sections, we will discuss in detail the methods and procedures through which network data can be obtained from groups.

Sources and tools for data collection

One of the commonly used techniques to collect social network data is survey and questionnaire methods (Marsden, 2005). Traditionally, pen and paper-based surveys were widely used for respondents to mark and report their relationships with each other by thumbing through the hard copies. Since the inception of the World Wide Web, online network surveys have become increasingly popular and desirable. In recent years, there has been a rapid development of advanced web tools to collect social network data. Such web-based software is not only a data collection portal, but can also be a data visualizer and analytic tool. C-IKNOW (Cyber-infrastructure for Inquiring Knowledge Networks on the Web) is a tool that we have developed to support our research on networks in groups (Contractor, 2009a).

We decided to use online network survey tools over paper-based and traditional online non-network surveys for three reasons. First, respondents can enter their attribute and relational data via an interactive web interface. When answering network questions in the online survey, respondents are able to select their relational contacts by filtering the target person's attributes (e.g., one's organizational or group affiliation) or searching the target person's name (see Figure 15.1 for an illustration of such features in C-IKNOW). In subsequent questions, the online survey will only display those selected contacts rather than repeatedly displaying all respondents listed in the survey. This filtering mechanism is especially helpful and desirable when respondents are connected with only a small portion of a very large network. In addition, if a respondent communicates with a person who is not on the contact list in the survey, the respondent can add this person into the

FIGURE 15.1 C-IKNOW interface: selecting relational contacts in the network.

network question. Then other respondents have the option to log back into the survey and report their network connections to this person.

Second, after the network data are collected, we have used C-IKNOW to provide respondents with network visualizations and algorithm-based recommendations based on the data they have provided. One critical challenge to network data collection is to obtain complete and quality data from group members. One novel solution to this challenge is to give respondents some potential payoff for providing complete and quality data. In one study we conducted at a large food and beverage products firm, we were interested in helping assess the effectiveness of distributed teams that were charged with the design of new food products. The design of the study required each member of the team to answer several questions about their own areas of expertise and their network relationships (such as prior or current collaboration) with other members of the team. Following the online survey, and with prior agreement from all group members, each member of the team was given the opportunity to log back into C-IKNOW and use it to identify who on the distributed team had expertise on a particular topic. Further, they could visualize how they might be directly or indirectly connected through network relationships with this individual. Clearly the quality of search results provided to the team member would depend on the quality of data entered by the members of the team. Thus it was in the team members' individual and collective interest to provide high-quality data as part of the survey. More generally, in our past experiences, the provision of network visualizations, access to metrics and recommendations incentivize respondents to provide accurate data. Of course, as mentioned in the above example, there needs to be a prior agreement about which responses provided by members will be shared among all members.

Third, respondents to network surveys are more likely to experience physical and mental fatigue due to the extended length and complexity of data inquiries. We designed the online survey to make the web interface as simple, visually appealing, and user-friendly as possible. The survey also prompts respondents to take breaks during the process and makes it easier for them to resume the survey from the point where they have left off.

The above online network survey tools are suitable for collecting whole-network data or egocentric network data. However, there are other computer programs specifically designed for collecting egocentric network data. For example, EgoNet (2011) is an open-source software for collecting egocentric network data developed by Christopher McCarty and his colleagues at the University of Florida. Researchers can set up network surveys by using EgoNet. In addition, EgoNet provides basic network metrics and data matrices which can be analyzed in other visual-analytic programs of social networks.

Although the survey method may be the easiest and most straightforward way to identify network connections in a group of individuals, it only collects subjective and self-reported data from the respondents. Usually these data are provided in retrospect and mediated by respondents' memory. In addition, the survey method is inadequate in capturing large-scale network data and in rich format. To overcome these limitations, we have joined with others who have a growing interest in exploring *observational* and *archival* approaches to collect more objective and dynamic network data in group settings.

First, researchers can acquire network data through observational coding. Here is a simple scenario: researchers join a group meeting of a software development team, and take notes on who is talking to whom as well as the frequency and length of each conversation. However, when studying larger, media-supported groups that may be geographically co-located or dispersed, there is a new generation of observational technologies that hold a lot of promise for capturing rich network data in teams. GroupScope (Poole et al., 2009) is an example of a new generation of an observational suite of tools that is being designed to include a multitude of high-definition video cameras, audio recorders, infrared sensors, accelerometers, RFIDs, and other observational instruments, to automate procedures to collect, annotate, and code large quantities of video and audio data generated by groups. Sandy Pentland at MIT, James Kitts at Columbia, and Tanzeem Choudhury at Dartmouth, and their colleagues have been at the forefront of developing these tools and utilizing them in their research (Wu, Waber, Aral, Brynjolfsson, & Pentland, 2008; Wyatt et al., 2011). Commodified versions of some of these observational technologies are now becoming available for use in research laboratories (Pentland, 2008).

An additional benefit of using observational technologies is to broaden our vision of what constitutes network data within groups. While survey methods typically provide data at one or a few points in time, observational technologies provide network data at intervals of a second or even less. These high-resolution network data, sometimes referred to as network event data, open up the possibility of developing new theories as well as methods for understanding the emergence and outcomes of group processes. The data collected from observational technologies may not be relational in nature. For example, observational technologies, such as RFIDs, might provide positional data for each group member. Additional processing would then be required to infer the distance between any two group members. Thus researchers need to utilize precise algorithms to identify network connections from observational data. For example, Mathur, Poole, Pena-Mora, Contractor, and Hasegawa-Johnson (2009) have developed an algorithm to map network linkages from video data combined with transcriptions of interactions within groups.

Another effective method is to collect *archival* data from groups by harvesting group members' digital traces from information systems that record members' behaviors (Lazer et al., 2009). For instance, as mentioned earlier, we are part of a large interdisciplinary effort to study teams within massively multiplayer online role-playing games (MMORPGs). MMORPGs serve as an excellent context in which to study how individuals (or more accurately their characters or avatars) with different skill sets need to come together in teams in order to accomplish quests and raids to kill monsters or obtain resources. This study relies heavily on our getting access to anonymized server logs maintained by the developers of these games. These logs chronicle every single action (such as making a product or moving to a location), interaction (such as who is chatting with whom or broadcasting a message to a team), and transactions (such as buying a weapon or gifting a wardrobe item to another player) carried out in the game. These digital traces can be extremely large in size. Our team is working with the dataset that is over 40 terabytes! Here again we face challenges in developing algorithms to extract network relationships accurately from the corpus of digital traces. This research has provided new insights into why people choose to team up with specific other individuals and with what implications for their performance (Williams, Contractor, Poole, Srivastava, & Cai, 2011).

Finally, we have also explored understanding the dynamics of teams by harvesting archival network data from publicly available digital sources such as links among individuals' websites, bibliometric databases, and text-mining documents written by individuals. As more research in various fields of science and engineering in the past few years are being carried in teams, there has been a growing interest in understanding and enabling "team science" (Börner et al., 2010). This field of inquiry, sometimes referred to as the Science of Team Science, is particularly focused on trying to explain why some teams are more effective than others based on their affiliations (reflected, for instance, by links among their websites), prior collaborations (reflected, for instance, by co-authorship gleaned from bibliometric databases), and common interests (reflected, for instance, by similar use of concepts obtained by text mining their documents). This research illustrates the potential of leveraging external digital data that are available on the Internet such as bibliometric, web crawling, and text mining of transcripts.

Survey data collection procedures

Before the actual data collection procedures start, the boundary of the network to be studied needs to be defined (Marsden, 2005). That is, how do we decide who is considered as a member of the network? Monge and Contractor (1988) observed that this boundary could be based on space and time. They proposed three criteria for who to include based on the space dimension: common attributes such as membership and affiliations, participating in a particular type of relationship, and common activities. In the time dimension, they distinguished between cross-sectional and longitudinal network research. We have used two approaches to administer longitudinal network surveys. One is to aggregate the number of group interactions periodically (i.e., at equal time intervals). For instance, we have collected information retrieval network data among established teams in the online *World of Warcraft* game at three points in time at monthly intervals (Wotal, Green, Williams, & Contractor, 2006). This enables us to understand the emergence of experts in the team. A second approach is to collect data at

292   Noshir S. Contractor and Chunke Su

specific stages or cycles of the group. For instance, we have used this approach to study the network structure of teams in online games when they first form and compare it to the teams' network structure at the conclusion of joint combat activities.

The above procedure is relatively straightforward if we are studying a formally assembled, well-defined, and pre-existing group. However, we need to be more cautious when we are examining ad-hoc, emergent, and bona-fide groups or where we are collecting network data to study group formation. Such groups have permeable boundaries, dynamic goals, and flexible group structures (Putnam & Stohl, 1996). Thus, it is more challenging to make a clear-cut decision on who should or should not be included in the network. Particularly if we are investigating the group creation process, we need to make sure to update the network formation continuously. Whenever a new member joins the group, we need to remind participants to provide their relational data with this new member in the survey. When someone exits the group, we may want to withdraw her or his relational data with others from the survey. However, we might want to retain information about those who exit the team if the research question is to understand why they may have left the team voluntarily or involuntarily.

Pre-survey interview

An additional strategy we have found useful to help researchers define the network boundary is to set up interviews with one or more members of the group (preferably the leaders or supervisors of the group) prior to data collection. Even when the network boundary has already been defined, the pre-survey interview can help verify the accuracy and validity of the determined boundary. In some cases it might reveal the need to include in the network some key individuals who are not technically on the team but have crucial interactions with the team.

Typically, we gather the following information about the group in the pre-survey interview: the name of each member (including individuals' nicknames if those are used widely at work), the basic structure of the group, the major tasks of the group, the primary knowledge areas required to complete group tasks (this is particularly applicable if we are studying information retrieval and allocation and want to ask questions about specific areas of expertise), the timeline of group work, the technology and resources utilized in the group (for multidimensional network research), the relative amount of interaction (e.g., daily, weekly, monthly, etc.) and other key information that might inform the design of specific questions. These meetings might also be used to discuss if and how much of the network data that is collected would be shared with the participants or their supervisors. As mentioned earlier, in some cases individuals' responses can be used to provide the team with a recommender system that can be used by the team to help them identify appropriate experts. While these systems will encourage respondents to provide more accurate data, it also means that some of their responses will be shared with other members of the team. These issues need to be negotiated prior to the design of the survey, and need to be included in any consent form that will be signed by respondents. Finally a pre-survey meeting is also helpful in enlisting a letter mailed from an influential individual in the organization encouraging participants to complete the survey.

As discussed elsewhere, unlike most other surveys, network surveys are only valid if the response rate is 100 percent or very close to it. This is because in a network survey, each respondent is providing information not only about themselves but also about every other person in the network. Therefore, a single missing respondent affects the data for all respondents.

Customization of survey

Based on the information garnered from the pre-survey interview, we create a survey customized for each group. If an online network survey is to be utilized, we need to add all participants' contact information to the survey database, such as their names, departmental affiliations, and email addresses. As mentioned previously, a major advantage of the online survey is to minimize the effort of each respondent. Therefore, it is always a good idea to pre-populate into the online survey as much information about respondents as we are able to collect in advance. This will give respondents a chance to review the material and modify it only if they identify certain errors. We then provide each participant with a unique login and password to access the survey online. Systems like C-IKNOW automate the procedure of emailing the URL of the survey to participants with their login information. Right after the opening welcome screen introducing the survey, participants must be presented with a consent form. The consent form should state clearly if some of their responses will be revealed in post-survey visual-analytics to group managers or all group members (e.g., the recommendation system mentioned earlier in this chapter).

Based on our own research experiences, for a group of 18 participants, a single network question would take a participant approximately five minutes to finish. Thus the entire survey may take a group member several hours to complete. As a result, we have on occasion given participants a generous time span (from days to weeks) to finish the survey at one's own pace. One advantage of online surveys is the ability for an individual to complete part of it at one time and then return to complete the rest at a later time. C-IKNOW provides the researcher with a dashboard indicating at any point in time how many questions have been completed by each respondent. Because the response rate is so crucial, we routinely and periodically send out reminders to participants encouraging them to complete their surveys.

The network survey is distinguished from most other surveys by its focus on relational questions. In a network survey, we are often interested in asking about different types of relationships between group members: interpersonal communication, trust, information retrieval and allocation, perception of expertise, advice-seeking, affect, collaboration, workflow, etc. (Krackhardt, 1992). This enables us to answer questions about how one relationship (such as trust) between two group members might influence a second relationship (such as information retrieval) between them. Later in this chapter we will discuss how to conduct these analyses.

After deciding on the specific relations one might want to measure, we next need to decide on the scales we use. We can use different scales and instruments to collect different kinds of network data: binary data (representing the presence and absence of certain relationships), continuous or valued data (differentiating degrees of certain relationships), and cognitive social structure data (which collects the perceptions of each respondent about relations among all members in the network).

The relational questions can be further categorized into sublevel context specific questions. For example, researchers can ask respondents to report their information retrieval behavior in a specific knowledge domain and repeat the same question for every other knowledge domain.

It is crucial to pay special attention to the importance and consequences of phrasing relational questions. For example, a question asking about "how often do you talk to your group members" would lead to a directional network of intragroup communication, whereas a question asking about "how often do you talk with your group members" results in a nondirectional network. This illustrates how what might appear to be a relatively trivial choice in wording can yield two very different kinds of network data. Further, relational questions can be phrased differently to elicit respondents' *desired* relationships or *actual* relationships. For example, the question "how often would you retrieve information from your group leader" might reflect a desired relationship and the question "how often did you retrieve information from your group leader" would imply an actual relationship. Likewise, there is a difference between *abstract* vs. *concrete* questions. An example of an abstract relational question would be "In a typical week, how often do you retrieve information from each group member?" A concrete question would be "In the past week, how often did you retrieve information from each member in the group?" An abstract question might be more appropriate if one is looking for general trends in the network that do not fluctuate dramatically. A concrete question might be more appropriate if one is looking for more accurate responses over a shorter (more recent) time frame.

Just as in non-network surveys, researchers should be cognizant of the challenges posed by confounding effects of social desirability. It is possible that respondents are giving researchers simply "what researchers want to hear" or "what make them look good" instead of genuinely reporting their perceptions and behaviors. Further, we have found that, in many cases, respondents are more hesitant to provide candid responses when answering network questions (especially on sensitive relationships such as personal affect and trust), because they are asked to reveal their perceptions of someone with whom they work or interact closely.

To alleviate these concerns, researchers should reiterate for the respondents the confidentiality and anonymity of survey data prior to data collection. This is a substantial challenge that is not always overcome. For instance, in a study we conducted among members on an emergency responders team, several participants refused to rate the extent to which they trusted other members because they did not feel "comfortable" sharing that information even with assurances of confidentiality.

Another strategy we have used to minimize socially desirable responses is to consider the ordering of questions carefully. For instance, it is not a good idea to ask respondents which members they retrieve information from on a particular topic, and follow that with another question asking them to rate the expertise of each member on the same topic. In order to reduce their cognitive dissonance, respondents might be tempted to rate highly the expertise of those from whom they reported retrieving information. This would contaminate the validity and reliability of the findings in the relationship between the two variables. One way to overcome such problems is to ensure that such questions are spaced far apart within the survey. We have also found it useful to encourage respondents to take breaks when answering a lengthy network survey. This helps mitigate respondent fatigue and improves overall completion rate.

If the data are collected online, it is critical that the survey portal directs respondents to where they have left off when they log back into the survey after taking the break. Finally, another strategy to reduce socially desirable responses is to make sure that we state the purpose of the research project to respondents in fairly general terms without making specific reference to research goals and research questions.

Administering data collection

To facilitate the data collection process and enhance the data quality, our first preference is to assemble all respondents in one room and administer the network survey physically in person. It is important to provide each respondent sufficient space so that they have privacy while responding to their surveys. Even if the network survey is to be completed online or in electronic forms, we have found that a face-to-face administration (in a room that has computers or where respondents bring their laptops) greatly increases the likelihood of collecting quality and complete data from participants. If a face-to-face meeting with respondents is not possible (as in the case with distributed teams), we have administered the online survey collectively at a scheduled time where we communicate with all respondents via conference call and stay on the line to answer any questions and offer clarifications. Even with the best of intentions, we have always encountered a few individuals who are unable to participate in a collective session. In such cases, we have invested the time and effort to schedule a one-on-one meeting (in person or via the phone) with individual participants to walk them through the survey questions. While these approaches might seem fairly labor-intensive, the critical importance of obtaining a high response rate justifies the return of investment.

At the beginning of the survey administration, in person or collectively, online or offline, we begin by briefly explaining the general goal of the research project and the procedures of survey completion. Next we ensure that all respondents have reviewed and approved the consent form. If the survey is administered online, respondents can indicate their willingness to "sign" a consent form by clicking on a button that says "Agree." Most of the respondents in our surveys have not previously encountered network questions. Since many of the group members are not accustomed to reporting relational data, it is crucial to clarify the privacy and confidentiality of the data they provide. This is particularly important if researchers are collecting sensitive relational data such as interpersonal trust, affect, or preferential choice. In cases where participants are given the option to access and review network visualizations or other network metrics following the survey, we make sure orally that they are aware of the relevant text in the consent form prior to them signing it.

Many of the strategies outlined above are motivated by the importance of a 100 percent response rate in network research. The 100 percent response rate refers to all respondents' completion of all survey questions, including individual-based and relational questions. In non-network research, there are standard protocols to deal with missing data without causing significant data loss both conceptually and statistically. However, as network data are relational in nature, if some participants do not respond, researchers would lose not only their data, but also the relational data they report about all other participants in the group. Hence, the lack of response by participants would render all their reported relationships with others incomplete and difficult to interpret. Clearly a small amount of missing data in network research would lead to considerable data loss. In addition, most social network analysis techniques do not have standard procedures for handling missing data. Any missing information in the data input would be invalid and cause errors in the analysis. Therefore, while a 100 percent response rate is not strictly required in traditional non-network research, researchers should make every effort to collect as complete network data as possible.

Of course, a 100 percent response rate cannot always be guaranteed in reality. Should researchers have to deal with missing network data, they can use some data manipulation methods to mitigate the negative impact of missing data on data analysis and interpretation, which will be discussed in a later section of this chapter.

Dealing with large samples

Groups vary in their sizes. In network terms, large samples could refer to either or both of the following situations: a network composed of one group with a large number of members, and a network composed of a large number of groups. Generally speaking, using the survey method to collect network data from large samples is extremely difficult and challenging. As the size of the network increases, the length of the relational questions in the survey expands considerably. Consequently, the data collection process becomes more time-consuming, and respondents are less willing and able to provide quality and complete data.

The large sample problem is especially salient in collecting whole-network data. One way to help resolve the large sample problem is to begin by focusing on only a small number of key members in the group. Then by using the respondent-driven sampling method (RDS; Heckathorn, 1997), researchers can invite these key members to identify other members with whom they are connected in a larger network. Further, the procedure can be repeated to survey even more members in the extended network. In this way, researchers can collect a large volume of network data without burdening every individual member for data input. In addition, the RDS approach is particularly helpful when investigating groups (such as "underground" groups) that might have a vested interest to remain concealed. In such cases, RDS provides an excellent strategy for researchers to develop trusting relationships with participants and utilize their network contacts to identify other members within the group.

The second method to help collect network data from large samples is to utilize diverse data collection methods and "mash" all the data into a coherent and meaningful data structure. When studying a large group, researchers can supplement survey methods with capturing group members' digital traces such as server log data and online behaviors (e.g., bibliometrics for scientific and research groups). These digitally generated data can be "mashed" with survey and observational data to provide a more comprehensive and enriched view of the group. For instance, in our study of groups in massively multiplayer online games, we invited players to complete an online survey. Since they logged into the game to complete their surveys, we were able to "mash" their survey responses with their online data obtained from server logs. In practice, the networks generated from each of these sources (surveys, server logs, bibliometrics) are stored in separate matrices where the rows and the columns represent the nodes in the network. We might conclude that each of these networks provides an important but incomplete indication of some underlying relationships (for instance, collaboration). In that case, "mashing" the three networks would imply adding the cell entries in the three matrices to generate a new network that might offer a more complete representation of the underlying relationships. The next section will discuss in detail how to mash and manipulate raw network data prior to data visualization and data analysis.

Manipulation of Network Data

After network data have been collected, researchers need to manipulate the raw network data to prepare them for visual-analytics. Manipulation typically refers to the process by which the "raw" network data are converted into the form which can be input directly into visualization and analysis software to explore specific research questions. Different visual-analytic tools may require different data inputs. Therefore, it is a common practice to manipulate the raw network data to make them suitable for a specific kind of analytic program. In some cases, researchers need to dichotomize the valued network data into binary data (either 1 or 0), because certain analytic programs or procedures require the input data to be binary. The cutoff value can be set to the mean score of the network, or the median score of the scales. It is worth noting that, in many instances, we are tempted to collect valued data from our respondents only to dichotomize them before conducting any analysis. If we can anticipate that the analysis we might want to conduct would only require binary data, we could have saved the respondent the additional effort in providing valued data. In other cases, researchers need to add multiple networks together, subtract one network from another, conduct cell by cell multiplications, and matrix multiplications.

We have used addition when we intended to combine two relations (such as advice and friendship) to generate a general measure of a "close" multiplex social tie. We have used subtraction where one of the relations we measured was the total amount of communication among team members, and the second relation we measured was the amount of task-related communication among team members. In this case, we subtract the latter from the former to generate a measure of non-task-related communication among team members.

We have used cell by cell multiplications when one of the relations measured was the extent to which each group member rated every other member's expertise on a topic, and the second relation measured was the frequency with which each member retrieved information on the same topic from every other member in the group. Cell by cell multiplication would provide a measure of the extent to which group members were retrieving information from those they considered knowledgeable.

Finally, we have used matrix multiplication in cases where we have group members reporting on their retrieval of information from multiple knowledge repositories. In this case the network is represented as a matrix where the rows refer to group members and the columns refer to knowledge repositories. In this so-called "bimodal" network, a cell entry of 1 in Row *i* and Column *j* indicates that the group member in Row *i* retrieved information from the knowledge repository in Column *j*. By multiplying this matrix with its transpose (where the matrix is flipped so that the rows now represent knowledge repositories and the columns represent the group members), we generate a new matrix where the rows and columns both represent group members and the cell entries represent the number of knowledge repositories from which they both retrieved information. The matrix algebra procedures to manipulate network data can be performed using a social network analysis software program such as UCINET (Borgatti, Everett, & Freeman, 2002) or by using R packages for Statnet (Handcock, Hunter, Butts, Goodreau, & Morris, 2003). The former program, which runs on Windows, is largely menu driven and has a low learning curve. The R packages for Statnet are Unix based and therefore platform independent. It requires a modest level of syntax writing and as a result has a relatively steep learning curve. But the tool has a great deal of flexibility and can be used on local computers as well as on higher performance cluster computing environments.

Dealing with incomplete network data

In practice, especially when collecting network data from a large group or a number of large groups, missing data are sometimes inevitable despite the best efforts of researchers. A government analyst who studies terrorist groups once remarked, "It is difficult to get terrorists to complete our network surveys."

When there is only an insignificant proportion of missing data, there are several remedies to minimize the loss of information in the data. Depending on the theoretical and conceptual nature of the variable being measured, we can recode the missing value into a new value that would be meaningful and valid for data analysis. For example, if group member A reports a friendship tie with member B in the survey, but member B does not respond to the survey, we might choose to infer that a friendship tie exists from member B to member A. The rationale for this type of recoding is based on the reciprocal nature of friendship relationships. We adopt this strategy when we believe that it is more likely for respondents to commit an error of omission rather than an error of commission.

In other cases, we have chosen to recode the missing value to 0 to signify the absence of a friendship from B to A. We adopt this strategy when we believe that it is more likely for respondents to overstate their friendship relationships, perhaps motivated by social desirability. If we have no plausible intuition about respondents' motivation to respond in a certain fashion, we have assigned a random value drawn from a distribution with the mean and standard deviation of all the values reported in the network. By doing so, we acknowledge that the missing values might in fact be in error but the errors are randomized across all missing values and hence would not systematically bias the results of any subsequent analysis.

Finally, if the recoding scheme is hard to justify based on one of the rationales outlined above, we have considered the option of removing the nonrespondent participants from the network. While the reduced network will now have complete data, we run the risk of excluding certain key members who did not respond but might have been the recipient of network ties from several respondents. In more than one of our studies we have identified key members who were "just too busy" to complete our network survey. Removing them from the network would clearly be counterproductive. Therefore the removal of missing data should be cautiously and deliberately used.

Visual-analytics of Network Data

After the raw network data have been manipulated, they are ready to be visualized and analyzed. The visual-analytics of network data are the ultimate instrument – a "macroscope" – to uncover the signature structures of network data. Broadly speaking, we undertake three tasks in this realm: visualization, descriptive metrics, and inferential statistics.

Visualization

Network visualization is a graphic illustration of the nodes and their linkages embodied in the network data. It serves as a visual aid to uncover the network structures, as well as a basic diagnostic tool to check the validity and accuracy of the network data. There are a number of network visualization programs that allow researchers to visualize their network data in customized layouts, such as different nodal sizes (to visualize continuous nodal attributes such as level of expertise), nodal colors (to visualize categorical nodal attributes such as areas of expertise), link widths (to visualize the strength of the network link), and network layout (to visualize clustering or other macro patterns in the network).

Huisman and Van Duijn (2005) provide a comprehensive and critical review of several network visualization tools. A recent addition to the suite of visualization tools is NodeXL (Hansen, Shneiderman, & Smith, 2010), which is a template for Excel 2007 and 2010 that lets you enter a network edge list, click a button, and see the network graph, all in the Excel window. Most network visualization programs offer limited analytic capabilities, but can import and export data to other network analytic programs to enable a seamless visual-analytic process.

We often conduct some network visualizations before network analytics to discern the basic network structure prior to data analysis. This procedure is also useful to make sure the data appear to be valid in light of all the manipulations we discussed earlier. But we also find considerable merit in utilizing visualization tools after conducting the analysis. The post-analytic visualization enables the incorporation into the visualization of metrics computed as part of the network analysis. For example, in NetDraw (Borgatti, 2002), a visualization tool that is built into UCINET, researchers can choose to display the size of the nodes in the network to represent degree centrality (the number of links connected to the node). The nodal color could indicate membership in a cluster identified by the network analysis, and the width of the link could represent the structural equivalence between two nodes (the structural equivalence is a network metric that indicates the extent to which the two nodes have similar patterns of interaction with all other nodes in the network).

In addition, network visualization can help researchers drill down into interesting facets or subregions of the network configuration and better understand the analytic results. For example, if a network analysis shows that a specific member has the highest betweenness centrality in the network, the visualization would be the most illustrative way to demonstrate the brokerage role of this member in the group (i.e., by connecting those members who are not directly connected with each other).

Descriptive metrics

Network scientists have developed a suite of descriptive metrics to analyze various properties of a social network at five distinctive levels: the individual, the dyad, the triad, the subgroup, and the global level (for a review, see Easley & Kleinberg, 2010; Wasserman & Faust, 1994). At each level, network analysis focuses on different descriptive metrics to measure different facets of network properties.

At the *individual* level, the key descriptive statistics include degree, betweenness, and closeness centralities of an individual member. Degree measures the extent to which a group member has a large number of direct network links. Betweenness measures the extent to which a group member connects group members who are not directly or weakly connected with one another. Closeness measures the extent to which a group member can reach all other group members via direct or indirect network links. Very often researchers will compute individual level network metrics and then use those as dependent or independent variables in non-network analytic procedures such as regression or ANOVA. For instance, researchers have used the degree centrality of an individual in the network as one of several variables to predict their level of leadership in the group (Huffaker, 2010).

At the *dyadic* level, the focus is placed on the relational properties of a pair of nodes in the network, such as reciprocity, redundancy, and structural equivalence. For example, we can measure the extent to which group members mutually seek advice from one another, by computing the ratio of the number of observed reciprocal ties (where A and B seek advice from one another) as a proportion of the number of possible reciprocal ties which is $n*(n-1)$ for a network of size n.

The *triadic* level focuses on metrics of three nodes and their relationships at a time, including transitivity and cyclicality. For instance, we can measure the extent to which if in a group, A trusts B and B trusts C, then A also trusts C. This can be computed by calculating the ratio of the number of observed transitive triads as a proportion of the total number of transitive triads. A researcher might posit that groups with higher levels of transitivity are more likely to experience higher levels of team identification.

At the *subgroup* level, the components and cliques metrics are calculated to measure the extent to which subgroups of individuals are cohesively connected in a network. For instance, a subgroup level analysis of the information retrieval network might reveal the presence of clear factions resulting in a fractured group where two sets of individuals only retrieve information from others within their own sets but not from the other set. A researcher might posit that groups that can be partitioned into factions based on their information retrieval network will underperform as compared to groups that are more cohesively connected.

Finally, the *global* level considers the network as a whole and examines the properties of the entire network such as density and network centralizations. For instance, a group would be highly centralized if one member is connected to all other members but the rest of the members are only connected to this one person who would then be the star of the network. The group would have low centralization if, for instance, each member of the network only has links with two other members. Some classic studies conducted by Bavelas (1948) over six decades ago have shown that highly centralized groups outperform decentralized groups on simple tasks. However, members in these highly centralized groups report on average lower levels of satisfaction than those in decentralized groups. As mentioned above, these descriptive metrics can be utilized to augment the illustrative power of network visualizations. Further, these metrics can be used as independent or dependent variables, or both, for other types of non–network analysis.

Inferential statistics

Visualizations and descriptive metrics are necessary but not sufficient tools to understand fully the antecedents and consequences of the structural signatures embedded in the network. For instance, descriptive network statistics discussed above can provide us with a measure of the extent to which there is reciprocity, transitivity, or centralization in the network. But what it does not provide is a statistically defensible measure of whether the observed reciprocity, transitivity, or centralization is significantly more than what we would expect by chance. This is where we turn to inferential statistics. The descriptive network statistics are analogous to measures of central tendency, such as the mean, in non–network analysis. Inferential network statistics are analogous to parametric tests such as the *t*-test or nonparametric tests such as the chi-square test in non–network analysis.

Unfortunately, most of the techniques used to compute inferential statistics in non–network analysis cannot be applied to network analysis. This is because a large proportion of inferential statistics used in non–network analysis make the assumption that the data are independently and identically distributed. But network data observations are not independent of one another. That is, the presence of a communication tie between individual A and B could conceivably impact the presence of a communication tie between individual A and some other individual C.

Most standard statistical analyses that focus on attributes of (rather than relations among) individuals are premised on the assumption that the data are drawn from a distribution where the observations are independent. For instance, the height of an individual A does not impact the height of an individual B. Thus, many of the standard statistical techniques used to analyze attribute social scientific data are not appropriate for analyzing network data. As a result, inferential statistics for network data are unable to use techniques that could violate the assumption of independence. Thus it is imperative to use specialized social network analytic techniques rather than traditional statistical methods for inferential hypothesis testing.

One common genre of hypotheses that is of considerable interest to group researchers is the extent to which one network relation among group members is positively or negatively associated with other network relations among group members. For example, we have examined the extent to which if A trusts B, A is more or less likely to retrieve information from B. In this case, we compute a simple correlation to measure the extent to which the trust link between two members in the network is accompanied by an information retrieval link.

Let us assume, that the correlation coefficient was 0.35. In order to test our hypothesis, we would need to establish if this value is significantly greater than 0. This would not be a problem in non-network analysis where the correlation coefficient would be accompanied with a P value indicating the likelihood that this value is greater than 0. However, since this correlation was computed on network data (which violate assumptions of independence), we cannot use the significance test provided with the correlation coefficient. Instead, we have to draw upon one of several specific analytic techniques developed by network statisticians.

Quadratic Assignment Procedure (QAP) is one popular technique to test the significance (Krackhardt, 1987b). To assess the relationships between more than two networks, researchers can use Multiple Regression Quadratic Assignment Procedure (MRQAP) (see e.g., Doerfel & Barnett, 1999; Krackhardt, 1988). QAP and MRQAP, both of which are available in network analysis software programs such as UCINET and StatNet, are reasonable approaches to test hypotheses about similarity among two or more network relations. But what if we are interested in assessing the extent to which there is a higher than expected level of transitivity in a single network (such as the advice network discussed earlier)? Or, what if we are interested in hypothesizing that an information-retrieval relation from group member A to B is explained not only by the extent to which A trusts B, but also the extent to which A trusts other members in the group who in turn trust B?

Recent developments in ERGM (Exponential Random Graph Modeling) analysis (also known as $p*$ analysis) provide a promising framework to test complex network hypotheses such as these (Frank & Strauss, 1986; Robins & Pattison, 2005; Wasserman & Pattison, 1996). In essence, ERGM/$p*$ analyses test the likelihood for the theoretically hypothesized structural properties to occur in the observed network (Robins, Pattison, Kalish, & Lusher, 2007). Researchers (Robins et al., 2007; Shumate & Palazzolo, 2010) have described how ERGM/$p*$ analyses can be used to uncover structural signatures in the observed network, thus reflecting the underlying social processes that generate such network structures.

Limitations, Challenges, and the Future

As we close this chapter, we must acknowledge the presence of a very large "elephant in the room" – the ethical challenges of network approaches. Unlike non-network research, a network study can never be truly anonymous. It makes little sense for respondents to report who they communicate with if we cannot establish the identity of the respondents! As a result, group researchers utilizing network approaches bear an additional burden in terms of meeting ethical standards. Indeed, over the years, proposals for network research projects have been met with more than their share of skepticism by members of Institutional Review Boards (IRBs) who have a commitment to protect human subjects. It is therefore not surprising that strategies to meet the requirements of the IRB have been the topic of discussion at several gatherings of researchers interested in network approaches.

While anonymity can never be upheld for the reasons outlined above, network researchers also bear a special burden in meeting requirements of confidentiality. That is, what results might one share with the respondents which would both be perceived as useful and not violating confidentiality? Ironically, the problems of confidentiality are greatest in small groups.

Consider the case where a faculty member conducted a "confidential" network analysis among a dozen students as part of a graduate seminar discussing network methods. Prior to taking a break during the three-hour seminar, students were asked to complete a confidential network survey listing whom they considered as their friends in the class. During the break, the faculty member drew a network visualization of the friendship network on the board without including the names of any of the students. As students returned from the break, they began to discuss the visualization on the board. They were drawn to the fact that one node in the network had listed all the other nodes in the network as friends, but none of the other nodes had reported a friendship link to this node. Even as the students reconvened for the second part of the seminar, many had made educated guesses about the identity of this node. There was no discussion specifically about the identity of the node during the seminar. However, for reasons that may or may not have been triggered by this event, the student did not return to class in the following days and ended up dropping out of the graduate program. This case illustrates how, despite the best of intentions and safeguards, network approaches still require the researcher to be extremely vigilant about potential ethical breaches.

A second potential ethical "landmine" deals with the use of archival digital trace data. Consider the case of the data we analyzed from a MMORPG. One of the games we are investigating is EverQuest II developed by Sony Online Entertainment. We presented a paper based on some of our results at a recent annual meeting of the American Association for the Advancement of Science (AAAS). In our presentation at the AAAS, we had indicated that all the data we were provided was anonymized and that we did not have access to any content of the chat. Given the wide audience for this meeting, it was not surprising that the findings were picked up by the popular press and by the blogosphere. Some of the stories reporting our findings failed to mention that the data were anonymized and did not include the content of the chat. We were in for an unpleasant surprise when we discovered that these stories had created quite a furor on some of the forums frequented by EverQuest II players who were understandably irate that Sony Online Entertainment might have contributed to an ethical breach by sharing with our research team personal and private information about the players without their permission. Even though no ethical breach was conducted, it heightened both Sony Online Entertainment's and our research team's sensitivity about the player's concerns.

Armed with this greater appreciation of the ethical challenges, we hope this chapter has illustrated why and how we have found network methodology to be an important "arrow" in the quiver of tools to advance our understanding of groups. The use of network approaches to study groups is by no means a recent phenomenon. As we mentioned at the start of this chapter, Alex Bavelas founded the Small Group Networks Laboratory at MIT shortly after World War II. After an initial flurry of activity, network approaches to the study of groups languished for several decades. But in the past decade, there has been a resurgence of interest in the use of network approaches to studying groups.

There are at least four reasons that explain this renewed interest. *First*, there is a much greater intellectual interest spurred by the societal appreciation of the role of networks as the primordial soup from which groups emerge. The trend from formal, long-term and heavily structured teams towards more agile, distributed, and ad-hoc teams in the contemporary workforce have underscored the role of networks. *Second*, the increasing prevalence of digital traces makes it much easier to capture copious amounts of network data through observational and archive methods. This mitigates one of the perennial challenges of social network approaches that rely heavily on labor-intensive (in particular, respondent-intensive) network surveys. *Third*, the recent methodological development in inferential statistics for network data outlined earlier in this chapter have finally enabled network researchers to augment exploratory network analysis (based on descriptive statistics) with the ability to test complex network hypotheses using confirmatory network analysis. *Finally*, recent developments in computational infrastructure from the desktop all the way to petascale computing and cloud computing have been crucial enablers in conducting network analyses.

As mentioned earlier, network analyses cannot rely on many of the standard statistical techniques developed for non-network data where one can make the assumption of independent observations. Instead, the statistical techniques developed specifically for network data tend to be very computationally intensive. It is not uncommon for sophisticated statistical models analyzing networks in relatively small groups to take up to an hour on the state of the art desktop machine. It is therefore not surprising that many of us have begun to exploit high-performance computing to conduct network analyses.

These four developments – renewed intellectual interest, new forms of digital data, recent developments in network methods, and advances in computational capabilities – argue well for the utilization of network approaches to advance contemporary group research. These developments also hold the promise for helping reconceptualize our notion of the group. Traditionally, the nodes in social network research are restricted to human members only, given its focus on "social" structures as opposed to impersonal networks such as the computer network or electric power grids. In empirical group research, the social network approach has been employed to examine the information retrieval relationship among group members (Palazzolo, 2005), the structures of information sharing and their effects on group member satisfaction (Su, Huang, & Contractor, 2010), and the effects of network structures on group performance (Rulke & Galaskiewicz, 2000). However, given the fast advancement of new media and web-based information technologies, there is an increasing demand for considering the "nonhuman" nodes when studying groups as social networks (Contractor, Monge, & Leonardi, 2011; Hollingshead & Contractor, 2002; Su & Contractor, 2011).

In recent years, we have begun to witness a transformation in our conceptualization of group to include not only human members but also digital agents such as Web 2.0, the Semantic Web (Shadbolt, Hall, & Berners-Lee, 2006) and Cyberinfrastructure (Atkins, 2003). The integration of both human and nonhuman nodes in the network inspires and requires researchers to conceptualize networks in a new way: as multidimensional networks. Contractor (2009b) defines a multidimensional network as a collection of multiple types of nodes together with multiple types of network ties among them. The nodes in a multidimensional network are "resources", including people, documents, datasets, analytic tools, instruments, concepts, and keywords (Hollingshead & Contractor, 2002).

The network ties represent different types of relationships between people and people, people and nonhuman nodes, and amongst nonhuman nodes themselves (Contractor, 2009b). For example, a multidimensional network of a software development team could include team members collaborating with each other, team members writing and publishing codes on the team intranet, the intranet reporting debugging procedures of the software, and the software being tested by different tools and by different members (Poole & Contractor, 2011). The inclusion of nonhuman nodes in the multidimensional network makes the data collection process even more complicated and time consuming. For example, in the human-only information retrieval network, researchers may only need to know "who retrieves information from whom" in the group. However, in the multidimensional network, it is important to collect data on "who is retrieving information from whom and/or which data repository." In short, the multiplicity of nodal types and their relationships in the multidimensional network demand some creative and innovative approaches to collection and collation of network data. We expect that in the future network approaches will be increasingly influential in helping us understand and enable groups conceptualized from this multidimensional perspective.

Acknowledgments

The authors wish to acknowledge the following funding sources that contributed to the development of materials presented in this chapter: Army Research Laboratory under Cooperative Agreement Number W911NF-09-2-0053; Air Force Research Laboratory FA8650-10-C-7010 and National Science Foundation Grants: BCS- 0940851, CNS-1010904, OCI-0904356, IIS-0838564, IIS-0841583. The views and conclusions contained in this document are those of the authors and should not be interpreted as representing the official policies, either expressed or implied, of the Army Research Laboratory, Air Force Research Laboratory, the National Science Foundation or the US Government. The US Government is authorized to reproduce and distribute reprints for Government purposes notwithstanding any copyright notation here on.

References

Atkins, D. (2003). *Revolutionizing science and engineering through cyberinfrastructure.* Report of the National Science Foundation Blue-Ribbon Advisory Panel on Cyberinfrastructure.

Balkundi, P., & Harrison, D. A. (2006). Ties, leaders, and time in teams: Strong inference about network structure's effects on team viability and performance. *Academy of Management Journal, 49*(1), 49–68.

Bavelas, A. (1948). A mathematical model for group structure. *Applied Anthropology, 7,* 16–30.

Borgatti, S. (2002). *NetDraw: Graph visualization software.* Harvard, MA: Analytic Technologies.

Borgatti, S., Everett, M. G., & Freeman, L. C. (2002). *Ucinet 6 for Windows: Software for social network analysis.* Harvard, MA: Analytic Technologies.

Börner, K., Contractor, N., Falk-Krzesinski, H. J., Fiore, S. M., Hall, K. L., Keyton, J., et al. (2010). A multi-level systems perspective for the science of team science. *Science Translational Medicine.* 2:49cm24.

Burke, C. S., Fiore, S. M., & Salas, E. (2003). The role of shared cognition in enabling shared leadership and team adaptability. In C. L. Pearce & J. A. Conger (Eds.), *Shared leadership: Reframing the hows and whys of leadership* (pp. 103–121). Thousand Oaks, CA: Sage.

Casciaro, T., & Lobo, M. S. (2005). Competent jerks, lovable fools, and the formation of social networks. *Harvard Business Review, 83*(6), 92–100.

Contractor, N. (2009a). *C-IKNOW: Cyber-infrastructure for inquiring knowledge networks on the Web*. Evanston, IL: Science of Networks in Communities (SONIC), Northwestern University.

Contractor, N. (2009b). The emergence of multidimensional networks. *Journal of Computer-Mediated Communication, 14*, 743–747.

Contractor, N. S., & Monge, P. R. (2002). Managing knowledge networks. *Management Communication Quarterly, 16*(2), 249–259.

Contractor, N., Monge, P., & Leonardi, P. (2011). Multidimensional networks and the dynamics of sociomateriality: Bringing technology inside the network. *International Journal of Communication, 5*, 1–20.

Contractor, N., Wasserman, S., & Faust, K. (2006). Testing multi-theoretical, multilevel hypotheses about networks: An analytic framework and empirical example. *Academy of Management Review, 31*(3), 681–703.

Cross, R., & Borgatti, S. (2004). The ties that share: Relational characteristics that facilitate information seeking. In M. H. Huysman & V. Wulf (Eds.), *Social capital and information technology* (pp. 137–161). Boston, MA: MIT Press.

Cross, R., & Parker, A. (2004). *The hidden power of social networks*. Boston, MA: Harvard Business School Press.

Cummings, J. N., & Kiesler, S. (2005). Collaborative research across disciplinary and organizational boundaries. *Social Study of Science, 35*(5), 703–722.

Doerfel, M. L., & Barnett, G. A. (1999). A semantic network analysis of the international communication association. *Human Communication Research, 25*, 589–603.

Easley, D., & Kleinberg, J. (2010). *Networks, crowds, and markets: Reasoning about a highly connected world*. New York: Cambridge University Press.

EgoNet (2011). EgoNet software. University of Florida. Available online at: http://sourceforge.net/projects/egonet/.

Frank, O., & Strauss, D. (1986). Markov graphs. *Journal of the American Statistical Association, 81*(395), 832–842.

Guimerà, R., Uzzi, B., Spiro, J., & Amaral, L. A. N. (2005). Team assembly mechanisms determine collaboration network structure and team performance. *Science, 308*, 697–702.

Handcock, M. S., Hunter, D. R., Butts, C. T., Goodreau, S. M., & Morris, M. (2003). *Statnet: An R package for the statistical modeling of social networks*. http://csde.washington.edu/statnet/.

Hansen, D., Shneiderman, B., & Smih, M. (2010). *Analyzing social media networks with NodeXL: Insights from a connected world*. New York: Morgan-Kaufmann.

Heald, M., Contractor, N., Koehly, L. M., & Wasserman, S. (1998). Formal and emergent predictors of coworkers' perceptual congruence on an organization's social structure. *Human Communication Research, 24*, 536–563.

Heckathorn, D. D. (1997). Respondent-driven sampling: A new approach to the study of hidden populations. *Social Problems, 44*(2).

Hollingshead, A. B., & Contractor, N. S. (2002). New media and organizing at the group level. In L. Lievrouw & S. Livingstone (Eds.), *Handbook of new media* (pp 221–235). London: Sage.

Huffaker, D. (2010). Dimensions of leadership and social influence in online communities. *Human Communication Research, 36*(4), 593–617.

Huisman, M., & Van Duijn, M. A. J. (2005). Software for social network analysis. In P. J. Carrington, J. Scott, & S. Wasserman (Eds.), *Models and methods in social network analysis* (pp. 270–316). New York: Cambridge University Press.

Jones, B. F., Wuchty, S., & Uzzi, B. (2008). Multi-university research teams: Shifting impact, geography, and stratification in science. *Science, 322*, 1259–1262.

Katz, N., Lazer, D., Arrow, H., & Contractor, N. (2004). Network theory and small groups. *Small Group Research, 35*(3), 307–332.

Kilduff, M., & Tsai, W. (2003). *Social networks and organizations.* London: Sage.

Krackhardt, D. (1987a). Cognitive social structures. *Social Networks, 9,* 104–134.

Krackhardt D. (1987b). QAP partialling as a test of spuriousness. *Social Networks, 9,* 171–186.

Krackhardt, D. (1988). Predicting with networks: Nonparametric multiple regression analyses of dyadic data. *Social Networks, 10,* 359–382.

Krackhardt, D. (1992). The strength of strong ties: The importance of philos in organizations. In N. Nohria & R. Eccles (Eds.), *Networks and organizations: Structure, form and action* (pp. 216–239). Boston, MA: Harvard Business School Press.

Lazer, D., Pentland, A., Adamic, L., Aral, S., Barabasi, A.-L., Brewer, D., et al. (2009). Social science: Computational social science. *Science, 323*(5915), 721–723.

Marsden, P.V. (2005). Recent developments in network measurement. In P. J. Carrington, J. Scott, & S. Wasserman (Eds.), *Models and methods in social network analysis* (pp. 8–30). New York: Cambridge University Press.

Mathur, S., Poole, M. S., Pena-Mora, F., Contractor, N., & Hasegawa-Johnson, M. (2009). *Detecting interaction links in a collaborating group using manually annotated data.* Working paper, National Center for Supercompting Applications, University of Illinois Urbana-Champaign, Urbana, IL.

Monge, P., & Contractor, N. (2003). *Theories of communication networks.* New York: Oxford University Press.

Monge, P. R., & Contractor, N. S. (1988). Measurement techniques for the study of communication networks. In C. Tardy (Ed.), *A handbook for the study of human communication: Methods and instruments for observing, measuring, and assessing communication processes* (pp. 107–138). Norwood, NJ: Ablex.

Palazzolo, E. (2005). Organizing for information retrieval in transactive memory systems. *Communication Research, 32*(6), 726–761.

Pentland, A., (2008) *Honest signals: How they shape our world.* Cambridge, MA: MIT Press,

Poole, M. S., Bajcsy, P., Contractor, N., Espelage, D., Fleck, M., Forsyth, D., et al. (2009). *GroupScope: Instrumenting research on interaction networks in complex social contexts.* Working paper, National Center for Supercompting Applications, University of Illinois Urbana-Champaign, Urbana, IL.

Poole, M. S., & Contractor, N. S. (2011). Conceptualizing the multiteam system as a system of networked groups. In Zaccaro, S. J. Marks, M. A., & L. A. DeChurch (Eds.), *Multiteam systems: An organizational form for dynamic and complex environments* (pp. 193-224). Routledge Academic.

Putnam, L., & Stohl, C. (1996). Bona fide groups: An alternative perspective for communication and small group decision making. In R. Y. Hirokawa & M. S. Poole (Eds.), *Communication and group decision making* (pp. 179–214). Thousand Oaks, CA: Sage.

Robins, G., & Pattison, P. (2005). Interdependencies and social processes: Dependence graphs and generalized dependence structures. In P. J. Carrington, J. Scott, & S. Wasserman (Eds.), *Models and methods in social network analysis* (pp. 192–213). New York: Cambridge University Press.

Robins, G., Pattison, P., Kalish, Y., & Lusher, D. (2007). An introduction to exponential random graph (p*) models for social networks. *Social Networks, 29*(2), 173–191.

Rulke, D. L., & Galaskiewicz, J. (2000). Distribution of knowledge, group network structure, and group performance. *Management Science, 46*(5), 612–625.

Scott, J. (2000). *Social network analysis: A handbook* (2nd ed.). Newbury Park, CA: Sage.

Shadbolt, N., Hall, W., & Berners-Lee, T. (2006). The semantic web revisited. *IEEE Intelligent Systems, 21*(3), 96–101.

Shumate, M., & Palazzolo, E. T. (2010). Exponential random graph (p*) models as a method for social network analysis in communication research. *Communication Methods and Measures, 4*(4), 341–371.

Su, C., & Contractor, N. (2011). A multidimensional network approach to studying team members' information seeking from human and digital knowledge sources in consulting firms. *Journal of the American Society for Information Science and Technology, 62*(7), 1257–1275.

Su, C., Huang, M., & Contractor, N. (2010). Understanding the structures, antecedents and outcomes of organisational learning and knowledge transfer: A multi-theoretical and multilevel network analysis. *European Journal of International Management, 4*(6), 576–601.

Wasserman, S., & Faust, K. (1994). *Social network analysis: Methods and applications.* New York: Cambridge University Press.

Wasserman, S., & Pattison, P. (1996). Logit models and logistic regressions for social networks: An introduction to Markov graphs and p*. *Psychometrika, 61*(3), 401–425.

Wellman, B. (1988). Structural analysis: From method and metaphor to theory and substance. In B. Wellman & S. Berkowitz (Eds.), *Social structure: A network approach* (pp. 19–61). Cambridge: Cambridge University Press.

Williams, D., Contractor, N., Poole, M. S., Srivastava, J., & Cai, D. (2011). The virtual worlds exploratorium: Using large-scale data and computational techniques for communication research. *Communication Methods and Measures, 5*(2), 163–180.

Wotal, B., Green, H., Williams, D., & Contractor, N. (2006). *WoW!: The dynamics of knowledge networks in Massively Multiplayer Online Role Playing Games (MMORPG).* Paper presented at the Annual Social Network Sunbelt Conference, Vancouver, Canada.

Wu, L., Waber, B., Aral, S., Brynjolfsson, E., & Pentland, A. (2008) Mining face-to-face interaction networks using sociometric badges: predicting productivity in an IT configuration task. *Proceedings of the International Conference on Information Systems*, Paris, France. December 14–17, 2008.

Wyatt, D., Choudhury, T, Bilmes, J., & Kitts. J. A. (2011). Inferring collocation and conversational networks using privacy-sensitive audio. *ACM Transactions on Intelligent Systems and Technology*, 2:1.

16

ANALYZING GROUP DATA

Deborah A. Kashy

MICHIGAN STATE UNIVERSITY

Nao Hagiwara

WAYNE STATE UNIVERSITY

Human beings are inherently social animals, and most of what we do involves participation in groups. Starting at birth, we are members of families; as we grow, we become members of friendship groups, classrooms, sports teams, to name a few; in adulthood we often become members of new family groups as well as work groups, religious groups, and so on. In each of the groups to which we belong, our behavior is likely to be influenced by other group members. Even young babies show evidence of this interconnectedness. For example, babies who receive consistent warmth and attention from their parents tend to develop into secure adults. In school, children's learning can be affected by other students in the class as well as by their teachers. For example, having a very disruptive child in the class may negatively impact all students' learning, but having a highly motivated teacher can raise all of his or her students' learning. Likewise, in adulthood, people's productivity in the workplace can be affected by the quality of their relationships with co-workers, the leadership style of their manager, or even the broader corporate culture.

In each of these examples, the groups clearly vary on many attributes, such as group size and structure, but the fundamental aspect of all of them is that the outcomes for members of these groups are linked. In some cases these links may reflect actual interpersonal influence, but in other cases the similarity in outcomes may result because group members share the same environment (Kenny, Mannetti, Pierro, Livi, & Kashy, 2002). We conceptualize these links broadly as *nonindependence*: The degree to which outcomes for persons who are in the same group are more similar (or dissimilar) to one another than are outcomes for persons from two different groups. The goal of this chapter is twofold: (a) to highlight the data analytic challenges and opportunities involved in conducting research with small groups; and (b) to introduce three data analytic models that can help researchers understand the ways that group members affect one another's behavior.

In this chapter we first discuss a series of basic definitions and methodological issues in group research, and we argue that the relatively new data analytic technique known as multilevel modeling (MLM; aka hierarchical linear modeling) is a tool that is indispensable for studying groups. We then present overviews of three methodological models that can be used to assess patterns of influence in small groups: the Actor–Partner Interdependence model (APIM); the One-with-Many design (OWM); and the Social Relations Model (SRM). Our aim for this chapter is to introduce these models conceptually, and to demonstrate their potential utility for group researchers. We do not provide a step-by-step tutorial for how these analyses would be implemented; instead we provide citations to papers that detail the data analytic procedures.

Some Basic Nuts and Bolts: Distinguishability, Types of Predictor Variables, and Levels of Measurement for Outcomes

Before jumping into analyzing group data, researchers must first consider several important factors that determine which data analytic approaches and models are appropriate for their research design. One important factor in group research is whether group members are distinguishable as a function of clearly identifiable "roles" within the group. Families are a prime example of distinguishable group members because each family may have a mother, father, older sibling, and younger sibling. Moreover, in families the relationship between mothers and fathers is likely qualitatively different from the relationships between parents and children, as well as sibling relationships. In other words, distinguishability implies that the relationships between predictor and outcome variables may differ depending on the roles of the individuals involved. More formally, distinguishability implies that individuals in the different roles are sampled from different populations.

On the other hand, there are many groups in which members can be said to be indistinguishable. Students participating in work teams or children who are members of friendship networks are examples of indistinguishable group members. In these cases, individuals within a group can have different qualities (e.g., mixed sex groups or high/low status), but they are sampled from a single population. Our experience suggests that the majority of small group research involves indistinguishable rather than distinguishable group members. The distinction between distinguishable and indistinguishable groups is important to make because data analytic procedures often differ depending on this factor. In this chapter we limit our discussion to the indistinguishable case. For a detailed discussion of analyses involving distinguishable group members, we refer readers to Kenny and Kashy (2011) and Kenny, Kashy, and Cook (2006).

We also need to discuss the nature of the independent or predictor variables in group research. There are three types of independent variables that can be differentiated by the degree to which they vary from group to group on average and from individual to individual within each group. A *between-groups* independent variable is one that varies from group to group, but within each group every individual is associated with the same score. For instance, in a study of leadership and team productivity (say that each team has four workers and one leader), the predictor variable might be the leader's number of years of experience. This variable is the same for every member of a particular team but can vary across teams such that some teams have highly experienced leaders and others have relative novices. When the independent variable is *within-groups*, its value varies from person to person within the group, but its average value is the same across the group. For example, on basketball teams, the percentage of points scored by each of five starting members during a game would be a within-groups variable, such that some team members score higher than others within a team, but the average percentage of points scored by the members is 20 per cent across the five-person teams. Another example of a within-groups variable would be gender if each six-person group is comprised of three men and three women. Finally, the independent variable can be a *mixed* variable that varies both between-groups and within-groups. To continue the basketball example, a mixed predictor variable could be motivation, because within a team some players are more motivated than others, and some teams have higher average motivation than others. Likewise, in the six-person group example, gender would be a mixed variable if gender composition varied from group to group.

A third important distinction in group research concerns the level at which the outcome variable is assessed. Outcome scores from group studies can be measured at (at least) three different levels: group, individual, and dyad within a group; and the level of measurement is an important factor in determining the appropriate data analytic approach for a given study. For a group-level measure, each group provides only a single outcome score (e.g., the total number of games won in a season), and so the same value is associated with every member of the group. Other common group-level variables include measures of overall group productivity or cohesiveness.

Group data can be also measured at the individual level such that each group member provides a score. For example, instead of measuring the total number of wins in a season for the whole team, we could measure each player's average points per game for the season. Thus, the individual level of measurement differs from the group level because each group member has a unique score. Finally, data from group research can be obtained at the dyad level within a group, as would be the case if we measured the average number of passes each player made to each of their team members in a season.

These three levels of measurement result in very different numbers of outcome scores. Group-level outcomes provide only one score per group regardless of group size. In contrast, individual-level outcomes provide n outcomes per group, where n equals the number of individuals in the group. Finally, dyad-level outcomes can provide as many as $n(n-1)$ outcomes per group.

Some Nonindependence Basics

When we say that an outcome score is nonindependent within groups, what we mean is that the scores for people within the same group are related to one another. Most often nonindependence results in a positive correlation between group members' scores. This occurs when an outcome is structured such that if one group member has a high score, other group members also have relatively high scores. For example, in studies of group productivity, having highly productive members in one's group may increase a person's own productivity.

Researchers sometimes fail to realize that nonindependence can also result in a negative correlation between group members' scores. This occurs when an outcome is structured such that if one group member has a high score, other group members have relatively low scores. The percentage of points scored in a basketball game is one example of this: If the team has a star player who scores a large percentage of the points, by necessity the other players will have lower percentages. The *intraclass correlation* (for computational details, see Kashy & Kenny, 2000) is an index of the degree of similarity (or dissimilarity) between group members' scores, and it is typically used to assess the direction and degree of nonindependence. More specifically, the intraclass correlation measures the degree to which scores within the same group are more similar to one another than scores from different groups.

If the key outcome is measured at the group level, then each individual within the group is associated with the same outcome score. This implies that the intraclass correlation for that variable will be exactly 1.0. In this case the problem posed by nonindependence is not complex, as the appropriate analysis simply involves treating each group as an individual data point. For example, if there are 25 groups that each include six participants, the analysis would be based on only 25 observations, not 150 observations. It would be a grave error to do the analysis treating each individual as a data point (i.e., with 150 observations) since individuals within a group provide completely redundant data.

When outcomes are measured at the individual or dyad levels, nonindependence poses somewhat more complex statistical challenges (Kashy & Kenny, 2000). Consider as an example a study examining gender differences in self-disclosure by individuals in 20 four-person, gender-homogeneous groups (i.e., ten groups of women and ten groups of men; group size $n = 4$), and so there are a total of 80 students in the sample. In the study the group members interact while being video taped and then coders rate how much each group member self-disclosed during the interaction. Thus, each group member has a self-disclosure score. The research question of interest would be whether there is a mean difference in the average self-disclosure as a function of gender. A common mistake would be to treat the 80 self-disclosure scores as data points in a between-subjects ANOVA or an independent groups t-test contrasting scores from women with those from men.

The issue is that these statistical tests assume that each outcome score is independent of every other outcome score (i.e., the independence assumption). Our example likely violates this assumption because the amount of self-disclosure for individuals in the same group is likely to be correlated. However, unlike the previous example in which the intraclass correlation was 1.0, here the intraclass correlation would likely be a smaller (but still positive) value. That is, some groups may establish a norm for high levels of self-disclosure, but in others no such norm may exist. In this case there would be relatively large differences in the amount of disclosure between groups and relatively small differences within groups. This type of nonindependence results in biased inferential statistics and ultimately may lead to bias in Type I error rates. That is, our statistical test that ignores the nonindependence might result in a $p < 0.05$, suggesting a statistically significant difference, when in fact, the correct analysis that takes interdependence into account would show a nonsignificant result (i.e., $p > 0.05$). Thus we might conclude that women disclose "significantly" more than men when there is no such sex difference in the population.

Multilevel Modeling as a Critical Tool for Group Research

In our minds, multilevel modeling is a very useful tool for group research because it is designed to handle hierarchically nested data (e.g., players within teams, students within work groups). This approach has a natural fit with group research because most group data have a hierarchical structure – individuals are nested within groups. Moreover, MLM can incorporate predictor variables at multiple levels of analysis (e.g., individual-level and group-level) while handling problems inherent when outcome scores are not independent.

Although MLM can be used for highly complex data analyses, at heart it can be viewed as a form of multiple regression (with a fancy error term; Bickel, 2007) in which outcome scores measured for each individual are predicted to be a function of both individual-level (i.e., within-groups or mixed) predictors and group-level (i.e., between-groups) predictors. For example, we can predict the average points per game for each basketball player to be a function of individual-level predictor variables such as player's motivation (a mixed predictor variable) and group-level predictor variables such as the number of years of the head-coach's experience (a between-groups predictor). In addition, MLM allows cross-level interactions; in the example, it may be that the effects of motivation on performance are stronger when the team has a more experienced coach.

In this example players are nested within teams, and so in MLM terms, player is the *lower-level unit* whereas team is the *upper-level unit*, and the outcome (the player's average points scored) is collected for each lower-level unit. Note that for the purposes of this example (and as a recommendation in general) continuous predictor variables that do not have a meaningful zero value (e.g., ratings of motivation on a scale of one to seven) should be grand-mean centered. That is, the mean motivation score across the entire sample has been subtracted from each player's motivation score. This redefines zero for motivation to be the average motivation score. In contrast, a zero for the number of years of the coach's experience is meaningful, and so this variable need not be centered.

Multilevel modeling is often described as a two-step process in which a "lower-level" regression is first computed separately for each "upper-level" unit. In the current example, this can be understood in conceptual terms to mean that a separate regression is computed *for each team*, and in each of these regressions the individual's performance or points scored is predicted as a function of that individual's motivation score. More formally, the lower level model for player i on team j would be

$$Points\ Scored_{ij} = b_{0j} + b_{1j}Motivation_{ij} + e_{ij},$$

where b_{0j} represents the predicted number of points scored for team j by a player who is average in motivation (recall that motivation is grand-mean centered), and b_{1j} represents the change in the number of points scored as motivation increases by one unit for team j.

The second step of the analysis involves treating the slopes and intercepts that were computed for each group as outcome scores in two "upper-level" regressions. In these regressions, group-level variables (e.g., coach's experience) can be used to predict the intercepts for each group (i.e., predicted points scored for the team for a player average on motivation), and the slopes for each group (i.e., the points scored–motivation relationship). That is, the first-step regressions generate an intercept for each team and a slope for each team. The second step in the analysis is to see whether these intercepts and slopes vary from team to team, and whether the variation from team to team is related to the coach's years of experience. More formally, in these upper level analyses, the regression coefficients from the first step are assumed to be a function of our group-level predictor, the number of years of the coach's experience. These two equations would be

$$b_{0j} = a_0 + a_1 CoachExperience_j + d_j$$

$$b_{1j} = c_0 + c_1 CoachExperience_j + f_j$$

The first equation predicts the intercepts from the lower-level analysis as a function of the upper-level predictor: coach's experience. For the example, a_0 is the predicted points scored for teams with new and inexperienced coaches (i.e., coach has 0 years of experience), and a_1 estimates whether individuals on teams that had more experienced coaches, on average, scored more points. Likewise, the second equation treats the first-step regression coefficients as a function of the upper-level predictor, coach's experience. Here c_0 estimates whether players higher in motivation scored more points on average, and c_1 estimates whether the effects of motivation on player performance differs as a function of the coach's experience. Note that c_1 is the test of the interaction between the two predictors: player's motivation and coach's experience.

The intercepts and slopes from the second step regressions, a_0, a_1, c_0, and c_1 are called fixed effects, and they summarize the overall relationships between the predictors and the outcome. MLM also provides estimates of random effects, or effects that vary from group to group after taking the effects of the predictor variables into account. There are three random effects represented in the three MLM equations. First, there is the error component, e_{ij}, in the lower-level or first-step equation. This represents variation in the number of points scored from player to player, after controlling for the effects of the players' motivation. The variance of these error components can be represented as σ_e^2. There are also random effects in each of the two second-step regression equations. The random effect d_j in the first of the second-step regressions represents variation in the intercepts that is not explained by the coach's experience. For the example, d_j represents variation in the average number of points scored from team to team that is not explained by the coach's experience. The variance in d_j is a combination of σ_d^2, which can be referred to as group variance, and σ_e^2.

One key element of MLM that is of particular use to group researchers is that it can be used to estimate and test the intraclass correlation. Recall that the intraclass correlation measures the degree to which scores within the same group are more similar to one another than scores from different groups. Furthermore, the MLM analysis automatically adjusts statistical significance tests to incorporate the degree of nonindependence in the data. The intraclass correlation that measures the degree of nonindependence of outcome scores within groups is then defined as ρ or rho:

$$\rho = \frac{\sigma_d^2}{\sigma_d^2 + \sigma_e^2}$$

For the example, this intraclass correlation measures the degree to which scores for players who are on the same team are more similar to one another than are scores for players who are on different teams after controlling for motivation effects.

The random effect in the second of the second-step equations is f_j and represents the degree to which the size of the points scored-motivation relationship varies from team to team after controlling for coach's experience. It may be that in some groups there is a strong tie between motivation and actual performance, but in other groups motivation has little impact on performance.

A complete treatment of MLM is clearly beyond the scope of this chapter. Indeed, in this very brief introduction to MLM, we have only briefly defined the key ideas involved in this data analytic approach. Our goal in including the section is to demonstrate that MLM solves many of the problems associated with analyzing group data. It naturally incorporates nonindependence, it allows researchers to test the effects of variables at both the individual and group levels, and it can also be used to specify and test cross-level interactions. We strongly encourage readers who are interested in conducting group research to acquaint themselves with (and ultimately become experts in) MLM techniques. Interested readers should see Bickel (2007) for a basic introduction, Hox (2002) or Snijders and Bosker (1999) for more technical discussions. Researchers can use MLM as a tool to estimate each of the three models we introduce below.

Models of Interdependence for Groups Research

Group researchers study groups because they believe that being a member of a group has an effect on individuals' behavior. Indeed, if this were not the case, then group researchers would almost certainly prefer to simplify both their data collection and analyses by studying individuals. So what makes groups special? We would argue that it is interdependence (our preferred term for nonindependence). Interdependence among group members may reflect a range of interpersonal processes including influence, reciprocity, conformity, similarity, and consensus, to name only a few. Thus, the most interesting part of group data (to us, anyway) is the interdependence itself, and so rather than focusing on statistical methods that can be used to reduce bias in traditional statistical analyses, in the remainder of this chapter we focus on three models of interdependent data, the APIM, the OWM, and the SRM.

As we will describe, the focus of the APIM is on predicting an individual's outcomes as a function of that individual's inputs as well as the average inputs of the other group members. Thus this model is generally used when both predictor and outcome scores are measured at the individual level. In contrast, the OWM and SRM designs focus on dyad-level measures within the group, and a primary goal of these two models is to estimate the degree to which these outcomes are affected by group, individual, and dyad-specific factors.

Actor–partner interdependence model

The basic assertion of the APIM is that, when individuals are members of a group, their outcomes are affected by both their own inputs as well as the inputs of the other group members. This model has been used extensively in dyadic research (i.e., when group size equals 2) to study topics ranging from emotion to relationship violence (Berg, Trost, Schneider, & Ethan, 2001; Butler et al., 2003; Butterfield, 2001; Campbell, Simpson, Kashy, & Rholes, 2001; Kenny & Acitelli, 2001; Kurdek, 2000; Lakey & Canary, 2002; Moffitt, Robins, & Caspi, 2006). For example,

Campbell et al. (2001) predicted interpersonal behavior in dating couples as a function of attachment avoidance. They found that more avoidant individuals behaved more negatively to their partners. In addition, they found that individuals with more avoidant partners also behaved more negatively to their partners. In the dyadic APIM, the effect of the person's predictor on the person's own outcome is called an *actor effect*, and the effect of the partner's predictor on the person's outcome is called a *partner effect*.

The APIM for small groups is a fairly straightforward extension of the dyadic model. Indeed the actor effect has the same definition: It is the effect of the person's own predictor on his or her own outcome. The partner effect has a somewhat different definition relative to the dyadic case. For small groups, the partner effect is the effect of the *average of the other group members' predictor scores* on the person's outcome (see Figure 16.1). Continuing with the basketball team example in which the outcome is the player's average points scored per game in a season and the predictor is the player's motivation, this model estimates the actor effect as the effect of the player's own motivation on the average points scored by that individual. In contrast, the partner effect is the effect of the average motivation level of the other players on the team on the number of points scored by the individual. This might show that having motivated team members, regardless of the player's own motivation, is a good predictor of the player's performance. Group researchers typically examine actor effects but often ignore partner effects. Yet it is partner effects that capture interdependence within groups because the presence

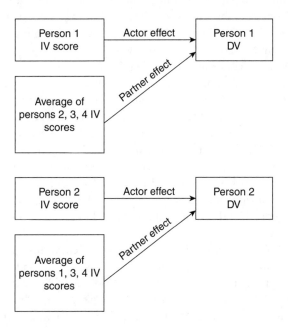

FIGURE 16.1 Actor–partner interdependence model.

of partner effects indicates that a person's response depends on characteristics and behaviors of the other group members.

Bonito (2000) used the APIM in a study examining the correspondence between perceived and actual group participation in three-person groups. He found that a person's actual contributions to a discussion positively predicted that person's own self-evaluation of participation in discussion (i.e., evidence of an actor effect), whereas the average contributions made by other group members did not predict the person's self-evaluation of participation (i.e., no evidence of a partner effect). In contrast, he found evidence of a negative actor effect and a positive partner effect when he predicted perceptions of *other* group members' participation: individuals who actually participated more perceived that others were less involved in the group interaction, and when other group members actually participated more, the individual perceived that the other group members were more active in the interaction. Similarly, Reid and Ng (2006) used actor–partner analyses in research with six-person groups to examine participation and perceived status in an intergroup setting.

In addition to estimating actor and partner effects, the APIM can be used to estimate the effects of actor–partner interactions. Actor–partner interactions suggest a synergy between actor and partner effects, and they can be specified in a number of ways. The most common type of interaction involves the product of the actor and partner effects. For example, having a set of highly motivated team members may moderate the relationship between a person's own motivation and number of points scored. That is, if other members of the group are highly motivated, then being a player who is relatively low on motivation may not have as much of a negative effect on that player's performance as might occur when the other team members' motivation is also low.

Bonito, DeCamp, Coffman, and Fleming (2006) examined actor–partner interactions in their study of group participation. In this study they predicted participation in a group discussion as a function of actor and partner effects for group members' information quantity, and actor and partner effects for group members' perception of interpersonal control. In this case an actor effect for quantity suggested that individuals with more information participated more, but there was no evidence of a corresponding partner effect. Instead, they found evidence of several interactions between actor and partner effects. For example, they found that, when an individual had greater control and the other group members had more information, then the individual participated in group discussion in a more substantive way.

One final note about including interactions – whenever the effects of actor–partner interactions are estimated, the main effects of actor and partner effects should be included in the model. Kenny et al. (2002) provide a detailed discussion of the APIM analysis for small groups using multilevel modeling, and syntax to specify this model using SAS or SPSS is available in Kashy and Donnellan (2012).

One-with-many design

The hallmark of the OWM design is that individuals are linked together as members of a group because each person is tied to the same focal individual. This data structure is traditionally referred to as a "wheel" in the sociometric literature (e.g., Mulder, 1960; see Figure 16.2). In this chapter, we refer to the person who has multiple partners (the "one") as the *focal person* and to the multiple others (the "many") as the *partners*. For instance, a manager (the focal person) may interact with many employees (partners), a teacher (the focal person) may interact with many students (partners), or a therapist (the focal person) may interact with many clients (partners). In this design there may be no direct relationship between the partners beyond their ties to the same focal person.

As an example, consider a small group study of leadership effectiveness in which one individual is assigned to the leader role, and the leader directs and coordinates the four other group members' activities. At the end of the study the leader might rate each group member on their performance, and each group member might rate the leader's performance. As this example illustrates, the scores obtained in the OWM design can be provided by either the one (e.g., the leader's ratings of the workers), the many (e.g., the workers ratings of the leader), or both. When the data come only from the focal persons, it is called a *one-perceiver-many-targets* design. When the data come only from the partners, it is called a *many-perceivers-one-target* design. Finally, when the data come from both the focal person and the partners, as in our example, it is called a *reciprocal* design. In the OWM design, interdependence occurs when scores for two partners who are tied to the same focal person are more similar to one another than are

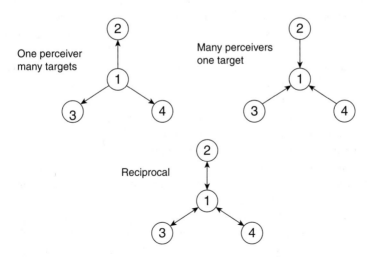

FIGURE 16.2 One-with-many design.

scores for partners who are tied to two different focal persons. It is important to note that the meaning of this interdependence depends on who generates the scores.

In the one-perceiver-many-targets design, there are many targets (i.e., workers), but only one perceiver (i.e., all of the scores come from the leader), allowing for an estimation of the degree to which a leader rates each of his or her workers in a similar way. Here the nonindependence occurs because the focal person's ratings may reflect his or her tendency to see all partners in a similar fashion. This is typically referred to as a *perceiver effect*, and variation in perceiver effects across groups suggests that there may be assimilation on the part of the focal persons. For instance, high levels of perceiver variance in the leader example would indicate that some leaders tend to report that all of their workers performed well, but other leaders report that none of their workers did well. Scores in the one-perceiver-many-targets design also reflect factors specific to the unique combination of a particular partner with the focal person. In other words, the leader may rate Bob's performance as exemplary, and this high rating may result from two elements: the leader tends to evaluate everyone's performance positively (the perceiver effect already discussed), and the leader thinks that Bob's performance was exceptionally strong.

In contrast, in the many-perceivers-one-target design, there are many perceivers (i.e., all of the scores come from the workers), but only one target (i.e., the leader). In the example, each worker rates his or her leader's performance, and so the nonindependence occurs because the workers' ratings of the leader may be similar. When multiple perceivers report on their perceptions of the same target, we can estimate *target effects*. When there is large variation in target effects, the implication is that some leaders are seen as performing well by all of their workers, but other leaders' performances are rated as inferior by all of their workers. This variation is sometimes referred to as consensus; it measures the degree to which each perceiver responds in a similar manner with the focal person. In the many-perceivers-one-target design, each score may reflect more than the target effect – there may be a unique component to the rating. For example, Bob may view his leader as highly competent whereas other group members see the leader's performance more negatively.

The reciprocal OWM design consists of both the one-perceiver-many-targets design and the many-perceivers-one-target design, and so it allows for estimation of both perceiver and target effects. That is, in a single study we can estimate the tendency for a leader to rate all of her or his workers' performances positively, and we can also estimate the tendency of the workers to agree in their ratings of that leader's performance. Thus, in both cases the focus is on the focal person, and so the reciprocal design allows researchers to examine the degree to which these two effects correspond with one another. In the example, if the correspondence is positive, it would indicate that leaders who generally perceive their workers performed well are generally viewed as performing well by those workers. This correspondence has been called *generalized reciprocity*, and it is estimated as the correlation between the perceiver and target effects.

The reciprocal design also allows us to examine dyad-level correspondence in ratings. *Dyadic reciprocity* measures the correspondence between the two unique effects in the reciprocal design: If the leader sees Bob's performance as especially strong (more so than other workers), does Bob see the leader's performance as especially strong (again, more so than other workers)? Dyadic reciprocity often occurs on affective measures such as liking. A detailed discussion of the OWM design and its analysis using SPSS can be found in Marcus, Kashy, and Baldwin (2009) and Kashy and Donnellan (2012).

Although the OWM design allows for estimation of consensus, assimilation, and reciprocity, it has some limitations as well. Continuing with the example, because each worker has only one leader, the worker's positive perception of the leader's performance may reflect the fact that they truly think that their particular leader did well, but it might also reflect the fact that the worker is a positive person who would think that almost any leader did well. In order to separate these factors, each individual must participate in multiple dyads, which leads us to our final methodological model: the social relations model.

The social relations model

The SRM, developed by Kenny and his colleagues (Kenny, 1994; Kenny & La Voie, 1984; Warner, Kenny, & Stoto, 1979), is a model of social behavior and interpersonal perception that can be applied in research contexts in which each person participates in more than one dyad within their group. The most common research design used with the SRM is called a round-robin design in which every member of the group interacts with or rates every other individual in the group (see Figure 16.3; Kenny, 1994). As we will describe, the SRM and OWM share many attributes, but the SRM has some advantages and can provide more precise estimates of perceiver, target, and relationship effects.

Consider as an example a study of newly acquainted college room mates living in four-person suites. In the study, each room mate rates how much he or she likes

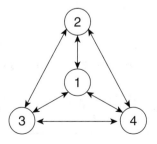

FIGURE 16.3 The social relations model – a round-robin design.

every other room mate in their suite. For instance, if the suite includes Ethan, Mike, James, and Landon, then a round-robin data structure for this group would generate 12 scores (i.e., Ethan's liking of Mike, Ethan's liking of James, Ethan's liking of Landon, Mike's liking of Ethan, and so on). This type of data allows researchers to examine the extent to which liking is determined by the unique relationship between two individuals. If Ethan were to report only on his liking of Mike, then we would not have enough information to establish whether Ethan's liking of Mike represents truly unique liking. That is, this liking score may occur if Ethan's suite is highly cohesive so everyone in the suite likes everyone else. Alternatively, Ethan may be a "liker" such that he likes everyone. Similarly, it may be that Mike is simply likeable and is liked by everyone. Finally, it may be the case that liking is in fact relationally determined and that ratings of liking within dyads are unique: Ethan likes Mike more than he likes his other room mates and more than his other room mates like Mike.

In order to separate these factors, each individual must participate in more than one dyad. Note that this is the primary difference between a SRM design and an OWM design, since the partners in the OWM design participate in only a single dyad with the focal person. With multiple interactions, the degree to which a person is a "liker" can be assessed by looking at whether that person generally likes everyone with whom he or she interacts. Similarly, the degree to which a person is "likeable" can be assessed by looking at whether everyone who interacts with that person likes him or her. Finally, if there is evidence that one person likes a particular partner over and above the person's tendency to be a "liker," and over and above the partner's tendency to be liked, then there is evidence that liking is uniquely determined by the specific relationship.

Moving now to a more formal definition of the SRM factors, according to the SRM each dyadic score may be comprised of four components. Consider as an example of Ethan's rating of how much he likes Mike. Figure 16.4 presents the SRM breakdown of this dyadic score. As mentioned, it may be that in Ethan's suite all the students like one another, and so this first component is called the *group mean* and reflects the average level of the outcome score for the group. Next, at the individual level, Ethan may tend to like everyone and so part of Ethan's liking of Mike may be a function of his general tendency to like people.

Score	=	Group Mean	+	Ethan's Actor Effect	+	Mike's Partner Effect	+	Ethan's Relationship Effect with Mike
Ethan's liking of Mike	=	Group Mean for liking	+	Ethan's tendency to like all of his roommates	+	Mike's tendency to be liked by all of his roommates	+	Ethan's unique liking of Mike

FIGURE 16.4 Social relations model components.

The tendency for a person to exhibit a consistent level of response across all inter-action partners is generally called a *perceiver effect*. The *target effect* is also an individual-level effect, and it measures the tendency for others to be consistent with a particular partner. Thus, for Ethan's liking of Mike the target effect measures the tendency for Mike to be liked by all of the other room mates in his suite. The *relationship effect* is at the dyad level. For Ethan's liking of Mike, the relationship effect measures the degree to which Ethan especially likes Mike, over and above his general tendency to like others and over and above Mike's tendency to be liked by others. Thus, the relationship effect reflects the unique combination of two individuals after removing their individual-level tendencies.

In the SRM, the focus is not on the size of perceiver, target, or relationship effects for any particular person or dyad. Instead, the focus is on the extent to which individuals vary in their perceiver or target effects, and whether dyads vary in their relationship effects. Thus, the perceiver variance measures the degree to which some individuals rate all interaction partners high on a specific outcome variable and other individuals rate all interaction partners low on the outcome variable. In the example, perceiver variance occurs if some individuals like all of their room mates, but other individuals do not like any of their room mates. Target variance measures the degree to which some individuals are rated high on a particular outcome variable by all interaction partners and other individuals are rated low on the outcome variable by all interaction partners. For instance, some room mates may be liked by everyone, and others may be uniformly dis-liked. Relationship variance measures the degree to which ratings vary depending upon the specific individuals in the dyad after removing variance due to those individuals' perceiver and target effects. For the liking data, the relationship vari-ance would measure the degree to which liking is unique to the particular dyadic combinations.

As was the case for the OWM, the perceiver variance reflects the degree of assimilation. In this case we define assimilation as the tendency to see all partners in the same way. However, in the OWM design, the assimilation was an attribute of the focal person (e.g., some leaders think all of their workers did well, but other leaders think that all of their workers did poorly), whereas in the SRM it is a general attribute that refers to all group members' perceptions. In other words, since each person in the SRM provides ratings of multiple targets, every group member has a perceiver effect, and so in the room mate example, assimilation is a general tendency for some individuals to be "likers" and others to be "dislikers." Similarly, the target variance for the SRM reflects the degree of consensus, as it did for the OWM; but in the OWM design, consensus referred specifically to agreement between the partner's perceptions of the focal person, and in the SRM it reflects a more general attribute of all individuals' perceptions of one another. Again, since each person in the SRM is the target of ratings by multiple perceivers, every group member has a target effect, and so in the room mate example, con-sensus is a general tendency for some individuals to be likeable and others less so.

Finally, as with the reciprocal OWM design, the SRM can be used to measure two types of reciprocity: generalized reciprocity and dyadic reciprocity. Recall that in the OWM design generalized reciprocity referred specifically to a correlation between the focal person's perceiver effect and the focal person's target effect. In the SRM, generalized reciprocity refers to all group members (since each person has his or her own perceiver effect and target effect), and so it is based on the correlation between each group member's perceiver and target effects. For instance, in the liking example, generalized reciprocity measures whether "likers" are more likeable. Dyadic reciprocity is measured by correlating the two group members' relationship effects. Thus dyadic reciprocity would emerge if two room mates feel uniquely similar levels of liking for one another (e.g., if Ethan especially likes Mike, does he feel the same way?). The SRM and OWM definitions of dyadic reciprocity are similar, except for the fact that, in the OWM design, one of the two dyad members is always the focal person, whereas in the SRM it is a property of every dyad within the group.

Over 200 research articles and chapters and more than 35 dissertations have applied the SRM to dyadic data within groups. One example of this is provided by Livi, Kenny, Albright, and Pierro (2008), who examined group members' perceptions of leadership using data from several existing studies. They found that group members agree on the degree of leadership displayed by each individual in their group (i.e., target variance). In contrast, they found relatively small amounts of perceiver variance, indicating that group members do differentially rate the degree of leadership displayed by other individuals in the group. A second example is a longitudinal study by Back, Schmukle, and Egloff (2008) in which individuals introduced themselves to other group members during an initial encounter and then sat in either neighboring seats (proximity), the same row (same group), or different rows (different group). A year after the initial encounter (with no intervening interaction), participants returned to the laboratory and were asked to rate photographs of the other participants from their original session on friendship desire. Results showed being near or in the same group with people during the initial encounter led to higher ratings of friendship desire with those people one year later, relative to those in a different group. Another example is a study involving four-person families (two parents and two adolescents) who rated their attachment relationships with each of the other family members (Buist, Reitz, & Dekovic, 2008). This research found that both the adolescent's internal working model of attachment (i.e., perceiver effect) and the characteristics of the unique attachment relationship (i.e., relationship effect) explain differences in quality of attachment. Kenny and Kashy (2011) provide a discussion of how the SRM parameters can be estimated for round-robin designs using MLM. More notably, David Kenny maintains a very useful website that provides links to a bibliography of all SRM studies as well as data analysis programs specifically designed for SRM analyses at http://davidakenny.net/srm/srm.htm.

Summary and Conclusion

In this chapter, we have highlighted both the data analytic challenges and opportunities that small groups researchers encounter. We argued that interdependence in small group research is important not only because it may result in biased statistical tests, but also because it likely reflects the kinds of interpersonal processes that draw investigators into the study of group behavior. Our discussion focused primarily on introductions to three methodological models of interdependent data: the APIM, OWM design, and SRM. The APIM can be used to predict an individual's outcomes as a function of both that individual's inputs, as well as the average inputs of the other group members. In contrast, the OWM design and SRM focus on estimating the degree to which outcomes are affected by group-, individual-, and dyad-specific factors. The major difference between the OWM and SRM is that in the OWM partners interact with only one focal person, whereas in the SRM individuals interact with multiple partners within their group.

Our goal in this chapter was to introduce these models and to argue that they allow groups researchers to ask unique and interesting questions. We hope that making future groups researchers aware of these models will motivate them to adventure into these kinds of sophisticated methods for studying group process. Finally, we hope that interested researchers will use the citations provided in this chapter to learn more about these models conceptually, as well as ways to implement them.

References

Back, M. D., Schmukle, S. C., & Egloff, B. (2008). Becoming friends by chance. *Psychological Science, 19*, 439–440.

Berg, E. C., Trost, M., Schneider, I. E., & Allison, M. T. (2001). Dyadic exploration of the relationship of leisure satisfaction, leisure time, and gender to relationship satisfaction. *Leisure Science, 23*, 35–46.

Bickel, R. (2007). *Multilevel analysis for applied research: It's just regression!* Guilford Press.

Bonito, J. A. (2000). The effect of contributing substantively on perceptions of participation. *Small Group Research, 31*, 528–553.

Bonito, J. A., DeCamp, M. H., Coffman, M., & Fleming, S. (2006). Participation, information, and control in small groups: An actor–partner interdependence model. *Group Dynamics: Theory, Research, and Practice, 10*, 16–28.

Buist, K. L., Reitz, E., & Dekovic, M. (2008). Attachment stability and change during adolescence: A longitudinal application of the social relations model. *Journal of Social and Personal Relationships, 25*, 429–444.

Butler, E. A., Egloff, B., Wilhelm, F. H., Smith, N. C., Erickson, E. A., & Gross, J. J. (2003). The social consequences of expressive suppression. *Emotion, 3*, 48–67.

Butterfield, R. M. (2001). Health-related social control and marital power: A test of two models. *Dissertation Abstracts International: Section B: The Sciences and Engineering, 61*, 6757.

Campbell, L., Simpson, J. A., Kashy, D. A., & Rholes, W. S. (2001). Attachment orientations, dependence, and behavior in a stressful situation: An application of the actor–partner interdependence model. *Journal of Social and Personal Relationships, 18*, 821–843.

Hox, J. (2002). *Multilevel analysis: Techniques and applications.* Mahwah, NJ: Lawrence Erlbaum Associates.

Kashy, D. A., & Donnellan, M. B. (2012). Conceptual and methodological issues in the analysis of data from dyads and groups. In K. Deaux & M. Snyder (Eds.), *The Oxford handbook of personality and social psychology* (pp. 209–238). New York: Oxford University Press.

Kashy, D. A., & Kenny, D. A. (2000). The analysis of data from dyads and groups. In H.T. Reis & C. M. Judd (Eds.), *Handbook of research methods in social psychology.* Cambridge: Cambridge University Press.

Kenny, D. A. (1994). *Interpersonal perception: A social relations analysis.* New York: Guilford.

Kenny, D. A., & Acitelli, L. K. (2001). Accuracy and bias in the perception of the partner in a close relatinoship. *Journal of Personality and Social Psychology, 80,* 439–448.

Kenny, D. A., & Kashy, D. A. (2011). Dyadic data analysis using multilevel modeling. In J. Hox and J. K. Roberts (Eds.), *The handbook of advanced multilevel analysis* (pp. 335-370). London: Taylor & Francis.

Kenny, D. A., Kashy, D. A., & Cook, W. L. (2006). *Dyadic data analysis.* Guilford Press.

Kenny, D. A., & LaVoie, L. (1984). The social relations model. In L. Berkowitz (Ed.), *Advances in experimental social psychology* (Vol. 18, pp. 142–182). Orlando, FL: Academic Press.

Kenny, D. A., Mannetti, L., Pietro, A., Livi, S., & Kashy, D. A. (2002). The statistical analysis of data from small groups. *Journal of Personality and Social Psychology, 83,* 126–137.

Kurdek, L. A. (2000). Attractions and constraints as determinants of relationship commitment: Longitudinal evidence from gay, lesbian, and heterosexual couples. *Personal Relationships, 7,* 245–262.

Lakey, S. G., & Canary, D. J. (2002). Actor goal achievement and sensitivity to partner as critical factors in understanding interpersonal communication competence and conflict strategies. *Communication Monographs, 69,* 217–235.

Livi, S., Kenny, D. A., Albright, L., & Pierro, A. (2008). A social relations analysis of leadership. *The Leadership Quarterly, 19,* 235–248.

Marcus, D., Kashy, D., & Baldwin, S. (2009). Studying psychotherapy using the one within many design: The therapeutic alliance as an exemplar. *Journal of Counseling Psychology, 56(4),* 537–548.

Moffitt, T. E., Robins, R. W., & Caspi, A. (2006). A couples analysis of partner abuse with implications for abuse-prevention policy. *Criminology and Public Policy, 1,* 5–36.

Mulder, M. (1960). Communication structure, decision structure and group performance. *Sociometry, 23,* 1–1.

Reid, S. A., & Ng, S. H. (2006). The dynamics of intragroup differentiation in an intergroup social context. *Human Communication Research, 32,* 504–525.

Snijders, T. B. A., & Bosker, R. J. (1999). *Multilevel analysis: An introduction to basic and advanced multilevel modeling.* Sage Publication Inc.

Warner, R. M., Kenny, D. A., & Stoto, M. (1979). A new round robin analysis of variance for social interaction data. *Journal of Personality and Social Psychology, 37,* 1742–1757.

17

CODING GROUP INTERACTION

Renee A. Meyers

UNIVERSITY OF WISCONSIN AT MILWAUKEE

David R. Seibold

UNIVERSITY OF CALIFORNIA—SANTA BARBARA

In the early 1980s, several group communication scholars at the University of Illinois (Dean Hewes, Bob McPhee, Scott Poole, and the second author) and their graduate students (including the first author) sought to peer deeper into "the black box" of group interaction processes. Their work was both theoretical (Structuration Theory perspective: Poole, Seibold, & McPhee, 1985; Socio-Egocentric Model: Hewes, 1986) and empirical (coding group argument, group development, group decision-making, group valence). Graduate courses, research team projects, and collegial conversations centered on how best to analyze and explain communicative processes in decision-making groups. The methodological solution to wide-ranging questions in this vein almost always involved coding group interaction. The questions could not be answered adequately and/or only by predicting from inputs to outputs, or by querying group participants about what they would say (or said they did) *if* they were in a group setting, or by asking students to write communicative responses to scenarios. In order to understand the complexity and seeming ambiguity of group communicative processes, it was necessary to scrutinize the data produced during members' discussions.

This commitment to coding group interaction has framed our research program for over two decades. We still believe that one of the best ways to understand group communication is to code the discourse. Knowing that the majority almost always wins in group decision-making interaction (Davis, 1973) provides only half a picture. We need to know why – exactly *how* is it that they accomplish "winning" *communicatively*? And if the minority should prevail, we need to know how they persuaded the majority to change its stance (Gebhardt & Meyers, 1995; Meyers, Brashers, & Hanner, 2000). Similarly, as Poole (Poole, 1981, 1983a, 1983b; Poole & Baldwin, 1996) has so elegantly demonstrated, we cannot assume that groups go through predictable stages of development until we have thoroughly examined how development is constituted in, and through, the group's interaction.

In short, coding group interaction provides a method for examining deeper-level communicative processes that help explain surface-level input–output predictions. A useful way for thinking about these layers is offered by Prosser and Trigwell (1999). They posit that both surface- and deep-level comprehension are necessary for learning about a phenomenon, but when taken together the greatest insight is realized. For example, when we discover that an input predicts a group output (e.g., group member expertise predicts a group outcome; Woolley, Gerbasi, Chabris, Kosslyn, & Hackman, 2008), we understand this phenomenon primarily on a surface level. That is, we know that this prediction will hold true much of the time. However, if we wish to understand more fully how experts in the group (those members with more knowledge or skill) accomplish this task, we must look below the surface and rigorously examine what occurs in their group decision-making discussions. What we might find are several different interactive paths that group experts and nonexperts co-construct to produce outcomes. As we discover and uncover these paths, and determine their effectiveness, we build both theoretical and practical knowledge to explain the initial input–output relationship.

Researchers who code group interaction do so because they ask questions that require rigorous observation of group communicative processes. How do group members argue? How do groups communicate in conflict? How do group members share (or not) information? How are participative comments connected (or not) to other comments in group discussion? How do members influence others with verbal messages in the course of the group's symbolic exchange? Moreover, they do this work because they want to know how communicative processes impact (or do not impact) group outcomes.

In this chapter, we describe how to code group interaction. We focus primarily on content analytic methods (rather than qualitative coding procedures) since these are the methods we most often employ in our own research. We provide detailed descriptions of the coding procedures so that readers can replicate them. To prevent induction of insomnia, however, we also highlight these descriptions with examples of our own experiences (successes and failures) using these methods. After explaining the mechanics of how to code group interaction, we discuss its benefits and drawbacks, and we close by identifying innovative practices for future research. In many ways our chapter can be read as a companion to the treatment of quantitative coding of negotiation behavior provided by Weingart, Olekalns, and Smith (2006).

Procedures for Coding Group Interaction

As previously noted, the decision to code group interaction is predicated on the research question. Questions about the functions, distribution, patterns, and structures of group communication invite the close observation that coding allows. Bakeman and Gottmann (1986) described this form of systematic observation:

> This approach typically is concerned with naturally occurring behavior observed in naturalistic contexts. The aim is to define beforehand various forms of behavior – behavioral codes – and then ask observers to record whenever behavior corresponding to the predefined codes occurs. A major concern is to train observers so that all of them will produce an essentially similar protocol, given that they have observed the same stream of behavior.
> *(Bakeman & Gottmann, 1986, p. 4)*

Coding group communication involves at least five steps: (a) transcribing the discussion data; (b) unitizing the interaction data; (c) developing a coding scheme; (d) coding the data; and (e) determining coding reliability. Another step, although one that is less often undertaken by content analytic researchers, is determining the validity of the coding. Each of these procedures is detailed next, augmented by examples of our successes and our struggles with these methods.

Transcribing the discussion data

In order to transcribe, either audio-taped or video-taped group discussion data must be available. Video tapes provide a more complete picture because they afford accurate identification of speakers. Moreover, although it is possible to code directly from audio tape or video tape, it is much easier to code from transcriptions. So after collecting the data on tape, transcription can begin.

Transcribing group discussion data typically is time consuming and laborious. It is especially difficult to transcribe from videotape, so you may need to transfer video-taped data to audio tapes. We did this for a large dataset that we collected, and although it took a great deal of time, it made the transcribing process much easier. Hiring expert transcribers is the most efficient method for completing this task, but they are often quite expensive. We have used student transcribers in some of our investigations, utilizing payment or extra credit (in group communication classes) as enticements. Depending upon the competence and motivation of the students, this practice has proven both successful and disastrous for us. We have had students do an expert job (this happened more often when we were paying them), and we have had students return the video tapes un-transcribed or transcribed so poorly they were unusable. The lesson learned – if you are going to utilize students, especially undergraduates – is to identify competent, motivated, and conscientious individuals whom you trust to perform the task to your standards. One way to accomplish this is to invite the best students from your class one semester to serve as undergraduate research assistants for you the following semester. Meeting regularly with them as a group throughout the research process, and allowing them to share their insights and ideas regarding the research, fosters greater commitment and involvement from them, and often, a passion for research that they never imagined.

In addition, if student transcribers (or even experts for that matter) are employed, it is essential to provide very detailed instructions for accomplishing the transcription task (see Appendix A for an example of instructions we have used). We also found it useful to transcribe at least some of the data ourselves. Although we did not relish this lengthy and laborious task, it turned out to be quite important. Doing transcription illuminates the data in ways that even a close reading of the ensuing transcript may miss, and we think it benefits all researchers studying group discussion to complete at least some transcription of their own data.

To ease the cognitive load of transcribing, we typically do not ask transcribers (especially students) to identify the name of the speakers, nor do we require them to sort out complex multiple-speaker episodes. After the transcriptions are completed, we view the video tape with transcript in hand and insert the name of the speaker next to each turn-at-talk. To the best of our ability, we sort multiple-speaker episodes, especially those involving fast-paced interruption sequences, and talk-over message acts, by reading backwards and forwards in the transcript to identify potential speakers in these episodes. When this process proves futile, the turn is assigned as a generic "multiple speakers" unit.

The final stage of transcribing requires punctuating the data. Expert transcribers do this as a matter of course, but you may want to recheck their interpretations. If you have employed student transcribers, you certainly should verify their punctuation choices. We watch the video tape with the transcript in hand. Using members' natural pausing, voice inflections, and intonation to determine sentences, questions, and exclamations, we insert periods, commas, capitalization, question marks, and exclamation points at appropriate places in the text. Although there is some debate as to whether this practice influences unitizing, Auld and White (1956) found that researchers who unitized a punctuated and capitalized transcript yielded unitized data that was reliable at 0.93 with other researchers who unitized a nonpunctuated transcript.

Unitizing the discussion data

Once the group communication dataset is transcribed and punctuated, the next step is to unitize the data. Unitizing is the process of identifying units to be categorized or rated (Folger, Hewes, & Poole, 1984), and it occurs in several steps

Specifying the discourse unit

The first step in unitizing discussion data is to identify the unit that best fits the research question, coding scheme, and data analytic tools to be employed (Folger et al., 1984; Guetzkow, 1950). In much of our research, we study members' arguments in group discussion (for a summary, see Seibold & Meyers, 2007), so we unitize as close to natural talk as possible.

In specifying the discourse unit, it is important to note both grammatical and functional considerations. Relying too heavily on functional considerations places greater interpretive demands on the coders (Auld & White, 1956; Hatfield & Wieder-Hatfield, 1998; McLaughlin, 1984), so we first defined our unit according to grammatical descriptors. Recognizing that group talk is often neither grammatically correct nor bound by grammatical rules, however, we also developed functional guidelines. We found that the discourse unit that best fit our parameters was the utterance or thought unit (McLaughlin, 1984). This discourse unit recognizes grammatically correct rule-bound statements co-equal with functionally appropriate, rule-independent structures like incomplete sentences, interrupted statements, co-produced agreements, functional dependent clauses, and singular words that function as complete thoughts. Since all of these structures are found in group argument discourse, the thought unit was deemed most appropriate for our research objectives (e.g., see Meyers, Seibold, & Brashers, 1991).

Specifying unitizing rules

Once the unit is determined, grammatical and functional unitizing rules are specified. Especially pertinent for determining thought units are rules about when to separate, and when to allow, run-on statements because more than one thought unit can occur in a single sentence. Grammatically, we identified two transition markers (after brushing up on our English grammar) as especially important to this task – coordinating and subordinating conjunctions. If definitions for these grammatical markers no longer come immediately from memory, as is the case for us, consult Appendix B. These types of conjunctions were identified as key for determining sentence division.

We identified sentences containing these types of conjunctions as illustrating functioning independent clauses (see Appendix B for examples). Hence sentence structures where two clauses were joined by parallel or syllogistic construction (e.g., if/then, on the other hand) remained as single units because the two parts of the statement did not function as independent clauses. We also developed rules about stand-alone utterances, false starts, introductory phrases, and interruptions (see Appendix B).

Identifying units

Once the unitizing rules are specified, unitizers (at least two individuals unfamiliar with the objectives of the research) are trained to identify the discourse units. The unitizers must first familiarize themselves with the unitizing rules, and then practice identifying units on discussion data similar to, but not included in, the final dataset. In the early days, our unitizers worked on paper copies of transcripts, placing a slash mark after each unit. Today, our unitizers identify the units in an electronic file by placing a keyboard return after each unit. Unitizers must work independently on the sample transcript. When the unitizing task is complete, they meet to talk over their unitizing decisions. Discussion at these meetings centers on sorting out differences, but this discussion process also is useful for reinforcing the reasoning behind similarities in unit identifications. Once 80 per cent reliability is reached in practice, each unitizer is given the final data and asked to identify the units. A note of caution. We have learned from experience that, although unitizing is not a difficult task, it is quite monotonous. So it is important to ask unitizers to do this work in increments and to stop when they feel fatigued.

Unitizing reliability

When the unitizing task is completed, it is time to compute reliability between the unitizers. The most common formula for determining unitizing reliability is Guetzkow's (1950) index of unitizing disagreement. It is based on the premise that two unitizers (A and B) each unitize a text into specifiable units (O). The formula is $U = (O_A - O_B)/(O_A + O_B)$, and it indicates the discrepancy between either unitizer and the best estimate of the *true* number of units (the average of the two unitizers' estimates).

Folger et al. (1984) contended this formula fails to quantify *unit by unit agreement* between coders. They argued, "Guetzkow's index only shows the degree to which two coders identify the *same number of units* in a text of fixed length, not whether those units were in fact the *same units*" (p. 123, emphasis added). They proposed an alternative method for computing unitizing reliability which involved segmenting the text into objective units that are smaller than the actual units. By segmenting more finely than the majority of actual units, the possibility of having two or more actual units occur within one objective unit is minimized. When the text has been objectively segmented, each objective unit is scrutinized to see if the unitizers agreed on the existence of an actual unit within that objective unit. If both coders agreed that an actual unit occurred, it is counted as an agreement. Reliability is then computed utilizing an index based on coder disagreement such as Scott's (1955) pi.

Folger et al. (1984) also suggested that it may be unnecessary to compute unit-by-unit reliability if "one is using an exhaustive coding scheme and Guetzkow's (1950) index is quite low, perhaps .10 or below" (p. 124). Such a score indicates little overall disagreement between the two unitizers. For example, we found that a score of 0.03 using Guetzkow's formula yielded a reliability of 0.90 using the Folger et al. procedure and Scott's (1950) pi. Our reading of much of the content analysis literature indicates that most researchers use only Guetzkow's formula to determine unitizing reliability, and that most unitizing reliabilities fall below the 0.10 criterion.

At this point in the process, the data are transcribed and unitized, and you are now ready to construct the coding scheme and complete the coding tasks. In the next section, we take you through that process.

Developing the Coding Scheme

Examination of relevant literature

Developing a coding scheme is a theoretical act and represents what the investigator thinks should be extracted from the discussion data (Bakeman & Gottman, 1986). As Bakeman and Gottman explain, "It is, very simply, the lens with which he or she has chosen to view the world" (p. 19). A vital part of the development of any coding scheme within the content analytic tradition is to become familiar with relevant literature so as to build upon previous work. Sometimes a literature search reveals an existing scheme that fits your research purposes, or a scheme that can be adapted to fit. At other times, no relevant coding schemes emerge. When this happens (a generally common occurrence), it is necessary to create your own scheme. This is a creative, innovative, and intellectually challenging process.

The first step in creating your own coding scheme is to develop a familiarity with the principal theoretical and conceptual strands found in your literature review, and to draw those out in an organized form. In early development work on the Conversational Argument Scheme (CAS; see Appendix C), Canary, Seibold, and colleagues (Canary, Ratledge, & Seibold, 1982; Seibold, Canary, & Tanita-Ratledge, 1983; Seibold, McPhee, Poole, Tanita, & Canary, 1981) began by reading three prominent and representative argument theories: Toulmin (1958), Perelman and Olbrechts-Tyteca (1969), and Jackson and Jacobs (1980). In addition, when Meyers (1987) joined the research team, cognitive theories of argument in psychology and in communication were consulted (e.g., Burleson, 1981; Burnstein, 1982; Hample, 1985; Vinokur, Trope, & Burnstein, 1975). Taken together, this literature provided a strong foundation for conceptualizing group argument, and for developing a scheme that would capture that representation.

Developing the scheme

Once the relevant literature is digested, it is time to sketch out a tentative coding scheme. This scheme sets out initial categories based on your reading of the literature and your conceptions of the discourse unit of interest. This preliminary scheme is then used for an initial coding of the data. Revisions are made as deemed appropriate. It is often helpful to ask a colleague to work with you during this process so that ideas for categories and revisions can be discussed. This coding and revision process continues until you (and your colleague) have constructed what you believe to be an exhaustive coding scheme. Working independently, the two of you use this final scheme to code a sample of group discussion data. When finished, compare your coding choices, talk through similarities and differences, and make revisions to the scheme if necessary. If revisions are made, you must repeat the coding process. When no revisions are needed, you have a final scheme that can be used for training coders.

The goal is to develop a coding scheme that is exhaustive (contains a category for all possible units in your data) and exclusive (contains no overlapping categories). Most coding schemes are designed to place each unit into only one category. It is possible to ask coders to place content into more than one category, but this places greater interpretive burdens on the coders. If you determine that multiple coding of single units is necessary, explicit coding rules must be provided to help coders navigate that process. An "Other" category is often added to schemes for placement of units that do not fit elsewhere.

Finally, it is important to develop category definitions and rules to help coders interpret the categories reliably. It is helpful to capture these definitions and rules in a single document (Canary, 1992). See Appendix C for CAS category definitions, and Appendix D for examples of some of the coding rules that were created to help coders manage the coding task.

Determining validity of the coding

Poole and colleagues (Folger, Hewes, & Poole, 1984; Poole & Folger, 1981; Poole, Folger, & Hewes, 1987; Poole, Keyton, & Frey, 1999) have long advocated the importance of determining the validity of coding. Yet many content analytic researchers overlook this task, and in truth, we too have seldom focused on determining the validity of our coding.

Although there are many types of validity (see Folger & Poole, 1980), one that is particularly relevant to coding group interaction is representational validity – verifying that categories reflect meanings that are present in the culture/group being investigated (Poole & Folger, 1981). Poole (1987) distinguished observer-privileged meanings from subject-privileged meanings. Observer-privileged meanings are those available to observers from the outside (e.g., researchers or "blind" coders), and subject-privileged meanings are those available to insiders and participants. Establishing categories that reflect subject-privileged meanings is paramount to establishing representational validity. Of course, as Poole et al. note, "Clearly, a coding scheme designed to capture subject-privileged meanings is harder to design than an observer-privileged system" (Poole et al., 1987, p. 106). One method they have advocated for establishing representational validity is using multidimensional scaling for paired comparisons of interactive passages (for a more complete explanation of this method, see Poole & Folger, 1981).

An example of establishing representational validity from our research would include asking research participants to define assertions (statements of fact or opinion). If they chose terms similar to those of the researchers, there would be greater assurance that the researched and the researchers understood assertions in the same way. This category would be said to have representational validity because it would depict a concept similarly for both parties in the research process.

Researchers may be reluctant to determine the validity of their coding because this task adds additional work to what is already a fairly onerous task. Moreover, representational validity should be re-assessed each time the scheme is applied to a new interactive context. Yet, as Poole and Folger (1981) indicated, it is "precisely because there is such a tremendous investment of time and effort in coding, (that) validity is a crucial issue" (p. 39). Indeed, by verifying coding validity, a researcher can establish greater confidence in the coded data and conclusions drawn from it.

Coding process

Training coders

The complexity of the scheme and the competence of the coders will dictate the length and difficulty of the coder training process. In past work employing the CAS, training has typically taken 50–60 hours. This scheme admittedly is complex, and we often use graduate student coders as well as senior-level undergraduates. Our experience indicates that, with proper training, both sets of students make competent coders. We typically train four coders for data sets of 40 or more group discussions.

The first step in training is familiarization with the coding scheme. We usually ask coders to do background reading on the research topic prior to working with the scheme. Content knowledge is an asset. We have found that students who have debated or studied argumentation theory made good coders with the CAS. We also require coders to read through the scheme, category definitions, and coding rules carefully. In the first training session, we discuss the coders' understanding of the scheme, address their questions, and work to shape consensual interpretations of the categories. Then we give each coder an identical excerpt of data that is similar to, but not included in, the final dataset, and we ask each coder to code that data independently before the next training meeting. We code these data too. At the next session, we compare all codes (including our codes). Differences are discussed and revisions are made to the scheme categories or rules when all coders agree that the revision is necessary, and when it does not deviate from the theoretical underpinnings of the scheme. Coders then receive another excerpt and the cycle is repeated. Our experience with the CAS training is that coders spent approximately ten hours in private coding each week, and discussion sessions lasted approximately four hours per week over a five-week period.

After each coding interval, simple percentage of agreement reliability checks are computed. In our training with the CAS, reliability levels began at 45 per cent agreement and rose to 80 per cent by the end of the five weeks. At this level, we decided that coders were adequately prepared, and training sessions were terminated. Each coder was provided with a final revised copy of the coding scheme, the coding rules, coding protocols (either hard copy or electronic), and half of the transcripts and video tapes. Coders were instructed to read through the coding scheme categories and rules before coding each transcript and to access the video tape if needed. They were asked to return two coded transcripts each week until the task was completed. This schedule was used to insure that coders would not forget the rules or categories, but it also ensured a pace that would guard against coder fatigue. When each coder had finished coding all the transcripts, they were compared for points of disagreement. All disagreements were clearly marked on the coding sheet and returned to the coders. They discussed each disagreement until a consensual agreement on a final single code was reached.

One of our early disappointments with use of the CAS was that coders were only able to achieve moderate category-by-category reliabilities (Meyers & Brashers, 1995). Moreover, they appeared to be simplifying the coding process by reducing the number of utilized categories (Meyers et al., 1991). Low reliabilities pose a central problem in this type of research because they indicate that the scheme could not be used by others to attain similar results. Moreover, if coders were dealing with the coding complexities by reducing the number of categories they utilized, then the validity of our results was also in question. So we entertained modifications to the coding procedures and created a multistage coding process for the CAS (Meyers & Brashers, 1995) that involved first parceling the interaction data and then coding them in successive iterations. This created a more prolonged coding process, but was less frustrating for the coders and resulted in improved reliability.

Multistage coding procedures

The initial task in the multistage procedure is to parcel the data so that a more coherent picture of the group's argument, in our research, is available. This task involves three levels of parceling. First, the nonargument statements are sorted from the argument statements. At the second level, all argument statements are separated according to the final decision alternative they support. Decision alternatives are identified initially, and trained coders next read through the transcripts and code each statement according to the decision alternative it favors.

At the third level of data partitioning, messages are further distinguished according to lines of argument (based on similar content features). This stage of parceling is accomplished in two steps. First, a category system identifying various lines of argument is constructed. In the initial investigation, we derived lines of argument by asking group participants, prior to entering group discussion, to generate lists of arguments that pertained to the task. Three judges then sorted these arguments into content categories and labeled each category. If two of three judges agreed that a content category existed, we treated it as a separate category; these consensual, labeled categories became the coding scheme for identifying lines of argument in this dataset. Alternatively, these categories could be deductively derived from the task scenario using the procedures described above for creating coding schemes (Lemus & Seibold, 2008).

Trained coders, using this set of argument content categories, classified each argument unit in the group discussion. Once they completed the coding, we used low-tech highlighters to color-code each content message unit. In more recent investigations, we have used computer highlighting to accomplish the same task. The color highlighting provided a visual picture of how group members moved from one content topic to another, and indicated when arguments were new or merely continuations of arguments offered earlier in the discussion. This procedure helped coders sustain a cognitive representation of the entire argument as it developed and persisted over a given period of time. We also have used text-based software to provide coders with these options in our analyses of argument in computer-mediated groups (Lemus & Seibold, 2008).

Successive coding iterations

Once the data were parceled so that the structure and organization of the groups' arguments were clear, further coding unfolded in six iterative sessions (refer to Appendix C for category names). First, coders placed each message statement into one of the four global-level categories contained in the scheme – Arguables, Convergence Markers, Disagreement-relevant Intrusions, or Delimitors. (They had done coding of the Nonarguables at an earlier stage). Second, the coders returned to the data to categorize each Arguable statement into one of the six subcategories – Assertion, Proposition, Elaboration, Response, Amplification, or Justification. Third, they returned to the data to code all Convergence Marker statements as Agreements or Acknowledgements. Fourth, coders recoded all Disagreement-relevant Intrusions into Objections or Challenges. Fifth, they recoded Delmitors as Frames, Forestall-secure, or Forestall-remove. Finally, they recoded Nonarguables as Process, Unrelated Statements, or Incompletes.

For each iteration, the coders practiced with data extraneous to the investigation, and coding choices were discussed until they were able to apply the codes reliably. For each set of tasks, coders returned to the same transcripts but focused on different aspects of the group argument. They not only fractionated their task into manageable parts, but with each additional reading of the transcript they became increasingly familiar with the complete discussion. Appendix E offers a short example of the final coded results.

Employing these multistage procedures required that more time be devoted to the coding process. However, we were happy to discover that they also resulted in improved reliabilities (Meyers & Brashers, 1995, 1998). In the next section, we discuss the process of determining coder reliability.

Determining reliability

Scholars debate the best basis for computing coding reliability (Krippendorff, 2004; Lombard, Snyder-Duch, & Bracken, 2002, 2004). Most researchers use one of three formulas: Cohen's kappa (1960), Scott's (1955) pi, or Krippendorff's alpha (1980, 2004). All of these measures provide a more conservative estimate of inter-coder reliability than does percentage agreement. Although there is no firmly established tradition for what constitutes acceptable reliability, most researchers would agree that 0.80 or higher (using one of these three formulas) is clearly acceptable. Depending upon the complexity of the data, the scheme, and the consequences of being wrong, reliabilities between 0.67 and 0.80 are considered moderately acceptable (Krippendorff, 2004). Reliabilities below those levels raise questions as to whether further use of the scheme could yield consistent results, as well as the representativeness of the coded data.

In sum, coding group interaction is a complex, time-consuming, but intellectually stimulating process. We aver that it is one of the best ways to get a firm grasp on what is happening in the group's discussion. Coding interaction provides opportunities to study discourse patterns, distributions, and structures. It brings greater coherence to seemingly chaotic conversations, and suggests linkages to group outcomes. Perhaps most important, coding group interaction stimulates new research questions, poses new communicative puzzles to solve, and uncovers often hidden elements of group discussions. In the next section, we reflect more fully on the benefits and drawbacks of this method.

Critical Reflection on Coding Group Interaction

Given the daunting details of interaction coding, you may be asking yourself, "Why would I want to use this method? Aren't there easier and less time consuming methods that involve fewer challenges?" Of course there are (see review in McGrath & Altermatt, 2001). Both of us have used such other methods at various times in our research careers. But when we are curious about what group communication really looks like, or wonder about how it manifests in team situations, and/or have questions about whether communication occurs as theorists have hypothesized, we feel compelled to do a close analysis of actual group interaction. When our research objective is to discover the possibilities of group communication in all its complexity, messiness, and sedimented nature, we always return to interaction coding.

Benefits of coding group interaction

We find three primary benefits from coding group interaction: (a) it provides a picture of the distribution of communicative acts; (b) it showcases the interactive structure of the discourse; and (c) it makes detection of communicative patterns and sequences possible. Identifying distributions, structures, and patterns in discussions helps us to understand both the development and predictability of interaction processes. In addition, they help us to explain unexpected interaction functions or outcomes (see description of process statements and humor sequences below), and/or to rule out alternative explanations for group decisions.

Distribution of communicative acts

Much of our work using the CAS has focused on identifying the distribution of discrete argument acts in group discussions (Seibold & Meyers, 2007). Coding argumentative discourse in groups, thought unit by thought unit, has allowed us to obtain a more exact picture of this distributive structure. As previously mentioned, we initially were surprised, and a bit disappointed, to find that student groups discussing hypothetical tasks produced a simple, and relatively simplistic, distribution of argument acts (Assertions, Elaborations, Agreement). This finding raised new questions for our research program. Do groups argue simplistically? Is this a function of their student status and/or the hypothetical task? Is this distribution related to the coding scheme or to group processes?

As indicated, the complexity inherent in the CAS influenced our decision to first focus on the coding scheme and procedures associated with its use. We constructed multistage coding procedures that resulted in a more complex distribution of argument acts. We believe that some of the early distributive simplicity was due to coder confusion and fatigue. But more recent investigations suggest additional answers. Coding of online student groups working on consequential tasks also showed a more complex distribution of argument acts (Lemus et al., 2004). So perhaps some of the earlier distributive simplicity was due to task type.

Recently we have begun work coding an actual jury discussion using the CAS, and initial findings suggest that the distribution of argument acts is much more complex, and may even support revisions to the present version of the CAS (Huber, Johnson, Hill, Meyers, & Seibold, 2007; Kang, Meyers, & Seibold, 2008; Meyers & Brashers, 2010; Meyers, Seibold, & Kang, 2010). We have discovered forms of Process statements that we have not seen elsewhere. For example, although the jury produced traditional types of Process statements (orienting the group to its task or specifying the process the group should follow), they also generated argument-relevant process statements. For example, jury members discussed how legal terms could or should be defined, how the arguments should be considered in time, and how legal definitions and restrictions could or should be used. These Process statements certainly were not employed to organize and facilitate group decision-making (as traditional Process statements do). Rather, they functioned to explore definitional possibilities, identify viewpoints, and set the groundwork for the group to be able to do its *arguing* work. Hence, we think there may be varying forms of Process statements. We currently are puzzling over how to code these statements and whether to add additional Process categories to the scheme.

Interactive structures

Coding interaction also provides an avenue for observing group communication structures. Early work by Canary, Brossmann, and Seibold (1987) revealed four group argument structures: simple, compound, eroded, and convergent. Simple arguments followed a straightforward argument pattern (assertion, elaboration, amplification, and so forth). Compound arguments included extended arguments, embedded arguments, and parallel arguments. Eroded arguments dissembled or fell apart. Convergent arguments used others' points to create an argument through agreement or tag-team communication. Moreover, Canary et al. found that groups reaching consensus had greater proportions of convergent argument structures than did dissensus groups, in which eroded structures were more prominent.

Similarly, in a study of differences and similarities in subgroup argument, Meyers, Brashers, & Hanner (2000) found that majority and minority subgroups produced different argument structures. Majorities were more likely than minorities to build their argument structures around convergence statements (and tag-team arguments), and they were less likely to disagree. Minority subgroups produced arguments with more disagreement messages to defend their positions against the unified majority. These differing subgroup structures suggest that some patterns may be unique to the interactive status of the group members.

Finally, Lemus et al. (2004) coded computer-mediated group (CMG) interactions to test the predictive utility of argument structures. Based on analyses of 477 distinct argument structures across eleven CMGs, the researchers found that the development of argument structures was a significant predictor of the success or failure of decision proposals. When argument structures in support of a decision proposal were more argumentatively developed than were argument structures against a decision proposal, CMG members were likely to endorse the decision proposal. Conversely, when argument structures in opposition were more argumentatively developed than argument structures in support of the decision proposals, CMG members were not likely to endorse the decision proposal. This work has been extended in subsequent studies (see review in Seibold, Lemus, & Kang, 2010).

Although coding group interaction can be time consuming, it also provides exciting insights that are potentially unavailable using other methods. For example, in coding German work groups' decision making, we found participants complained frequently and that complaining encouraged more of the same thereby producing a cycle of complaining behavior (Kauffeld & Meyers, 2009; Lehmann-Willenbrock & Kauffeld, 2010). The prominence of this unhappy discourse surprised and interested us. We think that other methods would not have enabled us to uncover complaining behaviors in quite the same way. Would team members responding to a survey, or a focus group, or an interview admit that "yes, I complain all the time." Would they be able to recall what they complain about, the form of those complaints, or how others in the group spur production of complaining cycles? Coding the actual interaction allowed us to view complaint behavior as it occurred, unmediated by members' recall, biases, or perceptions of prosocial norms.

Likewise, in an investigation of minority subgroup influence in teams (Meyers et al., 2000), we wanted to know what these subgroups can do communicatively to get their proposals accepted by the group. To discover the answer to this question, we had to analyze (code) the actual group interaction. What did we find when we did this close analysis? Minority subgroups can "win" by maintaining, and sustaining, a consistent line of argument throughout discussion. Refusing to change direction was a strategy that worked. These results have important applications for social justice and ethical decision-making and are simple strategies we can teach our students. Only by coding group interaction could we best understand how group members use communication to fashion a winning proposal (even when they are in the underdog position).

Communication patterns and sequences

Although much of our work has been focused on argument distribution and structures, researchers using the CAS in other communicative domains have attended more to identifying sequences of argument (see Canary & Sillars, 1992; Canary, Brossmann, Sillars, & LoVette, 1987; Canary, Weger, & Stafford, 1991; Ellis & Maoz, 2002). Recent work on complaints in work groups also is germane. Using Kauffeld's (2006) act4teams® scheme to code organizational group decision-making interaction, Kauffeld & Meyers (2009) found that complaints followed by a supportive statement beget yet another complaint, resulting in a repetitive complaining sequence. The discussion becomes increasingly negative. Alternatively, when complaints received no support or were followed by statements that moved the group back to its task, the complaining stopped.

Another example of how coded interaction can lead to discovery of communicative sequences comes from a recent examination of humor in these same work groups. Using data coded with the act4teams® scheme (Kauffeld, 2006), Hebl at al. (2009) showed that humor most often occurs in sequences of humor statements–laughter–humor statements. Less common, but significant in their occurrence in these work groups, were sequences of humor–laughter–terminating discussion or humor–laughter–empty talk. Hence the sequences discovered in these data suggest that humor can serve both positive and inhibitive functions. Coding the interaction and subjecting it to sequential analysis allowed us to explore the sequences and patterns that are shaped by, and shape, group humor.

Limitations of coding group interaction

Several limitations are evident in the preparation of data and the coding process. First, and as we noted, transcription is a lengthy, and often tedious, task. Second, development of one or more coding schemes, and attendant rule books, is a large undertaking. As Bakeman and Gottman (1986) state, "developing an appropriate scheme (or schemes) is often an arduous task. ... There is no reason to expect this process to be easy" (p. 46). Third, training coders is neither simple nor quick, especially in projects involving large datasets of groups. Such time and resource requirements give many researchers pause. Fourth, achieving acceptable reliabilities can be difficult if the coding scheme is complex or highly interpretive. The reputation of content analysis rests on acceptable reliability, so if you find you have not achieved that, revision to the coding scheme or training process is typically required. Fifth, data from the coding process is often nominal in form. This can limit the types of statistical analysis that can be performed on the data.

As with any method, coding group interaction has benefits and drawbacks. Yet we think that the complexity of group interaction is best illuminated when investigated with commensurate tools. Coding group interaction is one method that enables us to explore group interaction in all its complexity and to discover its structures, distributions, sequences, and links to group outcomes.

However, it *is* possible to simplify this process. One option may be to investigate communication produced in online environments. Online interactions offer immediate transcriptions of team members' statements, and remove the tedium and/or expense involved in transcribing face-to-face (f2f) group discussions. In addition, there are no interruptions, talkovers, or incomplete statements in online data, which are often difficult to code. In these ways (and others), coding online discussions may be less time consuming and easier than coding f2f discussions. Conversely, in online discourse, it is harder to interpret emotion or paralanguage (laughter, for example). Emoticons can help but not everyone uses them, or uses them in the same way. Still, given current trends toward more global and dispersed teams, we must continue to investigate both f2f and online groups if we are to best understand communication practices in teams.

Constructing simpler coding schemes is another way to address some of the complexity issues. For example, Poole, McPhee, and Seibold (1982) utilized a coding scheme with only two categories (positive and negative valence) to code comments in group decision-making interactions. This simple coding scheme yielded important information about the amount of this type of support (or lack thereof) for specific decision proposals. So simple coding schemes can also provide very useful information about communication in groups.

Constructing simpler coding schemes is particularly pertinent if you want to code interaction *in situ*. Coding group interaction as it occurs demands a scheme with fewer categories that address very specific communication behaviors. Suppose, for example, you wished to code 'humor' in team meetings and no recording equipment was permitted to be used to capture the data. You might develop a coding scheme of three categories: (a) positive humor, (b) negative humor, and (c) participant identification. This very narrow set of codes may allow for 'on the fly' coding but you would still want to assign two coders to code the discussion so as to check reliability of the codes later. If your definitions of positive and negative humor were well honed, and coders could reliably identify these two types of humor, you could answer some very interesting questions from these three categories alone. Who most often initiates humor in these groups? What types of humor are most common? Do all members contribute to humor production or is the distribution skewed? Are there positive and negative humor leaders? Do groups differ in frequency and type of humor production? All of these questions, and others, could be answered with this simpler category system.

If you were using the CAS, and you wanted to simplify the process, you could employ the five primary categories only (Arguables, Reinforcers, Promptors, Delimitors, and Nonarguables) as your coding scheme, thereby making coding much less complex. Indeed, in cases where the answers to your research questions do not depend on fine descriptions of the data, this is both a viable, and more efficient, process to follow. Coding with these five categories can still produce interesting findings regarding group argument (albeit at a more macro-level). Moreover, struggles with intercoder reliability should be markedly reduced.

As is surely evident, there are always tradeoffs in the research process when coding is involved. How can you best answer your research question versus how much time and effort can you afford? What is the best way to code the data versus how many resources can you muster? Answers to these and many other conflicting questions will frame your decisions about scheme development and use. Regardless of whether your coding scheme is simple or complex, micro-level or macro-level, the end goal for all content analytic group communication researchers is the same – understanding and explaining group interaction practices.

Innovations to Advance Future Research

Three innovations would greatly enhance this form of research: computerized transcription of data, coding via computer software and/or by a computer, and development of a cyberspace structure for archiving and retrieving group data and research tools. We hope that each of these innovations will come to fruition soon, and we speculate on that potential in this final section.

As we discussed, one of the most time-consuming processes involved in coding group interaction is data transcription. It is sometimes possible to code from actual video tapes, but it is not easy to do so. Hence, it would be particularly helpful if software that transcribed video-taped interactions was produced. Although voice recognition software is currently available, it is not accurate enough to transcribe group discussions. If computer scientists, working with group communication specialists, could develop software to accomplish this task accurately, the coding of group interaction would be significantly enhanced.

Second, coding itself is difficult and time consuming. However, recently developed computer software programs now make it possible for researchers to code transcribed or video data more efficiently at the computer. For example, the INTERACT system designed by a German firm, Mangold International (Mangold, 2005; www.mangold-international.com), allows a researcher to view a video of a group discussion and code directly from a customized keyboard. Figure 17.1 depicts a screenshot of the software with the coding units, video, time duration of each unit, identification of group member speaking, and the category assigned by the coder (this figure is taken, with permission, from Lehmann-Willenbrock & Kauffeld, 2010). The keyboard in the bottom right corner is programmed to contain the coding categories, group members' identifications, and some keys for cutting and editing the video.

If needed, the coder can stop the videotape or replay sections. This system works best if the unit of analysis is the sentence, turn-at-talk, or other larger unit, so that unitizing and categorizing can occur at the same time. If the unit selected is smaller than the sentence, it may be necessary to unitize the data prior to the computerized coding task. For more information, and relevant citations, see Kauffeld, 2006; www.mangold-international.com/en/service/publications/some-citation-references.html.

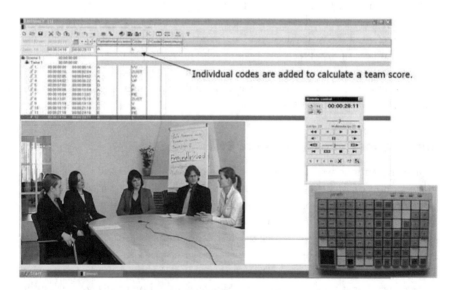

Individual codes are added to calculate a team score.

FIGURE 17.1 INTERACT Coding System
(from Lehmann-Willenbrock & Kauffeld, 2010).

Such computer software programs can help streamline the research process. Even more useful would be a software program that could directly assign units into relevant categories. If this were possible, the lengthy tasks of training coders and of coding the interaction would become unnecessary. Currently, the second author is working with Noshir Contractor and Scott Poole on a project that would use the Structuration Argument Theory version of CAS to test this possibility.[1]

Finally, it would be useful for group researchers to have access to datasets of group discussions. Finding sets of groups (especially naturally occurring groups), and getting permission to video tape them, is increasingly difficult. Currently, the first author and two other communication colleagues (Joe Bonito, John Gastil) have begun work on development of a GroupBank in cyberspace where all things group-related could be housed, including group data, coding schemes, coded data, measures of group process and outcomes, among other materials. This project is still in its early stages, but if it comes to fruition, it will offer a place where group researchers from any discipline can access group data and coding schemes.

This GroupBank would make the study of group processes easier and more efficient, and hopefully more enticing for faculty and graduate students alike. It would also allow for greater collaboration among group researchers across disciplines. Investigators could share findings, combine results, add to data, work together on datasets, and develop an interdisciplinary learning community to extend, and enhance, the current Interdisciplinary Network for Group Research venue.

Conclusion

In this chapter, we described how to code group members' communication. We provided descriptions of coding procedures and highlighted these details with examples of our successes and struggles using these methods. We discussed the benefits and limitations associated with this method, and closed by identifying innovations related to coding that could advance research in the future.

We continue to believe that coding group interaction is one of the best ways to investigate group discussion. Although this method is not without its drawbacks (especially time and resources), it affords opportunities to view communicative distributions, discourse sequences, and interaction structures that other methods do not illuminate. Choice of method is always predicated on the research question being asked, and this method is especially suited to group communication puzzles and challenges.

Note

1 Poole and Contractor are working with colleagues to develop GroupScope, an analytical tool that reduces the task of studying large dynamic groups (LDGs) to manageable proportions. Advances in computational video, audio, and text analysis,

and in middleware are enabling these researchers to construct an integrated analytical environment for management and analysis of the huge and complex datasets needed to study LDGs. The authors of this chapter, and other colleagues, will be aiding their study of human interaction systems by making the Conversational Argument Coding Scheme (CACS; Canary & Seibold, 2010) among the GroupScope multiple coding options. The argument coding processes noted in this chapter will be facilitated through first-order annotation procedures. Transcripts of group discussions will be annotated by human coders, and machine learning will utilize this coding to associate various first-order cues with classifications in the CACS usually accomplished through the iterative procedures we have described.

References

Auld, F., & White, A. M. (1956). Rules for dividing interviews into sentences. *Journal of Psychology, 42*, 273–281.

Bakeman, R., & Gottman, J. M. (1986). *Observing interaction: An introduction to sequential analysis.* Cambridge: Cambridge University Press.

Burleson, B. R. (1981). A cognitive-developmental perspective on social reasoning processes. *Western Journal of Speech Communication, 45*, 133–147.

Burnstein, E. (1982). Persuasion as argument processing. In H. Brandstatter, J. H. Davis, & G. Stocker-Kreichgauer (Eds.), *Group decision making* (pp. 103–124). New York: Academic Press.

Canary, D. J. (1992). *Manual for coding conversational arguments.* Department of Speech Communication, Pennsylvania State University, University Park, PA.

Canary, D. J., Brossmann, B. G., & Seibold, D. R. (1987). Argument structures in decision-making groups. *Southern Speech Communication Journal, 53*, 18–37.

Canary, D. J., Brossmann, B. G., Sillars, A. L., & LoVette, S. (1987). Married couples' argument structures and sequences: A comparison of satisfied and dissatisfied dyads. In J. W. Wenzel (Ed.), *Argument and critical practices: Proceedings of the fifth SCA/AFA conference on argumentation* (pp. 475–484). Annandale, VA: SCA.

Canary, D. J., Ratledge, N. T., & Seibold, D. R. (1982). *Argument and group decision-making: Development of a coding scheme.* Paper presented at the annual meeting of the Speech Communication Association, Louisville, KY.

Canary, D., & Seibold, D. R. (2010). Origins and development of the conversational argument coding scheme. *Communication Methods and Measures, 4*(1–2), 7–26.

Canary, D. J., & Sillars, A. L. (1992). Argument in satisfied and dissatisfied married couples. In W. L. Benoit, D. Hample, & P. J. Benoit (Eds.), *Readings in argumentation* (pp. 737–764). New York: Foris.

Canary, D. J., Weger, H., Jr, & Stafford, L. (1991). Couples argument sequences and their associations with relational characteristics. *Western Journal of Speech Communication, 55*, 159–179.

Cohen, J. (1960). A coefficient of agreement for nominal scales. *Educational and Psychological Measurement, 20*, 37–46.

Davis, J. H. (1973). Group decision and social interaction: A theory of social decision schemes. *Psychological Review, 80*, 97–125.

Ellis, D. G., & Maoz, I. (2002). Cross-cultural argument interactions between Jews and Palestinians. *Journal of Applied Communication Research, 30*, 181–194.

Folger, J. P., Hewes, D. E., & Poole, M. S. (1984). Coding social interaction. In B. Dervin & M. Voight (Eds.), *Progress in the communication sciences* (Vol. 4, pp. 115–161). Norwood, NJ: Ablex.

Folger, J. P., & Poole, M. S. (1980). Relational coding schemes: The question of validity. In M. Burgoon (Ed.), *Communication yearbook 5* (pp. 235–247). Newbury Park, CA: Sage.

Gebhardt, L. J., & Meyers, R. A. (1995). Subgroup influence in decision-making groups: Examining consistency from a communication perspective. *Small Group Research, 26,* 147–168.

Guetzkow, H. (1950). Unitizing and categorizing problems in coding qualitative data. *Journal of Clinical Psychology, 6,* 47–58.

Hample, D. (1985). A third perspective on argument. *Philosophy and Rhetoric, 18,* 1–22.

Hatfield, J. D., & Weider-Hatfield, D. (1978). The comparative utility of three types of behavioral units for interaction analysis. *Communication Monographs, 45,* 44–50.

Hebl, M., Pederson, J., Hill, R., Meyers, R. A., Kauffeld, S., & Lehmann-Willenbrock, N. (2009). *Exploring humor in task groups.* Paper presented at the annual conference of the International Communication Association, Chicago.

Hewes, D. E. (1986). A socio-egocentric model of group decision making. In R.Y. Hirokawa & M. S. Poole (Eds.), *Communication and group decision-making* (pp. 265–291). Beverly Hills, CA: Sage.

Huber, J., Johnson, M., Hill, R., Meyers, R. A., & Seibold, D. R. (2007). *Examining the argument process in jury decision making.* Paper presented to the Group Communication Division, National Communication Association, Chicago.

Jackson, S., & Jacobs, S. (1980). Structure of conversational argument: Pragmatic cases for the enthymeme. *Quarterly Journal of Speech, 66,* 251–265.

Kang, P., Meyers, R. A., & Seibold, D. R. (2008). *Examining argument in naturally occurring jury deliberations.* Paper presented at the Third Annual Conference of the Interdisciplinary Network for Group Research (INGRoup), Kansas City, KS.

Kauffeld, S. (2006). *Kompetenzen messen, bewerten, entwickeln* [Measuring, evaluating, and developing competencies]. Stuttgart: Schäffer-Poeschel.

Kauffeld, S., & Meyers, R. A. (2009). Complaint and solution-oriented circles: Interaction patterns in work group discussions. *European Journal of Work and Organizational Psychology, 18,* 267–294.

Krippendorff, K. (1980). *Content analysis: An introduction to its methodology.* Beverly Hills, CA: Sage.

Krippendorff, K. (2004). Reliability in content analysis: Some common misconceptions and recommendations. *Human Communication Research, 30,* 411–433.

Lehmann-Willenbrock, N., & Kauffeld, S. (2010). The downside of group communication: Complaining cycles in group discussions. In S. Schuman (Ed.), *The handbook for working with difficult groups: How they are difficult, why they are difficult and what you can do about it* (pp. 33–53). San Francisco: Jossey-Bass/Wiley.

Lemus, D. R., & Seibold, D. R. (2008). Argument development versus argument strength: The predictive potential of argument quality in computer-mediated group delibera-tions. In T. Suzuki, T. Kato, & A. Kubota (Eds.), *Proceedings of the 3rd Tokyo conference on argumentation: Argumentation, the law and justice* (pp. 166–174). Tokyo: JDA.

Lemus, D. R., Seibold, D. R., Flanagin, A. J., & Metzger, M. J. (2004). Argument in computer-mediated groups. *Journal of Communication, 54,* 302–320.

Lombard, M., Snyder-Duch, J., & Bracken, C. C. (2002). Content analysis in mass communication research: An assessment and reporting of intercoder reliability. *Human Communication Research, 28,* 587–604.

Lombard, M., Snyder-Duch, J., & Bracken, C. C. (2004). A call for standardization in content analysis reliability. *Human Communication Research, 30,* 434–437.

Mangold, P. (2005). *Interact handbook.* Arnstorf: Mangold Software & Consulting.

McGrath, J. E., & Altermatt, T. W. (2001). Observation and analysis of group interaction over time: Some methodological and strategic choices. In M. A. Hogg & R. S. Tindale (Eds.), *Blackwell handbook of social psychology: Group processes* (pp. 525–556). Malden, MA: Blackwell.

McLaughlin, M. L. (1984). *Conversation: How talk is organized.* Beverly Hills, CA: Sage.

Meyers, R. A. (1987). Argument and group decision-making: An interactional test of persuasive arguments theory and an alternative structurational perspective. (Doctoral dissertation, University of Illinois, 1987). *Dissertation Abstracts International, 49,* 12.

Meyers, R. A., & Brashers, D. E. (1995). Multi-stage versus single-stage coding of small group argument:A preliminary comparative assessment. In S.Jackson (Ed.), *Argumentation and values: Proceedings of the ninth SCA/AFA conference on argumentation* (pp. 93–100). Annandale,VA: SCA.

Meyers, R. A., & Brashers, D. E. (1998). Argument and group decision-making: Explicating a process model and investigating the argument-outcome link. *Communication Monographs, 65,* 261–281.

Meyers, R. A., & Brashers, D. E. (2008). *Extending the conversational argument coding scheme: Categories, units, and coding procedures.* Paper presented at the annual meeting of the National Communication Association, San Diego, CA.

Meyers, R. A., & Brashers, D. E. (2010). Extending the conversational argument coding scheme:Argument categories, units, and coding procedures. *Communication Methods and Measures, 4*(1–2), 27–45.

Meyers, R.A., Brashers, D. E., & Hanner, J. (2000). Majority/minority influence: Identifying argumentative patterns and predicting argument-outcomes links. *Journal of Communication, 50,* 3–30.

Meyers, R. A., Seibold, D. R., & Brashers, D. (1991). Argument in initial group decision-making discussions: Refinement of a coding scheme and a descriptive quantitative analysis. *Western Journal of Speech Communication, 55,* 47–68.

Meyers, R. A., Seibold, D. R., & Kang, P. (2010). Analyzing argument in a naturally occurring jury deliberation. *Small Group Research, 41,* 452–473.

Perelman, C. H., & Olbrechts-Tyteca, L. (1969). *The new rhetoric: A treatise on argumentation.* (J. Wilkinson & P. Weaver, Trans.). Notre Dame, IN: University of Notre Dame Press.

Poole, M. S. (1981). Decision development in small groups I:A comparison of two models. *Communication Monographs, 48,* 1–24.

Poole, M. S. (1983a). Decision development in small groups II:A study of multiple sequences in decision-making. *Communication Monographs, 50,* 206–232.

Poole, M. S. (1983b). Decision development in small groups III:A multiple sequence theory of decision development. *Communication Monographs, 50,* 321–341.

Poole, M. S., & Baldwin, C. (1996). Developmental processes in group decision making. In R.Y. Hirokawa & M. S. Poole (Eds), *Communication and group decision making* (2nd ed., pp. 215–241). Thousand Oaks, CA: Sage.

Poole, M. S., & Folger, J. P. (1981). A method for establishing the representational validity of interaction coding systems: Do we see what they see? *Human Communication Research, 8,* 26–42.

Poole, M. S., Folger, J. P., & Hewes, D. E. (1987). *Analyzing interpersonal interaction.* In M. E. Roloff & G. R. Miller (Eds.), *Interpersonal processes: New directions in communication research* (pp. 220–256). Newbury Park, CA: Sage.

Poole, M. S., Keyton, J., & Frey, L. R. (1999). *Group communication methodology: Issues and considerations.* In L. R. Frey, D. S. Gouran, & M. S. Poole (Eds), *The handbook of group communication theory and research* (pp. 92–112). Thousand Oaks, CA: Sage.

Poole, M. S., Seibold, D. R., & McPhee, R. D. (1985). Group decision-making as a structurational process. *Quarterly Journal of Speech, 71,* 74–102.

Prosser, M., & Trigwell, K. (1999). *Understanding learning and teaching: The experience in higher education.* Buckingham, UK: SRHE and Open University Press.

Scott, W. (1955). Reliability of content analysis: The case of nominal scale coding. *Public Opinion Quarterly, 17,* 321–325.

Seibold, D. R., Canary, D. J., & Tanita-Ratledge, N. (1983). *Argument and group decision-making: Interim report on a structurational research program.* Paper presented at the annual meeting of the Speech Communication Association, Washington, DC.

Seibold, D. R., Lemus, D. R., & Kang, P. (2010). Extending the conversational argument coding scheme in studies of argument quality in group deliberations. *Communication Methods and Measures, 4*(1–2), 46–64.

Seibold, D. R., McPhee, R. D., Poole, M. S. Tanita, N. E., & Canary, D. J. (1981). Argument, group influence, and decision outcomes. In C. Ziegelmueller & J. Rhodes (Eds.), *Dimensions of argument: Proceedings of the second SCA/AFA summer conference on argumentation* (pp. 663–692). Annandale, VA: SCA.

Seibold, D. R., & Meyers, R. A. (2007). Group argument: A structuration perspective and research program. *Small Group Research, 38,* 312–336.

Toulmin, S. E. (1958). *The uses of argument.* Cambridge, UK: The University Press.

Vinokur, A., Trope., Y., & Burnstein, E. (1975). A decision-making analysis of persuasive argumentation and the choice-shift effect. *Journal of Experimental Social Psychology, 11,* 127–148.

Weingart, L. R., Olekalns, M., & Smith, P. L. (2006). Quantitative coding of negotiation behavior. In P. Carnevale & C. K. W. de Dreu (Eds.), *Methods of negotiation research* (pp. 105–119). Leiden: Martinus Nijhoff.

Woolley, A. W., Gerbasi, M. E., Chabris, C. F., Kosslyn, S. M., & Hackman, J. R. (2008). Bringing in the experts: How team composition and collaborative planning jointly shape analytic effectiveness. *Small Group Research, 29,* 352–371.

Appendix A: Transcription Instructions (Meyers, 1987)

1. Transcribe the group discussion exactly as you hear it on the tape. Transcribe each word even if the sentence does not make sense to you. Be as complete as possible.
2. Each time a different speaker talks, start a new line on the transcription sheet – even if the person just says "yes" or "no."
3. If one group member interrupts another, place three dots (…) at the point in the sentence where the person is interrupted, and transcribe the interruption on the next line. If the first person (the member who was interrupted) continues the earlier statement, start a new line with three dots again (…) to indicate completion of the earlier statement and finish transcribing the interrupted members' statement on that line.

   Example
   John: I think we should advise him to board the plane because if he …
   Tim: I disagree completely with that idea.
   John: … doesn't take the trip, he will always regret it.

4. If two or more people talk at once (which is common in group discussion), transcribe each person's remarks to the best of your ability. Put each person's statement on a separate line and use quotation marks at the beginning and end of each statement to indicate that the statements are simultaneous.

   Example
   John: "Right, that makes sense to me."
   Mary: "Sure I think that's OK."
   Tom: "I guess I can go along with that."

5. Do not worry about which member is talking at any given time. When you have finished transcribing the discussion discourse, I will go back through the transcripts while watching the video tape and place members' names next to each transcribed line.

6. Finally, remember that some parts of the group conversation may not appear to make sense or it may appear unorganized. Do not worry about that. Group discussion sometimes appears disjointed and muddled. Just transcribe the conversation as you hear it as completely and carefully as you can.

Appendix B: Unitizing Rules (Meyers, 1987)

1. A unit is any statement that functions as a complete thought or change of thought.

2. A unit is typically defined as any statement that contains a subject (explicit or clearly implied) and predicate/verb (explicit or clearly implied) and/or can stand alone as a complete thought (including terms of address, acknowledgments, nonrestrictive dependent clauses, etc.) as indicted next.

3. *Simple sentences* constitute separate units. They contain a subject and predicate and constitute a complete thought.

   He should go to the doctor.
   She should go to University Y.

4. *Independent clauses* constitute separate units. They are a subset of a sentence, contain a subject and predicate, and can stand alone as a complete thought. Divide compound sentences into separate units when independent clauses are connected with coordinating conjunctions such as those that follow, or if the two parts of the sentence can stand alone as two complete thoughts.

   Additive: and, also, besides, moreover, furthermore, in addition, etc.
   Opposing: but, yet, however, rather, nevertheless, instead, on the contrary, on the other hand, etc.
   Alternative: or, either/or, nor, neither/nor, etc.
   Temporal: then, next afterwards, previously, now, meanwhile, subsequently, later, thereafter, henceforth, etc.
   Causal: for, so therefore, thus, consequently, hence, accordingly, as a result, otherwise, perhaps, indeed, surely, clearly, etc.

   Example
   He should go to the doctor and he should postpone his vacation.
   This sentence contains two independent clauses and should be unitized as two units:
   He should go to the doctor
   And he should postpone his vacation.

5. *Functioning independent clauses* constitute separate units. In group discussion, individuals often make statements that function as complete and independent thoughts (i.e., serve as independent clauses) even though grammatically they would not be classified as such. These statements often begin with dependent clause conjunctions – because, like, since, so – and are therefore, in a strict grammatical sense, dependent, rather than independent clauses. But when these types of clauses function in group talk as complete and independent thoughts, they should be unitized as separate units. Consider as separate utterances these types of functioning independent clauses which are joined with explanatory subordinating dependent conjunctions such as the following:

    when, whenever, because, just because, like, since, although, though, while, as, after, before, unless, until, in order than, so, so just, it's like, etc.

    Example
    I think he should go to the hospital, just because I think he is seriously ill. This statement contains one clear independent clause, and one "functioning" independent clause and should be unitized as two separate units:
    I think he should go to the hospital
    Just because I think he is seriously ill

    Example
    I think he should go to University Y, because, it's like he would have so much pressure at the other university.
    This statement contains a clear independent clause, and a "functioning" independent clause. It should be unitized as two separate units:
    I think he should go to University Y
    Because, it's like, he would have so much pressure at the other university.

6. *Agreement/disagreement* (yeah, right, no, no way) is counted as a separate unit if it stands alone and functions as a complete and independent thought (i.e., it is not part of a connecting statement that contains a subject and verb).

    Example
    No way should he go to University X – is unitized as a single unit.
    No way! He should go to University X – is unitized as two units.

7. *Multiple agreement/disagreement* spoken in immediate succession by the same person (yeah, right, uh-huh) should be unitized as a single unit.
8. *False starts or introductory phrases* do not count as separate units, and should be unitized with the next complete statement.

    Example
    Well, I put, I put, I think I, I put 4 in 10 for this one – is unitized as a single unit.

9. *Phrases* like "you know," "I guess," I mean," and "isn't it" when preceding a statement or added onto the end of a statement are not considered as separate units.

10. *Interruptions* are considered as separate units if they contain a complete thought. If a statement is interrupted and a complete statement is evident both before and after the interruption, it is unitized as two units. If a statement is interrupted, and only one complete statement is evident — what precedes the interruption or what follows the interruption does not constitute a complete unit — it is unitized as only one unit.

> Example
> Ann: He should board the plane because …
> Vic: I don't think that's a good idea.
> Ann: … because he needs a vacation
> This sequence contains three separate units. Both statements before and after the interruption are complete independent thoughts.

> Example
> Ann: He should board the plane …
> Vic: I don't think that's a good idea.
> Ann: … right away.
> This sequence contains only two units. Following the interruption, Ann merely completes her initial statement and does not produce a second independent thought.

Appendix C: Conversational Argument Scheme (CAS) (from Meyers & Brashers, 2008, Figure 2)

I. Arguables

A. *Generative mechanisms*
  1. *Assertions*: Statements of fact or opinion.
  2. *Propositions*: Statements that call for support, action, or conference on an argument-related statement.
B. *Reasoning activities*
  3. *Elaborations*: Statements that support other statements by providing evidence, reasons, or other support.
  4. *Responses*: Statements that defend arguables met with disagreement.
  5. *Amplifications*: Statements that explain or expound upon other statements in order to establish the relevance of the argument through inference.
  6. *Justifications*: Statements that offer validity of previous or upcoming statements by citing a rule of logic (provide a standard whereby arguments are weighed).

II. Convergence seeking activities (reinforcers)

7. *Agreement*: Statements that express agreement with another statement.
8. *Acknowledgment*: Statements that indicate recognition and/or comprehension of another statement, but not necessarily agreement with another's point.

III. Disagreement-relevant intrusions (promptors)

9. *Objections*: Statements that deny the truth or accuracy of any arguable.
10. *Challenges*: Statements that offer problems or questions that must be solved if agreement is to be secured on an arguable.

IV. Delimitors

11. *Frames*: Statements that provide a context for and/or qualify arguables.
12. *Forestall/secure*: Statements that attempt to forestall refutation by securing common ground.
13. *Forestall/remove*: Statements that attempt to forestall refutation by removing possible objections.

V. Nonarguables

14. *Process*: Non-argument related statements that orient the group to its task or specify the process the group should follow.
15. *Unrelated*: Statements unrelated to the group's argument or process (tangents, side issues, self-talk, etc.).
16. *Incompletes*: Statements that do not contain a complete, clear idea due to interruption or a person discontinuing a statement.

Appendix D: Coding Rules for Using the CAS (Meyers, 1987)

1. If the function of the statement is clear, code it into the appropriate category using the number code.
2. If the function of the statement is not immediately clear, coding should precede along the following sequence:
   - Arguables
   - Reinforcers
   - Promptors
   - Delimitors
3. Attributions of meaning should be limited to the text as much as possible. If a cogent idea is readily inferred from the statement in the text, code it into the appropriate category. When meaning is not evident in a given

utterance, read ahead in the transcript to ascertain the meaning assigned to the utterance by the group, or read previous parts of the transcript to determine if prior conversation provides a context. If a statement is not cogent or is impossible to interpret, do not infer its meaning. Instead code it in the Non-arguable category.

4. Questions should be coded according to their function in the group's argument.

    a. Questions which call for conferral, support, or action on an argument-related issue should be coded under the category Proposition. These include:

        i. Requests for additional information, clarification, justification, or support
            1. How do you know that is true?
            2. Do you have any evidence for that?
            3. What do you say that?

        ii. Requests for direct action
            1. Why don't we talk about this argument a little more?
            2. Do you think we should consider Tom's argument valid?
            3. What do you think about Sam's statement?

    b. Questions that reflect statements of the speaker's opinion should be coded in the appropriate category. These are usually indirect Assertions that state the speaker's opinion and should be coded in the Assertion category.

        i. You don't really believe he should have the operation, do you?
        ii. C'mon, how can you really think he should board the plane?

    c. Questions that relate to non-argument related issues (how to organize the discussion, simple requests for repetition, off-the-trace questions, etc.) should be coded in the Non-Arguable category.

Note: Additional coding rules can be found in Canary (1992).

Appendix E: Sample Coded Transcript Using Multistage Procedures (from Meyers & Brashers, 1995)

A/NA code	DA code	Content code	CAS global code	CAS specific code	Turn	Speaker	Discourse
A	C	3	ARG	ASRT	044a	Jim	You could look at it another, I mean maybe there's not connecting flights and stuff overseas

(Cont'd)

A/NA code	DA code	Content code	CAS global code	CAS specific code	Turn	Speaker	Discourse
A	C	3	ARG	ASRT	044b	Jim	So maybe if he's willing, he goes to the hospital and it's a stomachache,
A	C	3	ARG	ELAB	044c	Jim	It might take – really screw up his vacation, but …
A	C	3	ARG	ELAB	045	Ann	He can always get another flight.
A	C	3	ARG	ELAB	046	Kay	There's so many planes that fly out.
A	C	3	ARG	ELAB	047	Jim	… but seriously, there' a lot of little things like that.
A	C	3	CONV	AGRE	048	Ann	Yeah
A	C	1	PROM	CHAL	049a	Jim	Well, yeah, but the bottom line being that it's overseas.
A	C	1	ARG	ASRT	049b	Jim	So if he gets sick, they can't even make an emergency landing
	C	1	ARG	ELAB	050	Kay	Would have to crash into a mountain.
A	C	5	ARG	ASRT	051	Jim	Chances are, it's, you know, now I can, if it's the first time you're flying, you could be nervous and stuff.
A	C	5	CONV	AGRE	052	Lee	Uh-huh.

A/NA indicates Argument/Non-Argument message code.
DA indicates Decision Alternative code. In this case, there were three decision alternatives: Risky (R), Cautious (C), and Neutral (N).
In the transcript, each Content code would be highlighted in a different color.

18

THE ANALYSIS OF GROUP INTERACTION PROCESSES

Dean E. Hewes

UNIVERSITY OF MINNESOTA

Marshall Scott Poole

UNIVERSITY OF ILLINOIS URBANA-CHAMPAIGN

Group interaction is a process. It is not merely a set of messages, nor is it only a series of messages. It is a series of messages that influence subsequent group inter- action and/or reflect underlying rules of interaction such as phases that sequen- tially structure group interaction (cf. Hewes, 2009d; Poole, 1983b). This was recognized by some of the original framers of group behavior (Bales & Strodbeck, 1951; Fisher, 1970; McGrath & Altman, 1966) and it was showcased in classic, if formidable essays on the mathematics of group processes (Arrow, Karlin, & Suppes, 1960; Coleman, 1964). If temporal patterns of interaction are central to the study of groups, then to understand groups fully, it is important to have methods for characterizing and testing theories of group interaction.

As easy as it may be to say this, when we set about to identify temporal patterns in interaction, we find that most commonly used analytical methods, for example, analysis of variance for experimental data, regression for survey data, and non- parametric statistics, are simply not geared for the task. To study temporal patterns in group interaction requires us to do two things: (a) identify possible interaction patterns, and (b) conduct tests of hypotheses about those patterns. For example, a common temporal model of group decision-making posits that groups go through a sequence of phases during the decision process. In their classic model, Bales and Strodtbeck (1951), for example, posited that groups solve problems in a three- stage process composed of (a) an orientation phase dominated by information sharing, fact-finding, and characterization of the problem, followed by (b) an eval- uation phase in which members considered alternative solutions to the problem and conflicts over which alternative should be chosen occurred, concluding in (c) a control phase in which members come to a common decision, exerting control over one another and over their common environment. To assess whether this model fits the group's interaction we must first find a way to identify these three phases (if they occur at all) and then find a way to test for whether the observed sequence of phases fits this pattern.

When we first started studying group interaction in the early 1970s (for Hewes) and the late 1970s (for Poole), there were few widely accepted methods for the analysis of temporal patterns. Most researchers improvised and devised ways to get at temporal patterns that utilized traditional methods. For example, when Bales and Strodtbeck (1951) tested their problem–solving phase model, they devised a way to code behavior corresponding to what would be expected for each of their three phases (orientation, evaluation, and control), namely the famous Interaction Process Analysis coding system (Bales, 1950). They coded live discussions (audio recorders were not available then!) using this system and ended up with a series of coded statements. They then divided their discussions into three equal segments (corresponding to their three phases) and conducted t-tests to compare the levels of each type of code for the first, second, and third segments, respectively. Bales and Strodtbeck found that there were more orientation acts in the first segment, more disagreement and opinion acts in the second segment, and more solution and agreement acts in the third segment, which they took as evidence in favor of their model. Most studies of group interaction in the 1970s utilized improvised methods, which had the disadvantage of lack of standardization and thus might not yield comparable results across studies. During the 1980s and subsequently, scholars began to systematize their methods for interaction analysis, to the point where Poole, Van de Ven, Dooley, and Holmes (2000) could describe four different approaches to the analysis of processes, along with methods of capturing process data and statistical methods for analyzing it.

This chapter will discuss two major methods for the analysis of interaction, specifically models of sequential contingencies, such as Markov process models and lag-sequential analysis, and phasic analysis. Both methods facilitate inquiry into the patterns of sequential dependencies between and among coded communication acts.

This essay will focus mainly on general descriptions of these methods rather than the details of actually conducting the analysis. These details can be found in other sources (Bakeman & Gottman, 1997; Hewes, 1980; Poole et al., 2000). Group processes (and all temporal processes) are typically more complicated than static data. For this reason there is a need to adapt and improvise methods for process analysis. So there are no "cookbooks" for process analysis, the way there are for analysis of experiments or survey data (although things are becoming somewhat standardized and maybe there will be in the future). In this chapter we will try to give you a sense of the state of the current art in interaction analysis of group processes, as well as a glimpse of the future.

In the next section we define process and consider the specific questions we must ask to study processes. Subsequent sections address these questions, including a brief section on coding and categorizing the events that describe the process, followed by sections on methods for identifying and describing patterns in interaction processes, and concluding with a section on explaining why patterns occur. Specifically we will discuss sequential contingency analysis and phasic analysis.

What is a Process?

What is a process? Nicholas Rescher (1996; see also Teichmann, 1995) offers a succinct and inclusive definition:

> A process is a coordinated group of changes in the complexion of reality, an organized family of occurrences that are systematically linked to one another either causally or functionally ... A process consists in an integrated series of developments unfolding in joint coordination in line with a definite program. Processes are correlated with occurrences or events: Processes always involve various events, and events exist only in and through processes.
>
> *(p. 38)*

This definition has several implications. First, processes involve change and unfold over time, which necessitates research designs involving longitudinal study of one or more meetings or discussions. Second, processes are indicated by one or more series of events. An event is a "happening, occurrence or episode ... a change ... or composite of changes" (Mackie, 1995, p. 253). Teichmann (1995, p. 721) comments, that "'process' is to 'change' or 'event', rather as 'syndrome' is to 'symptom'." A process underlies a collection of events or changes, providing "some sort of unity or unifying principle to it" (Teichmann, 1995, p. 721). To infer that a process is the unifying principle underlying a sequence of events, it is necessary to identify patterns in the events that reflect the process in question and test whether those patterns as opposed to other possible patterns hold.

For example, Bales and Strodtbeck's problem-solving model is an example of what has been termed a *unitary sequence* (Poole, 1981) or *life-cycle* (Poole & Van de Ven, 2004) model of group process. This model assumes that the phases of the process will occur in a set order because of logical necessity or institutional rules that govern the problem-solving and decision-making process. For instance, it is logical to assume that we cannot develop solutions for a problem before we have characterized it and identified relevant facts, so it is first necessary to orient the group before moving to a phase of debate about solutions (evaluation). In the same vein, it is necessary to debate solutions before coming to a final solution in the control phase. This logical sequence serves as an underlying generative mechanism of the process that produces a three-phase sequence of activities (orientation–evaluation–control), and so accounts for the observed series of events. (A generative mechanism refers to rules or other factors that produce a particular effect; in our case, the observed patterns in group interaction processes.

As we describe more of these, you will notice that each explanation for group processes uses somewhat different elements in its generative mechanism.) Another generative mechanism that could produce a unitary sequence is a set of institutional rules that require the group to engage in activities in a certain order. For example, juries are required to first decide on guilt or innocence before deciding on a sentence for a defendant.

Mohr (1982) originally differentiated variance and process approaches in social scientific research. In general terms, a *variance theory* explains change in terms of relations among independent variables and dependent variables, while a *process theory* explains how a sequence of events leads to some outcome. Figure 18.1 shows a pictorial comparison of the two approaches, which are described and distinguished in greater detail in Poole et al. (2000; see also Poole, 2007). Variance and process approaches require us to adopt quite different research strategies and methods of analysis.

Explanations in variance theories take the form of causal models that incorporate these variables (e.g., X causes Y which causes Z). A variance theory can be tested using well-known experimental or survey approaches (see Chapter 2, this volume). A variance theory based on the functional theory of group decision, for example, would explain the effectiveness of group decisions as a function of variables such as the amount of evaluation of solutions and task complexity (Gouran & Hirokawa, 1996; Hollingshead et al., 2005). Functional theory posits that the amount of positive and negative analysis of consequences of solutions a group conducts should positively affect decision-making effectiveness. Task complexity should have a negative relationship with effectiveness and should interact with problem analysis so that more problem analysis for complex problems will enhance effectiveness (Gouran & Hirokawa, 1996; Orlitsky & Hirokawa, 2001).

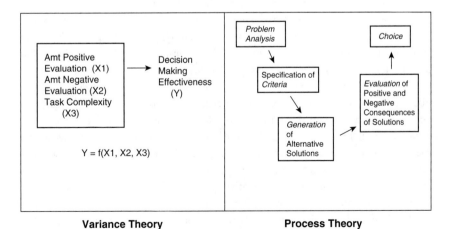

FIGURE 18.1 Variance and process theories exemplifying the decision functions theory.

To test this theory we could set up an experiment with two conditions, one where groups were given a high-complexity task and one where they were given a low-complexity task, holding other elements of the task constant. Effectiveness of group decision-making could be measured by comparing the actual decisions the groups made in each condition with a normatively correct decision as determined by outside task experts. We could measure solution evaluation either by having subjects rate the amount of each of these that their groups engaged in (a post-test) or by recording the group discussions, coding them for problem analysis and solution evaluation, and then taking the total number of statements of each type as measures of problem analysis (observational measurement). Standard statistical analysis could be employed to determine whether relationships among variables were consistent with those hypothesized by the theory.

In contrast, a process theory focuses on a series of events that bring about or lead to some outcome and attempts to specify the generative mechanism that could produce the event series. Explanations in process theories take the form of theoretical narratives that account for how one event led to another and that one to another, and so on to the final outcome. A process theory is tested by identifying or measuring observable events and determining whether the relations among events are what would be expected if the generative mechanism in the process theory was in operation.

As depicted in Figure 18.1, a process theory based on functional decision-making theory would posit that groups make a decision by engaging in a series of phases of activity that begins with problem analysis, then transitions to criteria specification, then to alternative solution generation, to positive and negative evaluation of solution consequences (in light of criteria), and, finally, to a choice of the best decision (we will call this a "unitary sequence" model, as opposed to a "multiple sequence" model in which groups might pass through several different sequences of phases). The generative mechanism that determines the order in which these activities are undertaken by the group is the principle of logical necessity, as described above. The degree to which the group adhered to this order and also carried out the activities in each phase completely and effectively is what determines the ultimate effectiveness of the decision.

To test this process theory of group decision-making, we could record the discussions of groups making in the experiment just described. Performance of decision functions would be measured using a coding system that identified each function. To ascertain whether the group performed the functions in the specified order, the discussion could be divided into five segments, and the relative proportion of acts corresponding to each of the five functions (problem analysis, criteria specification, alternative generation, etc.) that occurred in each segment. If a group's process was generated by the hypothesized logical necessity model, then there should be relatively more problem analysis acts than any other type in the first segment, more criteria development acts than any other type in the second segment, more solution development acts than any other type in the third segment, and so on. The degree to which a group's relative proportion of acts in each segment was consistent with this pattern could be calculated. The process theory could then be tested by ascertaining whether consistency with the hypothesized pattern was positively related to decision-making effectiveness.

We could go further and determine whether level of task complexity led to differences in group decision processes. For example, the groups engaged in a highly complex task might be expected to deviate more from the unitary sequence of phases in the logical necessity model than groups engaged in a task low in complexity. In this case we might test for whether low complexity groups adhered to the unitary sequence, whereas high complexity groups exhibited multiple sequences.

As this example illustrates, process theories are tested by identifying *patterns* in the temporal sequencing of group interaction and then evaluating whether these patterns are consistent with those that would be expected if the generative mechanism posited by the theory were in operation. This emphasis on the study of temporal patterns rather than relationships among variables is what distinguishes process research from variance research.

Analysis of group interaction processes is guided by four questions that aid in matching descriptions of patterns in group processes to the theories that might account for them. (1) What facets of interaction (types of events) should we measure? (2) Can we measure them reliably and validly? (3) What temporal patterns are there in the observed sequence of events? (4) What kind of processes account for these temporal patterns and what generates these processes? In the next section we will address the first two questions, which are well covered by Meyers and Seibold in this volume (Chapter 17), only insofar as required to set the stage for this chapter. Our primary focus will be methods for addressing questions 3 and 4, which will be discussed in subsequent sections.

Getting the Data: Coding Social Interaction

The first step in interaction analysis is to identify the events that make up the sequence by coding group interaction. Meyers and Seibold (this volume) give a detailed discussion of the coding process; see also Folger, Hewes, and Poole (1984), Neuedorff (2002), Krippendorf (2004) and Krippendorff & Bock (2009). It is important that the coding be reliable and the coding system valid, as discussed in their chapter.

Reliability and validity of codings are not just important for their own sake, they are required to meet the assumptions of interaction analysis methods. Sequential contingency analysis hinges on the identification of sequential relationships among acts, and it assumes that each category of act is coded with high reliability. Hence reliability must be determined in terms of individual categories in order to detect potentially serious sources of bias in sequential patterns (Hewes, 1985). Unitizing reliability is also critical, as Meyers and Seibold point out.

Phasic analysis assumes that phases are indicated by coding categories, so if the categories are not reliable and valid, there will be error in phase identification.

These concerns were remainder of this section will describe an example we will use throughout this chapter. Poole and Dobosh (2010) analyzed conflict management in two jury deliberation sessions, the first being the trial phase, in which the jury determines guilt or innocence on the various counts registered against the defendant, and the second the penalty phase, in which the jury determines the penalty that should be applied to the guilty party. The case involved murder and the defendant was eligible for the death penalty, so there was the potential for considerable tension and conflict in the deliberations (see SunWolf, 2007, for a more complete description of the trial).

Poole and Dobosh coded transcripts of the two jury deliberations with a coding system designed to capture the climate of decision-making interaction, the Group Working Relationships Coding System (GWRCS; Poole & Roth, 1989a). An abridged set of categories from this system are shown in Table 18.1. The GWRCS was derived through detailed analysis of group decision-making sessions coded with multiple category systems (Poole, 1983b). Rather than coding at the act level, units are defined in terms of a set time period such as 30 seconds, or, as in this case, ½ page of transcript. A time interval instead of specific thought or idea units is employed because the climate of interaction can best be identified by considering how members act and react toward each other; hence, coding based on extended intervals of interaction in which there are interchanges among members is required. Poole and Dobosh found 99 per cent agreement on unitizing reliability. Interrater reliability measured with Cohen's kappa was 0.97. There is also evidence for the validity of the GWRCS because it has been shown to have systematic relationships to related categories in task and conflict coding systems (Poole, 1983a; Poole & Roth, 1989a; Poole, Holmes, & DeSanctis, 1991). The analysis in Poole and Dobosh employed both sequential and phasic analyses and simplified versions of their analysis will be used to illustrate the methods discussed in subsequent sections.

Table 18.1 The Group Working Relationships Coding System (GWRCS)

1. *Focused work*: periods when members are primarily task-focused and do not disagree with one another, instead working together with little expression of conflict
2. *Critical work*: periods when members disagree with each other, but the disagreements are centered on ideas, and no opposing sides are differentiated
3. *Opposition*: periods in which disagreements are expressed through the formation of opposing sides; the existence of a conflict or disagreement is openly acknowledged during these periods
4. *Open discussion*: a mode of resolution of opposition that involves mutual engagement of parties in problem-solving discussions, negotiation, or compromise
5. *Relational integration*: periods when the group is not task-focused; these exhibit tangents, joking, and positive socioemotional interaction

Table 18.2 Distributional structure of the working relationships in Deliberations 1 and 2

	Deliberation 1	Deliberation 2
Focused work (FW)	188 (42.2%)	34 (6.0%)
Critical work (CW)	146 (32.7%)	147 (26.3%)
Opposition (OPP)	30 (6.7%)	127 (22.5%)
Open discussion (OD)	21 (4.7%)	217 (38.8%)
Integration (INT)	61 (13.7%)	11 (2.0%)

Before proceeding to consider various methods of analyzing group processes, let us first present the distributional structure of the various types of interaction that occurred in the two deliberations. Distributional structure refers to the total numbers of acts in each category (i.e., in how the interaction is distributed across the categories). It collapses the process into a summary picture of the discussion, and thus provides useful background to process analysis, much as a table of descriptive statistics does for a more sophisticated statistical analysis. The distribution of acts across categories for the two deliberations is shown in Table 18.2. As the table shows, there is more focused work and integration in Deliberation 1 than in Deliberation 2. On the other hand, there is more opposition and open discussion in the Deliberation 2 than Deliberation 1. The analysis of processes presented below will shed some light on the meaning of these differences.

Identifying Patterns in Group Interaction

Recall that our third question was: What temporal patterns are there in the observed sequence of events? Broadly, there are two approaches to answering this question: *sequential contingency analysis* (which includes Markov chain analysis, semi-Markov processes, and lag-sequential analysis) and *phasic analysis*. The two genres of techniques differ in that sequential contingency analysis focuses on patterns among individual events at the micro-level, while phasic analysis focuses on larger segments of interaction with common functions. We will discuss them in turn and then in the next section turn to explaining the patterns that we identify.

Sequential contingency analysis

The most widely used sequential analytic technique is sequential contingency analysis which was introduced quite early in the study of group behavior (Bales, 1950; Leik & Meeker, 1975). Sequential contingency analysis describes group interaction in terms of conditional probabilities, the probability that one type of event or act will follow another type of event. For example, what is the probability that a focused work act will be followed by an opposition act? If that probability differs from chance, then there is a sequential contingency relationship between the events.

There are several methods of doing sequential analysis, including Markov process models (Hewes, 1980), an extension of them called semi-Markov process models (Hewes, Planalp & Streibel, 1980), and lag-sequential analysis (Bakeman & Gottman, 1997).

We will primarily discuss Markov process models since they are the foundation for the others. Markov process models take a set of possible events or acts (in this case the categories of the GWRCS) and model the odds that various sequences of acts occur in the group interaction. For example, what are the odds that a period of focused work will be followed by a period of critical work and then that there will be a period of opposition? Markov process models can be constructed to describe the probability that every possible sequence of events of various lengths (two, three, four, etc.) will occur. These models identify some sequences as highly probable and some as having low probability of occurrence. This depicts the pattern of group interaction at the micro-level, where acts are related to other acts preceding and following them.

To define Markov process models somewhat more formally, they are used to predict the probability distribution of a set of events (in this case occurrence of the five interaction types) at time $t + k$ based on the probability distribution of the same set of events at time t. So in this case we will use the probability distribution of the five GWRCS acts at time t to predict the probability distribution of the five GWRCS acts at a future time $t + k$. The model is portrayed in a *transition matrix* (T) that indicates the probabilities of transition from one interaction type to another over time. Table 18.3 shows a transition matrix for the GWRCS categories. The types along the side represent the events at time 1 and the types along the top the events at time 2. So in Table 18.3, the element q_{12} represents the probability that a unit of focused work (at time 1) is followed by critical work

Table 18.3 First-order markov transition matrix for the Group Working Relationships Coding System, predicting probability of transition from unit at time 1 to unit at time 2

	FW_2	CW_2	OPP_2	OD_2	INT_2
FW_1	q_{11}	q_{12}	q_{13}	q_{14}	q_{15}
CW_1	q_{21}	q_{22}	q_{23}	q_{24}	q_{25}
OPP_1	q_{31}	q_{32}	q_{33}	q_{34}	q_{35}
OD_1	q_{41}	q_{42}	q_{43}	q_{44}	q_{45}
INT_1	q_{51}	q_{52}	q_{53}	q_{54}	q_{55}

FW, focused work; CW, critical work; OPP, opposition; OD, open discussion; INT, integration; subscript 1 = time 1; subscript 2 = time 2.

(at time 2), while the element q_{11} represents the probability that a unit of focused work is followed by a second unit of focused work. Thus, this model describes sequential interdependencies among units, a description of the local structure of action in terms of which units tend to lead to (or be responded to by) other units. The probabilities in each row must sum to one, since each previous unit must be followed by some other unit (except for the very last unit in the sequence).

Markov chain models are only valid representations of sequential dependencies if they can satisfy three assumptions: the assumptions of order, stationarity, and homogeneity. For the model to fit, all three assumptions must be satisfied. We will briefly discuss how these assumptions were tested, referring the reader to the discussion in Hewes (1980) and Poole et al. (2000); for a more technical discussion see Bishop, Fienberg, and Holland (1975).

Before turning to the three critical tests, we will describe how the Markov transition matrix T is computed from the coded data. Since a Markov chain models the dependence of subsequent units on prior units, the sequence of coded units is lagged one unit and then the lagged sequence is cross-tabulated with the original sequence to produce a matrix in which the rows are the lagged interaction units and the columns are the original sequence, as shown in Table 18.3. Then the entry in each row of the cross-tabulated matrix is divided by the row sum, giving a probability that the unit at time 1 will be followed by each of the seven units at time two (note that these probabilities sum to one). This gives us a first-order matrix, in which each unit at time 2 is dependent only on the distribution of units at time 1. If a first-order matrix adequately describes the data, it means that the each interval of interaction is influenced only by the interval immediately preceding it.

It is also possible that a unit is dependent on the distribution of the preceding two units, which represents a second-order process. In this case we would cross-tabulate the lag 2 sequence, the lag 1 sequence, and the original sequence (usually all possible combinations of the acts at time 1 and time 2 would be ranged along the side to form the rows and the final act in the sequence would be across the top as the columns). Table 18.4 shows a partial second-order transition matrix for the GWRCS. The entire matrix would contain 125 cells. This could be repeated for cases where a unit is dependent on the distribution of the preceding three acts (a third-order process, which would have 625 cells), four acts (a fourth-order process, which would have 3125 cells!), and so on. Eventually the matrix would have so many cells that there would not be enough data to estimate the probabilities within the cells; studies suggest that the statistics for testing the model perform well with expected values as low as 1 per cell. So with five categories we would need at least 25 acts to estimate the matrix in Table 18.3, and it would be better to have more than that. As you can imagine, we would need a *very* long meeting to have enough acts to estimate the probabilities for the fourth-order Markov process.

Table 18.4 A partial table for a second-order Markov process

	FW_3	CW_3	OPP_3	OD_3	INT_3
FW_1-FW_2					
FW_1-CW_2					
FW_1-OPP_2					
FW_1-OD_2					
CW_1-FW_2					
CW_1-CW_2					
CW_1-OPP_2					
CW_1-OD_2					
CW_1-INT_2					
OPP_1-FW_2					
OPP_1-CW_2					
......					

FW, focused work; CW, critical work; OPP, opposition; OD, open discussion; INT, integration; subscript 1 = time 1; subscript 2 = time 2.

Order

The first assumption that must be tested to fit a Markov chain is that the process has a definite order, as defined in the previous paragraph. To fit models of different orders, it is necessary to be able to model dependencies between time 1, time 2, time 3, and so on. If the unit at time 2 is dependent only on the distribution of units at time 1, then the data fit a first-order process; if the unit at time 3 is dependent on the distribution of units at times 1 and 2, then the data fit a second-order process; if the unit at time 4 depends on the distribution of units at times 1, 2, and 3, then the data fit a third-order process, and so on.

It is important to have a hypothesis about the order of the process. For instance, our previous example of the unitary model of group decision-making (driven by logical necessity in which problem analysis must come first, and only then can we specify criteria, and then we are in a position to develop solutions, etc.) suggests that we should have a first-order process. Each functional statement of problem definition or solution development is either preceded by an occurrence of that same type of event, indicating there a group is still performing the same function, or one from the immediately following function in the sequence (e.g., a criteria specification statement should follow a problem analysis statement). All other sequences of events should be much less likely. Lower probability sequences would be solution development followed by criteria specification or problem analysis. This reasoning can be extended for each temporally adjacent pair of acts. Further, problem analysis should have low probability of being preceded by any other functional event, since it begins the sequence theoretically.

The logic of the test for order is to compare the fit of models of successive order. The fit of the first-order model is compared to that of the zeroth-order model (a model that assumes no sequential structure in the event sequence). Then the fit of the second-order model is compared to that of the first-order model, the third-order model to the second-order model, and so on. A number of specific tests for the assumptions of Markov chains, but the most straightforward approach uses loglinear models (Bishop, Fienberg, & Holland, 1975).[1]

The order of the conditional probabilities is important both theoretically and descriptively. If the zero-order model fits best, then that indicates that there is no sequential pattern, a result that would run contrary to hypotheses concerning the group phases as illustrated above. It would also indicate that there was no reciprocity or connection between group members' statements. First- and second-order processes indicate, among other things, that members are responding to one another. For instance, a second-order process suggests that there is a response to the first member's statement and that there is then a response to the first two statements. This suggests that members are paying attention to the discussion, because their response takes the preceding two statements into account. Third- and higher order processes suggest even more complicated relationships. To our knowledge, however, no study of interaction structure has identified processes beyond the third order, even when there was a sufficient number of acts to test for higher orders. This may be due to (a) the nature of conversational rules, which specify that we should attend to immediately preceding statements, and (b) limitations in short-term memory that prevent people from holding more than a few statements in mind at a time.

Stationarity

The second assumption necessary for a Markov process to hold, stationarity, is that the same transition matrix T operates throughout the entire discussion. Logically, T can only be used to model the event series if it does not change over the course of time. The logic of the test for stationarity is as follows. First, the sequence of units is divided into shorter segments and transition matrices are computed for each segment. Typically the test is done by dividing the sequence in half; sometimes it is divided into thirds or quarters or even more segments; the only requirement is that the segments be long enough to estimate the Markov transition matrices for each. Second, these transition matrices are compared to each other. The null hypothesis for this test is that any differences between matrices are due to chance alone. If the null cannot be rejected, then the assumption of stationarity is supported. On the other hand, if we reject the null, it implies that the nature of dependencies among units changes as the discussion proceeds, and the Markov chain does not offer an adequate representation. Loglinear analysis can also be used to test for stationarity.[2]

Homogeneity

The final assumption of a Markov process is that the same model holds for all subgroups of the sample; this is termed the assumption of homogeneity. Generally, homogeneity is evaluated by comparing the transition matrices of subgroups that might differ, with the null hypothesis that there is no difference between subgroups. Procedurally, the test for homogeneity would first partition the sample into meaningful subgroups. Then contingency and transition matrices can then be computed for each subgroup and compared across subgroups. Again, loglinear analysis could be used to conduct these comparisons. The null hypothesis in this test is that there is no difference across subgroups, that is, that the Markov process is homogeneous. For example, one might compare the sequential structure for groups who differ in terms of their adherence to the unitary sequence (logical necessity), as in our example earlier. Groups with highly complex tasks may have different transition matrices from those carrying out tasks lower in complexity. If so, representing group interaction with a single transition matrix is biased and obscures real processes.

Details

Before wrapping up our discussion of the assumptions of sequential dependence analysis, an important question should be raised. In what order should these three assumptions be tested? They are like a house of cards in that if any one assumption is violated, the model does not hold. Despite the fact that all of these three assumptions can be tested separately, it is better to test them together because that would let us pick up possible interaction effects among these assumptions. To give an example of one possible interaction effect, the order of the process for high complexity groups might not be the order for the low complexity groups. In this case there is an interaction between the order and homogeneity assumptions. No group studies to our knowledge have tested for these interaction effects among the three assumptions, even though it would be simple to use loglinear models to do so (Hewes, 2009d).

An example

Table 18.5a shows the Markov process model for Deliberation 1 (D1, the trial phase) in the Poole and Dobosh (2010) study, while Table 18.5b shows the model for Deliberation 2 (D2, the penalty phase). Evaluating the assumptions of Markov models indicated that both deliberations were best modeled as a first-order Markov process that was stationary. The two deliberations, however, were not

Table 18.5 First-order Markov transition matrices for jury Deliberation 1

(a) For D1

	FW_2	CW_2	OPP_2	OD_2	INT_2
FW_1	0.65	0.17	0.02	0.00	0.16
CW_1	0.19	0.67	0.04	0.00	0.10
OPP_1	0.00	0.00	0.77	0.23	0.00
OD_1	0.05	0.00	0.14	0.67	0.14
INT_1	0.53	0.23	0.00	0.02	0.22

(b) For D2

	FW_2	CW_2	OPP_2	OD_2	INT_2
FW_1	0.53	0.35	0.06	0.00	0.06
CW_1	0.04	0.86	0.10	0.00	0.00
OPP_1	0.00	0.00	0.74	0.26	0.00
OD_1	0.00	0.00	0.12	0.86	0.02
INT_1	0.36	0.00	0.18	0.18	0.28

FW, focused work; CW, critical work; OPP, opposition; OD, open discussion; INT, integration; subscript 1 = time 1; subscript 2 = time 2.

homogeneous, and so it was not possible to develop a single Markov model for both deliberations. The relative magnitudes of the probabilities in the two matrices give us some indication of the nature of the group interaction in each and also possible differences. Here we will venture a single interpretation and refer you to the full article for additional detail.

D1 and D2 show clear differences in how conflict was handled by the group. Focused work was more likely to sustain itself in D1 than in D2. In the transition matrix for D1, the most probable transitions for focused work were into more focused work or into integration, which was likely to transition back into focused work. By contrast, the D2 transition matrix shows a 0.41 probability that focused work would transition to either critical work or opposition, and a smaller probability that it would transition to integration and from integration back into focused work. This suggests that D1 sustained cooperation more than D2. It also suggests that conflicts may have been suppressed in D1. Opposition in D1 was most likely to lead to tabling and open discussion, but the distributional structure shown in Table 18.2 suggests that tabling was more common than open discussion, suggesting avoidance of conflicts. In D2, on the other hand, there was a much greater probability that opposition would sustain itself and move into open discussion. This suggests that in D2, while there was more conflict, it was generally routed in constructive directions through open discussion.

This is an example of what we can learn through modeling sequential depend-encies in group interaction. If you compare the tables some more, you may well see other differences, some of which are discussed in Poole and Dobosh (2010).

Other methods for studying sequential contingencies

The basic three assumptions for Markov chain analysis apply equally to several other forms of sequential analysis that allow scholars to address additional ques-tions about group interaction. *Semi-Markov processes* model sequential dependen-cies like Markov processes do, but they also include the actual durations of periods between acts. In any group discussion there are lulls or periods when the interac-tion picks up speed. Semi-Markov analysis allows researchers to include this in the model. This enables researchers to study nonverbal effects, such as pacing of group discussions, on group effectiveness. Semi-Markov models have been shown to model group decision-making better than regular Markov models do (Hewes et al., 1980).

Lag-sequential analysis has been used extensively in social psychology and other areas to model sequential dependencies. As its name implies, this technique is concerned with lags. For example, for a lag-one analysis we examine the odds that one type of event is to precede the same or some other type of event immediately (a first-order process). For a lag-two analysis we look at the odds that some type of event is preceded by some type of event two intervals in the pass (not a second-order process), and so on for higher lags. So, for example, we might find a two-lag relationship between problem analysis and criteria specification. Any effect the intervening act might have on the relations between the lagged act and its "partner" is disregarded by lag sequential analysis. So the act in between the problem analysis act and the criteria development act is assumed to have no effect on their relation.

Advocates for lag-sequential analysis such as Bakeman and Gottman (1997) argue that lag-sequential analysis is simpler than Markov and semi-Markov proc-ess models because there is no need to assess the assumptions of order, homogene-ity, and stationarity. We would, however, caution that this is not actually the case. Any probabilistic model of group behavior (or anything else for that matter) has to establish that it fits the data and this requires tests for the assumptions of Markov models. Lag relationships are embedded in interactions that are modeled by Markov processes and therefore they are simply taken out of context when a sin-gular lagged relationship is identified. It is more advisable, we believe, to fit the appropriate Markov model and interpret lagged relationships in terms of the larger structure of interaction.

Another of sequential analysis is *moderated dependency analysis*. This relatively new method describes the connections between coded events in terms of the mental processes (cognitive, emotional, etc.) of individual group members. It assumes that the probability of an evaluation statement following an orientation statement, for example, is dependent on some underlying mental process, such as rule-following, that may be dynamic and undetectable through analysis of observed coded behavior alone. When the underlying mental process guiding members' contributions to the group interaction is shared, as in the case of a shared mental model of how decisions should be made (Klimoski & Mohammed, 1994; Langan-Fox, 2003), then hypotheses like those we advanced previously can be tested using coded data only. One way to account for group interaction unfolding according to the unitary model is to posit that members have a shared mental model of logical reasoning that guides their behavior (Honeycutt & Poole, 1994; Pavitt & Johnson, 2001).

However, it is often the case that members do not share the same rules or mental processes. Some members might hold the logical reasoning model, while others hold a model that decisions are really occasions for bargaining. Such members could be expected to interject comments that are not "logical" given the current flow of discussion. So we would expect "fuzzy" phases or even periods in which no coherent phase structure occurred; Poole and Roth (1989a) observed exactly this type of noncoherent period in the phases that they mapped. Over time, members might adjust their models or rules and interaction might become more coherent.

Moderated dependency analysis would still focus on sequential dependencies, but it also requires researchers to have a model of what interaction would occur if members with a given set of rules participated in the discussion. Since this cannot be constructed from the data, it requires building a simulation model of what the dependencies would look like if members with the hypothesized mental models interacted with each other and gradually adjusted their models to one another (see Larson, this volume). Hewes (2009a, 2009b, 2009c, 2009d, 2009e) discusses moderated dependency analysis in more detail.

Limitations of sequential contingency analysis

The various forms of Markov techniques offer important insights into the nature of group interaction. Some limitations, however, must be noted. In groups, as opposed to dyadic interaction, an individual's remarks may not be in response to the immediately previous remarks (Hewes, 2009a). Since individual group members do not have complete control over when they get a turn to talk, they may be responding to events not in the immediate past. They may instead have waited for their turn to speak. Sequential contingency techniques cannot describe or test for this aspect of group interaction. Second, the sequential analysis techniques discussed so far assume influence between events moves "from left to right." Events a at $t1$ are said to engender b's at some later point in the discussion, moving from left to right as we read a page in English, with each later event determined only by the preceding few events. An alternative approach supposes that group members are working from a socially shared script or mental model such as the logical sequence (cf. Bales & Strodbeck, 1951; Hewes, 2009d; Poole & Baldwin, 1996). In this case, group communication might be viewed as unfolding based on group members' knowledge of that script to which they refer while discussing. This is a hierarchical, rather than a left to right, organization, in that members are not only reacting to preceding statements, but trying to form the discussion based on this more general model. The large literature on shared mental models in groups suggests that this is a plausible alternative or addition to sequential structuring. If so, then phasic analysis is an appropriate alternative or addition.

Phasic analysis

The hypothesis that group processes such as decision making or long-term group development occur through a series of phases has a long and varied history (see, e.g., Bales & Strodtbeck, 1951; Fisher, 1970; Hirokawa, 1985; Poole, 1981, 1983b; Poole & Baldwin, 1996; Poole & Dobosh, 2010; Poole & Roth, 1989a, 1989b; for studies of decision-making phases; Wheelan, 2005, provides a good summary of work on group development). A phase is defined as a coherent period of group interaction and activity which serves an identifiable function, such as a period of problem definition, solution evaluation, integration or conflict.

As we have noted, many theories of group processes posit a unitary sequence of phases which all groups are presumed to follow, such as the normative sequence for group problem-solving (problem analysis, criteria definition, solution development, decision, implementation) or Tuckman's forming–storming–norming–performing sequence for long-term group development. As was previously discussed, the generative mechanism behind these sequences is logical necessity (a group has to form before conflicts can emerge, then it has to resolve its conflicts by coming to agreement on norms, etc.) or institutional rules. However, a good deal of empirical research indicates that group processes sometimes follow multiple paths (Poole & Baldwin, 1996; Poole & Dobosh, 2010). The unitary sequences seem to be normative ideals that group members try to follow in organizing their activities. In studies of multiple sequences in group decision-making, about 30 per cent of groups are observed to follow simple, normative sequences, 25 per cent focus mainly on solutions, while the remainder follow more complex decision paths, often recycling to previous phases or taking phases "out of order". Both the nature of the group task and social factors such as group size and cohesiveness are related to the complexity of group decision paths, with social factors accounting for a greater share of the variance (Poole & Roth, 1989b).

How do we identify phases in group processes? Most scholars rely on direct analysis of group interaction. Phases are higher order constructs that are indicated by the behaviors that typically occur during the phase. So, for example, in an orientation phase we might expect to observe a lot of questions, suggestions about how to tackle the task and organize the group, and expression of uncertainty.

Relevant coding systems are typically utilized to code the group interaction, resulting in a string of coded acts. This string is then partitioned into phases based on some criterion and function of the phases identified from the particular combinations of acts that occur within them.

One common way to partition strings of interaction into phases is to divide the string into the same number of equal length segments as phases in the theoretical model. So Bales and Strodtbeck (1951) divided their coded discussions into three segments and then tested for expected differences between segments in acts that indicated the three phases of orientation, evaluation, and control. The pattern of differences supported their prediction, so Bales and Strodtbeck concluded that their model of problem-solving fitted the data.

Partitioning group interaction into equal length segments is a workable approach to phasic analysis. However, if groups follow several possible sequences of phases or if they "loop back" and revisit earlier phases (e.g., as they attempt to decide guilt or innocence, jurors realize they do not know the law that is at the basis of their decision, so they loop back to orientation to familiarize themselves with the law, then proceed with their decision-making), then simply dividing the group discussion into equal segments is likely to cover over complexities and lead to misleading conclusions. In addition, even if there is a single sequence of phases, if they are of different lengths (e.g., a long orientation phase and a short criteria specification phase), taking equal length segments may also result in errors in identifying the sequence of phases.

To handle this problem, Poole and Holmes developed *flexible phase mapping* (Holmes & Poole, 1991; Poole & Roth, 1989a). Flexible phase mapping makes no assumptions about the number of types of sequences which will be found; only one type may be found, or many types may emerge, depending on the diversity of activities in the groups. Phase mapping is carried out through a series of incremental steps of data transformation and parsing. Coded interaction is transformed into phase indicators. The sequence of phase markers is then parsed into a phase map by an algorithm that basically "crawls" along the coded string and marks places at which indicators of a phase different from the current phase begin to occur. This yields a phase map with some long phases and, often, numerous short "phases" of four or fewer acts. The phase map is then smoothed to eliminate very short "phases" and to yield a map with more substantial phases. These steps are governed by precise rules for the data transformations at each step and an application, WinPhaser, is available to conduct the analysis (Holmes, 2000; for more detail, see Holmes & Poole, 1991).

In their phasic analysis, Poole and Dobosh first used the codings as direct indicators of a phase. So Focused Work indicated a phase of Focused Work, Opposition and Opposition phase, and so on. With more granular coding systems, several different codes and even combinations of codes occurring within a few acts of each other can be used as phase indicators. For example, Poole and Roth (1989a) used combinations of codes from two contiguous acts as phasic indicators.

They utilized a ten-category coding system and so there were 100 possible combinations, each of which was an indicator of one of seven phases.

Poole and Dobosh used a first pass of the phase definition algorithm to divide the two deliberations into a primary set of phases. In a second pass, the phase data was smoothed in two respects. First, short phases of two or fewer units that were surrounded by a single type of phase were merged into that phase. Second, where relatively short phases alternated, they were merged into a phase that was identified as the combination of the two units. So, for example, if a 30-unit period of critical work was broken by several periods of focused work of three or four units, it was labeled "critical work-focused work." This resulted in a layered analysis in which the basic phase sequence and then the smoothed phase sequence are displayed. It should be noted that in some cases flexible phase analysis will also demarcate periods when no coherent phases can be identified due to admixture of disparate and unrelated phasic indicators; these are termed "null" or nonorganized periods. Owing to the nature of the GWRCS, there were no null periods in the deliberations.

In addition to delimiting phases, it is also often useful to mark "breakpoints" (Poole, 1983b), such as procedural discussions, votes, meals, or temporary adjournments. Breakpoints (Fisher & Stutman, 1987: Poole & DeSanctis, 1992; Poole & Roth, 1989a) have been shown to offer opportunities for groups to make discontinuous shifts in their approach to their tasks and relationships.

High-level phase maps of the two deliberations studying by Poole and Dobosh (2010) are shown in Figure 18.2. As the maps indicate, there were fewer and longer phases in the trial deliberation than in the penalty deliberation. Most of the trial deliberation had relatively low levels of conflict, because of the predominance of Critical Work and Focused Work–Critical Work phases (the Focused Work–Critical Work phase consisted of a number of cycles of the two activities).

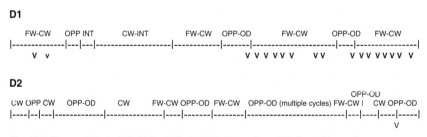

Key: FW=Focused Work; CW=Critical Work; OPP=Opposition; OD=Open Discussion; INT=Integration; V = Decision Point; Combination phases are indicated by dashes, e.g., FW-CW

FIGURE 18.2 Phase sequences for D1 and D2 (normalized to the same length) with phases in proportion to their length in the original. FW, focused work; CW, critical work; OPP, opposition; OD, open discussion; INT, integration; V, decision point; combination phases are indicated by dashes (e.g., FW-CW).

There were only a few, short, open oppositions in the trial phase. By contrast deliberations in the penalty phase exhibited a great deal of opposition (which signals open conflict and confrontation), which tended to be handled through open discussion. In general there was more variability among phase in the penalty deliberation than in the trial deliberation.

Differences between the two deliberations may be traceable to the different tasks they involved. In the trial phase, the jury had to make determinations on more than 20 counts (the points at which they did so are indicated by "v"s on the timeline. This enabled jurors to focus initially on those they could agree on, building a sense of progress and perhaps a degree of group cohesiveness. When there was opposition on a count, the jury tended to drop it and go on to an item they could agree on, then circle back to those they could not, saving the most contentious issue for last. This is reflected in the cycling in much of the discussion and in the brief integration periods which often marked a decision on a count, a sort of "celebration" before moving on to the next count. In the penalty phase there was a single decision – death penalty or an alternative life sentence – and the only alternative to discuss was whether there were mitigating circumstances, a matter tied directly to sentencing. Given different positions on the major task at hand, this deliberation exhibited open conflict throughout, as jurors grappled with their difference and tried to find solutions. Ultimately they could not agree and so the defendant received a life sentence instead of the death penalty.

One of the strengths of phasic analysis is that it enables us to get a "bird's eye" view of the decision process. Differences due to task, group composition, and other variables can be related to process in order to test their impact (see Poole & Roth, 1989b, for an example of this). But as the previous discussion indicates, phasic analysis can be even more informative if other information, such as the content of the discussion or key breakpoints, are combined with the information from the phasic analysis.

The jury deliberation example compares only two group decision processes, but a number of studies have mapped and compared larger samples (Nutt, 1984; Poole & Roth, 1989a). In such cases it is helpful to characterize the sequences so they can be empirically compared. At least three types of characterizations are useful. First, the phase sequences can be sorted into a typology that differentiates them qualitatively. For example, Poole and Roth (1989a) found three major types of decision paths in a sample of 47 diverse decisions: unitary, solution-centered, and complex. Typologies are often derived via the researcher's qualitative analysis of the paths, as in Nutt (1984). There are also empirical methods, such as optimal matching, that calculate the similarity of phase sequences (Abbott, 1990; Sankoff & Kruskal, 1983). This similarity data can then be statistically analyzed to derive clusters of similar paths that can form the basis for identification of types. These types can then become dependent variables, which are predicted by independent variables such as task or level of group cohesiveness (Poole & Roth, 1989b) or independent variables used to predict outcomes such as effectiveness and satisfaction (Nutt, 1984; Sambamurthy & Poole, 1992).

A second useful property of sequences are indices that measure the acts that occur in them, such as the level of idea development, the proportion of conflict in the sequence, or whether criteria defined early in a session were used to evaluate solutions later on. Many hypotheses about group processes involve predictions about relative levels of various acts. For example, Tuckman (1965) posited that groups that did not carry out their developmental phases (forming, storming, norming, and performing) adequately were destined to repeat them in the future in order to complete unfinished work in building the group. It would be possible to test this hypothesis by assessing the amount and proportion of time spent by a sample of groups in each phase of the group development sequence. Groups that devoted a good deal of their time to each phase and had no proportionately short phases would be expected to be more cohesive and effective than groups that gave short shrift to certain phases.

A third useful type of variable measures summary properties of sequences, such as how long they are, the degree to which they match a particular ideal type sequence, or the complexity of the sequences. Such variables can be used to characterize the process and also enable distinct event sequences to be compared. For example, Poole and Roth (1989b) assessed the "unitariness" of decision-making paths – that is, the degree to which they resembled the ideal decision-making sequence – and used this as a dependent variable, finding that task and level of group cohesiveness were good predictors of the degree to which a decision path fit the normative unitary sequence.

Phasic analysis, then, gives us a more macro-level view of group process. It traces the broader functional contours of a process and gives us a purchase on the question of whether a process unfolds as it "should" according to normative models. Many normative models of processes follow the recipe: first you should do this, then you should do this, then you should do this, etc. These are fairly high level, granular statements in that they do not often tell one exactly how to do things at the level of execution (possibly because there is more than one way to "do this" well or correctly). Phases are fairly coarse, granular constructs and so phase maps offer a connecting point between normative models of a process and how that process is actually executed by a group. Phasic analysis can shed light on the question of whether normative models of how group processes should unfold correspond to how they actually unfold.

How Do We Explain Observed Patterns?

Once we have identified one or more patterns in group interaction the next question is: What kind of generative mechanisms and factors account for these temporal patterns? Having worked with and taught interaction analytic techniques for decades, we have observed that those versed in more traditional methods of experimental and survey analysis have some difficulty thinking of hypotheses related to temporal patterns. Most of us tend to think of variables as states of behavior, personality, attitudes, beliefs, values, intentions, or states of groups (cohesiveness, motivation, etc.) rather than as temporal patterns or sequences of those states, yet developing thinking sequentially is crucial to analyze group interaction effectively. One must be able to ask and answer why-questions to explain sequential patterns or their role in determining group outcomes. Why do phases come in some specified order, or in no particular order? Why do cycles occur and what, if anything, causes them to stop or start? Why do non-stationary transition probabilities, changes in the order of those processes, or their nonhomogeneity occur?

Many studies simply identify patterns empirically, as described in the previous section. They use *ex post facto* narratives to explain them. This is fine as a first step, but not for a last. The next step is to identify the causal factors and/or generative mechanisms that engender those patterns. In the remainder of this section we discuss how to advance and specify generative mechanisms to explain patterns in interaction.

One approach to explaining interaction patterns is to identify the "motors" that shape the overall pattern of group interaction. Poole and Van de Ven (2004) and Van de Ven and Poole (1995) defined four basic generative mechanisms that explain how processes, including group interaction processes, unfold over time. Two of these have been alluded to already in our discussion of the unitary and multiple sequence models of phase development, and here we will briefly define the four models in more general terms.

First, a *life-cycle* model depicts the process of change as progressing through a necessary sequence of phases. The order and content of these phases is prescribed and regulated by logic or by norms prefigured at the beginning of the sequence. The unitary sequence model we have discussed is a life-cycle model.

A *teleological* model views group process as the product of a cycle in which members formulate goals, then take action based on those goals, evaluate the results, and modify their actions or goals in order to stay on track toward their desired end (McGrath & Tschan, 2004). The observed sequence of interaction that emerges from this cycling process will vary depending on the adjustments that are made by members as the session proceeds. The multiple sequence model discussed previously is a product of a teleological model. Members have a goal (e.g., to make a decision) and mental models of how to reach that goal. If all members share the same goal and model, then the group discussion will follow the unitary sequence (provided the model held by members is the logical one). If the group runs into a problem or a conflict breaks out, then the sequence may be more complex. The sequence will also be complex if members have different goals or mental models.

A *dialectical* model of development is generated by conflicts that emerge when a thesis and antithesis are produced that collide to produce a synthesis, which in

380 Dean E. Hewes and Marshall Scott Poole

time becomes the thesis for the next cycle of a dialectical progression. For example, a group may become too cohesive and integrated (thesis), which results in the inability to think creatively in order to craft an effective response to some problem the group faces (antithesis – note it is in contradiction with the thesis) (Sawyer, 2007). The group's attempt to remain in its comfort zone of integrated cohesiveness lowers its creativity, which results in a major failure. As a result of this several members are terminated and the group has to reconstitute itself so that it can be more flexible and creative while maintaining trusting relationships (synthesis). The conflict that drives the dialectical model is not simple interpersonal conflict or arguments over ideas. It stems from tensions and oppositions between conflicting demands on the group, such as the need to integrate versus the need for members to have some independence or the need to have structure versus the need to adapt to changing circumstances (Johnson & Long, 2002).

Finally, an *evolutionary* model of development consists of a repetitive sequence of variation, selection, and retention events in the group (for an application of this thinking in organizations, see Monge & Poole, 2008). We might, for example, consider solution options as generated and selected through an evolutionary process. Ideas would be suggested and would compete against other ideas in the group's discourse. Variation in an idea would occur during the discussion and there might even be a sort of cross-fertilization as ideas were combined and extended. Some ideas would drop out (be selected out), while others would thrive and be retained by the group in its final solution and in the memory of members. When a similar situation occurs in the future, the same idea might be revived as part of the population of ideas the group was entertaining.

Of these four models, only the first two have been actively applied to the study of group processes, but it is clear that the remaining two could be applied. Poole et al. (2000) defined empirical criteria that could be used to determine if a given model held. For example, for a life-cycle motor to hold, there must be a single, invariant sequence of phases and we must be able to identify the logic, norm, shared mental model or other structure that specifies and enforces the sequence. For a dialectical model to hold, there must be two competing demands that can be empirically documented and, usually, subgroups within the group that emphasize them. The resolution of the tension cannot be the "victory" of one or the other demand, but must instead be something novel that may contain aspects of the demands, but represents an emergent result. The various criteria defined in Poole et al. (2000) refer in part to properties of the interaction patterns, but also require additional evidence. The moderated dependency sequential model outlined above incorporates these directly into the developmental model, but for the other models defined by Poole and colleagues, the other factors operate in addition to the sequential model.

It is also possible that combinations of the four motors may influence group processes. For example, a group might apply a shared mental model of the logical sequence as it made a decision, resulting in a unitary sequence, but the content of the decision might be shaped by an evolutionary process in which various ideas compete for acceptance in each phase. In this case the life-cycle model sets the overall course of the decision process, while an evolutionary model governs specific micro-level decisions that determine the content of the final decision.

An alternative to fitting entire models is to posit hypotheses about variables that might influence sequential dependencies. This is a less ambitious strategy that can yield more definitive results with less effort and time. One type of hypothesis is to *make theoretical predictions that explain why a sequential process should be homogeneous, and/or some specified order, and/or stationary.* Poole and Dobosh expected that the two deliberations they studied would be second order, that is, that the sequential structure of the discussions would consist of three contiguous statements. They posited this because earlier work by Karl Weick (1979) and others proposed that the double interact, a sequence composed of an act, a response, and a response was the basic organizing unit of interaction. It turned out, as we saw above, that this hypothesis was not borne out.

A second type of hypothesis is to *make theoretical predictions that anticipate violations of the assumptions of a sequential mode that result from static input values.* For example, Poole and Dobosh expected the Markov processes and phase models for D1 and D2 to differ because in D1 the jury had to make decisions about more than 15 individual counts against the defendant, whereas in D2 it had to make only two decisions, would they impose the death penalty and, if not, what penalty would they impose on the defendant? The structural differences between tasks should make the two sequences nonhomogeneous. Poole and Dobosh also expected D1 to be nonstationary because of all the decisions required of the group, but it turned out it was in fact stationary.

Third, researchers can *make theoretical predictions about dynamic variables that cause changes in stationarity and order.* Rather than say that groups differ in the degree of stationarity based on some property that precedes group discussion, for instance, one might posit that sequential patterns of interaction may change as goals are met or not during the interaction or as the psychological or social emotional states of the group change. For example, Poole and Dobosh might have posited that the longer it takes a jury to make progress on a decision, the lower the morale of that group (cf. Hewes, 2009d; SunWolf, 2007). As morale drops, jury members might disengage from one another, resulting in lowering the order of the sequential process from a first-order process, where members are influencing each other, to a zero-order process, where individuals are not reacting to one another. This would make the deliberation nonstationary. To provide evidence that morale was related to the nonstationarity, the jury's interaction could be coded for statements that reflect levels of morale. The same reasoning could be applied to issues of order and interactions between those two assumptions and homogeneity.

The approaches discussed in this section are certainly not the only possible ones. What they do illustrate, though, is how far researchers can go beyond simply describing sequences. They also illustrate how sequential techniques can be integrated with theory and how sequential thinking can produce new directions for small group research.

Conclusion

Interaction analysis methodologies offer a broad range of possibilities for studying group interaction patterns. As this chapter shows, the logic behind interaction analysis is different from that for the analysis of experiments and surveys. Whereas the latter rely on traditional statistical techniques such as ANOVA, analysis of interaction processes requires describing and explaining patterns over time. To identify and explain patterns adequately requires special methods such as the various types of sequential dependency analysis and phasic analysis. These methods, while not that difficult to master, require us to learn different ways of thinking about group processes. We believe, however, that the effort is well worth it, because these methods can divulge a whole new world in group dynamics.

Notes

1 To test for order using loglinear analysis, we would fit models incorporating three terms, U_1, U_2, and U_3, where U_1 represents the time 1 units, U_2 the time 2 units, and U_3 the time 3 units. If a zeroth-order process holds, then the best fitting model in a hierarchical loglinear analysis would be $[U_1][U_2][U_3]$; the notation for this model indicates that units at all lags are independent of each other. For the first-order process the hypothesized model is $[U_1U_2][U_3]$, which indicates that each unit is interdependent only with the immediately preceding unit. For the second-order process the hypothesized model is $[U_1U_2U_3][U_1U_2][U_2U_3]$, which indicates that units at time 3 are dependent on the distributions of units at times 1 and 2; the first-order terms $[U_1U_2]$ and $[U_2U_3]$ also are included in the model because second-order processes also include first-order dependencies.

2 To test for stationarity using loglinear analysis, the first step is to segment the sequence of interaction units (henceforth referred to simply as a "sequence") into several pieces and compute a transition matrix for each sequence as described above. Once this has been done, a statistical test for the assumption of stationarity can be conducted by fitting a loglinear model for the $U_1 \times U_2 \times T$ contingency table formed by stacking the contingency matrices for the three segments according to temporal order. In this table U_1 represents the rows (prior events, time 1) of the table, U_2 the columns (second events, time 2) of the table, and T (time) the number of segments (where segments are arrayed in the order of temporal occurrence). The model to be fit is

$$L = [U_1U_2][U_1T]$$

This model is missing the term $[U_1U_2T]$, which would indicate dependency between time and the structure of the contingency matrices, that is, nonstationarity. The term $[U_1T]$ is included in the model because the row probabilities must sum to 1 for each time period; this creates an artifactual association between time and row values that this term models. If the model fits the data, then the assumption of stationarity is supported.

References

Abbott, A. (1990). A primer on sequence methods. *Organization Science, 1*, 375–392.

Arrow, K. J., Karlin, S., & Suppes, P. (1960). *Mathmatical methods in the social sciences.* Stanford, CA: Stanford University Press.

Bakeman, R., & Gottman, J. M. (1997). *Observing interaction.* Cambridge: Cambridge University Press.

Bales, R. F. (1950). *Interaction process analysis.* Reading, MA: Wesley.

Bales, R. F., & Strodtbeck, F. L. (1951). Phases in group problem-solving. *Journal of Abnormal and Social Psychology, 46,* 485–495.

Bishop, Y. M., Fienberg, S. E., & Holland, P. W. (1975). *Discrete multivariate analysis: Theory and practice.* Cambridge, MA: MIT Press.

Coleman, J. A. (1964). *Introduction to mathematical sociology.* New York: Free Press.

Fisher, B. A. (1970). Decision emergence: Phases in group decision-making. *Communication Monographs, 7,* 53–66.

Fisher, B. A., & Stutman, R. K. (1987). An assessment of group trajectories: Analyzing developmental breakpoints. *Communication Quarterly, 35,* 105–124.

Folger, J. P., Hewes, D. E., & Poole, M. S. (1984). Coding social interaction. In B. Dervin & M. Voight (Eds.) *Progress in communication sciences* (Vol. 4, pp. 115–161). New York: Ablex.

Gouran, D.S., & Hirokawa, R.Y. (1996). Functional theory and communication in decision-making and problem-solving groups: An expanded view. In R. Y. Hirokawa & M. S. Poole (Eds.), *Communication and group decision-making* (2nd ed., pp. 55–80). Thousand Oaks, CA: Sage.

Hewes, D. E. (1980a). Analyzing social interaction: Some excruciating models and exhilarating results. In D. I. Nimmo (Ed.) *Communication yearbook IV* (pp. 123–141). New Brunswik, NJ: Transaction Press.

Hewes, D. E. (1980b). Stochastic modeling of communication processes. In P. R. Monge & J. N. Cappella (Eds.), *Multivariate techniques in human communication research* (pp. 393–427). New York: Academic Press.

Hewes, D. E. (1985). Systematic biases in coded social interaction data. *Human Communication Research, 11,* 554–574.

Hewes, D. E. (2009a). The influence of communication processes on group outcomes: Antithesis and thesis. *Human Communication Research, 35,* 249–271.

Hewes, D. E. (2009b). *Dual-level connectionist models of group communication: Formalism, justifications and unanswered questions.* Paper presented at the National Communication Association Convention, Chicago, IL.

Hewes, D. E. (2009c). *Developmental processes in group decision making: A dual-level connectionist theory.* Paper presented at the National Communication Association Convention, Chicago, IL.

Hewes, D. E. (2009d). *Emotional dynamics in group communication: A dual-level connectionist theory* Paper presented at the National Communication Association Convention, Chicago, IL.

Hirokawa, R.Y. (1985). Discussion procedures and decision-making performance: A text of a functional perspective. *Human Communication Research, 12,* 203–224.

Hirokawa, R. Y. (1990). The role of communication in group decision-making efficacy: A task contingency perspective. *Small Group Research, 21,* 190–204.

Hollingshead, A. B., Wittenbaum, G. M., Paulus, P. B., Hirokawa, R. Y., Ancona, D. G., Peterson, R. S., Jehn, K. A., & Yoon, K. (2005). A look at groups from the functional perspective. In M. S. Poole & A. Hollingshead (Eds.) *Theories of small groups: Interdisciplinary perspectives* (pp. 21–63). Thousand Oaks, CA: Sage.

Holmes, M. (2000). *WinPhaser,* program available from Michael Holmes, Ball State University, Muncie, IN.

Holmes, M., & Poole, M. S. (1991). The longitudinal analysis of interaction. In B. Montgomery & S. Duck (Eds.) Studying interpersonal interaction (pp. 286–302). New York: Guilford.

Honeycutt, J., & Poole, M. S. (1994). *Procedural schemata for group decision-making.* Paper presented at the National Communication Association Convention, New Orleans, LA.

Klimoski, R., & Muhammad, S. (1994). Team mental model: Construct or metaphor? *Journal of Management, 20,* 403–437.

Krippendorff, K. (2004). *Content analysis: An introduction to its methodology* (2nd ed.). Thousand Oaks, CA: Sage.

Krippendorff, K., & Bock, M. A. (2009). *The content analysis reader.* Los Angeles: Sage.

Johnson, S. D., & Long, L. M. (2002). "Being a part and being apart": Dialectics and group communication. In L. R. Frey (Ed.) *New directions in group communication* (pp. 25–42). Thousand Oaks, CA: Sage.

Langan-Fox, J. (2003). Skill acquisition and the development of a team mental model. In M. A. West, D. Tjosvold, & K. G. Smith (Eds.) *International handbook of organizational teamwork and cooperative working* (pp. 321–359). London: Wiley.

Leik, R. K., & Meeker, B. F. (1975). *Mathematical sociology.* Englewood Cliffs, NJ: Prentice-Hall.

Mackie, P. (1995). *Event.* In T. Honderichs (Ed.) *The Oxford companion to philosophy* (p. 253). New York: Oxford University Press.

McGrath, J. E. & Altman, I. (1966). *Small group research: A synthesis and critique of the field.* New York: Holt, Rinehart & Winston.

McGrath, J. E., & Tschan, F. (2004). *Dynamics in groups and teams: Groups as complex action systems.* In M. S. Poole & A. H. Van de Ven (Eds.) *Handbook of organizational change and innovation* (pp. 50–72). New York: Oxford University Press.

Mohr, L. (1982). *Explaining organizational behavior.* San Francisco: Jossey-Bass

Monge, P. R., & Poole, M. S. (2008). The evolution of organizational communication. *Journal of Communication, 58*(4), 679–692.

Nutt, P. C. (1984). Types of organizational decision processes. *Administrative Science Quarterly, 29,* 414–450.

Orlitsky, M., & Hirokawa, R. Y. (2001). To err is human, to correct for it divine: A meta-analysis of research testing the functional model of group decision-making effectiveness. *Small Group Research, 32,* 313–341.

Pavitt, C. & Johnson, K.K. (2001). The association between group procedural MOPs and group discussion procedure. *Small Group Research, 32,* 595–623.

Poole, M. S. (1981). Decision development in small groups I: A test of two models. *Communication Monographs, 48,* 1–24.

Poole, M. S. (1983a). Decision development in small groups: II. A study of multiple sequences in group decision making. *Communication Monographs, 50,* 206–232.

Poole, M. S. (1983b). Decision development in small groups III: A multiple sequence theory of decision development. *Communication Monographs, 50,* 321–341.

Poole, M. S. (2007). Generalization in process theories of communication. *Communication Methods and Measures, 1,* 181–190.

Poole, M. S., & DeSanctis, G. (1992). Microlevel structuration in computer-supported group decision-making. *Human Communication Research, 19,* 5–49.

Poole, M. S., & Dobosh, M. (2010). Exploring conflict management processes in jury deliberations through interaction analysis. *Small Group Research, 41,* 408–426.

Poole, M. S., Holmes, M., & DeSanctis (1991). Conflict management in a computer-supported meeting environment. *Management Science, 37,* 926–953.

Poole, M. S., & Roth, J. (1989a). Decision development in small groups IV: A typology of group decision paths. *Human Communication Research, 15,* 323–356.

Poole, M. S., & Roth, J. (1989b). Decision development in small groups V: Test of a contingency model. *Human Communication Research, 15,* 549–589.

Poole, M. S., Seibold, D. R., & McPhee, R. D. (1985). Group decision-making as a structurational process. *Quarterly Journal of Speech,* 71, 74–102.

Poole, M. S., Siebold, D. R., & McPhee, R. D. (1996). The structuration of group decisions. In R. Y. Hirokawa & M. S. Poole (Eds.), *Communication and group decision-making* (2nd ed., pp. 114–146). Thousand Oaks, CA: Sage.

Poole, M. S. & Van de Ven, A. H. (2004). Theories of organizational change and innovation processes. In M. S. Poole & A. H. Van de Ven (Eds.). *Handbook of organizational change and innovation* (pp. 374–397). New York: Oxford University Press.

Poole, M. S., Van de Ven, A. H., Dooley, K., & Holmes, M. E. (2000). *Organizational change and innovation processes: Theory and methods for research.* New York: Oxford University Press.

Rescher, N. (1996). *Process metaphysics: An introduction to process philosophy,* Albany, NY: State University of New York Press.

Sambamurthy, V. & Poole, M. S. (1992). The effects of variations in capabilities of GDSS designs on management of cognitive conflict in groups. *Information Systems Research, 3,* 224–251.

Sankoff, D., & Kruskal, J. B. (1983) (Eds.). *Time warps, string edits, and macromolecules: The theory and practice of sequence comparison.* Reading, MA: Addison-Wesley.

Sawyer, K. (2007). *Group genius: The creative power of collaboration.* New York: Basic Books.

Sun Wolf (2007). *Practical jury dynamics 2.* Charlottesville, VA: Lexis-Nexis.

Teichmann, R. (1995). Process. In T. Honderichs (Ed.) *The Oxford companion to philosophy* (p. 721). New York: Oxford University Press.

Tuckman, B. W. (1965). Development sequence in small groups. *Psychological Bulletin, 63,* 384–399.

Wheelan, S. A. (2005). The developmental perspective. In S. A. Wheelan (Ed.) *The handbook of group research and practice* (pp. 119–132). Thousand Oaks, CA: Sage.

Weick, K. (1979). *The social psychology of organizing.* Boston, MA: Addison-Wesley Publications.

19

MEASURING TEAM DYNAMICS IN THE WILD

Michael A. Rosen, Jessica L. Wildman and Eduardo Salas

DEPARTMENT OF PSYCHOLOGY, AND INSTITUTE FOR SIMULATION AND TRAINING, UNIVERSITY OF CENTRAL FLORIDA

Sara Rayne

NAVY PERSONNEL RESEARCH, STUDIES, AND TECHNOLOGY

Teams are a way of life in modern organizations. It is easy to take this for granted, but the safety and well-being of people in many industries and those they serve rely on effective communication, collaboration, and coordination. Good teamwork in the cockpit has helped to make commercial flights safer than the highways. Poor teamwork contributes heavily to the estimated 98,000 deaths a year caused by preventable medical errors in the US. For these reasons, we (along with many others) have dedicated our professional careers to understanding and improving team performance where it counts – in high-stakes industries. We have found that team performance measurement is central to understanding and building high-performance teams. It is critical for building and testing new theory and for systematically applying the science of teams to improve productivity, safety, and quality through better teamwork. However, measuring team performance in the field can be very challenging. Organizations have many moving parts, and practical constraints such as time, access, and control over confounding variables frequently threaten to undermine the meaning of any measurements.

This chapter attempts to provide an introduction to some of these real-world challenges involved in measuring team performance in, well, the real world. Specifically, we address four goals. First, we describe features of organizational environments that can complicate the process of measuring team dynamics and introduce several examples from our work of teams operating in these conditions. These examples will be referenced throughout the chapter to illustrate the principles discussed. Second, we provide a brief review of the main methods available. Third, we provide a summary of major challenges to team performance measurement in the wild. Fourth, we discuss strategies for managing the tradeoffs inherent in designing measurement systems when dealing with the challenges in the field. We hope readers see these challenges as we do: opportunities to solve creatively and adaptively unique problems impacting the quality of life of many workers.

Description of the "Wild:" Challenging Characteristics of Teams and Organizations

One of the great rewards of being an applied scientist is the ability to be an "occupational tourist" to some extent, learning about and getting to know the people in a variety of complex domains. There are many differences across work teams in different industries; however, there are also some unifying features. In this section we present a description of some of these factors as well as examples of teams presenting tough cases for performance measurement.

Features of the team, organizational, and environmental context

Teams are made up of individual members, all of whom can (and frequently do) have very different backgrounds, experiences, and expertise. They are embedded within organizations with different norms, policies, and cultures. Some team members will be a part of multiple teams at once and have to manage and prioritize their contributions across these teams – not to mention finding time to complete their own individual work. While there is no one framework that accounts for all of these differences, field researchers working across domains such as aviation, healthcare, the military, and power generation have developed a common set of organizational and environmental descriptors outlining challenging real-world contexts (Cannon-Bowers, Salas, & Pruitt, 1996; Orasanu & Connolly, 1993). These features include: ill-structured problems; uncertain dynamic environments; shifting, ill-defined, or competing goals; action/feedback loops; time stress; high stakes for errors; multiple players or stakeholders in outcomes; organizational goals and norms; expertise levels of the team members; and task characteristics such as information quantity and decision complexity. Table 19.1 provides examples the challenges some of these factors pose for team performance measurement. However, in general, they outline a dynamic environment demanding adaptive responses. This changing nature of tasks, environmental conditions, and performance processes is one of the core complications for conducting team performance measurement in the field. Defining the content of a measuring system is relatively straightforward in stable tasks and environments. Unfortunately, the real world does not stand still for measurement.

We have found that the features of the team's task as well as its structure or design are strong influences on what good and poor team performance will look like for a given team. As such, it is a good starting point for thinking about team performance measurement.

First, you have to understand the work a team is accomplishing – what task is the team performing? Developing this understanding involves clarifying issues of

Table 19.1 Features of field settings that complicate team performance measurement

Feature of the environment	Issues posed for team performance measurement	Tips
Ill-structured problems	When the task is ill-defined, it is challenging to develop a model of what 'good performance' looks like and consequently difficult to evaluate a team relative to a standard. Performance processes will naturally be different when the task changes. Different performance strategies can develop between teams and assessing whether one or the other is better or there is an equifinality involved can be difficult.	Capture information about what the team is doing concurrently with information about team processes. This will help you to understand different aspects of teamwork during different tasks or phases of performance.
Uncertain dynamic environments	When outcomes are unclear and probabilistic, it is difficult to make connections between the team's performance processes (i.e., what they did) and the team's outcome.	As much as possible, identify the other factors at play and measure those as well. For example, the patient's status upon arrival plays a large role in that patient's outcomes at a trauma center. If severity data are captured on patients, it can be statistically controlled in analyses.
Shifting, ill-defined, or competing goals	Performance outcomes can only be judged relative to a criterion based on the team's goals. If goals change rapidly, are not defined clearly, or conflict, developing a sense of whether or not the team is meeting a valued goal is a challenge.	When this is a primary environmental condition, focusing on the team's ability to identify and communicate goals, short or longer term, can be an effective strategy.
High stakes	Access to teams performing in high stakes environments can be limited for safety and security reasons.	Leave no pre-existing source of information unturned. Use document reviews, interviews, case reports, existing training and any other documentation available to make sure you have the best possible understanding of the work. You'll need this to make the most of the limited time you'll have.
Level of expertise of members	Teamwork and individual level taskwork are interdependent and reciprocally causative. Differences in how team members perform their individual tasks have implications for what effective and ineffective teamwork looks like.	As clearly as possible, draw distinctions between individual and team level performance (e.g., what an individual does, and how individuals interact as a unit). Keep track of who is on the team for each performance episode so that it can be linked back to individual level information.

task type and *task complexity*, as well as the *external context* in which the task is performed (McGrath, 1984; Strubler & York, 2007). Essentially, you need to clarify the problem the team is addressing and the conditions under which they have to work. Understanding characteristics of the task will help draw connections between previous research and the present context. This is critical for setting expectations of the types of teamwork behaviors that will contribute to effective performance.

Second, you need to understand the way in which the team is configured to address this task – what is the team's structure? The team's design or structure can be thought of as the organization's solution to the problem (i.e., the task). This includes dimensions such as leadership and communication structure (Dyer, 1984). Structural aspects of a team influence how the members interact. For example, differences in role division and interdependence will change the amount of communication required to be effective (e.g., higher interdependence and role specialization may require more communication as members must rely more intensely on others with different specialties). Table 19.2 provides a description and relevant literature on the dimensions of team task and team design.

Table 19.2 Overview of different team characteristics that have implications for team performance

Team task		
Task type	The nature of the work performed by the team	McGrath (1984), Cohen and Bailey (1997), Driskell, Salas, and Hogan (1987), Mattson, Mumford, and Sintay (1999), Saavedra Earley, and Dyne (1993), Sundstrom, De Meuse, and Futrell (1990)
Task complexity	The extent to which the task places high cognitive demands on the task-doer	Campbell (1988), Jehn (1994), Kankanhalli, Tan, and Wei (2006)
Task identity	The degree to which the team works on a problem from beginning to end	Abbott, Boyd, and Miles (2006), Strubler and York (2007)
Task environment	The characteristics of the environment in which the team task is performed including environmental uncertainty, dynamism, stakes for errors, multiple stakeholders, or conflicting goals	Duncan (1972), Hough and White (2004), Lipshitz and Strauss (1997), Locke, Smith, Erez, Chah, and Schaffer (1994), Priem, Rasheed, and Kotulic (1995), Shi and Tang (1997)
Size	A structural variable of a team describing the number of member directly involved in the team's primary goals and tasks	Dyer (1984), Sundstrom, et al. (1990)

(continued)

Table 19.2 (*Cont'd*)

	Team design	
Technology dependence	The degree to which team activities are constrained by technological resources such as communication systems, machines, tools, or specialized equipment	Devine (2002), Sundstrom et al. (1990)
Interdependence	The nature of the interconnections between members of the team including goal, task, and feedback interconnections	Bell and Kozlowski (2002), Cohen and Bailey (1997), Mattson et al. (1999), Saavedra, Earley, and Dyne (1993)
Distribution	The degree to which the team members are spread out across time (temporal distribution) and space (physical distribution)	Bell and Kozlowski (2002), Kirkman and Mathieu (2005)
Leadership structure	The configuration of leadership within the team, which can generally be categorized into basic structures: external manager, designated leader, temporary designated leader, task-based team leader, and distributed team leadership	Barry (1991), Erez, LePine, and Elms (2002), Gronn (2002), Klein, Ziegert, Knight, and Xiao (2006), Morgeson (2005), Yang and Shao (1996)
Role division	The way the team divide work among members, which can generally be categorized into two basic structures: functional and divisional	Harris and Raviv (2002), Moon et al. (2004)
Autonomy	Level of control the team has over its own design, structure, and accomplishment of work that can be divided into three levels: semi-autonomous, self-regulating, and self-designing	Abbott et al. (2006), Cohen and Bailey (1997), Sundstrom et al. (1990)
Communication structure	The pattern of both verbal and nonverbal communication within the team that can generally be categorized into three patterns: hub-and-wheel, star, and chain	Dyer (1984)
Temporal structure	The aspects of the team focused specifically on time such as team lifespan, performance episode duration, performance episode frequency, and continuity of membership	Devine (2002)

In sum, teams can differ in terms of the task they perform, how they are structured to complete this task, and the organizational context in which they are embedded. All of these factors need to be considered when developing measurement protocols for teams in context. Before discussing some measurement methods, specific challenges and strategies that work, we provide a few examples of teams we've worked with.

Example teams in context

The following sections provide brief descriptions of real teams we have encountered as team researchers. These teams posed significant challenges for measurement, and are vastly different than the three to four person teams performing a well-defined task within a laboratory setting.

Multidisciplinary trauma teams

At a minimum, multidisciplinary trauma teams usually consist of surgeons, emergency medicine physicians, nurses, technicians, and first responders as well as the patient. Frequently, residents at various levels of experience are included as well. There are large differences in level and type of expertise of members. These teams assemble rapidly to care for critically injured patients. They are under extreme time pressure and have the highest consequences for errors. Quite literally, people's lives depend on how they perform their technical skills and how they work together as a team. There are multiple transitions of care – critical points where information and authority are transferred between team members (e.g., first responders to stabilization team and subsequently to surgery and the inrtensive care unit). Leadership (or ultimate responsibility for the patient) changes with these transitions and consequently there can be competing subgoals on the team as well as disagreement on how to prioritize injuries and treatments.

One of the many challenges for measurement posed by this team involves understanding the complexity of the domain and gauging effectiveness. First, teamwork and taskwork (i.e., the parts of a team member's job that are not directly dependent on other team members) are intertwined. Effective communication is, in part, about *how* team members communicate (e.g., clarity and structures such as closed-loop communication) but it is also about *what* and *when* they communicate. Understanding the effectiveness of team communication processes in terms of content and timing requires an understanding of the domain, in this case trauma medicine. Learning the fundamentals of trauma is no small task, and trying to focus your attention on teamwork in the presence of life-and-death situations was difficult for our observers. In one project, our goal was to develop measurement protocols that helped instructors provide diagnostic feedback to team members on the quality of their team processes during trauma cases. Several features of our solution involved: (a) tying measurement to a phase structure for a trauma case;

(b) focusing on critical tasks that occur for every patient, regardless of conditions; and (c) clearly defining team membership and roles.

First, every trauma case tends to unfold in phases (e.g., pre-arrival information from first responders, arrival and handoff, primary survey, secondary survey, etc.). Team performance tends to vary over time (i.e., sometimes a team will communicate effectively; other times they will not). If global or overall ratings of a team's performance are made, this dynamic aspect of a team's interaction is lost. By structuring measurement around the temporal flow of a team's task, observers are capturing smaller chunks of performance. They are measuring at a higher temporal resolution.

Second, we concretely identified critical, recurring team interdependencies. In each phase of performance, we found that there were very specific tasks where teamwork mattered. For instance, during primary survey (i.e., an initial inspection of a patient's injuries), close-loop communication was critical to ensure the team leader heard and understood what the primary surveyor was finding. At a different phase, the leader's ability to articulate a clear plan of care for the patient was the critical indicator of effectiveness. Uncovering these very specific team task elements within each phase helped to focus observers' attention – they knew when to look for what – and it helped trainers to provide effective, process-oriented feedback because they had rich detail about what happened.

Third, we developed a map of the team's role structure. By incorporating the key individual clinical task responsibilities into the measurement tool, drawing distinctions between deficiencies in team interaction and deficiencies in clinical execution became possible. This was necessary for our purposes of providing systematic feedback on teamwork. It was only through creating a highly structured tool that we were able to make sense of the technical complexity occurring during trauma cases.

As frequently happens in applied research projects, the development of a measurement tool becomes an intervention in its own right. It is an opportunity for the experts within a domain to reflect on their processes and come to consensus on key issues (e.g., a defined role structure). Our work with these teams led not only to the tool, but to several clarifications about roles in addition to a shared expectation for what good teamwork is on the trauma team.

Navy security detachments

The US Navy is full of teams doing various types of work. In a project aimed at identifying the basic characteristics of US Navy teams for the purposes of improving selection and training for those teams, we had the opportunity physically to observe a security detachment team in a training exercise. The primary mission of the team is to provide any and all security services to other Navy groups. This mission can include a variety of activities such as providing security watches and patrols for groups embedded downrange in temporary bases, providing security on deployed ships, or more short-term assignments such as escorting vehicles through hostile territory. These teams are much larger than the well-known three and four person teams that most researchers focus on, often consisting of 70 or 80 members that identify with one another as a team. The overall mission of the team often requires for the group to split off into multiple subgroups, and the roles within the team are very unstable with team members often rotating in and out of tasks depending on the situation. Every member of the team is trained to have the same set of security-related skills such as weapons training, combat skills, and fine-tuned situation awareness. By the very nature of their work, these teams are expected to encounter unexpected life-or-death situations and to be prepared to engage in enemy combat on a moment's notice. The consequences of their work are extremely high – the success of the Navy groups they are protecting depends on their ability to provide security services successfully.

There are several unique challenges within US Navy security teams that make it difficult to measure their performance accurately. First, the extreme nature of the work setting makes it difficult to observe natural team performance without putting the researcher in danger. Few people want to risk being caught in a fire fight for the sake of research, and the Navy is not exactly willing to put researchers out where they can get in the way of their soldiers either. Second, because of the sheer size of the team, it is nearly impossible to identify the boundaries of the team clearly and to observe every member simultaneously. We observed a team of 75 individuals engaged in a 16-hour overnight field training exercise which included simulated attack sequences such as detecting a "bomb" attached to a visitor to the simulated camp and responding to small attacks to the camp's perimeter. Just trying to identify where the action was taking place at any given time was a challenge. Luckily, the goal of our observation was to get a general understanding of the structure and the nature of the team, so the specific events that occurred were less important than the overall approach the team took to address their work.

The first step toward developing a measurement tool for these teams was to build a literature-based set of team characteristics that we were interested in understanding. From this list of characteristics, an interview protocol was developed that probed team experts in an open-ended manner regarding the structure and nature of their team's interactions (e.g., what tasks does your team engage in? How does your team communicate?) The findings from these interviews were used to develop grounded observational checklists outlining a variety of observable characteristics for the team such as task type, leadership structure, task interdependence levels, team processes, and physical distribution type. These observation checklists were used as tools to gather information regarding the security detachment while observing their training exercise.

As expected, the gathering of information regarding the characteristics and performance of the security detachment was less than straightforward. For example, it was nearly impossible to describe the physical distribution of the team at any given point in time as the physical proximity of the team members differed dramatically depending on what task they were engaging in (i.e., some were co-located together in the base's command tent while others were in small groups patrolling the perimeter), which members of the team were being considered at the time, and whether or not electronic communication was considered. The best conclusion we could come to is that their distribution is generally mixed, which is less than ideal in terms of specificity. In another example, the leadership structure of the team also changed dramatically over time. The team does have a formally defined leader, but in one simulated situation, that leader was "injured" and leadership was shifted immediately to the next qualified team member. Furthermore, when subgroups of the team would go out on patrol, each of those patrol groups would have a temporarily assigned leader who controlled the moment-by-moment movements of the patrol group while still reporting directly to the detachment's formal leader. The point being, the complexity of the security detachment made it very difficult for us to describe the team using the more clear-cut approaches that have been developed in traditional team science settings.

Methods of Team Performance Measurement in Field Settings

As with designing any measurement system, decisions about the content (i.e., what to measure) and the method (i.e., how to measure it) are central to building a team performance measurement system. Questions of when to measure are equally important (Wildman, Bedwell, Salas, & Smith-Jentsch, 2010) and will be addressed later in this chapter. Additionally, the purpose of the measurement system, or answering the question of why (e.g., research questions, validation/ evaluation of an intervention, certification as in aviation and military teams, feed-back during training or continuous improvement) impacts decisions about what, how, and when to measure. We present a brief discussion of content and method below. For more detailed discussions of these and related issues, see Cannon-Bowers and Salas (1997); Salas, Priest, and Burke (2005); Kendall and Salas (2004); and, Rosen, Salas, Lazzara, and Lyons (in press).

Content: what is team performance?

The content of team performance measurement systems should be rooted in a theory of teamwork. The Input-Process-Output (IPO) framework and its recent adaptations (e.g., Ilgen, Hollenbeck, Johnson, & Jundt, 2005; Kozlowski & Klein, 2000; Marks, Matheiu, & Zaccaro, 2001) has proven to be a valuable tool in our work. Input factors (e.g., member and task characteristics) influence the processes teams engage in (e.g., the interaction of members) as well as emergent states (see Marks et al., 2001) to determine team outcomes. Team performance is the sum of individual and team level actions taken to reach a shared goal. It is a process, and not an outcome (Campbell, 1990). However, in naturalistic settings, the team's processes are not the only topic of interest. It is the linking of team performance (processes) to team effectiveness (an evaluation of outcomes) that organizations and researchers are usually interested in. Team effectiveness has been defined as a judgment or evaluation relative to some set standards of the products or outputs of team performance (Salas et al., 2007). This includes evaluations of quality and quantity of team outputs, member satisfaction with team processes, and the degree to which the team's interactions strengthened or weakened the team's ability to continue to work together in the future (Hackman, 1987).

These ideas drive much of our work. From them, we have learned the importance of distinguishing and subsequently drawing connections between team performance and effectiveness, that is, the processes and outcomes of teams (Cannon-Bowers & Salas, 1997; Salas, Burke, & Fowlkes, 2006). Looking at one in isolation from the other can be misleading. There are numerous theories of team performance or components of team performance to choose from when developing a measurement system (for recent reviews, see Kozlowski & Ilgen, 2006). However, these theories are cast in generalizable terms; that is, they describe what team performance looks like in a very abstract way. This is beneficial and a fundamental part of the scientific method, but it requires that descriptions of teamwork from these theoretical frameworks be contextualized – or made specific – for the team(s) of interest (Salas et al., 2007). For example, back-up behavior in a team involves one team member stepping in to provide assistance to another team member having difficulty completing his or her task. This is a general team process behavior linked to good performance (Salas, Sims, & Burke, 2005); however, the legitimacy of need is a critical factor in understanding if the back-up behavior is an effective or ineffective instance of that process (Porter et al., 2003).

For an observer rating team performance, a contextualized understanding of what is happening with a given team is necessary in order to make judgments about the observed process behavior. In the trauma team example describe above, a team member stepping and taking over another's task could be an indicator of good teamwork if the person receiving the help was having difficulty completing their task (e.g., less experienced team members having problems with a difficult intubation will often trade out with other team members with more skill). However, if there was no real need, this can be a very disruptive behavior that undermines trust on a team. Therefore, creating a measurement tool that grounds the generalizable and theoretically based process behaviors with a team's specific context can greatly increase the reliability and validity of the tool (e.g., discriminating between good and bad back-up behavior). To achieve this, a variety of methods can be employed including interviews, focus groups, informal or unstructured observations, and document reviews (for a review of these methods, see Rosen, Salas, Lazzara, & Lyons, in press).

Method: what are the main methods for measuring team performance in the field?

In field settings, observation is still the workhorse of performance measurement systems (Cannon-Bowers & Salas, 1997). Automated performance measurement and communication analysis systems exist (e.g., Dorsey et al., 2009; Foltz & Martin, 2009); however, these are not widely used, and are generally developed for very specific applications. Most researchers and practitioners working in the field are not in a position to spend the time and other resources needed to take advantage of these technologies. Consequently we focus on methods of observation here. Choosing a specific method for an observational protocol always involves tradeoffs. There is no one best universal solution, but there will be solutions that are more effective in specific cases than others. Table 19.3 provides a summary

Table 19.3 Summary of main observational performance measurement methods

Method	Description and examples	Strengths/weaknesses	Citations
Behaviorally anchored rating scales (BARS)	Brief descriptions of effective and ineffective team behaviors are used as anchors associated with each dimension of team performance being measured. *Example:* Rating the quality of a team's mutual support during a trauma resuscitation from 1 (team members did not ask for or provide task assistance) to 5 (team members asked for and provided task assistance as needed).	*Strengths* Captures information about the quality of teamwork behaviors. Concrete descriptions of teamwork process behaviors facilitate interrater reliability. *Weaknesses* Temporal information can be lost as ratings are summated across time.	Kendall and Salas (2004)
Behavioral observation scales (BOS)	Likert-type scales are used to rate the frequency of team process behaviors. *Example:* Rating the frequency of closed-loop communication in a trauma case on a scale from 1 (never) to 5 (always).	*Strengths* Captures information about the frequency of teamwork behaviors. *Weaknesses* While temporal information is captured, it is summative in nature and does not capture the sequence of behaviors. Relies on human capacity of frequency estimation which can be flawed.	Kendall and Salas (2004)

Table 19.3 (*Cont'd*)

Method	Description and examples	Strengths/weaknesses	Citations
Behavioral markers/ event-based methods	Behavioral marker measurement systems use descriptions of team process behaviors linked to trigger events (i.e., task or environmental changes requiring a team response). *Example:* A behavioral marker of leadership could be a trauma team leader verbalizing a clear plan of care for the patient to all team members after a secondary survey has been completed.	*Strengths* Behavioral marker and event-based methods are capable of capturing performance over time (e.g., how teams respond to changes in their environment). Interrater reliability can be easier to develop and maintain than methods requiring more abstract ratings. *Weaknesses* Event-based methods are most useful in simulations where the events can be controlled.	Flin and Martin (2001), Fowlkes, Dwyer, Oser, and Salas (1998), Rosen et al. (2008)

of the main types of observational methods and their associated strengths and weaknesses. We have found that managing these tradeoffs is the key to developing good measurement tools.

In addition to the scoring method and content, it is critical that the measurement system be implemented in a systematic way. This involves training raters to use the structure protocols, assessing interrater reliability, and developing supporting materials (e.g., manuals and scoring guides). Additionally, it has often been noted that it takes a team to observe a team. Because of the complexities of team performance, one person will not likely be able to capture all of what is happening. Dividing the observational workload is a key strategy for success. In the following section, we describe some of the main challenges to implementing the methods described above.

Challenges

The preceding discussion has hopefully made salient both the importance and challenging nature of team performance measurement in the wild. In this section, we provide an overview of some of the tough problems researchers have to address when developing a team performance measurement system.

Some aspects of team performance are not directly observable

As described above, theoretical models of teamwork are most commonly built around IPO frameworks. Team performance is the process component of these frameworks. It involves the interdependent actions the team members make to meet its goals. It has been noted that understanding aspects of team performance is easier than individual performance because much of the team's work is external and observable (in comparison to the internal cognition involved in individual performance; Cooke, Salas, Kiekel, & Bell, 2004). While this is very true, it is not always the case that a full understanding of a team's performance can be developed strictly from observable processes. Implicit group processes are critical to performance outcomes in many situations (Entin & Serfaty, 1999; MacMillan, Entin, & Serfaty, 2004). Expert team performance is often as much about what the team members *do not* have to communicate explicitly as it is about observable processes (Salas, Rosen, Burke, Goodwin, & Fiore, 2006). A well-executed blind pass in basketball is the perfect example of implicit coordination. One player is able to pass to another in the absence of any communication.

To complicate the matter further, teams will develop different coordination strategies (i.e., mixes of implicit and explicit coordination) based on differences in input variables such as team characteristics (e.g., distribution), technology in use, and task and organizational characteristics (Espinosa, Lerch, & Kraut, 2004). Consequently, identifying the set of coordination behaviors representing 'good' team performance (i.e., process behaviors linked to effective outcomes) is problematic. There are no 'one size fits all' team performance measurement systems, out of the box, or off the shelf solutions. As observation-based methods are still the primary means of measuring team performance in the wild, these balances between implicit and explicit coordination strategies pose a major challenge. The best solution for a given situation usually involves a mix of methods, with teamwork behaviors captured through observation and unobservable aspects of performance captured through other means such as self-report. This is the solution we adopted in a study of operating room (OR) teams. Team knowledge at attitudes where capture via survey at different points in time (some measures taking after each operation), and behaviors were observed by external raters.

Identifying boundaries

Knowing who is on the team is critical for focusing observation sessions. Many times, however, defining the boundaries of team membership is not as simple as it sounds. Disentangling teams from their surroundings or mapping out the interdependencies of members can prove quite challenging. If an organization is represented as a network with people as nodes and task interdependencies as links, the problem usually becomes clear. Finding where the team begins and ends is difficult, and with any densely connected network, drawing boundaries is somewhat arbitrary.

For example, even in something as tightly constrained as an OR, the boundaries of team membership can become blurred. Within the actual room during procedures, there are usually groups of people performing the procedure (i.e., the surgeon, assistant, surgical technician), managing the patients airway and sedation (i.e., anesthesiologist, nurse anesthetist), and a person managing the overall work-flow (i.e., a scrub nurse documenting and managing). This can be viewed as one complex team; however, the interdependencies do not stop with these groups of people. There are several other groups of staff tightly coupled to the immediate OR team, including support staff involved in room turnover in between procedures (i.e., room cleaning and sterilization; room turnover is a tightly monitored metric of efficiency in most ORs), surgical supply personnel responsible for stocking a room with the necessary equipment for a given proce-dure, and OR department administration responsible for scheduling and ensuring appropriate resources are available. While none of these groups of people are present during an actual surgery, their work can directly impact the work of the OR team.

The same difficulty applies to large teams such as the US Navy security detach-ment. This group of 70 or more members is formally identified as a unit and trains together as an intact group, but much of the work they are engaging in is seg-mented into multiple smaller units. Within each perimeter patrol team, two or three team members are tightly coupled and act independently until there is an event to report back to the command team, which is co-located and tightly cou-pled within the central command center in the base. These subgroups can be seen as parts of a larger complex team or as interconnected teams of their own – the divisions are quite subjective.

Along these lines, it has been noted that not all team members contribute equally to the team's processes and outcomes (Humphrey, Morgeson, & Mannor, 2009). Some members are more central than others to performance outcomes, and consequently should be represented more in the measurement of processes. In order to deal with this issue, careful attention needs to be paid to the purpose of measurement. Clearly articulating a purpose for measurement is the logical first step, but one that is usually not given due attention. A measurement system cannot capture everything. The focus – including the team members targeted for measurement – is determined by the questions being asked.

Changes over time

All teams, regardless of differences such as type, size, or composition, develop, perform, and change over time. Therefore, it can be challenging to capture the true characteristics or dynamics of a team when observing or measuring for only a short duration. For example, even if a team is observed for an entire perform-ance episode, that particular performance episode may not be representative of the team's overall performance. They may have been influenced by the observer's presence and driven to perform at their maximum level rather than their typical level, or something about that particular performance episode could have differed drastically from the average performance episode (e.g., there was a rare change in the environment).

In order to get a true understanding of a team's average performance, measurement must span over a significant amount of time, which can be difficult if not impossible in a practical sense. Furthermore, team composition and structure characteristics often change over time as well. Some team members leave and new ones come in and have to be socialized and trained, creating changing social dynamics and coordination issues that can influence team dynamics. Changing environments and task requirements cause the team to change aspects such as communication and leadership structure in response. These changes can become very difficult to capture in the field when performance is sampled at a 'low frame rate' (i.e., small observation periods with large gaps in between). As described above, we usually attempt to uncover some type of temporal structure to a team's work (e.g., phases of performance, or critical events or tasks). For example, when observing the Navy security team engaged in the training exercise, we discovered that when a security threat occurred, the leadership structure would shift from more formal, designated leadership to a task-based leadership in which team members who have the most expertise in an area took the lead to solve the threat. Once the threat was handled, the leadership structure returned to a formal external leader. This understanding of the temporal structure helps to anchor assessments of teamwork across time and create a profile or pattern of performance as opposed to a single snapshot.

Balancing methodological rigor and practicalities

The reliability and validity of the measurement tools used in the field is of utmost concern. With poorly designed or implemented measurement systems, data collections are at best a waste of time in that the data are unusable and at worst actually influence answers to research questions or inform organizational decisions based on biased or otherwise compromised data (Brannick & Prince, 1997). In field research, especially in applied communities, there are many constraints and pressures threatening to undermine the ideal of performance measurement system design and implementation. For example, there frequently will not be open-ended opportunities to perform observations. Access to teams in field settings is almost always limited. Consequently, all of the time necessary for the traditional process of iterating the development of tools and evaluating the psychometric properties of an observation protocol in context will not usually be available. Obtaining the necessary reliability and validity evidence involves managing an imperfect situation and finding creative ways to meet the constraints inevitably placed upon the field researcher. Developing 'quick start' observer training using prerecorded videos of teams performing to establish interrater reliability initially, and ongoing monitoring of rater drift are strategies we have found to be invaluable.

What Works: Strategies for Success

As discussed previously, developing a team performance measurement system for field settings always involves making decisions about which methods to use, what content to focus on, and when to collect the data. All of these decisions are bound by the constraints of the field and developing a measurement system involves balancing the tradeoffs of different approaches with the uniqueness of the situation. In this section, we provide several guiding strategies we follow when entering into a new domain. These strategies are summarized in Table 19.4.

Table 19.4 Summary of strategies for success

What works?	*Tips and considerations*
1. Start with a clear understanding of the why, what, and how of your measurement	What purpose will the measurement data serve in the end? What aspects of performance need to be captured? What measurement method is best suited for that content? What are the practical constraints on performance measurement?
2. Capturing the dynamics of team dynamics … measure team performance over time	What aspects of team structure and composition need to be measured over time? What aspects of performance are inherently time-based?
3. Get the most data in the least amount of time: use structured protocols	Take the time to plan your measurement approach before you begin Make measurement tools as detailed and clear as possible to maximize efficiency Use structured protocols to prioritize measurement goals in case of unexpected changes
4. Make your measurement diagnostic: capture performance at multiple levels	Remember that measurement should go beyond description: it should evaluate and diagnose the causes of performance as well Link processes to outcomes in order to uncover the underlying causes of performance Link multiple levels to uncover how individual performance influences team-level performance
5. Teams don't perform in a vacuum: capture contextual influences to get the big picture	Consider top-down influences on team performance: organizational and environmental factors Use team classification schemes to identify potential contextual factors and measure those influences in order to take into account top-down influences

Begin with a clear understanding of the why, what, and how of the measurement

It is critical to have a clear purpose in mind when undertaking any team performance measurement procedure. Like good theory, the purpose drives the entire
measurement process. The purpose of performance measurement determines a
variety of decisions regarding the measurement approach such as whether single
or multiple measures are necessary, the processes and outcomes to be measured,
and how those constructs will be captured.

When designing a measurement system, you should always be able to answer
the following question: what is the intended outcome of the measurement? In
other words, what purpose will the performance measurement data serve in a
practical sense? For example, in our trauma team example described above, the
data capture was intended to drive decisions about the type of feedback the team
needed as well as whether or not they need some type of team training. In the
Navy security team example, the data were aimed at describing the nature of the
teams in a specific enough manner to match team member knowledge, skills,
and abilities to the teams for selection and training purposes. More generally, performance measurement data may be used as part of a training needs analysis to
develop training for the teams, as evaluative data aimed at providing the team
members with feedback (e.g., Pritchard, Youngcourt, Philo, McMonagle, & David,
2007) and making human resource decisions or programmatic decisions (e.g.,
Tannenbaum, 2006), or more basically as scientific research data aimed at a better
understanding of this particular team in the field.

Answering the *why* question clearly and early in the measurement design process
will help to determine the answer to the next critical question: what specific content of team dynamics will be measured? As described above, this will involve things
such as team performance behaviors and team effectiveness outcomes. We have
found that being as concrete and specific about the content of the measurement
tool is almost always a productive endeavor. For example, we were only able to judge
the quality of the trauma team's communication when we had a detailed mapping
of what they should be communicating and when the communication should occur
(e.g., when a leader needs to verbalize a clear plan of care for the patient). If we
simply tried to rate 'team communication' on a scale from 1 to 5 (highly ineffective
to highly effective), we would not have been able to do that reliably. We needed to
be very specific about what good and bad communications were in order to
rate them. It is important to pinpoint what aspects of team performance are to be
captured before beginning a measurement procedure, as the content of the measurement will dictate the answer to the third critical consideration: which measurement tool or approach is most appropriate for any given team dynamic construct?

Different measurement approaches are more or less appropriate for capturing different aspects of performance such as teamwork-related behaviors and
taskwork-related behaviors (Cannon-Bowers, Burns, Salas, & Pruitt, 1998).

For example, if the purpose of the measurement is to develop training to improve the communication practices within a team (i.e., a teamwork behavior), then the team's existing communication patterns would be a critical component of performance to capture. In this situation, the measurement is aimed at training of communication skills, and therefore using audio-recording equipment to capture communication over time that can be analyzed using communication coding schemes later may be the most appropriate approach.

Conversely, if the purpose of performance measurement is to evaluate the team's overall effectiveness and implement a reward system for achieving the team's primary goal (i.e., a taskwork behavior), then the content of the measurement may only need to capture the outcomes of the team's performance considered important by the stakeholders (e.g., final sales, number of products completed). In a more basic research-oriented situation, the purpose of measurement may be to capture a variety of theoretically driven antecedents, processes, and consequences related to team performance. This purpose would likely require the measurement system to capture multiple aspects of team performance simultaneously (e.g., cohesion, communication, coordination, overall effectiveness), which may require multiple measurement techniques or approaches.

Finally, it is important to consider the practical constraints on performance measurement in the field early in the decision process. Specifically, regardless of the purpose of your measurement and the corresponding ideal measurement method, unless you have the resources available to proceed with the ideal method, a less ideal path may be the only available option. Perhaps you do not have access to enough observers to perform any direct observational methods, or you need results immediately and therefore do not have time to transcribe and code communication data. In this case, the performance measurement system should be designed to capture the most important aspects of the team's performance with the most robust method that the practical constraints will allow. The key, however, is to identify all practical constraints early on in the performance measurement system design process in order to avoid delays and setbacks once measurement has started.

Frequently, when measuring team performance in the wild, the purpose on some level will be to improve that performance. Salas and colleagues (2009) have proposed a set of best practices in the management of team performance organized around the adaptive, leadership, management, and technical capacities underlying organizational effectiveness (Letts, Ryan, & Grossman, 1998). As detailed in Table 19.5, these best practices can be used to help focus the development of a team performance measurement system focused on increasing effectiveness.

Capturing the dynamics of team dynamics ... measure team performance over time

As the phrase "team dynamics" implies, a static snapshot of a team is usually insufficient to generate a meaningful understanding of a team. The nature and quality

Table 19.5 Summary of best practices for team performance management (from Salas, Weaver, Rosen, & Smith-Jentsch, 2009)

Best practice	Tips	Selected references
Adaptive capacity		
1. Build flexible and adaptable team players	Build mutual performance monitoring and back-up behavior skills in team members using cross training and other methods. Build mutual trust among team members.	Burke, Fiore, and Salas (2003), Porter et al. (2003), Salas, Sims, and Burke, (2005)
2. Build a big play book – encourage a large team-task strategy repertoire	Provide a safe environment to practice new performance strategies (e.g., use simulation-based training).	Orasanu (1990), Salas, Priest, Wilson, and Burke (2006)
3. Create teams that know themselves and their work environment	Team cue recognition training. Perceptual contrast training. Build team communication skills (information exchange, closed-loop communication).	Salas, Cannon-Bowers, Fiore, and Stout (2001), Wilson, Burke, Priest, and Salas (2005)
4. Build teams that can tell when the usual answer isn't the right answer	Develop team planning skills. Use guided error training to promote an understanding of when the routine solution is not the appropriate solution.	Lorenzet, Salas, and Tannenbaum (2006)
5. Develop self-learning teams – train teams to help themselves	Team self-correction training; team leader debrief skills. Foster a team learning orientation, psychological safety.	Bunderson and Sutcliffe (2003), Edmondson (1999), Smith-Jentsch et al. (1998)
6. Don't let the weakest link have the strongest voice – build teams that take advantage of their resources	Develop a strong team orientation in team members. Promote assertiveness. Build diversity of expertise and transactive memory.	Eby and Dobbins (1997), Hollenbeck, Sego, Ilgen, and Major (1997)
Leadership capacity		
7. Articulate and cultivate a shared vision which incorporates both internal and external clients	Ask how the team will make a difference for internal and external clients. Establish measurable indicators of team success. Determine what team hopes to accomplish in its wildest dreams.	Briner, Hastings, and Geddes (1996), Christenson and Walker (2004), Williams and Laugani (1999)

Table 19.5 (*Cont'd*)

Best practice	Tips	Selected references
	Adaptive capacity	
8. Create goals the team can grow with: build hierarchically aligned goals with malleability and flexibility at both the individual and team level	Include all team members in goal generation. Set team and individual level goals which are aligned with upper level goals. Allow overall goals to have wiggle room and build flexibility into subgoals. Ensure that there are multiple strategies to reach the goal.	Getz and Rainey (2001), Locke and Brian (1967)
9. Build motivation into the performance management process – make clear connections between actions, evaluations, and outcomes	Team members should be encouraged and rewarded for praising colleague accomplishments and being supportive during setbacks. Only utilize group-level incentives and rewards for work performance. Create opportunities for taking major responsibility for some elements of the task are available for each member. Make the connections between actions, results, evaluations, and outcomes clear.	Oser, McCallum, Salas, and Morgan (1989), Pritchard and Ashwood (2008), Swezy and Salas (1992)
10. Team leaders must champion coordination, communication, and cooperation	Build the team to reflect the various forms of expertise required by the tasks at hand. Foster the use of external sources (i.e., temporary members, consultant team members) if the expertise is not inherent in the team. Divide tasks to suit individual expertise, but do allow opportunities for growth. Remember that leader does not equal expert, defer to those with the expertise (see Best Practice # 5)	Dyer (1984), Salas, Wilson, Murphy, King, and Salisbury (in press), Zalesney, Salas, and Prince (1995)
11. Understand the "why": examine both failures and successes during debriefs	Review instances of both effective and ineffective behavior during feedback sessions. Recognize failures as learning opportunities.	Ellis and Davidi (2005), Zakay, Ellis, and Shevalsky (2004)

Table 19.5 (*Cont'd*)

Best practice	Tips	Selected references
	Management capacity	
12. Clearly define what to measure: Develop and maintain a systematic and organized representation of performance	Develop a document or set of documents explicitly linking KSAs to performance metrics, feedback, and outcomes (e.g., reinforcement, promotion, pay). The purpose of measurement should drive measure development.	Bartram (2005), Kurtz and Bartram (2002), Stevens and Campion (1994)
13. Uncover the 'why' of performance: develop measures which are diagnostic of performance	Foster an understanding of why performance was effective or ineffective. Incorporate measures which include outcomes and processes. The purpose of measurement should drive development. Avoid 'easy' measures which miss large amounts of performance related information. Measure performance from multiple perspectives. Solicit input from team members (e.g., using 360° feedback). Develop a discipline of pre-brief–performance–debrief.	Cannon-Bowers and Salas (1997)
14. Measure typical performance continuously	Measure performance over time. Choose to measure what employees "will do." Automate as much of the performance monitoring process as possible. Provide ongoing, diagnostic feedback which identifies and removes roadblocks to effective performance.	Klehe and Anderson (2007), Sackett, Zedeck, and Folgi (1988)
	Technical capacity	
15. Include teamwork competencies in formal performance evaluations	Offer both team and individual level reinforcement (both formal and informal)	Murphy and Cleveland (1995), Salas, Kosarzycki, Tannenbaum, and Carnegie (2005)

Table 19.5 (*Cont'd*)

Best practice	Tips	Selected references
	Technical capacity	
16. Have a plan for integrating new team members, and execute it	Clearly define teamwork and taskwork competencies needed for effective performance and ensure new team members possess these KSAs.	Cannon-Bowers and Salas (1997), Levine and Choi (2004)
17. Assess and foster shared mental models	Measure and provide feedback (cue–strategy associations). Cross-training, interpositional knowledge training. Encourage a culture of learning. Develop a strong sense of 'collective,' trust, teamness and confidence.	Blickensderfer, Cannon-Bowers, and Salas (1998), Cannon-Bowers, Salas, and Converse (1993), Cooke, Gorman, Duran, and Taylor (2007), Mohammed and Dumville (2001)
18. Develop or select for individual personal discipline and organizational skills	Include these skills in KSA and competency definition. Ensure modes of distributed communication, information systems, and access to necessary organizational materials remotely.	Ancona and Caldwell (2007)
19. Communicate the "big picture:" facilitate a global awareness of competing goals and deadlines of all teams	Coordinate meetings of team leaders to discuss multiple deadlines. Create global Gantt chart with real-time updates if possible.	Mortensen, Woolley, and O'Leary (2007)
20. Maturity counts – recognize that a multiteam framework works best for mature projects	Apply MTM to mature teams or projects. Have at least one member 100% dedicated to a single team during the kickoff period to ensure continuity.	Mortensen, Woolley, and O'Leary (2007)
21. Foster trust – cultivate a culture of information sharing	Foster information sharing. Cultivate a culture of error reporting and feedback, which focuses on learning from mistakes, not punishment.	Salas, Sims, and Burke (2005), Webber (2002)

KSA = Knowledge, Skills, and Attitudes; MTM = Multi-team Management.

of a team's performance can vary greatly at different phases or points in their performance cycle. The structure of the team may change over time as well (e.g., leadership structure, communication structure) or the composition of the team may change as new team members replace old members leaving. Some teams may vary more over time than others, but all teams encounter temporal factors that influence their performance, such as changing deadlines and time pressure.

Furthermore, some aspects of team dynamics, such as coordination and entrainment processes, are inherently temporal in that they are focused on the synchronization and timing of the team's actions. Marks, Mathieu, and Zaccaro (2001) suggested that teams cycle through action and transition phases throughout their life as a team. In other words, teams go through a series of input–process–output episodes, some episodes focused on planning and preparation activities (i.e., transition phases), and others focused on actually enacting the previously created plans (i.e., action phases). This framework suggests that if team performance measurement was to only capture a snapshot of team performance, it could only capture one of these two phases. In order to capture the pattern of and interaction between action and transition cycles in a team, it is important to measure their performance over time. Additionally, team adaptation, or the process of adjusting and changing functioning over time in response to dynamic environmental cues (Burke, Stagl, Salas, Pierce, & Kendall, 2006), inherently cannot be measured at one point in time.

Get the most data in the least amount of time: use structured protocols

When trying to capture team dynamics in the wild, it can be tempting simply to gather informal observations of performance, conduct a few informal interviews, and consider the job done. However, we have found that an upfront investment is required to ensure a high-quality performance measurement system (see also Salas, Burke, & Fowlkes, 2006). Specifically, a good performance measurement system cannot be developed haphazardly or at the last minute, and informal observations are not enough. The design of any measurement tool requires ample time, labor, and expertise in order to ensure that the protocol is as structured, straightforward, and intuitive as possible. In other words, when designing the tools for performance measurement, such as researcher observation protocols or communication coding schemes, these tools should provide a detailed, uniform template that ensures each observer or coder captures all desired aspects of performance in the same way, and that interpretations are made in a consistent manner. This ensures that the data captured will be as useful and usable as possible, and the process of performance measurement will be efficient and precise. If measurement approaches such as observations or communication analysis are left too vague or open to an individual researcher's whim, the data gathered across sources will not be consistent enough to combine in any meaningful way, and data collection may take more time than necessary, resulting in wasted resources. Therefore, the more clearly the measurement protocol describes to the observer or coder (a) what dimensions of performance to capture and (b) how exactly to record and interpret these data, the better. For example, in the Navy security team observation, the protocol was designed in a relatively simple, multiple-choice structure (e.g., leadership structure is hierarchical, shared, emergent, or other) with very detailed descriptions accompanying each choice to aid the rater in making accurate judgments.

Another advantage to structuring performance measurement protocols is the prioritization of measurement goals. More specifically, if the performance measurement system is structured in such a way that the most critical aspects of the team's dynamics are captured first, and then other "wish list" items are collected as opportunity allows, then when problems arise or constraints appear (as is often the case in the field), the measurement approach can be adjusted as appropriate while retaining the most critical aspects of performance. In the ideal situation, all aspects of performance would be captured. However, in the event that the performance episode being observed is unexpectedly cut short, at the very least the observer should capture the more important aspects of performance as dictated by the prioritization. Thus, the structuring of performance measurement protocols can ensure that captured data will still be usable even when things do not go quite as planned.

Make your measurement diagnostic: capture performance at multiple levels

Performance measurement is always a means to an end. The data are destined for some purpose ranging from improving understanding to designing training or management interventions. Regardless of the specific purpose, all performance measurement systems should serve three core purposes: describing, evaluating, and diagnosing the team's performance. Description of team performance is necessary, but not sufficient for useful performance measurement data. Without evaluating or diagnosing the causes underlying performance outcomes, no measurement system can be used to develop training, serve as an assessment tool, or truly inform the science of teams.

Diagnosing the causes of effective and ineffective performance is perhaps the most important component in the performance measurement process because without an understanding of the causes underlying performance, the development of feedback and training becomes difficult and suboptimal, if not impossible. Identifying deficiencies in performance is not very useful unless you can also identify the underlying causal mechanisms to change in order to rectify those deficiencies. Diagnosing the underlying causes of effective and ineffective performance is the only way performance measurement can be used to manage and improve performance. The utility of linking specific performance outcomes to specific causal mechanisms in order to achieve effective performance measurement has been called to attention by other organizational researchers (e.g., Ittner & Larcker, 2003).

In order for any performance measurement system to provide the most accurate description, evaluation, and diagnosis of performance, it should take an integrative, multilevel approach to measurement. Specifically in terms of team performance measurement, this means measurement should capture both individual and team level processes and outcomes (Cannon-Bowers & Salas, 1997). Process measures are focused on strategies and procedures used to accomplish a task, while outcome measures are focused on quantifying the end result of those processes. Outcome measures alone are not diagnostic of performance as the process measures are what provide an explanation of the underlying causes. Furthermore, team-level measures must be supplemented with individual-level measures as individual behavior can influence team-level processes and outcomes. This position has been also been advocated quite strongly throughout the team literature (e.g., Salas, Burke, Fowlkes, & Priest, 2003). In order to diagnose and manage team performance accurately, both individual- and team-level processes and outcomes must be captured, and the linkages between them must be delineated.

Teams don't perform in a vacuum: capture contextual influences to get the big picture

In the previous section, the influence of individual-level processes and outcomes on team performance was discussed, with an emphasis on how lower-level performance can influence performance in a bottom-up direction. However, there are also influences that can impact team performance from a top-down direction. We cannot fully understand the dynamics of various teams without capturing how the surrounding context impact processes and performance. Additionally, not all teams operate in the same environment, meaning the way in which environmental factors influence team processes and outcomes differs across teams. In other words, the differing impact of contextual factors may cause different teams to engage in extremely different sets of processes. Thus, it is integral that performance measurement systems capture the differing impact of environmental context on team dynamics for each individual measurement situation.

A recent review of the team classification literature delineated seven underlying contextual dimensions critical to the classification of teams: (1) fundamental work cycle; (2) physical ability requirements; (3) temporal duration; (4) task structure; (5) active resistance; (6) hardware dependence; and (7) health risk (for full descriptions, see Devine, 2002). For example, military teams often perform under conditions of gunfire and other potentially life-threatening occurrences (i.e., health risk). This contextual influence would quite dramatically alter team processes and performance (e.g., stress, handling injuries) and therefore should be captured as part of the performance measurement system in order to take these effects into account. Organizational and environmental variables such as those described by Devine (2002) can have a very real impact on the processes and outcomes of team performance, and should be included in any performance measurement system.

Concluding Remarks

Field settings pose major challenges for researchers and practitioners seeking to understand and improve team functioning. However, to answer the important questions in the science of teams and to guide application, an increasingly more sophisticated understanding of team dynamics in the wild must be developed. We hope this chapter has helped to bring to light some of the fundamental issues in capturing team performance in what is frequently a messy or difficult environment for measurement. The strategies offered are only a start and it is our hope that others continue to add to the dialogue and generate new approaches, techniques, tools, and methods to augment the current state of the science.

Acknowledgment

This work was supported by the Navy Personnel Research, Studies and Technology Department under the auspices of the US Army Research Office Scientific Services Program administered by Battelle (Contract No. W911NF-07-D-001, TCN 09059). The views presented in this paper are those of the authors are do not represent the views of the Navy Personnel Research, Studies and Technology Department or the U.S. Army Research Office. At the time of writing this chapter, Michael A. Rosen and Jessica Wildman were graduate student at UCF. Michael Rosen is now an Assistant Professor at the Armstrong Institute for Patient Safety and Quality, and the Department of Anesthesiology and Critical Care Medicine, The Johns Hopkins University School of Medicine (email: mrosen44@jhmi.edu). Jessica Wildman is now an Assistant Professor in the College of Psychology and Liberal Arts, Florida Institute of Technology (jwildman@fit.edu)

References

Abbott, J. B., Boyd, N. G., & Miles, G. (2006). Does type of team matter? An investigation of the relationships between job characteristics and outcomes with a team-based environment. *Journal of Social Psychology, 146*, 485–507.

Ancona, D. G., & Caldwell, D. (2007). Improving the performance of new product teams. *Research-Technology Management, 50*(5), 37–43.

Barry, D. (1991). Managing the bossless team: Lessons in distributed leadership. *Organizational Dynamics, 20*, 31–47.

Bartram, T. (2005). Small firms, big ideas: The adoption of human resource management in Australian small firms. *Asia Pacific Journal of Human Resources, 43*(1), 137–154.

Bell, B. S., & Kozlowski, S. W. J. (2002) A typology of virtual teams: Implications for effective leadership. *Group and Organization Management, 27*(1), 14–49.

Blickensderfer, E., Cannon-Bowers, J. A., & Salas, E. (1998). Cross training and team performance. In J. A. Cannon-Bowers & E. Salas (Eds.), *Making decisions under stress: Implications for individual and team training* (pp. 299–311). Washington, DC: American Psychological Association.

Brannick, M. & Prince, C. (1997). An overview of team performance measurement. In M. Brannick, E. Saas & C. Prince (Eds.) *Team performance assessment and measurement: Theory, methods, and applications* (pp. 3–16). Mahwah, NJ: Lawrence Erlbaum Associates.

Briner, W. Hastings, C. & Geddes, M. (1996). *Project leadership* (2nd ed.). Gower Publishing Company.

Burke, C. S., Stagl, K. C., Salas, E., Pierce, L., & Kendall, D. L. (2006). Understanding team adaptation: A conceptual analysis and model. *Journal of Applied Psychology, 91*, 1189–1207.

Bunderson, J. S. & Sutcliffe, K. M. (2003). Management team learning orientation and business unit performance. *Journal of Applied Psychology, 88*(3), 552–560

Burke, C. S., Fiore, S. M., & Salas, E. (2003). The role of shared cognition in enabling shared leadership and team adaptability. In J Conger & C. Pearce (Eds.), *Shared leadership: Reframing the hows and whys of leadership* (pp. 103–122). London: Sage Publishers.

Campbell, D. J. (1988). Task complexity: A review and analysis. *Academy of Management Journal, 13*(1), 40–52.

Campbell, J. P. (1990). Modeling the performance prediction problem in Industrial and organizational psychology. In M. D. Dunette & L. M. Hough (Eds.), *Handbook of industrial and organizational psychology*. Palo Alto, CA: Consulting Psychologists Press.

Cannon-Bowers, J. A., Burns, J. J., Salas, E, & Pruitt, J. S. (1998). Advanced technology in decision-making training. In J. A. Cannon-Bowers & E. Salas (Eds.), *Making decisions under stress: Implications for individual and team training* (pp. 365–374). Washington, DC: APA Press.

Cannon-Bowers, J. A. & Salas E. (1997). A framework for developing team performance measures in training. In M. T. Brannick, E. Salas, & C. Prince (Eds.), *Team performance assessment and measurement: Theory, methods, and applications* (pp.45–62). Mahwah, NJ: Lawrence Erlbaum Associates.

Cannon-Bowers, J. A., Salas, E., & Converse, S. A. (1993). Shared mental models in expert decision-making teams. In N. J. Castellan (Ed.), *Current issues in individual and group decision making* (pp. 221–246). Hillsdale, NJ: Erlbaum.

Cannon-Bowers, J. A., Salas, E., & Pruitt, J. S. (1996). Establishing the boundaries of a paradigm for decision-making research. *Human Factors, 38*(2), 193–205.

Christenson, D. & Walker, D. H. T. (2004). Understanding the role of "vision" in project success. *Engineering Management Review, 32*(4), 57–73.

Cohen, S. G. & Bailey, D. E. (1997). What makes teams work: Group effectiveness research from the shop floor to the executive suite. *Journal of Mangement, 23*(3), 239–290.

Cooke, N. J., Gorman, J. C., Duran, J. L., & Taylor, A. R. (2007). Team cognition in experienced command-and-control teams. *Journal of Experimental Psychology: Applied, 13*(3), 146–157.

Cooke, N. J., Salas, E., Kiekel, P. A., & Bell, B. (2004). Advances in measuring team cognition. In E. Salas & S. M. Fiore (Eds.), *Team cognition: Understanding the factors that drive process and performance* (pp. 83–106). Washington, DC: American Psychological Association.

Devine, D. J. (2002). A review and integration of classification systems relevant to teams in organizations. *Group Dynamics: Theory, Research, and Practice, 6*(4), 291–310.

Dorsey, D., Russell, S., Keil, C., Campbell, G., Van Buskirk, W., & Schuck, P. (2009). Measuring teams in action: Automated performance measurement and feedback in simulation-based training. In E. Salas, G. F. Goodwin & C. S. Burke (Eds.), *Team effectiveness in complex organizations: Cross-disciplinary perspectives and approaches* (pp. 351–381). New York: Routledge.

Driskell, J. E., Salas, E. & Hogan, R. (1987). *A taxonomy for composing effective naval teams* (Technical Report Number 87-002). Orlando, FL: US Naval Training Systems Center Technical Reports.

Duncan, K. (1972). Strategies for analysis of the task. In J. Hartley (Ed.), *Strategies for programmed instruction: An educational technology* (pp. 19–81). London: Butterworths.

Dyer, J. L. (1984). Team research and team training: A state of the art review. In F. A. Muckler (Ed.), *Human factors review* (pp. 285–323). Santa Monica: Human Factors Society.

Eby, L. T. & Dobbins, G. H. (1997). Collectivistic orientation in teams: An individual and group-level analysis. *Journal of Organizational Behavior, 18*(3), 275–295.

Edmondson, A. (1999). Psychological safety and learning behavior in work teams. *Administrative Science Quarterly, 44*(2), 350–383.

Entin, E. E., & Serfaty, D. (1999). Adaptive team coordination. *Human Factors, 41*(2), 312–325.

Ellis, S., & Davidi, I. (2005). After-event reviews: Drawing lessons from successful and failed experience. *Journal of Applied Psychology, 90*(5), 857–871.

Erez, A., LePine, J. A., & Elms, H. (2002). Effects of rotated leadership and peer evaluation on the functioning and effectiveness of self-managed teams: A quasi-experiment. *Personnel Psychology, 55*, 929–948.

Espinosa, J. A., Lerch, F. J., & Kraut, R. E. (2004). Explicit versus implicit coordination mechanisms and task dependencies: One size does not fit all. In E. Salas & S. M. Fiore (Eds.), *Team cognition: Understanding the factors that drive process and performance* (pp. 107–129). Washington, DC: American Psychological Association.

Flin, R., & Martin, L. (2001). Behavioral markers for crew resource management: A review of current practice. *International Journal of Aviation Psychology, 11*(1), 95–118.

Foltz, P. W., & Martin, M. J. (2009). Automated communication analysis of teams. In E. Salas, G. F. Goodwin & C. S. Burke (Eds.), *Team effectiveness in complex organizations: Cross-disciplinary perspectives and approaches* (pp. 411–431). New York: Routledge.

Fowlkes, J. E., Dwyer, D. J., Oser, R. L., & Salas, E. (1998). Event-based approach to training (EBAT). *The International Journal of Aviation Psychology, 8*(3), 209–221.

Getz, G. E., & Rainey, D. W. (2001). Flexible short-term goals and basketball shooting performance. *Journal of Sport Behavior, 24*.

Gronn, P. (2002). Distributed leadership as a unit of analysis. *Leadership Quarterly, 13*, 423–451.

Hackman, J. R. (1987). The design of work teams. In J. Lorsch (Ed.), *Handbook of organizational behavior* (pp. 315–342). New York: Prentice Hall.

Harris, M., & Raviv, A. (2002). Organization design. *Management Science, 48*, 852–865.

Hollenbeck, J., Sego, D., Ilgen, D., & Major, D. (1997). Team decision-making accuracy under difficult conditions: Construct validation of potential manipulations using TIDE2 simulation. *Team performance assessment and measurement: Theory, methods, and applications* (pp. 111–136). Mahwah, NJ: Lawrence Erlbaum Associates Publishers.

Hough, J. R., & White, M. A. (2004). Scanning actions and environmental dynamism: Gathering information for strategic decision making. *Management Decision, 42*, 781–793.

Humphrey, S. E., Morgeson, F. P., & Mannor, M. J. (2009). Developing a theory of the strategic core of teams: A role composition model of team performance. *Journal of Applied Psychology, 94*(1), 48–61.

Ilgen, D. R., Hollenbeck, J. R., Johnson, M., & Jundt, D. (2005). Teams in organizations: From input-process-output models to IMOI models. *Annual Review of Psychology, 56*, 517–543.

Ittner, C. D., & Larcker, D. F. (2003). Coming up short on nonfinancial performance measurement. *Harvard Business Review*, 88–95.

Jehn, K. A. (1994). Enhancing effectiveness: An investigation of advantages and disadvantages of value-based intragroup conflict. *Journal of Conflict Management, 5*(3), 223–238.

Kankanhalli, A., Tan, B. C. Y., & Wei, K. (2006). Conflict and performance in global virtual teams. *Journal of Management Information Systems, 23,* 237–274.

Kendall, D. L., & Salas, E. (2004). Measuring team performance: Review of current methods and consideration of future needs. In J. W. Ness, Tepe, V., and Ritzer, D. (Ed.), *The science and simulation of human performance* (pp. 307–326). Boston: Elsevier.

Kirkman, B., & Mathieu, J. (2005). The dimensions and antecedents of team virtuality. *Journal of Management, 31,* 700–718.

Klehe, U., & Anderson, N. (2007). Working hard and working smart: Motivation and ability during typical and maximum performance. *Journal of Applied Psychology, 92*(4), 978–992.

Klein, K., Ziegert, J. C., Knight, A. P., & Xiao, Y. (2006). Dynamic delegation: Shared, hierarchical and deindividualized leadership in extreme action teams. *Administrative Science Quarterly, 51,* 590–621.

Kozlowski, S. W. J., & Ilgen, D. R. (2006). Enhancing the effectiveness of work groups and teams. *Psychological Science in the Public Interest, 7*(3), 77–124.

Kozlowski, S. W. J., & Klein, K. J. (2000). A multilevel approach to theory and research in organizations: Contextual, temporal, and emergent processes. In K. J. Klein & S. W. J. Kozlowski (Eds.), *Multilevel theory, research, and methods in organizations: Foundations, extensions, and new directions* (pp. 3–90). San Francisco, CA: Jossey-Bass.

Kurz, R., & Bartram, D. (2002). Competency and individual performance: Modelling the world of work. In I. T. Robertson, M. Callinan, & D. Bartram (Eds.), *Organizational effectiveness. The role of psychology* (pp. 227–255). Chichester, UK: Wiley.

Letts, C. W., Ryan, W. P., & Grossman, A. (1998). *High performance nonprofit organizations: Managing upstream for greater impact.* New York: John Wiley & Sons, Inc.

Levine, J. M., & Choi, H. (2004). Minority influence in work teams: The impact of newcomers. *Journal of Experimental Social Psychology, 40,* 273–280.

Lipshitz, R., & Strauss, O. (1997). Coping with uncertainty: A naturalistic decision-making analysis. *Organizational Behavior and Human Decision Processes, 69,* 149–163.

Locke, E. A., & Brian, J. F. (1967). Performance goals as determinants of level of performance and boredom. *Journal of Applied Psychology, 51*(2), 120–130.

Locke, E. A., Smith, K. G., Erez, M., Chah, D., & Schaffer, A. (1994). The effects of intra-individual goal conflict on performance. *Journal of Management, 20,* 67–91.

Lorenzet, S. J., Salas, E., & Tannenbaum, S. I. (2006). Benefitting from mistakes: The impact of guided errors on learning, performance, and self efficacy. *Human Resource Development Quarterly. 16,* 301–322.

MacMillan, J., Entin, E. E., & Serfaty, D. (2004). Communication overhead: The hidden cost of team cognition. In E. Salas & S. M. Fiore (Eds.), *Team cognition: Understanding the factors that drive process and performance* (pp. 61–82). Washington, DC: American Psychological Association.

Marks, M. A., Mathieu, J. E., & Zaccaro, S. J. (2001). A temporally based framework and taxonomy of team processes. *Academy of Management Review, 26,* 356–376.

Mattson, M., Mumford, T. V., & Sintay, G. S. (1999). *Taking teams to task: A normative model for designing or recalibrating work teams.* Paper presented at the Academy of Management.

McGrath, J. E. (1984). *Groups: Interaction and performance.* Englewood Cliffs, NJ: Prentice Hall.

Mohammed, S., & Dumville, B. C. (2001). Team mental models in a team knowledge framework: Expanding theory and measurement across disciplinary boundaries. *Journal of Organizational Behavior, 22*(2), 89–106.

Moon, H., Hollenbeck, J. R., Humphrey, S. E., Ilgen, D. R., West, B., Ellis, A. P. J., et al. (2004). Asymmetric adaptibility: Dynamic team structures as one-way streets. *Academy of Management Journal, 47,* 681–695.

Morgeson, F. P. (2005). The external leadership of self-managing teams: Intervening in the context of novel and disruptive events. *Journal of Applied Psychology, 90,* 497–508.

Mortensen, M., Woolley, A. W., & O'Leary, M. (2007). Conditions for enabling effective multiple team membership. In K. Crowston, S. Sieber, & E. Wynn (Eds.). IFIP, *Virtuality and Virtualization* (Vol. 236, pp. 215–228). Boston: Springer.

Murphy, K. R., & Cleveland, J. N. (1995). *Understanding performance appraisal: Social, organizational, and goal-based perspectives.* Thousand Oaks, CA: Sage.

Orasanu, J. (1990). *Diagnostic approaches to learning: Measuring what, how, and how much: Comments on chapters 12, 13, and 14.* Hillsdale, NJ: Lawrence Erlbaum Associates, Inc.

Orasanu, J., & Connolly, T. (1993). The reinvention of decision making. In G. Klein, J. Orasanu, R. Calderwood & C. E. Zsambok (Eds.), *Decision making in action: Models and methods* (pp. 3–20). Norwood, CT: Ablex.

Oser, R. L., MacCallum, G. A., Salas, E., & Morgan, B. B., Jr (1989). *Toward a definition of teamwork: An analysis of critical team behaviors.* (Technical Report 89-004). Orlando, FL: Naval Training Systems Center.

Porter, C. O., Hollenbeck, J.R., Ilgen, D.R., Ellis, A.P., West, B.J., & Moon, H. (2003). Backing up behaviors in teams: the role of personality and legitimacy of need. *Journal of Applied Psychology, 88*(3), 391–403.

Priem, R. L., Rasheed, A. M. A., & Kotulic, A. G. (1995). Rationality in strategic decision processes, environmental dynamism and firm performance. *Journal of Management, 21,* 913–929.

Pritchard, R. & Ashwood, E. (2008). *Managing motivation: A manager's guide to diagnosing and improving motivation.* New York: Routledge, Taylor & Francis Group.

Pritchard, R. D., Youngcourt, S. S., Philo, J. R., McMonagle, D., & David, J. H. (2007). The use of priority information in performance feedback. *Human Performance, 20*(1), 61–83.

Rosen, M. A., Salas, E., Lazzara, E. H., & Lyons, R. (in press). Cognitive task analysis: methods for capturing and leveraging expertise in the workplace. In M. A. Wilson, R. J. Harvey, G. M. Alliger & W. Bennett, Jr (Eds.), *The handbook of work analysis: The methods, systems, applications, & science of work measurement in organizations.*

Rosen, M. A., Salas, E., Wu, T. S., Silvestri, S., Lazzara, E. H., Lyons, R., et al. (2008). Promoting teamwork: An event-based approach to simulation-based teamwork training for emergency medicine residents. *Academic Emergency Medicine, 15*(11), 1190–1198.

Saavedra, R., Earley, R. C., & Dyne, L. (1993). Complex interdependence in task-performing groups. *Journal of Applied Psychology, 78*(1), 61–72.

Sackett, P. R., Zedeck, S., & Folgi, L. (1988). Relations between measures of typical and maximum job performance. *Journal of Applied Psychology, 73,* 482–486.

Salas, E., Burke, C. S., & Fowlkes, J. E. (2006). Measuring team performance "in the wild:" Challenges and tips. In W. Bennet, Jr, C. E. Lance & D. J. Woehr (Eds.), *Performance measurement: Current perspectives and future challenges* (pp. 245–272). Mahwah, NJ: Erlbaum.

Salas, E., Burke, C. S., Fowlkes, J. E., & Priest, H. A. (2003). On measuring teamwork skills. In J. C. Thomas & M. Hersen (Eds.), *Comprehensive handbook of psychological assessment* (pp. 427–442). Indianapolis, IN: Wiley Publishing, Inc.

Salas, E., Cannon-Bowers, J. A., Fiore, S. M., & Stout, R. J. (2001). Cue-recognition training to enhance team situation awareness. In M. McNeese, E. Salas, & M. Endlsey, (Eds.), *New trends in collaborative activities: Understanding system dynamics in complex environments* (pp. 169–190). Santa Monica, CA: Human Factors and Ergonomics Society.

Salas, E., Kosarzycki, M. P., Tannenbaum, S. I., & Carnegie, D. (2005). Aligning work teams and HR practices: Best practices. In R. J. Burke & C. L Cooper (Eds.), *Reinventing human resource management: Challenges and new directions* (pp. 133–149). New York: Taylor & Francis Group.

Salas, E., Priest, H. A., & Burke, C. S. (2005). Teamwork and team performance measurement. In J. R. Wilson & N. Corlett (Eds.), *Evaluation of human work* (3rd ed., pp. 793–808). Boca Raton, FL: Taylor & Francis.

Salas, E., Priest, H. A., Wilson, K. A., & Burke, C. S. (2006). Scenario-based training: Improving military mission performance and adaptability. In T. Britt, A. Adler, C. Castro & T. Britt (Eds), *Military life: The psychology of serving in peace and conflict* (Vol. 2, *Operational stress*, pp. 32–53). Westport, CT: Praeger Security International.

Salas, E., Rosen, M. A., Burke, C. S., & Goodwin, G. F. (2009). The wisdom of collectives in organizations: An update of the teamwork competencies. In E. Salas, G. F. Goodwin, & C. S. Burke (Eds.), *Team effectiveness in complex organizations: Cross-disciplinary perspectives and approaches* (pp. 39–79). New York: Routledge.

Salas, E., Rosen, M. A., Burke, C. S., Goodwin, G. F., & Fiore, S. (2006). The making of a dream team: When expert teams do best. In K. A. Ericsson, N. Charness, P. J. Feltovich & R. R. Hoffman (Eds.), *The Cambridge handbook of expertise and expert performance* (pp. 439–453). New York: Cambridge University Press.

Salas, E., Rosen, M. A., Burke, C. S., Nicholson, D., & Howse, W. R. (2007). Markers for enhancing team cognition in complex environments: The power of team performance diagnosis. *Aviation, Space, and Environmental Medicine (Special Supplement on Operational Applications of Cognitive Performance Enhancement Technologies), 78*(5), B77–85.

Salas, E., Sims, D. E., & Burke, C. S. (2005). Is there a big five in teamwork? *Small Group Research, 36*(5), 555–599.

Salas, E., Stagl, K. C., Burke, C. S., & Goodwin, G. F. (2007). Fostering team effectiveness in organizations: Toward an integrative theoretical framework of team performance. In R. A. Dienstbier, J. W. Shuart, W. Spaulding, & J. Poland (Eds.), *Modeling complex systems: Motivation, cognition and social processes. Nebraska Symposium on Motivation* (Vol. 51, pp. 185–243). Lincoln, NE: University of Nebraska Press.

Salas, E., Weaver, S. J., Rosen, M. A., & Smith-Jentsch, K. A. (2009). Managing team performance in complex settings: Research-based best practices. In J. W. Smither & M. London (Eds.), *Performance management: Putting research into practice* (pp. 197–232). San Francisco, CA: Jossey-Bass.

Salas, E., Wilson, K. A., Murphy, C., King, H., & Salisbury, M. (in press). Communicating, coordinating and cooperating when the life of others depends on it: Tips for teamwork. *Joint Commission Journal on Quality and Safety.*

Shi, Y., & Tang, H. K. (1997). Team role behaviour and task environment. *Journal of Managerial Psychology, 12,* 85–94.

Smith-Jentsch, K. A., Zeisig, R. L., Acton, B., & McPherson, J. A. (1998). Team dimensional training: A strategy for guided team self-correction. In J. A. Cannon-Bowers & E. Salas (Eds.), *Making decisions under stress: Implications for individual and team training* (pp. 271–298). Washington, DC: American Psychological Association.

Stevens, M. J., & Campion, M. A. (1994). The knowledge, skill, and ability requirements for teamwork: Implications for human resource management. *Journal of Management, 20*(2), 503–530.

Strubler, D. C., & York, K. M. (2007). An exploratory study of the team characteristics model using organizational teams. *Small Group Research, 38,* 670–695.

Sundstrom, E., De Meuse, K. P., & Futrell, D. (1990). Work teams: Applications and effectiveness. *American Psychologist, 45,* 120–133.

Tannenbaum, S. I. (2006). Applied performance measurement: Practical issues and challenges. In W. Bennett, C. E. Lance, & D. J. Woehr (Eds.), *Performance measurement:*

Current perspectives and future challenges (pp. 297–318). Mahwah, NJ: Lawrence Erlbaum Associates.

Webber, S. (2002). Mapping a path to the empowered searcher. In C. Graham (Ed.), *Online Information: Proceedings* (pp. 3–5). Oxford.

Wildman, J. L., Bedwell, W. L., Salas, E., & Smith-Jentsch, K. A. (2010). Performance measurement at work: A multilevel perspective. In S. Zedeck (Ed.), *APA handbook of industrial and organizational psychology*. Washington, DC: American Psychological Association.

Williams, G., & Laugani, P. (1999). Analysis of teamwork in an NHS community trust: An empirical study. *Journal of Interprofessional Care, 13,* 19–28.

Wilson, K. A., Burke, C. S., Priest, H. A., & Salas, E. (2005). Promoting health care safety through training high reliability teams. *Quality and Safety in Health Care, 14,* 303–309.

Yang, O., & Shao, Y. E. (1996). Shared leadership in self-managed teams: A competing values approach. *Total Quality Management, 7,* 521–534.

Zakay, D., Ellis, S., & Shevalsky, M. (2004). Outcome value and early warning indications as determinants of willingness to learn from experience. *Experimental Psychology, 51*(2), 150–157.

20

INTERVENTIONS IN GROUPS

Methods for Facilitating Team Development

David R. Seibold

UNIVERSITY OF CALIFORNIA–SANTA BARBARA

Renee A. Meyers

UNIVERSITY OF WISCONSIN, AT MILWAUKEE

Situating Our (Team) Work

In the course of the past three decades, working alone and together, we have devoted an average of a day per week working with some 100 organizations in the private and public sectors, at more than 150 of their sites, and with at least 4000 persons from nearly 50 countries. These engagements involved many different activities (e.g., facilitating small and large group meetings and retreats, training, coaching, conducting formative and summative evaluation studies, and process consultations), including *three methods for team development interventions* – our focus in this chapter. Typically, the groups and teams whom we assist are work units (or subgroups within them) that function to accomplish formal tasks, although we also have worked with cross-functional groups created for short terms to deal with specific problems of concern to the entire organization or to the units from which members are drawn (Devine, Clayton, Philips, Dunford, & Melner, 1999; Greenbaum & Query, 1999). Many of the groups we assist are *teams*, either because members refer to themselves that way to capture a high level of cohesiveness they feel they possess or because they possess the structural criteria for that type of group (Arrow, McGrath, & Berdahl, 2000; LaFasto & Larson, 2001).

We will say more in the next section about the types of organizations in which these groups and teams are embedded, and especially about other contextual issues that situate our interventions with the teams (e.g., contacts with the organizations, our relationships with the teams, ethical issues). However, in order to offer context for our practices and research with the three methods for facilitating team development, some examples of the *range of team interventions* to which we refer in this chapter include: team building with research and development teams of scientists in the health and energy sectors; assisting with the implementation of self-directing work teams in manufacturing plants, financial services firms, and government agencies; supporting a hospice care team concerned with volunteer turnover; assisting engineers with team process problems in their project groups; facilitating goal setting among teams of staff, faculty, and administrators focused on quality of work life issues on their campus; addressing intragroup cooperation and intergroup coordination among technicians and supervisors in five departments of a hospital laboratory; supporting team development with groups of senior executives and administrators; creating a cross-functional team of professionals from four locations in a children and family services county agency; and helping interdisciplinary groups of faculty from 13 campuses in a state-wide university system conduct research on teaching and learning.

We refer to our "team interventions" in the senses that Cummings and Worley (2005) discuss intervention: a sequence of purposeful events, activities, and behaviors designed to help a group or organization improve its processes and outcomes. As Bartunek, Austin, and Seo (2008) observe, interventions can vary from brief to lengthy, be relatively simple to quite complex, involve few to many participants, and focus on one to multiple levels of an organization. The three intervention methods we describe range from extended to relatively brief yet all include complex sequences of events, activities, and actions. And although the focus in all three methods usually is a single natural work group with six to 15 members, the examples above attest that we have used these methods with cross-functional groups as large as 50 members, with participants from multiple levels of an organization, with several interdependent groups at the same time, and even with involvement from stakeholders outside the organizations in which the focal group is embedded (e.g., its clients, suppliers, and distributors, and in other cases both community members and representatives of other agencies). The vast majority of our projects have been the first type of group-focused interventions described by Hackman and Edmondson (2008): seeking to improve the functioning of existing teams through process-focused methods (supplemented by diagnostic-based assessments, group-based training, individual coaching, and system-wide consultation). Less often, our engagements have been of the second type noted by Hackman and Edmondson: creating new teams to solve existing organizational problems.

Overview

In the remaining four sections we discuss three team development methods that we use with group-focused interventions designed to enhance teamwork, and we address numerous issues associated with them. First, we clarify the range of organizations with whom we have worked, and we treat key practical matters: our roles and motivations concerning these interventions, principles and ethical issues, organizations' contact with us and vice versa, and conducting research with and in these interventions. Second, we discuss the focus of our interventions with teams – team development and team building – including the assumptions and objectives of such interventions. We discuss ten qualities of groups with teamwork and four dimensions undergirding them, and how our efforts at team development along those dimensions align with four established approaches to team building. Third, we explicate the methods we use to facilitate the development of teamwork in three types of group interventions: (a) implementing – over time and within intact groups – interventions for enhancing team development and performance; (b) implementing – in brief periods and with either an intact team or with multiple groups simultaneously – interventions focused on helping members identify problems in their unit(s) that members may choose to confront and how they will do so; (c) implementing – through processes involving critical praxis and reflexivity – improved versions of either of the two team development interventions above. Although we treat theses methods separately in order to explain each clearly, they can be used jointly in many team interventions. In addition, the order in which we discuss the three methods can be read as a chronology of our development of them and, in many ways, our own professional development (so we will note what "worked" and what did not). Fourth, we conclude with how team development practice and research can be integrated.

Before turning to those four sections, however, we acknowledge that group intervention typically is considered a *method of practice* rather than a *method of research*. Readers may wonder why a chapter on team intervention methods appears in a volume on research methods for studying groups. However, we have found these two types of methods to be mutually informing, especially in the context of our larger efforts to bridge theory and practice in our engaged scholarship. First, our group interventions have led us to conduct research on the methods themselves (Meyers, 2006; Meyers & Johnson, 2008; Seibold, 1995; Seibold & Kang, 2008), and we will draw upon each of these works to illustrate the team intervention methods we discuss. Second, in making decisions about team intervention methods of practice, we have turned in the past 30 years to research that was current then about the utility and implementation of those methods (e.g., Austin & Bartunek, 2003; Buller & Bell, 1986; Dyer, 1995; Lawler, 1995; Rousseau, Aubé, & Savoie, 2006; Schein, 1988).

Third, in the course of using these methods, we draw on theory and research to supplement the team intervention. For example, when we intervened to enhance team processes in organizations that were transitioning from traditional to team-based structures, we relied upon the work of Lawler (1995) to assess whether there was sufficient infrastructure at the organizational level to support teams. With other groups, we have aided members to adapt Poole's (1991) procedures for managing group meetings as well as procedures reviewed by SunWolf and Seibold (1999). We also have noted Tompkins and Cheney's (1985) paradox of concertive control in conversations with members about the normative pressures they created in their self-managed teams. Indeed, the roots of our approaches to team development are in the theoretical and applied research of Kurt Lewin,

Chris Argyris, Rensis Likert, Douglas McGregor, and Richard Hackman (see Boss & McConkie, 2008). Fourth, we do not simply bring theory *to* each engagement. The process is reciprocal: occasions for theory development arise *in* and *from* the engagement. As Seibold (2005) pointed out, and as we develop more fully in the final section, we often "discover" relationships that can be tested in the context of the engagement and which – if supported – advance knowledge in established areas of scholarship concerning groups (for examples, several of which included intervention methods in this chapter, see Berteotti & Seibold, 1994; Franken & Seibold, 2010; Krikorian, Seibold, & Goode, 1997; Seibold, 1990).

Situating Our (Teamwork) Engagements

Just as our research has reflected joint commitments to theory development (Seibold & Meyers, 2007) and to applied scholarship concerning group communication (e.g., Considine, Meyers, & Timmerman, 2006; Kauffeld & Meyers, 2009; Lehmann, Meyers, Kauffeld, & Lehmann-Willenbrock, 2009; Meyers, Seibold, & Kang, 2010; Seibold, 2005), our careers have included deep *engagement* with groups and teams in many settings. We noted at the outset the numbers of organizations and wide variety of projects with which we have been involved. Perhaps 60 per cent of these have been with for-profit organizations ranging from minority-owned small enterprises to *Fortune 100* corporations that produce food, clothing, equipment, and power, and that provide financial services, telecommunications, hospitality, entertainment, and insurance. Thirty per cent of our work has been with federal/state/municipal government and nonprofit organizations focused on health and human services, environmental protection, education, philanthropy, transportation, international aid and development, and with professional and religious affiliations. The other 10 per cent have been projects in which we and our students offered services to institutions with insufficient resources to undertake them (e.g., charities, shelters, civic organizations, and hospices).

We have evolved a set of *principles* to guide our interventions with teams and organizations. They also reflect our attempts to deal with *ethical aspects* of our interventions. We do not become involved in projects unless we think we can aid team members – no matter how enticing the project may be to either of us. That commitment carries an additional responsibility: preparing thoroughly concerning the goals and practices of the team(s) thorough personal and group interviews, observations, use of quantitative measures and surveys, and archival work. We also monitor our involvement to ensure we have done no harm – especially through unintended consequences. For example, we rely on "evaluation (sub)teams" to poll their colleagues frequently and provide us with feedback. Increasingly, that has given way to reflections with the entire team about our practices, as we describe in Method 3 below and the critical praxis at its core.

If problems arise, our first priority is to remedy them (which offers an opportunity for all participants in the process to learn from the experience and to develop skills for coping with other problems that invariably arise when we are not the source nor available). We hold ourselves accountable not only to the group members with whom we are intervening, but to the entire system in which participants are embedded. For that reason, we decline projects in which the participant(s) cannot openly discuss why we are assisting them and what members wish to accomplish. Rather, we routinely request permission to seek additional information that will illuminate the team problem(s): speaking with persons at multiple levels of the organizational hierarchy, and interviewing across lateral relationships with peers, other teams, even clients when appropriate. In that same spirit of candor, we encourage participants at all levels – especially administrators – to engage in "open book" management. Through our diligence, availability, expertise, candor, confidentiality, and concern for members' needs individually and collectively, we attempt to create relationships with teams that meet the standards of all good personal relationships: integrity, acceptance, respect, trust, and interdependence (moving toward teams' independence rather than their dependence on us). Finally, we are drawn to interventions with teams in organizations whose products and services improve society, and that evidence social responsibility. Conversely, we do not become engaged with organizations (or with organizations who own them) whose products or services make us uncomfortable – especially those that adversely affect the health and vitality of our society and our world.

Our *roles* in these engagements have been diverse: as university teachers offering service learning experiences for college students; as university administrators and project directors working with our own or another organization's members and stakeholders; as members of the community served by the group(s); as consultants (working alone or under the auspices of a consulting firm contracted to the organization); as researchers interested in studying team development processes and interventions (or as scholars returning to study other group or organizational processes that we observed during interventions but that prompted theoretical questions outside the purview of this volume such as strategy formulation and strategic communication, users' modifications of planned change programs, participation systems, risk and crisis communication). Our *motivations* for involving ourselves in many projects that led to published research and in many more that did not, to paraphrase those outlined by Seibold (2005), were to assist the teams "for the experience" (a new problem, new participants); "for the course" (to develop learning aids, or to create a meaningful pedagogical and service experiences for students); "for the cause" (to aid those who sought assistance and whose mission we embraced); "for the participants" (especially the teams of employees); and, yes, "for the reward" (appreciation, advancement, compensation).

Given the various roles and motivations that have linked us with these teams and organizations, the manner in which we have been *contacted by them* – or have approached them *when we initiated contact* – also has varied widely. When our primary motivations have been to conduct research, we secured approval of review boards at our institutions; developed population lists and sampled systematically (supplemented with snowball and accidental sampling); approached as scholars interested in data collection (but always with the potential to improve practices in the organization); found our way through contacts to gatekeepers with the power to provide access; negotiated relationships with team members as research participants and secured informed consent; participated fully through the intervention methods described later; debriefed following data collection and subsequently provided reports to the team(s) and organization(s) – which sometimes led to continuing relationships with the teams.

At the other end of the continuum, organizations have approached us – as faculty willing to perform service on behalf of the university, as teachers interested in involving students in projects, as compensated consultants (directly or through firms for whom we have been subcontractors), or as community members interested in helping with technical assistance or helping the cause – and our interventions have been limited to those relationships. Even in those instances we frequently have conducted research *with* the team (rather than *about* the team) concerning problems of concern to members or their managers, for assessment of the team, to create baselines to judge changes after the intervention, and for feedback concerning individual dispositions (useful for supplementary coaching of individuals). In these relationships, any data collected with the group(s) are reported back to the members and are confidential. In between these poles, however, are times when multiple roles have emerged, and when we see the potential for academic research even when we are not engaged with the team as researchers. Sometimes our relationships with the group (i.e., mutual respect, trust, and delivery of a sound service) led its members to be willing to participate in research for a scholarly audience, at which time we turn to institutional review procedures. We thus seek to balance our commitment to academic scholarship with intensive organizational engagement and service work, and to integrate those pursuits as much as possible.[1]

Situating Our (Team-building) Interventions

Our interventions with groups and teams involve three *team-building* methods for aiding their members to develop teamwork. In groups or teams whose practices reflect *teamwork, ten qualities are present*:

(1) members share and can articulate a *team vision* (above and beyond specific task goals for the aggregate);

(2) members have defined, valued, and accepted *role expectations* (which may be more or less than the specific jobs they perform);

(3) members have considerable role-related *autonomy* (besides their formal task duties);

(4) members tend to develop *high standards for themselves* and exert considerable control over the group or team and its work environment (in contrast to only managers' expectations and control);

(5) members tacitly or explicitly *develop a structure* that is responsive to environmental demands, yet appropriate for whatever the organization considers necessary;

(6) members conduct significant types and portions of *decision making within the team* (rather than having all decisions made by others outside the team or atop it);

(7) members *share leadership* to some extent and/or have a formal team leader who empowers members and works to secure resources that the team needs to excel;

(8) members freely *share information and interpretations* with each other (including about nontask matters);

(9) members acknowledge and reinforce each other's *contributions and supportiveness*; and

(10) members convey and *display mutual respect and trust* with one another (Hackman, 1990; Seibold, Kang, Gailliard, & Jahn, 2009).

As Boss and McConkie (2008) note, the *objectives* of team building are to improve team and organizational effectiveness through a set of *mediating processes*. When the methods employed are successful (including cycles of data collection, data analysis, data feedback, and action planning), team effectiveness is improved via task skill building and increased *member competence*, greater *openness* in problem solving and in relationships, members' increased *concern for one another*, their willingness to hold themselves *accountable for commitments* made during the intervention, and the stronger *trust that emerges within the team*. According to Boss and McConkie, the potential for increased organizational effectiveness results when the stronger team also develops a *climate* in which problems are acknowledged and solved, it assumes *ownership* of organizational goals and thus increased commitment, there is a spillover of *collaboration* among interdependent groups, the team's *awareness of group processes* has performance implications in other areas of organizational functioning, and when the team development yields personal and team *empowerment* to address other organizational matters. The *assumption* is that a team's participation in its own problem diagnosis and action planning will increase members' commitment to those processes. The first two methods we report – an extended team intervention, and a brief "workout" – are quite consistent with the characterization offered by Boss and McConkie of the assumptions, objectives, and mediating processes of team-building interventions.

We have found that the ten qualities of teamwork introduced in this section reflect four *dimensions*: vision, roles, processes, and relationships. *Vision* includes the group's goals and objectives but also members' team identity (for themselves and for outsiders). Second, members of groups or teams characterized by high levels of teamwork also have *roles that may be more or less than their jobs*. Role-related dynamics leading to teamwork entail how each member comes to understand what other members expect of him or her. Third, *processes* in groups with teamwork are characterized by flexibility and responsiveness to the changing environment, more so than "standard operating procedures" implemented by managers. Furthermore, there are sufficient resources (financial, personnel, technology, and material) to sustain teamwork, as well as reward, training, and information systems that enable and facilitate members' strong teamwork (Hackman, 1990). Fourth, the *relationships* dimension of teamwork typically reveals members' communication to be characterized by respectful and open sharing of information, by perspective taking and valuing difference, and by allowance for both supportive and constructive negative feedback.

Each of these four dimensions along which we seek to facilitate teamwork corresponds to one of the four *approaches* to team building originally classified by Beer (1976). Although Beer treated them as different "team-building designs," our first two methods below incorporate all four approaches within each intervention. First, traditional *goal-setting* approaches focus on redefining goals, from which effectiveness flows via enhanced member awareness and commitment as well as strengthened team culture. In our work on building team *vision*, members focus on whether they share the same beliefs about what the group seeks to accomplish, how they wish to be known, and whether they articulate that vision in the same terms.

Second, team development approaches to fostering clearer *roles* among members assume that if role clarity increases (thru role negotiation and definition), team effectiveness will improve via members' performance of perceived roles. In our focus on helping members to have defined, valued, and accepted *roles*, the team is concerned with whether each member understands what other members expect of her (which may be more or less than that member's formal job). Is each member's role perception consistent with others' expectations for that role? Does each member feel valued by others in the group for the role she or he plays? Third, *problem-solving* approaches to team building focus on having members solve task challenges together (through jointly generating and analyzing data, planning action, and implementing changes they design). Team effectiveness follows from members' experience of collaboration on work problems they share. In our team interventions, members focus on difficulties associated with *processes* related to operations, procedures, and resources in the group or team. Has the team developed operational practices and structures to ensure success? Are there sufficient resources (e.g., financial, personnel, technology) for the group to achieve its goals (independent of members' level of commitment, communication, and collaboration)?

Fourth, team-building designs focused on improving members' *interpersonal relations* propose that team effectiveness will increase if members' relationships are strengthened via greater trust and mutual support. Our approaches to team development *combine* this focus on *members' relationships* with the three other foci above. Our methods encourage and enable members to raise and answer the following questions. Does communication in the group reflect open sharing of information and interpretations? Are members' messages mutually respectful? Have members developed ways of communicating support, appreciation, and negative feedback constructively? Is there trust based on competence, consistency, candor, and concern for others?

Challenges

Incorporating all four foci into each of our interventions does not imply that they are, can, or should be dealt with simultaneously. Like others (Dyer, 1995), we have struggled over which dimension of team effectiveness to address *first* and *in what order* the others should then become focal: vision? roles? processes? relationships? In our earliest projects, we focused on achieving better teamwork through first addressing members' relationships with each other. No doubt this resulted from our own disciplinary roots as well as what research revealed about the importance of strong relational communication in successful groups (see summary in Barker, Abrams, Tiyaamornwong, Seibold, et al., 2000). However, even when members had the interactional skills to deal with relationship "issues" in the group, they found those difficulties often were rooted in deeper problems with the direction of the group (or lack thereof), confusion or disagreement about their roles relative to those goals, and/or processes rooted in structural and resource problems with which they struggled continuously (and around which relational issues flared up).

Therefore, and relying on the rationale for the importance of goal-setting designs (Buller & Bell, 1986), a little later in our careers we tended to emphasize the vision and roles dimensions first in our interventions. We conjoined those two dimensions because we found that team members did not deal with vision-related processes without talking about roles – those they sought to play and those expected of others. These interventions were more successful than those in which we had addressed relationships first, largely because members could focus on something "out there" (i.e., problems other than their relationships with each other). However, we again found members returning to the structural and resource-based process problems that were the bane of their existence.

Indeed, it was not until we helped the groups(s) *first* to focus on those operational/procedural/structural/resources problems that we became confident in the methods we report next. Research had suggested that successful groups have these structural factors in place for the most part (Hackman, 1990), especially reward, training, and information systems, material resources, and effective formal leadership. Especially when our relationships with team members were still nascent, members were most willing to participate in team development interventions that would at least improve their own work conditions, independent of any reluctance they had about any other aspects of the intervention designed to foster teamwork (particularly dealing with their relationships with each other). Most importantly, in working together to resolve work *process* problems associated with the group's operations, structure, and resources, a crucible was created within which members learned the values of collaboration, of assuming responsibility for solutions to their problems, of making self-interest secondary to securing resources, and of setting aside relational issues until work problems were resolved. This was a key to the success of these interventions, since "teamwork" was recognized by members as the basis for their preliminary "wins" in improving their work processes and conditions. In turn, these initial team-based successes motivated members toward further work together on matters that might improve team functioning. As will be evident from our treatment of these methods next, we learned that members were *then* more willing to engage a shared *vision* and their *roles* in it. And by the time their work along those dimensions was completed, addressing *relationships* in the group also became easier because members already had clear examples of the value of feedback, supportiveness, respect, and trust from their work together on issues related to the three other dimensions.

Methods of Team Development

Improved teamwork is not only an end-state for these interventions (assuming team members develop consensus that *they* wish to become a group with the ten teamwork qualities noted earlier), but the processes of teamwork also are woven into these team development methods. On the first count, these interventions do not represent actions we do *to* teams; they are sets of activities that we complete *with* teams. Our involvement may be triggered by members' recognition of problems with goals, roles, procedures, and relationships; by managers' concerns about motivational or performance issues; by referrals to the team or to managers of third parties inside and outside the organizations with whom we have worked and who believe we might be able "to help" the team develop stronger teamwork.

In many instances, the team already evidences high levels of teamwork but simply seeks to be stronger. Hence, skepticism about us is minimal because we are seen as partners with members in *their* process of developing better teamwork. Given members' centrality to the processes in each method, and our increasing reliance (via Method 3) on all parties' reflexivity about the intervention, we do not find ourselves as "diagnosing problems," nor deciding unilaterally on courses of action *for* the team, nor making "recommendations" that an organization "does not want to hear." Rather, through interviews, surveys, measures, archives, and observations we first surface data, then cluster them along the four dimensions of teamwork, next facilitate members' sensemaking about them, and ultimately provide a set of structured activities in each method within which members work on problems they prioritize. The processes in which members engage lead to solutions that make teamwork more likely, and provide members with opportunities to solve problems through greater teamwork.

To preview, the three methods we use to facilitate the development of teamwork include:

Method 1 – "process consultations" with intact groups that occur over extended periods of time and include activities to develop teamwork along each of the four dimensions discussed earlier but in the order noted above (i.e., processes, then goals/roles, and then relationships); or

Method 2 – "workouts" with intact groups, cross-functional teams, or multiple groups simultaneously that occur in brief periods of time and include activities that are focused on helping members identify problems in their unit(s) that members may choose to confront and how they will do so after the session; or

Method 3 – enhanced versions of either of these two team development interventions through processes involving members and our own "critical praxis and reflexivity."

The choice of method is dependent on some of the factors inherent to each method and as reflected in the differences just described: length of time that members can commit to team building and the number and range of issues they wish to engage (Method 1 vs. Method 2); how long our involvement is sought or possible (Method 1 vs. Method 2); and the amount of reflection and degree of control for the process of team building that participants themselves are willing to assume (Method 3 vs. Methods 1 and 2).

Method 1: TEAM PROCESS CONSULTATION

Our first method of working with some groups involves extended interventions: implementing – over time and within an intact group – an intervention for enhancing team development and performance. Typically, this method of engagement involves the authors' immersion into the group on a frequent (weekly) and extended (three or four months) basis. It must be sufficiently long to aid team members: to recognize the ways in which their interactional processes contribute to their problems as well as to their strengths; to work within those same processes to identify causes and determine solutions to the problems members jointly agree upon; and to facilitate team-based learning of the skills and processes employed through the facilitative relationship, so that members can utilize them on their own in dealing with problems in the future. The method involves elements of process consulting (Schein, 1988) and aspects of team building (Dyer, 1995), and one of us has characterized it as "team process consultation" (Seibold, 1995).

One example of Method 1 conducted by Dave (first author) took place over several months with the members of teams in a team-managed plant that manufactures oil filters for diesel engines in heavy construction equipment. Most of the members were engineers or highly trained technicians employed to support the automation systems in plant, and the majority had been hired because they had experience working in other team environments. So the intervention, invited by the members and supported by the parent companies that supported this joint venture (called BFSI), really was one of "adding strength to strength." We draw upon selected portions of that intervention to illustrate the steps in it, but a full treatment of the case and the method can be found in Seibold (1995).

First, since team process consultation emanates from a series of assumptions concerning people problems and change processes, how "outsiders" like us can be helpful with both, and the conditions under which success is most likely, these assumptions were discussed with the teams at BFSI. Concerning people and change, Dave noted findings that people do not resist change so much as they resist the feeling they are being changed. Personal commitment is a more powerful motivator than external reward or punishment. Focused feedback and coaching can effect more enduring change than criticism. Personal and systemic change are more likely when members feel valued by others. These conversations make transparent the facilitator's values, members' values, and some basis for building trust.

Second, the following tenets of team facilitation also were discussed as part of orienting the teams to what could transpire through the intervention and why. Members may be motivated to change but may not recognize systemic problems, nor what to do about them. Through observation, data collection, and discussion, "outsiders" can help members to focus their attention on previously unseen patterns. Given the time needed for insight and trust to develop, team members must come to their own understanding of "the problem" and to their own solutions. Since no remedy will be perfect or permanent because new problems emerge, team members must also learn how to monitor, interpret, analyze, solve, and implement decisions continuously about their own problems. This discussion was met with some surprise, as it often is in other groups, as members began to see (if not yet fully accept) the need to share responsibility for the project.

Third, assumptions about preconditions for success of team building were discussed too (with some treatment of supporting research). Success of team building is most likely when there is the existence of internal tensions and/or formal group problems (their struggles with several technical problems that were delaying production as well as coordination difficulties between shifts); commitment of the group's designated leader to the intervention (the plant manager in this case); support from informal leaders in the group and their full involvement in team development; willingness of members to resolve problems and to be accountable for the results (which reinforced the discussion above); realistic expectations concerning the team development process and its outcomes; and technically competent team members who inspire each other's respect and who are capable of enacting changes that emerge from the intervention (for a recent summary, see Boss & McConkie, 2008).

Implicit in these three assumptions concerning team process consultation are *values* that we believe should be part of team interventions of this sort: promoting a culture of collaboration, engendering ownership of process and outcome, creating openness in communication, increasing personal and group effectiveness and efficiency, and supporting curiosity and continuous learning. We therefore find it necessary and most productive to work with members collectively to understand team processes involved in problem solving, integrating resources, sharing information, and dealing with interpersonal difficulties. Although some attention is given to enhancing individuals' skills (through training and coaching), our principal focus is on developing a common conception of "teamwork" that captures many of the characteristics with which we began this chapter. We attempt to capture them in members' terms. For example, at BFSI one team's credo to "communicate honestly" noted the need for sharing information and interpretations freely that is part of our literature. Or a team's appropriation of "continuous improvement"– part of a Total Quality Management program in which they were involved – reflects *our* criterion of members' high standards for themselves but in a way that signals where *they* stand.

Consistent with the ordering of teamwork dimensions noted above, our team process consultations proceed through the following *stages* – nearly all of which were performed in their entirety at BFSI (see Seibold, 1995). First, we work with each group to create an "agenda" for its work by categorizing *problems* the group faces. Using methods that are both quantitative (e.g., established research measures as diagnostic instruments) and qualitative (e.g., members' responses to open-ended questions such as "What is preventing this team from accomplishing all that it is capable of?"), members then elaborate on them in joint sessions we facilitate. We categorize the problems in terms of the challenges they reveal about the teamwork dimensions of vision, roles, processes, and relationships but they are their problems that they recognize.

Second, we then rely upon members' involvement to improve *processes* related to the team's structure, operations, and procedures. From the list in the first step, members identify operational/procedural problems they feel they can resolve quickly and on their own (without reliance on a supervisor). This involvement (at BFSI as two ad-hoc task forces, utilizing portions of formal group meetings each Monday, and informal discussions during lunches and between shifts) ensures that problems most important to the members themselves are addressed first, and that members take ownership of results that have the potential to improve their personal and collective situation. Increased commitment to the group and to the rest of the team-building process usually follows, as members see they are capable of effecting change concerning matters they face and consider important.

Third, with our assistance members then revisit the group's goals and begin to create discursive bases for a shared *vision*. Discussion centers around goals that have been set for the group: do members know them and do they concur? Conversations shift toward whether members feel they are capable of more than has been asked of them, or than they have produced, and how realistic their goals are. This usually leads to not only what "the team" wishes to accomplish, but to how its members wish to be known. At BFSI these discussion over many meetings proved to be especially important, for team members at this "green field" (new) plant had not only to deal with their nascent status but with how they wished to be seen by each of their parent companies. Since members stood in for the plant manager at many meetings with customers, the outcome of this step had implications for their ability and facility at speaking as "one" for the plant.

Fourth, members invariably consider *role* dynamics associated with their emergent and nascent vision for the team. Do they understand and accept others' expectations of them? How will members' need for performing outside those role constraints be met? What are the implications of these role expectations for any status hierarchy that results? How will members deal with that structure when it is at odds with the presumed egalitarianism that has been an undercurrent in their dialogue? Most of these matters were moot at BFSI, where members' experiences in teams in prior jobs socialized them to the importance of accepting roles for the good of the team.

Finally, we endeavor to aid members to improve *relationships* within the team. What are the ongoing relational problems in the group? Many, if not most, of those relationship issues identified in the first step have been worked through (or found not to be as serious as thought) as members successfully collaborated on the other issues during each of the preceding steps. Broader questions arise: how can interpersonal and team-wide communication be improved in ways that strengthen members' relationships? This may involve training or coaching in areas such as listening, communicating non-defensively, offering negative feedback, supportiveness, and appreciative inquiry. At BFSI, stylistic differences between a couple of key members (and their consequence in having supporters of each person form cliques that were not always cooperative) were matters that needed to be addressed. Following two or three mediated sessions between the members, and resultant "behavioral contracts" with each other concerning what they would and would not do (as well as next steps if either felt aggrieved), a group session was held during which the two members acknowledged the implications of their relationships on the team and worked to bridge their supporters.

Method 2: TEAM WORKOUT

Method 2 involves "workouts" with intact groups, cross-functional teams, or multiple groups simultaneously that occur in brief periods of time and include activities that are focused on helping members identify problems in their unit(s) that members may choose to confront and how they will do so after the session. One of our more recent and continuing team interventions employing (primarily) Method 2 has been in the service of groups of researchers themselves (Meyers, 2006). Since 2003, Renee (second author) has worked with groups of interdisciplinary faculty from University of Wisconsin System universities (13 colleges spread throughout Wisconsin) to conduct research on teaching and learning issues (e.g., Ciccone, Meyers, & Waldmann, 2008; Ferrante et al., 2008; Lau & Meyers, 2007; for additional information on this initiative, see www.sotl.uwm.edu). Faculty researchers (either teams or individuals) come together several times over a two-year period: (a) to discuss and select a teaching and learning research question; (b) to learn how to conduct this type of research (frequently scientists, engineers, anthropologists, music and art faculty – they are expert in conducting disciplinary research but know little about how to investigate student learning or the links between teaching and learning); (c) to explore forms of data relevant to answering their research question (i.e., student written or oral assignments, student interviews, focus groups, or surveys, among other types of data); and (d) to learn about ways to analyze these data (using either quantitative and qualitative methods or both). Between face-to-face meetings, in which Method 2 is employed three or six times, researchers are supported via email, conference calls, and interactive websites. These links are utilized to discuss the problems encountered, to encourage researchers, to allow for mutual learning, and to work through team issues.

As is evident, this second method of team development with some groups, including these interdisciplinary faculty groups, involves a brief approach to group intervention: implementing – in a short period and with either an intact team or, occasionally, with multiple groups simultaneously – an intervention focused on helping members identify problems their team(s) may wish to address and potential means for redressing those issues. In most instances, we use this method instead of the extended team development method described above because the organization in which the group is embedded does not wish members to be involved in the lengthier and more involved ways just noted. However, we may employ this method of team development with a group with whom we are working (as a focused part of the extended intervention) or have already worked (as part of the group's desire to monitor its progress and to target recent problems). These functions also reveal why we refer to this method as a "workout."[2]

In other interventions where we have employed Method 2, the team development process is centered on a one- or two-day retreat attended by all members and held away from their work area. It is preceded by our interviews with each team member, from which we summarize strengths and problems they believe are undermining teamwork. The off-site meeting begins with discussion of team strengths identified by members during our interviews (and developing a consensus-based final list). Acknowledgments of all members' contributions to those team strengths are then provided by each other member, which we facilitate in a round-robin. This usually leaves each member feeling supported by the rest of the team.

We then treat the attributes of "teamwork" that we reviewed at the outset of this chapter. This is yoked to members' conversation about whether they believe those characteristics exist in their group, and whether members wish to pursue attributes of teamwork they do not currently possess. We distribute a list of the issues/weaknesses that surfaced during individual interviews, and we compare those problems to any gaps in teamwork the members have just identified. We use subgroup discussions to clarify, extend, and finalize the list of "team issues." This summary is utilized in subsequent parts of the session and as an agenda for members' joint efforts at team development after we are gone, since one session can be but part of that process.

In a following one- or two-hour session, team members participate in a structured discussion of personal actions in which they *each* will engage in order to redress issues individually that the team confronts and to improve teamwork. This portion of the team's "workout" usually proves to be quite important for members. First, social comparison processes operate. Members realize that if another member commits to an action that all recognize will require great effort or sacrifice, they cannot avoid comparisons concerning how much they promise to do. Second, the session is structured so that members not only listen to what others commit to improve, but others can suggest additional actions the focal individuals might undertake to improve the team. These comments usually reflect role expectations, and ensuing discussions serve as forums for role negotiation. Third, public commitments can serve as bases for positive confrontations after the session, if team members feel an individual has not followed through on these commitments. Fourth, many of the "issues" on the team's list of problems/weaknesses have emerged from the members themselves, and members recognize that those issues often can be solved through their own actions. Most members realize their interdependence and the necessity of joint communication, commitment, and collaboration for success in almost all consequential aspects of team functioning.

During the final portion of the retreat, team members identify persons beyond the group whose actions are needed to redress problems that are beyond members' control and yet are undermining teamwork and limiting team effectiveness. Members jointly discuss what resources are needed to improve the team, and whose help is needed to secure them. Administrators/managers are invited to attend a final session, to listen to members' requests for their assistance in securing resources or meeting with outside agents, and to make their own commitments concerning what they will do to aid members' team development efforts. We capture on our laptops all commitments made during the workout, and we send to the entire team a summary of everyone's actions. The lists of team issues and of commitments are foundational for continuing work by the team members themselves, a plan for which is developed before members leave the retreat. We also have used this approach with multiple (sub)groups from the same organization working simultaneously and in parallel through these steps across two days − part of an organizational transformation effort and large group intervention.

Method 3: CRITICAL PRAXIS AND REFLEXIVITY

The two team-building methods we have outlined thus far fall within first-generation and second-generation planned change interventions in organizations (Austin & Bartunek, 2003; Seo, Putnam, & Bartunek, 2004). Our third method for team development, a modification to the previous two methods, is representative of third-generation approaches to interventions discussed by Bartunek, Austin, and Seo (2008). Specifically, the method involves implementing – through critical praxis and reflexivity – enhanced versions of either of the two team interventions above.

The essential feature of critical praxis *is continuous reflection about practice* (Pedlar, 2005; Revans, 1998). Because it can be an interpersonal and group activity as much as it includes personal reflection, critical praxis also provides each participant a voice in addressing the problems that are uncovered. This is especially salient for understanding and facilitating *teamwork.* We do not utilize critical praxis as a specific set of steps or stages that are qualitatively different from each other, as with Methods 1 and 2. In this sense it is less a method than a stance, one that can be adopted concerning any practice, including the other methods.

We have gravitated toward critical praxis through conscious commitment to ongoing reflection on what, why, and how *we* practice team facilitation and whether, why, and in what ways *members* engage teamwork processes (those we seek to facilitate and their own). This usually occurs through routines involving structured activity, evaluation/reflection, and interaction. Critical praxis thus encourages continuous questioning, including evaluating teamwork processes and structures. It also includes attention to values and issues that surface as a result of teamwork practice. It underscores the importance of team members' concerns, not merely their contributions. In this sense, critical praxis creates a teamwork experience in its own right: as a practice it facilitates teamwork processes about which members are in dialogue, but the practice of using this approach (Holmes, Cockburn-Wootten, Motion, Zorn, & Roper, 2005) may itself foster a teamworking process.

Seibold and Kang (2008) provide an extended case analysis of a municipal human services agency in which members of a support group were involved in improving teamwork. Within the context of the first author's use of both team intervention methods above with this support team (SST; i.e., extended team development that included a team workout) members' reflexivity led to a dozen changes in how those two methods unfolded with the SST.

For example, the *impetus* for the team development intervention itself came from a direct request to the facilitator from the team members (as he was working with the professionals they supported), not from their managers (who had contracted for teamwork with the professionals' team). During team discussions, and because members are encouraged to question any and all practices, SST members reflected upon whether managers were valuing them as much as valuing the professionals whom they supported. In turn, the facilitator was led to consider whether his own engagements in this and other organizations were reproducing managerial bias (Cunliffe, 2004).

To further illustrate how critical praxis functioned in this example, during preparations for the SST members' workout retreat, discussions among the members about their responsibility for the team intervention (relative to the facilitator's) also led to a series of modifications of Method 2. At members' request, preliminary interviews were conducted with *members as a group* rather than with individuals alone. *Members* created the *agenda and procedures* for the day away, not the facilitator. *Members* proposed *outcomes* from the retreat that they would consider most meaningful for the team, not (only) those of the facilitator. As *members* also assumed responsibility for preparing some of the *procedures and structured experiences* they wished to utilize in the retreat, the facilitator's role changed from de facto leader to co-leader and collaborator, to providing feedback, and to assisting with gathering resources. At the *members'* request, SST managers also participated in discussion in which established practices were critiqued. As a direct result of reflecting on their own assumptions about the importance of teamwork for all groups in the agency (not simply the professionals whom they had originally sought to aid), the managers increased their commitment to the SST's development (and even to teamwork in their own management team).

After the retreat and during the course of the first author's extended team process consultation with the SST, intentionally reflexive discussions with its members (during established times) led to modifications of Method 1. The planning (sub)team for the workout session remained in force; its members led weekly follow-ups, not the facilitator. Over time, all members of the SST took turns in rotating through membership on the planning team and its efforts to guide the extended team-building process. Indeed, the facilitator's role changed to observing and reinforcing the ways in which members' efforts were indicative of high levels of teamwork. Most important, SST members' processes of structured activity, evaluation/reflection, and interaction led to awareness of their potential to be reorganized into a single team and to their call for change from the managers in the organization. Their discussions also had the unintended consequence of fostering tension about this proposal. Fortunately, by this time members also had developed competencies for managing this intragroup conflict (although it has never been fully resolved).

Many of the changes noted by Seibold and Kang (2008) are now becoming part of how we proceed with the first two methods, although even they may change at any time if our own or members' reflexivity reveals other matters that encourage modification of our customary procedures.

Practice ↔ Research

Group interventions involving team development can be mutually informing as methods of practice and as methods for research, as we have demonstrated at various points in this chapter with our own and with others' engagements and research. We elaborate on the recursive relationship between research and practice in this conclusion. We note instances of their joint embodiment in researchers-as-practitioners like ourselves, and in other cases when the researchers and the practitioners are different.

In most of our engagements, the data we gather with the team(s) as a whole or with individual members are confidential. When our relationships with those teams and their members have led to research reports for audiences of scholars, our publications have been case studies for the most part (for team development interventions, see Meyers & Johnson, 2008; Seibold, 1995; Seibold & Kang, 2008). This is not unusual for this genre. Frey's (1995) edited volume on innovations in facilitation methods with groups in natural settings is comprised entirely of case studies. Case studies focus on a single entity (the organizational team in our studies), but they admit of the researchers' detailed account and analysis – as informed by data collected through a variety of methods and over a sustained period of time (Cresswell, 1994).

Even if they are restricted to single instances, the potential "meaningfulness" and "richness" of case study findings (Hartley, 1994) invite comparisons with the findings from major reviews of multiple studies of multiple groups that may prove heuristic (in the area of teamwork, cf. Kozlowski & Ilgen, 2006). Practice-based case studies also can generate research. Our immersion in groups and teams for extended periods of time has led us to investigate subgroup influence (Gebhardt & Meyers, 1995), to a line of research on "innovation modification" by teams participating in organizations' planned change programs (Lewis & Seibold, 1993), and to develop a model of the "dark side" of teams (Seibold et al., 2009). Our extended, numerous engagements also have enabled publications analyzing our practices (Seibold, 2005) relative to broader accounts of organizational development interventions (e.g., third-generation approaches) and relative to modes of inquiry (e.g., critical praxis), as noted earlier. Methods of practice also are likely to sensitize researchers in ways that enable them to shore up their own conceptual and theoretical stances. For example, Seibold (1998) was led to emphasize the central role of groups in mediating individual-organization relationships (a position consistent with that of Poole, 1998). In turn, our theoretical position concerning members' structuring activities and group structuration (Seibold & Meyers, 2007) have sensitized us as practitioners to the complexities of team development to which our methods must also be sensitive.

In some instances, the researcher-as-practitioner may have access to sufficient numbers of groups and can design more comprehensive studies of the effects of those interventions or of theoretically important dynamics across groups (Lehmann et al., 2009). But most of our team-development projects have been singular, separated, and serial in nature, so we have not been able to create large datasets of multiple teams. When the unit of analysis has been the individual, we have been able to conduct panel (Cooper, Seibold, & Suchner, 1997) and quasi-experimental studies (Seibold, Kudsi, & Rude, 1993) in reporting quantitative assessments of the effectiveness of organizational interventions.

There are innumerable times when researchers who are immersed in practical engagements appropriate theory and empirical findings from their own and others' academic research to aid their own and team members' sensemaking about teamwork, just as we earlier noted several of the many ways in which we have done so. Indeed, the researcher-as-practitioner recognizes the value of the parallels, intersections, and integration between basic and applied research and can thus speak more easily to both audiences (e.g., Seibold, Lemus, Ballard, & Myers, 2009).

Researchers-as-practitioners also have ready access to *research measures* and can employ those instruments to supplement portions of their team development intervention methods involving cycles of data collection, data analysis, data feedback, and design. For example, we have utilized the Small Group Relational Satisfaction Scale (Anderson, Martin, & Riddle, 2001), the Small Group Socialization Scale (Riddle, Anderson, & Martin, 2000), the Organizational Temporality Scale (Ballard & Seibold, 2004), the Organizational Listening Survey (Cooper & Buchanan, 1999), as part of the multimethod first step described in connection with the extended team process consultation (Method 1). Data from these and other measures that both meet acceptable standards of validity and reliability in the research community, yet target problematic areas of team relationships and interactions, have enabled us to offer sensitizing feedback to individuals and to create team-level diagnostics that help "unfreeze" the group (especially when their members are used to dealing with aggregated data, statistical displays, and population norms). We also have used these measures to evaluate overtime changes in a team. With our small sample sizes, however, we have not been able to use the data from these measures to conduct the multilevel analyses encouraged by Poole, Keyton, and Frey (1999).

There is still a dearth of research concerning the effectiveness of *team communication* facilitation, and Hartwig and Frey (2007) offer means for filling that gap. Nonetheless, we note in closing that the group researcher–practitioner (at his or her best) possesses expertise and skills that strengthen and develop team task and relational environments. With attention to method, careful planning, proper assessment, mutual respect, credible execution, wisdom and experience, facilitators can provide valuable insight, practical interventions, and often-successful solutions to team development puzzles.

Notes

1 Some of our engagements fall under the umbrella of action research, "a participatory process concerned with developing practical knowledge in the pursuit of worthwhile human purposes ... (and that) brings together action and reflection, theory and practice, in participation with others ..." (Reason & Bradbury, 2001, p. 1). As in other types of action research, our projects are usually rooted in participants' needs

and undertaken in partnership with them. Furthermore, the third approach to team development interventions that we note later in this chapter – critical praxis and reflexivity – relies on cycles of reflection that are core to many forms of action research. Our methods of data collection also involve insider/outsider participation in team development, which can be a key feature of action research designs. However, the three forms of team intervention we discuss in this chapter seek to enhance *groups'* teamwork rather than altering *individuals'* personal theories of action (for which group methods require considerable time and commitment according to Argyris, as noted by Hackman & Edmondson, 2008).

2 We are indebted to Robert L. Husband for this term, and for his work with us in developing some of the steps and structured experiences we use with this second method.

References

Anderson, C. M., Martin, M. M., & Riddle, B. L. (2001). Small group relational satisfaction scale: Development, reliability, and validity. *Communication Studies, 52*, 220–233.

Arrow, H., McGrath, J. E., & Berdahl, J. L. (2000). *Small groups as complex systems: Formation, coordination, development, and adaptation.* Thousand Oaks, CA: Sage.

Austin, J. R., & Bartunek, J. M. (2003). Theories and practices of organizational development. In W. Borman, D. Ilgen, & R. Klimoski (Eds.), *Handbook of psychology: Industrial and organizational psychology* (Vol. 12, pp. 309–332). New York: John Wiley & Sons.

Ballard, D. I., & Seibold, D. R. (2004). Organizational members' communication and temporal experience: Scale development and validation. *Communication Research, 31*(2), 135–172.

Barker, V. E., Abrams, J. R., Tiyaamornwong, V., Seibold, D. R., Duggan, A., Park, S. H., et al. (2000). New contexts for relational communication in groups. *Small Group Research, 31*, 470–503.

Bartunek, J. M., Austin, J. R., & Seo, M. G. (2008). Conceptual underpinnings of intervening in organizations. In T. G. Cummings (Ed.), *Handbook of organizational development* (pp. 151–166). Los Angeles, CA: Sage.

Beer, M. (1976). The technology of organization development. In M. D. Dunnette (Ed.), *Handbook of industrial and organizational psychology* (pp. 937–994). Chicago: Rand-McNally.

Berteotti, C. R., & Seibold, D. R. (1994). Coordination and role-definition problems in health care teams: A hospice case study. In L. R. Frey (Ed.), *Group communication in context: Studies of natural groups* (pp. 107–131). Hillsdale, NJ: Lawrence Erlbaum.

Boss, R. W., & McConkie, M. L. (2008). Team building. In T. G. Cummings (Ed.), *Handbook of organizational development* (pp. 237–259). Los Angeles, CA: Sage.

Buller, P. F., & Bell, C. H. (1986). Effects of team building and goal setting on productivity: A field experiment. *Academy of Management Journal, 29*, 305–328.

Ciccone, A. A., Meyers, R. A., & Waldmann, S. (2008). What's so funny? Moving students toward complex thinking in a course on comedy and laughter. *Arts and Humanities in Higher Education, 7*, 308–322.

Considine, J., Meyers, R. A., & Timmerman, C. E. (2006). Evidence use in group quiz discussions: How do students support preferred choices? *Journal for Excellence in College Teaching. 17*, 65–89.

Cooper, L. O., Seibold, D. R., & Suchner, R. (1997). Listening in organizations: An analysis of error structures in models of listening competency. *Communication Research Reports, 14*, 312–320.

Cresswell, J. W. (1994). *Research design: Qualitative and quantitative approaches.* Thousand Oaks, CA: Sage.

Cummings, T. G., & Worley, G. (2005). *Organization development and change* (8th ed.). Cincinnati, OH: Southwestern.

Cunliffe, A. (2004). On becoming a critically reflexive practitioner. *Journal of Management Education, 28*, 407–426.

Devine, D. J., Clayton, L. D., Philips, J. L., Dunford, B. B., & Melner, S. B. (1999). Teams in organizations: Prevalence, characteristics, and effectiveness. *Small Group Research, 30,* 678–711.

Dyer, W. G. (1995). *Team building: Current issues and new alternatives* (3rd ed.). Reading, MA: Addison-Wesley.

Ferrante, K., Olson, K. M., Castor, T., Hoeft, M., Johnson, J. R., & Meyers, R. A. (2008). Students' metaphors as descriptors of effective and ineffective learning experiences. *Practice and Evidence of Scholarship of Teaching and Learning, 3*, 103–128.

Franken, L., & Seibold, D. R. (2010). Business process modeling at the Internal Funding Office: Structuring group interaction processes to structure business processes. In L. Black (Ed.), *Group communication: Cases for analysis, appreciation, and application* (pp. 17–24). Dubuque, IA: Kendall Hunt.

Frey, L. R. (Ed.) (1995). *Innovations in group facilitation techniques: Case studies of applications in naturalistic settings.* Cresskill, NJ: Hampton Press..

Gebhardt, L. J., & Meyers, R. A. (1995). Subgroup influence in decision-making groups: Examining consistency from a communication perspective. *Small Group Research, 26,* 147–168.

Greenbaum, H. H., & Query, J. L. (1999). Communication in organizational work groups: A review and analysis of natural work groups. In L. R. Frey, D. S. Gouran, & M.S. Poole (Eds.), *The handbook of group communication theory and research* (pp. 539–564). Thousand Oaks, CA: Sage.

Hackman, J. R. (1990). *Groups that work (and those that don't): Creating conditions for effective teamwork.* San Francisco: Jossey-Bass.

Hackman, R. J., & Edmondson, A. C. (2008). Groups as agents of change. In T. G. Cummings (Ed.), *Handbook of organizational development* (pp. 167–186). Los Angeles, CA: Sage.

Hartley, J. F. (1994). Case studies in organizational research. In C. Cassell & G. Symon (Eds.), *Qualitative methods in organizational research: A practical guide* (pp. 208–229). London: Sage.

Hartwig, R. T., & Frey, L. R. (2007). *Facilitating team communication facilitation.* Paper presented at the annual meeting of the National Communication Association, Chicago.

Holmes, P., Cockburn-Wootten, C., Motion, J., Zorn, T. E., & Roper, J. (2005). Critical reflexive practice in teaching management communication. *Business Communication Quarterly, 68,* 247–256.

Kauffeld, S., & Meyers, R. A. (2009). Complaint and solution-oriented circles: Interaction patterns in work group discussions. *European Journal of Work and Organizational Psychology, 18,* 267–294.

Kozlowski, S. W. J., & Ilgren, D. R. (2006). Enhancing the effectiveness of work groups and teams. *Psychological Science in the Public Interest, 7*(3), 77–124.

Krikorian, D., Seibold, D. R., & Goode, P. L. (1997). Re-engineering at LAC: A case study of emergent network processes. In B. D. Sypher (Ed.), *Case studies in organizational communication* (2nd ed., pp. 129–144). New York: Guilford.

LaFasto, F., & Larson, C. (2001). *When teams work best.* Thousand Oaks, CA: Sage.

Lau, A., & Meyers, R. A. (2007). *Student perceptions of classroom group work: The good, the bad, and the ugly.* Paper presented at the annual meeting of the National Communication Association, Chicago.

Lawler, E. E. (1995). *Creating high-performance organizations.* San Francisco: Jossey-Bass.

Lehmann, M., Meyers, R. A., Kauffeld, S., & Lehmann-Willenbrock, N. (2009). *Transforming negative communication in German decision-making teams: An examination of reflexivity training.*

Paper presented at the annual meeting of the National Communication Association, Chicago.

Lewis, L. K., & Seibold, D. R. (1993). Innovation modification during intra-organizational adoption. *Academy of Management Review, 18*, 322–354.

Meyers, R. A. (2006). *Facilitating interdisciplinary and intercampus faculty research groups: Exploring similarities and differences in scholarly approaches.* Paper presented at the annual meeting of National Communication Association, San Antonio.

Meyers, R. A., & Johnson, J. R. (2008). Facilitating the design of a campus leadership team. *Communication Education, 57*, 472–481.

Meyers, R. A., Seibold, D. R., & Kang, P. (2010). Analyzing argument in a naturally occurring jury deliberation. *Small Group Research. 41*, 452–473.

Pedlar, M. (2005). A general theory of human action. *Action Learning: Research and Practice, 2,* 127–132.

Poole, M. S. (1991). Procedures for managing meetings: Social and technological innovation. In R. A. Swenson & B. O. Knapp (Eds.), *Innovative meeting management* (pp. 53–109). Austin, TX: 3M Meeting Management Institute.

Poole, M. S. (1998). The small group should be *the* fundamental unit of communication research. In J. S. Trent (Ed.), *Communication: Views from the helm for the twenty-first century* (pp. 94–97). Needham Heights, MA: Allyn & Bacon.

Poole, M. S., Keyton, J., & Frey, L. R. (1999). Group communication methodology: Issues and considerations. In L. R. Frey, D. S. Gouran, & M. S. Poole (Eds.), *The handbook of group communication theory and research* (pp. 92–112). Thousand Oaks, CA: Sage.

Reason, P., & Bradbury, H. (Eds.) (2001). *Handbook of action research: Participative inquiry and practice.* London: Sage.

Revans, R. (1998). *ABC of action learning.* London: Lemos & Crane.

Riddle, B. L., Anderson, C. M., & Martin, M. M. (2000). Small group socialization scale: Development and validity. *Small Group Research, 31,* 554–572.

Rousseau, V., Aubé, C., & Savoie, A. (2006). Teamwork behaviors: A review and an integration of frameworks. *Small Group Research, 37*, 540–570.

Schein, E. H. (1988). *Process consultation: It roles in organizational development* (2nd ed.). Upper Saddle River, NJ: Prentice-Hall.

Seibold, D. R. (1990). Management communication issues in family businesses: The case of Oak Ridge Trucking Company. In B. D. Sypher (Ed.), *Case studies in organizational communication* (pp. 163–176). New York: Guilford.

Seibold, D. R. (1995). Developing the "team" in a team-managed organization: Group facilitation in a new plant design. In L. R. Frey (Ed.), *Innovations in group facilitation techniques: Case studies of applications in naturalistic settings* (pp. 282–298). Cresskill, NJ: Hampton.

Seibold, D. R. (1998). Groups and organizations: Premises and perspectives. In J. S. Trent (Ed.), *Communication: Views from the helm for the twenty-first century* (pp. 162–168). Needham Heights, MA: Allyn & Bacon.

Seibold, D. R. (2005). Bridging theory and practice in organizational communication. In J. L. Simpson & P. Shockley-Zalabak (Eds.), *Engaging communication, transforming organizations: Scholarship of engagement in action* (pp. 13–44). Cresskill, NJ: Hampton.

Seibold, D. R., & Kang, P. (2008). Using critical praxis to understand and teach teamwork. *Business Communication Quarterly, 71*(4), 421–438.

Seibold, D. R., Kang, P., Gailliard, B. M., & Jahn, J. (2009). Communication that damages teamwork: The dark side of teams. In P. Lutgen-Sandvik & B. Davenport Sypher (Eds.), *Destructive organizational communication: Processes, consequences, and constructive ways of organizing* (pp. 267–289). New York: Routledge/Taylor & Francis.

Seibold, D. R., Kudsi, S., & Rude, M. (1993). Does communication training make a difference? Evidence for the effectiveness of a presentation skills program. *Journal of Applied Communication Research, 21*, 111–131.

Seibold, D. R., Lemus, D. R., Ballard, D. I., & Myers, K. K. (2009). Organizational communication and applied communication research: Parallels, intersections, integration, and engagement. In L. R. Frey & K. N. Cissna (Eds.), *Routledge handbook of applied communication research* (pp. 331–354). New York: Routledge/Taylor & Francis.

Seibold, D. R., & Meyers, R. A. (2007). Group argument: A structuration perspective and research program. *Small Group Research, 38,* 312–336.

Seibold, D. R., Meyers, R. A., & Shoham, M. D. (2010). Social influence in groups and organizations. In C. R. Berger, M. E. Roloff, & D. Roskos-Ewolsen (Eds.), *Handbook of communication science* (2nd ed., pp. 237–253). Thousand Oaks, CA: Sage.

Seo, M., Putnam, L. L., & Bartunek, J. M. (2004). Dualities and tensions of planned organizational change. In M. S. Poole & A. H. Van de Ven (Eds.), *Handbook of organizational change and innovation* (pp. 73–107). New York: Oxford University Press.

SunWolf, & Seibold, D. R. (1999). The impact of formal procedures on group processes, members, and task outcomes. In L. R. Frey (Ed.), *The handbook of group communication theory and research* (pp. 395–431). Thousand Oaks, CA: Sage.

Tompkins, P. K., & Cheney, G. (1985). Communication and unobtrusive control in contemporary organizations. In R. D. McPhee & P. K. Tompkins (Eds.), *Organizational communication: Traditional themes and new directions* (pp. 179–210). Newbury Park, CA: Sage.

AUTHOR INDEX

SUBJECT INDEX

aggression 174
artifacts: material artifacts 219
avatars 176, 185, 188–91

behavioral markers see event-based
  methods
bona fide group perspective 211–6, 219,
  220, 222–5, 229, 231: challenges 215–6;
  definition 211; methodologies 212,
  tenets of 213–4

children 235, 240–1, 244
circumplex models of mood 162
collective induction 35–8;
commitment acts 14
coding: coding schemes/systems 159, 237,
  241, 244, 255, 335–6, 341; 342–43,
  363–364; discourse units 332–4;
  innovations 345–7; limitations 344–5;
  online discussions 344; process 68;
  procedures 330; reliability 333, 340,
  363–4; software 346; training coders
  337–8; transcribing 331–332; unitizing
  332–3, 363–364; validity 336–7, 364;
cognitive consensus 134–5:
  measurement 141
computational modeling see computer
  simulation
computer-mediated groups 218, 239
computer simulation 79–104: advantages
  of 80–2; agent-based modeling
  approach 92–7; challenges 97–101;

formula translation approach 82–6;
  generative process modeling approach
  86–92; purpose of 80; vs. mathematical
  theories 80; vs. natural language
  theories 80; See also group discussion,
  group problem solving
concertive control 229
concept mapping 144
confederates 42, 46, 51, 180
confidentiality 229–30
content analysis see theme analysis
conversational analysis 220
counterfactual thinking 248–9

data aggregation 271
data analysis 311–327: actor-partner
  interdependence model (APIM) 312,
  318–320; between groups 313, 315;
  determining appropriate approach
  312–3; homogeneity 370; lag-
  sequential analysis 372–3; models of
  interdependence 318–27; moderated
  dependency analysis 373; multilevel
  modeling 315–8; nonindependence 311,
  314–5; one-with-many design (OWM)
  312, 321–3; sequential contingency
  analysis 365ff, social relations model
  (SRM) 312, 323–6; stationarity 369–370,
  transition matrix 366–8; unitariness
  378–379; within groups 313, 315
data collection: multiple sources 222;
  network 286–297